Towards Understanding

Qur'ānic Arabic

A Manual
Teaching Arabic Through the Qur'ān
(Elementary)

**WITH FREE DVDS COVERING ALL 16
LESSONS**

DR MUHAMMAD IBRAHIM H. I. SURTY

QAF QUR'ĀNIC ARABIC FOUNDATION
552B Coventry Road, Small Heath,
Birmingham, B10 0UN (U.K)
e-mail: qaf@blueyonder.co.uk

www.qaf.org.uk

Cover designed by Prof. Aftab Ahmad Gharda.

Published by:
QAF: Qur'ānic Arabic Foundation,
552B Coventry Road,
Small Heath,
Birmingham B10 0UN,
England,
United Kingdom.

British Library Cataloguing in Publication Data
Surty, Muhammad Ibrahim Hafiz Ismail
Towards Understanding Qur'ānic Arabic
(A manual teaching Arabic through the Qur'ān)
            (Elementary)
1. Arabic, Koran, Language, Islam

ISBN 978-1-898596-65-3

Printed and bound in Great Britain by
The Cromwell Press Ltd. Aintree Avenue
White Horse Business Park Trowbridge
Wiltshire BA14 0XB

Introduction

(The best among you is one who learns and teaches the Qur'ān – *Hadīth*)

Views of the Muslim Scholars

"I consider the noble endeavors of Dr Surty to teach Arabic, the language of the Noble Qur'ān, which remained alive among Arabs for more than fourteen centuries, as praise worthy. It is also the language of the Traditions of the Messenger of Allah ﷺ and from where stems all the Islamic *Sharī'ah* which is followed by Muslims throughout the world.

Among the tasks which Dr Surty accomplished is compiling a book comprising of lessons to teach Qur'ānic Arabic based on introducing its vocabulary and expanding its meaning to the students in a simple direct method taking into consideration the context and atmosphere of Britain and Western countries. Two aims have been achieved by his approach: teaching Arabic language in general and Qur'ānic terms in particular.

His attempt deserves recognition and admiration. I am hopeful that students who wish to learn Arabic will find the book very useful. In collaboration with Dr Surty and on his request, I am contributing this introduction to his book."

Shaykh Sayyid Abul Hasan Ali Nadwi - Chairman of the Board of Trustees, Oxford Center for Islamic Studies, St. Cross College, Oxford, U.K.

"I am much obliged to Dr Surty who kindly showed me his book and explained its teaching methodology. I found the book and its methodology a new approach to facilitate the teaching of the language of the Qur'ān. I am hopeful that this novel book will promote its universal usage and help teachers of Arabic as a second language to follow his new methods. Any efforts in this direction will be very rewarding since teaching Qur'ānic Arabic is certainly included in the saying of the Prophet ﷺ: 'the best of you is he who learns and teaches the Qur'ān'."

Professor Dr Shaykh Idris - Institute of Islamic and Arabic Sciences of America, USA

"Arabic language has been honoured to be the language of the Noble Qur'ān. Beginners always find difficulties in the comprehension of this language which increases the need to

5

develop new methods of teaching it. This big challenge has been confronted by the author who compiled this valuable and extremely useful work based on his long experience and aptitude of research. He has succeeded in its presentation as he has selected its examples and applications mainly from the Qur'an, in addition to some extracts from *Ḥadīth*, proverbs and wise sayings."

Professor Dr Ahmed Ali al-Imam, Vice Chancellor, Qur'ānic University and Islamic Sciences, Omdurman, Sudan.

"Having gone through the work, I have found it to be unique. It is a book seeking to teach Arabic with the Holy Qur'ān as its focus. Every word used in this important book is to be found in the Holy Qur'ān and in the *Ḥadīth* of the Prophet Muḥammad ﷺ. By the time one reads this book through, one would end up not only learning Arabic vocabulary and grammar, but becoming very well acquainted with the teachings of Islam.
In this well researched work, Dr Surty, no doubt putting to good use his long experience in teaching Arabic to non-Arabs, has started with the assumption that the reader is an absolute beginner. This book is a must for all those who wish to learn Qur'anic Arabic without tears. I commend it to all non-Arabic speaking people who want to learn Qur'ānic Arabic easily."

Professor Dr Abubakar A. Gwandu - Vice Chancellor, Usman Danfodio University, Sokoto, Nigeria.

"It is a great monumental work based on several years of teaching experience at University level as well as at the Muslim Community. This work provides an opportunity to millions who are not versed in the Arabic language to comprehend the Qur'ān in its revealed language. The teachers of Arabic will find great comfort. I strongly recommend the course and pray for its success."

Dr S. M. Darsh - President, *Sharī'ah* Council, London

"Undoubtedly, there is a great need for text books which introduce Qur'ānic Arabic to English speakers. I studied Dr Surty's book with interest and found it a pioneer work in its field which excels most of the literature available before it. I am very sure that beginners will find the book extremely useful."

Dr Bustami Khir - Senior Lecturer, Westhill College, Birmingham, U.K.

"This book fills a major gap in the field of Arabic language teaching. Very well written, systematically compiled to make Qur'ānic Arabic easy to learn and a joy to teach. The author manages in this work to combine a scholar's depth with Arabic teacher's skills to produce a masterpiece in Qur'ānic studies that make the eyebrows of all experts rise."

Dr Mawil Izzi Dien, Reader St. David's University College, University of Wales, U.K.

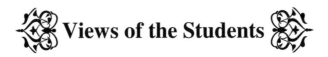 **Views of the Students**

"Clear graded progression facilitates rapid learning, specially written texts highlight grammatical themes, and lead smoothly into the student being able to tackle Qur'ānic texts directly. Grammatical themes are backed up by clear reference tables that keep consolidation of lessons. Wherever possible new rules are presented in a systematic way that aids assimilation."

Lucy Hudson - M.A Student, CSIC, University of Birmingham, U.K.

"This book is logical, clear and well presented with relevant and interesting exercises and extracts. The methodology is well defined and demonstrates an organised progression which facilitates learning and enables very fast progression to be made. Following the course was very enjoyable and has stimulated me to continue my further study of Arabic."

Clair Norton – Graduate Student, Department of Byzantine Studies, University of Birmingham, U.K.

"I am an English Muslim. I have made several attempts to teach myself Arabic but by far the best method I have come across is Dr Surty's course 'Towards Understanding Qur'ānic Arabic.'

Jannat Al-Haddad – Wisbech

"I have attended Dr Surty's classes on Qur'ānic Arabic at the Oxford Center for Islamic Studies and I was amazed at how much we had learnt and managed to remember from each lesson!
The method is very clear and easy to follow. I recommend the course to everyone for self study and teaching.

D. K. Maryam – Oxford

"I found the book to be very helpful in learning the Qur'ānic language and grammar. I am also involved with a small group of ladies who are learning Qur'ānic Arabic, and we have found Dr Surty's course to be of enormous help. For basic *Tajweed* the cassettes are really helpful."

Rashda Ali - London

"This course enables people who want to read and understand the Qur'ān (from Arabic), an opportunity to develop a strong foundation. With this, the student can develop the interest and confidence to go further. I recommend the course as a stepping stone to deeper understanding of the Arabic language."

M. Yusuf – Walsall

Contents

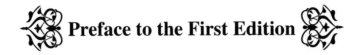

Preface to the First Edition

Qur'ānic Arabic has been and remains the standard of excellence in literary Arabic. This Elementary course in Qur'ānic Arabic is the result of several years of research and practical teaching both at University level and to the Muslim community at the principal mosques in the city of Birmingham, England. The QAF: Qur'ānic Arabic Foundation presents this course with pleasure and plans, *in shā'Allāh*, in future to publish on a similar pattern Intermediary and Advanced courses with the assistance of scholars of international repute.

The introduction contains two sections. Section One provides a number of reasons for the study of Qur'ānic Arabic and Section Two explains the methodology of the course which is the key to success.

This Elementary course contains four phases. The First Phase begins with the letters of the Arabic alphabet, teaches the Qur'ānic script with the help of modern methods and provides a range of exercises. Two three hour long cassettes accompany the course and will assist in the pronunciation of Arabic letters and the learning of the Arabic script and provide help with some of the exercises of the lessons.

The Second Phase includes seven lessons and is strictly confined to the singular form of nouns, First Form verbs, and other themes. Each lesson contains a few units. These grammatical themes are accompanied by extensive Arabic text. This is a most effective method in explaining the theme/s of the unit and also assists in revision and recapitulation of themes introduced previously. Furthermore examples from the text are analysed, and where necessary grammatical rules formed; a numerical order is retained for ease of reference and for full thematic explanations. The glossary, extensive exercises and methodology for teachers are a supplement to each lesson. From Lesson Five onwards an attempt has been made to provide many examples from the Qur'ān which can be understood within the framework of the grammatical themes introduced. The text for the final lessons 13 - 16 is confined to the Qur'ān. In Phase Two alone there are one hundred and sixty-nine Qur'ānic textual references providing examples in the singular form alone. Vocabulary for these references is provided. The text of the lessons is also supported by a few *Aḥādīth*, the sayings of the Prophet Muḥammad (peace be upon him) and by the use of Arabic proverbs.

The Third Phase deals with the Dual, Sound Plural and Derived Forms of verbs II and IV. It includes two lessons and follows the same pattern as outlined in Phase Two.

The Plural, the Derived Forms of verbs III, V-X together with other themes are included in the Fourth Phase. These are accompanied by Qur'ānic textual references to each lesson and also includes an extensive selection of Qur'ānic text for recapitulation of all the grammatical themes introduced. The course includes over 500 references to the Qur'ān. A few tables frequently referred to in the work.

All in all it is a ninety hour course presented systematically and structured to facilitate careful graded progression. It is nevertheless a step by step long climb up hill, progress to the next step being conditional upon confidence with the step preceding it. The climb should not however be seen as threatening, rather with each step so short and allowing a secure foothold before the next is attempted, it represents an ideal invitation. The course was designed for the graduating students at Sokoto. Furthermore it has been very rewarding, stimulating interest towards the comprehension of the Qur'ān among post-graduate students at CSIC, University of Birmingham, undergraduates at various colleges at the Center for Islamic Studies, St. Cross College, Oxford and among a large number of professionals, businessmen, general workers and housewives in Birmingham, UK.

QAF is planning to begin a teachers' training course so that this attempt to generate an understanding of the language of the Qur'ān here in Birmingham can be spread far and wide.

QAf may in the future provide a teaching kit and training video to facilitate further comprehension of the Word of Allah.

We look forward to all your suggestions and assistance for the teaching and learning of the Qur'ān. As the Prophet Muḥammad 🕌 once said: " The best among you is one who learns and teaches the Qur'ān."

Tāj Cottage,
Birmingham, U.K.   **Muhammad Ibrahim H. I. Surty**
Muḥarram 1414 A.H

Preface to the Second Edition

Praise be to Allah that the first edition assisted a large number of people to basic Qur'ānic Arabic. A few Arabic teachers have been teaching the course in their institutions. The view of the students who studied the course in 90 contact hours are very encouraging and indicate clearly that this experience is successful. I wish to express my gratitude to a Palestinian scholar Mr Fuad Husain who has meticulously studied the book, taught the course and pointed out a few typographical errors which are corrected in this edition. We hope that Arabic teachers and Islamic institutions the world over will extend their support for the spread of this course and assist us with their valuable advice. May Allah accept this humble effort for His pleasure alone.

Tāj Cottage,
Birmingham, U.K.   **Muhammad Ibrahim H. I. Surty**
Jumada al-Ula 1416 A.H

Preface to the Third Edition

By the grace of Allah it is a pleasure to witness the success of this course. It has been taught at a number of places and the comments of both teachers and students have been very encouraging.

It also gives me great pleasure to state that as a result of a collaboration between the Qur'ānic Arabic Foundation (QAF) of UK and the Islamic Research Foundation (IRF) of India, the entire course has been recorded as seventy-seven half hour episodes on Betacom broadcasting quality video in a classroom setting. Over a thousand visual aids have been used, carefully prepared over several years of teaching. These videos are currently being edited and *inshā'Allah* an album will be available sometime in the future. Every attempt has been made to strictly follow the textual course which will *inshā'Allah* go a long way in assisting students who wish to comprehend Qur'ānic Arabic.

As the first phase of the course deals with the Qur'ānic script, it was deemed appropriate to show children being taught Qur'ānic script in a classroom setting using modern pedagogical methods. Such pedagogy is needed especially in the west where qualified teachers in Qur'ānic Arabic are so few compared to the ever increasing number of pupils who need to be taught the Qur'ānic script.

In fact, almost all Muslim parents living in the west consider this as a challenge and witness difficulties and problems in this aspect of their children's upbringing. In order to help alleviate this problem QAF has decided to design a special course by taking the first phase of the present course and converting it into twelve half hour video recordings accompanied by a text book. The text is presented in graded progression using tried and tested methods. Necessary visual aids are judiciously being used and these, I believe, will *inshā-'Allah* enable children to learn the script in a remarkably short period of time. Interested persons can obtain the course from QAF.

In this edition an appendix has been added which contains the English translation of the Qur'ānic text quoted in this course, *Traslation and Commentary*, by *Shaykh* 'Abdul-Mājid

Daryabadi, with an introduction by *Shaykh* Abul Hasan 'Ali Nadawi, Islamic Fondation, Leicester, 2001. This particular translation is used, as in my humble opinion, it is very close to the Arabic Qur'ānic text. This will make it easier for the beginner to find the meaning to the corresponding Arabic words. I wish to register my gratitude to The Islamic Foundation for granting permission for the publication of extracts from this work.

A glossary of grammatical terms in English, guidelines to the beginners and a key to Phase One exercises 1-18 'write in Arabic' are also included in this edition.

The presentation of this edition has also benefited from a complete re-formatting on computer. Bilingual publications (especially with Arabic) pose difficult problems. I wish to acknowledge with thanks the suggestions and assistance provided by Mr H. Cengez, Mr Abdul Basit, Mr M. Rayyan, Mr M. bin Faredj, Mr M. Muktar, Mr N. Qaddoura, Ms. C. Bebawi, Mrs A. Hasan, Mr M. Abd al-Rahman, Mr M. Yusuf, Mr M. Khan, and Dr Manzoor Alam.

Readers are kindly requested to point out errors and make suggestions for the future improvement of the course.

Tāj Cottage,
Birmingham, U.K.   **Muhammad Ibrahim H. I. Surty**
Rabī'al-Thānī 1422 A.H.

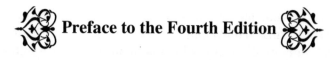

Preface to the Fourth Edition

Almighty Allah by His Grace provided me an opportunity to produce the fourth edition and also teach successively to the students both at the University of Birmingham and at QAF: Qur'ānic Arabic Foundation in the city of Birmingham, England to a large number of the members of the community both male and female all along twenty years successively. In teaching, the spirit of this course is its methodology, which has been developed over the years and Almighty Allah has enabled me to protect it by recording at IRF: Islamic Research Foundation Mumbai Studio in seventy seven episodes by establishing an interaction in a classroom with the students. *al-ḥamd li Allāh* serial programmes on Qur'ānic Arabic have been telecasted by peace TV covering the entire world and this noble venture is enabling thousands of interested people the world over to learn Qur'ānic Arabic. In view of ever increasing and pressing demands from the viewers, QAF has an honour to present with this edition free DVDs covering all 16 lessons of the course.

QAF has already published a hard back A4 size in full colour illustrated book with twelve episodes on two free DVDs for children and beginners. This course covers the first phase of the Qur'ānic Arabic text book. Interested people can obtain the course from QAF (www.qaf.org.uk).

It gives us great pleasure to know that a number of classes are organised for the teaching of Qur'ānic Arabic in which this text book has been used. With the availability of the DVDs, the first of its kind in the world for such course in the English language, we believe, the task of both teaching and learning will become easy. DVDs will provide an ample opportunity to the students to revise and learn rapidly. Through this method students can solve the difficulties and remove their anxieties. Teachers can also change their method of teaching. The judicious use of audio visual aids with colour coding will facilitate them to explain the difficulties in relation to the comprehension of Qur'ānic Arabic themes.

The methodology for the teaching of all lessons mentioned in the text book is meticulously followed and accuracy has been retained in recording of the programmes. The viewers are requested to point out the lapses.

In this edition an attempt has been made to provide the key to 35 exercises which cover both, the designed text and also the Qur'ānic text. Students are adviced to follow the method from the beginning for the writing of the Arabic script and try to complete the exercises by themselves without referring to the key. This method will create confidence in them.

I seize this oppurtunity to thank all those who have assisted me for this revised and enlarged edition. Mr. Muhammad Yunus Khan assisted immensly to this edition. I sincerely thank him for his dedication. I thank *al-Shaykh* Dr. Ijaz Mian for proof reading. I express my thanks to Mr. Akram Abdul Basit for redesigning the title cover of the book, Mr. M. Muntazir, Mr. Allaedin Adawi, Mr. Jasri Jamal and Mr Mohammed Salem for type setting.

Based on my 30 years of teaching experience of the course, I am optimistic that the course will go a long way in assisting the seekers of Qur'ānic Arabic to come closer to the language of the Qur'ān. An attempt will *in shā Allāh* be made to fulfil our promise to present both intermediary and advanced courses in the Qur'ānic Arabic.

Muhammad Ibrahim H.I. Surty
Tāj Cottage
Birmingham
Muḥarram 1428 A.H.

Transliteration Table

(Alif)	١			*(Fā')*	ف	f
(Hamzah)	ء	'		*(Qāf)*	ق	q
(Bā')	ب	b		*(Kāf)*	ك	k
(Tā')	ت	t		*(Lām)*	ل	l
(Thā')	ث	th		*(Mīm)*	م	m
(Jīm)	ج	j		*(Nūn)*	ن	n
(Ḥa')	ح	ḥ		*(Wāw)*	و	w
(Khā')	خ	kh		*(Hā')*	ه	h
(Dāl)	د	d		*(Yā')*	ي	y
(Dhāl)	ذ	dh		*Tā'Marbūṭah*	ة	ah/at
(Rā')	ر	r		*Tā'al-Ta'nīth*	ة	ah/at
(Zāy)	ز	z			ـَ	a
(Sīn)	س	s			ـِ	i
(Shīn)	ش	sh			ـُ ـَا	u ā
(Ṣād)	ص	ṣ			ـِي	ī
(Ḍād)	ض	ḍ			ـُو	ū
(Ṭā')	ط	ṭ			ـَىْ	ay
(Ẓā')	ظ	ẓ			ـَوْ	aw
('Ayn)	ع	'			آ	ā
(Ghayn)	غ	gh				

Abbreviation

ج	Plural
ح	*Ḥadīth*
م	*Mathal* (proverb)

Sing.	Singular
Pl.	Plural
P.	Page
Lit.	Literary
III M^1	Third Person Masculine singular
III M^2	Third Person Masculine dual
III M^{3+}	Third Person Masculine Plural
III F^1	Third Person Feminine singular
III F^2	Third Person Feminine dual
III F^{3+}	Third Person Feminine Plural
II M^1	Second Person Masculine singular
II M^2	Second Person Masculine Dual
II M^{3+}	Second Person Masculine Plural
II F^1	Second Person Feminine Singular
II F^2	Second Person Feminine Dual
II F^{3+}	Second Person Feminine Plural
I M^1	First Person Masculine Singular
I M^2	First Person Masculine Dual
I M^{3+}	First Person Masculine Plural
I F^1	First Person Feminine Singular
I F^2	First Person Feminine Dual
I F^{3+}	First Person Feminine Plural
AP$^{2-10}$	Active Participle. 2-10 indicates the numbers of the Derived Forms
PP$^{2-10}$	Passive Participle. 2-10 indicates the numbers of the Derived Forms
VN$^{2-10}$	Verbal Nouns. 2-10 indicates the numbers of the Derived Forms
N	Noun
SP	Sound plural
BP	Broken plural

Ad	Adverb
Adj	Adjective
CP	'Construct Phrase'
TA	Table A1-18
TB	Table B
TC	Table C
TD	Table D

وَمَا تَوْفِيقِي إِلَّا بِاللَّهِ 11:88

24

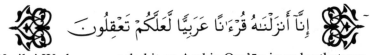

Verily! We have revealed it an Arabic Qur'ān in order that you
reflect (**12**:2)[*]

WHY QUR'ĀNIC ARABIC?

The Qur'ān is the first, the oldest and the most unique book
of the Arabic language. All schools of Muslim thought
throughout the ages have been unanimous in their acceptance
and veneration of its revealed Arabic text. It is the most
renowned masterpiece of the Arabic language and a classic the
world over. Its excellent and most appropriate wording, its
clarity, and well balanced verses, its impressive and inimitable
eloquence, its gentle and majestic style penetrate deep into a
person's heart stimulating age old human values and wisdom.
Its innate melody, beauty and grace provide a spiritually
soothing therapy and ensure tranquillity and peace of mind. The
Qur'ān without any dispute is the fountainhead of numerous
branches of Arabic literature and its decisive influence over the
origin and development of Arabic literature is incalculable. The
Qur'ānic text has been and remains the standard of excellence in
literary Arabic, and its authority continues to be decisive for
many linguistic disputes. Throughout the course of fourteen
centuries this set standard of excellence has never permitted any
deviation in literary Arabic at any time. As a result of this
unique consistency, literary Arabic has been closely associated
with the Qur'ānic standard. This standard provides ease and
comfort for scholars and students alike to comprehend what is
an extremely rich literature base. Perhaps in other languages of
the world this consistency does not exist.

Indeed, the idol worshippers of Makkah who were extremely
hostile to the mission of the Qur'ān did their best to safeguard
their religious and commercial interests. They clearly saw in the
success of this message the decline of their power and glory. At
that time they loved and respected the Arabic language and its
eloquence and regarded these as the criteria for the supremacy
of one tribe over another. They were however, helpless in face

---

[*] See also the Qur'ān, **13**:37; **15**:13; **16**:163; **26**:193-195; **27**:1; **36**:69; **39**:28;
41:3, 44; **44**:7; **43**:1-3; **46**:12

of the unique style and teachings of this Qur'ānic Arabic, unable despite their joint efforts and repeated invitations[1], of producing anything to match it.

History testifies that their efforts to prevent people from either listening to or reciting 'the marvelous message' of the Qur'ān proved futile. People were attracted towards the Qur'ān and most of them after their listening to or reciting of its passages were captivated by its marvel, wisdom and noble messages.[2]

A systematic campaign to codify the exegesis of the Qur'ān, Islamic sciences and various branches of Arabic language and literature began in the ninth century C.E[3]. This immense codification task required a large number of distinguished and competent scholars who had deep rooted grounding in Arabic and other related disciplines. The arena was also left open for non-Arabs to produce celebrated and authentic works on a variety of disciplines. These non-Arab Muslim scholars from the common strata of people from different parts of the Muslim world, had learned Arabic for the sake of the Qur'ān. Their deep rooted understanding of different branches of learning enabled them along with their Arab brothers to successfully accomplish this codification task and to become indisputable authorities on various branches of learning.

This systematic, painstaking endeavor and dedication has produced celebrated treatises on various disciplines. Each discipline witnessed a considerable number of books, which were later regarded as masterpieces and sources for related disciplines. Almost all treatises compiled during this period frequently quoted verses from the Qur'ān with great veneration and regarded it as the fountainhead of all learning. Had there been no al-Qur'ān, these remarkable pieces of Arabic literature would never have seen the light of day.

The Qur'ān constantly encourages human beings to use their wisdom and intellect for the conquest of the forces of nature for the service of mankind.[4] It invites *tadabbur* (contemplation), *tafaqquh* (comprehension), *tafakkur* (reflection) and *ta'aqqul* (seeking wisdom) from man such that he can observe how well

---

[1] The Qur'ān, **2**:23-24; **11**:13; **52**:34; **10**:37-38; **17**:88
[2] *ibid.* **72**:2
[3] Christian Era.
[4] The Qur'ān, **16**:2

26

measured and divinely guided the natural phenomena are.[5] According to the Qur'ān, knowledge and righteousness must go hand in hand.[6] It promises good rewards and high rank for those who possess knowledge coupled with faith and practice.[7]

It is evident from Qur'ānic principles that the progress of any person on earth lies in the knowledge of created things and in careful utilisation of the hidden forces of nature. This is possible only through exploration, observation and experimentation.

Inspired by this Qur'ānic concept, Muslims began their efforts to assimilate the ancient heritage of mankind. During the reigns of al-Ma'mūn and al-Mu'taṣim (ninth century C.E) many books dealing with philosophy, logic, ethics, alchemy, medicine, astrology and mathematics were translated into Arabic. The flexible nature of the language was invaluable in expressing both concrete and abstract ideas.

Muslim scholars preserved much of the Greek sciences which might otherwise have been lost or remained hidden for many centuries preceding the intellectual reawakening in Europe and the political superiority of the European powers.

Soon the process of dissemination in various disciplines connected with human progress began. Many Muslim scientists, philosophers, historians, geographers, astronomers, physicians, chemists, botanists, linguists, jurists etc. were born and through lifelong study, research, devotion and constant endeavor became universally acknowledged authorities in the knowledge of created things. They were able to utilise, through their researches, the hidden forces of nature for the service of mankind. They always found in the Qur'ān clear encouragement and support for their intellectual pursuits. They frequently quoted verses from the Qur'ān closely related to their disciplines in their epoch-making treatises and they made this remarkable contribution in the language of the Qur'ān, i.e. Arabic.

---

[5] *Ibid.* **16**:44; **13**:8; **8**:35; **36**:33-40. It is to be noted that out of 6,616 *āyāt*, verses of the Qur'ān, around 800 verses cover such themes.
[6] *Ibid.* **3**:16
[7] *Ibid.* **58**:2; **29**:20; **10**:101; **50**:6; **3**:190-191; **2**:169; **41**:52; **51**:20-22; **7**:179; **22**:40; **45**:13 and many more.

The richness of Muslims' intellectual and scientific contributions can be assessed from the fact that the process of compilation of Arabic manuscripts is not yet complete. Libraries in the Muslim world are busy in this exercise and every day new manuscripts are discovered. Thousands of important works have been lost during the vicissitude of time. It is to be noted that so far around 3 million Arabic manuscripts have been catalogued. Today, there is a tremendous scope for researches and scholars in this extremely rich field. Looking at the size of the Muslim contribution it is not an exaggeration to state that the world history of the medieval period will remain incomplete if the historian is either ignorant of or prejudiced against Arabic.

The Qur'ānic sciences have been able to preserve the vast and ancient world heritage in Arabic. The richness of this preservation can be assessed by the fact that commentaries written on the Old and New Testaments during the eighteenth, nineteenth, and twentieth centuries benefited considerably from Arabic material.

'Since the beginning of the nineteenth century', writes Alfred Guillaume, ' there has been constant recourse to Arabic for the explanation of rare words and forms in Hebrew; for Arabic, though more than a thousand years junior as a literary language, is the senior philosophically by countless centuries. Perplexing phenomena in Hebrew can often be explained as solitary and archaic survivals of forms, which are frequent and common in the cognate Arabic. Words and idioms, whose precise sense had been lost in Jewish tradition, receive a ready and convincing explanation from the same source. Indeed, no serious student of the Old Testament can afford to dispense with first-hand knowledge of Arabic. The pages of any critical commentary on the Old Testament will illustrate the depth of the Biblical exegesis owes to Arabic.'[8]

For an assessment of the outstanding characteristics of the Arabic language and its position among the existing and extinct major languages of the world it is essential to study briefly the development of the major languages.

---

[8] Alfred Guillaume in his preface to *The Legacy of Islam*, Oxford, 1931 p. ix.
S. Inayatullah, *Why We Learn the Arabic Language?*, Lahore, 1963, pp.12, 13. The first thesis on this theme was contributed by the Dutch scholar Albert Schulton, *The Use of Arabic in the Interpretation of Scripture*.

Arabic is the youngest language of the Semitic group. Other principal members are Hebrew, Aramaic, Syriac, Ugaritic, Accadian and the Semitic languages of Ethiopia, Tigre, Tigina, Amharic and Geez.

The Ugaritic and Acadian languages are long since dead. Aramaic, the lingua franca of Western Asia for many centuries, survives only in vestigial form, as does Syriac. Hebrew, one of the oldest members of the Semitic family, suffered from neglect for centuries before and after the Prophet Jesus (peace be upon him) and during the days of Greek and Roman power. After the rise of Christianity it was confined to a very small minority. The rise and spread of Islam almost eclipsed the language, which somehow remained alive for centuries and eventually found official shelter in Israel. Ethiopian Semitic languages remained confined to Ethiopia.

The major languages of other groups suffered the same fate as the Semitic group. Latin, which played such a decisive role in medieval Europe, is a rich classical language but it finds little modern colloquial usage. Greek, with its classical richness, was the most universal language of the ancient period but cannot successfully be maintained by the small state of Greece with its neighboring states busy patronising and elevating their own languages. The ancient Indian language of Sanskrit, like Latin, finds little use today.

In terms of classical importance, richness and continuous progress and prosperity from the time of its origin up to the present day only the Chinese language can be placed along side Arabic. But its influence is largely confined to China while Arabic is studied even in China by millions of Chinese Muslims and a considerable number of the Chinese business community.

This brief survey of the scope of the major languages of the world reveals the following facts:

(a) Most of the celebrated classical languages either perished or were eclipsed for centuries.
(b) A few classical languages witnessed political victimisation and managed to remain alive only among a few groups of people.
(c) When languages were eclipsed for several centuries their progress was adversely affected.

(d) Not a single language served as a lingua franca right from the time of its maturity till the present day.
(e) Even if a classical language has managed to stay alive from its origin till the present day it has nevertheless remained confined to a single nation and race.
(f) The progress of the Arabic language never eclipsed even for a single day right from the time of its maturity as a living language of the world and lingua franca of Muslims.

The grammatical structure of the Arabic language is highly developed, systematic and scientific. From the root, many words of different meanings can be easily coined by strict adherence to set etymological tables. For example, from the tri-consonant root k, t, b, which denotes the meaning of writing, many words can be formed with different meanings, such as *kataba* meaning to write; *kitāb* book; *kutubī* bookseller; *kuttāb* Qur'ānic school; *kitābah* script; *maktab* office; *miktab* type writer; *maktabah* library; *maktūb* written; *mukātabah* correspondence; *kātib* scribe; and in the passive form *kutiba*, it was written; plus many other examples. The grammatical structure of Arabic throughout fourteen hundred years has remained remarkably the same as displayed in the Qur'ān.

Most words in the Qur'ān provide a number of comprehensive meanings. It is humanly impossible to translate it faithfully into any other language because neither the exact meaning is expressed nor the comprehensive scope of the original word covered. Therefore the real charm and marvel always remains hidden, to be comprehended and properly enjoyed only in Arabic. Even celebrated translators of the Qur'ān always faced this problem and admitted their inability to render its meaning faithfully into any other language.

In a very concise way extensive and deep ideas and thoughts are manifested in the Qur'ān. Frequently, a word will open new horizons in the mind of the reader and the reader will feel neither heaviness nor frustration, but rather each repetition of the word increases his thought, bewilderment and faith.

Take for example the word *rabb* in the Qur'ān which means Nourisher, Sustainer, Guide, Protector, Lord, etc. The term *rubūbiyyah* in the opinion of some leading lexicographers, means 'to develop a thing from stage to stage in accordance with its inherent aptitudes, needs and its different aspects of existence and also in a manner affording the requisite freedom to attain its full stature.'[9]

Sadly, however, some educated Muslims in the modern world are content with poor Qur'ānic translations. This attitude can cause great deficiency in the comprehension of the true concepts of the Qur'ān and is indeed fraught with danger.

Human progress, success and prosperity at all times depends largely on the careful utilisation of space, time and energy. The Qur'ānic script on account of its unique nature economises considerably on all three accounts. Other scripts of the world's languages generally require independent consonants and vowels for the composition of a word. In Arabic script a word is composed by the reduction of most of its consonants into one third of its size. When for the composition of a word a double consonant is required in Arabic either a one third or full consonant accomplishes the function of a double consonant. For example if the word 'Muḥammad' is written in Roman script or any other script for that matter the consonants and vowels from M to D need to be full, but in Arabic script the consonants *mīm* will be used as one third, *ḥā'* as one third, next *mīm* will stand for two *mīm*s, and *dāl* independent. Again, the short vowels in Arabic are just brief signs, which are not required when the script is learnt properly. More than two thirds of the space, time and energy can be saved in writing the name 'Muḥammad' and this is equally true of many words in Arabic script.

Arabic script and its profusely rich vocabulary, has enriched some linguistically different languages of the world such as Persian, Urdu, Turkish, Malay, Berber, Hausa, Pushto and Javanese. '...Arabic is unique', writes a Western Professor of Arabic, Hamilton Gibb, 'in having carried over its super luxuriant vocabulary to play an important part in the literature of a highly developed civilization'. He further says '...an exceedingly rich development of language in the realm of material life. Not only do synonyms abound but every variety of natural phenomenon, however complex is expressed by a term proper to itself.'[10]

---

[9] Abul Kalam Azad, *The Tarjumān al-Qur'ān*, edited and translated by Sayed Abdul Latif. Vol. 1, *Sūrat al-Fātiḥah*, Sind Sagar Academy, Lahore 1968, p.19
[10] *Arabic Literature*, Oxford, 1963, p.4

Nobody can ever comprehend the inherent values of Muslim society, nor can the great variety of the elements of Islamic civilisation be fully understood without a sound knowledge of Arabic. Only through the medium of Arabic can one successfully establish links with the foundations of Islamic culture for the future progress and prosperity of Muslim society.

Furthermore Arabic is one of the leading languages of the world. It is one of the six official languages of the United Nations and many independent nations have accepted it as their official language. More than three-quarters of a billion multilingual Muslims throughout the world have deep veneration for it as the medium through which they can reach the principal sources of Islam - the Qur'ān and the *Sunnah* - which are such an integral part of their lives. They offer their Prayers in Qur'ānic Arabic which is the lingua franca of the Muslim world.*

* See DVD 1 episode no. 1 in *Learn Qur'ānic Script Rapidly*.

32

# Methodology

Since oil was discovered in the Muslim world, vigorous attempts have been made to learn the Arabic language for various reasons, whether for use in trade and commerce, industrial establishments, technological developments, job opportunities, news media, tourism and academic pursuits. This has resulted in the publication of a large number of books in different languages all aimed at teaching the Arabic language. These books are designed to meet the demands of the market. They use material that may well be relevant for the purpose of commerce, news media, and tourism, etc., but are so lacking in Qur'ānic vocabulary that they are of little use in this regard. It is very likely, therefore, that students may lose their enthusiasm for learning Qur'ānic Arabic.

Each aspect mentioned above has its own peculiar and distinctive feature, which must be taken into consideration before one embarks on teaching of Arabic. Teaching a language is a continuous process, in which the aims are developed from beginning to end in such a way that at the final stage the desired goal is achieved. A tourist, for example, is more interested in conversing in vocabulary, which may help him to locate places and manage his affairs during his short stay in a foreign Arab land. He is not concerned about the marvels of the Arabic language manifested in the Qur'ān and *Ḥadīth* literature. Similarly, one who is interested only in industrial or commercial ventures will confine his language to these fields.

From the aforesaid it follows that there is a great need to teach Arabic in a way which will help in the comprehension of the Qur'ān.

The greatest difficulty which beginners studying the Arabic language encounter is the recognition of various forms of nouns and verbs. Nouns exist in three numbers, e.g. singular, dual and plural; two genders, masculine and feminine. The dual as found in Arabic is usually something with which students are not acquainted because it does not exist in most other languages. The Plural in Arabic is formed by adopting different methods, and nouns in all three exist in the nominative, accusative and genitive cases. If nouns and pronouns in their singular, dual and plural numbers, two genders and then three cases are presented simultaneously, it causes confusion in the minds of the beginners and they tend to lose interest in learning Arabic.

The same is true for verbs. Again there are three numbers: singular, dual and plural, two genders: masculine and feminine; two tenses: used for first person, second person and third person. Furthermore verbs are either active or passive, and have derived forms. Naturally, if all these patterns are presented together, then it will create confusion, especially for beginners. Conversely this method may not be very effective for those whose mother tongue is Arabic; they may not find these variations difficult in view of their familiarity with them. But certainly for beginners it can be something of a maze.

In view of the problems identified above, the present course is divided into four phases. The First Phase deals exclusively with the letters of the Arabic alphabet and Qur'ānic script. The Second Phase gradually introduces in The First Form of the verbs 'Five Pillars ' e.g. (1) Perfect (2) Imperfect (3) Verbal Nouns (4) Active Participles (5) Passive Participles. These are deliberately called 'Pillars' because of their extensive use in the text. In view of their very good effects for rapid comprehension of Arabic, Table 5 in appendix E has been presented which includes most of the triliteral verbs both sound and weak used in the first seven lessons in 'Five Pillars'. If the readers refer this table when the 'Pillars' are introduced in the lessons through graded progression, experience suggests, that they will find very useful. Table 6 in the appendix F presents a table which includes most of the Derived Forms used in the lessons 8-16 through graded progression. This table will assist greatly towards the comprehension of the 'Five Pillars' in the Derived Forms. Teachers should try to photocopy these two sets of tables on two different colour cards. As the roots are presented in numerical order in both tables it will be easier to refer to these roots in the class-room encouraging students to comprehend 'Five Pillars'. The Third Phase introduces the Dual and other themes and the Fourth Phase deals with the Plural and other themes. In the Third and the Fourth Phases while introducing the Derived Forms of the verbs gradually the 'Five Pillars' are also presented in each Derived Form and in such a way that students can easily identify them and recognise their roots. For this purpose Tables B, C and D in the Appendix are frequently referred to. At the final stage the passive forms in the Perfect and in the Imperfect are presented. Experience suggests that these 'Five Pillars' both in the First Form and the Derived Forms of the verbs help students to comprehend the text, to build confidence and enable them to construct many new words and employ these in sentences. The *Amr*, the Imperative, and the *Nahy*, the Prohibitive, are used frequently in the Qur'ān. These are not however used in the earlier lessons because their formation requires the comprehension of the Imperfect Jussive form; in the graded progression afforded by this course this cannot be taught in the earlier lessons.

The Basic structure of Qur'ānic Arabic

For effective teaching of the basic structures of Qur'ānic Arabic, three areas of work can be distinguished;
1. Vocabulary
2. The Text and Grammatical Themes
3. Exercises

1. Vocabulary

The right vocabulary for this course comes, necessarily, from the Qur'ān itself. A little over one thousand words from the Qur'ān are taught, their selection being determined by (a) the frequency of their occurrence in the Qur'ān; (b) their effectiveness for explaining the grammatical themes: and (c) their suitability for developing familiarity with the subject matter of the text. As to the rate of assimilation: experience has shown that students can retain an average of twelve words per hour of teaching.

Initial lessons incorporate carefully selected and easy words, which help students to comprehend the grammatical rules, which can be extremely useful for the future development of the text. For example, in Lessons 1 and 2 such words are selected which represent through the letters of their beginning all 28 letters of the Arabic alphabet and which help to learn the Sun and the Moon letters when these nouns are definite. (See Units 7 and 8).

In view of the limited time, space and energy all modern words and terminology which have no relevance for the comprehension of the Qur'ān are avoided. For example modern words such as *sayyārah* (car), *ṭayyārah* (plane), *maṭār* (airport), *jawāz al-safar* (passport), *jumruk* (customs), *ta'shīrah* (visa), *hātif* (telephone), *barīd* (post) and the like which cannot be found in the Qur'ān, can be conveniently learnt when more time is available. In any case the basic structure of literary Arabic is absolutely Qur'ānic.

A good teacher is familiar with the basic problems, aptitude and background knowledge of his students. In order to create confidence among them, their existing knowledge of Arabic must be fully explored and carefully utilised. Muslim students who practice Islam are quite familiar with certain Arabic words, phrases and sentences frequently used at home and in society generally. Such Arabic material must be presented to them in a compiled form to stimulate their interest in learning the Arabic language.

For example: *Bismillāh irrahmānir raḥīm* (in the name of Allah the Merciful the Mercy Giving). *Lāilāha illallāhu Muḥammadur Rasūlullāh* (There is no god except Allah, Muḥammad is the Messenger of Allah); *Subḥānallāh* (Glory be to Allah); *Alḥamdulillāh* (Praise be to Allah); *Allāhu Akbar* (Allah is Great); *In shā' Allāh* (Allah willing); *Māshā Allāh* (what Allah wills); *Astaghfirullāh* (I seek forgiveness from Allah); *Asslāmu 'alaykum* (peace be on you); *al-Ḥayāt* (life); *al-Mawt* (death); *Kitāb* (book); *Qalam* (pen); *al-Jannah* (Paradise); *al-Nār* (Hell); *al-Qiyāmah* (the Day of Judgment); *Malā'ikah* (angels); *Rūḥ* (spirit); *as-Ṣalāh* (Prayer); *az-Zakāh* (Welfare due) and many others. Furthermore there are a few local languages spoken by a large part of the multilingual Muslim world, which incorporate an extremely rich vocabulary of Arabic words and usages. Prominent among these are Persian, Urdu, Turkish, Hausa, Swahili, Malay, Berber and Javanese.

A few examples are provided from the Hausa language. Similar examples can be cited from other languages mentioned above.

(a) Arabic words used in Hausa without any alteration in composition and meaning:

Hausa	Arabic	Meaning
sa'a	*sa'ah*	hour
amana	*amānah*	trust
kabila	*qabīlah*	tribe
nasiha	*naṣīhah*	advice
dunya	*dunyā*	world

(b) Some phonological differences are made in Arabic words to suit Hausa pronunciation but the meaning remains the same:

Hausa	Arabic	Meaning
masifa	*musibah*	calamity
aljihu	*al-jayb*	the pocket
alkama	*qamḥ*	wheat
allo	*lawḥ*	board
alura	*ibrah*	needle

(c) The origin of the word is Arabic but is used to convey a different meaning:

Hausa	Meaning	Arabic	Meaning
al majiri	beggar	*al-muhājir*	immigrant
ajali	death	*ajal*	instant of death
albashi	salary	*al-ma'āsh*	subsistence
kalu-bale	challange	*qālū balā*	they said yes

Usage of some words is localised, while the basic form of some other words is slightly modified to suit the requirements of the local language. If all such words are properly classified and presented to the students, this exercise will encourage them. They will realise that they are not learning Arabic from scratch but that there is a concrete foundation on which they can endeavor to construct an edifice.

2. *The Text and Grammatical Themes*

Systematic presentation and very carefully graded progression are the keys for effectiveness with the text and grammar. Each "theme" is taught as a short unit (represented as a distinct numbered unit in the teaching material), and is comprised of an extensive text. The illustrative examples from the text are analysed fully. Considerable attention has been given to the way in which the text revises and recapitulates the work that precedes it. No grammatical theme, as far as possible, is presented in the text, which is neither taught before nor fully explained. The purpose for the selection from the Qur'ān is to emphasise the grammatical themes so far presented. In such selection, other Qur'ānic literary aspects are not presented at this elementary stage. These will be covered, *in shā' Allāh* in the intermediary and advanced courses. What is required at this stage is to find a few examples for grammatical themes and comprehend them. For example, all lessons in Phase Two are strictly confined to the singular and the First Form of the verb. No trace can be found of the Dual, Plural and any Derived Form of those verbs; it is as if at that stage they do not exist. The purpose for adopting this method is to provide the students with the opportunity to comprehend the singular forms and other themes presented in this Phase fully, to remove their fear and develop confidence in them towards learning a new language. Experience suggests that students at all levels take a keen interest in learning the language.

Arabic is a systematic language, which is governed by grammatical rules. Much effort has gone into forming the grammatical rules for each unit and these are presented in numerical order throughout the work.

Interrogation is one of the most common features of the Qur'ānic text. There are some one thousand examples of such constructions in the Qur'ān. It is introduced in the text from the beginning in the following gradual stages.

i. *mā, a, hal, man*
ii. *bimā, mimmā, mimman, fīmā, limā, liman, 'alāmā, min ayna*
iii. *kayfa*
iv. *amā, alaysa, alam, etc.*

Emphasis is another important feature of the Qur'ān. There are over five thousand occasions where emphasis is employed in the Qur'ān. These are also presented in the text gradually.

3. *Exercises*

Exercises are essentially a supplement to the taught lesson. They follow on from, and rehearse the theme taught beforehand and already practiced through drill in class. The broad principles followed in the exercise material are:

(a) not to transgress the boundaries established by the unit divisions of the course.

(b) first to consolidate, then to extend.

Effectively by the end of this course of exercises students will be equipped to write Arabic albeit, always, as an aid to reading the Qur'ān.

The text and the method are the backbone of this course. The result is a course providing a systematic presentation and graded progression of the grammatical themes through the vehicle of the text in ninety contact hours. It is also suitable for students of different age groups, levels and abilities. Over the years considerable improvements have been made both in the teaching method and the text after making careful assessment of students' progress, their fears and anxieties, difficulties and enquiries. All these factors have been taken into account for the purpose of this course.

The foregoing methodology for teaching Arabic for the comprehension of the Qur'ān is only a skeleton. It is for the teachers to provide flesh and blood. The more they work the healthier the body they make. Success will depend largely on how effectively the glossary, the themes, the text, and the exercises are introduced and taught.

Guidelines for Beginners

- Phase One is based on the Qur'ānic script. Arabic text is presented systematically in graded progression and in 13 themes, which include 18 exercises. The text is articulated by an Arab *Qārī* providing students an opportunity to correct the articulations while learning the script. There is great need to take maximum advantage because correct articulation is one of the essential requirements of the Qur'ānic sciences.

- The transliteration system presented in the transliteration table is strictly adhered to in this book. This can enable the beginners to recognise each Arabic consonants. An attempt is made to provide in the appendix a key in Arabic for exercises 1–18 where only transliteration is provided and the beginner is asked to write in Arabic. This may enable beginners to assess.

- In Phase Two through graded progression nouns, pronouns and verbs are presented in singular form only. It is advisable not to incline towards comprehension of dual and plural in nouns, pronouns and verbs at this stage.

- Try to concentrate on the grammar which is introduced through the vehicle of designed text and from lesson five onwards it includes selected text from the Qur'ān.

- The course is divided into 63 units which incorporate 93 grammatical rules. As the course is closely knitted each unit must be fully comprehended. All rules are analysed with the examples taken from the lessons. Negligence or weakness in any unit may hinder further progress.

- Practical efforts should be made to memorise new words as soon as the reader is acquainted with them. If these are deferred for some reason, their number will increase and this can become threatening and compel the beginner to give up the course.

- Each lesson includes a vocabulary. For self assessment of the spelling of Arabic words cover the column in Arabic and write Arabic words by referring to the translation in English.

- Try to work in the exercises provided at the end of each lessons. A key to exercises 1 to 35 has been provided in appendixs 9 I. This will grant extra strength in the comprehension of elementary Arabic, consolidate confidence and remove anxieties and fear.
- For language learning it is always better not to remain confined to the texts provided in the lessons. It is always beneficial to construct new sentences through the vehicle of gradually introduced grammar and vocabulary. Arabic grammar is fortunately well structured, systematic and scientific. This special feature of the language compliments all such efforts.
- The language can be learned either through the vehicle of text or grammar. In this course both venues are kept wide open. The designed text is grammar oriented and basic grammatical rules are also presented simultaneously, both are complementary to each other.
- Commencing from lesson 2 based on graded progression 'Five Pillars' e.g. Perfect, Imperfect, Verbal Noun, Active Participle and Passive Particle are presented in the First Form covering both sound and weak roots refer table D in the appendix. 'Five Pillars' are very important. Further progress in Phase Three and Four is focused on these pillars. Derived forms in graded progression from II to X are presented starting from lesson 8 to 16. 'Five Pillars', are judiciously used in all derived forms refer table E in the appendix. At an advanced stage the passive forms of Perfect and Imperfect are introduced. There is great need to comprehend the derived forms and their significance because these are frequently used in the text.
- Always consult a dictionary especially to learn the wide range of derivations from the root as well as different shades of meaning words provide which can be used in different contexts. For beginners one of the best dictionaries is Hans Wehr, *A Dictionary of Modern Written Arabic* edited by J. M. Cown, Otto Harrass Owitz, Wiesbaden, 1966. Some of the prominent patterns used in this dictionary are incorporated in the book. This can facilitate comprehension.

- From the beginning, it is beneficial to develop the habit of computing as many words as possible from the root. This practice will accelerate the learning process.
- In Arabic each word has its own distinct characteristic, which needs to be identified in terms of its formation, which is either based on the responsible internal or external factors. The more a person comprehends the grammar the more it is possible for him/her to realise such change.
- Never memorise the translation of sentences without comprehending the words which the sentence is composed of. Try to avoid writing the translation in between the space of Arabic text. This may create a false image for the comprehension of the text.
- It is better to avoid your own free translation of the quotations to the Qur'ān. Because only such pieces of text are selected which are complimentary to the progress so far made in grammar. Since the Qur'ān is the Word of Allah, it is safe to rely on translations from those scholars who are knowledgeable in Qur'ānic sciences and again such translations are contextual. The principal purpose for the use of selected Qur'ānic text is to consolidate the base of the grammar. At this elementary stage it is difficult for the beginners to comprehend the literary *I'jāz* inimitability of Qur'ānic Arabic.
- Consult the translation of the text in English in the appendix.
- In the course all attempts have been made to make the foundation strong and enable the beginner to comprehend, with the help of a dictionary, unseen Arabic texts. The greatest advantage is that the Qur'ān has miraculously set a standard for Arabic and even enabled Arab nations to accept one language and that is Arabic.
- Try to reflect over the grammatical structures you may have already studied in your private recitation of the Qur'ān. This may increase your confidence and enthusiasm to learn more.
- It has been observed that many beginners do not comprehend grammatical terms. Referring to

42

grammatical terms in the appendix 5 can solve such difficulties.

- The selected Qur'ānic script will assist beginners in their recitation of the Qur'ān according to '*ilm al-tajwīd*, the science of reciting the Qur'ān.

- The designed Arabic text and the selection of the texts from the Qur'ān, the *Sunnah* Arab proverbs and wise sayings through graded progression provide a unique opportunity not only to learn the Arabic language but to open a flood gate of Islamic vision and ethics, noble values and profound thoughts for character building. The deeper reflection in these aspects shall be extremely fruitful for the beginner.

(**15: 9**)

QUR'ĀNIC ARABIC SCRIPT

(a) The Formation of the Arabic Alphabet

The familiarisation of the following shapes can assist a beginner before he/she embarks on learning the Arabic alphabet.

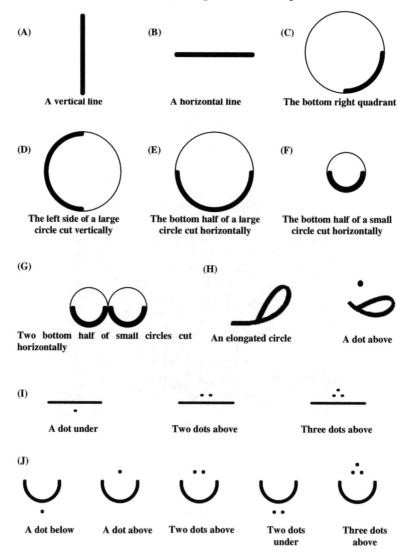

(A) A vertical line

(B) A horizontal line

(C) The bottom right quadrant

(D) The left side of a large circle cut vertically

(E) The bottom half of a large circle cut horizontally

(F) The bottom half of a small circle cut horizontally

(G) Two bottom half of small circles cut horizontally

(H) An elongated circle   A dot above

(I) A dot under   Two dots above   Three dots above

(J) A dot below   A dot above   Two dots above   Two dots under   Three dots above

The Arabic alphabet makes use of twenty eight consonants. All consonants are formed of a circle or a straight line or a combination thereof. These twenty eight characters can be divided (see Table b) into eight groups A - H and a further ninth group miscellaneous. In A - H the basic character of the consonants remains the same. With the addition of a dot or dots a number of additional consonants can be formed.

It has been established through experience that for rapid learning all Arabic consonants should be recognized by applying a short Arabic vowel *fatḥah* ‒ a. For example the consonant ب *Bā* hall be articulated as *Ba'*.

From group A to F the principal shape of the consonants remains the same in each group, they however, change their character with the application of dot/dots. Their divisions in three groups assist a beginner to recognize them easily, articulate them and finally write them.

Group A

Group A includes three consonants. These are formed with a horizontal line and two short vertical lines.

 From right to left

(i) A dot under the long horizontal line forms the consonant: *ba'* (like *b* in baby).

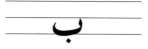

(ii) Two dots above the long horizontal line forms the consonant: *ta'* (like t in tree).

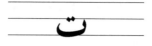

(iii) Three dots above the horizontal line form the consonant: *tha'* (no equivalent can be found in English, although the pronunciation of *th* in *thorn* and *thumb* does assist somewhat.

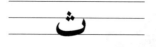

Exercise No. 1

(1) Read:

(2) Write in Arabic:

   ba', tha', ta', tha', ba', ta'

Group B

Group B includes three consonants. These are formed with a long horizontal line (____) and a long semicircle.

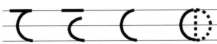

(i)   When a dot is added to the middle of the semicircle in the above mentioned character it becomes *jīm*. (for the convenience of reading Arabic script it may be pronounced *ja'* as with the letter *j* in the English *John* or *Jack*).

(ii)   If the above mentioned character appears without a dot it should be taken as the consonant: *ḥa'* (There is no equivalent in English. *Ḥa'* is pronounced by means of a strong sound from the middle of the throat.)

(iii)   A dot above the long horizontal line forms: *kha'* (The pronunciation is close to *ch* in Scottish *loch*).

Exercise No. 2

(1)   Read:

(2)   Write in Arabic:

        ḥa', ta', tha', ja', kha', ba', ḥa', tha', ta'

Group C

Group C contains two consonants. A short horizontal line and a short vertical line meeting to form an angle.

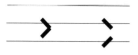

(i)   When this character appears without a dot it should be taken as: *da'* (softer than the English *d*).

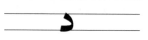

(ii)   A dot above the consonant makes: *dha'*
(there is no equivalent in English).

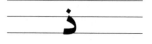

Exercise No. 3

(1)   Read:

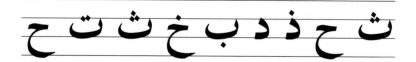

(2)   Write in Arabic:

dha', ta', da', ḥa', tha', kha', dha', da', tha', kha'

Group D

Group D includes two consonants.
A quadrant

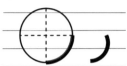

(i)   When it is without a dot it is: *ra'* (like the *r* in road).

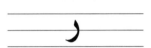

(ii)   A dot above the *ra'* forms: *za'* (like the *z* in *zenith*).

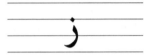

Exercise No. 4

(1)   Read:

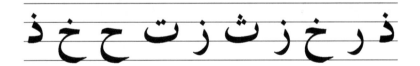

(2)   Write in Arabic:

za', ḥa', da', dha', ra', ta', tha', ja', ba', kha', za'

49

Group E

Group E includes two consonants. Two small semicircles joined together (ᴗᴗ) with a large semicircle.

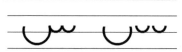

(i)   When this character appears without a dot it is: *sīn* (like the *ss* in *kiss*). [*sa'*]

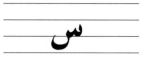

(ii)   Three dots above two small semicircles will form: *shīn* (like the *s* in *sugar* and the *sh* in *wash* or *brush*). [*sha'*]

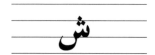

Exercise No. 5

(1) Read:

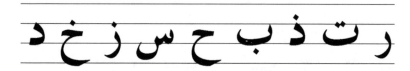

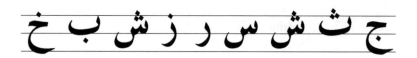

(2)   Write in Arabic:

kha', sa', sha', ba', da', tha', dha', ba', ḥa', za', sha', ba', dha', ta', sa', sha', ḥa', kha', ja', ra',

Group F

Group F contains two consonants. An elongated circle ()
and a large semicircle joins it.

(i)   When the above character appears without a dot it is: *ṣād*
      (no English equivalent) [*ṣa'*]

(ii) A dot above the circle makes: *ḍād*
      (again, there is no English equivalent) [*ḍā'*].

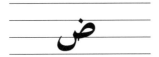

Exercise No. 6

(1)   Read:

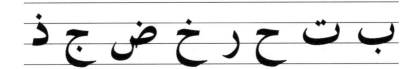

(2)   Write in Arabic:

> *sa', ṣa', da', ḍa', ta', tha', ja', ḥa', ba', kha', sha',
> dha', ra', za', tha', ḥa', kha', ra', za', ja', da',
> dha', ṣa', ḍa', sa', sha', ba', ta'*

51

Group G

Group G includes two consonants. A circle () and a long vertical line.

(i)   When the character is without a dot it is: [ṭa']
        (ṭa' is pronounced with a long tongue.)
        (There is no English equivalent.)

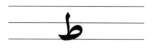

(ii)   A dot above the circle forms: [ẓa']
        (ẓa' is pronounced with a long tongue).
        (There is no English equivalent.)

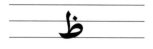

Exercise No. 7

(1) Read:

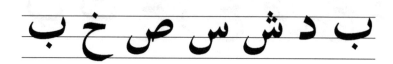

(2)   Write in Arabic:
        ḍa', ra', za', ba', ta', sa', sha', kha', tha', ja', ḥa',
        ẓa', ṭa'

Group H

Group H contains two consonants. A small semicircle (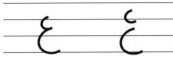) joins with a large semicircle.

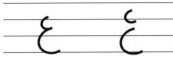

(i)   When the character appears without a dot it is: *'ayn* [*'a*] (close to the pronunciation of ح without aspirate).

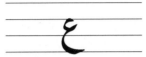

(ii)   A dot above the semicircle forms: *ghayn* [*gha'*] (the sound is close to the sound made when one is gargling).

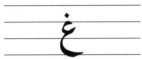

Exercise No. 8

(1) Read:

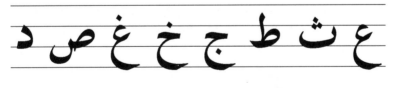

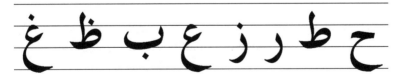

(2)   Write in Arabic:

ta', ba', tha', gha', da', dha', sa' sha', ṭa', ẓa', ḥa', za', ḍa', ṭa', kha'

Group Miscellaneous

Group M includes the remaining ten consonants. Although these consonants are not similar to each other, they are formed with a circle and a line.

(1)   A long vertical line forms *Alif.* It does not provide any sound.

ا

(2)   A long horizontal line and a long vertical line meet at point (⎣) in the centre, a small semicircle (ﻉ) joined with a small horizontal line (ﻉ forms: *kāf* [ka']
(like the *k* in *yoke*).

ك

(3)   A long vertical line continues in a semicircle to form: *lām* [*la'*] (like the *l* in *umbrella*).

ل

(4)   A small extended circle (ﻭ) is joined with a long horizontal line and a dot above the circle forms: *fa'* (like the *f* in *fig*).

ف

(5)   A small circle (O) is joined with a large semicircle and two dots above the small circle forms: *qāf* [*qa'*]

ق

(There is no English equivalent.)

(6)   Two small circles make: *ha'* (like the *h* in *hurry*).

ه

(7) A small elongated circle (م) and a large vertical line form: *mīm* [*ma'*] (like the *m* in *mother*).

م

(8) A small elongated circle (ـو) and a quadrant form: *wāw* [*wa'*] (like the *w* in *work*). It is written as it is pronounced by making both lips round and then opening them.

و

(9) A large semicircle and a dot in its center make: *nūn* [*na'*] (like the *n* in *noon*).

ن

(10) A small semicircle and a large semicircle and two dots under the large semicircle form: *ya'* (like the *y* in *yes*).

ي

Exercise No 9.

(1)   Read:

م ح ل ج ق ث ك ت ف ب

ا ي ز ه ر و ذ د ن خ

ط ي ه و م ن ف ك ل ق

(2)   Write in Arabic:

fa', ka', qa', la', ma', na', wa', ḥa', ya', 'a, 'a, gha', ṭa', ẓa', ṣa', ḍa', ta', tha', kha', ha', wa'

The Alphabet

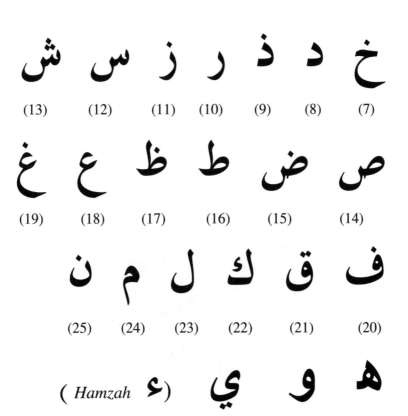

ح ج ث ت ب ا

(6)   (5)   (4)   (3)   (2)   (1)

ش س ز ر ذ د خ

(13)   (12)   (11)   (10)   (9)   (8)   (7)

غ ع ظ ط ض ص

(19)   (18)   (17)   (16)   (15)   (14)

ن م ل ك ق ف

(25)   (24)   (23)   (22)   (21)   (20)

ه و ي (ء *Hamzah*)

(28)   (27)   (26)

(1) *Alif*	(2) *Bā*	(3) *Tā*	(4) *Thā*	(5) *Jim*
(6) *Hā*	(7) *Khā*	(8) *Dāl*	(9) *Dhāl*	(10) *Rā*
(11) *Zāy*	(12) *Sīn*	(13) *Shīn*	(14) *Ṣād*	(15) *ḍād*
(16) *Ṭā'*	(17) *Ẓā'*	(18) *'Ayn*	(19) *Ghayn*	(20) *Fā*
(21) *Qāf*	(22) *Kāf*	(23) *Lām*	(24) *Mīm*	(25) *Nūn*
	(26) *Hā'*	(27) *Wāw*	(28) *Yā'*	

Hamzah gives a sound when one of three *ḥarakāt* is placed (*fatḥa*, *ḍammah* or *kasrah*). These three *ḥarakāt* are used in Arabic as short vowels.

(b) Alphabet and Articulation (places of Origin)

Group I	*Al-Ḥurūf al-Hawā'iyyah* The Areial letters	(1)	‍ـَا
		(2)	ـِ ي
		(3)	ـُ وْ

(1)	a	
(2)	i	From the cavity of the mouth and throat the air comes out while making the required sound.
(3)	u	

II	*Al-Ḥurūf al-Shafawiyyah* The Labial letters	(1)	ب
		(2)	م
		(3)	و
		(4)	ف

(1)   (*Ba'*) When the wet portion of the lips meet and then separate while pronouncing the letter.

(2)   (*Ma'*) When the dry portions of the lips meet and then separate while pronouncing the letter.

(3)   (*Wāw*) When the sides of the lips meet, making a round shape. The round shape is retained while pronouncing the letter.

(4)   (*Fā'*) When the upper incisors hold the wet portion of the lower lip and the incisors are released while pronouncing the letter.

III	*Al-Ḥurūf al Ḥalqiyyah* The Gutteral letters	(1)	ء ه
		(2)	ع ح
		(3)	غ خ

(1) (*'A, Hā'*) The sound comes from the bottom of the throat (larynx).

(2) (*'Ayn, Ḥā'*) The sound comes from the middle portion of the throat.

(3) (*Ghayn, Khā'*) The sound comes from the upper portion of the throat.

IV	*Al-Ḥurūf al-Lahawīyah* The Velar letters	(1)	ق
		(2)	ك

(1) (*Qāf*) By blocking the passage of the throat with the dead end of the tongue touching the opposite portion of the hard palate.

(2) (*Kāf*) The dead end of the tongue touches the portion of the hard palate at a slight distance to the portion for *Qāf*.

V	*Al--Ḥurūf al-Shajriyyah* The Orificial letters.	ي، ش، ج

(*Jīm, Shīn, Yā'*) The middle portion of the tongue touches the opposite portion of the hard palate.

VI	*Al-Ḥurūf al Dhawlaqiyyah* The Liquids	(1)	ر
		(2)	ن
		(3)	ل

(1)   (*Rāʾ*) The tip of the tongue touches the opposite portion of the hard palate.

(2)   (*Nūn*) The tip of the tongue touches the portion between the root of the upper incisor and the place of origin of the letter *Rāʾ*.

(3)   (*Lām*) The upper portion of the left side of the tongue touches the root of the upper incisors.

VII	*Al-Ḥurūf al-Niṭʿiyyah* The Interdental letters	ط, ت ،د

(*Ṭāʾ, Dāl, Tāʾ*) The tip of the tongue touches the root of the upper incisors.

VIII	*Al-Ḥurūf al-Lithawiyyah* The Gingival letters	ظ ذ، ث

(*Thāʾ, Dhāl, Ẓāʾ*) The tip of the tongue touches the edge of the upper incisors.

IX	*Al-Ḥurūf al-Asaliyyah* The Apical letters	ص، ز، س

(*Sīn, Zāʾ, Ṣād*) The tip of the tongue touches the root of the lower incisors.

| X | *Ḥarf al-Ḍād*
The letter *Ḍād* | ض |

(*Ḍād*) The lower portion of the twisted left side of the tongue touches the edges of the upper left molars.

Example Analysis:

Group I:

These are long vowels which should be stretched to the measure of two *Ḥarakah*.

Group II - X:

The most suitable method for familiarizing and recognizing the correct *makhraj*, the place of origin, of a letter is to keep it *sākin*, quiescent, and add before it *Alif maftūḥ*, *Alif* having *fatḥah*. All the alphabet mentioned in groups II - X in the table are kept *sākin*, quiescent, for this purpose.[*]

---

[*] For the articulation of all Arabic consonants and for the pronunciation of their original sound see my work, *A Course in 'Ilm al-Tajwīd. The Science of Reciting The Qur'ān*, Islamic Foundation, Leicester, Reprint, 2005 with three audio CDS, pp.43-56. This course is comprised of a book and two audiocassettes. The book includes exercises for the pronunciation of the Arabic alphabet and these are recited on the audiocassettes.

Group I

ـَ ا   ـِ ي   ـُ وْ

Group II

أَبْ أَبْ أَبْ			أَمْ أَمْ أَمْ		
أَفْ أَفْ أَفْ			أَوْ أَوْ أَوْ		
أَوْ أَفْ أَوْ أَفْ			أَبْ أَمْ أَبْ أَمْ		
أَبْ أَوْ أَمْ أَفْ			أَبْ أَوْ أَمْ أَفْ		

Group III

ءَ ءَ ءَ	أَهْ أَهْ أَهْ
ءَ أَهْ ءَ أَهْ	ءَ أَهْ ءَ أَهْ
أَعْ أَعْ أَعْ	أَحْ أَحْ أَحْ
أَعْ أَحْ أَعْ أَحْ	ءَ أَعْ ءَ أَعْ
أَهْ أَحْ أَهْ أَحْ	ءَ أَحْ ءَ أَحْ
أَغْ أَغْ أَغْ	أَخْ أَخْ أَخْ
أَغْ أَخْ أَغْ أَخْ	أَهْ أَخْ أَهْ أَخْ

Group IV

أَقْ أَقْ أَقْ

أَقْ أَكْ أَقْ أَكْ

أَكْ أَكْ أَكْ

أَكْ أَقْ أَكْ أَقْ

Group V

أَجْ أَجْ أَجْ

أَيْ أَيْ أَيْ

أَشْ أَيْ أَجْ

أَشْ أَشْ أَشْ

أَيْ أَجْ أَشْ

أَيْ أَشْ أَجْ

Group VI

أَرْ أَرْ أَرْ

أَلْ أَلْ أَلْ

أَلْ أَنْ أَرْ

أَنْ أَنْ أَنْ

أَلْ أَنْ أَرْ

أَلْ أَرْ أَنْ

Group VII

أَذْ أَذْ أَذْ

أَتْ أَتْ أَتْ

أَذْ أَتْ أَطْ

أَطْ أَطْ أَطْ

أَطْ أَذْ أَتْ

أَتْ أَطْ أَذْ

Group VIII

أَذْ	أَذْ	أَذْ		أَتْ	أَتْ	أَتْ
أَظْ	أَظْ	أَظْ		أَتْ	أَذْ	أَظْ
أَذْ	أَظْ	أَتْ		أَظْ	أَتْ	أَذْ

Group IX

أَسْ	أَسْ	أَسْ		أَزْ	أَزْ	أَزْ
أَصْ	أَصْ	أَصْ		أَسْ	أَزْ	أَصْ
أَزْ	أَصْ	أَسْ		أَصْ	أَسْ	أَزْ

GroupX

أَضْ	أَضْ	أَضْ		أَضْ	أَضْ	أَضْ

Exercise

أَبْ	أَتْ	أَثْ	أَجْ	أَحْ	أَخْ	أَدْ
أَذْ	أَرْ	أَزْ	أَسْ	أَشْ	أَصْ	أَضْ
أَطْ	أَظْ	أَعْ	أَغْ	أَفْ	أَقْ	أَكْ
أَلْ	أَمْ	أَنْ	أَوْ	أَهْـ	أَيْ	ءَ

أَطْ	أَهْ	أَبْ	أَرْ	أَعْ	أَقْ	أَجْ
أَوْ	أَعْ	أَكْ	أَيْ	أَضْ	أَسْ	أَثْ
أَمْ	أَحْ	أَشْ	أَصْ	أَظْ	أَتْ	أَلْ
أَخْ	أَفْ	أَغْ	أَزْ	أَذْ	أَدْ	أَنْ

وَبَشِّرِ الصَّابِرِينَ 2:155

(c) *Ḥarakāt*, *Short Vowels*

(i) *Fatḥah* [_́ (a) as the articulation of *u* in shut]: A flat sign

above the consonant adds a flat sound to the original sound
of the consonant.
For the sake of rapid progress in the reading of Arabic script
all consonants are introduced with the addition of this flat
sound.

Practice Text:

، أَ ، تَ ، بَ ، طَ ، غَ ، ظَ ، عَ ، ضَ ، صَ ، شَ

قَ ، فَ ، رَ ، ذَ ، زَ ، دَ ، ثَ ، جَ ، خَ ، لَ ، مَ ، نَ ، حَ

(ii) *Kasrah* [_ (i) as *i* in tin]: A sign placed under the
consonant brings the original sound of the consonant down.

جِ	بِ	قِ	عِ	سِ	طِ	دِ	كِ	تِ
(ji)	*(bi)*	*(qi)*	*('i)*	*(si)*	*(ṭi)*	*(di)*	*(ki)*	*(ti)*

فِ	يِ	حِ	غِ	ثِ
(fi)	*(yi)*	*(ḥi)*	*(ghi)*	*(thi)*

Practice Text:

لِ ، رِ ، ضِ ، نِ ، مِ ، ذِ ، شِ ، ظِ ، صِ

صِ ، ءِ ، خِ ، زِ ، هِ

(iii) *Ḍammah* [$\_$ (u) as *u* in bull]: This mini (*wāw*) above the consonant raises the original sound of the consonant up.

شُ   حُ   ظُ   فُ   كُ   طُ   عُ   صُ   بُ

(shu)   (ḥu)   (ẓu)   (fu)   (ku)   (ṭu)   ('u)   (ṣu)   (bu)

مُ   ثُ   ذُ

(mu)   (thu)   (dhu)

Practice Text:

صُ   سُ   رُ   ذُ   زُ   دُ   بُ   تُ   أُ

يُ   هُ   وُ   نُ   لُ   قُ   غُ   طُ   ضُ

Exercise No. 11

(1) Read:

سُ سِ سَ   عُ عِ عَ   قُ قِ قَ   بُ بِ بَ   جُ جِ جَ

يُ يِ يَ   فُ فِ فَ   كُ كِ كَ   دُ دِ دَ   طُ طِ طَ

ظُ ظِ ظَ   صُ صِ صَ   ثُ ثِ ثَ   غُ غِ غَ   حُ حِ حَ

مُ مِ مَ   أُ إِ أَ   وُ وِ وَ   ذُ ذِ ذَ   شُ شِ شَ

ءُ ءِ ءَ   خُ خِ خَ   زُ زِ زَ   هُ هِ هَ   لُ لِ لَ

(2) Write in Arabic:

(1) *ja*	(2) *'u*	(3) *bi*	(4) *dhu*	(5) *thi*
(6) *sha*	(7) *si*	(8) *su*	(9) *ki*	(10) *wu*
(11) *qa*	(12) *fi*	(13) *zu*	(14) *ya*	(15) *wi*
(16) *lu*	(17) *mu*	(18) *hu*	(19) *kha*	(20) *ḥi*
(21) *ghi*	(22) *na*	(23) *ku*	(24) *ẓa*	(25) *qu*
(26) *khi*	(27) *mi*	(28) *ṭa*	(29) *ḍu*	(30) *dha*
(31) *hi*	(32) *ḥa*	(33) *wa*	(34) *tu*	(35) *ṭi*
(36) *ṣa*	(37) *shi*			

(d) The composition of Words

With the exception of six consonants ا ، د ، ذ ، ر ، ز ، و

The remaining twenty two consonants can be reduced to a quarter of their original independent size. There are four possibilities for all Arabic consonants when they are used in the formation of a word: (1) independent (2) initial (3) medial (4) final (see table (b) columns 6 - 9). This means that all together in the Arabic script one has to recognize 96 different characters. However only 38 characters are required to be familiarised, the remainder being generated by adding one or more dots in the correct place. The linking forms are integral to the shape of the Arabic characters (they are not an external ornament), and the script is capable of extra ordinary grace, energy, beauty and brevity.

TABLE (b) ARABIC ALPHABET

1	2	3	4	5	6	7	8	9
Group	Letters without dots	Letters with one dot	Letters with two dots	Letters with three dots	Independent	Initial	Medial *	Final **
A		Bāʼ ب	Tāʼ ت	Thāʼ ث	ب	بـ	ـبـ	ـب
B	Ḥāʼ ح	Khāʼ خ Jīm ج			ح ج	جـ جـ	ـجـ ـجـ	ـح ـج
C	Dāl د	Dhāʼ ذ			د	د	ـد	ـد
D	Rāʼ ر	Zāʼ ز			ر	ر	ـر	ـر
E	Sīn س			Shīn ش	س	سـ	ـسـ	ـس
F	Ṣād ص	Ḍād ض			ص	صـ	ـصـ	ـص
G	Ṭāʼ ط	Ẓāʼ ظ			ط	طـ	ـطـ	ـط
H	ʿAyn ع	Ghayn غ			ع	عـ	ـعـ	ـع

TABLE (b) ARABIC ALPHABET

1	2	3	4	5	6	7	8	9
Group	Letters without dots	Letters with one dot	Letters with two dots	Letters with three dots	Independent	Initial	Medial	Final
M		Fā' ف			ف	ﻓ	ﻔ	ﻒ
	Kāf ك				ك	ﻛ	ﻜ	ﻚ
			Qāf ق		ق	ﻗ	ﻘ	ﻖ
	Lām ل				ل	ﻟ	ﻠ	ﻞ
	Mīm م				م	ﻣ	ﻤ	ﻢ
		Nūn ن			ن	ﻧ	ﻨ	ﻦ
	Hā' ه				ه	ﻫ	ﻬ	ﻪ
	Wāw و				و	و	ﻮ	ﻮ
			Yā' ي		ي	ﻳ	ﻴ	ﻲ
	Alif ا				ا	ا	ﺎ	ﺎ
	Hamzah ء				ء / ئ	ء / ئ		ء

Note:

i. When preceeded by a non-conecting letter, the letters in the medial position are the same as when they are initial.

ii. When preceeded by a non-conecting letter, these letters in their final position are the same as when they are independent.

iii. The *hamzah* is written in different ways governed by a number of phonological rules.

71

ا إ أ آ اً ب ب بب

ث ث ثث ج ج جج

ذ ذ ر ز شش شش شش

ض ضضض غ غغغ

ف ففف ق ققق

ك كك لل لل م مم

ن نن ه هة ة

و و ي يي

Six consonants remain independent when they appear at the beginning of a word:

$$أَمِنَ \quad = \quad نَ \quad ــِم \quad أَ \quad (١)$$

$$ن \quad مِ \quad أَ$$

(amina) = (na) (mi) (a)

$$دَفَعَ \quad = \quad ـعَ \quad فَـ \quad دَ \quad (٢)$$

$$عَ \quad فَ \quad دَ$$

(dafa'a) = ('a) (fa) (da)

$$ذَخِرَ \quad = \quad ـرَ \quad ـخِ \quad ذَ \quad (٣)$$

$$رَ \quad خِ \quad ذَ$$

(dhakhira) = (ra) (khi) (dha)

$$رَضِىَ \quad = \quad ـىَ \quad ـضِ \quad رَ \quad (٤)$$

$$ىَ \quad ضِ \quad رَ$$

(radiya) = (ya) (di) (ra)

$$زَلَلَ \quad = \quad ـلَ \quad ـَل \quad زَ \quad (٥)$$

$$لَ \quad لَ \quad زَ$$

(zalala) = (la) (la) (za)

(٦)   وَ   صَ ـ ل = وَصَلَ

وَ   صَ   لَ

(wa)   (ṣa)   (la)   =   (waṣala)

(final)	(initial)	(independent)
ـنَ	مِـ	أ
ـعَ	فَـ	دَ
رَ	خِـ	ذَ
ئ	ضِـ	رَ
لَ	لَـ	زَ
ـلَ	صَـ	وَ

(ا ، د ، ذ ، ر ، ز ، و) When they appear in a word as the final consonant, they are joined with the preceding consonants. (See table b column 9)

74

جَعَلَ	ضُرِبَ	مَزَحَ	سُطِرَ	عَقَلَ
جَـعَـلَ	ضُـرِبَ	مَـزَحَ	سُـطِـرَ	عَـقَـلَ
(ja'ala)	(ḍuriba)	(mazaḥa)	(suṭira)	('aqala)

يَسَرَ	فَتَحَ	تَحِرَ	طَوَفَ	قَصَرَ
يَـسَـرَ	فَـتَـحَ	تَـحِـرَ	طَـوَفَ	قَـصَرَ
(yasara)	(fataḥa)	(taḥira)	(ṭawafa)	(qaṣara)

طَيَرَ	ضَخِرَ	غُفِرَ	حَنَقَ	بُنِيَ
طَـيَـرَ	ضَـخِـرَ	غُـفِـرَ	حَـنَـقَ	بُـنِـيَ
(ṭayara)	(ḍakhira)	(ghufira)	(ḥanaqa)	(buniya)

خُفِضَ	ضَبَطَ	نَهَشَ	شَكَرَ	ظُلِمَ
خُـفِـضَ	ضَـبَـطَ	نَـهَـشَ	شَـكَـرَ	ظُـلِـمَ
(khufiḍa)	(ḍabaṭa)	(nahasha)	(shakara)	(ẓulima)

كُذِبَ	خَشِيَ	هَدِمَ	لَوَمَ
كُـذِبَ	خَـشِـيَ	هَـدِمَ	لَـوَمَ
(kudhiba)	(khashiya)	(hadima)	(lawama)

Exercise No. 12

(1) Read:

عَلِمَ، نُصِرَ، كَرُمَ، جُعِلَ، أَثِمَ، تَوَبَ، تُرِكَ، مَنَعَ، جُمِعَ،
خَسِرَ، دُفِعَ، ذُكِرَ، رُفِعَ، قَعَدَ، عُقِلَ، ظُفِرَ، قَنَطَ، يَسَرَ، فَهِمَ،
رُزِقَ

75

Write in Arabic:

(1) *basaṭa*   (2) *naẓara*   (3) *ḍaḥika*   (4)   *ṭami'a*

(5) *tubi'a*   (6) *thamara*   (7) *jahila*   (8) *'arafa*

(9) *ḥanatha*   (10) *khayara* (11) *dasira*   (12) *dhawaqa*

(13) *ṣadafa*   (14) *raḥima*   (15) *razaqa*   (16) *suṭira*

(17) *futiḥa*   (18) *ḍubiṭa*   (19) *shariba* (20) *'akala*

(e) The Sukūn, Vowellessness / Quiescent

Either of these signs [-' -] a mini circle or a mini semi circle indicate that the consonant is vowel less. It means that the consonant is immobile but is willing to accept the sound of the preceding consonant which carries a short vowel and is therefore mobile and ends with its own articulation (original sound).

قُلْ   كَمْ   إِنْ   قَدْ   لَمْ   لَنْ   عَنْ   مِنْ

qu+l   ka+m   i+n   qa+d   la+m   la+n   'a+n   mi+n

(qul) (kam) (in)   (qad) (lam) (lan) ('an) (min)

أُنْزِلَ   أَظْلَمَ   نَعْبُدُ   كُنْتُمْ   مِنْهُمْ

أُ نْ زِلَ   أَظْ لَمَ   نَـعْ بُدُ   كُنْ تُمْ   مِنْ هُمْ

(unzila) (aẓlama) (na'budu) (kuntum) (minhum)

76

لَمْ يَلِدْ	لَمْ يَكْذِبْ	لَمْ يَفْعَلْ	يَضْرِبُ
لَمْ يَـ لِدْ	لَمْ يَكْـ ـذِبْ	لَمْ يَفْـ ـعَلْ	يَضْـ ـرِبُ
(lamyalid)	(lamyakdhib)	(lamyaf'al)	(yaḍribu)

سَمِعْتُمْ	نَسْتَغْفِرُكَ	فَهِمْتُمْ	عَلِمْتُمْ
سَمِعْـ ـتُمْ	نَسْـ تَغْـ ـفِرُكَ	فَهِمْـ ـتُمْ	عَـ لِمْـ ـتُمْ
(sami'tum)	(nastaghfiruka)	(fahimtum)	('alimtum)

أَلَمْ نَشْرَحْ لَكَ صَدْرَكَ

(alam nashraḥ laka ṣadraka)

Exercise No.13

(1) Read:

(٤) لَمْ يَزِدْ	(٣) لَيْسَتْ	(٢) عَيْنَيْنِ	(١) يَسْتَغْفِرْ لَكُمْ
(٨) قَدْ قَسَت	(٧) لَكُنْتُمْ	(٦) نَقْصُصْ	(٥) يُضْرَبُ
(١٢) طِبْتُمْ	(١١) شِئْتُمْ	(١٠) نَدْعُ	(٩) نَعْبُدُ
(١٦) يُوَسْوِسُ	(١٥) قُتِلْتُمْ	(١٤) نَحْنُ	(١٣) يَدَيْهِ
(٢٠) غُلِبَت	(١٩) قُلْتُكُمْ	(١٨) هَدَيْتَ	(١٧) يُدْخِلْكُمْ

77

(2) Write in Arabic:

(1) *qara'tum*   (2) *sata'lamu*   (3) *jahluka*   (4) *qaḍayta*

(5) *kam labithtum* (6) *'abduka*   (7) *naḥmaduka*

(8) *min qablikum*   (9) *arsaltum*   (10) *faraghtum*

(11) *amintum*   (12) *lam aḍrib* (13) *lam yakdhib*

(14) *amrukum*   (15) *ajrukum*

(f) *Long Vowels*

(1) The consonant *Alif* vowelless / quiescent [–ا = ā] if preceded by a consonant which carries *fatḥah* [–] becomes a long vowel. It increases its value of stretch from one *ḥarakah* [–ˊ (*a*)] to two [–ˊ (*a*) + –ˊ (*a*)]. For such a long vowel in the Qur'ānic script *Alif* [ا] and a short [–ˊ] (This short *Alif* is also known as dagger *Alif*.) are placed on the consonant which carries *fatḥah*.

، أ / ءُ	، بَ / بـُ	، جَ / جـُ	، دَ / دُ ،
(ā)	(bā)	(jā)	(dā)
، سَ / سـُ	، عَ / عـُ	، غَ / غـُ	، كَا / كـُ ،
(sā)	('ā)	(ghā)	(kā)
	، لَّ / لاَ / لـُ	يَا / يـُ	
	(lā)	(yā)	

78

(5) وَعَدْنَا	(4) إِسْحْقُ	(3) أَبْصَرُهُمْ	(2) رَزَقْنَهُمْ	(1) ذَ لِكَ
وَاعَدْنَا	إِسْحَاقُ	أَبْصَارُهُمْ	رَزَقْنَاهُمْ	ذَالِكَ

(10) أَرْسَلْنَكَ	(9) سُبْحَنَكَ	(8) تَلهَا	(7) كَذَلِكَ	(6) فَجَعَلْنَهَا
أَرْسَلْنَاكَ	سُبْحَانَكَ	تَلَاهَا	كَذَالِكَ	فَجَعَلْنَاهَا

(15) مَاوْى	(14) هُدْى	(13) مَتْى	(12) نَرْى	(11) بَلْى
مَاوَا	هُدَا	مَتَا	نَرَا	بَلَا

(In the six words (11-15) used above (ى) yā' is written, but not pronounced.

Exercise No. 14

(1) Read

(5) عَسْى	(4) دَعْوَاهُمْ	(3) سُفْلَى	(2) مَعِيشْ	(1) خَلَقْنَكُمْ
(10) أَنْعَامَكُمْ	(9) طَغْى	(8) هَذَا	(7) قُرْبى	(6) إِنْسَنْ
(15) أَفْضَى	(14) أَخْوَاتُكُمْ	(13) حُسْنى	(12) يَمْرَيمُ	(11) رَمى
(20) سُفْلَى	(19) لَسَحِرَنْ	(18) كَفَى	(17) أَوْلَادَكُمْ	(16) نَسْعْى
(25) كَانْ	(24) جَعَلْنَا	(23) أَهْلَكْنَا	(22) أَنْزَلَنَا	(21) سَمِعْنَا

(2) Write in Arabic:

(1) ahalalnā (2) akalahā   (3) arḍinā   (4) bisiḥrihim

(5) takādu   (6) baynahumā (7) idhā   (8) lānā

(9) bimā   (10) tabsuṭhā (11) 'araḍnā (12) ghazalahā

(13) aṣwāfihā (14) awbārihā (15) ash'ārihā

79

(2) The consonant *yā'* [ى] vowelless / quiescent [— ى = ī] if

preceded by a consonant which carries kasrah [—] becomes a

long vowel. It increases its value of stretch / prolongation from

one harakah [— (i)] to two [— (i) + — (i)].

ضِيْ	سِيْ	فِيْ	لِيْ	قِيْ	عِيْ	تِيْ	بِيْ	إيْ
		فِيْمَا	قِيْلَ	فِيْهَا				

(4) شٰكِرِيْنَ	(3) خٰسِرِيْنَ	(2) مٰكِرِيْنَ	(1) يُرِيْدُ
(8) صٰدِقِيْنَ	(7) حٰكِمِيْنَ	(6) مُهْتَدِيْنَ	(5) غٰفِلِيْنَ
(12) بِمُزَحْزِحِه	(11) بَعْدِه	(10) إيْمٰنُهُمْ	(9) كٰذِبِيْنَ
	(15) عَلَى بَصَرِه ـ	(14) عَلَى مِثْلِه ـ	(13) تُرْزَقٰنِه ـ
	(18) عِنْدَ قَوْمِه ـ	(17) فِيْ قَلْبِه ـ	(16) عَلَى سَمْعِه ـ
(22) بِه ـ	(21) عَنْ سَبِيْلِه ـ	(20) مِنْ فَوْقِه ـ	(19) مِنْ فَضْلِه ـ

With examples 11-22, some published copies of the Qur'ān
place a short *Alif* or dagger *Alif* under the consonant (ha) [هٰ]

achieve the (hī) sound instead of a mini *yā'* quiescent (حـ)

after the consanant (ha) هـ / هـ حـ written above for this (hi)

sound. (See examples 13-22)

(16) عَلَى سَمْعِهِ	(15) عَلَى بَصَرِهِ	(14) عَلَى مِثْلِهِ	(13) تُرْزَقِهِ
(20) مِنْ فَوْقِهِ	(19) مِنْ فَضْلِهِ	(18) عِنْدَ قَوْمِهِ	(17) فِيْ قَلْبِهِ
		(22) بِهِ	(21) عَنْ سَبِيْلِهِ

Exercise No. 15

(1) Read:

(١) ثِيْ (٢) جِيْ (٣) حِيْ (٤) خِيْ (٥) رِيْ (٦) دِيْ

(٧) ذِيْ (٨) زِيْ (٩) شِيْ (١٠) صِيْ (١١) طِيْ (١٢) ظِيْ (١٣) غِيْ

(١٤) كِيْ (١٥) مِيْ (١٦) نِيْ (١٧) وِيْ (١٨) هِيْ

(١٩) سَجِدِيْنَ (٢٠) صَبِرِيْنَ (٢١) خَشِعِيْنَ (٢٢) ظَلِمِيْنَ

(٢٣) إِبْرَهِيْمَ (٢٤) عِيْسَى (٢٥) لَعِبِيْنَ (٢٦) خَلِدِيْنَ

(٢٧) مُّسْرِفِيْنَ (٢٨) مُجْرِمِيْنَ (٢٩) دُوْنِهِ (٣٠) أَمْرِهِ

(٣١) رُسُلِهِ (٣٢) مُفْسِدِيْنَ (٣٣) مُدْبِرِيْنَ

(2) Write in Arabic:

(1) nāṭiqīna   (2) muslimīna (3) qāniṭīna   (4) yū'idu
(5) mushrikīna (6) nāṣirīna   (7) min ba'dihī (8) bi'ibādihī
(9) jāhilīna   (10) ẓahrihī   (11) ba'da ẓulmihī

81

(3) the consonant *waw* [و] vowelless / quiescent if preceded by a consonant which carries *ḍammah* [ُ] becomes a long vowel [و ُ = *ū*]. It increases its value of stretch from one *ḥarakah* [ُ (*u*)] to two [ُ (*u*) + ُ (*u*)].

أُوْ   بُوْ   تُوْ   عُوْ   قُوْ   فُوْ   ذُوْ   يُوْ

(yū)   *(dhū)*   *(fū)*   *(qū)*   *('ū)*   *(bū)*   *('ū)*   *('ū)*

(٤) يُشْرِكُوْنَ   (٣) لَغَفِلُوْنَ   (٢) يَخْتَلِفُوْنَ   (١) خَلِدُوْنَ

(yushrikūna)   *(laghāfilūna)*   *(yakhtalifūna)*   *(khālidūna)*

(٨) يُبْصِرُوْنَ   (٧) كَرِهُوْنَ   (٦) يَعْمَلُوْنَ   (٥) تَعْقِلُوْنَ

(yubṣirūna)   *(kārihūna)*   *(ya'malūna)*   *(ta'qilūna)*

(١٢) تَسْخَرُوْنَ   (١١) يَفْعَلُوْنَ   (١٠) يُجَهِدُوْنَ   (٩) تُرْجَعُوْنَ

(taskharūna)   *(yaf'alūna)*   *(yujāhidūna)*   *(turja'ūna)*

(١٦) مُوْسَى   (١٥) دَاوُرْدُ   (١٤) مُفْتَرُوْنَ   (١٣) تُجْرِمُوْنَ

(mūsā)   *(dāwūdu)*   *(muftarūna)*   *(tujrimūna)*

(٢٠) أَزْوَجُهُ   (١٩) أَخْرَجَهُ   (١٨) سُبْحَنَهُ   (١٧) أَمْرُهُ

(azwājuhū)   *(akhrajahū)*   *(subḥānahū)*   *(amruhū)*

(٢٤) كَلِمَتُهُ   (٢٣) عِلْمُهُ   (٢٢) رَسُوْلُهُ   (٢١) عِنْدَهُ

(kalimātuhū)   ('ilmuhū)   (rasūluhū)   ('indahū)

(٢٥) غَيْرُهُۥ   (٢٦) طِلَلُهُۥ   (٢٧) وَجْهَهُۥ   (٢٨) صَدْرُهُۥ (٢٩) بَصَرُهُۥ

(baṣaruhū)   (ṣadruhū)   (wajhahū)   (ṭilāluhū)   (ghayruhū)

In examples 17-29, some published copies of the Qur'ān place an inverted *ḍammah* [ʿ] above the consonant to achieve the (*hū*) sound instead of a mini *wāw* quiescent immediately after the consonant as written above.

(١٧) أَمْرُهُ،   (١٨) سُبْحَنَهُ،   (١٩) أَخْرَجَهُ،   (٢٠) أَزْوَاجُهُ،

(azwājuhū)   (akhrajahū)   (subḥānahū)   (amruhū)

(٢١) عِنْدَهُ،   (٢٢) رَسُوْلُهُ،   (٢٣) عِلْمُهُ،   (٢٤) كَلِمَتُهُ،

(kalimātuhū)   ('ilmuhū)   (rasūluhū)   ('indahū)

(٢٥) غَيْرُهُ،   (٢٦) طِلَلُهُ،   (٢٧) وَجْهَهُ،   (٢٨) صَدْرُهُ، (٢٩) بَصَرُهُ،

(baṣaruhū)   (ṣadruhū)   (wajhahū)   (ṭilāluhū)   (ghayruhū)

Exercise No. 16

(1) Read:

طُوْ (7)	ضُوْ (6)	رُوْ (5)	خُوْ (4)	جُوْ (3)	دُوْ (2)	ذُوْ (1)
تُفْلِحُوْنَ (11)	أَطِيْعُوْنَ (10)	يَكْتُمُوْنَ (9)	مُوْ (8)			
كَفِرُوْنَ (14)	يَعْتَدُوْنَ (13)	تُحْشَرُوْنَ (12)				
خَسِرُوْنَ (17)	غَلِبُوْنَ (16)	يَعْمَلُوْنَ (15)				
يُوْقِنُوْنَ (20)	تَخْتَلِفُوْنَ (19)	يَصْنَعُوْنَ (18)				
بَيْتِهٖ (24)	فَضْلُهٗ (23)	كُتُبِهٖ (22)	رِضْوَانُهٗ (21)			
عَذَبِهٖ (28)	مَغْفِرَتُهٗ (27)	رَحْمَتُهٗ (26)	سَبِيْلُهٗ (25)			

(2) Write in Arabic:

(1) thū   (2) zū   (3) sū   (4) shū   (5) ṣū   (6) ẓū   (7) ghū   (8) lū

(9) nū   (10) tufliḥūna   (11) dākhilūna   (12) yaṣna'ūna

(13) yunẓarūna   (14) yastahziūna   (15) yash'urūna

(16) yulḥidūna   (17) yubṣirūna   (18) muslimūna   (19) darajātuku

(20) 'amaluhū   (21) fikruhū   (22) nūruhū   (23) yastaghfirūnakum

(24) shahādatahū   (25) qawmuhū

(g) *Hamzah* [ء] *Glottal Stop*

Hamzah gives a sound when either a short vowel or a *sukūn*, quiescent sign is placed on it.
There are two kinds of *hamzahs* in Arabic:

(1) *Hamzat al waṣl*, Connecting *hamzah* [أ] and

(2) *Hamzat al-qaṭ'*, Disjunctive *hamzah* [أ].

(1) The Connecting *hamzah* should be dropped when the preceding consonant bearing a short vowel joins the word which begins with the Connecting *hamzah*..

[Here it should not be recited because *ka* joins with *lām*.]

(*dhālikal kitābu*) ذَلِكَ الْكِتَبُ when it is independent.

(2) *Hamzat al-qaṭ'*, the Disjunctive *hamzah* unlike *Hamzat al-waṣl* is recited.

(٥) ذَرَأَكُمْ   (٤)نَبَأَهُمْ   (٣) جِئْتَ   (٢) أَرْسَلَ   (١) يَأْكُلُ

(dhra'akum) (naba'ahum) (ji'ta)   (arsala)   (ya'kulu)

(٩) اسْتُهْزِئُ   (٨) قَرَأْتَ   (٧) الْمُؤْمِنِينَ   (٦) نَبَأَهُمْ

(istuhzi'u)   (qara'ta) (almuminīna) (naba'ahum)

(١٣) سَأَلَ   (١٢) الْبُؤُوْسُ   (١١) الْبِئْرُ   (١٠) بِئْسَ

(sa'ala)   (al bu'ūsu)   (al bi'ru)   (bi'sa)

(١٦) مِنَ الْحَرَمِ   (١٥) مِنَ الْمَسْجِدِ   (١٤) مِنَ الْبَيْتِ

(minal ḥarami)   (minal masjidi)   (minal bayti)

(١٨) اسْمَعْ كَلَامِي   (١٧) مِنَ الْأَرْضِ

(isma' kalāmī)   (minal 'arḍi)

(٢٠) انْصُرْ أَخَاكَ   (١٩) ارْجِعْ إِلى الْمَسْجِدِ

(unṣur akhāka)   (irji 'ilal masjidi)

(٢١) اُخْرُجْ مِنَ الْمَدْرَسَة   (٢٢) إِنْ شَاءَ   (٢٣) يَشَاءُ

(ukhruj minal madrasati)   (in shā'a)   (yashā'u)

It is evident from examples 1-13 above that the Disjunctive *hamzah*, at times, needs a base of any one of the following:

(i) a little loop (   ) (see nos. 3, 10 and 11),
(ii) a consonant *alif* (ا) (see nos. 1, 2, 4, 5 and 6),
(iii) a consonant *wāw* (و) (see no.12),
(iv) a consonant *yā'* (ى) (see no.9).
It also appears without any base (see no.s 22 and 23).
   The connecting *hamzah* is not recited in example nos. 14-17 because the preceding consonant *Nūn* carries a short vowel and joins with the consonant *Lām*.

   The sentences in examples 19-22 begin with *hamzat al-waṣl*, connecting *hamzah* اِسْمَعْ and اِرْجِعْ should be read with *kasarah* under *hamzah* and in examples 22 and 23 اُخْرُجْ and اُنْصُرْ should be read with *ḍammah*. The reasoning behind the insertion of either *kasrah* or *ḍammah* on the *hamzah* is provided in lesson 14 unit 53.

(h) Dipthongs وْ — *(aw)* ىْ — *(ay)*

" A combination of two distinct vowel sounds, uttered in rapid succession, one of which is more strongly stressed than the other and is done syllabic, so that they constitute together only a single syllable."

(١) بَوْ   (٢) أَيْ   (٣) دَوْ   (٤) شَيْ   (٥) رَوْ   (٦) جَيْ

(baw)   (ay)   (daw)   (shay)   (raw)   (jay)

(٧) سَوْ   (٨) رَيْ   (٩) ضَوْ   (١٠) سَيْ   (١١) طَوْ

(saw)   (ray)   (ḍaw)   (say)   (ṭaw)

(١٢) ضَيْ   (١٣) ذَوْ   (١٤) طَيْ   (١٥) فَوْ   (١٦) عَيْ

(ḍay)   (dhaw)   (ṭay)   (faw)   ('ay)

(١٧) قَوْ   (١٨) غَيْ   (١٩) لَوْ   (٢٠) فَيْ   (٢١) مَوْ

(qaw)   (ghay)   (law)   (fay)   (maw)

(٢٢) بَيْ   (٢٣) نَوْ   (٢٤) طَوْ   (٢٥) الْمَوْتُ   (٢٦) الْبَيْتُ

(bay)   (naw)   (ṭaw)   (almawtu)   (albaytu)

(٢٧) الْجَيْبُ   (٢٨) الْعَيْنُ   (٢٩) الْفَوْزُ   (٣٠) الْعَيْبُ

(aljaybu)   (al'aynu)   (alfawzu)   (al'aybu)

(i) Shaddah [ّ] Double Consonants

[ّ] This sign above the consonant always accommodates one of the short vowels *fathah* ◌َ ,*kasrah* ◌ِ or *dammah* ◌ُ .

Any consonant that carries *shaddah* has a dual role to play. Firstly it should remain vowelless and secondly it should be read with the short vowel sign which it carries.

←

$$\text{أَبْ} + \text{بَ} = \text{أَبَّ} \quad (abba)$$

$$\text{ضُبْ} + \text{بُ} = \text{ضُبُّ} \quad (dubbu)$$

$$\text{عَدْ} + \text{دِ} = \text{عَدِّ} \quad ('addi)$$

87

(٤) شَقَّ   (٣) دَقَّ   (٢) سَبَّ   (١) تُبَّ

(شَقْ+قَ)   (دَقْ+قَ)   (سَبْ+بَ)   (تُبْ+بَ)

(shaqqa)   *(daqqa)*   *(sabba)*   *(tubba)*

(٨) الرَّحْمَنُ   (٧) الرَّحِيْمُ   (٦) حُبَّ   (٥) وُدَّ

(اَرْرَحْمَانُ)   (اَرْرَحِيْمُ)   (حُبْ+بَ)   (وُدْ+دَ)

(arrahmānu)   *(arrahīmu)*   *(hubba)*   *(wudda)*

In the examples 7-24 the letter does not carry any short vowel, in this case it will remain silent and *alif* shall be combined with the letter which carries *shaddah*. See rule No. 14.

(١٢) الْمُعِزُّ   (١١) الْوَهَّابُ   (١٠) الْقُدُّوْسُ   (٩) الصَّبُوْرُ

(الْمُعِزْزُ)   (الْوَهْـ هَابُ)   (الْقُدْدُوْسُ)   (اَصْ صَ بُوْرُ)

(al-mu'izzu)   *(al-wahhābu)*   *(al-quddūsu)*   *(assabūru)*

(١٦) الْقَيُّوْمُ   (١٥) الشَّكُوْرُ   (١٤) الْعَلِيُّ   (١٣) السَّمِيْعُ

(الْقَيْ يُوْمُ)   (اَشْ شَ كُوْرُ)   (الْعَلِيْ يُ)   (اَسْ سَ مِيْعُ)

(al-qayyūmu)   *(ashshakūru)*   *(al'aliyyu)*   *(assami'u)*

(٢٠) الزَّكَوةُ   (١٩) الصَّلَوةُ   (١٨) الرَّشِيْدُ   (١٧) الْحَيُّ

(اَزْزَكَاةُ)   (اَصْ صَ لَاةُ)   (اَرْرَشِيْدُ)   (الْحَيْ يُ)

(azzakātu)   *(assalātu)*   *(arrashīdu)*   *(al-hayyu)*

(٢٤) الصَّمَدُ   (٢٣) التَّوَّابُ   (٢٢) الأَوَّلُ   (٢١) الْمُؤَخِّرُ

(الْمُؤَخِّرُ) (الْـأَوْوَلُ) (اَتْتَوْوَابُ) (اصْ صَمَدُ)

(aṣṣamadu) *(attawwābu)* *(al'awwalu) (almu'akhkhiru)*

Exercise No.17

(1) Read:

(١) السَّلَامُ (٢) الْجَبَّارُ (٣) الْمُتَكَبِّرُ (٤) الْوَلِيُّ

(٥) الشَّهِيْدُ (٦) الْقَوِيُّ (٧) الْفَتَّاحُ (٨) الظَّاهِرُ

(٩) الْبَرُّ (١٠) الْعَلَمُ (١١) الشَّاكِرُ (١٢) الْمَنَّانُ

(١٣) الْمُصَوِّرُ (١٤) الْغَفَّارُ (١٥) الْقَهَّارُ (١٦) الْوَهَّابُ

(١٧) الرَّزَّاقُ (١٨) الْعَفُوُّ (١٩) الْغَنِيُّ (٢٠) الرَّبُّ

(2) Write in Arabic:

(1) *assamāwātu* (2) *addīnu* (3) *aljinnu* (4) *ashshamsu*

(5) *sakhkhara* (6) *yunajjīkum* (7) *aẓẓālimūna*
(8) *albarru* (9) *annāsu* (10) *annūru* (11) *adhdhākirūna*

(12) *aḍḍlālu* (13) *alḥaqqu* (14) *yuḥibbūnahum*

(15) *innakum* (16) *yaẓunnūna* (17) *'allama* (18) *ḥarramnā*

(19) *bimu'adhdhibīna* (20) *ḥajja* (21) *jahannama*

(j) *Tanwīn*, Nunation [اً an, اٍ in, اٌ un]

[اً (*an*)] A double *fatḥah* sign on the consonant means *fatḥah* plus 'n' sound of the *tanwīn*. Generally *alif* is added at the end.

(٤) سَعِيْراً	(٣) مَسْرُوْرَاً	(٢) نَفْعَاً	(١) ضَبْحَاً
سَعِيْرَنْ	مَسْرُوْرَنْ	نَفْعَنْ	ضَبْحَنْ
(sa'īran)	(masrūran)	(naf'an)	(ḍabḥan)

(ii)

[— (in)] A double *kasrah* sign under the consonant means *kasrah* plus 'n' sound of the *tanwīn*.

جِ	بِ	إِ
(ji+n=jin)	(bi+n=bin)	(i+n=in)

قِ	رِ	سِ
(qi+n=qin)	(ri+n=rin)	(si+n=sin)

(٤) مَسْكُوْب	(٣) مَمْدُوْد	(٢) مَنْضُوْد	(١) مَخْضُوْد
مَسْكُوْبِنْ	مَمْدُوْدِنْ	مَنْضُوْدِنْ	مَخْضُوْدِنْ
(maskūbin)	(mamdūdin)	(manḍūdin)	(makhḍūdin)

(iii)

[ُ — (un)] A double *ḍammah* sign above the consonant means *ḍammah* plus 'n' sound of the *tanwīn*.

أُ	بُ	جُ
(u+n=un)	(bu+n=bun)	(ju+n=jun)

قُ	رُ	سُ
(qu+n=qun)	(ru+n=run)	(su+n=sun)

(٥) خَبِيْرٌ	(٤) عَلِيْمٌ	(٣) لَشَدِيْدٌ	(٢) لَشَهِيْدٌ	(١) لَكَنُوْدٌ
خَبِيْرُنْ	عَلِيْمُنْ	لَشَدِيْدُنْ	لَشَهِيْدُنْ	لَكَنُوْدُنْ

90

(khabīrun) ('alīmun) (lashadīdun) (lashahīdun) (lakanūdun)

Exercise No. 18

(1) Read:

(١) عَزِيْزاً (٢) حَقٌّ (٣) ظَاهِرٌ (٤) حَكِيْماً (٥) لَطِيْفٌ

(٦) بَاطِنٍ (٧) بَصِيْراً (٨) لَطِيْفٌ (٩) وَكِيْلٌ

(١٠) خَبِيْراً (١١) عَظِيْمٍ (١٢) نَصِيْرٍ (١٣) مُؤْمِناً

(١٤) غَفُورٌ (١٥) قَدِيرٍ (١٦) خَالِقاً (١٧) كَبِيْرٌ

(١٨) كَفِيْلٍ (١٩) كَبِيْراً (٢٠) خَالِقٌ (٢١) مَتِيْنٍ

(٢٢) كَرِيْماً (٢٣) حَفِيْظٌ (٢٤) غَالِبٍ

(2) Write in Arabic:

(1) raqīban (2) qadīrun (3) qābiḍin (4) mujīban

(5) mubīnan (6) jalīlin (7) wārithūna (8) wāsi'an

(9) jamī'in (10) ḥaqqan (11) jamī'an (12) ghāfirin

91

(k) *The Use of Ta'al-Ta'nīth* [ة / ـة] *Feminization*.

(١) رَحْمَةٌ   (٢) الزَّكَوةُ   (٣) الْحِكْمَةُ   (٤) الْحَيَوةُ
(rahamatun)   (azzakātu)   (alḥikmatu)   (alhayātu)

(٥) نِعْمَةٌ   (٦) قُرَّةٌ   (٧) رِسَالَةٌ   (٨) مُسْفِرَةٌ
(ni'matun)   (qurratun)   (risālatun)   (musfiratun)

(٩) نَاعِمَةٌ   (١٠) ذَرَّةٌ   (١١) الْبُقْعَةُ   (١٢) دَعْوَةٌ
(nā'imatun)   (dharratun)   (albuq'atu)   (da'watun)

(١٣) الْجَنَّةُ   (١٤) مُبَرَكَةٌ   (١٥) مَرَّةٌ   (١٦) ذِلَّةٌ
(aljannatu)   (mubārakatun)   (marratun)   (dhillatun)

(١٧) جَدِيدَةٌ   (١٨) الْوَاقِعَةُ   (١٩) شَدِيدَةٌ   (٢٠) اللَّوَّامَةُ
(jadīdatun)   (alwāqi'atu)   (shadīdatun)   (allawwāmatu)

(٢١) كَبِيرَةٌ   (٢٢) مُهِمَّةٌ   (٢٣) الْجَهلِيَّةُ   (٢٤) ءَايَةٌ
(kabīratun)   (muhimmatun)   (aljāhiliyyatu)   (āyatun)

(٢٥) الصَّرَانِيَّةُ   (٢٦) الْقَدِيمَةُ   (٢٧) الْقَرْيَةُ   (٢٨) الْحُطَمَةُ
(annaṣrāniyyatu)   (alqadīmatu)   (alqaryatu)   (alḥuṭamatu)

(٢٩) مَرْفُوعَةٌ   (٣٠) خَلَّةٌ
(marfū'atun)   (khallatun)

(l) *Madd* prolongation [~]

The length of the duration is either 4-5 (*ḥarakāt*) a+a+a+a+a=a^6 or 5-6 *ḥarakāt* i.e. a^7. It means the consonant which carries the *madd* should be prolonged up to the length referred to above.

(١) قٓ (٢) صٓ (٣) الٓرٰ (٤) حمٓ (٥) طسٓ

(٦) عٓسٓقٓ (٧) كٓهيعٓصٓ (٨) ٱلسَّمَآءَ (٩) شَآءَ

(١٠) سَوَآءٌ (١١) السُّفَهَآءُ (١٢) مَرِيٓئًا (١٣) هَنِيٓئًا

(١٤) ٱلنِّسَآءُ (١٥) جَزَآءٌ (١٦) دُعَآءٌ (١٧) نِدَآءٌ

(١٨) شُهَدَآءُ (١٩) هَؤُلَآءِ (٢٠) إِنَّآ أَعْطَيْنٰكَ

(٢١) إِنَّآ أَنْزَلْنٰهُ (٢٢) وَمَآ أَدْرٰـكَ (٢٣) وَلَآ أَنْتُمْ

(٢٤) مَآ فِيْ أَنْفُسِكُمْ (٢٥) واعْلَمُوٓآ أَنَّ اللّٰهَ

(٢٦) قُوٓآ أَنْفُسَكُمْ (٢٧) وَمَآ أَرْسَلْنٰكَ

(٢٨) فَتُوبُوٓآ إِلَى بَارِئِكُمْ (٢٩) إِنَّآ أَوْحَيْنَآ إِلَيْكَ

(٣٠) قَالُوٓآ أَنُؤْمِنُ كَمَآ آمَنَ الْسُّفَهَاء

قُولُوٓاْ ءَامَنَّا بِٱللّٰهِ وَمَآ أُنزِلَ إِلَيْنَا وَمَآ أُنزِلَ إِلَىٰ إِبْرَٰهِـۧمَ

1.   Children throughout the world at a certain early age all make scribbles similar to this:

    From these early efforts it is possible to identify to the child a circle and vertical and horizontal lines. The child should then be informed that with this combination of a circle and a line it is possible to form all Arabic consonants. Experience suggests that with this method not only do children become interested in learning Arabic consonants but also their confidence develops quickly in writing these consonants.

2.   The formation of the letters in Groups A-M is based entirely on this method. The teacher should introduce a number of new letters in one contact hour such that students are able to group and become aware that in different groups the placement of dots forms new letters.

3.   Columns 7, 8, and 9 in table B show the full number of shapes possible for the alphabet characters in different positions in the word. The teaching and learning of the shapes of the characters is greatly facilitated by drawing on the black board and getting students both to recognise and to copy them down. Pronunciation of the characters can be taught simultaneously.

    For the presentation of the initial, medial and final forms of the characters, a little physical activity on the teacher's part helps to impress the lesson on the students' memories.

Six consonants (namely ا ، د ، ذ ، ر ، ز ، و) are described as being unable to extend the left "arm". All other consonants are willing to extend both arms whenever needed.

The teacher can now use his/her arms to show how the consonants are joined: for example by inclining the head to the right for *fatḥah (a)*, raising the head for *ḍammah (u)*, and bending the knees a little for *kasrah (i)*.

4. By adopting this most effective method the articulation of all 28 letters of the Arabic alphabet is made clear on the DVDs. Teachers should gradually introduce the groups mentioned in Exercise 10 and provide students with ample opportunity to listen and pronounce each letter.
Learn Arabic Qur'ānic Rapidly with 12 DVDs episode in 2 DVDs mentioned in preface will assist greatly for rapidly learning. Studend can be shown episode through graded progression.

وَرَحْـمَتِي وَسِعَتْ كُلَّ شَيْءٍ 7:156

Phase Two

قُل كُلٌّ يَعمَلُ عَلَىٰ شَاكِلَتِهِ فَرَبُّكُم أَعلَمُ بِمَن هُوَ أَهدَىٰ سَبِيلًا 17:84

﷽ الدَّرْسُ الأَوَّلُ ﷽
1

﷽ UNIT 1 ﷽

(١)   كِتَابٌ وَزَهْرَةٌ.

(٢)   قَلَمٌ وَ عَيْنٌ.

(٣)   كُرْسِيٌّ وَ سَمَاءٌ.

(٤)   بَابٌ وَ غُرْفَةٌ.

(٥)   خُبْزٌ وَ شَمْسٌ.

(٦)   طَرِيقٌ وَ مَائِدَةٌ.*

(٧)   مَالٌ وَ يَدٌ.

(٨)   وَلَدٌ وَ بِنْتٌ.

(٩)   أَبٌ وَ أُمٌّ.

(١٠)   رَجُلٌ وَامْرَأَةٌ.

---

* Only those nouns are selected in the book which are to be found in the Qur'ān and the *Sunnah*.

هَذَا كِتَابٌ.	مَا هَذَا ؟ (١)
هَذَا قَلَمٌ.	مَا هَذَا ؟ (٢)
هَذَا كُرْسِيٌّ.	مَا هَذَا ؟ (٣)
هَذَا بَابٌ.	مَا هَذَا ؟ (٤)
هَذَا خُبْزٌ.	مَا هَذَا ؟ (٥)
هَذَا طَرِيقٌ.	مَا هَذَا ؟ (٦)
هَذَا مَالٌ.	مَا هَذَا ؟ (٧)
هَذَا رَجُلٌ.	مَنْ هَذَا ؟ (٨)
هُوَ أَبٌ.	مَنْ هُوَ ؟ (٩)
هُوَ وَلَدٌ.	مَنْ هُوَ ؟ (10)

❀ UNIT 3 ❀

هَذِهِ زَهْرَةٌ.	مَا هَذِه ؟ (١)
هَذِهِ سَمَاءٌ.	مَا هَذِه ؟ (٢)
هَذِهِ عَيْنٌ.	مَا هَذِه ؟ (٣)
هَذِهِ غُرْفَةٌ.	مَا هَذِه ؟ (٤)
هَذِهِ شَمْسٌ.	مَا هَذِه ؟ (٥)

هَذه مَائدَةٌ.	(٦) مَا هَذه ؟
هَذه يَدٌ.	(٧) مَا هَذه ؟
هَذه امْرَأَةٌ.	(٨) مَنْ هَذه ؟
هِيَ أُمٌّ.	(٩) مَنْ هِيَ ؟
هِيَ بِنْتٌ.	(١٠)مَنْ هِيَ ؟

❀ UNIT 4 ❀

نَعَمْ، هَذا كِتَابٌ.	(١) أَهَذَا كِتَابٌ؟
نَعَمْ، هَذه زَهْرَةٌ.	(٢) هَلْ هَذه زَهْرَةٌ ؟
نَعَمْ، هَذا قَلَمٌ.	(٣) أَهَذَا قَلَمٌ ؟
نَعَمْ، هَذه عَيْنٌ.	(٤) هَلْ هَذه عَيْنٌ ؟
نَعَمْ، هَذا كُرْسِيٌّ.	(٥) أَهَذَا كُرْسِيٌّ ؟
نَعَمْ، هَذه غُرْفَةٌ.	(٦) أَهَذه غُرْفَةٌ ؟
نَعَمْ، هَذه طَرِيقٌ.	(٧) هَلْ هَذه طَرِيقٌ ؟
نَعَمْ، هَذه مَائدَةٌ.	(٨) أَهَذه مَائدَةٌ ؟
نَعَمْ، هَذا مَالٌ.	(٩) هَلْ هَذا مَالٌ ؟
نَعَمْ، هَذه يَدٌ.	(١٠) هَلْ هَذه يَدٌ ؟
نَعَمْ، هُوَ رَجُلٌ.	(١١) أَهُوَ رَجُلٌ ؟
نَعَمْ، هِيَ امْرَأَةٌ.	(١٢) هَلْ هِيَ امْرَأَةٌ ؟

99

(١٣) أَهِيَ بِنْتٌ ؟	نَعَمْ، هِيَ بِنْتٌ.
(١٤) هَلْ هُوَ وَلَدٌ ؟	نَعَمْ، هُوَ وَلَدٌ.
(١٥) أَهِيَ أُمٌّ ؟	نَعَمْ، هِيَ أُمٌّ.
(١٦) هَلْ هُوَ أَبٌ ؟	نَعَمْ، هُوَ أَبٌ.

❈ UNIT 5 ❈

(١)	مَنْ أَنْتَ ؟	أَنَا رَجُلٌ.
(٢)	مَنْ أَنْتِ ؟	أَنَا امْرَأَةٌ.
(٣)	مَنْ أَنْتَ ؟	أَنَا أَبٌ.
(٤)	مَنْ أَنْتِ ؟	أَنَا أُمٌّ.
(٥)	مَنْ أَنْتَ ؟	أَنَا وَلَدٌ.
(٦)	مَنْ أَنْتِ ؟	أَنَا بِنْتٌ.
(٧)	أَأَنْتَ أَبٌ ؟	نَعَمْ، أَنَا أَبٌ.
(٨)	أَأَنْتِ أُمٌّ ؟	نَعَمْ، أَنَا أُمٌّ.
(٩)	هَلْ أَنْتَ رَجُلٌ ؟	نَعَمْ، أَنَا رَجُلٌ.
(١٠)	أَأَنْتِ امْرَأَةٌ ؟	نَعَمْ، أَنَا امْرَأَةٌ.
(١١)	أَأَنْتَ وَلَدٌ ؟	نَعَمْ، أَنَا وَلَدٌ.
(١٢)	هَلْ أَنْتِ بِنْتٌ ؟	نَعَمْ، أَنَا بِنْتٌ.

(١)   أَهَذَا كِتَابٌ ؟   لاَ، هَذَا قَلَمٌ.

(٢)   هَلْ هَذَا مَالٌ ؟   لاَ، هَذَا بَابٌ.

(٣)   أَهَذه مَائدةٌ ؟   لاَ، هَذه يَدٌ.

(٤)   هَلْ هَذه غُرْفَةٌ ؟   لاَ، هَذه شَمْسٌ.

(٥)   هَلْ هَذَا كُرْسِيٌّ ؟   لاَ، هَذَا كِتَابٌ.

(٦)   هَلْ هَذه زَهْرَةٌ ؟   لاَ، هَذه سَمَاءٌ.

(٧)   أَهَذَا خُبْزٌ ؟   لاَ، هَذه طَرِيقٌ.

(٨)   أَهِيَ بِنْتٌ ؟   لاَ، هِيَ أُمٌّ.

(٩)   هَلْ هُوَ وَلَدٌ ؟   لاَ، هُوَ أَبٌ.

(١٠)   هَلْ هِيَ بِنْتٌ ؟   لاَ، هِيَ أُمٌّ.

(١١)   هَلْ هُوَ رَجُلٌ ؟   لاَ، هُوَ وَلَدٌ.

(١٢)   أَأَنْتِ أُمٌّ ؟   لاَ، أَنَا بِنْتٌ.

(١٣)   أَأَنْتَ أَبٌ ؟   لاَ، أَنَا وَلَدٌ.

(١٤)   هَلْ أَنْتِ بِنْتٌ ؟   لاَ، أَنَا أُمٌّ.

(١٥)   هَلْ أَنْتَ وَلَدٌ ؟   لاَ، أَنَا أَبٌ.

101

GLOSSARY LESSON 1

كِتَابٌ	(M¹) book	مَائِدَةٌ	(F¹) table
زَهْرَةٌ	(F¹) flower	أَبٌ	(M¹) father
قَلَمٌ	(M¹) pen	أُمٌّ	(F¹) mother
عَيْنٌ	(F¹) eye	مَالٌ	(M¹) wealth
كُرْسِيٌّ	(M¹) chair	يَدٌ	(F¹) hand
سَمَاءٌ	(F¹) sky	هُوَ	(III M¹) he
بَابٌ	(M¹) door	هِيَ	(III F¹) she
غُرْفَةٌ	(F¹) room	أَنْتَ	(II M¹) you
خُبْزٌ	(M¹) bread	أَنْتِ	(II F¹) you
شَمْسٌ	(F¹) sun	أَنَا	(M¹+F¹) I
رَجُلٌ	(M¹) man	هَذَا	(M¹) this
امْرَأَةٌ	(F¹) woman	هَذه	(F¹) this
وَلَدٌ	(M¹) boy	مَنْ؟	(M¹+ F¹) who?
بِنْتٌ	(F¹) girl	أَ / هَلْ؟	Is?
طَرِيقٌ	(M¹+ F¹) road	لَا	No
كَأْسٌ	(F¹) glass	نَعَمْ	yes

🕸 GRAMMATICAL THEMES 🕸

🕸 UNIT 1 🕸

الأَسْمَاءُ : تَنْكِيرٌ ، تَذْكِيرٌ وَتَأْنِيثٌ

Nouns: Indefinite and Genders

Rule No. 1

With some exceptions generally, the final consonant of a noun, if it is indefinite carries a *tanwīn*, nunation. *mostly dhumma/tain*

[˵ _ ، _]

Example Analysis:

كِتَابٌ (a book)

In this word (بٌ) is the final consonant of a noun كِتَابٌ

and it carries a *tanwīn* [˵] therefore, it is indefinite. It means a book.

Rule No. 2

Generally nouns ending in [ـة / ة] are feminine.

Example Analysis:

(1) غُرْفَةٌ (a room)   (2) مَائِدَةٌ (a table)

The first noun غُرْفَةٌ ends with [ـة] and the second noun [مَائِدَةٌ] ends with [ة] therefore both are feminine.

Both carry *tanwīn* [˵], therefore, both are indefinite.

خَلِيفَةٌ ends in (ـة) but since it refers to a masculine noun therefore it is masculine. Similarly the proper noun طَلْحَة .

Rule No. 3

Parts of the human body, which are in pairs, are, according to Arabic usage, regarded as feminine.

Example Analysis:

(1) عَيْنٌ (an eye)   (2) يَدٌ (a hand)

An eye and a hand are parts of the human body. A person possesses two eyes and two hands, therefore, both nouns are feminine.

Rule No. 4

Some nouns do not end in [ـة / ة] i.e. a feminine ending, but because of their feminine usage they are regarded as feminine.

Example Analysis:

(1) سَمَاءٌ (a sky)[1]   (2) شَمْسٌ (a sun)[2]

Historically, both nouns were originally used as feminine.

Note two nouns are connected with a particle [وَ] which

means (and) قَلَمٌ وَ عَيْنٌ (a pen and an eye).

Here the first noun قَلَمٌ   is connected by the particle [وَ   ]

with the second noun عَيْنٌ .

---

[1] سَمَاءٌ was originally سُمَيَّة with (ـة) feminine ending.

[2] شَمْسٌ was originally شُمَيْسَة with (ـة) feminine ending.

[Note the first noun is masculine and the second is feminine and they are connected with a particle [وَ] which means 'and'.]
(See the text on Unit 1)

Note there are a few nouns in Arabic which can be treated both as masculine and feminine. The noun طَرِيقٌ in this unit can be used for both genders

The love of Allah

UNIT 2

حُرُوفُ الاسْتِفْهَامِ وَالضَّمَائِرِ
Interrogation and personal pronouns

Rule No. 5

The particles مَا (what?) and مَنْ (who?) are used for interrogation. مَا is used for masculine and feminine inanimate nouns and مَنْ is used for masculine and feminine nouns, used for human beings.

Rule No. 6

هَذَا (this) is a singular masculine (M[1]) demonstrative pronoun for demonstration when the object for demonstration is very close.

Rule No. 7

هُوَ (he) is the third person singular masculine personal pronoun (III M [1]).

Example Analysis: *Rules 5-7*

(i) If a masculine inanimate object كِتَابٌ (a book) is identified as near by, the interrogation is raised with مَا (what?) and هَذَا (this) مَا هَذَا ؟ (What is this?). The answer for the interrogation is هَذَا كِتَابٌ (this is a book).

N.B. Is in the above sentence is automatically understood. There is no special word in Arabic for is.

(ii) مَنْ هُوَ (who is he?)

As مَنْ (who?) is a particle and is used for the interrogation of masculine and feminine nouns used for human beings. Hence it is used with the masculine pronoun هُوَ (he).

(2) مَنْ هُوَ (who is he?)

مَنْ can be used for interrogation with هَذَا provided the object for demonstration is a human being singular and masculine.
In both these interrogations if the object is a man then the answer will be هَذَا رَجُلٌ (this is a man).

N.B. : All nouns used in this unit are masculine.

✿ UNIT 3 ✿

Rule No. 8

هَذه (this) is a singular feminine demonstrative pronoun when the object is near/close.

Rule No. 9

هِيَ (she) is the third person singular feminine (III F [1]) personal pronoun.

Example Analysis: *Rules 9-10*

(i) If a feminine inanimate object زَهْرَةٌ (a flower) is shown as nearby, the interrogation is raised with مَا (what?).

مَا هَذه (What is this [feminine]?)

The answer is:

هَذه زَهْرَةٌ (This is a flower.)

(ii) مَنْ هِيَ (Who is she?)

هِيَ بِنْتٌ (She is a girl.)

N.B. :Note all nouns in this unit are feminine.

✾ UNIT 4 ✾

Rule No. 10

هَلْ / أَ (Is?) are the particles used for interrogation for masculine and feminine nouns. Both can be used interchangeably.

Example Analysis:

أَهَذَا كِتَابٌ؟ (Is this a book?)

If the answer is in the affirmative, نَعَمْ (yes) is placed before the sentence.

نَعَمْ ، هَذَا كِتَابٌ (Yes, this is a book.)

N.B. :Note in this unit all answers are in the affirmative.

UNIT 5

Rule No. 11

أَنْتَ (you) is used for the second person singular masculine pronoun (II M[1]) and أَنْتِ (you) for the second person feminine singular (II F[1]).

Rule No. 12

أَنَا (I) is used for both the singular masculine and feminine first person (I M[1] + F[1]).

Example Analysis: *Rules 11-12*

If the question is raised to a man:

مَنْ أَنْتَ ؟ (Who are you?)

The answer is:

أَنَا رَجُلٌ (I am a man.)

The second person personal pronoun helps to develop conversation and dialogue.

UNIT 6

Note the answer is in the negative, لَا (no) is placed before the sentence.

أَهَذَا كِتَابٌ؟ (Is this a book?)

لاَ ، هَذَا قَلَمٌ (No, this is a pen.)

❦ METHOD OF TEACHING ❦
LESSON 1

Audio Visual Aids:
Overhead Projector and Screen.
Magnetic Board.
Flip chart / Black Board.
Markers (various colours).
Acetates for the first textual lesson.
6" x 4" Cards.
Pointer.
Cassette Tape Recorder.

Phase I

Steps:

1. Demonstrate to the students a card on which a figure of a book is drawn.

2. Demonstrate the other side of the card on which كِتَابٌ is written. كِتَابٌ is written in black ink and (‗) *tanwīn* is written in red ink.

3. Ask all the students to read these words. Ask a few individual students to read the noun in Arabic.

4. Turn over the card and let the students say كِتَابٌ after looking at the figure.

5. Place the card on the magnetic board making the side on which the figure is drawn visible.

6. Use a card for the consonant ' وَ ' which means 'and' and place it on the magnetic board.

7. Demonstrate another noun زَهْرَةٌ with a figure of a flower and repeat steps 1-5 above.

8. Now read زَهْرَةٌ وَ كَتَابٌ . Make sure that the students can read in Arabic. Ask them to translate into English.

9. Gradually introduce the cards with figures for all nouns in UNIT 1 and place them on the magnetic board.

10. Read the nouns with a pointer in sequence. Break the sequence and point out different nouns making sure that the students recognise these nouns.

Phase II: Reading UNIT 1 of the Arabic Text

Making visible only UNIT 1 of the Arabic text on the screen. Ask the students to read in Arabic. Correct the pronunciations. Provide individual attention if the class is small. Repeat the reading exercise until you are satisfied that the students can read the text correctly.

Phase III: Grammatical Themes UNIT 1

Project on the screen Rule No. 1 and its Example Analysis. Explain the rule. Raise relevant questions making sure that the students understand the rule. Repeat this treatment for all rules in UNIT 1.

(Bearing in mind the variation in the themes of the remaining units, the presentation can be modified in all three phases mentioned above and still fulfil the requirements of the units.)

Phase IV: Exercises

All exercises should be marked if the group is small. In the case of a fairly large group, the key should be provided in the classroom enabling students to correct mistakes themselves.

Students should be asked to refer appendix H number 8 for correction of their exercises.

Phase V Dictation

In order to make sure that students write all new words in Arabic correctly, efforts should be made to dictate all such words and correct their exercise books.

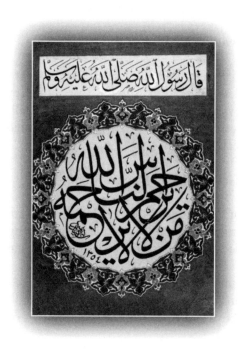

Lesson 1

Exercise No. 19

(1) Construct sentences by selecting appropriate nouns from the following tables: -

قَلَمٌ ، بَابٌ ، رَجُلٌ ، غُرْفَةٌ ، مَائِدَةٌ ، وَلَدٌ ، امْرَأَةٌ ، كِتَابٌ ، كُرْسِيٌّ ، بِنْتٌ ، سَمَاءٌ ، أَبٌ ، زَهْرَةٌ ، شَمْسٌ ، أُمٌّ ، يَدٌ	هَذَا	أ
	هَذِه	هَلْ

رَجُلٌ، امْرَأَةٌ ، أَبٌ ، أُمٌّ ،	هُوَ
بِنْتٌ ، وَلَدٌ .	هِيَ

(2) Translate into Arabic:

(1) Is he a man?

(2) Yes, he is a man.

(3) Is this a flower?

(4) Yes, this is a flower.

(5) Is this an eye?

(6) No this is a hand.

(7) Who is this?

(8) This is a man.

(9) Who is she?

(10) She is a mother.

(11) Is this a door?

(12) No, this is a glass.

(13) Is she a girl?

(14) No, she is a woman.

(15) She is a mother and he is a father

113

الدَّرْسُ الثَّانِي

2

✾ UNIT 7 ✾

(١) أَلْأَبُ وَ الْبَابُ.

(٢) الْجَنَّةُ وَ الْحَرْثُ.

(٣) الْخُبْزُ وَ الْعَيْنُ.

(٤) الْغُرْفَةُ وَ الْفُلْكُ.

(٥) الْقَلَمُ وَ الْكَأْسُ.

(٦) الْمَالُ وَ الْوَلَدُ.

(٧) الْهُدَى وَ الْيَدُ.

✾ UNIT 8 ✾

(١) التُّرَابُ وَ الثَّوْبُ.

(٢) الدُّنْيَا وَ الذَّهَبُ.

(٣) الرَّجُلُ وَ الزَّهْرَةُ.

(٤) السَّمَاءُ وَ الشَّمْسُ.

(٥) الصِّرَاطُ وَ الضَّوْءُ.

(٦) الطَّعَامُ وَ الظُّلْمَةُ.

(٧) اللَّيْلُ وَ النَّهَارُ.

115

(١) هَذَا قَلَمٌ وَ ذَلِكَ ثَوْبٌ.

(٢) هَذِه جَنَّةٌ وَ تِلْكَ غُرْفَةٌ.

(٣) هَذَا كُرْسِيٌّ وَ ذَلِكَ كِتَابٌ.

(٤) هَذِه شَمْسٌ وَ تِلْكَ نَارٌ.

(٥) هَذَا حَرْثٌ وَ تِلْكَ كَأْسٌ.

(٦) هَذِه دُنْيَا وَ تِلْكَ ظُلْمَةٌ.

(٧) هَذَا بَابٌ وَ ذَلِكَ كِتَابٌ.

(٨) هَذِه عَيْنٌ وَ تِلْكَ أُمٌّ.

(٩) هَذَا طَعَامٌ وَ ذَلِكَ خُبْزٌ.

(١٠) هَذِه مَائِدَةٌ وَ تِلْكَ بِنْتٌ.

(١) مَنْ عَلِمَ؟

هُوَ عَلِمَ، ٱلْأَبُ عَلِمَ، اَلرَّجُلُ عَلِمَ، الْوَلَدُ عَلِمَ، مُوسَى عَلِمَ.

(٢) مَنْ عَلِمَتْ؟

هِيَ عَلِمَتْ، ٱلْأُمُّ عَلِمَتْ، الْمَرْأَةُ عَلِمَتْ، الْبِنْتُ عَلِمَتْ، مَرْيَمُ عَلِمَتْ.

(٣) مَنْ جَهِلَ؟

هُوَ جَهِلَ، جَهِلَ ٱلْأَبُ، جَهِلَ الرَّجُلُ، جَهِلَ الْوَلَدُ، زَيْدٌ جَهِلَ.

(٤) مَنْ جَهِلَتْ؟

هِيَ جَهِلَتْ، جَهِلَتِ الْأُمُّ، جَهِلَتِ الْمَرْأَةُ، جَهِلَتِ الْبِنْتُ، زَيْنَبُ جَهِلَتْ.

(٥) مَنْ صَدَقَ؟

صَدَقَ اللهُ وَ صَدَقَ الرَّسُولُ (ﷺ).

(٦) مَنْ كَتَبَ وَ مَنْ قَرَأَ؟

كَتَبَ ٱلْأَبُ وَ قَرَأَ الْوَلَدُ.

(٧) هُوَ دَخَلَ ثُمَّ خَرَجَ.

(٨) هِيَ دَخَلَتْ ثُمَّ خَرَجَتْ.

(٩) ٱلْأَبُ دَخَلَ ثُمَّ أَكَلَ.

(١٠) اَلْأُمُّ دَخَلَتْ ثُمَّ أَكَلَتْ.

(١١) قَرَأَ ٱلْأَبُ وَ سَمِعَ ٱلْوَلَدُ.

(١٢) قَرَأَتِ ٱلْأُمُّ وَ سَمِعَتِ ٱلْبِنْتُ.

(١٣) مَنْ ذَهَبَتْ؟ اَلْأُمُّ ذَهَبَتْ وَ ٱلْبِنْتُ ذَهَبَتْ.

(١٤) مَنْ ضَعُفَ؟ ضَعُفَ ٱلْأَبُ.

(١٥) هَلِ ٱلْبِنْتُ ضَعُفَتْ؟ لاَ، ضَعُفَتِ ٱلْأُمُّ.

🌸 UNIT 11 🌸

(١) أَكَتَبْتَ؟ نَعَمْ، كَتَبْتُ.

(٢) هَلْ سَمِعْتَ؟ نَعَمْ، سَمِعْتُ.

(٣) هَلْ أَكَلْتَ؟ نَعَمْ، أَكَلْتُ.

(٤) هَلْ ذَهَبْتَ؟ نَعَمْ، ذَهَبْتُ.

(٥) هَلْ قَرَأْتَ وَ عَلِمْتَ؟
نَعَمْ، قَرَأْتُ وَعَلِمْتُ.

(٦) هَلْ دَخَلْتَ؟
نَعَمْ، دَخَلْتُ ثُمَّ خَرَجْتُ وَ ذَهَبْتُ.

(٧) أَشَرِبْتَ؟
نَعَمْ، أَكَلْتُ وَ شَرِبْتُ.

118

(٨) هَلْ جَهِلْتَ؟

نَعَمْ، جَهِلْتُ.

(٩) هَلْ كَتَبْتَ؟

نَعَمْ، كَتَبْتُ ثُمَّ قَرَأْتُ وَ عَلِمْتُ.

(١٠) هَلْ جَلَسْتَ؟

نَعَمْ، جَلَسْتُ ثُمَّ أَكَلْتُ.

❁ UNIT 12 ❁

(١) صَدَقَ اللهُ وَ صَدَقَ الرَّسُولُ (ﷺ).

(٢) اللهُ صَادِقٌ وَ الرَّسُولُ (ﷺ) صَادِقٌ.

(٣) صَدَقَتِ الْأُمُّ وَ كَذَبَتِ الْبِنْتُ.

(٤) الْأُمُّ صَادِقَةٌ وَ الْبِنْتُ كَاذِبَةٌ.

(٥) عَلِمَ الْأَبُ وَ جَهِلَتِ الْأُمُّ.

(٦) الْأَبُ عَالِمٌ وَ الْأُمُّ جَاهِلَةٌ.

(٧) قَرَأَ الْوَلَدُ

(٨) الْوَلَدُ قَارِئٌ وَ الْبِنْتُ سَامِعَةٌ.

(٩) أَأَنْتِ كَاتِبَةٌ؟

نَعَمْ، أَنَا كَاتِبَةٌ.

(١٠) هَلْ قَرَأْتَ وَ عَلِمْتَ؟

نَعَمْ، قَرَأْتُ وَ عَلِمْتُ.

(١١) أَأَنْتِ صَادِقَةٌ وَ هِيَ كَاذِبَةٌ؟

نَعَمْ، أَنَا صَادِقَةٌ وَ هِيَ كَاذِبَةٌ.

(١٢) هَلْ أَنْتِ عَالِمَةٌ؟

نَعَمْ، أَنَا عَالِمَةٌ.

(١٣) كَتَبَ الْعَالِمُ وَ قَرَأَ الْجَاهِلُ.

(١٤) قَرَأَ الْعَالِمُ وَ سَمِعَتِ الْجَاهِلَةُ.

(١٥) دَخَلَ الصَّادِقُ وَ خَرَجَ الْكَاذِبُ.

(١٦) الْجَاهِلُ دَخَلَ ثُمَّ خَرَجَ وَ ذَهَبَ.

(١٧) الْكَاتِبَةُ كَتَبَتْ وَ الْعَالِمَةُ قَرَأَتْ وَعَلِمَتْ.

(١٨) اَلْأَبُ ضَعِيفٌ وَ اَلْأُمُّ ضَعِيفَةٌ.

(١٩) اللهُ سَمِيعٌ عَلِيمٌ.

120

GLOSSARY
LESSON 2

جَنَّةٌ	(F¹) garden	ثُمَّ	Then
حَرْثٌ	(M¹) field	عَالِمٌ	(M¹) scholar
فُلْكٌ	(F¹) ship	عَالِمَةٌ	(F¹) scholar
هُدىً	guidance	عَلِمَ	(III M¹) to know
تُرَابٌ	(M) soil	عَلِمَتْ	(IIIF¹) she knew
ثَوْبٌ	(M) garment	عَلِمْتَ	(IIM¹) you knew
دُنْيَا	(F) world	عَلِمْتِ	(IIF¹) you knew
ذَهَبٌ	(M) gold	عَلِمْتُ	(IM¹+F¹) I knew
صِرَاطٌ	(M¹) road	جَهِلَ	to remain ignorant
ضَوْءٌ	light	صَدَقَ	to speak truth
طَعَامٌ	(M¹) food	كَتَبَ	to write
ظُلْمَةٌ	darkness	قَرَأَ	to read
لَيْلٌ	(M¹) night	دَخَلَ	to enter
نَهَارٌ	(F¹) day	خَرَجَ	to come out
نَارٌ	(F) Fire	أَكَلَ	to eat
شَرِبَ	to drink	كَذَبَ	to speak lie
سَمِعَ	to listen to	جَلَسَ	to sit
ضَعُفَ	become weak	ذَهَبَ	to go

كَيفَ أدعوكَ وأنا عَاص
وكَيفَ لا أدعوكَ وأنت كَريمُ

❧ GRAMMATICAL THEMES ❧
LESSON 2
UNIT 7 – 8

الْحُرُوْفُ الشَّمْسِيَّةُ وَالْحُرُوفُ القَمَرِيَّةُ وَالمَعْرِفَةُ

The Sun and the Moon Letters and Definite Nouns

Rule No. 13

All twenty eight Arabic consonants are divided on phonetic grounds into two equal groups. Fourteen are known as *al-Ḥurūf al-Qamariyyah,* **The Moon letters[1]:**

ا، ب، ج، ح، خ، ع، غ، ف، ق، ك، م، هـ،، و، ي

and the remaining fourteen are *al- Ḥurūf ash Shamsiyyah,* **The Sun letters[2]:**

ت، ث، د، ذ، ر، ز، س، ش، ص، ض، ط، ظ، ل، ن

Rule No. 14

When the article "*al***"** اَلْ **is placed at the beginning of an indefinite noun it makes it definite and the** *tanwīn,* **nunation confines it to a** *ḥarakah,* **a short vowel.**

Example Analysis:

بَابٌ (a door) الْبَابُ (the door)

---

[1] These letters are named as moon letters because the noun الْقَمَرُ (the moon) provides a pattern for articulation for all such nouns.

[2] These letters are named as sun letters because the noun الشَّمْسُ provides a pattern for articulation for all such nouns.

بَابٌ Is indefinite because the final consonant *bā'* carries a *tanwīn* [ُ] (see Rule No. 1) when the article "*al*" اَل is placed at the beginning of the noun the *tanwīn* of the final consonant *bā'* is confined to a *ḥarakah ḍammah* [ُ] because it was carrying *ḍammah tanwīn* [ٌ] previously.

N.B. : when an indefinite noun is changed into a definite with the article "<u>al</u>" اَل, the definite noun should NEVER carry a <u>tanwīn</u>.

Rule No. 15

When an indefinite noun begins with one of the Moon letters and is changed into a definite noun by placing "*al*" اَلْ at the beginning, the *lām* of "*al*" اَلْ should be recited.

الْبَابُ (*al-bābu*) The door.

الْجَنَّةُ وَالْحَرْثُ (*al-jannatu walḥarthu*)

All fourteen nouns in this unit begin with one of the Moon letters and all include the article "*al*" اَلْ. Therefore, *lām* of "*al*" should be recited and all become definite.

N.B. :The underlined consonants in this unit are all the fourteen Moon letters.

Rule No. 16

When an indefinite noun begins with one of the Sun letters and it is changed into a definite noun by placing "al" اَل at the beginning, the *lām* of "al" should be assimilated with the Sun letter.

(The *kasrah* ⎯ is placed under the *shaddah* (ّ) in الصِّرَاطُ. It is followed in the designed text).

Example Analysis:

التُّرَابُ (*atturābu*) The soil.

The sound of the letter *lām* should be assimilated with the Sun letter *tā'* with which the noun begins. There are fourteen nouns in this unit which begin with one of the Sun letters and include"al" اَل. Therefore, *lām* of "al" should be assimilated with the Sun letter.

N.B. The underlined consonants in this unit are all the fourteen Sun letters.

UNIT 9

Rule No. 17

ذَلِكَ (that) [M¹] is a singular masculine demonstrative pronoun and تِلْكَ (that) [F¹] is a singular feminine demonstrative pronoun. Both are used when the object for demonstration is far away.

ذَلِكَ ثَوْبٌ (That is a cloth.)

تِلْكَ غُرْ فَةٌ (That is a room.)

UNIT 10

الْفِعْلُ الْمَاضِيْ

The Verb: Perfect

Verbs in Arabic are mostly triliteral (containing three radical letters) but there are a few quadriliteral (containing four radical letters) verbs. They include two tenses: the Perfect(past tense) and the Imperfect (present and future tenses).

Some Arabic grammarians use the verb فَعَلَ (he did), the third person singular masculine IIIM[1], as a root and also as an example pattern. This pattern is frequently used in this work. It is therefore, necessary to understand it.

The initial radical letter in فَعَلَ is *Fā*, the medial is *'Ayn* and the third radical letter is *Lām*. The medial radical *'Ayn* in a triliteral Perfect verb may carry *fatḥah* —— , *kasrah* —— or *dammah* —— but the radical *Fā'* and *Lām* only carry *fatḥah* in all roots. The following three verbs give examples of the three possibilities for the radical *'Ayn*.

(1)

فَـ ـعَـ ـلَ
⇓ ⇓ ⇓
كَـ ـتَـ ـبَ

The radical *Kāf* stands for *Fā*, the radical *Tā'* stands for the medial radical *'Ayn* and *Bā'* stands for the third radical *Lām*. (He wrote) is the third person singular masculine.(III M[1])

(2)

فَـ ـعـ ـلَ
⇓ ⇓ ⇓
جَـ ـهـ ـلَ

The radical *Jīm* stands for *Fā*, the radical *Hā* stands for *'Ayn* which carries *kasrah* —— and *Lām* stands for the third radical *Lām*. جَهِلَ (He remained ignorant) is (III M[1]).

(3)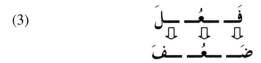

The radical *Ḍā'* stands for *Fā*, the radical *'Ayn* stands for *'Ayn*
which carries *ḍammah* ＿ and *Fā* stands for the third radical

Lām ضَعُفَ (He became weak) is (III M[1]).

[Note in all three examples the radicals *Fā* and *Lām* carry
fatḥah but the radical *'Ayn* carries either *fatḥah*, *kasrah* or
ḍammah. فَعُلَ]

N.B. *The radical* **'ayn** *in* فَعَلَ *root carries fatḥah only. The
remaining two vowels kasrah and ḍammah are deliberately
placed for the sake of example so that it can be used as a pattern
for all such roots in which radical 'ayn carries either kasrah
and ḍammah.*

Arabic verbs are either transitive (requiring a direct object to
complete the sense) or intransitive (which does not take a direct
object) and a few others are both transitive or intransitive
depending on their use.

(1) The pattern فَعَل generally retains the transitive character as
in كَتَبَ (he wrote) or أَكَلَ (he ate) but there are a few roots
which although they share the same pattern (i.e. فَعَلَ) retain
their intransitive character such as جَلَسَ (he sat).

(2) The pattern فَعِل generally gives intransitive significance as
in عَلِمَ (he knew) جَهِلَ (he remained ignorant).

(3) The pattern فَعُلَ is intransitive in its character and indicates a permanent state or inherent quality as in ضَعُفَ (he became weak)

(4) Certain verbs depending on their use are either transitive or intransitive as in سَمِعَ (he heard).

Rule No. 18

If the مُبْتَدَأ subject *fā'il* is third person masculine singular (III M¹) the verb ends with (⎯ a).

Example Analysis:

(1) مُوسَى عَلِمَ (Mūsā knew.)

In the above example مُوسَى is third person masculine singular (III M¹) and he is also the subject therefore, عَلِمَ ends with (⎯ a).

In examples 3, 5, 6, 7, 8, 11, and 14 all verbs end with (⎯ a) and all are (III M¹). In the above example مُوسَى is the مُبْتَدَأ، subject and عَلِمَ the خَبَرٌ predicate and it is a nominal sentence.

N.B. The predicate agrees with the subject in case, gender an number.

Rule No. 19

If the subject is third person feminine singular (III F¹) the verb ends with (ـتْ ⎯).

Example Analysis:

(2) مَرْيَمُ عَلِمَتْ (Maryam knew.)

مَرْيَمُ is third person singular feminine (III F¹) and she is the subject of the verb عَلِمَتْ which ends with (ـَ تْ).

In example no's. 2, 4, 8, 10, 12, 13 and 15 all verbs end with (ـَ تْ) because their subject is feminine.

Note the particle ثُمَّ is employed for connection. It connects two actions with some duration of time. It also signifies gradation.

(7) هُوَ دَخَلَ ثُمَّ خَرَجَ (He entered, then he came out.)

UNIT 11

Rule No. 20

If a particle, a noun or a verb ends with a quiescent consonant and the following word begins with a *hamzat al-waṣl* [آ], the connecting *hamzah* then generally *kasrah* is added to the quiescent consonant enabling it to join with the following word.

Example Analysis:  جَهِلَتِ الْأُمُّ

The verb جَهِلَتْ ends with the quiescent (تْ) because its subject is الْأُمُّ (III F¹). This quiescent (تْ) joins with الْأُمُّ which begins with *hamzat al-waṣl*, the connective *hamzah*. A *Kasrah* is added to the quiescent (تْ) enabling it to join with the *Lām* of الْأُمُّ .

Note this kasrah can be called kasrah of convenience which provides convenience when two words are connected with each other in the articulation. The verb usually precedes the subject. Such verbal sentences need no subject pronoun.

(١٥) هَلِ الْبِنْتُ ضَعُفَتْ ؟

The particle هَلْ ends with the quiescent (لْ) and the next word الْبِنْتُ begins with *hamzat al waṣl*, the connecting *hamzah*. A *kasrah* is added to the consonant *Lām* enabling it to join with the *Lām* of الْبِنْتُ .

Rule No. 21

If the subject is second person masculine singular (II M¹) the verb ends in (تَ) keeping its radical letter *Lām* quiescent.

Example Analysis:

(1)   أَأَنْتَ كَتَبْتَ؟ (Did you write?)

The subject of the verb كَتَبْتَ is أَنْتَ which is second person masculine singular (II M¹). Therefore, it ends with (تَ). The radical letter *Lām* in this verb is *Bā* therefore it is kept quiescent.

In examples 5 and 6 the verbs end in (تَ) leaving the radical *Lām* quiescent.

Rule No. 22

If the subject is second person feminine singular (II F¹) the verb ends in (تِ) keeping its radical letter Lām quiescent.

Example Analysis:

هَلْ أَنْتِ سَمِعْتِ ؟ (Did you (F¹) listen?)

The subject of the verb سَمِعْتِ is أَنْتِ which is second person feminine singular (II F¹). Therefore, it ends in (تِ). The radical letter *Lām* in this verb is '*a*' therefore it remains quiescent.

In examples 2, 3, 6 and 9 verbs دَخَلْتِ، أَكَلْتِ، سَمِعْتِ

and كَتَبْتِ end in (تِ) leaving the radical letter *Lām* quiescent.

N.B. Note in Rule No. 20 the radical Lām is not quiescent as it carries fathah. The kasrah is placed under Tā' for convenience only. In this Rule No. 22 Tā' carries kasrah but the radical Lām is quiescent.

Rule No. 23

If the subject is first person singular masculine and feminine (IM¹+ I F¹) the verb ends with تُ keeping its radical letter *Lām* quiescent.

Example Analysis:

أَنَا كَتَبْتُ (I [M¹+F¹] wrote.)

The subject of the verb كَتَبْتُ is أَنَا which is first person singular masculine and feminine (I M¹+I F¹). Therefore , it ends with (تُ). The radical letter *Lām* in this verb is *Bā'* therefore it remains quiescent.

Examples 1- 10 end in (تُ) leaving the radical letter *Lām* quiescent.

UNIT 12

اسْمُ فَاعِلٍ

Active participle (AP)

Rule No. 24

Each verb stands for a specific action. The Active Participle indicates the doer of the action. It may be treated either as a noun or as an adjective.

The method of forming an Active Participle (M^1) is as follows:

(1) Add *Alif* after the radical letter *Fā'*.
(2) Place *kasrah* under the radical letter *'Ayn*.
(3) As AP is a noun the radical letter *Lām* in case of indefiniteness shall carry a *tanwīn* and if definite it shall carry a *ḥarakah* short vowel.

فَاعِلٌ (doing / doer) = فَ ا عِ لٌ فَعَلَ

كَاتِبٌ (writing /writer) = كَ ا تِ بٌ كَتَبَ

سَامِعٌ (listening / listener) = سَ ا مِ عٌ سَمِعَ

Rule No.14 applies when an indefinite Active Participle is made definite.

For feminine (F^1) ـة / ة added to the radical letter *Lām*, which then takes *fatḥah*.

فَاعِلٌ	فَاعِلَةٌ
كَاتِبٌ	كَاتِبَةٌ

132

سَامِعٌ   سَامِعَةٌ

N.B. Each verb stands for a specific action. The Active participle indicates the doer of the action. It may be treated either as a noun or an adjective.

The Active Participle is also formed on the pattern of فَعِيْلٌ.

Generally this position is used for adjectives and attributes of Allah.*

(Hearing) سَمِعَ ← سَمِيْعٌ

(Knowing) عَلِمَ ← عَلِيْمٌ

N.B. When the radical letter 'Ayn of a verb carries __dammah__ فَعُلَ the Active Participle can be formed on the pattern of فَعِيْلٌ.

الأَبُ ضَعِيْفٌ وَالأُمُّ ضَعِيْفَةٌ. (the father is weak and the mother is weak.)

---

*It reflects the intensity of an action.

133

METHOD OF TEACHING
LESSON 2

(A) Units 7-9

1. Write on 6cm x 4cm cards all the nouns so far introduced indefinite form using red ink for الْ and *dammah* ُ .

2. The methods indicated in phases 1-3 in Lesson 1 are useful for teaching these units.

(B) Units 10-12

1. Preparation of 12cm x 6cm cards is recommended for all verbs introduced in this lesson.

2. Select three colours for the radical letters *Fā', 'Ayn* and *Lā* and retain these colours strictly for the roots throughout the course.

3. Use Master Root فَعَلَ by preparing three cards for each letter. Use the same colours as selected in (2) above.

4. Use the fourth colour for all additions and retain the colour strictly for all conjugated as well as derived forms.

5. Display to the students all the cards on which the verbs are written one after the other and ask the students to read and translate.

6. For each verb invent a demonstrative sign with your actions close to the actions which the verbs demand and which the students can easily understand. Introduce all verbs through your actions enabling the students to give you the verb in Arabic through your actions.

7. Write هُوَ، هِي، أَنْتَ، أَنْتِ، أَنَا on five cards and fix them on the magnetic board. Exhibit one after the other the cards on which the verbs are written pointing to personal pronouns and asking the students to give the conjugated forms.

8. Introduce the Active Participle in four colours, three for the roots and one for the additions. It is also better to pin this sheet at the back of the card which contains the same root.

9. From experience, if the endings of the Perfect for five conjugated forms ('a, 'at, ta, ti, tu) are said in chorus, this will enable the students to use them for the conjugations of the roots.

10. The following table may assist students in their familiarisation of the Moon letters and the Sun letters.

The Sun Letters	The Moon Letters
ت ث	أ ب
د ذ ر ز	ج ح خ
س ش ص ض ط ظ	ع غ ف ق ك
ل	م
ن	ه و ي

Lesson 2

Exercise No. 20

(1) Construct sentences by using appropriate nouns and verbs from the following tables:

	هَذَا	
الــتُّرَابُ، الثَّوْبُ، الْجَنَّةُ، الْحَرْثُ		
	هَذه	أ
النَّهَارُ، اللَّيْلُ، الْفُلْكُ،		
	ذَلِكَ	
الظُّلْمَةُ، الطَّعَامُ، الصِّرَاطُ، الذَّهَبُ		
الدُّنْيَا	تِلْكَ	هَلْ

فَعَلَ، فَاعِلٌ، ذَهَبَتْ، سَمِعْتَ، جَاهِلَةٌ، جَلَسَ	هُوَ
قَرَأْت، صَادِقٌ، أَكَلْتُ، كَاذِبٌ، شَرِبْتُ، دَخَلَ	هِيَ
قَارِئٌ، خَرَجَتْ، سَامِعَةٌ، صَدَقْت، صَادِقَةٌ	أَنْتَ
كَذَبْتَ، عَالِــمٌ، صَدَقْتَ، كَاتِبٌ، عَالِمَةٌ	أَنْتِ
ضَعُفَ، جَلَسْتَ، عَلِمْتُ، جَهِلْت، جَاهِلٌ	أَنَا

(2) Translate into Arabic:

1. This is the soil and that is the garden.
2. This is the cloth and that is the ship.
3. This is the darkness and that is the light.
4. This is the hand and that is the gold.
5. That is the glass and this is a flower.
6. This is the world and that is the sky.

136

7. This is a road and that is a ship.
8. Allah knew and the messenger ﷺ knew.
9. She ate and she drank.
10. The father read and the daughter listened.
11. Did you (M[1]) write and read?
12. Yes, I wrote and read.
13. The liar came out and went.
14. The girl is a reader and the boy is a listener.
15. The scholar wrote and the writer read

(3) Give the active participate singular, masculine, feminine, definite and indefinite from the following roots.

فَعَلَ، قَرَأَ، سَمِعَ، عَلِمَ، جَهِلَ، كَتَبَ، صَدَقَ، كَذَبَ،

أَكَلَ ، شَرِبَ، جَلَسَ

(68: 4)

137

الدَّرْسُ الثَّالِثُ
3

❈ UNIT 13 ❈

(١) هَلْ هُوَ أَبٌ؟

نَعَمْ، هُوَ أَبٌ.

(٢) أَيْنَ هُوَ؟

هُوَ فِي الْغُرْفَةِ.

(٣) مَنْ هِيَ؟

هِيَ أُمٌّ.

(٤) أَيْنَ هِيَ؟

هِيَ فِي الْبَيْتِ، وَ هِيَ جَالِسَةٌ عَلَى الْكُرْسِيِّ.

(٥) أَأَنْتِ بِنْتٌ؟

نَعَمْ، أَنَا بِنْتٌ.

(٦) أَيْنَ أَنْتِ؟

أَنَا فِي الْمَدْرَسَةِ، وَ أَنَا كَاتِبَةٌ بِالْقَلَمِ.

(٧) مَنْ أَنْتَ؟

أَنَا وَلَدٌ.

(٨) أَيْنَ أَنْتَ؟

أَنَا فِي الْمَدْرَسَةِ، وَ أَنَا جَالِسٌ عَلَى الْكُرْسِيِّ.

(٩) يَا مُوسَى! أَيْنَ أَنْتَ؟

أَنَا فِي الْمَسْجِد.

(١٠) يَا مَرْيَمُ! أَيْنَ أَنْتِ؟

أَنَا فِي الْبَيْت.

(١١) يَاأَيُّهَا الْوَلَدُ! هَلْ أَنْتَ ذَاهِبٌ إِلَى الْمَدْرَسَة؟

لاَ، أَنَا ذَاهِبٌ إِلَى الْمَسْجِد لِلصَّلاَة.

(١٢) يَاأَيَّتُهَا الْبِنْتُ! هَلْ أَنْتِ ذَاهِبَةٌ إِلَى الْبَيْت؟

نَعَمْ، أَنَا ذَاهِبَةٌ مِنَ الْمَدْرَسَةِ إِلَى الْبَيْت.

(١٣) يَاأَيُّهَا الرَّجُلُ! مَا هَذَا؟

هَذَا قَلَمٌ وَ هُوَ عَلَى الْمَائِدَة.

(١٤) يَاأَيَّتُهَا الْمَرْأَةُ! مَا هَذه؟

هَذه زَهْرَةٌ وَ هِيَ فِي الْكَأْس.

(١٥) يَا وَلَدُ! مَا هَذه؟

هَذه مَائِدَةٌ.

(١٦) مِنْ أَبٍ لِوَلَد.

(١٧) مِنْ بَيْتٍ إِلَى مَسْجِد.

(١٨) الأَرْضُ لِلّه وَ الْمُلْكُ لِلّه وَ أَنَا لِلّه.

(١)   بِمَ؟ = [بِ + مَا]

(٢)   مِمَّ؟ = [مِنْ + مَا]

(٣)   مِمَّنْ؟ = [مِنْ + مَنْ]

(٤)   فِيمَ؟ = [فِي + مَا]

(٥)   لِمَنْ؟ = [لِ + مَنْ]

(٦)   لِمَ؟ = [لِ + مَا]

(٧)   عَلَامَ؟ = [عَلَى + مَا]

(٨)   مِنْ أَيْنَ؟

(٩)   عَلِمَ اللهُ وَ هُوَ الْعَالِمُ.

(١٠)   صَدَقَ الرَّسُولُ (ﷺ) وَ هُوَ الصَّادِقُ.

(١١)   مَنِ الْخَالِقُ؟   اللهُ هُوَ الْخَالِقُ.

(١٢)   أَأَنْتَ خَالِقٌ؟   لَا، اللهُ خَالِقٌ.

(١٣)   بِمَ كَتَبْتَ؟   كَتَبْتُ بِالْقَلَمِ.

(١٤)   عَلَى مَنْ قَرَأْتَ؟   قَرَأْتُ عَلَى الْأَبِ.

(١٥)   مِمَّ شَرِبْتَ؟   شَرِبْتُ مِنَ الْكَأْسِ.

(١٦)   لِمَنْ هَذَا الْحَرْثُ؟   هَذَا الْحَرْثُ لِلْأَبِ.

(١٧)   أَيْنَ الطَّعَامُ؟   الطَّعَامُ عَلَى الْمَائِدَةِ.

(١٨)   أَيْنَ الْفُلْكُ؟   الْفُلْكُ فِي الْبَحْرِ.

(١٩) مِنْ أَيْنَ دَخَلَ الْوَلَدُ؟ دَخَلَ الْوَلَدُ مِنَ الْبَابِ ثُمَّ خَرَجَ مِنَ الْبَيْتِ وَ ذَهَبَ إِلَى الْحَرْثِ.

(٢٠) ذَهَبْتُ مِنَ الْمَسْجِدِ إِلَى الْبَيْتِ.

(٢١) ذَهَبْتُ إِلَى الْبَيْتِ وَ جَلَسْتُ عَلَى الْكُرْسِيِّ وَ أَكَلْتُ عَلَى الْمَائِدَةِ.

(٢٢) مَنْ كَفَرَ بِاللهِ؟

الشَّيْطَانُ كَفَرَ بِاللهِ وَ الْكَافِرُ كَفَرَ بِاللهِ.

(٢٣) مَنْ فَهِمَ وَ مِنْ أَيْنَ فَهِمَ؟

فَهِمَ الْوَلَدُ مِنَ الْكِتَابِ.

(٢٤) عَلَامَ جَلَسَتِ الْأُمُّ؟

جَلَسَتِ الْأُمُّ عَلَى الْكُرْسِيِّ.

(٢٥) لِمَنِ الْأَرْضُ وَ السَّمَاءُ؟

اَلْأَرْضُ وَ السَّمَاءُ لِلَّهِ.

(٢٦) لِمَنِ الْمُلْكُ؟

اَلْمُلْكُ لِلَّهِ.

(٢٧) هَلِ الْمُلْكُ لِلْإِنْسَانِ؟

لَا، الْمُلْكُ لِلَّهِ.

(٢٨) مَا نَزَلَ مِنَ السَّمَاءِ؟

نَزَلَ الْقُرْآنُ مِنَ السَّمَاءِ، وَ نَزَلَتِ التَّوْرَاةُ مِنَ السَّمَاءِ، وَنَزَلَ الْإِنْجِيلُ وَ الزَّبُورُ مِنَ السَّمَاءِ.

(٢٩) عَلَى مَنْ نَزَلَ الإِنْجِيلُ؟

نَزَلَ الإِنْجِيلُ عَلَى عِيسَى (عَلَيْهِ السَّلَام)

(٣٠) عَلَى مَنْ نَزَلَ الْقُرْآنُ؟

نَزَلَ الْقُرْآنُ عَلَى مُحَمَّدٍ (ﷺ).

(٣١) هَلْ ذَهَبْتَ إِلَى الْمَسْجِدِ؟

نَعَمْ ذَهَبْتُ إِلَى الْمَسْجِدِ للصَّلَاةِ.

(٣٢) هَلْ فِي الأَرْضِ بَحْرٌ؟

نَعَمْ، فِي الأَرْضِ بَحْرٌ.

(٣٣) مَنْ لِلْفُلْكِ فِي الْبَحْرِ؟

اللهُ لِلْفُلْكِ فِي الْبَحْرِ.

(٣٤) مَنْ فَهِمَتْ مِنَ الْقُرْآنِ؟

الأُمُّ فَهِمَتْ مِنَ الْقُرْآنِ.

❀ UNIT 15 ❀

(١) مِنْهُ. مِنْهَا. مِنْكَ. مِنْكِ. مِنِّي.

(٢) بِهِ. بِهَا. بِكَ. بِكِ. بِي.

(٣) لَهُ. لَهَا. لَكَ. لَكِ. لِي.

(٤) عَلَيْهِ. عَلَيْهَا. عَلَيْكَ. عَلَيْكِ. عَلَيَّ.

(٥) إِلَيْهِ. إِلَيْهَا. إِلَيْكَ. إِلَيْكِ. إِلَيَّ.

(٦) فِيهِ. فِيهَا. فِيكَ. فِيكِ. فِيَّ.

(٧) أَيْنَ هُوَ؟ هُوَ فِي الْمَسْجِد.

هَلْ هُوَ فِيه؟ نَعَمْ، هُوَ فِيه.

(٨) أَيْنَ هِيَ؟ هِيَ فِي الْفُلْك.

هَلْ هِيَ فِيهَا؟ نَعَمْ هِيَ فِيهَا.

(٩) هَذِه غُرْفَةٌ وَ الْأَبُ جَالِسٌ فِيهَا.

(١٠) هَلْ هَذَا الْكِتَابُ لِيْ؟

نَعَمْ، هَذَا الْكِتَابُ لَكَ.

(١١) اللهُ رَبٌّ وَ مُحَمَّدٌ (ﷺ) رَسُولٌ.

(١٢) هَلْ قَرَأْتَ وَعَلِمْتَ مِنَ الْقُرْآن؟

نَعَمْ، قَرَأْتُ وَعَلِمْتُ مِنْهُ.

(١٣) يَا وَلَدُ! هَلْ كَتَبْتَ بِالْقَلَمِ؟

نَعَمْ، كَتَبْتُ بِالْقَلَمِ.

(١٤) هَلْ هَذَا مِنْكَ؟

نَعَمْ، هَذَا مِنِّي.

(١٥) مِمَّنْ هَذَا؟

هَذَا مِنْهُ وَ مِنْهَا.

(١٦) هَذِه الدُّنْيَا لِلَّه، فِيهَا خَيْرٌ وَ شَرٌّ.

144

GLOSSARY
LESSON 3

رَبٌّ	Nourisher, Cherisher, Sustainer, Lord	خَلَقَ	to create
مُلْكٌ	(M[1]) Kingdom	نَزَلَ	to descend
أَرْضٌ	(F[1]) earth	كَفَرَ	to reject, to disbelieve
مَسْجِدٌ	(M[1]) mosque	شَرِبَ	to drink
صَلاةٌ	(F[1]) Prayer	فَهِمَ	to understand
خَيْرٌ	virtue, good	رَجَعَ	to return
شَرٌّ	evil, vice	مِنْ	from
شَيْطَانٌ	(M[1]) Satan	إِلَى	to
بَيْتٌ	(M) house	بِـ	with
مَدْرَسَةٌ	(F[1]) school	لِ	for
بَحْرٌ	(M[1]) sea	عَلَى	on
يَا	(M+F) O!	فِي	in
أَيُّهَا	(M) O you!	عَنْ	from
أَيَّتُهَا	(F) O you!	تَوْرَاةٌ	Torah
أَيْنَ	where	إِنْجِيلٌ	Gospel
		زَبُورٌ	Psalm

145

GRAMMATICAL THEMES

Lesson 3

The text of lessons 1 and 2 provide good examples of the nominative case. Nouns in the nominative case end with a short vowel *dammah* ُ — or *dammah tanwīn* ٌ — depending on their form. Nouns remain in this case unless there is a good reason to change the case.

UNIT 13

حَالَةُ الْجَرِّ

Genitive Case

Rule No. 25

Seventeen particles are used in Arabic as prepositions. If one of them appears before a noun it changes the noun into the genitive case. In the genitive case, nouns accept either

kasrah (ِ) **or** *kasrah tanwīn* (ٍ) **depending on whether they are definite or indefinite.**

Example Analysis:

In the glossary the words عَنْ to مِنْ are prepositions and when they occur before a noun the noun becomes genitive.

هُوَ فِي الْغُرْفَةِ (He is in the room.) (2).

The preposition فِي appears before the noun الْغُرْفَة and is one of the particles which requires the genitive case. Therefore, ة (ta) of الْغُرْفَة carries *kasrah* without *tanwīn* because the noun is definite.

(17) مِنْ بَيْتٍ إِلَى مَسْجِدٍ (From a house to a mosque.)

مِنْ (from) and إِلَى (to) are prepositions and requires the genitive particles appear before the nouns بَيْتٍ and مَسْجِدٍ respectively.

As both these nouns are indefinite, their final consonants, therefore, carry *kasrah tanwīn*.

حُرُوْفُ النِّدَاءِ

Interjection / Vocative particles: [يا (O!) (M¹+F¹)]

أَيُّهَا (O you! M) أَيَّتُهَا (O you! F)

In their daily conversation Arabs use interjection particles for inviting the attention of person/s.

Rule No. 26

The particle for interjection يَا (O! M¹+F¹) cannot be followed by a noun with a definite article أَلْ (*al*). This particle can also be used for both genders.

Example Analysis:

يَاوَلَدُ ! مَا هَذه؟ (O boy! What is this (F[1]) ?) The particle for

interjection يَا is followed by the noun وَلَدُ. Although the definite

article (اَل) is not applied after يَا , the noun is construed as

definite because the speaker is addressing a specific person

therefore it is written without *tanwīn*.

Rule No. 27

The particles for interjection أَيُّهَا **and** أَيَّتُهَا **are**

always followed by nouns with the definite article (اَل)

(al).

UNIT 14

The Combination of Interrogative Particles:

The interrogative particles هَلْ ، أَ ، مَا **and** مَنْ are

introduced in Lesson No.1. They are combined with the

prepositions in this lesson and one more interrogative particle

أَيْنَ (Where ?) is added.

In Arabic some interrogative particles can be combined with

prepositions. (See UNIT 14 examples 1-8)

(1) بِمَ   With what ?

(2) مِمَّ   From what ?

(3) مِمَّنْ   From whom ?

(4) فِيْمَ   In what ?

(5) لِمَنْ   For whom ? To whom, whose?

(6) لِمَ   For what ? (why ?)

(7) عَلَامَ   On what ?

(8) مِنْ أَيْنَ   From where ?

Rule No. 28

If an interrogative particle is combined with a preposition the preposition will not have any genitive effect on the interrogative particle because interrogative particles are indeclinable.

Example Analysis:

In example no (5) لِمَنْ the preposition (لِ) is combined with

مَنْ The final consonant ن will remain *sākin* quiescent unless there is a need to join it with another noun which begins with *Hamzat al-waṣl*, the connecting *hamzah* (see Rule No.20) as it happens in example no (26) لِمَنِ الْمُلْكُ؟ Here مَنْ carries *kasrah* because it is combined with الْمُلْكُ but in example no. (16) لِمَنْ هَذَا الْحَرْثُ it retains its *sākin* quiescent form.

150

UNIT 15

ضَمِيرٌ مُتَّصِلٌ
Pronoun Suffix

The following are the singular pronoun suffixes:

هَا ــ (III F¹)   ــهُ (III M¹)

كِ (II F¹)   كَ (II M¹)

ي / نِي (I M¹ + F¹) (see appendix TA 18)

Rule No. 29

Pronoun suffixes can be combined with prepositions. When these are combined they give the meaning of both the pronoun suffixes and the prepositions employed.

Example no. 1

مِنْ (from) + ــهُ (him)   = مِنْهُ from him

مِنْ (from) + هَا (her)   = مِنْهَا from her

مِنْ (from) + كَ (you II M¹)   = مِنْكَ from you

مِنْ (from) + كِ (you II F¹)   = مِنْكِ from you

مِنْ (from) + نِي (me I M¹+F¹) = مِنِّي from me

On phonetical grounds there is a need to place نِي after مِنْ

151

When the quiescent نْ is joined with the following noun which

starts with *hamzat al-waṣl*, the connecting *hamzah* نْ quiescent

will carry *fatḥah* ــَ as in example no. 12,

أَنَا ذَاهِبَةٌ مِنَ الْمَدْرَسَةِ إِلَى الْبَيْتِ .   Here the quiescent

consonant of نْ will carry *fatḥah* in order to join with the noun

الْمَدْرَسَة.

In example no. 2 the preposition إِلَى is combined with ـهُ .
On phonetical grounds it is pronounced and written as *ilayhi*
instead of *ilayhu.*

In example no. 3 إِلَى + ـهُ = إِلَيْهِ is pronounced as *ilayhi*

and إِلَى + ي = إِلَيَّ as *ilayya.*

In example no. 4 عَلَى + ـهُ = عَلَيْهِ is pronounced as *'alayhi*

and عَلَى + ي = عَلَيَّ as *'alayya.*

In example no. 3 إِلَى + ـهُ = إِلَيْهِ is pronounced as *ilayhi*

and إِلَى + ـي = إِلَيَّ is pronounced as *ilayya.*

In example no. 6 فِي + ـهُ = فِيْهِ is pronounced as *fīhi* and

فِي + ي = فِيَّ is pronounced as *fiyya..*

152

METHOD OF TEACHING
LESSON 3

1. Explain the Genitive case with the use of cards for prepositions as well as using a few masculine and feminine nouns.

2. Explain the various forms of particles for interjection with cards on the magnetic board.

3. The combination of interrogative particles with prepositions can be explained by shifting the cards on the magnetic board.

4. Similarly, the combination of prepositions with pronoun suffix can be explained. Make sure that the students understand the variations in the pronunciations of a few such combinations.

5. Use the method for the introduction of rules and example analysis already explained and introduced rules (no. 25 -28).

6. Create the atmosphere of speaking Arabic by raising appropriate questions and allowing the students to give their replies in Arabic. Correct their mistakes by means of class discussions.

Lesson 3

Exercise No. 21

(1) Select the correct word(s) from the parentheses to fill in the blanks in the following sentences:

١. هِيَ كَاتِبَةٌ .... الْقَلَمِ

(فِي، لِـ، إِلَى، بِـ، عَلَى)

٢. ذَهَبْتُ .... الْبَيْتِ .... الْمَسْجِدِ.

(فِي، بِـ، لِـ، مِنْ، إِلَى، عَلَى)

٣. قَرَأْتُ .... الْكِتَابِ

(فِي، بِـ، لِـ، إِلَى، مِنْ، عَلَى)

٤. الْوَلَدُ خَرَجَ .... الْبَيْتِ

(فِي، بِـ، لِـ، مِنْ، إِلَى، عَلَى)

٥. الْفُلْكُ .... الْبَحْرِ.

(فِي، بِـ، لِـ، مِنْ، إِلَى)

٦. الْكَأْسُ .... الْمَائِدَةِ.

(لِـ، فِي، بِـ، عَلَى، إِلَى، مِنْ)

٧. الْعَالِمُ جَالِسٌ .... الْكُرْسِيِّ.

(لِـ، فِي، بِـ، عَلَى، إِلَى)

٨. هُوَ أَكَلَ .... الْيَدِ.

(لِـ، فِي، بِـ، عَلَى، إِلَى)

154

٩. أَنَا جَالِسٌ .... الْمَسْجِد.

(لِـ، فِي، بِـ، عَلَى، إِلَى)

(2) Translate the following sentences into Arabic.

1. Where is the girl? The girl is in her room.
2. Allah is the Creator and He is the Knower and I am an ignorant.
3. From where did you (M[1]) come out from the house? I came out from the door.
4. Who are you (F[1])? Who is he and who is she?
5. With what did you write? I wrote with the pen.
6. The earth is for Allah and I am for Allah.
7. O you boy! From where did you go?
8. I returned to the house and sat on the chair.
9. On what did you (M[1]) sit? I sat on the chair in my room.

Sūrat al-Ikhlās (No. 110)
Calligrapher: 'Azīz al-Dīn Wakīlī

(١) كِتَابُ اللّٰه   (٢) سُورَةُ الْقُرْآن

(٣) سُورَةُ الرَّحْمٰن   (٤) بَيْتُ اللّٰه

(٥) مَسْجِدُ الرَّسُوْل (ﷺ)   (٦) عَبْدُ اللّٰه

(٧) صَلَاةُ الْعَبْد   (٨) قَلَمُ الْبِنْت

(٩) ظُلْمَةُ اللَّيْل   (١٠) ضَوْءُ النَّهَار

(١١) فَاعِلُ الْخَيْر   (١٢) أَرْضُ اللّٰه

(١٣) مَالُ الْأَب   (١٤) فُلْكُ الْبَحْر

(١٥) كُرْسِيُّ الْبَيْت   (١٦) تُرَابُ الْحَرْث

(١٧) مَائِدَةُ الطَّعَام   (١٨) ثَوْبُ الْوَلَد

(١٩) عَالِمُ بَلَد   (٢٠) كِتَابُ أَب

(٢١) زَهْرَةُ أُمٍّ   (٢٢) غُرْفَةُ بِنْت

(٢٣) بَيْتُ رَجُلٍ   (٢٤) مَسْجِدُ بَلَد

(٢٥) كِتَابُهُ، كِتَابُهَا، كِتَابُكَ، كِتَابُكِ، كِتَابِيْ.

(٢٦) جَنَّتُهُ، جَنَّتُهَا، جَنَّتُكَ، جَنَّتُكِ، جَنَّتِيْ.

(٢٧) اللّٰهُ إِلَهُ الْأَرْضِ وَإِلَهُ السَّمَاء. اللّٰهُ إِلَهِيْ وَرَبِّيْ.

(٢٨) مُحَمَّدٌ (ﷺ) عَبْدُ اللّٰه وَرَسُوْلُ اللّٰه . مُحَمَّدٌ (ﷺ) عَبْدُهُ وَرَسُوْلُهُ.

(٢٩) اللهُ خَالِقُ السَّمَاءِ وَخَالِقُ الأَرْضِ.

(٣٠) الْقُرْآنُ كِتَابُ اللهِ.

(٣١) كُلُّ شَيْءٍ فِي الدُّنْيَا هَالِكٌ.

(٣٢) مَنْ تِلْكَ؟ تِلْكَ بِنْتٌ وَاسْمُهَا زَيْنَبُ وَهِيَ شَارِبَةٌ مِنَ الْكَأْسِ.

🏵 UNIT 17 🏵

(١) يَاعَبْدَ اللهِ! كَيْفَ حَالُكَ؟ أَنَا بِخَيْرٍ، الْحَمْدُ للهِ.

(٢) يَامَرْيَمُ! كَيْفَ حَالُكِ؟ أَنَا بِخَيْرٍ، الْحَمْدُ للهِ.

(٣) كَتَبْتُ بِسْمِ اللهِ.

(٤) جَلَسْتُ فِي بَيْتِ اللهِ.

(٥) نَزَلَ الْقُرْآنُ عَلَى رَسُوْلِ اللهِ (ﷺ).

(٦) مَا ذَلِكَ؟ ذَلِكَ كِتَابٌ.

(٧) عِنْدَ مَنْ ذَلِكَ الْكِتَابُ؟ ذَلِكَ الْكِتَابُ عِنْدَ الْوَلَدِ.

(٨) ثَوَابُ الْجَنَّةِ مِنْ عِنْدِ اللهِ وَكَذَلِكَ عَذَابُ النَّارِ مِنْ عِنْدِ اللهِ.

(٩) مِنْ أَيْنَ ذَهَبْتَ وَإِلَى أَيْنَ ذَهَبْتَ؟ ذَهَبْتُ مِنْ حَرْثِ الأَبِ إِلَى بَيْتِ الأَخِ.

(١٠) هَلْ كَتَبْتَ؟

نَعَمْ، كَتَبْتُ لِأَخِيهِ وَلِأُمِّهَا.

(١١) لِمَنْ قَرَأْتَ؟

قَرَأْتُ لِأَبِيهِ.

(١٢) مَا اسْمُكَ؟

اسْمِيْ إِبْرَاهِيْمُ.

(١٣) هَل اسْمُهَا فَاطِمَةُ؟

لَا، اسْمُهَا مَرْيَمُ.

(١٤) يَا كَافِرُ! أَنْتَ كَفَرْتَ بِخَالِقِكَ وَإِلَهِكَ.

(١٥) اللهُ خَالِقِي وَرَبِّي وَأَنَا عَبْدُهُ.

(١٦) أَيْنَ بِنْتُكَ؟

هِيَ فِيْ غُرْفَةِ أَبِيهَا.

(١٧) هَلْ أَكَلْتَ مَعَ الْأَبِ فِيْ غُرْفَةِ الطَّعَامِ؟

نَعَمْ، أَكَلْتُ مَعَهُ فِيْ غُرْفَةِ الطَّعَامِ.

(١٨) هَلْ عِنْدَكَ كِتَابُ وَلَدِهِ؟

لَا، عِنْدِي قَلَمُ وَلَدِهِ.

(١٩) بِمَ كَتَبْتَ؟

كَتَبْتُ بِقَلَمِه.

(٢٠) هَذَا أَبُوْهُ وَهَذَا أَخُوْهُ.

(٢١) هَذَا الْكِتَابُ لِأَبِيْهِ وَذَلِكَ الْكِتَابُ لِأَخِيْهِ.

(١) قَالَ، قَالَتْ، قُلْتَ، قُلْتِ، قُلْتُ، قَائِلٌ.

(٢) هَلْ صُمْتَ لله؟ نَعَمْ، قَدْ صُمْتُ لله.

(٣) قَالَ لِيْ أَبِيْ: قَدْ قَامَتِ الصَّلَاةُ فَقُمْتُ لِلصَّلَاة.

(٤) قُمْتُ فِي مَسْجِدِ بَلَدِيْ وَقُلْتُ: كُنْتُ فِي مَسْجِدِ الرَّسُوْل (ﷺ).

(٥) هَلْ هِيَ ذَاهِبَةٌ إِلَى مَسْجِدِ الرَّسُوْل (ﷺ)؟ نَعَمْ هِيَ ذَاهِبَةٌ إِلَى مَسْجِدِ الرَّسُوْل (ﷺ) لِلصَّلَاة.

(٦) هَذَا الرَّجُلُ كَأَبِيْ وَهَذِهِ الْبِنْتُ كَأُخْتِيْ.

(٧) كَانَ إِبْرَاهِيْمُ (عليه السلام) لله وَكَانَ اللهُ لَهُ.

(٨) هَلْ نِمْتَ قَبْلَ الصَّلَاةِ أَمْ بَعْدَ الصَّلَاةِ؟

(٩) نَامَتْ أُمِّيْ فِي بَيْتِ أَبِيْهَا وَنَامَ أَبِيْ فِي غُرْفَتِه.

(١٠) جَاءَ الْأَبُ مِنَ الْحَرْثِ إِلَى الْبَيْتِ وَجَلَسَ فِيْ غُرْفَة الطَّعَام.

(١١) قَالَ الْوَلَدُ: جِئْتُ مِنَ الْمَدْرَسَةِ وَجَلَسْتُ عَلَى الْكُرْسِيِّ.

(١٢) قَالَ اللهُ فِيْ كِتَابِه: " قَدْ سَمِعَ اللهُ ".

(١٣) اَلنَّدَمُ تَوْبَةٌ. "ح"

(١٤) كُلُّ مُسْكِرٍ حَرَامٌ.

(١٥) لِكُلِّ شَىءٍ زَكَوْةٌ وَ زَكَوْةُ الْجَسَدِ الصَّوْمُ.

GLOSSARY
LESSON 4

ثَوَابٌ	reward	حَمِدَ	to praise
عَذَابٌ	punishment	حَمْدٌ	praise
الْجَنَّةُ	Paradise	هَلَكَ	to perish
النَّارُ	Hell	هَالِكٌ	[AP] perishing
إِلَهٌ	(M¹) god	خَلَقَ	to create
سُورَةٌ	(F¹) Chapter of the Qur'ān	خَالِقٌ	[AP] creator
عَبْدٌ	(M¹) slave, servant	قَالَ	to say [TA1]
حَال	(M¹) condition	صَامَ	to fast [TA1]
اسْمٌ	(M¹) name	كَانَ	to be [TA1]
أُخْتٌ	(F¹) sister	قَامَ	to stand [TA1]
مَعَ	at, near, with, by, on (of place time and possession), upon, in the opinion of	نَامَ	to sleep [TA2]
كَيْفَ	how	جَاءَ	to come [TA2]
كُلُّ	all, each, every	عِنْدَ	with, together with, accompanied by, in company of
مُسْكِرٌ	intoxicative	ضِيَاءٌ	light
نَدَمٌ	remorse	شَيْءٌ	thing

160

		الرَّحْمَنُ	the Merciful
تَوْبَةٌ	repentance	حَرَامٌ	forbidden

GRAMMATICAL THEMES
LESSON 4

UNIT 16

الإِضَافَةُ

The 'Construct Phrase'

Rule No. 30

Iḍāfah consists of two nouns of any gender which are combined together in a phrase indicating their close relationship and generally imparting the meaning of possession. The first noun of the 'construct phrase' (*muḍāf*) provides the meaning of 'being possessed' and the second noun (*muḍāf ilayh*) denotes the 'possessor.'

(A)   The second noun '*muḍāf ilayh*':

i.   Always remains in genitive case.
ii.   It can remain either definite or indefinite.
iii.   It can be a pronoun suffix.

(B)   The first noun '*muḍāf*: the final consonant will carry
        — or a dhumma by itself.
        carries a tanwin

i.   Always appears as indefinite with a *harakah*, short
        vowel.   (carrying ُ)
ii.   Depending on its case it can remain in nominative,
        accusative or genitive form.
iii.   It agrees in meaning in both cases of definiteness and
        indefiniteness of the second noun.

Example Analysis:

(1) كِتَابُ اللهِ (The Book of Allah. / Allah's Book)

Both nouns كِتَابُ and اللهِ are closely related with each other and

this construction forms a phrase. The first noun كِتَابُ is written

and pronounced as indefinite with a *dammah* ـُ *harakah*

because it is in the nominative case but it gives the definite
meaning for its close relationship with the second noun of the
phrase Allah. The second noun is definite and it is in the
genitive case (carrying *kasrah*). See other examples 2 - 17.

In example no. 27 الْقُرْآنُ كِتَابُ اللهِ (The Qur'ān is the book of

Allah.) الْقُرْآنُ is subject and كِتَابُ اللهِ is predicate.

In example no. 19 عَالِمُ بَلَدٍ (A scholar of a town.), the second

noun is indefinite. It is in the genitive case carrying *kasrah
tanwīn*. Because of this the first noun is also indefinite, it is an
active participle and is in the nominative case.

كِتَابُهُ (His book), كِتَابُ is the first noun and ـهُ the pronoun

suffix stands for the second noun and is free from any genitive
effect. In the construct phrase the pronoun suffix becomes the
possessive pronoun.

❀ UNIT 17 ❀

Example (3) كَتَبْتُ بِاسْمِ اللهِ (I wrote in the name of Allah.).

Here كَتَبْتُ is the subject and بِسْمِ اللهِ (in the name of Allah) is

the predicate. This predicate is comprised of a construct phrase

اسْمُ اللهِ (the name of Allah), which is preceded by a preposition

163

ب (in / with). The second noun of the construct phrase الله is definite and it is in the genitive case (carrying *kasrah).* The first noun اسْمُ gives definite meaning, and is in the genitive case (carrying *kasrah)* because it is preceded by a preposition ب (with / in).

In the accusative case, nouns accept *fathah* or *fathah tanwīn* depending on their form. Lesson no. 6 deals with this but there is a need to understand the following rule.

Rule No. 31

If the first noun (*mudāf*) of a construct phrase (*idāfah*) is preceded by an interjection / vocative particle *yā* (يَا) then its case will be changed into the accusative (carrying a *harakah*

***fathah* _). The second noun always remains in the genitive case.**

Example Analysis:

(1) يَاعَبْدَ اللهِ! كَيْفَ حَالُكَ؟ (O! 'AbdAllâh how are you?)

عَبْدَ اللهِ is a construct phrase and the first noun (*mudāf*) عَبْدَ is preceded by يَا, a vocative, therefore it carries *fathah.* It is therefore in the accusative case and carries *fathah.*

Rule No. 32

A few nouns in Arabic including أَخٌ، أَبٌ on phonological grounds receive special treatment when any possessive pronoun is attached to them.

i. In the nominative case *Wāw* (و) is added between the noun and the possessive pronoun.

ii. In the genitive case *Yā'* (ي) is added between the noun and the pronoun suffix.

iii. In the accusative case *Alif* (ا) is added between the noun and the possessive pronoun.

Example Analysis:

هَذَا أَبُوهُ وَهَذَا أَخُوهُ (This is his father and this is his brother.)

أَخٌ and أَبٌ are in the nominative case, therefore *wāw* (وَ) is added between them and the pronoun suffix (هُ).

هَذَا الْكِتَابُ لِأَبِيْه وَهَذَا الْكِتَابُ لِأَخِيْه

(This book is for his father and this book is for his brother.)

In this sentence أَبٌ وَأَخٌ is preceded by the preposition (لِ)

(For), therefore they are in the genitive case. *Yā* (ي) is added between them and the possessive pronoun (ـِه).

(See next lesson for examples in the accusative case.)

مَعَ (with, together with / and عِنْدَ at, with) are prepositions which change the nouns into the genitive case.

ذَلِكَ الْكِتَابُ عِنْدَ الْوَلَد (That book is with the boy.)

The noun الْوَلَد is preceded by the preposition عِنْدَ (with), therefore it is in the genitive case and carries *kasrah*.

ثَوَابُ الْجَنَّة مِنْ عِنْد الله (The reward of Paradise is from Allah.)

عِنْدَ is preceded by one of the genitive particles مِنْ, therefore its

165

final consonant *Dāl* (د) carries *kasrah*. الله is preceded by عِنْدَ therefore it is in the genitive case.

هَلْ أَكَلْتَ مَعَ الأبِ في غُرْفةِ الطَّعامِ؟

(Did you eat in the dining room with your father?) The noun الأَبُ is preceded by مَعَ (with) therefore it is in the genitive case.

هَلْ عِنْدَكَ كِتَابُ وَلَدِهِ؟ (Do you have the book of his son ? / Do you have his son's book?) كِتَابُ here is the first noun of the first 'construct phrase'. وَلَد is the second noun of the 'construct phrase', therefore, it is in the genitive case. وَلَد again becomes the first noun of the second 'construct phrase' وَلَده (his son). The second noun of the second 'construct phrase' is the pronoun (ه) (his). In this case وَلَد retains its *kasrah* as well as the genitive case.

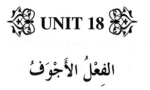

UNIT 18

الفِعْلُ الأَجْوَفُ

Hollow / Defective Verbs

All three radical letters remained intact and did not witness any change in the formation of the active participle and in the conjugation in all triliteral verbs introduced in Lessons 2 and 3. There are certain roots in which:

166

i. either one or two radical letters are vowels,

ii. or the first, second or third radical letters are *hamzah*, glottal stops,

iii. or the second and third radical letters are identical.

Such roots cause certain phonological changes in their forms and conjugations which beginners always find difficult. Experience suggests that if these are introduced systematically and gradually both in the text and example analysis, it greatly facilitates beginners to not only comprehend various changes but also gives them confidence to construct many words.

Various patterns of weak verbs are presented with capital letter A in numerical order. (A1-A11) and their full conjugations are presented in the appendix TA. Table D in the appendix includes the 'Five Pillars'.

A verb is called hollow because its medial radical letter is a

vowel. (ا و ى)

A1 (See table A for full conjugations)

Conjugations:

III M¹ remains as قَالَ (he said)

III F¹ becomes قَالَتْ (she said)

In these two forms the medial radical letter is identifiable.

These two forms in قَامَ, صَامَ becomes صَامَ and صَامَتْ, in

becomes قَامَتْ, in كَانَ becomes كَائَتْ.

II M¹ becomes قُلْتَ (you M¹ said)

II F¹ becomes قُلْتِ (you F¹ said)

and

I M¹ + F¹ becomes قُلْتُ (I M¹ + F¹ said)

In these three forms the medial radical letter is not identifiable.

167

It should be noted that there is a change in the initial radical letter (*Fā*), which is *Qāf*. Here, instead of carrying *fatḥah* it carries *ḍammah* and there is good reason for this. قَالَ is originally قَوَلَ the medial radical letter *wāw* which is dropped in these three forms is represented with *ḍammah* in the initial radical letter ق which becomes قُ.

These three forms in the root صَوَمَ becomes صُمْتَ (II M¹) صُمْت (II F¹) and صُمْتُ (I M¹+F¹); in the root قَوَمَ becomes قُمْتَ (II M¹) قُمْت (II F¹) and قُمْتُ (I M¹ + F¹); in the root كَوَنَ becomes كُنْتَ (II M¹) كُنْت (II F¹) and كُنْتُ (I M¹+F¹).

N.B. قَالَ *can be traced in an Arabic dictionary under* قَوَلَ

A2

The verb جَاءَ is doubly weak. Its medial radical letter is a vowel جَيِءَ (ی) and the final radical is (ء) *hamzah* a glottal stop.

In the third person forms *Alif* is retained.

(III M¹) remains as جَاءَ (he came)

(III F¹) becomes جَاءَتْ (she came)

In the second and first person (ی) is represented by a short vowel *kasrah*.

(II M¹) becomes جِئْتَ (you came)

(II F¹) becomes جِئْت (you came)

(I M¹ + F¹) becomes جِئْتُ (I came)

The initial radical letter (ح) in the above three conjugations carries *kasrah* instead of *fatḥah*. This *kasrah* represents the origin (ى) and *hamzah* the glottal stop remains quiescent.

Note there are a few exceptions to this method. For example نَامَ is originally نَوَمَ but its conjugations are as follows

III M¹ نَامَ (he slept)

III F¹ نَامَتْ (she slept)

II M¹ نِمْتَ (you slept)

II F¹ نِمْتِ (you slept)

I M¹ + F¹ نِمْتُ (I slept)

It is to be noted that in the glossary of each lesson different forms of weak verbs are indicated in the parenthesis by referring them to TA in the appendix.

The use of the particle قَدْ (verily) and كَانَ (he was)

The perfect tense presents a completed action in Arabic, which is determined and expressed by means of time scale in this lesson in the following ways:

i.   for the approximation of the past to the present (*māḍī qarīb*),

ii.   for the remote past (*māḍī baʿīd*),

iii.   Unrestricted past (*māḍī muṭlaq*)

Rule No. 33

If the particle قَدْ precedes the perfect it approximates the past to the present.

Example Analysis:

قَدْ قَامَتِ الصَّلَاةُ . (Indeed the Prayer has [just] started.)

قَدْ can be used with all conjugations of the perfect tense.

Rule No. 34

كَانَ and its conjugations give the meaning of remote past.

Example Analysis:

(١) كَانَ إِبْرَاهِيْمُ (الﷺ) لله وَكَانَ اللهُ لَهُ.

(Ibrāhīm (ﷺ) was for Allah so Allah was for him.)

Note all perfect verbs present the unrestricted past.

The Particle فَ (then, and, so)

This particle is used for a sequence of events (*tartīb*). In the above example no. 7 as the Prophet Ibrāhīm (ﷺ) dedicated his entire life for the sake of Allah, Allah in response to this supported him.

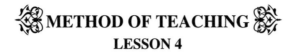 **METHOD OF TEACHING**
LESSON 4

1. Select a few 'construct phrases' with pairs of nouns and prepare the cards for each noun highlighting *ḥarakah*, the short vowels, in red for both nouns.

2. Place pairs of cards one after the other on the magnetic board and ask the students to read and translate them.

3. Rearrange the cards on the board constructing a few additional construct phrases from the cards.

4. There is good scope for the development of classroom conversation in Arabic by forming questions with the interrogative particles using vocabulary already introduced. Always correct students 'mistakes by seeking assistance from the students themselves if they fail, try to correct through guided questions.

5. Prepare the separate cards for each radical letter of the new verbs introduced in this lesson and compare these with the 'Master Root' cards of three radical letters.

6. Present the conjugations for the verbs on the magnetic board enabling the students to comprehend the variations in the conjugations.

Lesson 4

Exercise No. 22

(1) Construct five sentences using Construct phrase.

(2) Put *i'rāb*

(١)   ما اسمك؟

اسمي أحمد.

(٢)   الكافر من كفر بالله.

(٣)   هو أبوه وهو أخي.

(٤)   قرأت من كتاب الله.

(٥)   هذا الكتاب لمسجدي.

(٦)   أنا عبد الله وهو كافر بالله.

(٧)   من رب السماء ورب الأرض؟

(٨)   القرآن كتاب الله.

(٩)   أين مال الأب؟

مال الأب في بيته.

(١٠)   من ظلمة الليل إلى ضياء النهار.

(3) Translate into Arabic

   (1) Did you (M[1]) read from the Book of Allah? Yes, I read from the Book of Allah.

   (2) O boy! What is your name? Who are you and where is your house?

   (3) I am in my house and you (M[1]) are in your house.

   (4) Did you (M[1]) go to your brother's house?

   (5) I ate my food with my hand in the dining room.

   (6) The reward of Paradise and the punishment of Hell is from Allah.

   (7) I am with Allah and He is the Lord of the heaven and the earth.

   (8) I said: I am observing fast for the sake of Allah. He said: you are fasting.

   (9) The Messenger of Allah ﷺ said: the earth is a mosque.

   (10) He stood in the mosque of the Messenger ﷺ.

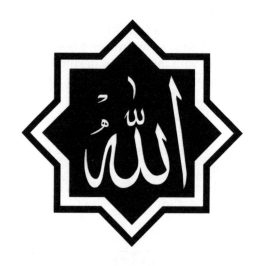

قَوْلٌ مَّعْرُوفٌ وَمَغْفِرَةٌ خَيْرٌ مِّن صَدَقَةٍ يَتْبَعُهَآ أَذًى وَٱللَّهُ غَنِيٌّ حَلِيمٌ

2:263

(١) السَّمَاءُ فَوْقَ الْأَرْضِ وَ الْأَرْضُ تَحْتَ السَّمَاءِ.

(٢) نَزَلَ الْإِنْجِيْلُ قَبْلَ الْقُرْآنِ وَ نَزَلَ الْقُرْآنُ بَعْدَ الْإِنْجِيْلِ.

(٣) ذَهَبْتُ إِلَى حَرْثِي قَبْلَ الصَّلَاةِ وَ رَجَعْتُ إِلَى الْبَيْتِ بَعْدَ الصَّلَاةِ.

(٤) الْمَسْجِدُ أَمَامَ بَيْتِي وَ حَرْثِي خَلْفَ بَيْتِي.

(٥) الْمَدْرَسَةُ بَيْنَ بَيْتِي وَ حَرْثِي.

(٦) هَلْ أَكَلْتَ قَبْلَ الصَّلَاةِ أَمْ بَعْدَ الصَّلَاةِ؟

(٧) أَكَلْتُ مَعَ أَبِي قَبْلَ الصَّلَاةِ عَلَى الْمَائِدَةِ فِي غُرْفَةِ الطَّعَامِ.

(٨) هَلْ ذَهَبْتَ مَعَ أَبِيكَ إِلَى الْمَسْجِدِ لِلصَّلَاةِ؟
نَعَمْ، ذَهَبْتُ مَعَ أَبِي إِلَى الْمَسْجِدِ لِلصَّلَاةِ.

(٩) مَا اسْمُ أُمِّكَ وَ أَيْنَ هِيَ؟
اسْمُ أُمِّي مَرْيَمُ وَ هِيَ فِي بَيْتِ زَيْدٍ.

(١٠) مَا اسْمُ أُخْتِكَ وَ أَيْنَ هِيَ؟
اسْمُ أُخْتِي زَيْنَبُ وَ هِيَ ذَاهِبَةٌ إِلَى الْمَدْرَسَةِ.

(١١) أَيْنَ مَدْرَسَتُهَا؟

مَدْرَسَتُهَا أَمَامَ حَرْثِي.

(١٢) أَيْنَ حَرْثُكَ؟

حَرْثِي بَيْنَ بَيْتِي وَمَدْرَسَتِي.

(١٣) ذَهَبْتُ إِلَى بَيْتِ اللهِ فِي مَكَّةَ مَعَ أَبِي وَ أُمِّي لِلْحَجِّ.

(١٤) دَخَلْتُ إِلَى مَسْجِدِ النَّبِيِّ (ﷺ) فِي الْمَدِينَةِ لِلصَّلَاةِ.

(١٥) كَفَرَ الْكَافِرُ فَقُلْتُ لَهُ: يَاأَيُّهَا الْكَافِرُ! كَفَرْتَ بِخَالِقِكَ وَ رَبِّكَ.

(١٦) اللهُ رَبِّي وَ رَبُّكَ وَ هُوَ وَاحِدٌ.

❀ UNIT 20 ❀

(١) دَعَوْتُ أَبِي إِلَى مَدْرَسَتِي.

(٢) كَفَرَ الْوَلَدُ بِاللهِ فَغَضِبَ أَبُوهُ عَلَيْهِ، ثُمَّ تَابَ الْوَلَدُ فَرَضِيَ أَبُوهُ عَنْهُ وَ دَعَا لَهُ.

(٣) الرَّسُولُ (ﷺ) دَاعٍ إِلَى الْجَنَّةِ وَ الشَّيْطَانُ دَاعٍ إِلَى النَّارِ.

(٤) الدَّاعِي إِلَى اللهِ فَازَ.

(٥) هَلْ سَعَيْتَ فِي الدُّنْيَا؟

(٦) السَّاعي فَازَ في الدُّنْيَا.

نَعَمْ، سَعَيْتُ في الدُّنْيَا وَ فُزْتُ.

(٧) سَعَتْ أُمِّي وَ فَازَتْ وَ لَهَا أَجْرٌ عِنْدَ رَبِّهَا.

(٨) أَنَا سَاعٍ وَ اللهُ هَادٍ.

(٩) تَابَتْ أُمِّي إِلَى اللهِ بَعْدَ الصَّلاةِ وَ تُبْتُ إِلَى اللهِ قَبْلَ الصَّلاةِ وَ بَعْدَ الصَّلاةِ.

(١٠) قَالَ قَائِلٌ: مَنْ صَامَ فَازَ.

(١١) صُمْتُ للهِ فَأَنَا صَائِمٌ.

(١٢) سَأَلْتُ أُمِّي: هَلْ أَنْتِ صَائِمَةٌ؟

قَالَتْ لِي: أَنَا صَائِمَةٌ وَ رَاضِيَةٌ باللهِ.

(١٣) هَلْ أَبُوكَ رَاضٍ عَنْكَ؟

نَعَمْ، أَبِي رَاضٍ عَنِّي.

(١٤) مَنْ قَائِمٌ أَمَامَكَ وَ مَنْ قَائِمَةٌ خَلْفَكَ؟

أَخِي قَائِمٌ أَمَامِي وَ أُخْتِي قَائِمَةٌ خَلْفِي.

(١٥) مَنْ قَائِمٌ بَيْنَكَ وَ بَيْنِي؟

زَيْدٌ قَائِمٌ بَيْنِي وَ بَيْنَكَ.

(١٦) مَنِ الْهَادِي؟

اللهُ هُوَ الْهَادِي.

(١٧) مَنِ الْفَانِي؟

الْإِنْسَانُ فَانٍ، وَ أَنَا فَانٍ وَ الدُّنْيَا فَانِيَةٌ.

(١٨) نَهَى اللهُ فِي الْقُرْآنِ عَنِ الشَّرِّ وَ أَمَرَ بِالْخَيْرِ.

(١٩) اللهُ نَاهٍ عَنِ الشَّرِّ وَ آمِرٌ بِالْخَيْرِ وَ الشَّيْطَانُ نَاهٍ عَنِ الْخَيْرِ وَ آمِرٌ بِالشَّرِّ.

(٢٠) كَانَتْ فَاطِمَةُ (رَضِيَ اللَّهُ عَنْهَا) بِنْتَ* الرَّسُولِ (ﷺ) وَ كَانَ الرَّسُولُ (ﷺ) قَدْ رَضِيَ عَنْهَا.

(٢١) فَاطِمَةُ (رَضِيَ اللَّهُ عَنْهَا) رَضِيَتْ بِالرَّسُولِ (ﷺ) وَ بِالْإِسْلَامِ.

(٢٢) الرَّسُولُ (ﷺ) فَازَ فِي الدُّنْيَا وَ الْآخِرَةِ.

* See Rule no 52

❁ UNIT 21 ❁

(١) يَا رَجُلُ! أَإِلَهَ مَعَ اللهِ؟
لَا إِلَهَ إِلَّا اللهُ.

(٢) أَهَذَا الْكِتَابُ أَمْ ذَلِكَ؟
لَا هَذَا وَ لَا ذَلِكَ.

(٣) يَا بِنْتُ! أَصَدَقْتِ أَمْ كَذَبْتِ؟
صَدَقْتُ.

(٤) يَاأَيُّهَا الْوَلَدُ! هَلْ أَكَلْتَ أَمْ شَرِبْتَ؟
قَدْ شَرِبْتُ.

(٥) هَلْ أَنْتَ دَخَلْتَ وَ خَرَجْتَ مِنَ الْغُرْفَةِ؟
لَا، مَا دَخَلْتُ وَ مَا خَرَجْتُ.

(٦) أَمَا ذَهَبْتَ؟

بَلَى، مَا ذَهَبْتُ.

(٧) أَمَا كَفَرْتَ بِالشَّيْطَانِ؟

بَلَى، كَفَرْتُ بِالشَّيْطَانِ.

(٨) أَمَا رَضِيتَ بِاللهِ؟

بَلَى، رَضِيتُ بِاللهِ.

(٩) أَمَا أَمَرَ الشَّيْطَانُ بِالشَّرِّ وَ نَهَى عَنِ الْخَيْرِ؟

بَلَى، أَمَرَ الشَّيْطَانُ بِالشَّرِّ وَ نَهَى عَنِ الْخَيْرِ.

(١٠) أَمَا أَمَرَ اللهُ بِالْخَيْرِ؟

بَلَى، أَمَرَ اللهُ بِالْخَيْرِ.

❀ UNIT 22 ❀

(١) الْكِتَابُ مَكْتُوبٌ وَ الثَّوبُ مَغْسُولٌ.

(٢) اَلِاسْمُ مَعْلُومٌ وَ الصِّرَاطُ مَجْهُولٌ.

(٣) الْوَلَدُ مَضْرُوبٌ وَ الْبِنْتُ مَرْضِيَّةٌ.

(٤) الْبِنْتُ مَقْتُولَةٌ.

(٥) أَيْنَ الْمَقْتُولَةُ؟

الْمَقْتُولَةُ فِي الْبَيْتِ.

(٦) الْإِثْمُ مَنْهِيٌّ عَنْهُ.

(٧) الْجَزَاءُ مَعْلُومٌ وَ كَذَلِكَ الْعَذَابُ مَعْلُومٌ.

(٨) الْمَاءُ مَشْرُوبٌ وَ كَذَلِكَ اللَّبَنُ مَشْرُوبٌ.

(٩) الطَّعَامُ مَأْكُولٌ وَ كَذَلِكَ اللَّحْمُ مَأْكُولٌ.

(١٠) الْإِنْسَانُ مَخْلُوقٌ وَ كَذَلِكَ الْأَرْضُ مَخْلُوقَةٌ.

(١١) مَنِ الْمَعْبُودُ؟

اللهُ هُوَ الْمَعْبُودُ.

(١٢) الصَّلَاةُ صِلَةٌ بَيْنَ الْعَبْدِ وَ الْمَعْبُودِ.

(١٣) "السَّلَامُ قَبْلَ الْكَلَامِ" "ح"

(١٤) "كُلُّ مَعْرُوْفٍ صَدَقَةٌ" "ح"

(١٥) "الصَّلَاةُ نُوْرُ الْمُؤْمِنِ" "ح"

(١٦) "يَدُ اللهِ مَعْ الْجَمَاعَةِ" "ح"

(١٧) مِفْتَاحُ الْجَنَّةِ الصَّلَاةُ ومِفْتَاحُ الصَّلَاةِ الْوَضُوْءُ "ح"

(١٨) مَنْ كَانَ فِي حَاجَةِ أَخِيْهِ كَانَ اللهُ فِي حَاجَتِهِ "ح"

(١٩) جَمَالُ الرَّجُلِ فَصَاحَةُ لِسَانِهِ "م"

(٢٠) هَلَكَ مَنِ اتَّبَعَ هَوَاهُ "م"

(٢١) اَلْهَوَى إِلَهٌ مَعْبُوْدٌ "م"

(٢٢) لِسَانُ التَّجْرِبَةِ أَصْدَقُ "م"

(٢٣) صَبْرُكَ عَلَى مَحَارِمِ اللهِ أَيْسَرُ مِنْ صَبْرِكَ عَلَى عَذَابِ اللهِ "م"

(٢٤) لَا طَاعَةَ لِمَخْلُوْقٍ فِي مَعْصِيَةِ الْخَالِقِ. "م"

(٢٥) بَيْنَ الرَّجُلِ وَبَيْنَ الْكُفْرِ تَرْكُ الصَّلَاةِ. "م"

GLOSSARY
LESSON 5

نَبِيٌّ	Prophet	بَيْنَ	in between
آخِرَةٌ	Hereafter	فَ	then, so
جَزَاءٌ	reward	بَلَى	yes indeed
مَاءٌ	water	أَمْ	or
لَبَنٌ	milk	أَوْ	or
لَحْمٌ	meat	أَمَرَ	to command
إِثْمٌ	sin	تَابَ	to repent
صِلَةٌ	link	فَازَ	to be successful
الْحَجُّ	the Pilgrimage	دَعَا	to call
وَاحِدٌ	one	دَعَا (ل)	to pray
قَبْلَ	before	دَعَا (عَلَى)	to curse
بَعْدَ	after	فَنِيَ	to perish
تَحْتَ	below	رَضِيَ (عَنْ)	to be pleased with
فَوْقَ	up, on top	سَعَى	to endeavor, struggle
خَلْفَ	at the back	هَدَى	to guide
أَمَامَ	in front	نَهَى	to prevent

182

غَسَلَ	to wash	سَأَلَ	to ask
قَتَلَ	to kill	أَيْنَ؟	Where?
عَبَدَ	to worship	سَلاَمٌ	salutation
كَلاَمٌ	speech	جَمَاعَة	community
صَدَقَةٌ		مِفْتَاحٌ	key
وَضُوْءٌ	ablution	مُؤْمِنٌ	believer
نُوْرٌ	light	جَمَالُ	beauty
أَصْدق	most truthful	فَصَاحَةُ	eloquence
صَبْرٌ	patience	لِسَانُ	tongue
مَحَارِمُ	forbidden	هَلَكَ	to perish
أَيْسَرُ	most easy	تَبِعَ	to follow
عَذَاب	punishment		
حَاجَةٌ	need	هَوَى	lust
طَّاعَةٌ	obedience	تَجْرِبَة	experience
مَعْصِيَةٌ	disobedience	إَلَه	god
كُفْرٌ	disbelief	مَعْرُوفٌ	acts agreed upon
تَرْكٌ	neglect	خَالِقٌ	creator

183

🏵 GRAMMATICAL THEMES 🏵
LESSON 5

🏵 UNIT 22 🏵

الظُّرُوْفُ

Rule No. 35   *Adverbs*

Nouns generally accept the genitive case if they are preceded by adverbs and prepositions.

Example Analysis:

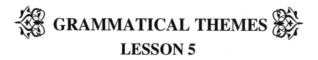

(١) السَّمَاءُ فَوْقَ الأَرْضِ وَالأَرْضُ تَحْتَ السَّمَاءِ .

(The sky is above the earth and the earth is below the sky.)

فَوْقَ (above) is followed by the noun الأَرْضِ and

تَحْتَ (below) is followed by the noun السَّمَاءِ.

Therefore both nouns are in the genitive case.

الأَسْمَاءُ : مُنْصَرِفٌ وَغَيْرُ مُنْصَرِفٍ

Perfectly Declinable (*Munṣarif*) nouns and nouns Declined without *Tanwīn* (*Ghayr munṣarif*)

Rule No. 36

Nouns, with regard to their vowel endings, are of two kinds: Perfectly Declinable and Declined without *tanwīn*. Perfectly Declinable nouns accept *tanwīn* depending on their case (__

___ ___), whereas nouns Declined without *tanwīn* (*ghayr*

***munṣarif*) accept only two short vowels *ḍammah* (___)**

184

when they are in the nominative case and *fatḥah* (___) for both the accusative and genitive cases.

Example Analysis:

اسْمُ أُمِّيْ مَرْيَمُ وَهِيَ فِي بَيْتِ زَيْدٍ.

The name of my mother is Maryam and she is in the house of Zayd.

The proper name Zayd, according to Arabic usage, is Perfectly Declinable (*munṣarif*) therefore it carries *tanwīn*. It is a *kasrah*

tanwīn because it is preceded by a preposition فِي .

مَرْيَمُ is a proper name and according to Arab usage is declined without tanwin (*ghayr munṣarif*). It is in the nominative case and therefore, carries *ḍammah*.

جَاءَ زَيْدٌ . (Zayd came) Zayd is in the nominative case therefore, it is carrying *ḍammah tanwīn*.

اسْمُ أُخْتِي زَيْنَبُ وَهِيَ ذَاهِبَةٌ إِلَى الْمَدْرَسَةِ .

The name of my sister is Zaynab and she is going to the school.
The proper name Zaynab according to Arabic usage is Declined without *tanwīn* (*ghayr munṣarif*) and is in the nominative case.

Therefore it carries *ḍammah* (___).

(١٣) ذَهَبْتُ إِلَى بَيْتِ اللهِ فِي مَكَّةَ مَعَ أَبِي وَأُمِّي لِلْحَجِّ .

I went to the House of Allah at Makkah with my father and mother for the pilgrimage.
Makkah according to Arabic usage is Declined without *tanwīn*. It is in the genitive case and carries *fatḥah* instead of *kasrah*.

185

UNIT 20

أَفْعَالٌ : مُعْتَلٌّ

Defective / Weak Verbs:

A few weak verbs are introduced in this lesson. The variation in their pattern and the formation of their different forms requires some familiarisation. For their full conjugations refer table A Appendix 1.

A3

رَضِيَ (عَنْ) (He became pleased with): Its final

radical letter is a vowel (ي) and its conjugation in five forms is

as follows:

(II M¹) رَضِيَ   (III F¹) رَضِيَتْ   (III M¹) رَضِيْتَ

(He became pleased) (She became pleased) (You became pleased)

(I M¹ + F¹) رَضِيْتُ   (II F¹) رَضِيْتِ

(You became pleased)   (I became pleased)

Active Participle: *Indefinite*: رَاضٍ (M¹)   رَاضِيَةٌ(F¹)

(pleasing)

Definite: اَلرَّاضِي (M¹)   اَلرَّاضِيَةُ (F¹)

Passive Participle: مَرْضِيٌّ (M¹)   مَرْضِيَّةٌ (F¹)

(pleased)

فَنِيَ (He perished): is a weak verb. Its final radical letter

is a vowel (ى) and again the conjugated forms are as follows:

186

فَنِيَ (III M[1])   فَنِيَتْ (III F[1])   فَنِيْتَ (II M[1])

(He perished)   (She perished)   (You perished)

فَنِيْت (II F[1])   فَنِيْتُ (I M[1] + F[1])

(You perished)   (I perished)

Active Participle: *Indefinite*: فَانٍ (M[1]) فَانِيَةٌ (F[1])

(Perishing)

Definite: الْفَانِي (M[1]) الْفَانِيَةُ (F[1])

A4

دَعَا (He called): It is a weak verb and its final radical letter is a

vowel (و) دَعَوَ .

Its five conjugated forms are as follows:

دَعَا (III M[1]) دَعَتْ (III F[1])   دَعَوْتَ (II M[1])

(He called)   (She called)   (You called)

دَعَوْت (II F[1])   دَعَوْتُ (I M[1] + F[1])

(You called)   (I called)

Active Participle: *Indefinite*:   دَاعٍ (M[1])   دَاعِيَةٌ (F[1])*

(Caller / calling)

Definite: الدَّاعِي (M[1]) الدَّاعِيَةُ (F[1])

Passive Participle: مَدْعُوٌّ (M[1]) مَدْعُوَّةٌ (F[1]) (Invited)

If دَعَا is followed by a preposition (لِ) it means to pray and

if it is followed by (عَلَى) it means to curse.

* Note this feminine form can be used for the masculine as well

187

A5

سَعَى (He strove) نَهَى (He prevented)

Both are weak verbs because their final radical letter is a vowel
(ى).

سَعَى Its conjugation in the five forms is as follows:

سَعَى (III M¹)   سَعَتْ (III F¹)   سَعَيْتَ (II M¹)

(He struggled)   (She struggled)   (You struggled)

سَعَيْت (II F¹)   سَعَيْتُ (I M¹ + F¹)

(You struggled)   (I struggled)

Active Participle: *Indefinite*: سَاعٍ (M¹) سَاعِيَةٌ (F¹)

(Struggler)

Definite: السَّاعِيَةُ (M¹) السَّاعِي (F¹)

نَهَى (He prevented) Its conjugations in the five forms is
as follows.

نَهَى (III M¹)   نَهَتْ (III F¹)   نَهَيْتَ (II M¹)

(He prevented)   (She prevented)   (You prevented)

نَهَيْت (II F¹)   نَهَيْتُ (I M¹ + F¹)

(You prevented)   (I prevented)

Active Participle: *Indefinite*: نَاهٍ (M¹) نَاهِيَةٌ (F¹)

(Preventer)

Definite: النَّاهِيَةُ (M¹) النَّاهِي (F¹)

Passive Participle: مَنْهِيٌّ (M¹) مَنْهِيَّةٌ (F¹)

(Prevented)

A6

هَدَى (He guided): This too is a weak verb. Its final

radical letter is a vowel (ى). The conjugation of the five forms

is as follows:

هَدَى (III M¹)　　　هَدَتْ (III F¹)　　　هَدَيْتَ (II M¹)

(He guided)　　　(She guided)　　　(You guided)

هَدَيْتِ (II F¹)　　　هَدَيْتُ (I M¹ + F¹)

(You guided)　　　(I guided)

Active Participle: *Indefinite*: هَادٍ (M¹) هَادِيَةٌ (F¹)

(Guide)

Definite:　　　الْهَادِي (M¹) الْهَادِيَةُ (F¹)

Passive Participle: مَهْدِيٌّ (M¹) مَهْدِيَّةٌ (F¹) (Guided)

A7

أَمَرَ (He commanded): is a defective verb. The initial

radical letter is *hamzah*, a glottal stop. The conjugation of the

five forms is as follows:

أَمَرَ (III M¹)　　　أَمَرَتْ (III F¹)　　　أَمَرْتَ (II M¹)

(He commanded)　　　(She commanded)　　　(You commanded)

أَمَرْتِ (II F¹)　　　أَمَرْتُ (I M¹ + F¹)

(You commanded)　　　(I commanded)

Active Participle: آمِرٌ (M¹) آمِرَةٌ (F¹)

(Commander)

Passive Participle: مَأْمُورٌ (Commanded)

Note two more verbs تَوَبَ = فَوَزَ (He repented) and تَابَ = فَازَ

(He succeeded) their conjugation is similar to (A¹)

189

Active Participle: فَازَ تَابَ

فَائِزٌ تَائِبٌ

 UNIT 21

The Particle أَمْ (or): is used for introducing the second member of an alternative question.

(٢) أَهَذَا الْكِتَابُ أَمْ ذَلِكَ؟ (Is this the book or that ?)

In the answer both are negated.

لاَ هَذَا وَلاَ ذَلِكَ. (Neither this nor that.)

The particle بَلَى (surely, yes indeed) is used in answering

a question when it is answered in affirmation with نَعَمْ yes).

But there also remains a possibility for a negative reply as in:

(١) يَا رَجُلُ! أَإِلَهٌ مَعَ اللهِ أَمْ أَنْتَ كَاذِبٌ ؟

O man! Is there any god beside Allah or are you a liar?

If the above question is answered with (نَعَمْ) yes there is

confirmation of another god beside Allah and confirmation also of a person as a liar. But when the answer for such a question is

given with بَلَى (yes indeed) the ambiguity for the confirmation

is removed.

مَاضٍ : نَفْيٌ

Perfect Negative

Rule No. 37

When the particle (مَا) precedes the perfect it becomes negative.

هَلْ أَنْتَ دَخَلْتَ وَخَرَجْتَ مِنَ الْغُرْفَةِ؟

لاَ، مَا دَخَلْتُ وَمَا خَرَجْتُ .

Did you enter and come out of the room? No, I neither entered nor came out.

It is evident from the meaning that when (مَا) precedes the perfect it provides a negative meaning. In the question two verbs دَخَلْتَ and خَرَجْتَ give a positive meaning but in the answer both are preceded by (مَا) and in both, therefore, facilitates its negative rendition.

(8)   بَلَى، رَضِيْتُ بِاللهِ.   أَمَا رَضِيْتَ بِاللهِ؟

Didn't you become please with Allah? Yes indeed, I became pleased with Allah.

The interrogative particle (أ) preceded مَا رَضِيْتَ Perfect Negative. With interrogative (أ) means (Didn't you become pleased?)

اِسْمٌ مَفْعُوْلٌ

Passive Participle

So far the Perfect, Perfect Negative and the Active Participle have been introduced and explained. In this lesson another noun pattern, which is closely related with the Passive Participle verb, is introduced and this is also known as the Objective noun. When the action, which the verb stands for, is performed it is referred to as the Passive Participle.

The method for making the Passive Participle from the sound root is as follows:

1. Prefixes: (1) مَ   (2) وُ ___ُ   (3) ___ٌ

2. Keep the initial radical letter *Fā'* quiescent.

3. Place the prefix (1) مَ before the initial letter *Fā'*.

4. Ignore the short vowel the medial radical letter *'Ayn* carries and insert prefix (2) (وُ ___) in its place.

5. Add prefix (3) *tanwīn* on the final radical letter *Lām* depending on its case.

مَــ ــفْـ ــعُـ ـوْلٌ

كَتَبَ (he wrote)   مَــ ــكْـ تُـ وْبٌ (written) (M¹)

قَرَأَ (he read)   مَــ ـقْـ رُ وْءٌ (read) (M¹)

Example Analysis:

(٩) الطَّعَامُ مَأْكُولٌ وَكَذَلِكَ اللَّحْمُ مَأْكُولٌ.

The food is eaten / edible and likewise the meat is eaten/ edible.

Note in كَذَلِكَ the preposition كَ   (like) is combined with

ذَلِكَ meaning (like that / likewise).

Note: For Qur'ānic Text readers are advised to consult an authentic translation of the Qur'ān. For the selected text the contextual translation is required to be referred to. For this purpose references are provided to each quotation. The reference **53**:7 means *Sūrah*, Chapter no.53 *āyah*, verse no.7.
Appendix F number 6 provides the translation on the Qur'ānic quotations used in the book.

النَّصُّ الْقُرْآنِيُّ

Lesson 5

١. هُوَ ٱلْأَوَّلُ وَٱلْأَخِرُ وَٱلظَّاهِرُ وَٱلْبَاطِنُ وَهُوَ بِكُلِّ شَيْءٍ عَلِيمٌ (٣: ٥٧)

٢. فِى ٱلسَّمَاءِ إِلَهٌ وَفِى ٱلْأَرْضِ إِلَهٌ (٨٤: ٤٣)

٣. وَكَلِمَةُ ٱللَّهِ (٤٠: ٩)

٤. وَرَبُّكَ عَلَى كُلِّ شَيْءٍ حَفِيظٌ (٢١: ٣٤)

٥. ٱللَّهُ خَالِقُ كُلِّ شَيْءٍ (٦٢: ٣٩)

٦. هَلْ مِنْ خَالِقٍ غَيْرُ ٱللَّهِ (٣: ٣٥)

٧. وَأَرْضُ ٱللَّهِ وَاسِعَةٌ (١٠: ٣٩)

٨. وَجَاءَتْ كُلُّ نَفْسٍ مَعَهَا سَائِقٌ وَشَهِيدٌ (٢١: ٥٠)

٩. جَاءَ أَمْرُ ٱللَّهِ (١٤: ٥٧)

١٠. وَجَاءَتْ سَكْرَةُ ٱلْمَوْتِ بِٱلْحَقِّ (١٩: ٥٠)

١١. كُلُّ نَفْسٍ ذَآئِقَةُ ٱلْمَوْتِ (185 :3)

١٢. وَدَخَلَ جَنَّتَهُ وَهُوَ ظَالِمٌ لِّنَفْسِهِۦ (35 :18)

١٣. أَنَا۠ يُوسُفُ وَهَـٰذَآ أَخِى (90 :12)

١٤. وَشَهِدَ شَاهِدٌ مِّنْ أَهْلِهَآ (26 :12)

١٥. ءَأَنتَ فَعَلْتَ هَـٰذَا (62 :21)

١٦. مُّحَمَّدٌ رَّسُولُ ٱللَّهِ (29 :48)

١٧. هَـٰذَا رَحْمَةٌ مِّن رَّبِّى (98 :18)

١٨. أَءِلَـٰهٌ مَّعَ ٱللَّهِ (27:63)

١٩. فِى سَبِيلِ ٱللَّهِ (154 :2)

QUR'ANIC TEXT
VOCABULARY
LESSON 5

الأَوَّلُ	The first	أَخٌ	(M¹) brother
الآخِرُ	The last	أَهْلٌ	household
الظَّاهِرُ	The Outward	فَعَلَ	to do
كَلِمَةٌ	(F¹) word	سَبِيلٌ	(M¹) path
حَفِظَ	to protect	نَفْسٌ	soul
حَفِيظٌ	[AP] protector	سَاقَ	to drive
غَيْرُ	other	سَائِقٌ	driver
وَسِعَ	to be wide, spacious	شَهِدَ	to be witness
وَاسِعٌ	[AP] spacious	شَاهِدٌ	[AP] witness
مَوْتٌ	death	أَمْرٌ	affair, matter
حَقٌّ	truth	سَكْرَةٌ	agony
ذَائِقَةٌ	(shall) taste	رَحْمَةٌ	mercy
ظَلَمَ	to oppress	رَسُولٌ	messenger [AP] (M¹)
		ظَالِمٌ	oppressor

196

 METHOD OF TEACHING
LESSON 5

1. Adverbs can be explained by carefully selecting and using some of the objects already available in the classroom. For example by placing a chair under the table, on the table, behind the table or in front of the table.

2. *Munṣarif* and *Ghayr Munṣarif* nouns generally cause confusion for beginners. This problem can be solved by giving some explanation but avoiding extensive grammatical details at this stage.

3. Various patterns of weak verbs, as they appear in the text are placed separately under capital A. This will enable both teachers and students to refer to them whenever such verbs appear in future.

4. After introducing each pattern with the help of cards and strictly adhering to the colour coding for the roots, let the students give the conjugations and construct Active Participles and Passive Participles.

5. Class conversation can be developed by raising questions with Perfect Negatives and different patterns of Active Participles and Passive Participles.

Lesson 5

Exercise No. 23

(1) From the following roots give III F^1, II M^1, II F^1,   I M^1+F^1

كَانَ، سَعَى، فَازَ، تَابَ، دَعَا، هَدَى، نَهَى.

(2) Select the correct word(s) from the parentheses to fill in the blanks in the following sentences.

(١)   أَكَلْتُ ...... الصَّلَاة .

(مَعَ، عِنْدَ، تَحْتَ، خَلْفَ، فَوْقَ، قَبْلَ)

(٢)   كِتَابِي ...... وَلَده .

(قَبْلَ، بَعْدَ، تَحْتَ، عِنْدَ)

(٣)   السَّمَاءُ ...... الأَرْضِ .

(مَعَ، عِنْدَ، تَحْتَ، قَبْلَ، فَوْقَ)

(٤)   الأَرْضُ ...... السَّمَاء .

(مَعَ، عِنْدَ، قَبْلَ، تَحْتَ، خَلْفَ، فَوْقَ)

(٥)   شَرِبْتُ ...... الطَّعَامِ .

(تَحْتَ، عِنْدَ، خَلْفَ، فَوْقَ، مَعَ)

(٦)   ذَهَبْتُ ...... وَلَدِي .

(عِنْدَ، مَعَ، تَحْتَ، فَوْقَ، خَلْفَ)

(٧)   الْمَسْجِدُ أَمَامَ بَيْتِي، وَحَرْثِي ...... بَيْتِي .

(مَعَ، عِنْدَ، تَحْتَ، فَوْقَ، خَلْفَ)

(3) Put *i'rab*

(١)   ذهبت إلى المسجد للصلاة مع أبي .

(٢)   هل رضيت بالله ؟

نعم، رضيت بالله وهو خالقي .

(٣)   السماء مخلوقة الله .

(٤)   ذهبت الى المسجد قبل الصلاة ورجعت الى البيت بعد الصلاة .

(٥)   الله هو المعبود وأنا عبد الله .

(٦)   أما نهيت ؟ بلى، نهيت .

(٧)   هل كتبت ؟ لا، ما كتبت .

(4) Construct five sentences using Passive Participle.

(5) Translate the following sentences into Arabic.
1. O Allah! You have created me and I am the created being.
2. My house is in front of the mosque and my field is behind the mosque.
3. Did you (M[1]) eat before Prayer or after Prayer ?
4. Above the ship is the sky and below the ship is water.
5. My book is with you. (M[1])
6. I went with my father to the garden.
7. I did not enter the field. I went to the mosque for Prayer.
8. Didn't he reject Satan? Yes indeed, he rejected him.
9. You (M[1]) commanded me towards virtue.
10. The book is written and read.

(6) Give Active Participle and Passive Participle [singular, masculine, feminine, definite, and indefinite] from the following roots.

فَعَلَ، قَرَأَ، سَمِعَ، عَلِمَ، جَهِلَ، كَتَبَ، صَدَقَ، كَذَبَ، أَكَلَ، شَرِبَ

(7) From the Qur'ānic text of Lesson 5 identify the 'construct phrases.'

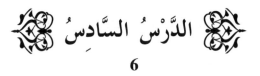

الدَّرْسُ السَّادِسُ

6

UNIT 23

(١) هَلْ أَكَلْتَ الطَّعَامَ؟

نَعَمْ، أَكَلْتُ الطَّعَامَ، وَشَرِبْتُ الْمَاءَ، فَالطَّعَامُ
مَأْكُولٌ وَالْمَاءُ مَشْرُوبٌ.

(٢) نَصَحَ الْأَبُ الْوَلَدَ وَأَمَرَهُ بِالْخَيْرِ، فَالْوَلَدُ
(٣) مَنْصُوحٌ وَمَأْمُورٌ بِالْخَيْرِ.

(٤) نَصَرْتُ الرَّجُلَ، فَأَنَا نَاصِرٌ وَالرَّجُلُ مَنْصُورٌ.

(٥) غَسَلَ الْوَلَدُ الثَّوْبَ بِالْمَاءِ، فَالثَّوْبُ مَغْسُولٌ.

(٦) قَتَلَ الْأَبُ الْقَاتِلَ، فَالْقَاتِلُ مَقْتُولٌ.

(٧) غَسَلَتِ الْبِنْتُ غُرْفَةَ الطَّعَامِ فَالْغُرْفَةُ مَغْسُولَةٌ.

(٨) حَفِظَ اللهُ الْقُرْآنَ فَالْقُرْآنُ مَحْفُوظٌ.

(٩) حَفِظْتُ بَيْتِي فَالْبَيْتُ مَحْفُوظٌ.

(١٠) هَلْ حَفِظْتَ مَالَكَ؟

نَعَمْ، حَفِظْتُ مَالِي فَالْمَالُ مَحْفُوظٌ.

(١١) فَتَحَ الْأَبُ بَابَ الْبَيْتِ فَالْبَابُ مَفْتُوحٌ.

(١٢) لَقِيتُ أَبَاكَ وَأَخَاكَ فِي الْحَرْثِ.

(١٣) فَتَحْتُ الْبَابَ وَدَخَلْتُ الْغُرْفَةَ.

201

(١٤) هَلْ أَكَلْتَ اللَّحْمَ وَشَرِبْتَ اللَّبَنَ؟

لَا، مَا أَكَلْتُ اللَّحْمَ وَمَا شَرِبْتُ اللَّبَنَ.

(١٥) مَا ضَرَبَ الْأَبُ ابْنَهُ.

(١٦) هَلْ كَتَبْتَ الْكِتَابَ؟

لَا، مَا كَتَبْتُ الْكِتَابَ.

(١٧) الْوَلَدُ فَرَّ مِنَ الْبَيْتِ فَهُوَ فَارٌّ.

(١٨) أَمَا فَرَّ الْوَلَدُ مِنَ الْبَيْتِ؟

بَلَى، فَرَّ الْوَلَدُ مِنَ الْبَيْتِ.

(١٩) أَمَا تَرَكْتَ الشَّرَّ؟

بَلَى، تَرَكْتُ الشَّرَّ وَتُبْتُ إِلَى اللهِ.

(٢٠) الرَّجُلُ مَرَّ عَلَى الْمَدِينَةِ مَعَ وَلَدِهِ.

(٢١) عَبَدْتُ اللهَ وَمَا عَصَيْتُ الرَّسُولَ (ﷺ).

(٢٢) مَنْ فَتَحَ مَكَّةَ؟

فَتَحَ الرَّسُولُ (ﷺ) مَكَّةَ.

(٢٣) قَرَأْتُ الْقُرْآنَ فِي الصَّلَاةِ فَفَهِمْتُ مَا قَرَأْتُ.

(٢٤) عُذْتُ بِاللهِ مِنَ الشَّيْطَانِ.

(٢٥) مَنْ نَصَرَكَ؟

نَصَرَنِي رَبِّي فَهُوَ نَاصِرِي.

(٢٦) فَتَحْتُ الْقُرْآنَ وَقَرَأْتُ، فَسَمِعَنِي أَبِي وَقَالَ:
أَنْتَ قَارِئٌ وَالْقَارِئُ فَائِزٌ فِي الدُّنْيَا وَالْآخِرَةِ.

(٢٧) سَأَلَ سَائِلٌ: مَنْ رَبُّكَ وَمَا دِينُكَ؟

قُلْتُ: اللهُ رَبِّي وَالْإِسْلَامُ دِينِي.

(٢٨) سَأَلَنِي زَيْدٌ عَنِ الْكِتَابِ.

(٢٩) خَلَقَ اللهُ الشَّمْسَ وَالْقَمَرَ وَالْأَرْضَ وَالسَّمَاءَ.

(٣٠) جَعَلَ اللهُ لِلْإِنْسَانِ السَّمْعَ وَ الْبَصَرَ وَالْفُؤَادَ، وَجَعَلَ بَيْنَ النَّاسِ مَوَدَّةً وَ رَحْمَةً.

(٣١) جَعَلَ اللهُ كُلَّ شَيْءٍ فِي الْأَرْضِ وَالسَّمَاءِ لِلْإِنْسَانِ، فَالْإِنْسَانُ خَلِيفَتُهُ فِي الْأَرْضِ.

❀ UNIT 24 ❀

(١) الْأَبُ يَأْكُلُ الطَّعَامَ وَبِنْتُهُ تَشْرَبُ اللَّبَنَ.

(٢) هِيَ تَأْكُلُ الطَّعَامَ وَأَنَا أَشْرَبُ اللَّبَنَ.

(٣) هَلْ تَأْكُلِينَ الطَّعَامَ؟

لَا، أَنَا أَشْرَبُ اللَّبَنَ.

(٤) هَلْ تَدْخُلِينَ الْبَيْتَ مِنَ الْبَابِ؟

نَعَمْ، أَدْخُلُهُ مِنَ الْبَابِ.

(٥) هَلْ تَغْسِلِينَ الثَّوْبَ بِالْمَاءِ؟

نَعَمْ، أَغْسِلُهُ بِالْمَاءِ.

(٦) أَنَا أَعْبُدُ اللهَ وَ أَقْرَأُ الْقُرْآنَ.

يَعْبُدُ الْكَافِرُ الْبَرَّ وَالْبَحْرَ وَأَنَا أَعْبُدُ اللهَ. (٧)

مَنْ يَنْصُرُكَ؟ (٨)

اللهُ يَنْصُرُنِي.

يَا اللهُ أَنَا أَعْبُدُكَ فِي النَّهَارِ وَفِي اللَّيْلِ. (٩)

هَلْ تَتْرُكِينَ اللهَ وَتَعْبُدِينَ نَفْسَكِ؟ (١٠)

لاَ، أَنَا أَعْبُدُ اللهَ.

مَنْ يَأْمُرُ الإِنْسَانَ بِالْخَيْرِ؟ (١١)

اللهُ يَأْمُرُ الإِنْسَانَ بِالْخَيْرِ.

هَلْ تَذْهَبِينَ إِلَى الْمَسْجِد لِلصَّلاَةِ؟ (١٢)

نَعَمْ، أَذْهَبُ إِلَى الْمَسْجِد لِلصَّلاَةِ.

هَلْ تَقْرَئِينَ الْقُرْآنَ فِي الصَّلاَةِ؟ (١٣)

نَعَمْ، أَقْرَأُ الْقُرْآنَ فِي الصَّلاَةِ.

خَلَقَ اللهُ آدَمَ مِنْ تُرَابٍ وَخَلَقَ النَّاسَ مِنْ أَبٍ وَاحِدٍ (١٤)
وَأُمٍّ وَاحِدَةٍ.

❀ UNIT 25 ❀

هَلْ أَنْتَ تَغْسِلِينَ غُرْفَةَ الطَّعَامِ؟ (١)

لاَ، أَنَا أَغْسِلُ ثَوْبِي.

هَلْ أَنْتَ تَعْبُدُ مَخْلُوقَ اللهِ؟ (٢)

لاَ، أَنَا أَعْبُدُ اللهَ وَهُوَ خَالِقِي وَ رَبِّي.

204

(٣) يَا رَجُلُ! اللهُ يَعْلَمُ وَأَنْتَ لاَ تَعْلَمُ.

(٤) أَلاَ تَقْرَأُ الْقُرْآنَ؟

بَلَى، أَقْرَأُ الْقُرْآنَ كُلَّ يَوْمٍ.

(٥) هِيَ تَعْصِي اللهَ وَالرَّسُولَ (ﷺ) وَلاَ تَخْشَى عَذَابَ الدُّنْيَا وَالآخِرَة.

(٦) تَفْنَى السَّمَاءُ وَالأَرْضُ وَيَبْقَى وَجْهُ رَبِّكَ.

(٧) إِبْرَاهِيْمُ يَفْتَحُ الْبَابَ وَيَدْخُلُ الْبَيْتَ وَيَقُولُ لِوَلَده: أَنْتَ تَفْعَلُ الشَّرَّ بِنَفْسِكَ فَلِمَاذَا تَلُومُ الشَّيْطَانَ؟

(٨) الآنَ أَلُومُ نَفْسِي عَلَى شَرِّي وَأَتُوبُ إِلَى اللهِ رَبِّي.

(٩) يَبْلُو اللهُ الإِنْسَانَ بِالْخَيْرِ وَالشَّرِّ وَيَفُوزُ الإِنْسَانُ فِي الدُّنْيَا وَالآخِرَة بِالْخَيْرِ.

(١٠) الأَبُ يَمُوتُ وَابْنُهُ يَبْكِي لِمَوْته.

(١١) هَلْ تَبْكِيْنَ لِمَوْتِ الْعَالِمِ؟

نَعَمْ، أَبْكِي لِمَوْتِ الْعَالِمِ، فَمَوْتُ الْعَالِمِ مَوْتُ الْعَالَمِ.

(١٢) هَلْ تَخْشَى الْمَوْتَ؟

لاَ، أَنَا لاَ أَخْشَى الْمَوْتَ.

(١٣) الْمَوْتُ مِنَ اللهِ وَكَذَلكَ الْحَيَاةُ مِنَ اللهِ.

(١٤) يَعُودُ الْوَلَدُ مِنَ الْمَدْرَسَةِ وَيَدْخُلُ الْبَيْتَ وَيَقْرَأُ دَرْسَهُ.

(١٥) هَلْ تَعُودُ الْبِنْتُ مِنَ الْمَدْرَسَة؟

نَعَمْ، تَعُودُ الْبِنْتُ مِنَ الْمَدْرَسَة.

(١٦) مَاذَا تَرْجِينَ مِنَ اللهِ؟

أَرْجُو مِنَ اللهِ خَيْراً.

(١٧) أَفْعَلُ الْخَيْرَ وَ أَتْرُكُ الشَّرَّ.

(١٨) أَلَا تَنْصُرُنِي وَتَكُونُ مَعِي؟

بَلَى، أَنْصُرُكَ وَأَكُونُ مَعَكَ.

(١٩) هَلْ تَرْضَى بِجَزَائِكَ؟

نَعَمْ، أَرْضَى بِجَزَائِي.

(٢٠) أَنَا أَسْعَى فِي الدُّنْيَا قَبْلَ الْمَوْتِ وَأَرْجُو الْجَزَاءَ مِنَ اللهِ بَعْدَ الْمَوْتِ.

(٢١) مَنْ يَرْزُقُكَ؟

اللهُ يَرْزُقُنِي وَهُوَ الرَّازِقُ.

(٢٢) مَنْ يَهْدِيكَ؟

اللهُ يَهْدِينِي وَهُوَ الْهَادِي.

(٢٣) اللهُ يَرَانِي وَلَا أَرَاهُ.

(٢٤) اَلْأَنَاةُ مِنَ اللهِ وَالْعَجَلَةُ مِنْ الشَّيْطَانِ "ح"

(٢٥) التَّائِبُ مِنَ الذَّنْبِ مَنْ لَا ذَنْبَ لَهُ "ح"

(٢٦) اَلْحَيَاءُ شُعْبَةٌ مِنْ الإِيمَانِ "ح"

(٢٧) اَلْحَيَاءُ لَا يَأْتِي إِلَّا بِخَيْرٍ "ح"

(٢٨) اَلْحَيَاءُ خَيْرٌ كُلُّهُ "ح"

(٢٩) الدُّعَاءُ مُخُّ الْعِبَادَة "ح"

(٣٠) الْجَاهِلُ يَرْضَى عَنْ نَفْسِه. "م"

(٣١) الْجَاهِلُ يَطْلُبُ الْمَالَ وَالعَاقِلُ يَطْلُبُ الْكَمَالَ. "م"

(٣٢) خَيْرُ النَّاسِ مَنْ يَنْفَعُ النَّاسَ. "م"

(٣٣) إِنَّ الَّذِي لَيْسَ فِي جَوْفِه مِنْ الْقُرْآنِ كَالْبَيْتِ الْخَرِب.

(٣٤) إِنَّ خَيْرَ حَدِيثٍ كِتَابُ الله وخَيْرَ الْهَدْيِ هَدْيُ مُحَمَّد (ﷺ) .

(٣٥) مَنْ قَالَ رَضِيْتُ بِالله رَبّاً وَبِالإِسْلامِ دِيناً وَبِمُحَمَّدٍ نَبِيّاً وَرَسُولًا وَجَبَتْ لَهُ الْجَنَّةُ.

207

GLOSSARY
LESSON 6

دِيْنٌ	religion	عَبَدَ/يَعْبُدُ	to worship
مَوَدَّةٌ	love	نَفَعَ/يَنْفَعُ	to benefit
مَدِيْنَةٌ	city	طَلَبَ/يَطْلُبُ	to seek
وَجْهٌ	face	تَرَكَ/يَتْرُكُ	to leave, renounce, give up
قَمَرٌ	moon	غَسَلَ/يَغْسِلُ	to wash
خَلِيْفَةٌ	vicegerent, deputy	جَعَلَ/يَجْعَلُ	to make
حَيَاةٌ	life	فَتَحَ/يَفْتَحُ	to open, to conquer
ابْنٌ	son	فَهِمَ/يَفْهَمُ	to understand, to comprehend
سَمْعٌ	hearing	فَرَّ/يَفِرُّ	to escape, to flee, to run away
بَصَرٌ	vision, eyesight	مَرَّ (بِـ)/ يَمُرُّ	to pass [with some one or something, go walk or pass]
فُؤَادٌ	heart	عَاذَ/يَعُوْذُ	to seek refuge (TA1)
كَمَالٌ	perfection	لَقِيَ/يَلْقَى	to meet (TA3)
عَاقِلٌ	wise	بَكَى/يَبْكِي	to cry (TA6)
نَاسٌ	people	عَصَى/يَعْصِي	to disobey (TA6)
لِمَاذَا؟	why?	أَنَاةٌ	forbearance
نَصَرَ/يَنْصُرُ	to help	عَجَلَةٌ	haste
رَزَقَ/يَرْزُقُ	to provide sustenance	ذَنْبٌ	sin

208

بَقِيَ / يَبْقَى	to remain, to survive (TA3)	شُعْبَةٌ	branch
نَسِيَ / يَنْسَى	to forget (TA3)	حَيَاءٌ	modesty
خَشِيَ / يَخْشَى	to be afraid (TA3)	أَتَى / يَأْتِي	to come
عَادَ / يَعُوْدُ	to return (TA1)	دُعَاءٌ	supplication
بَلاَ / يَبْلُو	to test (TA4)	مُخٌّ	essence
مَاتَ / يَمُوْتُ	to die (TA1)	عَبَادَةٌ	worship
رَأَى / يَرَى	to see (TA10)	تَائِبٌ	repenting
لاَمَ / يَلُوْمُ	to blame (TA1)	خَيْرٌ	good
رَجَا / يَرْجُو	to hope (TA4)	جَوْفٌ	inside

(3: 129) Calligraphy in the shape of a vase on papyri.

209

GRAMMATICAL THEMES
LESSON 6

مَفْعُوْلٌ: حَالَةُ النَّصْبِ
The Object: Accusative Case

In the previous lessons nouns are presented in either the nominative case or the genitive case (carrying *dammah* - or *kasrah* -). In this lesson nouns are given in the accusative case (carrying *fathah*) when they become the object. Transitive verbs need objects to give them full meaning.

Rule No. 38

An object which indicates the action of a verb in Arabic always remains in the accusative case i.e. (carrying *fathah*).

Example Analysis:

هَلْ أَكَلْتَ الطَّعَامَ؟

نَعَمْ، أَكَلْتُ الطَّعَامَ، وَشَرِبْتُ الْمَاءَ، فَالطَّعَامُ مَأْكُوْلٌ وَالْمَاءُ مَشْرُوْبٌ.

Did you eat the food ? Yes, I ate the food and I drank water so the food is eaten and water is drunk.

الطَّعَامَ and الْمَاءَ are objects, therefore, they carry *fathah* and مَأْكُوْلٌ and مَشْرُوْبٌ are Passive Participles.

210

قَتَلَ الْأَبُ الْقَاتِلَ فَالْقَاتِلُ مَقْتُولٌ The father killed the killer so the killer is killed.

The first noun الْقَاتِلَ is an Active Participle (APM[1]) and an object, therefore, it is in the accusative case (carries *fathah*). The second noun الْقَاتِلُ is in the nominative case, therefore, it carries *dammah*.

غَسَلَت الْبِنْتُ غُرْفَةَ الطَّعَامِ فَالْغُرْفَةُ مَغْسُوْلَةٌ.

The girl washed the dining room so the room is washed.

The first noun غُرْفَةَ is an object, therefore, it is in the accusative case and it is also the first noun of the construct phrase. The second noun الْغُرْفَةُ is in the nominative case, therefore, it carries *dammah*.

لَقِيْتُ أَبَاكَ وَأَخَاكَ فِي الْحَرْثِ.

I met your father and your brother in the field.

أَبٌ and أَخٌ are two of a handful of nouns which on phonetical grounds require special treatment. As both are objects, both are therefore in the accusative case.

أَبَاكَ وَأَخَاكَ *Alif* is added after the consonants ب and خ

جَعَلَ اللهُ لِلْإِنْسَانِ السَّمْعَ وَالْبَصَرَ وَالْفُؤَادَ، وَجَعَلَ بَيْنَ النَّاسِ مَوَدَّةً وَرَحْمَةً.

Allah has made for mankind the hearing, the sight and the heart and He has made between mankind love and mercy.

السَّمْعَ، وَالْبَصَرَ، وَالْفُؤَادَ are the definite nouns and these are objects. Therefore, they are in the accusative case (carrying *fatḥah*). مَوَدَّةً، وَرَحْمَةً are indefinite and both are objects, therefore, they carry *fatḥah tanwīn*.

UNIT 24

مُضَارِعٌ مَعْرُوفٌ

Imperfect Indicative

Rule No. 39

The imperfect in Arabic presents the incomplete action of a verb. It imparts the meaning of the present continuous and future tense. The context in which the imperfect is used indicates the future tense.

The Method for Making the Imperfect Sound Indicative

It has been made clear that for the formation of derived forms in Arabic the root is inevitable. The root can either be sound or weak. As has been indicated in Indicative Sound Perfect, there is the possibility for the radical medial *'Ayn* to accept either *fatḥah*, *kasrah* or *ḍammah* فَعَلَ، فَعِلَ، فَعُلَ Similarly, in the Imperfect, the radical *'Ayn* can either accept *fatḥah, kasrah or ḍammah* and it is not necessary that it should agree with the short vowel of the radical *'Ayn* of Imperfect.

I

فَعَلَ

(The medial radical is carrying *fatḥah*)

مَنَعَ	نَصَرَ	جَلَسَ
(Perfect Indicative)	(Perfect Indicative)	(Perfect ndicative)
(He prevented)	(He helped)	(He sat)
يَمْنَعُ	يَنْصُرُ	يَجْلِسُ
(Imperfect)	(Imperfect)	(Imperfect)
(He prevents)	(He helps)	(He sits)
[The medial *'Ayn* is carrying *fatḥah* in the Imperfect Indicative]	[The medial *'Ayn* is carrying *ḍammah* in the Imperfect Indicative]	The medial *'Ayn* carrying *kasrah* in the Imperfect Indicative]
(The third radical is a guttural letter.*)		

(Common in use) [spanning middle and right columns]

* There are six guttural letters and these are known in Arabic as الْحُرُوْفُ الْحَلَقِيَّةِ. They are: خ ، غ ، ح ، ع ، ــهـ ، ء .

---

* There are six gutteral letters and these are known in Arabic as *al-Hurūf al-Halqiyyah*. These are:

213

II

فَعِلَ

(The medial radical is carrying *kasrah*)

عَلِمَ	حَسِبَ
(Perfect Indicative)	(Perfect Indicative)
(He knew)	(He thought)
يَعْلَمُ	يَحْسَبُ
(Imperfect Indicative)	(Imperfect Indicative)
(He knows)	(He thinks)
[The medial radical in the	[The medial radical in the
Imperfect is carrying *fathah*]	Imperfect is carrying *fathah*]
(Common in Use)	

III

فَعُلَ

(The medial radical is carrying *dammah*)

كَرُمَ

(He respected)
(Perfect Indicative)

يَكْرُمُ

(He respects)
(Imperfect Indicative)

(Rare in use)

It is clear from the above analysis that the radical 'Ayn in the Perfect may carry either *fathah*, *kasrah* or *dammah*. For the determination by beginners of its exact short vowel in the Imperfect there is a need to refer to a good Arabic dictionary.

Generally, dictionaries will immediately after the triliteral roots provide a sign for the short vowel which the radical 'Ayn in the Imperfect will carry (for example Hans Wehr places either a, i, u, signs after the roots and other dictionaries place signs such as

(- - -)

Rule No. 40

When the medial radical *'Ayn* of the Perfect Indicative (III M¹) carries *fathah* in most of verbs then it accepts *kasrah* and *dammah* in the radical *'Ayn* of the Imperfect Indicative.

Rule No. 41

When the medial radical *'Ayn* of the Perfect Indicative (III M¹) carries *kasrah* in most of verbs then it accepts *fathah* in the radical *'Ayn* of the Imperfect Indicative.

Rule No. 42

When the medial radical *'Ayn* of the Perfect Indicative (III M¹) carries *dammah* then generally in the Imperfect Indicative it remains the same.

Rule No. 43

The Imperfect Indicative commonly retains the *fathah* of the Perfect if the second and third radical is a guttural letter.

Examples:

←

يَمْنَعُ / مَنَعَ   يَسْأَلُ / سَأَلَ

(He prevents) (He prevented) (He asks) (He asked)

215

$$\text{يَذْهَبُ} \quad / \quad \text{ذَهَبَ}$$

(He goes)   (He went)

The imperfect cannot be formed without four letter prefixes.

(1) أَ   (2) تَ   (3) ي   (4) ن

Imperfect Indicative

III M1:

(1) Keep the radical *Fā'* quiescent.

(2) Add / Prefix (3) ي (يَفْ)

(3) Place the short vowel which the radical *'Ayn* takes in the Imperfect Indicative. It takes *fathah* (يَفْعَ)

(4) Place on the final radical *Lām ḍammah* يَفْعَلُ (He does)

III F¹:

(1) 1 - 3 - 4 will remain the same as in III M¹

(2) Add the prefix (2) ت تَفْعَلُ (She does)

II M¹:

Will remain the same as III F¹ تَفْعَلُ (you (M¹) do)

II F¹:

(1) Keep the radical *Fā'* quiescent.

(2) Add Prefix (2) ت (تَفْ)

(3) Keep the vowel on the radical *'Ayn* which the Imperfect Indicative takes (تَفْعَ)

216

(4) Place *kasrah* under the radical *Lām* . (تَفْعَلِ)

(5) Add (3) ي   and (4) ن

(you (F¹) do) تَفْعَلِيْنَ

I M¹⁺F¹:

(1) 1 – 3 – 4 will remain the same as in III M¹
(2) Add Prefix (1) أ (أَفْعَلُ) (I [M¹⁺F¹] do)

Imperfect Weak Indicative:

The patterns of Imperfect Weak Indicative are presented here. This is achieved by following their Perfect patterns and retaining some capital letters which have been used for the Perfect.

A1*

قَوَلَ = قَالَ

The medial radical (و) appears in conjugations of the Imperfect Indicative.

III M¹ يَقُوْلُ (He says)   III F¹ تَقُوْلُ (She says)

II M¹ تَقُوْلُ (You say)   II F¹ تَقُوْلِيْنَ (You say)

I M¹⁺F¹ أَقُوْلُ (I say)

A2*

جَيَءَ = جَاءَ

The medial radical (ي) and the final radical (*ḥamzah*) glottal stop appear in conjugations of the Imperfect Indicative.

---

* See TA in the appendix

III M¹ يَجِيءُ (He comes)   III F¹ تَجِيءُ (She comes)

II M¹ تَجِيءُ (You come)   II F¹ تَجِيئِيْنَ (you come)

I M¹⁺ F¹ أَجِيءُ (I come)

نَامَ =(نَوَمَ)

The medial radical (و) changes into *Alif* in conjugations of the Imperfect Indicative.

III M¹ يَنَامُ (He sleeps) III F¹ تَنَامُ (She sleeps)

II M¹ تَنَامُ (You sleep) II F¹ تَنَامِيْنَ (You sleep)

I M¹⁺ F¹ أَنَامُ (I sleep)

A3

رَضِيَ

The final radical (ي) appears at the end.

III M¹ يَرْضَى (He becomes   III F¹ تَرْضَى (She becomes
              pleased)   pleased)

II M¹ تَرْضَى (You become   II F¹ تَرْضَيْنَ (You become
              pleased)   pleased)

I M¹⁺ F¹ أَرْضَى (I become pleased)

فَنِيَ

The final radical (ي) remains but is not pronounced in conjugations of the Imperfect except II F¹

III M¹ يَفْنَى (He perishes)   III F¹ تَفْنَى (She perishes)

II M¹ تَفْنَى (You perish)   II F¹ تَفْنَيْنَ (You perish)

I M¹ + F¹ أَفْنَى (I perish)

$$(لَقِيَ \; يَلْقَى)$$

A4

$$دَعَوَ = دَعَا$$

The final radical (و) appears in conjugations of the Imperfect Indicative with the exception of II F¹.

III M¹ يَدْعُو (He calls)   III F¹ تَدْعُو (She calls)

II M¹ تَدْعُو (You call)   II F¹ تَدْعِينَ (You call)

I M¹⁺ F¹ أَدْعُو (I call)

$$(رَجَا \; يَرْجُو)$$

(to hope)

A5

سَعَى (He struggled) / يَسْعَى

Its conjugations in the Imperfect Indicative is the same as in (A3) above.

A6

$$هَدَى \; [\; \_ِ \; ي \;]$$

The final radical (ي) remains and the medial radical carries *kasrah* in the conjugations of the Imperfect Indicative.

III M¹ يَهْدِي (He guides)   III F¹ تَهْدِي (She guides)

II M¹ تَهْدِي (You guide)   II F¹ تَهْدِينَ (You guide)

I M¹⁺ F¹ أَهْدِي (I guide)

$$(\text{عَصَى يَعْصِي})$$

Its conjugations in the Imperfect Indicative is the same as in
(**A6**) above.

A7

$$أَمَرَ$$

Ḥamzah, the glottal stop, remains in all conjugations of the
Imperfect Indicative.

III M[1] يَأْمُرُ (He commands)   III F[1] تَأْمُرُ (She commands)

II M[1] تَأْمُرُ (You command) II F[1] تَأْمُرِيْنَ (You command)

I M[1]+F[1] آمُرُ (I command)

The weak verbs which follow are presented in this lesson
for the first time. Their conjugations for the Perfect and
Imperfect Indicative are provided under (**A10**), and (**A11**).

A8

$$(\text{فَرَرَ}) \ \text{فَرَّ}$$ (He escaped)

In فَرَّ the second and third radical letters are identical. The

radicals *'Ayn* and *Lām* are the consonant (ر), therefore, both are

combined with *shaddah*.

Perfect Indicative:

III M[1] فَرَّ (He escaped)   III F[1] فَرَّتْ (She escaped)

II M[1] فَرَرْتَ (You escaped)   II F[1] فَرَرْتِ (You escaped)

I M[1]+F[1] فَرَرْتُ (I escaped)

Active Participle: فَارٌّ (escapee)

Imperfect Indicative:

III M¹ يَفِرُّ (He escapes)   III F¹ تَفِرُّ (She escapes)

II M¹ تَفِرُّ (You escape)   II F¹ تَفِرِّيْنَ (You escape)

I M¹⁺ F¹ أَفِرُّ (I escape)

(مَرَّ يَمُرُّ)

A9

سَأَلَ (He asked)

In سَأَلَ the medial radical 'Ayn is *ḥamzah*, a glottal stop, which is retained in all conjugations and derivations.

Perfect Indicative:

III M¹ سَأَلَ (He asked)   III F¹ سَأَلَتْ (She asked)

II M¹ سَأَلْتَ (You asked)   II F¹ سَأَلْتِ (You asked)

I M¹⁺ F¹ سَأَلْتُ (I asked)

Active Participle: سَائِلٌ (asking / a person who asks)

Passive Participle: مَسْؤُوْلٌ (asked)

Imperfect Indicative:

III M¹ يَسْأَلُ (He asks)   III F¹ تَسْأَلُ (She asks)

II M¹ تَسْأَلُ (You ask)   II F¹ تَسْأَلِيْنَ (You ask)

I M¹⁺ F¹ أَسْأَلُ (I ask)

A10

The verb رَأَى is a doubly weak verb. The medial radical is *ḥamzah*, a glottal stop, and the final radical is (ى). In the

221

conjugations of the Perfect Indicative both *ḥamzah* and (ى)
are recited and in the Imperfect Indicative (ى) is written but
not pronounced except in II F[1].

Perfect Indicative:

III M[1] رَأَى (He saw) III F[1] رَأَتْ (She saw)

II M[1] رَأَيْتَ (You saw) II F[1] رَأَيْتِ (You saw)

I M[1]+ F[1] رَأَيْتُ (I saw)

Active Participle: رَاءٍ (seer)

Passive Participle: مَرْئِيٌّ (seen)

Imperfect Indicative:

III M[1] يَرَى (He sees) III F[1] تَرَى (She sees)

II M[1] تَرَى (You see) II F[1] تَرَيْنَ (You see)

I M[1]+ F[1] أَرَى (I see)

A11

The verb وَقَى is a doubly weak verb. The first radical is
(و) and the final radical is (ى). In the conjugation of the
Perfect Indicative both (و) and (ى) are recited and in the
Imperfect Indicative (و) is deleted.

Perfect Indicative:

III M[1] وَقَى (He guarded) III F[1] وَقَتْ (She guarded)

II M[1] وَقَيْتَ (You guarded) II F[1] وَقَيْتِ (You guarded)

I M[1]+ F[1] وَقَيْتُ (I guarded)

Active Participle: وَاقٍ (guarding)

III M¹ يَقِي (He guards)   III F¹ تَقِي (She guards)

II M¹ تَقِي (You guard)   II F¹ تَقِيْنَ (You guard)

I M¹⁺ F¹ أَقِي (I guard)

Weak roots A1 – A11 presented in Unit 24 can be referred to in TA in the appendix.

UNIT 25

مُضَارِعٌ: نَفْيٌ

Imperfect Negative

Rule No. 44A

If the negative particle (لَا, not) in most cases and (مَا not) in some cases precedes the Imperfect Indicative it then makes it negative.

يَارَجُلُ! اللهُ يَعْلَمُ وَأَنْتَ لاَ تَعْلَمُ

O man! Allah knows and you do not know.

تَعْلَمُ is the Imperfect Indicative and is preceded by the negative particle (لاَ).   Therefore the Imperfect Indicative becomes negative.

223

النَّصُّ الْقُرآنِيّ

Lesson 6

١. وَمِنَ ٱلنَّاسِ مَن يَعْبُدُ ٱللَّهَ عَلَىٰ حَرْفٍ (22: 11)

٢. قَالَ رَبِّي يَعْلَمُ ٱلْقَوْلَ فِي ٱلسَّمَآءِ وَٱلْأَرْضِ (21: 4)

٣. إِنَّهُۥ يَعْلَمُ ٱلْجَهْرَ مِنَ ٱلْقَوْلِ (21: 110)

٤. يَعْلَمُ مَا يَلِجُ فِي ٱلْأَرْضِ وَمَا يَخْرُجُ مِنْهَا (34: 2)

٥. وَمَا تَسْقُطُ مِن وَرَقَةٍ إِلَّا يَعْلَمُهَا (6: 59)

٦. ٱللَّهُ يَعْلَمُ مَا تَحْمِلُ كُلُّ أُنثَىٰ (13: 8)

٧. وَمَا تَحْمِلُ مِنْ أُنثَىٰ وَلَا تَضَعُ إِلَّا بِعِلْمِهِۦ (41: 47)

٨. يَعْلَمُ مَا تَكْسِبُ كُلُّ نَفْسٍ (13: 42)

٩. وَمَا يَعْلَمُ تَأْوِيلَهُۥ إِلَّا ٱللَّهُ (3: 7)

١٠. تَعْلَمُ مَا فِي نَفْسِي وَلَآ أَعْلَمُ مَا فِي نَفْسِكَ (5: 116)

١١. وَلَا تَكْسِبُ كُلُّ نَفْسٍ إِلَّا عَلَيْهَا (6: 164)

١٢. وَأَمَّا مَنْ خَافَ مَقَامَ رَبِّهِ وَنَهَى ٱلنَّفْسَ عَنِ ٱلْهَوَى (79: 40)

١٣. لَّآ أَمْلِكُ لِنَفْسِى نَفْعًا وَلَا ضَرًّا إِلَّا مَا شَآءَ ٱللَّهُ (7: 188)

١٤. فَمَن يَنصُرُنِي مِنَ ٱللَّهِ إِنْ عَصَيْتُهُ (11: 63)

١٥. وَلَا يَظْلِمُ رَبُّكَ أَحَدًا (18: 49)

١٦. وَيَدْرَؤُا۟ عَنْهَا ٱلْعَذَابَ (24: 8)

١٧. وَمَا لِىَ لَآ أَعْبُدُ ٱلَّذِى فَطَرَنِى (36: 22)

١٨. يَوْمَ يَفِرُّ ٱلْمَرْءُ مِنْ أَخِيهِ ۞ وَأُمِّهِ وَأَبِيهِ (80: 34-35)

١٩. يَقُولُ ٱلْإِنسَٰنُ يَوْمَئِذٍ أَيْنَ ٱلْمَفَرُّ (75: 10)

٢٠. فَعَصَىٰ فِرْعَوْنُ ٱلرَّسُولَ (73: 16)

٢١. عُذْتُ بِرَبِّى (44: 20)

٢٢. فَمَن يَنصُرُنِي مِنَ ٱللَّهِ إِنْ عَصَيْتُهُ (11: 63)

٢٣. وَٱللَّهُ يَهْدِى مَن يَشَآءُ (2: 213)

٢٤. وَسِعَ رَبِّى كُلَّ شَىْءٍ عِلْمًا (6: 80)

٢٥. نُورٌ عَلَىٰ نُورٍ يَهْدِى ٱللَّهُ لِنُورِهِ مَن يَشَآءُ (24: 35)

٢٦. وَٱللَّهُ يَقُولُ ٱلْحَقَّ وَهُوَ يَهْدِى ٱلسَّبِيلَ (33: 4)

٢٧. ذَٰلِكَ هُدَى ٱللَّهِ يَهْدِى بِهِۦ مَن يَشَآءُ (6: 88)

٢٨. وَهُوَ ٱلَّذِى خَلَقَ ٱلَّيْلَ وَٱلنَّهَارَ وَٱلشَّمْسَ وَٱلْقَمَرَ (21: 33)

٢٩. وَٱللَّهُ خَلَقَ كُلَّ دَآبَّةٍ مِّن مَّآءٍ (24:45)

٣٠. وَجَعَلَ ٱلنَّهَارَ نُشُورًا (25: 47)

٣١. وَجَعَلَ فِيهَا سِرَٰجًا وَقَمَرًا مُّنِيرًا (25: 61)

٣٢. وَجَعَلَ ٱلشَّمْسَ سِرَاجًا (71: 16)

٣٣. جَعَلَ ٱلشَّمْسَ ضِيَآءً وَٱلْقَمَرَ نُورًا (10: 5)

٣٤. وَخَلَقَ كُلَّ شَىْءٍ وَهُوَ بِكُلِّ شَىْءٍ عَلِيمٌ (6: 101)

٣٥. وَخَتَمَ عَلَىٰ سَمْعِهِۦ وَقَلْبِهِۦ وَجَعَلَ عَلَىٰ بَصَرِهِۦ غِشَٰوَةً (45: 23)

٣٦. خَلَقَ مِنَ ٱلْمَآءِ بَشَرًا (25: 54)

٣٧. وَإِذَا مَرِضْتُ فَهُوَ يَشْفِينِ * (26: 80)

---

(37) * *Kasrah* under the consonant *Nūn* indicates Qur'ānic abbreviation of the pronoun suffix (ي) I M[1] + F[1].

QUR'ANIC TEXT
VOCABULARY
LESSON 6

حَرْفٌ	an edge (a point of turning)	هَوَى	lust
قَوْلٌ	word	مَلَكَ/يَمْلِكُ	to possess
جَهْرٌ	public, open	نَفْعٌ	benefit
وَلَجَ/يَلِجُ	to penetrate, enter, pass through	ضَرٌّ	hurt
سَقَطَ/يَسْقُطُ	to fall	دَرَأَ/يَدْرَأُ	to revert
وَرَقَةٌ	(F¹) leaf	مَرْءٌ/امرُؤٌ	man
حَمَلَ/يَحْمِلُ	to bear, carry, lift	يَوْمَئِذٍ	then on that day
أُنْثَى	female	مَفَرٌّ	fleeing
كَسَبَ/يَكْسِبُ	to earn	نُورٌ	light
إِلاَّ	except, save, unless	شَاءَ/يَشَاءُ	to will
تَأْوِيلٌ	interpretation	الْحَقُّ	the truth
خَافَ/يَخَافُ	to dread, fear	دَابَّةٌ	moving creature
مَقَامٌ	standing before, dignity	نُشُورٌ	resurrection
نَهَى/يَنْهَى	to prevent	سِرَاجٌ	lamp
غِشَاوَةٌ	covering	ضِيَاءٌ	glow, light
بَشَرٌ	human being	خَتَمَ/يَخْتِمُ	to seal
إِذَا	when	إِنْ	if

227

بَشَرٌ	man	فَطَرَ/يَفْطُرُ	to create out of nothing
مَرِض/يَمْرَضُ	to be sick	مُنِيرٌ	enlightening
شَفِي/يَشْفَي	to heal, cure		

وَرَحْمَتِي وَسِعَتْ كُلَّ شَيْءٍ 7:156

228

METHOD OF TEACHING
LESSON 6

1. With the display of intransitive verb cards on the magnetic board appropriate cards for nouns used as object can be placed against each verb card by seeking assistance from the students.

2. With the help of cards, the short vowel signs of two nouns of construct phrase when the first noun becomes an object can be explained.

3. The special forms of the nouns أَبٌ and أَخٌ in the accusative case need to be explained with the construction of sentences with cards.

4. The Imperfect Indicative can be effectively taught by adding four cards containing four letters as the signs of the Imperfect one after the other to the "Master Card" on the magnetic board.

5. Allow the students themselves to construct from the roots the different forms of the Imperfect Indicative.

6. Special care is needed to explain the various patterns of weak forms in the Imperfect. New patterns should not be introduced until the previous pattern is fully understood and sufficient drill has been done.

7. The Imperfect Active and Negative can be included in Arabic conversation in the classroom. Questions should be formed which enable the students to use these forms in their answers.

8. Students should be encouraged to form both Active Participles and Passive Participles from the sound as well as the weak roots.

Lesson 6

Exercise No. 24

(1) Select the correct word(s) from the parentheses to fill in the blanks in the following sentences:

(١) غَسَلْتُ الثَّوْبَ فَالثَّوْبُ ....
(مَأْكُوْلٌ، مَغْسُوْلٌ، مَضْرُوْبٌ، مَشْرُوْبٌ)

(٢) أَكَلْتُ الطَّعَامَ فَالطَّعَامُ ....
(مَشْرُوْبٌ، مَغْسُوْلٌ، مَأْكُوْلٌ، مَضْرُوْبٌ)

(٣) شَرِبْتُ الْمَاءَ فَالْمَاءُ ....
(مَكْتُوْبٌ، مَفْتُوْحٌ، مَشْرُوْبٌ، مَأْكُوْلٌ)

(٤) نَصَرْتُ الرَّجُلَ فَالرَّجُلُ ....
(مَضْرُوْبٌ، مَأْكُوْلٌ، مَنْصُوْرٌ، مَغْسُوْلٌ)

(٥) ضَرَبَ الْأَبُ الْوَلَدَ فَالْوَلَدُ ....
(مَأْكُوْلٌ، مَضْرُوْبٌ، مَغْسُوْلٌ، مَنْصُوْرٌ)

(٦) حَفِظَ الرَّجُلُ الْبَيْتَ فَالْبَيْتُ ....
(مَشْرُوْبٌ، مَضْرُوْبٌ، مَغْسُوْلٌ، مَحْفُوْظٌ)

(٧) كَتَبْتُ الْكِتَابَ فَالْكِتَابُ ....
(مَكْتُوْبٌ، مَشْرُوْبٌ، مَضْرُوْبٌ، مَحْفُوْظٌ)

(٨) فَتَحْتُ الْبَابَ فَالْبَابُ ....
(مَكْتُوْبٌ، مَغْسُوْلٌ، مَنْصُوْرٌ، مَفْتُوْحٌ)

230

(٩) غَسَلْتُ الْعَيْنَ فَالْعَيْنُ ....
(مَكْتُوبَةٌ، مَغْسُولَةٌ، مَفْتُوحَةٌ، مَضْرُوبَةٌ)

(١٠) فَرَّ الْوَلَدُ مِنَ الْبَيْتِ فَالْوَلَدُ ....
(مَشْرُوبٌ، مَغْسُولٌ، مَأْكُولٌ، فَارٌّ)

(2) Put i'rāb

(١) لقي زيد رجلا.

(٢) فتحت القرآن فالقرآن مفتوح.

(٣) هل قرأت الكتاب؟
ما قرأت الكتاب.

(٤) الولد يقرأ القرآن والأم تسمعه.

(٥) البنت تشرب الماء والولد يشرب اللبن.

(٦) أنت تذهب إلى المدرسة وأنت تأكلين الطعام.

(٧) أنا أكتب الكتاب وبنتي تجلس على الكرسي أمامي.

(٨) البنت تعود من المسجد وتقرأ القرآن في البيت.

(٩) النفس تلوم على الشر وترضى بالخير.

(١٠) هل أنت تعصين الله والرسول (ﷺ)؟

(١١) أنا أرجو منك خيرا.

(١٢) هو يتلو القرآن ويبكي.

(١٣) ترى في الدنيا خيرا وشرا.

(١٤) هل ترضى بجزائي لك؟

(١٥) أنت تموت والدنيا تفنى.

(١٦) هو يسعى ويقول: أنا فائز في الدنيا.

(١٧) يقول الانسان يومئذ أين المفر.

(3) Change the following Perfect into Imperfect.

(١) قَرَأْتَ (٢) كَتَبْتُ (٣) عَلِمَتْ (٤) فَهِمَ

(٥) سَمِعَتْ (٦) نَصَرْتُ (٧) جَهَلَتْ (٨) جَلَسَ

(٩) دَخَلْتَ (١٠) خَرَجْتِ (١١) تَلَوْتُ (١٢) قُلْتَ

(١٣) دَعَوْتُ (١٤) رَأَتْ (١٥) رَجَا (١٦) عَصَتْ

(١٧) خَشِيتَ (١٨) فَنِيَتْ (١٩) فُزْتَ (٢٠) سَعَيْتُ

(٢١) لُمْتَ (٢٢) هَدَى (٢٣) تُبْتُ (٢٤) بَكَيْتِ

(٢٥) مَاتَتْ (٢٦) رَضِيَ (٢٧) عُدْتُ (٢٨) كُنْتِ

(4) Translate into Arabic

(1) The food is eaten and the hand is washed.
(2) The mother drank the milk and the father drank the water.
(3) I am going to the mosque for Prayer.
(4) Are you (M[1]) reading the book?
(5) Are you (M[1]) washing the dining room?
(6) Are your father and his brother in the mosque?
(7) The name of the book of my Lord is the Qur'ān.
(8) I am worshipping Allah and He is my Lord.

232

(9) She writes and I read.

(10) I am entering my son's house.

(11) Do you (M[1]) read the Qur'ān in your house? Yes, I read the Qur'ān in my house.

(12) He cries and repents to Allah.

(13) Will you (M[1]) return to your house from the Prophetic mosque?

(14) Yes, I will return after Prayer.

(15) Do you (F[1]) disobey Allah and His Messenger () ? I do not disobey Allah and His Messenger()

(16) I read the Qur'ān and repent to Allah.

(17) The ignorant person seeks the world and feels pleased with the world.

(18) The scholar struggles for the Hereafter.

(19) He does not worship the creation of Allah.

(20) You (M[1]) worship Allah and will return to Him.

(5) From the Qur'ānic text of lesson 6 identify the following:

   (a) Imperfect verbs.
   (b) Objects.

الدَّرْسُ السَّابِعُ
7
UNIT 26

(١)   أَيْنَ الْبِنْتُ الْجَمِيلَةُ؟

الْبِنْتُ الْجَمِيلَةُ فِي الْغُرْفَةِ.

(٢)   هَلْ ذَهَبْتَ مَعَ الرَّجُلِ الْقَصِيرِ؟

نَعَمْ، ذَهَبْتُ مَعَ الرَّجُلِ الْقَصِيرِ.

(٣)   هَلْ رَأَيْتَ الْأُمَّ الْجَمِيلَةَ؟

لَا، مَا رَأَيْتُ الْأُمَّ الْجَمِيلَةَ.

(٤)   مَا يَفْعَلُ الْوَلَدُ الطَّوِيلُ فِي الْغُرْفَةِ؟

الْوَلَدُ الطَّوِيلُ يَقْرَأُ الْقُرْآنَ الْكَرِيمَ.

(٥)   يَذْهَبُ أَبٌ قَصِيرٌ مِنَ الْبَيْتِ إِلَى الْمَسْجِدِ لِلصَّلَاةِ.

(٦)   أُمٌّ عَالِمَةٌ خَيْرٌ مِنْ أُمٍّ جَاهِلَةٍ.

(٧)   أَيْنَ يَعْمَلُ الْوَلَدُ الْكَبِيرُ؟

الْوَلَدُ الْكَبِيرُ يَعْمَلُ فِي حَرْثِهِ.

(٨)   هَلْ تَقْرَأُ الْقُرْآنَ الْكَرِيمَ؟

نَعَمْ، أَقْرَأُ الْقُرْآنَ الْكَرِيمَ.

(٩)   هَلْ تَعْبُدُ اللهَ؟

نَعَمْ، أَعْبُدُ اللهَ الْعَظِيمَ السَّمِيعَ الْعَلِيمَ.

(١٠) أَنْتَ رَجُلٌ قَوِيٌّ تَعْمَلُ فِي حَرْثِكَ وَ أَنَا رَجُلٌ ضَعِيفٌ لَا أَعْمَلُ فِي حَرْثِي.

(١١) دَعَا زَكَرِيَّا رَبَّهُ.

(١٢) يَدُ الله فَوْقَ الْعَالِمِ.

(١٣) لَا يَكْذِبُ رَسُولُ الله (ﷺ).

(١٤) هَلْ أَنْتَ مَظْلُومٌ؟

نَعَمْ، أَنَا مَظْلُومٌ.

(١٥) إِلَهٌ بَاطِلٌ لَا يَضُرُّ وَ لَا يَنْفَعُ.

(١٦) أَنَا لَا أَشُكُّ فِي كِتَاب الله.

(١٧) أَتَشُكِّينَ فِي الله وَ هُوَ خَالِقُ الأَرْضِ وَ السَّمَاءِ؟

(١٨) أَنَا لَا أَشُكُّ فِي الله وَ هُوَ خَالِقِي وَ رَبِّي.

(١٩) قَتَلَ مُوسَى (عليه السلام) رَجُلًا عَاصِيًا.

(٢٠) أَلَا تَنْظُرُ إِلَى السَّمَاء كَيْفَ خَلَقَهَا اللهُ.

(٢١) يَكْسِبُ الْكَاذِبُ إِثْمًا عَظِيمًا وَ لِلْكَافِرِ عَذَابٌ أَلِيمٌ.

(٢٢) لِي نَفْسٌ لَائِمَةٌ عَلَى الشَّرِّ.

(٢٣) الأَرْضُ لِلَّه الْوَاحِدِ الْقَوِيِّ.

(٢٤) اللهُ لَا يَظْلِمُ الإِنْسَانَ، بَلِ الإِنْسَانُ يَظْلِمُ نَفْسَهُ.

(٢٥) أَقْرَأُ مِنْ كِتَاب الله الْعَزِيزِ الْحَكِيمِ.

(٢٦) بِسْمِ الله الَّذِي لَا يَضُرُّ مَعَ اسْمِهِ شَيْءٌ فِي الأَرْضِ وَ لَا فِي السَّمَاءِ وَ هُوَ السَّمِيعُ الْعَلِيمُ.

(١) إِنَّ الْقُرْآنَ الْكَرِيمَ كِتَابُ الله وَإِنَّهُ يَهْدِي إِلَى الْجَنَّة وَيَأْمُرُ بِالْخَيْرِ وَ الْحَسَنَة.

(٢) إِنَّ الْكَافِرَ لَيَقُولُ بَعْدَ مَوْتِه: لَيْتَنِي مَا كَفَرْتُ بِاللهِ وَلَيْتَنِي فَعَلْتُ الْخَيْرَ.

(٣) لَيْتَ الْقَائِلَ فَاعِلٌ.

(٤) لَعَلَّكَ تَفُوزُ لِأَنَّكَ تَسْعَى.

(٥) بِنْتُكَ لَا تَفُوزُ فِي الدُّنْيَا لِأَنَّهَا لَا تَسْعَى.

(٦) رَجَعَ الْوَلَدُ الَّذِي فَرَّ مِنَ الْبَيْتِ وَتَابَ إِلَى اللهِ.

(٧) أَرَأَيْتَ الظَّالِمَ الَّذِي يَظْلِمُ الْإِنْسَانَ؟

(٨) الظَّالِمُ يَظْلِمُ لِأَنَّهُ يَنْسَى اللهَ وَلَا يَخْشَى عَذَابَهُ.

(٩) مَنْ يَرْحَمُ الْإِنْسَانَ وَمَنْ يَظْلِمُ الْإِنْسَانَ؟ اللهُ يَرْحَمُ الْإِنْسَانَ وَالشَّيْطَانُ يَظْلِمُهُ.

(١٠) الْمَرْأَةُ الَّتِي تَقْرَأُ الْقُرْآنَ خَيْرٌ مِنَ الْمَرْأَةِ الَّتِي تَسْمَعُهُ.

(١١) إِبْرَاهِيمُ رَجُلٌ صَالِحٌ لِأَنَّهُ لَا يَكْذِبُ وَلَا يَأْمُرُ بِالشَّرِّ، وَلَكِنَّهُ يَأْمُرُ بِالْخَيْرِ وَالصَّلَاة.

(١٢) الدُّنْيَا مَتَاعٌ وَخَيْرُ مَتَاعِهَا الْمَرْأَةُ الصَّالِحَةُ.

(١٣) إِنَّ الْمَرْأَةَ الصَّالِحَةَ كَالْجَنَّةِ فِي الدُّنْيَا.

(١٤) إِنَّ رَبَّكَ يَعْلَمُ أَنَّكَ تَقُومُ فِي اللَّيْلِ لِلصَّلَاةِ وَأَنَّكَ عَلَى صِرَاطِه الْمُسْتَقِيمِ.

(١٥) إِنَّ رَبَّكَ لَيَعْلَمُ مَنْ أَنْتَ وَ مَا فِي قَلْبِكَ.

(١٦) إِنَّ اللهَ لاَ يَنْظُرُ إِلَى وَجْهِكَ وَ لاَ إِلَى ثَوْبِكَ وَ لَكِنَّهُ يَنْظُرُ إِلَى قَلْبِكَ.

(١٧) رَبُّكَ اللهُ الَّذِي خَلَقَكَ وَ هَدَاكَ إِلَى الصِّرَاطِ الْمُسْتَقِيمِ.

(١٨) إِنَّكَ عَلَى صِرَاطِ اللهِ الَّذِي لَهُ مَا فِي السَّمَاءِ وَالأَرْضِ.

(١٩) الإِنْسَانُ يَنَامُ وَلَكِنَّ اللهَ لاَ يَنَامُ وَهُوَ الْحَيُّ الْقَيُّومُ.

(٢٠) لَقَدْ هَدَانِي اللهُ إِلَى الصِّرَاطِ الْمُسْتَقِيمِ.

(٢١) لَقَدْ صَدَقَ اللهُ وَالرَّسُولُ (ﷺ).

(٢٢) إِنَّ اللهَ لَمَعَ الصَّادِقِ وَالصَّادِقَةِ.

(٢٣) هَلِ الْعَالِمُ حَيٌّ أَمْ مَيِّتٌ؟

(٢٤) الْعَالِمُ حَيٌّ لاَ يَمُوتُ بِالْمَوْتِ وَلَكِنَّ الْجَاهِلَ مَيِّتٌ.

(٢٥) إِبْرَاهِيْمُ يَعْبُدُ اللهَ كَأَنَّهُ يَرَاهُ.

قَالَ رَسُولُ اللهِ (ﷺ):

(٢٦) "مَثَلُ الَّذِي يَذْكُرُ رَبَّهُ وَالَّذِي لاَ يَذْكُرُ رَبَّهُ كَمَثَلِ الْحَيِّ وَالْمَيِّتِ".

(٢٧) "الطَّاعِمُ الشَّاكِرُ كَالصَّائِمِ الصَّابِرِ".

(٢٨) "الْمُؤْمِنُ لِلْمُؤْمِنِ كَالْبُنْيَانِ الْوَاحِدِ يَشُدُّ بَعْضُهُ بَعْضًا".

(٢٩) "هِجْرَةُ الْمُؤْمِنِ سَنَةً كَسَفْكِ دَمِهِ".

(٣٠) "الْيَدُ الْعُلْيَا خَيْرٌ مِنَ الْيَدِ السُّفْلَى".

(٣١) لاَ يَدْخُلُ الْجَنَّةَ قَاطِعٌ.

(٣٢) الدَّالُّ عَلَى الْخَيْرِ كَفَاعِلِهِ.

(٣٣) لاَ يَدْخُلُ الْجَنَّةَ نَمَّامٌ.

(٣٤) لاَ إِيمَانَ لِمَنْ لاَ أَمَانَةَ لَهُ وَلاَ دِينَ لِمَنْ لاَ عَهْدَ لَهُ.

(٣٥) قَالَ رَجُلٌ يَا رَسُولَ الله مَنْ أَحَقُّ بِحُسْنِ
صَحَابَتِي؟ قَالَ: أُمُّكَ. قَالَ ثُمَّ مَنْ؟ قَالَ:
أُمُّكَ. قَالَ ثُمَّ مَنْ؟ قَالَ: أُمُّكَ. قَالَ ثُمَّ مَنْ؟
قَالَ: أَبُوكَ.

(٣٦) "يَقُولُ الله عَزَّ وَجَلَّ: مَنْ جَاءَ بِالْحَسَنَةِ فَلَهُ عَشْرُ
أَمْثَالِهَا * وَأَزِيدُ وَمَنْ جَاءَ بِالسَّيِّئَةِ فَجَزَاءُ سَيِّئَةٍ
مِثْلَهَا أَوْ أَغْفِرُ ...."

(٣٧) كَانَ كَلاَمُ رَسُولِ الله (ﷺ) كَلاَمًا فَصْلٍ يَفْهَمُهُ كُلُّ مَنْ
يَسْمَعُهُ.

(٣٨) صَاحِبُ الْحَاجَةِ أَعْمَى.   "م"

(٣٩) الصِّنَاعَةُ فِي الْكَفِّ أَمَانٌ مِنَ الْفَقْرِ.   "م"

(٤٠) لِكُلِّ حَيٍّ أَجَلٌ.   "م"

(٤١) الرَّجُلُ مَنْ لَهُ رَأْيٌ صَائِبٌ.   "م"

(٤٢) عَيْنُ الْهَوَى لاَ تَصْدُقُ.   "م"

(٤٣) مَنْ فَعَلَ مَا شَاءَ لَقِيَ مَا سَاءَ.   "م"

(٤٤) إِنَّ مِنَ الْبَيَانِ لَسِحْرًا "م"

* 6 : 160

GLOSSARY
LESSON 7

جَمِيْلٌ	beautiful	لَكِنَّ	but
قَصِيْرٌ	short	لَعَلَّ	perhaps
طَوِيْلٌ	tall	الَّذِي	(M¹) which
كَرِيْمٌ	noble	مِثْلُ	like
كَبِيْرٌ	big	الَّتِي	(F¹) which
عَظِيْمٌ	great	لَـ	indeed
قَوِيٌّ	strong	رَجَعَ/يَرْجِعُ	to return
شَكَّ/يَشُكُّ	to doubt	نَسِيَ/يَنْسَى	to forget
أَلِيْمٌ	painful	رَحِمَ/يَرْحَمُ	to have mercy
عَزِيْزٌ	mighty	مَتَاعٌ	provision
حَكِيْمٌ	wise	صَلَحَ/يَصْلُحُ	to be good
مُسْتَقِيْمٌ	straight	صَالِحٌ	[AP M¹] virtuous
حَسَنَةٌ	good	الْقَيُّوْمُ	The Sustainer The Eternal
إِنَّ	verily	ذَكَرَ/يَذْكُرُ	to remember
أَنَّ	that	صَبَرَ/يَصْبِرُ	to exercise patience
كَأَنَّ	as if	صَابِرٌ	[AP M¹] patient
لَيْتَ	perchance	بُنْيَانٌ	building
بَاطِلٌ	[AP] false, vain	قَاطِعٌ	One who cuts the tie of relationship
شَدَّ/يَشُدُّ	to be or become firm	بَيَانٌ	speech
بَعْضٌ	some	سَحْرٌ	magic

هِجْرَةٌ	separation	نَمَّامٌ	slanderer
سَنَةٌ	year	أَمَانَةٌ	trust
سَفَكَ/يَسْفِكُ	blood shedding	عَهْدٌ	strict adherence
دَمٌّ	blood	أَحَقُّ	more deserving
عَالٍ	high, tall	حُسْنٌ	good conduct
سُفْلَى	lower part of something	صَحَابَةٌ	companionship
فَصْلٌ	parting	عَشْرٌ	ten fold
أَعْمَى	blind	زَادَ/ يَزِيدُ	to increase
أَمَانٌ	security	غَفَرَ/يَغْفِرُ	to forgive
فَقْرٌ	poverty	عَزَّ	Exalted
أَجَلٌ	death	جَلَّ	Glorified
دَالٌّ	indicator	جَزَاءٌ	reward
رَأْيٌ	opinion	سَيِّئَةٌ	evil
كَفٌّ	palm of the hand	صِنَاعَةٌ	art, skill, vocation

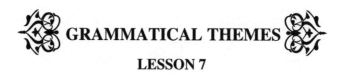

GRAMMATICAL THEMES

LESSON 7

UNIT 26

الصِّفَةُ

The Adjective

Rule No. 44B

Generally the adjective immediately follows the qualifying noun and agrees with it in number, gender, case and definiteness and indefiniteness.

Example Analysis:

أَيْنَ الْبِنْتُ الْجَمِيلَةُ؟

Where is the beautiful girl?

الْجَمِيلَةُ (The beautiful) is an adjective which agrees with its

qualifying noun الْبِنْتُ (the girl) :

in gender: both are feminine.

in case: both are in the nominative case and their case ending is

dammah (ُ),

in number: both are singular,

in definiteness: both are definite, both carry (اَلْ) the

definite article.

هَلْ ذَهَبْتَ مَعَ الرَّجُلِ الْقَصِيرِ؟

Did you go with the short man?

Because of the preposition مَعَ (with) the qualifying noun

الرَّجُلِ is in the genitive case (carrying *kasrah*). The adjective

الْقَصِيْرِ is in the genitive case, and therefore, agrees with the qualifying noun in its case. Both nouns are masculine, singular and definite.

هَلْ رَأَيْتَ الأُمَّ الْجَمِيْلَةَ؟

Did you see the beautiful mother?

The qualifying noun الأُمَّ (the mother) is an object which is in the accusative case (carrying *fathah*), therefore, its adjective

الْجَمِيْلَةَ (the beautiful) agrees with the qualifying noun in case, gender, number and definiteness.

أُمٌّ عَالِمَةٌ خَيْرٌ مِنْ أُمٍّ جَاهِلَةٍ.

A learned mother is better than an ignorant mother.

The adjective عَالِمَةٌ (a learned [F[1]]) is indefinite because its

qualifying noun أُمٌّ (a mother) is indefinite. Both agree in gender and number and both are in the nominative case.

هَلْ تَعْبُدُ اللهَ؟

نَعَمْ، أَعْبُدُ اللهَ الْعَظِيْمَ السَّمِيْعَ الْعَلِيْمَ.

Do you worship Allah? Yes, I worship Allah the Great, the All-Knowing, The All-Hearing.

اللهَ is a qualifying noun and is object. Therefore it is in the

accusative case (carrying *fathah*) الْعَظِيْمَ السَّمِيْعَ الْعَلِيْمَ are three successive adjectives they agree with the qualifying noun in all four agreements mentioned above.

Note there can be more than one adjective for a qualifying noun and all shall agree with the same case ending of a qualifying noun.

اللهُ رَبِّي وَ كِتَابُهُ الْعَزِيزُ فِي يَدِي وَ أَنَا أَقْرَأُ مِنْهُ.

(26) Allah is my Lord and His mighty book is in my hand and I am reading from it. كِتَابُهُ (His book) is a construct phrase.

الْعَزِيزُ (The mighty) is the adjective of كِتَابُ which is owing to (*iḍāfah*) a construct phrase which is definite. There is an agreement between the qualifying noun and the object in number, gender, case and definiteness.

۞ UNIT 27 ۞

The Particle إِنَّ and her sisters

Rule No. 45

(a) When إِنَّ (verily) and her sisters أَنَّ that, كَأَنَّ like that, لَيْتَ would that, لَعَلَّ perhaps, لَكِنَّ however, but, precedes the subject they change the subject into the accusative case.

(b) The Predicate remains in the nominative case and can be preceded by the particle (لَ indeed) for further emphasis.

(c) Pronominal suffixes can be attached with the particle إِنَّ and her sisters as subjects.

Example Analysis:

إِنَّ الْقُرْآنَ الْكَرِيْمَ كِتَابُ اللهِ وَإِنَّهُ يَهْدِي إِلَى الْجَنَّةَ وَيَأْمُرُ
بِالْخَيْرِ وَالْحَسَنَةِ.

Verily ! the noble Qur'ān is the book of Allah and it guides to Paradise and commands virtue and good [deeds]. الْقُرْآنَ

is the subject which is preceded by the particle إِنَّ therefore, the case of the Qur'ān will change into the accusative.

كِتَابُ اللهِ (the book of Allah) is a predicate, therefore, the case

ending of كِتَابُ is ḍammah , in the nominative case.

The particle أَنَّ (that) is used for the conjunction. The pronoun suffix هُ is attached with it أَنَّهُ = هُ + أَنَّ (that it) which refers to the Qur'ān.

بِنْتُكَ لاَ تَفُوزُ فِي الدُّنْيَا لِأَنَّهَا لاَ تَسْعَى وَتَنَامُ كُلَّ يَوْمٍ.

Your daughter will not succeed in the world because she does not struggle and sleeps the whole day.

لِأَنَّهَا = هَا + that, أَنَّ + for, لِـ (because she). The particle أَنَّ is

attached with the pronoun suffix هَا as well as the preposition (لِ) being attached with أَنَّ.

Note the first person pronoun suffix ي / ـِي can be attached with

إِنَّنِي = ي + إِنَّ and it can be إِنَّنِي = نِي + إِنَّ (verily I) إِنَّنِي أَنَا اللهُ
" (verily I am Allah.) (**20**: 14)

لَيْتَ الْقَائِلَ فَاعِلٌ

Would that the sayer is [also] a doer.

245

The particle لَيْتَ (would that) is the sister of إِنَّ and precedes the subject الْقَائِلَ (the sayer). Therefore الْقَائِلَ is in the accusative case and فَاعِلٌ (a doer) is the predicate, therefore, it is in the nominative case.

لَعَلَّكَ تَفُوزُ لِأَنَّكَ تَسْعَى

Perhaps you succeed because you struggle.

لَعَلَّ (perhaps) is one of the sisters of إِنَّ and كَ (you) is a pronoun suffix which is also subject.

إِنَّ اللهَ لاَ يَنْظُرُ إِلَى وَجْهِكَ وَلاَ إِلَى ثَوْبِكَ وَلَكِنَّهُ يَنْظُرُ إِلَى قَلْبِكَ.

Verily Allah neither looks at your face nor your clothing but He looks at your heart.

لَكِنَّ (but, however) is one of the sisters of إِنَّ and the pronoun suffix هُ is attached with it (لَكِنَّ + هُ) which is the subject.

إِبْرَاهِيمُ يَعْبُدُ اللهَ كَأَنَّهُ يَرَاهُ.

Ibrāhīm worships Allah as if he sees Him.

كَأَنَّ (as if) is one of the sisters of إِنَّ and the pronoun suffix (هُ) is attached with it (كَأَنَّ + هُ) which is the subject.

الَّذِي (M[1]) الَّتِي (F[1]) (who, that which, which, that) are the relative pronouns.

رَجَعَ الْوَلَدُ الَّذِي فَرَّ مِنَ الْبَيْتِ وَتَابَ إِلَى اللهِ عَلَى مَا فَعَلَ.

The boy who ran away from the house returned and he repented to Allah for what he did.

الْوَلَدُ who is related to the masculine singular therefore the masculine singular relative pronoun is used in this instance.

الْمَرْأَةُ الَّتِي تَقْرَأُ الْقُرْآنَ خَيْرٌ مِنَ الْمَرْأَةِ الَّتِي تَسْمَعُهُ.

246

The woman who recites the Qur'ān is better than the woman who listens to it.

الْمَرْأَةُ who is related to the feminine singular and therefore, the feminine singular relative pronoun is used.

إِنَّ رَبَّكَ لَيَعْلَمُ مَنْ أَنْتَ وَمَا فِي قَلْبِكَ.

Verily your Lord indeed knows who you are and what is in your heart.

The particle (لَـ) for emphasis is prefixed to the Imperfect

(لَـ + يَعْلَمُ) indeed he knows.

إِنَّكَ عَلَى صِرَاطِ الله الَّذِي لَهُ مَا فِي السَّمَاءِ وَالأَرْضِ.

Verily you are indeed on the path of Allah to Whom belongs whatever is in the heavens and the earth.

لَقَدْ هَدَانِي اللهُ إِلَى الصِّرَاطِ الْمُسْتَقِيْمِ.

Indeed Allah has guided me to the straight road.

The particle (لَ) is prefixed to قَدْ (لَ + قَدْ). As قَدْ

itself is used for emphasis after prefixing (لَ) it denotes a double emphasis which is difficult to translate into English because such expression does not exist in the English language.

إِنَّ اللهَ لَــمَعَ الصَّادق وَالصَّادقة.

Verily! Allah is indeed with the truthful man and truthful woman.

The particle (لَ) is prefixed to the preposition (مَعَ+ لَـ)

indeed with. For emphasis note that the particle (لَ) can be prefixed: to the personal pronoun III M¹ (لَهُوَ) (see Qur'ānic text **3**: 62), to the demonstrative pronoun (لَهَذَا), to the nouns

(لَذُوْ، لَسَمِيْعُ، لَحَقٌّ، لَقُرْآنٌ) (see Qur'ānic text **69**: 51, **56**: 77, **86**: 13, **40**: 61).

247

النَّصُ الْقُرْآنِيُ
Lesson 7

١.   بِسْمِ ٱللَّهِ ٱلرَّحْمَـٰنِ ٱلرَّحِيمِ (30 :27)

٢.   إِنَّ رَبِّى رَحِيمٌ وَدُودٌ (90 :11)

٣.   إِنَّهُ هُوَ ٱلتَّوَّابُ ٱلرَّحِيمُ (37 :2)

٤.   إِنَّ ٱللَّهَ بِٱلنَّاسِ لَرَءُوفٌ رَّحِيمٌ (65 :22)

٥.   إِنَّ رَحْمَتَ ٱللَّهِ قَرِيبٌ (56 :7)

٦.   إِنَّ رَبِّى عَلَىٰ كُلِّ شَىْءٍ حَفِيظٌ (57 :11)

٧.   إِنَّ ٱلْعِزَّةَ لِلَّهِ جَمِيعًا هُوَ ٱلسَّمِيعُ ٱلْعَلِيمُ (65 :10)

٨.   إِنَّ ٱلْأَمْرَ كُلَّهُ لِلَّهِ (154 :3)

٩.   وَأَنَّ ٱللَّهَ عِندَهُ أَجْرٌ عَظِيمٌ (28 :8)

١٠. وَمَا مِنْ إِلَـٰهٍ إِلَّا ٱللَّهُ وَإِنَّ ٱللَّهَ لَهُوَ ٱلْعَزِيزُ ٱلْحَكِيمُ (62 :3)

١١. إِنَّ ٱللَّهَ لَا يَخْفَىٰ عَلَيْهِ شَىْءٌ فِى ٱلْأَرْضِ وَلَا فِى ٱلسَّمَآءِ (5 :3)

١٢. وَمَن شَكَرَ فَإِنَّمَا يَشْكُرُ لِنَفْسِهِ ۖ وَمَن كَفَرَ فَإِنَّ رَبِّي غَنِيٌّ كَرِيمٌ (27: 40)

١٣. إِنَّ ذَٰلِكَ عَلَى ٱللَّهِ يَسِيرٌ (29: 19)

١٤. إِنَّ أَرْضِى وَاسِعَةٌ (29: 56)

١٥. تَخْلُقُ مَا يَشَآءُ ۚ وَٱللَّهُ عَلَىٰ كُلِّ شَىْءٍ قَدِيرٌ (5: 17)

١٦. لَهُ ٱلْمُلْكُ وَلَهُ ٱلْحَمْدُ ۖ وَهُوَ عَلَىٰ كُلِّ شَىْءٍ قَدِيرٌ (64: 1)

١٧. إِنَّ ٱللَّهَ لَا يَظْلِمُ مِثْقَالَ ذَرَّةٍ (4: 40)

١٨. وَٱللَّهُ يَهْدِى مَن يَشَآءُ إِلَىٰ صِرَاطٍ مُّسْتَقِيمٍ (2: 213)

١٩. وَأَنَّ ٱلْفَضْلَ بِيَدِ ٱللَّهِ (57: 29)

٢٠. وَلَوْ شَآءَ رَبُّكَ لَجَعَلَ ٱلنَّاسَ أُمَّةً وَاحِدَةً (11: 118)

٢١. كَيْفَ ضَرَبَ ٱللَّهُ مَثَلًا كَلِمَةً طَيِّبَةً كَشَجَرَةٍ طَيِّبَةٍ أَصْلُهَا ثَابِتٌ وَفَرْعُهَا فِى ٱلسَّمَآءِ (14: 24)

٢٢. وَمَا مِنْ غَآئِبَةٍ فِى ٱلسَّمَآءِ وَٱلْأَرْضِ إِلَّا فِى كِتَابٍ مُّبِينٍ (27: 75)

٢٣. ٱللَّهُ لَآ إِلَٰهَ إِلَّا هُوَ ٱلْحَىُّ ٱلْقَيُّومُ (2: 255)

٢٤. وَٱللَّهُ ذُو ٱلْفَضْلِ ٱلْعَظِيمِ (2: 105)

٢٥. لِلَّهِ ٱلْمَشْرِقُ وَٱلْمَغْرِبُ ۚ يَهْدِى مَن يَشَآءُ إِلَىٰ صِرَٰطٍ مُّسْتَقِيمٍ (142 :2)

٢٦. بِنَصْرِ ٱللَّهِ ۚ يَنصُرُ مَن يَشَآءُ ۖ وَهُوَ ٱلْعَزِيزُ ٱلرَّحِيمُ (5 :30)

٢٧. يَخْلُقُ مَا يَشَآءُ ۚ وَهُوَ ٱلْعَلِيمُ ٱلْقَدِيرُ (54 :30)

٢٨. خَلَقَ ٱلْإِنسَٰنَ مِن نُّطْفَةٍ فَإِذَا هُوَ خَصِيمٌ مُّبِينٌ (4 :16)

٢٩. أَلَا يَعْلَمُ مَنْ خَلَقَ وَهُوَ ٱللَّطِيفُ ٱلْخَبِيرُ (14 :67)

٣٠. وَيَتُوبُ ٱللَّهُ عَلَىٰ مَن يَشَآءُ ۗ وَٱللَّهُ عَلِيمٌ حَكِيمٌ (15 :9)

٣١. وَيَجْعَلَ ٱللَّهُ فِيهِ خَيْرًا كَثِيرًا (19 :4)

٣٢. جَعَلَ ٱللَّهُ ٱلْكَعْبَةَ ٱلْبَيْتَ ٱلْحَرَامَ قِيَٰمًا لِّلنَّاسِ (97 :5)

٣٣. قَالَ أَقَتَلْتَ نَفْسًا زَكِيَّةً بِغَيْرِ نَفْسٍ (74 :18)

٣٤. فِي جَنَّةٍ عَالِيَةٍ ۞ لَّا تَسْمَعُ فِيهَا لَٰغِيَةً (10-11 :88)

٣٥. وَإِذَا رَأَيْتَ ثَمَّ رَأَيْتَ نَعِيمًا وَمُلْكًا كَبِيرًا (20 :76)

٣٦. سَأَلَ سَآئِلٌ بِعَذَابٍ وَاقِعٍ (1 :70)

٣٧. ذَٰلِكَ هُوَ ٱلْفَوْزُ ٱلْعَظِيمُ (64 :10)

٣٨. إِنَّ فِي ذَٰلِكَ لَآيَةً لِّمَنْ خَافَ عَذَابَ ٱلْآخِرَةِ (103 :11)

٣٩. إِنَّهُ لَقَوْلُ رَسُولٍ كَرِيمٍ ۞ وَمَا هُوَ بِقَوْلِ شَاعِرٍ
(69: 40-41)

٤٠. إِنَّ رَبَّكَ يَبْسُطُ ٱلرِّزْقَ لِمَن يَشَآءُ وَيَقْدِرُ (17: 30)

٤١. أَنَّ ٱلْفُلْكَ تَجْرِى فِى ٱلْبَحْرِ بِنِعْمَتِ ٱللَّهِ (31: 31)

٤٢. قَالَتْ رَبِّ إِنِّى ظَلَمْتُ نَفْسِى (27: 44)

٤٣. قَالَ أَعْلَمُ أَنَّ ٱللَّهَ عَلَىٰ كُلِّ شَىْءٍ قَدِيرٌ (2: 259)

٤٤. كُلَّمَا دَخَلَ عَلَيْهَا زَكَرِيَّا ٱلْمِحْرَابَ وَجَدَ عِندَهَا رِزْقًا
قَالَ يَـٰمَرْيَمُ أَنَّىٰ لَكِ هَـٰذَا ۖ قَالَتْ هُوَ مِنْ عِندِ ٱللَّهِ ۖ إِنَّ ٱللَّهَ
يَرْزُقُ مَن يَشَآءُ بِغَيْرِ حِسَابٍ (3: 37)

٤٥. إِنَّ ٱلدِّينَ عِندَ ٱللَّهِ ٱلْإِسْلَـٰمُ (3: 19)

٤٦. إِنَّ ٱللَّهَ يَأْمُرُ بِٱلْعَدْلِ وَٱلْإِحْسَـٰنِ (16: 90)

٤٧. أَنَّ ٱلنَّفْسَ بِٱلنَّفْسِ وَٱلْعَيْنَ بِٱلْعَيْنِ وَٱلْأَنفَ بِٱلْأَنفِ
وَٱلْأُذُنَ بِٱلْأُذُنِ وَٱلسِّنَّ بِٱلسِّنِّ (5: 45)

٤٨. وَأَنَّ ٱللَّهَ بِكُلِّ شَىْءٍ عَلِيمٌ (5: 97)

٤٩. إِنَّ رَبِّى لَطِيفٌ لِّمَا يَشَآءُ ۚ إِنَّهُ هُوَ ٱلْعَلِيمُ ٱلْحَكِيمُ (12: 100)

٥٠. إِنَّ رَبَّكَ هُوَ ٱلْخَلَّـٰقُ ٱلْعَلِيمُ (15: 86)

٥١. ٱلْحَمْدُ لِلَّهِ ٱلَّذِى وَهَبَ لِى عَلَى ٱلْكِبَرِ إِسْمَعِيلَ وَإِسْحَقَ (39 :14)

٥٢. مَن ذَا ٱلَّذِى يَشْفَعُ عِندَهُۥ إِلَّا بِإِذْنِهِۦ (255 :2)

٥٣. هُوَ ٱللَّهُ ٱلَّذِى لَا إِلَهَ إِلَّا هُوَ عَلِمُ ٱلْغَيْبِ وَٱلشَّهَدَةِ (22 :59)

٥٤. مَن قَتَلَ نَفْسًا بِغَيْرِ نَفْسٍ أَوْ فَسَادٍ فِى ٱلْأَرْضِ فَكَأَنَّمَا قَتَلَ ٱلنَّاسَ جَمِيعًا (32 :5)

٥٥. فَمَن تَبِعَنِى فَإِنَّهُۥ مِنِّى وَمَنْ عَصَانِى فَإِنَّكَ غَفُورٌ رَّحِيمٌ (36 :14)

٥٦. وَلَوْ شَآءَ رَبُّكَ لَجَعَلَ ٱلنَّاسَ أُمَّةً وَٰحِدَةً (118 :11)

٥٧. أَنَّمَا ٱلْحَيَوٰةُ ٱلدُّنْيَا لَعِبٌ (20 :57)

٥٨. وَمَا رَمَيْتَ إِذْ رَمَيْتَ وَلَكِنَّ ٱللَّهَ رَمَىٰ (17 :8)

٥٩. إِنَّ ٱللَّهَ بِكُلِّ شَىْءٍ عَلِيمٌ (7 :58)

٦٠. إِنَّ قَرُونَ كَانَ مِن قَوْمِ مُوسَىٰ (76 :28)

٦١. إِنِّى ذَاهِبٌ إِلَىٰ رَبِّى (99 :37)

٦٢. إِنَّكَ لَرَسُولُهُۥ (1 :63)

٦٣. إِنَّ رَبِّى لَسَمِيعُ ٱلدُّعَآءِ (39 :14)

٦٤.   وَإِنَّهُ لَحَقُّ ٱلْيَقِينِ (69: 51)

٦٥.   إِنَّكَ لَفِى ضَلَٰلِكَ ٱلْقَدِيمِ (12: 95)

٦٦.   إِنَّ ٱلْإِنسَٰنَ لَفِى خُسْرٍ (103: 2)

٦٧.   إِنَّ عَذَابَ رَبِّكَ لَوَٰقِعٌ (52: 7)

٦٨.   لَقَدْ صَدَقَ ٱللَّهُ رَسُولَهُ ٱلرُّءْيَا بِٱلْحَقِّ (48: 27)

٦٩.   إِنَّهُ تَذْكِرَةٌ (74: 54)

٧٠.   إِنَّهُ لَقُرْءَانٌ كَرِيمٌ (56: 77)

٧١.   إِنَّهُ لَقَوْلٌ فَصْلٌ (86: 13)

٧٢.   إِنَّ ٱللَّهَ لَذُو فَضْلٍ عَلَى ٱلنَّاسِ (40: 61)

QUR'ANIC TEXT
VOCABULARY
LESSON 7

الرَّحْمَنُ	The Merciful	كَلِمَةٌ	word
الرَّحِيمُ	The Mercy Giving	طَيِّبٌ	good
رَؤُوْفٌ	Clement, Compassionate	أَصْلٌ	root
تَوَّابٌ	Ever Relenting	ثَابِتٌ	firm
قَرِيْبٌ	near	فَرْعٌ	branch
عِزَّةٌ	honour	غَائِبٌ	hidden
أَجْرٌ	reward	مُبِيْنٌ	clear
خَفِيَ/يَخْفَى	to be hidden, to be concealed	عَظِيْمٌ	great
شَكَرَ/يَشْكُرُ	to thank, be thankful	فَضْلٌ	beauty, grace
غَنِيٌّ	Self Sufficient	مَشْرِقٌ	east
يَسِيْرٌ	easy	مَغْرِبٌ	west
قَدِيْرٌ	Able to do	مُسْتَقِيْمٌ	straight
مِثقَالٌ	weight of	نَصْرٌ	help
ذَرَّةٌ	smallest particle	نُطْفَةٌ	drop of fluid
شَاءَ/يَشَاءُ	to wish	خَصِيْمٌ	opponent
أُمَّةٌ	community	لَطِيْفٌ	subtle
ثُمَّ	then, hence	خَبِيْرٌ	all aware
نَعِيْمٌ	bliss	حَرَامٌ	sacred standard,
مُلْكٌ	dominion	قِيَامٌ	maintenance
وَقَعَ/يَقَعُ	to come to pass	زَكِيَّةٌ	innocent

وَاقِعٌ	[AP] occurring	عَالِيَةٌ	elevated
فَوْزٌ	success	لاَغٍ	idle speech
خَافَ/يَخَافُ	to fear	سِنٌّ	tooth
كَرِيمٌ	generous	الْخَلاَّقُ	The most Powerful Creator
آيَةٌ	sign	وَهَبَ/يَهَبُ	to grant
شَاعِرٌ	poet	إِذْنٌ	permission
بَسَطَ/يَبْسُطُ	to spread	جَمِيعٌ	all, entire, whole
رِزْقٌ	sustenance	غَيْبٌ	hidden
قَدَرَ/يَقْدِرُ	to decree, ordain, decide	فَسَادٌ	corruption
جَرَى/يَجْرِي	to follow	تَبِعَ/يَتْبَعُ	to follow
نِعْمَةٌ	bounty	غَفُورٌ	Most Forgiving
مِحْرَابٌ	sanctuary, an apartment inside the sanctuary	ثَمَّ	there
وَجَدَ/يَجِدُ	to find	رَمَى/يَرْمِي	to throw (TA6)
أَنَّى	whence	يَقِينٌ	assured certainty
حِسَابٌ	measure	ضَلاَلٌ	aberration
عَدْلٌ	justice	قَدِيمٌ	old
إِحْسَانٌ	kindness, godliness	رُؤْيَا	dream
عَيْنٌ	eye	خَسِرَ	to incur loss
أُذُنٌ	ear	تَذْكِرَةٌ	admonition
أَنْفٌ	nose	فَصْلٌ	divisive

🕌 METHOD OF TEACHING 🕌
LESSON 7

1. The pattern an adjective phrase can be effectively explained if it is compared with a simple sentence comprising of a subject and a predicate. Like. زَيْدٌ عَالِمٌ
    Zayd is a scholar. The predicate agrees with the subject in gender and number but in an adjective phrase comprising of the qualifying noun and the adjective it can be used either as a subject or as a predicate in a sentence. Here the adjective agrees with the qualifying noun in case, number, gender and definiteness or indefiniteness.

2. The adjective phrase can further be explained with pairs of cards (adjectives and qualifying nouns) by shifting the cards on the magnetic board with the help of the students. Four areas of agreement can be presented by selecting one colour.

3. Six cards in one colour can be prepared for إِنَّ and its sisters and their accusative effect as agents in the sentences can be explained.

4. Similarly (لَ) can be made clear by affixing it to nouns, pronouns, verbs, prepositions and particles.

5. The selection in the Qur'ānic text is strictly confined to the themes so far introduced. A grammatical analysis of the Qur'ānic text at this stage will help in understanding the different form and will also create confidence among the students in the text of the Qur'ān.

Lesson 7

Exercise No.25

(1) Select the correct word(s) from the parentheses to fill in the
blanks in the following sentences:

(١)   هَذَا رَجُلٌ ....

(كَبِيرٌ، صَالِحٌ، الْقَصِيرُ، جَمِيلَةٌ)

(٢)   هَذِه الْبِنْتُ ....

(صَالِحٌ، كَبِيرٌ، جَمِيلَةٌ، الْقَصِيرِ)

(٣)   ذَهَبْتُ إِلَى الْمَسْجِدِ مَعَ رَجُلٍ ....

(جَمِيلَةٌ، الْقَصِيرُ، طَوِيلٍ، كَبِيرٌ)

(٤)   رَأَيْتُ الْبَيْتَ ....

(الْكَبِيرَ، صَغِيرًا، الْجَمِيلُ، طَوِيلَةٌ)

(٥)   كَتَبْتُ بِالْقَلَم ....

(الصَّغِيرِ، صَالِحَةٌ، صَادِقٌ، كَاذِبًا)

(2) Put *I'rāb*

(١)   تكسب الظالمة إثما عظيما.

(٢)   النفس المطمئنة خير من النفس اللائمة.

(٣)   هل تشكين في كتاب الله؟

(٤)   أنا لا أشك في كتاب الله.

(٥)   هل تحب الله الواحد؟

(٦)   أنا أحب الله السميع العليم.

(٧)   القرآن الكريم كتاب الله.

(٨) رجل قوي خير من رجل ضعيف.

(٩) بنت جميلة صادقة.

(١٠) الولد الصغير يقرأ كتاب الله في غرفته.

(١١) إن الله سميع عليم.

(١٢) ليتني سمعت قولك.

(١٣) إن ربك هو الذي خلق وهدى.

(١٤) إن المرأة الجميلة التي تقرأ القرآن تفوز في الدنيا والأخرة.

(١٥) إن الله لا يأمر بالشر ولكنه يأمر بالخير.

(١٦) لعل الولد الذي يسعى يفوز في سعيه.

(١٧) إن الله لمع الرجل الصالح.

(١٨) إن محمدا لرسول الله (ﷺ).

(١٩) أنا أعبد الله كأني أراه.

(٢٠) إن الله لا يظلم الإنسان ولكن الإنسان يظلم نفسه.

(3) Translate into Arabic:

(1) O My brother! Where are you going? Are you pleased with me?
(2) The health of my brother's son is good.
(3) The short boy reads the noble Qur'ān and his learned mother hears it.
(4) A tall father goes to the Prophetic mosque for Prayer.
(5) I saw the beautiful flower on the big table.
(6) She loves Allah, the All Hearing, the All Knowing.
(7) Zayd oppresses a tall man, his name is Aḥmad.
(8) Do you (M¹) have a doubt in the Book of Allah ?
(9) A learned boy is better than an ignorant boy.
(10) A beautiful girl reads the noble Qur'ān.
(11) A strong boy works in his father's field.
(12) The tranquil soul enters Paradise.

(13) Verily! Mūsā(عليه السلام) is the messenger of Allah.

(14) Certainly! Your (M¹)Lord indeed knows what you speak and listens.
(15) Verily! The scholar does not die with his death but the ignorant person dies.
(16) The woman who reads the Qur'ān is my sister.
(17) The tall boy who reads the Qur'ān is indeed successful.
(18) I love Allah and indeed! Allah is my Creator and your (M¹) Creator.

(4) From the Qur'ānic Lesson 7 identify the following:
(a) Adjectives.

(b) Predicates of إِنَّ and her sisters.

Phase Three

۞ UNIT 28 ۞

١. أَنَا أَشْكُرُ اللهَ شُكْراً كَثِيراً فِي اللَّيْلِ وَ فِي النَّهَارِ لِأَنَّهُ خَالِقِي وَ رَبِّي.

٢. نَصَرَ اللهُ الرَّسُولَ (ﷺ) نَصْراً عَزِيزاً.

٣. قُمْتُ فِي صَلَاةِ اللَّيْلِ قِيَاماً طَوِيلاً وَنِمْتُ فِي اللَّيْلِ نَوْماً قَلِيلاً.

٤. ذَكَرْتُ اللهَ ذِكْراً كَثِيراً.

٥. الظَّالِمُ يَظْلِمُنِي ظُلْماً كَثِيراً وَ أَصْبِرُ عَلَيْهِ صَبْراً جَمِيلاً.

٦. الصَّبْرُ عَادَةٌ مَحْمُودَةٌ.

٧. يَظْلِمُ الظَّالِمُ فِي الدُّنْيَا وَ لَكِنَّ اللهَ يَأْخُذُهُ أَخْذاً شَدِيداً.

٨. مَا الظُّلْمُ؟

الظُّلْمُ وَضْعُ الشَّيْءِ عَلَى غَيْرِ مَحَلِّهِ.

٩. مَنْ عَمِلَ عَمَلاً صَالِحاً فِي الدُّنْيَا فَلَهُ الْجَنَّةُ جَزَاءً فِي الآخِرَةِ.

١٠. كَذَبَ ابْنِي فَغَضِبْتُ غَضَباً شَدِيداً وَ نَصَحْتُهُ نُصْحاً جَمِيلاً.

١١. اللَّهُمَّ إِنِّي أَسْأَلُكَ عِلْماً نَافِعاً وَ عَمَلاً صَالِحاً وَ حِفْظاً قَوِيّاً وَ فَهْماً كَامِلاً وَ عَقْلاً سَالِماً.

١٢. اللَّهُمَّ أَنْتَ رَبِّي وَ أَنَا عَبْدُكَ، خَلَقْتَنِي وَ هَدَيْتَنِي فَأَنَا أَحْمَدُكَ عَلَى ذَلِكَ حَمْداً كَثِيراً.

١٣. الْمُسْلِمُ مَنْ سَلِمَ النَّاسُ مِنْ لِسَانِه وَ يَدِه.

١٤. الْكَافِرُ لاَ يَعْمَلُ عَمَلاً صَالِحاً وَ يَقُولُ عَلَى الله كَذِباً.

١٥. مَنْ يَفِرُّ مِنَ الْمَوْت؟
الْكَافِرُ يَفِرُّ مِنْهُ فِرَاراً

❀ UNIT 29 ❀

١. مَا هَذَان؟
هَذَانِ قَلَمَان. هَذَانِ كِتَابَان. هَذَانِ كُرْسِيَّان.
هَذَانِ بَحْرَان. هَذَانِ رَجُلَانِ قَصِيرَان.

٢. مَا هَاتَان؟
هَاتَانِ يَدَان.   هَاتَانِ بِنْتَان.
هَاتَانِ غُرْفَتَان.   هَاتَانِ زَهْرَتَان.
هَاتَانِ مَائِدَتَانِ صَغِيرَتَان.

٣. مَا ذَانِكَ؟
ذَانِكَ أَبَوَان.   ذَانِكَ كِتَابَان.
ذَانِكَ خُبْزَان.   ذَانِكَ كُرْسِيَّان.
ذَانِكَ وَلَدَانِ صَغِيرَان.

٤. مَا تَانِكَ؟

262

تَانِكَ عَيْنَانِ. تَانِكَ يَدَانِ. تَانِكَ جَنَّتَانِ.

تَانِكَ فُلْكَانِ. تَانِكَ زَهْرَتَانِ جَمِيلَتَانِ.

٥. هَذَانِ رَجُلَانِ ذَاهِبَانِ مِنْ بَيْتَيْنِ إِلَى حَرْثَيْنِ لِلْعَمَلِ.

٦. تَرَكْتُ زَهْرَتَيْنِ جَمِيلَتَيْنِ فِي كَأْسَيْنِ صَغِيرَتَيْنِ.

٧. قَرَأْتُ كِتَابَيْنِ فِي يَوْمَيْنِ.

٨. غَسَلْتُ يَدَيْنِ وَ رِجْلَيْنِ بِالْمَاءِ.

٩. دَخَلْتُ جَنَّتَيْنِ أَمَامَ بَيْتَيْنِ.

❈ UNIT 30 ❈

١. نَزَّلَ اللهُ الْقُرْآنَ تَنْزِيلاً.

٢. الرَّحْمَنُ ❈ عَلَّمَ الْقُرْآنَ ❈ خَلَقَ الإِنْسَانَ ❈ عَلَّمَهُ الْبَيَانَ (55: 1-4)

٣. الرَّسُولُ (ﷺ) عَلَّمَ الْقُرْآنَ وَ السُّنَّةَ.

٤. تَعْلِيمُ الْقُرْآنِ وَ تَبْلِيغُهُ عَمَلَانِ صَالِحَانِ عِنْدَ الرَّحْمَنِ.

٥. الرَّسُولُ (ﷺ) مُعَلِّمُ الْقُرْآنِ وَ مُبَلِّغُ الإِسْلَامِ.

٦. مَنْ يُعَلِّمُكَ الْقِرَاءَةَ وَ الْكِتَابَةَ؟
الْمُعَلِّمُ يُعَلِّمُنِي الْقِرَاءَةَ وَ الْكِتَابَةَ.

٧. هُوَ اللهُ الَّذِي يُقَرِّبُكَ إِلَى الْخَيْرِ وَ يُبَعِّدُكَ عَنِ النَّارِ وَ يُطَهِّرُ قَلْبَكَ مِنَ الشَّرِّ وَ الْفَسَادِ.

263

٨. الشَّيْطَانُ يُضِلُّ الإِنْسَانَ عَنْ صِرَاطِ الرَّحْمَنِ وَ
يُقَرِّبُهُ إِلَى الشَّرِّ وَ الْفَسَادِ.

٩. هَلْ تَشُكُّ في تَنْزِيلِ الْقُرْآنِ؟
أَنَا لاَ أَشُكُّ في تَنْزِيلِ الْقُرْآنِ.

١٠. الأَبُ يُعَلِّمُ الابْنَ تَرْتِيلَ الْقُرْآنِ.

١١. الابْنُ يُحِبُّ الْقُرْآنَ حُبًّا شَدِيداً.

١٢. هَلْ تُحِبُّ اللهَ؟
نَعَمْ، أُحِبُّ اللهَ حُبًّا شَدِيداً لأَنَّهُ خَالِقِي وَ رَبِّي ،
وَ لأَنَّهُ إِذَا مَرِضْتُ فَهُوَ يَشْفِينِي وَ إِذَا ضَلَلْتُ
فَهُوَ يَهْدِينِي.

١٣. صَدَّقَ أَبُو بَكْرٍ رَسُولَ اللهِ (ﷺ) فَعَزَّ وَ فَازَ،
وَ كَذَّبَهُ أَبُو لَهَب فَذَلَّ وَ خَسِرَ.

١٤. الصَّلَاةُ مُطَهِّرَةٌ مِنَ الْفَحْشِ وَ العِصْيَانِ.

١٥. مَنْ يُصَلِّي الصَّلَاةَ بِخُشُوعٍ يَفُوزُ في الدُّنْيَا وَ الآخِرَةِ.

١٦. صَلَّيْتُ في مَسْجِدِ النَّبِيِّ (ﷺ) فَدَعَوْتُ اللهَ
دُعَاءً طَوِيلاً.

١٧. أَنَا أُصَلِّي لأُطَهِّرَ قَلْبِي وَ أَثُوبَ إِلَى رَبِّي.

١٨. تَحْقِيرُ الإِنْسَانِ وَ تَذْلِيلُهُ عَمَلَانِ قَبِيحَانِ
عِنْدَ الرَّحْمَنِ.

١٩. مَنْ حَقَّرَ مُسْلِماً فَقَدْ ذَلَّ.

قَالَ رَسُولُ اللهِ (ﷺ):

٢٠. اَلْمَرْءُ مَعَ مَنْ أَحَبَّ. "ح"

٢١. الطُّهُورُ شَطْرُ الْإِيمَانِ. "ح"

٢٢. السِّوَاكُ مَطْهَرَةٌ لِلْفَمِ. "ح"

٢٣. كَلِمَتَانِ خَفِيفَتَانِ عَلَى اللِّسَانِ ثَقِيلَتَانِ فِي الْمِيزَانِ حَبِيبَتَانِ عِنْدَ الرَّحْمَنِ: سُبْحَانَ اللهِ وَ بِحَمْدِه سُبْحَانَ اللهِ الْعَظِيمِ. "ح"

٢٤. يُسَلِّمُ الصَّغِيرُ عَلَى الْكَبِيرِ وَالْمَاشِي عَلَى الْقَاعِدِ وَالْقَلِيلُ عَلَى الْكَثِيرِ.

٢٥. مَنْ يُرِدِ اللهُ بِهِ خَيْراً يُفَقِّهْهُ فِي الدِّينِ.

٢٦. يَأْتِي عَلَى النَّاسِ زَمَانٌ الصَّابِرُ فِيهِمْ عَلَى دِينِه كَالْقَابِضِ عَلَى الْجَمْرِ.

٢٧. الْمُؤْمِنُ مِرْآةُ الْمُؤْمِنِ.

٢٨. آفَةُ الْعِلْمِ النِّسْيَانُ. "م"

٢٩. اَلْجَهْلُ مَوْتُ الْأَحْيَاءِ. "م"

٣٠. الْعَاقِلُ تَكْفِيهِ الْإِشَارَةُ. "م"

٣١. الصَّبْرُ مِفْتَاحُ الْفَرَجِ. "م"

٣٢. الإِنْسَانُ عَبْدُ الإِحْسَانِ. "م"

٣٣. مَنْ جَدَّ وَجَدَ. "م"

٣٤. كُلُّ جَدِيدٍ لَذِيذٌ. "م"

٣٥. مَنْ قَلَّ حَيَاؤُهُ كَثُرَ ذَنْبُهُ. "م"

٣٦. مَنْ حَفَرَ بِئْراً لأَخِيهِ فَقَدْ وَقَعَ فِيْهِ. "م"

٣٧. شَرُّ السَّمَكِ يُكَدِّرُ الْمَاءَ. "م"

٣٨. مَنْ سَلِمَتْ سَرِيْرَتُهُ سَلِمَتْ عَلاَنِيَّتُهُ. "م"

٣٩. خَيْرُ الأَعْمَالِ أَدْوَمُهَا وإِنْ قَلَّ. "م"

٤٠. إِنَّ اللَّبِيْبَ مِنَ الإِشَارَةِ يَفْهَمُ . "م"

او اِذَا حَكَمْتُمْ بَيْنَ ٱلنَّاسِ أَن تَحْكُمُوا۟ بِٱلْعَدْلِ

4:58

267

نَوْمٌ	[VN] sleep	كَذِبٌ	lie
قَلِيلٌ	little	نَزَّلَ/ يُنَزِّلُ	II to reveal
كَثِيرٌ	much	تَنْزِيلٌ	[VN] revelation
عَادَةٌ	habit	عَلَّمَ/يُعَلِّمُ	II to teach
أَخَذَ/يَأْخُذُ	to take, to seize, to grab	تَعْلِيمٌ	[VN²] education
أَخْذٌ	seizure	بَيَانٌ	speech
شَدِيدٌ	strong	تَبْلِيغٌ	[VN²] propagation
وَضَعَ/يَضَعُ	to place	مُعَلِّمٌ	[AP²] teacher
وَضْعٌ	placement	مُبَلِّغٌ	[AP²] propagator
مَحَلٌّ	place, location	قِرَاءَةٌ	[VN] reading
غَضِبَ/يَغْضَبُ	to become angry	كِتَابَةٌ	[VN] writing
نَصَحَ/يَنْصَحُ	to admonish	قَرَّبَ/ يُقَرِّبُ	II to cause or allow someone to come near
نُصْحٌ	admonition	بَعَّدَ/ يُبَعِّدُ	II to cause or keep someone at a distance
عِلْمٌ	knowledge	طَهَّرَ/يُطَهِّرُ	II to purify
سَلِمَ/يَسْلَمُ	to protect	أَضَلَّ/يُضِلُّ	II to make someone loose his way
سَالِمٌ	[AP] protector	تَذْلِيلٌ	[VN²] humiliation

لِسَانٌ	tongue	قَبِيحٌ	ugly
رَتَّلَ/يُرَتِّلُ	II to recite [VN]	حَبِيبٌ	lovable
تَرْتِيلٌ	recitation	ثَقِيلٌ	heavy
أَحَبَّ/يُحِبُّ	II to love	مِيزَانٌ	balance
صَدَّقَ/يُصَدِّقُ	II to deem someone or something credible, accept something as true	خَفِيفٌ	light, subtle
كَذَّبَ/يُكَذِّبُ	II to accuse of lying, call someone a liar	سُبْحَانَ الله	praise be to Allah
ذَلَّ/يَذِلُّ	to be low	شَطْرٌ	portion
خَسِرَ/يَخْسَرُ	to incur a loss	إِيمَانٌ	faith
فُحْشٌ	indecency	السِّوَاكُ	cleaning of teeth
عِصْيَانٌ	disobedience, rebellion	مَطْهَرَةٌ	means of purification
خُشُوعٌ	humility	فَمٌ	mouth
حَقَّرَ/يُحَقِّرُ	II to degrade	آفَةٌ	calamity
تَحْقِيرٌ	[VN²] degradation	نِسْيَانٌ	[VN] oblivion, forgetfulness
عَزَّ/يَعِزُّ	to be become respected	كَفَى/يَكْفِي	to be sufficient
إِشَارَةٌ	pointing out	اللَّهُمَّ	O Allah
مِفْتَاحٌ	key	أَحْيَاءٌ	living
فَرَجٌ	freedom from grief, joy, relaxation, ease, relief	فِرَارٌ	escape

جَدَّ	to strive	شَرٌّ	evil
لَذِيذٌ	delicious	سَمَكٌ	fish
قَلَّ/يَقِلُّ	to be or become little	كَدَّرَ/يُكَدِّرُ	to turn muddy II
حَيَاءٌ	modesty	سَرِيرَةٌ	secret
ذَنْبٌ	sin	عَلَانِيَةٌ	manifest
حَفَرَ/يَحْفِرُ	to dig	عَقْلٌ	intellect
بِئْرٌ	well	زَمَانٌ	time
قَبَضَ	to hold	جَمْرٌ	live coal
مِرْآةٌ	mirror		

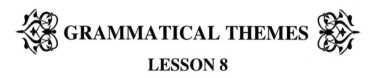
GRAMMATICAL THEMES

LESSON 8

UNIT 28

Verbal Noun

So far the Perfect, Active Participle (AP), Passive Participle (PP) and Imperfect have been introduced. Based on the opinions of Arabic grammarians IIIM[1] is used in the work as the root. There are, however, some Arabic grammarians who instead of using IIIM[1] regard the Verbal Noun as the root for derivation. Verbal Nouns are the fifth important theme in the first phase of this work and as such are considered to be one of the pillars for comprehension of the Arabic language. In view of the importance of Verbal Nouns they are mentioned in the Dictionaries along with the IIIM[1] roots in parenthesis. Some Verbal Nouns accept more than one pattern and these are also mentioned in the Dictionaries.

Verbal Nouns are derived from the verbs and have many patterns. Furthermore, in any one pattern there can be some exceptions. It is amazing that these various patterns which on the surface appear to be threatening nevertheless become spontaneously clear when extensive reading of Arabic text is undertaken. It has been noticed, for example that while reading the text in the class-room students can easily identify them. The construction of the sentence and the context distinctly indicates Verbal Nouns.

Grammarians have presented VN in accusative case because they regard it as the root. In this work it is deliberately presented in nominative case.

271

Rule No. 46

Each verb incorporates an action. The performance of such action is known as *isamfi 'l*, verbal noun.

Example: The root فَعَلَ to do, to act

Verbal Noun: فَعْلٌ doing, action.

There are over forty patterns provided by Arabic grammarians for the formation of Verbal Nouns derived from the First form of the verbs. In some of the patterns a few letters are added to the radical letter but the total number of letters in any pattern of a verbal noun including the radical letter does not exceed more than six letters. The most popular are the following patterns. It is to be noted, however, that even in these popular patterns there are a few exceptions for some roots.

(a) Many transitive verbs on the scale of فَعَلَ give a فَعْلٌ

   pattern to Verbal Nouns.

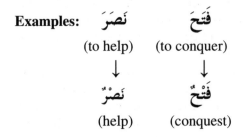

Examples: نَصَرَ   فَتَحَ

                (to help) (to conquer)

                   ↓   ↓

                نَصْرٌ   فَتْحٌ

                (help)   (conquest)

(b) Many transitive verbs on the scale of فَعَلَ give a فُعُولٌ

   pattern to Verbal Nouns.

Examples: جَلَسَ   خَرَجَ   سَجَدَ

             (to sit) (to come out) (to prostrate)

              جُلُوسٌ   خُرُوجٌ   سُجُودٌ

             (sitting)   (exit)   (prostration)

(c) Many intransitive verbs on the scale of فَعِلَ give a فَعَلٌ
   pattern to Verbal Nouns.

Example: فَرِحَ   مَرِضَ

(to become glad)   (to become sick)

فَرَحٌ   مَرَضٌ

(joy)   (sickness)

(d) Many intransitive verbs on the scale of فَعُلَ give a
فُعُولَةٌ pattern to Verbal Nouns.

Example: صَعُبَ   سَهُلَ

(to be hard)   (to be or become easy)

صُعُوبَةٌ   سُهُولَةٌ

(hardship)   (ease)

(e) فَعَالَةٌ is one of the popular patterns for Verbal Nouns.

Example: نَظُفَ   فَصُحَ

(to be clean)   (to be eloquent)

نَظَافَةٌ   فَصَاحَةٌ

(cleanliness)   (eloquence)

(f) The following patterns indicate special character or function
   in Verbal Nouns:

1. The pattern فُعَالٌ indicates the nature of ailment or a special
sound.

Examples: سُعَالٌ   بُكَاءٌ

(cough)   (cry)

2. فِعَالٌ indicates an obstinate nature.

Examples: إِبَاءٌ   نِفَارٌ

(dislike, pride)   (aversion)

3. فِعَالَةٌ indicates a profession.

Examples: قِرَاءَةٌ   كِتَابَةٌ   تِجَارَةٌ

(recitation of the Qur'ān) (penmanship) (merchandise)

4. فَعِيْلٌ indicates a kind of sound.

Examples: شَهِيْقٌ   زَفِيْرٌ

(sighing)   (moaning)

5. فَعَلَانٌ indicates abnormal behaviour.

Examples: هَيَجَانٌ   خَفَقَانٌ

(irritation)   (throbbing)

6. فُعْلَةٌ indicates colour.

Examples: صُفْرَةٌ   حُمْرَةٌ

(yellow colour)   (red colour)

Rule No. 47

An unrestricted object (*maf'ūl muṭlaq*) is always preceded by its closely related verb but for the Direct object (*maf'ūl bihī*) it is not necessary for a closely related verb to precede it.

Example Analysis:

مَنْ عَمِلَ عَمَلاً صَالِحًا فِي الدُّنْيَا فَلَهُ جَزَاءُالْجَنَّة فِي الآخِرَة.

(9) Whosoever does virtuous deed in this world for him there is a reward of Paradise in the Hereafter.

عَمَلاً (a deed) is a verbal noun. It is also an unrestricted object *(maf'ūl muṭlaq)* because it is preceded by its closely related verb عَمِلَ. The Active Participle صَالِحًا is its adjective which agrees with the qualifying noun عَمَلاً in case, gender, number and indefiniteness.

اللَّهُمَّ إِنِّي أَسْأَلُكَ عِلْماً نَافِعاً وَعَمَلاً صَالِحاً وَحِفْظاً قَوِيّاً وَفَهْماً كَامِلاً وَعَقْلاً سَالِماً.

O Allah! I ask from You beneficial knowledge and virtuous deeds and a strong memory and complete understanding and sound intellect.

The verbal nouns in the above sentence are عِلْماً عَمَلاً، حِفْظاً، فَهْماً and عَقْلاً and these are also *(maf'ūl bihī)* Direct objects because closely related verbs to these verbal nouns are not preceded. The adjectives for these verbal nouns, which are also qualifying nouns, are نَافِعاً، صَالِحاً، قَوِيّاً، كَامِلاً and سَالِماً because they agree with the qualifying nouns in number, gender, case and indefiniteness.

275

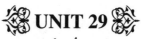

UNIT 29

الْأَسْمَاءُ: الْمُثَنَّى

Nouns: Dual

Rule No. 48

When اَن — in the nominative case and يْن — in the genitive and accusative cases are added to a singular noun then it becomes dual.

Example Analysis: مَا هَذَانِ؟ (١)

هَذَانِ قَلَمَانِ.   هَذَانِ كِتَابَانِ.   هَذَانِ كُرْسِيَّانِ.

هَذَانِ قَلَمَانِ.   هَذَانِ قَلَمَانِ.   هَذَانِ بَحْرَانِ.

هَذَانِ رَجُلَانِ قَصِيرَانِ.

(1) What are these two (M²)? These two are pens. These two are books. These two are chairs. These two are seas. These two are short men.

هَذَانِ = هَذَا + ـَ ان (these two M²)

قَلَمَانِ = قَلَم + ـَ ان (two pens M²)

All five nouns in no. 1 above are masculine and are in the nominative case. Therefore, they became dual with the addition of (ـَ ان).

The adjective قَصِيرَانِ = قَصِير + ـَ ان (two short M²). This adjective agrees with the qualifying noun رَجُلَانِ in number case, gender and indefiniteness, and both are dual. هَاتَانِ

(٢) مَا هَاتَانِ؟   هَاتَانِ مَائِدَتَانِ.   هَاتَانِ بِنْتَانِ.

هَاتَانِ زَهْرَتَانِ.

276

What are these two (F²)? These two are tables. These two are girls. These two are rooms. These two are flowers.

هَذه (this F¹) changes to the dual هَاتَان (these two F²)

مَائِدَة + ـ ان = مَائِدَتَان (two tables F²) The (ة) of

feminity remains and (ان ـ) is added.

What are these two (M²)? (٣) مَا ذَانِكَ؟

ذَلكَ (that M¹) becomes ذَانِكَ (those two M²)

What are those two (F²)? (٤) مَا تَانِكَ؟

تلْكَ (that F¹) becomes تَانِكَ (those two F²)

 UNIT 30

Verbs: Derived Forms:

In the previous lessons all verbs, whether sound or weak, are confined to the first indicative triliteral form. In Arabic from a few forms can be derived most of the roots but from some it is not possible to derive even a single form. This means that not all roots take all derived forms. There are 15 derived forms which clearly express the modification of the meaning imparted by the first form and which make the scope of the Arabic language wider.

Out of 15 derived forms 9 are included in the book. Among these 9, there are a few which are frequently used and these will be indicated later. In order to know how many derived forms a root accepts, consultation of an Arabic dictionary is inevitable. In some Arabic to English dictionaries these are introduced with Roman numerals and in this work, for the sake of convenience, the same method is employed.

Formation:

Derived forms are formed from the root III M[1] with certain prefixes. Unlike the first form they have one set pattern for the Perfect, Imperfect, Verbal Noun, Active Participle and Passive Participle and this makes recognition of their various forms easy. These 'Five Pillars' have been introduced through graded progression in the first seven lessons (phase two). In this lesson and the subsequent lessons these shall be used in Derived Forms altogether. (See Appendix TB.)

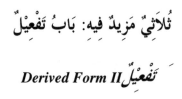

ثُلَاثِيٌّ مَزِيدٌ فِيهِ: بَابُ تَفْعِيْلٌ

Derived Form II تَفْعِيْلٌ

The second derived form principally has causative and intensive significance. Other significances, such as evaluation and estimation, are also apparent.

Formation:

Perfect:

III M[1]: This is formed from the first form III M[1] (فَعَلَ) The

radical *Fā'* letter remains unchanged (فَ). The radical *'Ayn*

letter is doubled (ـــعّـــ) and placed a *fatḥah*. The radical *Lām*

remains unchanged (لَ) فَعَّلَ

The root عَلِمَ in II becomes عَلَّمَ (he taught)

Other conjugations in the Perfect Indicative follow the

pattern عَلَّمَ and their endings are the same as the Perfect in the

First form. (See Appendix TC under II)

The five singular forms are as follows:

III M¹	عَلَّمَ	III F¹	عَلَّمَتْ
	(he taught)		(she taught)
II M¹	عَلَّمْتَ	II F¹	عَلَّمْتِ
	(you taught)		(you taught)

I M¹⁺F¹ عَلَّمْتُ

(I taught)

The formation of the Imperfect is based on the
III M¹ pattern

يُعَلِّمُ (he teaches). All prefixes and endings remain the same as
in the First form. (See Appendix TD under II)

III M¹	يُعَلِّمُ	III F¹	تُعَلِّمُ
	(he teaches)		(she teaches)
II M¹	تُعَلِّمُ	II F¹	تُعَلِّمِينَ
	(you teach)		(you teach)

I M¹⁺F¹ أُعَلِّمُ

(I teach)

Verbal Nouns:

The Verbal noun is formed on the pattern of تَفْعِيل.
There is no variation in this if it is derived from the sound
triliteral root. The Verbal Noun of عَلَّمَ, therefore, becomes

تَعْلِيمٌ (teaching, education).

If the final radical letter of the second derived form is *hamzah*,
a glottal stop, or a vowel then its verbal noun follows the
pattern of تَفْعِلَةٌ.

Examples: From قَوَّى (to make strong) the verbal noun

becomes تَقْوِيَةٌ (strengthening). From هَنَّأَ (to congratulate) the

Verbal Noun becomes تَهْنِئَةٌ (congratulation).

Active Participles:

The Active Participle is formed on the pattern of مُفَعِّلٌ.

The Active Participle of عَلَّمَ is مُعَلِّمٌ (a teacher).

Passive Participles:

The Passive Participle is formed on the pattern of مُفَعَّلٌ.

The Passive Participle for عَلَّمَ is مُعَلَّمٌ (taught).

Significances: Derived Form II
(a) Intransitive verbs, which become transitive.

First Form	Meaning	Second Form	Meaning
ضَعُفَ	(to become weak)	ضَعَّفَ	(to weaken)
سَلِمَ	(to be safe and sound)	سَلَّمَ	(to preserve, to surrender, to greet)
طَالَ	(to be or become long)	طَوَّلَ	(to make long or longer)

(b) Transitive verbs intensified.

عَلِمَ	(to know)	عَلَّمَ	(to teach)
رَكِبَ	(to ride)	رَكَّبَ	(to make someone ride)
سَمِعَ	(to hear)	سَمَّعَ	(to let someone hear)
خَافَ	(to be frightened)	خَوَّفَ	(to frighten)

280

First Form	Meaning	Second Form	Meaning
كَسَرَ	(to break)	كَسَّرَ	(to break into pieces)
غَسَلَ	(to wash)	غَسَّلَ	(to wash thoroughly)
مَنَعَ	(to prevent)	مَنَّعَ	(to fortify strengthen)
قَتَلَ	(to kill)	قَتَّلَ	(to massacre)

(c) To attribute the action with (something or someone)

First Form	Meaning	Second Form	Meaning
صَدَقَ	(to speak the truth)	صَدَّقَ	(to deem someone / something credible, accept someone / something as true)
كَذَبَ	(to speak a lie)	كَذَّبَ	(to accuse of lying, call someone a liar,)
كَفَرَ	(to cover, hide)	كَفَّرَ	(to disbelieve, to cover, hide something, seduce someone to unbelief)

(d) Gives new meaning.

صَلَّى (to pray)

Example Analysis:

(١) نَزَّلَ اللهُ الْقُرْآنَ تَنْزِيلاً.

Allah has revealed the Qur'ān piece meal.

نَزَّلَ is the second derived form from نَزَلَ (to descend) meaning he revealed. It becomes transitive and requires an

281

object. Its object is الْقُرآنَ, which is in the accusative case.

تَنْزِيْلاً is the verbal noun from نَزَّلَ and it is also an unrestricted object (*maf'ūl muṭlaq*). (see Table TB under II)

(٥) الرَّسُوْلُ (ﷺ) مُعَلِّمُ الْقُرْآنِ وَمُبَلِّغُ الإِسْلاَمِ

The Messenger (ﷺ) is the teacher of the Qur'ān and the propagator of Islam.

عَلَّمَ and مُبَلِّغٌ and مُعَلِّمٌ are the Active Participles from بَلَّغَ The second derived form and both are the first nouns of construct phrases. (See Table TB under II)

الْقُرْآنُ مُنَزَّلٌ مِنَ الله

The Qur'an was sent down from Allah.

مُنَزَّلٌ is the Passive Participle from the second derived form

نَزَّلَ

(See TB under II)

It is evident from the grammatical themes so far presented that the root (III M[1]) plays a decisive role in the formation of many words. Once it is determined and a person is acquainted with the grammatical structure, the task of finding out the meaning of any word from the dictionary becomes easy. This is because the roots are presented in the dictionary in alphabetical order rather than the word order. This system at first sight is both amazing and daunting to the beginner but as one starts to understand the basic structure of the Arabic language the roots gradually and spontaneously penetrate the mind of the learner.

With the exception of two consonants particles (e.g. مِنْ ، لَمْ في etc) and quadriliteral verbs (e.g. بَعْثَرَ ، دَحْرَجَ) it is difficult to use the dictionary without roots.

There are, however, nine additional letters commonly used along with the roots for the formation of many words. Grammarians have identified these as: (و , ت , م , ل, ا , س ,

ه, ي , ن). For the sake of remembrance two words can be formed (سَالِمْ، تَوْهِيْن).

Familiarisation of additional letters in different conjugated forms of the verbs including derived forms (see TA, TB, TC in the Appendix) and nouns facilitates the identification of the roots.

In weak verbs, as has been made clear, one of their radicals are vowels. These vowels for the use of the dictionary can either be (ي) or (و). For example قَالَ and بَاعَ are hollow verbs and their medial radical is a vowel and it can be (و) or (ي). For قَالَ it is (و) and for بَاعَ it is (ي).

النَّصُّ الْقُرْآنِيُّ
Lesson 8

١. مَن كَانَ عَدُوًّا لِّجِبْرِيلَ فَإِنَّهُ نَزَّلَهُ عَلَىٰ قَلْبِكَ بِإِذْنِ ٱللَّهِ مُصَدِّقًا لِّمَا بَيْنَ يَدَيْهِ (2: 97)

٢. وَهُوَ قَآئِمٌ يُصَلِّي فِي ٱلْمِحْرَابِ أَنَّ ٱللَّهَ يُبَشِّرُكَ بِيَحْيَىٰ مُصَدِّقًا بِكَلِمَةٍ مِّنَ ٱللَّهِ (3: 39)

٣. فَلَا صَدَّقَ وَلَا صَلَّىٰ ۝ وَلَٰكِن كَذَّبَ (75: 31-32)

٤. وَٱللَّهُ يُقَدِّرُ ٱلَّيْلَ وَٱلنَّهَارَ (73: 20)

٥. إِنَّهُ فَكَّرَ وَقَدَّرَ (74: 18)

٦. ٱلَّذِي خَلَقَ فَسَوَّىٰ ۝ وَٱلَّذِي قَدَّرَ فَهَدَىٰ (87: 2-3)

٧. سَبَّحَ لِلَّهِ مَا فِي ٱلسَّمَٰوَٰتِ وَٱلْأَرْضِ وَهُوَ ٱلْعَزِيزُ ٱلْحَكِيمُ (57: 1)

٨. وَيُسَبِّحُ ٱلرَّعْدُ بِحَمْدِهِۦ (13: 13)

٩. كُلٌّ قَدْ عَلِمَ صَلَاتَهُ وَتَسْبِيحَهُ (24: 41)

١٠. وَسَخَّرَ ٱلشَّمْسَ وَٱلْقَمَرَ كُلٌّ يَجْرِى إِلَىٰٓ أَجَلٍ مُّسَمًّى (31: 29)

١١. وَتُعِزُّ مَن تَشَآءُ وَتُذِلُّ مَن تَشَآءُ (3: 26)

١٢. وَٱلَّذِى جَآءَ بِٱلصِّدْقِ وَصَدَّقَ بِهِۦ (39: 33)

١٣. وَكَلَّمَ ٱللَّهُ مُوسَىٰ تَكْلِيمًا (4: 164)

١٤. تَنزِيلُ ٱلْكِتَٰبِ مِنَ ٱللَّهِ ٱلْعَزِيزِ ٱلْحَكِيمِ (46: 2)

١٥. أَنَّهُۥ مُنَزَّلٌ مِّن رَّبِّكَ بِٱلْحَقِّ (6: 114)

١٦. وَيُعَلِّمُهُ ٱلْكِتَٰبَ وَٱلْحِكْمَةَ وَٱلتَّوْرَىٰةَ وَٱلْإِنجِيلَ (3: 48)

١٧. وَٱلشَّمْسَ وَٱلْقَمَرَ حُسْبَانًا ذَٰلِكَ تَقْدِيرُ ٱلْعَزِيزِ ٱلْعَلِيمِ (6: 96)

١٨. فَمَا يُكَذِّبُكَ بَعْدُ بِٱلدِّينِ (95: 7)

١٩. يَوْمَ يَنظُرُ ٱلْمَرْءُ مَا قَدَّمَتْ يَدَاهُ (78: 40)

٢٠. يَقُولُ يَٰلَيْتَنِى قَدَّمْتُ لِحَيَاتِى (89: 24)

٢١. وَهَٰذَا كِتَٰبٌ مُّصَدِّقٌ لِّسَانًا عَرَبِيًّا (46: 12)

٢٢. وَيَنصُرَكَ ٱللَّهُ نَصْرًا عَزِيزًا (48: 3)

٢٣. إِنَّ لَكَ فِى ٱلنَّهَارِ سَبْحًا طَوِيلًا (73: 7)

٢٤. قَوْلٌ مَّعْرُوفٌ وَمَغْفِرَةٌ خَيْرٌ مِّن صَدَقَةٍ يَتْبَعُهَآ أَذًى

(2: 263)

٢٥. مَّا نَزَّلَ ٱللَّهُ بِهَا مِن سُلْطَنٍ (7: 71)

٢٦. لَا يُكَلِّفُ ٱللَّهُ نَفْسًا إِلَّا وُسْعَهَا (2: 286)

عَدُوٌّ	enemy	أَعَزَّ/يُعِزُّ	II to give honour
بَشَّرَ/يُبَشِّرُ	II to give glad tiding	أَذَلَّ/يُذِلُّ	II to abase
فَكَّرَ/يُفَكِّرُ	II to reflect, to ponder	صِدْقٌ	[VN] truthfulness, veracity, virtue, firmness
قَدَّرَ/يُقَدِّرُ	II to ordain, decree, dispose	كَلَّمَ / يُكَلِّمُ	II to speak
سَبَّحَ/يُسَبِّحُ	II to praise, to glorify Allah	تَكْلِيمٌ	[VN²] speaking
سَوَّى/يُسَوِّي	II to balance	تَنْزِيلٌ	[VN²] revelation
رَعْدٌ	thunder	مُنَزَّلٌ	[PP²] revealed
صَلَّى/يُصَلِّي	II to pray	حُسْبَانٌ	[VN] reckoning
سَخَّرَ/يُسَخِّرُ	II to subjugate, to bring under control	تَقْدِيرٌ	[VN²] disposition
جَرَى/يَجْرِي	to flow (water), to run	يَلَيْتَ	a particle used to express desire, I wish, would that
تَسْبِيحٌ	glorification of Allah	قَدَّمَ / يُقَدِّمُ	II to put forward
مُسَمَّى	[PP²] named	عَرَبِيٌّ	Arabic
مَعْرُوفٌ	[PP] known	سَبْحٌ	[VN] chain of business
صَدَقَةٌ	alms, charity	وُسْعٌ	capacity

287

تَبِعَ/يَتْبَعُ	to follow, serve, obey	سَوَّى / يُسَوِّي	II to form with just proportion
سُلْطَانٌ	authority	حَرَّمَ/يُحَرِّمُ	II to declare something sacred, inviolable
كَلَّفَ/يُكَلِّفُ	II to commission charge, entrust, assign someone		

METHOD OF TEACHING
LESSON 8

With the introduction of a few patterns students have so far been familiarised with the formation of Perfect, Imperfect, Active Participles and Passive Participles ['Five Pillars']. As there are many patterns for the formation of the Verbal Nouns these may naturally cause some confusion. It is to be stressed that a Verbal Noun is a noun. It accepts the *tanwin* when it is indefinite and the article (اَلْ) when it is definite. Although Verbal Nouns have many patterns if students have been acquainted with the set patterns of Active Participle and the Passive Participle then it will not be too difficult for them to recognise the Verbal Noun.

Let the students identify Verbal Nouns from the text and allow them to explain their reasoning for the same.

Only prominent patterns can be projected with an overhead projector. At this stage it is not advisable to give all the patterns of Verbal Nouns.

Indicate the roots and encourage the students to construct the Verbal Nouns.

Recapitulation of the formation of the Perfect, Imperfect, Active Participle, Passive Participle and Verbal Nouns from the roots already introduced will create confidence among the students. Five cards from each root can be prepared by retaining the same colour coding for the radicals and additional letters. For example

كَتَبَ، يَكْتُبُ، كِتَابَةٌ، كَاتِبٌ، مَكْتُوبٌ

and display each set for each root to the students asking them to read them and give their meanings.

The formation of dual nouns can be simplified by placing two cards for (ان __) and (يْنِ __) on the magnetic board. Cards

289

for the nouns can be placed against (اَنِ ـَـ) and (ـَـيْنِ)
enabling the students to change the singular noun into a dual
noun making sure that they understand the change in the
formation of the dual in the nominative, accusative and genitive
cases.

Thus far the students have been made familiar with the 'Five
Pillars' mentioned above. It is always useful to take advantage
of the students' previous knowledge. These 'Five Pillars' can be
incorporated gradually in the derived forms.

The formation of the derived form II by retaining the same
colours for radical and additional letters both on the magnetic
board and overhead projector for all 'Five Pillars' will enable
the students to understand them without any difficulty. Now
from the root (عَلِمَ) 10 cards can be prepared for the 'Five
Pillars'.
For example:

عَلِمَ يَعْلَمُ عِلْمٌ عَالِمٌ مَعْلُوْمٌ

عَلَّمَ يُعَلِّمُ تَعْلِيْمٌ مُعَلَّمٌ مُعَلِّمٌ

Let the students identify all derived forms from the text and ask
for their reasons for the same.

At this stage it is essential to teach the students how to use an
Arabic dictionary and to make sure that they have practical
experience of this.

290

Lesson 8

Exercise No. 27

(١) Construct five sentences using إِنَّ and its sisters.

(2)   Construct five sentences using the Second derived form فَعَّلَ.

(3) Construct the sentences from the following table.

	هَذَانِ
عَيْنَانِ، أَبَوَانِ، مَائِدَتَانِ، قَلَمَانِ، يَدَانِ، وَلَدَانِ، عَلاَمَتَانِ،	هَاتَانِ
كِتَابَانِ، جَنَّتَانِ، بِنْتَانِ، كَأْسَانِ، كُرْسِيَّانِ، فُلْكَانِ،	ذَانِكَ
خُبْزَانِ، غُرْفَتَانِ، بَحْرَانِ، زَهْرَتَانِ، رَجُلاَنِ، امْرَأَتَانِ	تَانِكَ

(3) Select the correct word(s) from the parentheses to fill in the blanks in the following sentences.

(١)   هُوَ يَشْكُرُ اللهَ شُكْرًا ....

(شَدِيدًا، كَثِيرًا، سَالِمًا، طَوِيْلاً)

(٢)   هُوَ يَقُوْمُ فِي صَلاَةِ اللَّيْلِ قِيَامًا ....

(شَدِيدًا، عَزِيْزًا، طَوِيْلاً، كَثِيرًا)

291

مَاتَ أَبِي فَصَبَرْتُ صَبْرًا ..... (٣)

(جَمِيلاً، شَدِيدًا، عَزِيزًا، طَوِيلاً)

حَفِظْتُ الْقُرْآنَ حِفْظًا .... (٤)

(قَوِيًّا، عَزِيزًا، طَوِيلاً، جَمِيلاً)

ذَكَرْتُ الله ذِكْرًا .... (٥)

(كَثِيرًا، جَمِيلاً، قَوِيًّا، عَزِيزًا)

(4) Put i'rāb

(١) قام أحمد في الليل وذكر الله ذكرا كثيرا.

(٢) الظالم يظلم ظلما كثيرا.

(٣) هاتان علامتان وهذان رجلان قصيران.

(٤) نزل الله القرآن تنـزيلا.

(٥) أنا معلم القرآن ومبلغ الإسلام.

(٦) هو يصلي الصلاة لذكر الله.

(٧) هل أنت تحب الله السميع العليم؟

(٨) أنا مدرس أدرس ابني القراءة والكتابة.

(٩) من يصلي الصلاة بخشوع يفوز في الدنيا والآخرة.

(١٠) القرآن تنـزيل من الله وأنا أحبه.

(5) Translate into Arabic.

1. Those two pens are on the table.

2. Two eyes are beautiful and big.

3. Two short boys are sitting on two tables.

4. I worship Allah because I love Allah much.

5. The Prayer is for the purification of the soul.

6. I became very angry because he told a lie.

7. Allah revealed the Qur'ān to His Messenger .

8. The humiliation of mankind is an ugly act.

9. The teaching of the Qur'ān is a beautiful act.

10. O Allah! I ask for patience.

(6) From the Qur'ānic text of Lesson 8 identify the Derived Form II: Perfects, Imperfects and Verbal nouns.

(١) هُمَا أَبَوَان

(٢) هُمَا ذَاهِبَان مِنْ بَيْتِهِمَا إِلَى الْمَسْجِد للصَّلَاة.

(٣) ذَانِكَ الأَبَوَان يَعْمَلَان فِي الْحَرْث وَتَانِكَ الْبِنْتَان ذَاهِبَتَان إِلَى الْمَسْجِد لِدَرْس الْقُرْآن.

(٤) الأُمُّ وَالْبِنْتُ ذَهَبَتَا مِنَ الْحَرْث إِلَى الْبَيْت فَشَرِبَتَا الْمَاءَ وَأَكَلَتَا الطَّعَامَ.

(٥) هَلْ ذَهَبْتُمَا مِنَ الْمَدْرَسَة إِلَى الْبَيْتِ؟ لا، مَا ذَهَبْنَا إِلَى الْبَيْت.

(٦) قَرَأْنَا الْقُرْآنَ فِيْ الْمَدْرَسَة عَلَى الْمُعَلِّم.

(٧) قَرَأْتُ الْكِتَابَيْن اللَّذَيْن تَرَكْتُهُمَا فِي الْغُرْفَة.

(٨) الزَّهْرَتَان اللَّتَان تَرَكْتَ فِي الْبَيْت جَمِيلَتَان.

(٩) الْبِنْتَان تَذْهَبَان إِلَى الْمَدْرَسَة مَعَ الْوَالِدَيْن.

(١٠) ذَانِكَ الأَبَوَان يَعْمَلَان فِي الْحَرْث وَتَانِكَ الْبِنْتَان تَرْجِعَان مِنَ الْمَدْرَسَة إِلَى الْبَيْت.

(١١) الأَبَوَان يَرْجِعَان إِلَى بَيْتِهِمَا بَعْدَ الصَّلَاة.

(١٢) هَلْ أَنْتُمَا تَقْرَءَان أَمْ تَكْتُبَان؟

(١٣) نَحْنُ نَقْرَأُ الْقُرْآنَ الكَرِيمَ.

(١٤) الأَبُ ذُو مَالٍ كَثِيرٍ وَالأُمُّ ذَاتُ أَخْلاقٍ كَرِيمَةٍ.

(١٥) أَنْتُمَا ذَوَا عِلْمٍ.

(١٦) لَقِيتُ رَجُلَيْنِ ذَوَيْ عِلْمٍ وَامْرَأَتَيْنِ ذَوَاتَيْ عِلْمٍ.

(١٧) مُوسَى وَعِيسَى (عَلَيْهِمَا السَّلاَمُ) رَسُولاَنِ مُصْلِحَانِ مَبْعُوثَانِ مِنْ عِنْدِ الرَّحْمَنِ.

(١٨) إِبْرَاهِيمُ وَإِسْمَاعِيلُ شَرِيكَانِ فِي بَيْتَيْنِ.

(١٩) مَائِدَتَا الْبَيْتِ كَبِيرَتَانِ وَجَمِيلَتَانِ.

(٢٠) كِتَابَايَ عِنْدَ صَدِيقَيْنِ حَمِيمَيْنِ.

(٢١) نَذْهَبُ مِنَ الْبَيْتِ إِلَى الْمَسْجِدِ وَسَنَأْكُلُ الطَّعَامَ بَعْدَ الصَّلاَةِ.

ﷺ UNIT 32 ﷺ

(١) الْمُسْلِمُ مَنْ أَسْلَمَ وَجْهَهُ لِلَّهِ.

(٢) آمَنْتُ بِمَا أَنْزَلَ اللَّهُ عَلَى مُحَمَّدٍ (ﷺ) وَبِمَا أَنْزَلَ عَلَى مَنْ قَبْلَهُ.

(٣) أَدْخَلَ اللَّهُ آدَمَ (عَلَيْهِ السَّلاَمُ) وَامْرَأَتَهُ الْجَنَّةَ فَضَلَّلَهُمَا الشَّيْطَانُ وَأَخْرَجَهُمَا مِنْهَا.

(٤) الْمُشْرِكُ لاَ يَفُوزُ فِي الآخِرَةِ لأَنَّهُ يُشْرِكُ بِاللَّهِ.

(٥) الْمُؤْمِنُ يُؤْمِنُ بِاللَّهِ أَنَّهُ وَاحِدٌ لاَ شَرِيكَ لَهُ.

(٦) اللَّهُ هُوَ الَّذِي يُحْيِي الإِنْسَانَ وَيُمِيتُهُ.

(٧) الشَّيْطَانُ يُزَيِّنُ لِلْمُشْرِكِ عَمَلَهُ فَيَظُنُّ أَنَّهُ يُحْسِنُ صُنْعاً.

(٨) الإِحْسَانُ عَمَلٌ عَظِيمٌ يُحِبُّهُ اللَّهُ.

(٩) إِنَّ اللَّهَ يُحِبُّ الْمُحْسِنَ.

(١٠) اللَّهُ لاَ يُحِبُّ مَنْ يُفْسِدُ فِي الأَرْضِ.

(١١) هَلْ تُحِبُّ الْمُفْسِدَ؟ أَنَا لاَ أُحِبُّ الْمُفْسِدَ وَلَكِنْ أُحِبُّ الْمُصْلِحَ.

(١٢) الإِصْلاَحُ والإِحْسَانُ عَمَلاَنِ حَبِيبَانِ عِنْدَ الرَّحْمَنِ.

(١٣) الرَّسُولُ (ﷺ) مُصْلِحُ الإِنْسَانِ.

(١٤) حَفِظْتُ الْقُرْآنَ فَفَرِحَ أَبِي وَدَعَا لِي بِالصَّلاَحِ وَالْفَوْزِ بِالْجَنَّةِ.

(١٥) قَدْ حَسَّنَ اللَّهُ صُوْرَتَهُ كَمَا حَسَّنَ سِيْرَتَهُ.

(١٦) قَالَ رَسُولُ الله (ﷺ):
إِنَّ اللَّهَ يُحِبُّ الرِّفْقَ فِي الأَمْرِ كُلِّهِ.

(١٧) الرَّغْبَةُ فِي الدُّنْيَا تُكْثِرُ الْهَمَّ وَالْحُزْنَ.

(١٨) صِلَةُ الرَّحِمِ تَزِيدُ فِي الْعُمْرِ.

(١٩) مَنْ سَرَّتْهُ حَسَنَتُهُ وَسَاءَتْهُ سَيِّئَتُهُ فَهُوَ مُؤْمِنٌ.

(٢٠) الْمُؤْمِنُ لِلْمُؤْمِنِ كَالْبُنْيَانِ يَشُدُّ بَعْضُهُ بَعْضاً.

(٢١) الْحِكْمَةُ ضَالَّةُ الْمُؤْمِنِ أَيْنَمَا وَجَدَهَا أَخَذَهَا.

(٢٢) حُبُّكَ الشَّيْءَ يُعْمِي وَ يُصِمُّ.

(٢٣) لاَ حَسَدَ إِلاَّ فِي اثْنَيْنِ رَجُلٌ آتَاهُ اللهُ الْقُرْآنَ فَيَقُوْمُ بِهِ آنَاءَ اللَّيْلِ وَآنَاءَ النَّهَارِ وَرَجُلٌ آتَاهُ اللهُ مَالاً فَيُنْفِقُ مِنْهُ آنَاءَ اللَّيْلِ وَآنَاءَ النَّهَارِ.

(٢٤) عَجَباً لِأَمْرِ الْمُؤْمِنِ إِنَّ أَمْرَهُ كُلَّهُ خَيْرٌ وَلَيْسَ ذَلِكَ لِأَحْدٍ إِلاَ لِلْمُؤْمِنِ إِنْ أَصَابَتْهُ سَرَّاءُ شَكَرَ فَكَانَ خَيْرًا لَهُ وَإِنْ أَصَابَتْهُ ضَرَّاءُ صَبَرَ فَكَانَ خَيْرًا لَهُ.

(٢٥) أَنَّ رَجُلاً سَأَلَ رَسُوْلَ اللهِ (ﷺ): أَيُّ الإِسْلاَمِ خَيْرٌ؟ قَالَ: تُطْعِمُ الطَّعَامَ وَتَقْرَأُ السَّلاَمَ عَلَى مَنْ عَرَفْتَ وَمَنْ لَمْ تَعْرِفْ.

(٢٦) نِعْمَ الْمُؤَدِّبُ الدَّهْرُ. "م"

(٢٧) النَّاسُ عَبِيدُ الإِحْسَانِ. "م"

(٢٨) وَمِنْ تَعْظِيْمِ الْعِلْمِ تَعْظِيْمُ الْكَتَابِ. "م"

(٢٩) الْكَسَلُ وَكَثْرَةُ النَّوْمِ يُبْعِدَانِ مِنَ اللهِ وَيُورِثَانِ الْفَقْرَ."م"

(٣٠) الدُّنْيَا تَمْنَعُ مِنَ الْخَيْرِ. "م"

(٣١) تَوْفِيْقُ الإِنْسَانِ للطَّاعَةِ نِعْمَةٌ مِنَ اللَّهِ. "م"

(٣٢) الإِنْسَانُ يُدَبِّرُ وَ اللهُ يُقَدِّرُ. "م"

(٣٣) إِذَا جَدَّ الْمَرْءُ وَ أَجَادَ عَزَّ وَ سَادَ . "م"

ذُوْ	possessor, holder, master, owner	سِيْرَةٌ	way of life, conduct
مُصْلِحٌ	[AP⁴] reformer	رِفْقٌ	kindness, gentleness
مَبْعُوثٌ	[PP] sent	رَغْبَةٌ	wish, desire, longing
شَرِيْكٌ	[AP] sharer, partner, associate	هَمٌّ	anxiety
صَدِيْقٌ	friend	حُزْنٌ	sadness, grief, sorrow
حَمِيْمٌ	bosom friend	صِلَةٌ	link, connection
مُشْرِكٌ	[AP⁴] polytheist	رَحِمٌ	womb
إِحْسَانٌ	[VN⁴] kindness, performance of good deeds	عُمْرٌ	life
مُحْسِنٌ	[AP⁴] kind, performer of good deeds	سَيِّئَةٌ	evil
مُفْسِدٌ	[AP⁴] one who spreads corruption	حِكْمَةٌ	wisdom
فَوْزٌ	success	ضَالٌّ	lost
صُوْرَةٌ	form, shape	نِعْمَ	what a perfect, wonderful, an excellent
أَسْلَمَ / يُسْلِمُ	IV to surrender	مُؤَدِّبٌ	[AP²] educator, teacher
سَلَّمَ / يُسَلِّمُ	II to preserve, protect from harm	أَفْسَدَ / يُفْسِدُ	IV to spoil someone or something

299

مُرْسَلٌ	[PP⁴] messenger, sent	حَسَّنَ / يُحَسِّنُ	II to beautify, put into better form
أَدْخَلَ / يُدْخِلُ	IV to make or let enter	أَكْثَرَ / يُكْثِرُ	IV to do much, to give much or frequently
ضَلَّلَ / يُضَلِّلُ	II to mislead, misguide	زَادَ / يَزِيدُ	to increase, to become more
أَخْرَجَ / يُخْرِجُ	IV to take out, to bring out	سَرَّ / يَسُرُّ	to make happy, gladden
أَحْيَى / يُحْيِي	IV to give life	زَيَّنَ / يُزَيِّنُ	II to adorn, decorate
أَمَاتَ / يُمِيتُ	IV to cause death	أَعْمَى/يُعْمِي	IV to make blind
آمَنَ / يُؤْمِنُ	IV to believe	أصم/يصمّ	IV to make deaf
أَشْرَكَ / يُشْرِكُ	IV to make someone a partner	عَزَّ /يَعِزُّ	to be respected
ضَالَّة	lost property	سَادَ/يَسُوْدُ	to be head
رِفْقٌ	kindness	حَسَدٌ	envy
بُنْيَانٌ	building	آتَى /يُوْتِي	to grant
دَهْرٌ	time, age	أَنْفَقَ/ يُنْفِقُ	to spend
عَبِيْدٌ	slaves	عَجَبٌ	astonishment
تَعْظِيمٌ	[VN²] glorification, respect	أَصَابَ/يُصِيْبُ	IV to hit
كَسَلٌ	laziness	سَرَّاءُ	prosperity
أَبْعَدَ / يُبْعِدُ	IV to go or move far away	ضَرَّاءُ	calamity
أَوْرَثَ / يُوْرِثُ	IV to possess as an inheritance something	صَبَرَ /يَصْبِرُ	to exercise patience

300

فَقْرٌ	poverty	حَسَدٌ	envy
تَوْفِيقٌ	[VN²] success, prosperity, good fortune	حِكْمَةٌ	wisdom
طَاعَةٌ	[VN] obedience	أَقَامَ / يُقِيْمُ	IV to establish
نِعْمَةٌ	life of ease, pleasure	آنَاءُ	during
دَبَّرَ / يُدَبِّرُ	II to prepare, plan, organise, design	أَنْفَقَ / يُنفِقُ	IV to spend
دَالٌّ	[AP] demonstrator	عَجَبٌ	strange
حَرَكَةٌ	Action	أَصَابَ / يُصِيْبُ	IV to afflict
بَرَكَةٌ	blessing	ضَرَّاءُ	calamity
أَجَادَ / يُجِيْدُ	IV to make good	جَدَّ	to struggle
سَادَ	to lead	أَطْعَمَ / يُطْعِمُ	IV to feed

301

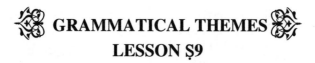

GRAMMATICAL THEMES
LESSON §9

الأَفْعَالُ: الْمُثَنَّى
Verbs: Dual

The Formation

Perfect:

IIIM¹ فَعَلَ	IIIM² فَعَلاَ	(they (two) did)
	(ا ‑) (ā) is prefixed at the end.	
IIIF¹ فَعَلَتْ	IIIF² فَعَلَتَا	(they (two) did)
	(ـتَا ‑) (tā) is prefixed at the end.	
IIM¹ فَعَلْتَ	IIM² فَعَلْتُمَا	(you (two) did)
	(تُمَا) (tumā) is prefixed at the end.	
IIF¹ فَعَلْتِ	IIF² فَعَلْتُمَا	(you (two) did)
	as in IIM²	
IM¹+F¹ فَعَلْتُ	IM²,³⁺ + F²,³⁺ فَعَلْنَا	(we did)
	(نَا) (nā) is prefixed at the end.	

[See TA.]

N.B. Note the first person dual and plural for both genders remains the same.

302

Imperfect:

IIIM¹ يَفْعَلُ   IIIM² يَفْعَلَانِ (they (two) do)

(ان-) (āni) is prefixed at the end.

IIIF¹ تَفْعَلُ   IIIF² تَفْعَلَانِ (they (two) do)

(ان-) (āni) is prefixed at the end.

IIM¹ تَفْعَلُ   IIM² تَفْعَلَانِ (you (two) do)

(ان-) (āni) is prefixed at the end.

IIF¹ تَفْعَلِينَ   IIF² تَفْعَلَانِ (you (two) do)
                    remains the same as in IIM²

IM¹+F¹ أَفْعَلُ   IM²,³⁺ + F²,³⁺ نَفْعَلُ (we do)

(ن) one of the signs of the
Imperfect is prefixed here.

[See TA]

*N.B. Note that as in the Perfect, the first person dual and plural
in the Imperfect and for both genders remains the same.*

Example Analysis:

(٢)   هُمَا ذَاهِبَانِ مِنْ بَيْتِهِمَا إِلَى الْمَسْجِد لِلصَّلَاةِ.

They (two) are going from their house to the mosque for Prayer.

ذَاهِبَانِ = ان + — ذَاهِبٌ (going) AP²

بَيْتِهِمَا = هُمَا + بَيْت (their (two) house)

(pronoun suffix dual)

303

الأُمُّ وَالْبِنْتُ ذَهَبَتَا مِنَ الْحَرْثِ إِلَى الْبَيْتِ فَشَرِبَتَا الْمَاءَ وَ أَكَلَتَا الطَّعَامَ.

The mother and the daughter went from the field to the house, then they drank the water and ate the food.

ذَهَبَتَا، شَرِبَتَا and أَكَلَتَا are the Perfect Indicative dual verbs as in IIIF[2].

Personal Pronouns:

هُوَ	(he)	هُمَا	(they (two) IIIM[2] + F[2])
هِيَ	(she)		
أَنْتَ	(you M[1])	أَنْتُمَا	(you (two) IIM[2] + F[2])
أَنْتِ	(you F[1])		
أَنَا	(I M[1]+ F[1])	نَحْنُ	(we I M[2,3+] + F[2,3+])

(See TA. 17)

Pronoun suffix:

ـهُ...	(his)	هُمَا..	(their (two) III M[2] + F[2])
هَا...	(her, its)		
كَ...	(your M[1])	كُمَا..	(your (two) II M[2] + F[2])
كِ...	(your F[1])		

$$ي/\text{ني (my M}^1 + \text{F}^1) \qquad \text{..نَا (our I M}^{2,3+} + \text{F}^{2,3+})$$

(See TA 18.)

$$هَلْ ذَهَبْتُمَا مِنَ الْمَدْرَسَةِ إِلَى الْبَيْتِ؟$$

$$لاَ ، مَا ذَهَبْنَا إِلَى الْبَيْتِ.$$

Did you (two) go from the school to the house? No, we did not go to the house.

ذَهَبْتُمَا (you (two) went) is IIM^2 + IIF^2 the Perfect Indicative

and can be used for both genders. ذَهَبْنَا (we went) is IM$^{2, 3+}$ + IF$^{2,3+}$ the Perfect Indicative.

$$ذَانِكَ الْأَبَوَانِ يَعْمَلاَنِ فِيْ الْحَرْثِ وَتَانِكَ الْبِنْتَانِ تَرْجِعَانِ مِنَ$$

$$الْمَدْرَسَةِ إِلَى الْبَيْتِ.$$

Those (two) fathers are working in the field and those (two) girls are returning from the school to the house.

يَعْمَلاَنِ (they (two) are working) is IIIM^2 the Imperfect

Indicative and تَرْجِعَانِ (they (two) are returning) is IIIF^2 also the

Imperfect Indicative. The context clearly suggests that it is used for IIIF^2.

$$نَذْهَبُ مِنَ الْبَيْتِ إِلَى الْمَسْجِدِ$$

We are going from the house to the mosque.

نَذْهَبُ (we are going) is IM$^{2,3+}$ + IF$^{2,3+}$ the Imperfect

Indicative.

Rule No. 49

When the dual noun becomes the first noun of the construct phrase its final (ن) is dropped.

    Example Analysis:

مَائِدَتَا الْبَيْتِ كَبِيرَتَانِ وَجَمِيْلَتَانِ.

Two tables of the house are big and beautiful.

    مَائِدَتَا becomes the first noun of the construct phrase therefore, (ن) is dropped. The *Alif* of مَائِدَتَا helps us to recognise that it is dual.

كِتَابَايَ عِنْدَ صَدِيْقَيْنِ حَمِيمَيْنِ.

My two books are with two close friends.

    كِتَابَانِ becomes the first noun of the 'construct phrase' therefore, (ن) is dropped.

لَقِيْتُ رَجُلَيْنِ ذَوَيْ عِلْمٍ وَامْرَأَتَيْنِ ذَوَاتَيْ عِلْمٍ.

I met two men possessors of knowledge and two women possessors of knowledge.

ذُوْ (possessor) M[1]   ذَوَا (possessors) M[2] in the accusative case.

ذَاتَ (possessor) F[1]   ذَوَاتَيْ (possessors) F[2] in the accusative case.

Rule No. 50

When سَ **and** سَوْفَ **are placed before the Imperfect then its meaning is confined to the future tense. At times it also imparts the meaning of the near future.**

Example Analysis:

(٢٠) نَذْهَبُ مِنَ الْبَيْتِ إِلَى الْمَسْجِدِ وَسَنَأْكُلُ الطَّعَامَ بَعْدَ الصَّلَاةِ.

We are going from the house to the mosque and we will eat the food after Prayer.

نَأْكُلُ is the Imperfect and when سَ— is prefixed it means (we will eat).

﷽ UNIT 32 ﷽

ثُلَاثِي مَزِيْدٌ فِيهِ: بَابُ إِفْعَال

Derived Form IV إِفْعَال

The fourth derived form has principally causative and factual significance.

Perfect:

The Formation:

It is formed from the First Form IIIM[1] (فَعَلَ) keeping the radical *Fā'* quiescent and prefixing (أ) أَفْعَلَ

عَلِمَ (to know)   عَلَّمَ (to teach)   أَعْلَمَ (to inform)

حَسَنَ (to be nice, handsome)   حَسَّنَ (to beautify)   أَحْسَنَ (to do well)

The other conjugations in the Perfect Indicative follow the pattern of أَفْعَلَ and their endings remain the same as the Perfect in the First Form. (See TC under IV.)

The five singular forms are as follows:

III M¹ أَعْلَمَ (He informed)   III F¹ أَعْلَمَتْ (She informed)

II M¹ أَعْلَمْتَ (You informed)   II F¹ أَعْلَمْتِ (You informed)

I M¹ + F¹ أَعْلَمْتُ (I informed)

Imperfect:

The formation of the Imperfect is based on the IIIM¹ pattern يُفْعِلُ and all prefixes and endings remain the same as in the First Form.
(See TD under IV.)

Verbal Nouns:

Verbal nouns are formed on the pattern of إِفْعَالٌ. There is no variation in this if it is derived from the sound triliteral root. The verbal noun of أَعْلَمَ is إِعْلَامٌ (information).

Active Participle:

The Active Participle is formed on the pattern of مُفْعِلٌ.
The Active Participle of أَعْلَمَ is مُعْلِمٌ (an informer).

308

Passive Participle:

The Passive Participle is formed on the pattern of مُفْعَلٌ .

The Passive Participle for أَعْلَمَ is مُعْلَمٌ (informed).

There are certain changes, however, which take place if the root is weak.

(a) The radical *Fā'* is a vowel:

(i) If the radical *Fā'* is a *hamzah* then two *hamzah* meet together and it becomes (آ — ā) e.g. from أَمِنَ (to be safe) it becomes آمَنَ (to believe).

(ii) If the radical *Fā'* is either (و) or (ي) both remain the same, e.g. from وَجَدَ (to find) it becomes أَوْجَدَ (to create) and from يَبِسَ (to become dry) it becomes أَيْبَسَ (to make dry).

(iii) In the Imperfect the vowels change into (و). آمَنَ in the Imperfect is يُؤْمِنُ . أَيْقَظَ (to wake up someone) in the Imperfect is يُوقِظُ .

(iv) In Active Participles where (ي) is replaced by (ـُ) مُؤْمِنٌ (believer) مُوقِظٌ (one who wakes up)
(v) In Passive Participles where the radical *Lām* carries *fathah* instead of *kasrah* as in Active Participles.
مُوقَظٌ (awakened)

309

(vi) In Verbal Nouns the vowel becomes (ي) إِيْمَانٌ

(belief) إِيْقَاظٌ (awakening) إِيْجَادٌ (invention)

(b) The radical *'Ayn* is a vowel:

    (i) طَالَ (to become long) becomes أَطَالَ (to make long or longer) and قَامَ (to get up) becomes أَقَامَ (to make someone rise).

    (ii) In the Imperfect the radical *'Ayn* changes into (ي) and the preceding letter carries *kasrah* from أَرَادَ (to desire) it becomes يُرِيْدُ .

    (iii) In Active Participles in place of (ي) (ـُ) is added and it becomes مُرِيْدٌ (disciple).

    (iv) In Passive Participles the radical *Lām* becomes الف مُرَادٌ (intention).

    (v) In Verbal Nouns the radical *'Ayn* is dropped and (ة) is added e.g. إِرَادَةٌ (intention).

(c) The radical *Lām* is a vowel:

    (i) If the radical *Lām* is either (و) or (ى) then for the Perfect and the Imperfect it follows the pattern of TA6. e.g. أَبْكَى / يُبْكِي (to make someone cry).

(ii) Active Participle	مُبْكٍ	
(iii) Passive Participle	مُبْكًى	
(iv) Verbal Noun	إِبْكَاءٌ	

Significances: Derived form IV

(a) An Intransitive verb becomes transitive.

First Form	Meaning	Fourth Form	Meaning
مَاتَ	(to die)	أَمَاتَ	(to make someone die)
ضَحِكَ	(to laugh)	أَضْحَكَ	(to let someone laugh)

(b) The transitive verb intensified.

عَلِمَ	(to know)	أَعْلَمَ	(to inform)
أَكَلَ	(to eat)	آكَلَ	to feed, to eat with someone

311

شَرِبَ (to drink)   أَشْرَبَ   (to give someone/
                                              something to drink)

(c) Sometimes, however, it gives the same meaning as the First Form. For example:

First Form	**Meaning**	**Fourth Form**	**Meaning**
ضَرَّ	(to cause harm)	أَضَرَّ	(to cause harm)
حَبَّ	(to love)	أَحَبَّ	(to love)
نَكِرَ	(not to know)	أَنْكَرَ	(not to know)

(d) Sometimes it gives new meaning and does not originate from the triliteral root.

أَعَانَ   (to help someone)

أَرْسَلَ   (to send out)

النَّصُّ الْقُرْآنِيُّ
Lesson 9

١. مَثَلُ الْفَرِيقَيْنِ كَالْأَعْمَىٰ وَالْأَصَمِّ وَالْبَصِيرِ وَالسَّمِيعِ
(11: 24)

٢. وَدَاوُۥدَ وَسُلَيْمَٰنَ إِذْ يَحْكُمَانِ فِي الْحَرْثِ (21: 78)

٣. وَجَعَلَ بَيْنَ الْبَحْرَيْنِ حَاجِزًا (27: 61)

٤. وَمِن ذُرِّيَّتِهِمَا مُحْسِنٌ وَظَالِمٌ لِّنَفْسِهِ مُبِينٌ (37: 113)

٥. بَلْ يَدَاهُ مَبْسُوطَتَانِ يُنفِقُ كَيْفَ يَشَاءُ (5: 64)

٦. الطَّلَٰقُ مَرَّتَانِ فَإِمْسَاكٌ بِمَعْرُوفٍ أَوْ تَسْرِيحٌ بِإِحْسَٰنٍ
(2: 229)

٧. أَتَجْعَلُ فِيهَا مَن يُفْسِدُ فِيهَا وَيَسْفِكُ الدِّمَاءَ (2: 30)

٨. وَقَالَ رَجُلٌ مُّؤْمِنٌ مِّنْ ءَالِ فِرْعَوْنَ يَكْتُمُ إِيمَٰنَهُۥ
(40: 28)

313

٩. فَلَوْلَا كَانَتْ قَرْيَةٌ ءَامَنَتْ فَنَفَعَهَآ إِيمَـٰنُهَآ إِلَّا قَوْمَ يُونُسَ

(10: 98)

١٠. هُوَ ٱللَّهُ رَبِّى وَلَآ أُشْرِكُ بِرَبِّى أَحَدًا (18: 38)

١١. ٱلْحَمْدُ لِلَّهِ ٱلَّذِىٓ أَنزَلَ عَلَىٰ عَبْدِهِ ٱلْكِتَـٰبَ (18: 1)

١٢. ٱللَّهُ ٱلَّذِىٓ أَنزَلَ ٱلْكِتَـٰبَ بِٱلْحَقِّ وَٱلْمِيزَانَ (42: 17)

١٣. ءَامَنتُ بِمَآ أَنزَلَ ٱللَّهُ مِن كِتَـٰبٍ (42: 15)

١٤. مَا كُنتَ تَدْرِى مَا ٱلْكِتَـٰبُ وَلَا ٱلْإِيمَـٰنُ (52: 39)

١٥. ذَٰلِكَ مِمَّآ أَوْحَىٰٓ إِلَيْكَ رَبُّكَ مِنَ ٱلْحِكْمَةِ (17: 39)

١٦. لَّـٰكِنِ ٱللَّهُ يَشْهَدُ بِمَآ أَنزَلَ إِلَيْكَ أَنزَلَهُۥ بِعِلْمِهِۦ (4: 166)

١٧. هَلْ جَزَآءُ ٱلْإِحْسَـٰنِ إِلَّا ٱلْإِحْسَـٰنُ (55: 60)

١٨. وَأَمَّا مَنْ ءَامَنَ وَعَمِلَ صَـٰلِحًا فَلَهُۥ جَزَآءً ٱلْحُسْنَىٰ (18: 88)

١٩. فَمَنْ عَفَا وَأَصْلَحَ فَأَجْرُهُۥ عَلَى ٱللَّهِ (42: 40)

٢٠. ثُمَّ تَابَ مِنْ بَعْدِهِۦ وَأَصْلَحَ فَأَنَّهُۥ غَفُورٌ رَّحِيمٌ (6: 54)

٢١. وَمَن قَتَلَ مُؤْمِنًا خَطَـًٔا فَتَحْرِيرُ رَقَبَةٍ مُّؤْمِنَةٍ (4: 92)

٢٢. إِنَّآ أَرْسَلْنَـٰكَ بِٱلْحَقِّ بَشِيرًا وَنَذِيرًا (35: 24)

٢٣. وَوَهَبْنَا لَهُۥ يَحْيَىٰ وَأَصْلَحْنَا لَهُۥ زَوْجَهُۥٓ (21: 90)

٢٤. إِنَّا أَنزَلْنَٰهُ فِى لَيْلَةِ ٱلْقَدْرِ (1 :97)

٢٥. وَمَآ أَدْرَىٰكَ مَا لَيْلَةُ ٱلْقَدْرِ (2 :97)

٢٦. وَكَذَٰلِكَ أَنزَلْنَٰهُ قُرْءَانًا عَرَبِيًّا وَصَرَّفْنَا فِيهِ مِنَ ٱلْوَعِيدِ (113 :20)

٢٧. وَأَنزَلْنَآ إِلَيْكَ ٱلْكِتَٰبَ بِٱلْحَقِّ مُصَدِّقًا لِّمَا بَيْنَ يَدَيْهِ مِنَ ٱلْكِتَٰبِ (48 :5)

٢٨. كَمَآ أَخْرَجَكَ رَبُّكَ مِنۢ بَيْتِكَ بِٱلْحَقِّ (5 :8)

٢٩. رَبِّ إِنِّى لِمَآ أَنزَلْتَ إِلَىَّ مِنْ خَيْرٍ فَقِيرٌ (24 :28)

٣٠. أَفَأَنتَ تُنقِذُ مَن فِى ٱلنَّارِ (19 :39)

٣١. مَّن ذَا ٱلَّذِى يُقْرِضُ ٱللَّهَ قَرْضًا حَسَنًا (11 :57)

٣٢. أَنَّىٰ يُحْىِۦ هَٰذِهِ ٱللَّهُ بَعْدَ مَوْتِهَا (259 :2)

٣٣. إِنَّ ٱللَّهَ يَفْعَلُ مَا يُرِيدُ (14 :22)

٣٤. إِنَّ ٱللَّهَ يَحْكُمُ مَا يُرِيدُ (1 :5)

٣٥. إِنْ هُوَ إِلَّا ذِكْرَىٰ (90 :6)

٣٦. وَٱللَّهُ أَنزَلَ مِنَ ٱلسَّمَآءِ مَآءً فَأَحْيَا بِهِ ٱلْأَرْضَ بَعْدَ مَوْتِهَآ (65 :16)

٣٧. وَلَقَدْ كَرَّمْنَا بَنِى ءَادَمَ (70 :17)

٣٨. قَالَ عَذَابِى أُصِيبُ بِهِۦ مَنْ أَشَآءُ ۖ وَرَحْمَتِى وَسِعَتْ كُلَّ

شَىْءٍ (7: 156)

٣٩. أَفَمَن شَرَحَ ٱللَّهُ صَدْرَهُۥ لِلْإِسْلَـٰمِ فَهُوَ عَلَىٰ نُورٍ مِّن رَّبِّهِۦ

(39: 22)

٤٠. هَلْ أَتَىٰكَ حَدِيثُ ضَيْفِ إِبْرَٰهِيمَ ٱلْمُكْرَمِينَ (51: 24)

٤١. وَمَآ أَرْسَلْنَا مِن رَّسُولٍ إِلَّا بِلِسَانِ قَوْمِهِۦ (14: 4)

٤٢. فَلَمَّا وَضَعَتْهَا قَالَتْ رَبِّ إِنِّى وَضَعْتُهَآ أُنثَىٰ وَٱللَّهُ أَعْلَمُ بِمَا

وَضَعَتْ وَلَيْسَ ٱلذَّكَرُ كَٱلْأُنثَىٰ ۖ وَإِنِّى سَمَّيْتُهَا مَرْيَمَ وَإِنِّىٓ

أُعِيذُهَا بِكَ وَذُرِّيَّتَهَا مِنَ ٱلشَّيْطَـٰنِ ٱلرَّجِيمِ (3: 36)

٤٣. وَنَادَىٰ فِرْعَوْنُ فِى قَوْمِهِۦ قَالَ يَـٰقَوْمِ أَلَيْسَ لِى مُلْكُ

مِصْرَ (43: 51)

٤٤. إِنَّمَآ أَنتَ نَذِيرٌ ۚ وَٱللَّهُ عَلَىٰ كُلِّ شَىْءٍ وَكِيلٌ (11: 12)

٤٥. وَمَا يُدْرِيكَ لَعَلَّ ٱلسَّاعَةَ قَرِيبٌ (42: 17)

٤٦. فَلَمَّآ أَحَسَّ عِيسَىٰ مِنْهُمُ ٱلْكُفْرَ قَالَ مَنْ أَنصَارِىٓ إِلَى

ٱللَّهِ (3: 52)

٤٧. مَن كَانَ يَرْجُواْ لِقَآءَ ٱللَّهِ فَإِنَّ أَجَلَ ٱللَّهِ لَـَٔاتٍ (29: 5)

٤٨. يَوْمَ لَا تَمْلِكُ نَفْسٌ لِّنَفْسٍ شَيْئًا ۖ وَٱلْأَمْرُ يَوْمَئِذٍ لِّلَّهِ

(82: 19)

٤٩. يَوْمَ تَجِدُ كُلُّ نَفْسٍ مَّا عَمِلَتْ مِنْ خَيْرٍ مُّحْضَرًا وَمَا عَمِلَتْ مِن سُوءٍ تَوَدُّ لَوْ أَنَّ بَيْنَهَا وَبَيْنَهُۥ أَمَدًا بَعِيدًا

(3: 30)

٥٠. وَمَن كَانَ فِى هَٰذِهِۦ أَعْمَىٰ فَهُوَ فِى ٱلْأَخِرَةِ أَعْمَىٰ

(17: 72)

٥١. مَن قَتَلَ نَفْسًا بِغَيْرِ نَفْسٍ أَوْ فَسَادٍ فِى ٱلْأَرْضِ فَكَأَنَّمَا قَتَلَ ٱلنَّاسَ جَمِيعًا (5: 32)

٥٢. قَالَ أَمَّا مَن ظَلَمَ فَسَوْفَ نُعَذِّبُهُۥ (18: 87)

٥٣. وَلَسَوْفَ يُعْطِيكَ رَبُّكَ فَتَرْضَىٰ (93: 5)

٥٤. سَيَجْعَلُ ٱللَّهُ بَعْدَ عُسْرٍ يُسْرًا (65: 7)

٥٥. وَسَنَقُولُ لَهُۥ مِنْ أَمْرِنَا يُسْرًا (18: 88)

QUR'ANIC TEXT
VOCABULARY
LESSON 9

مَثَلٌ	likeness	إِيمَانٌ	[VN⁴] faith
فَرِيقٌ	**party**	بَشِيرٌ	[AP] bringer of glad tiding
فَقِيرٌ	in need	نَذِيرٌ	[AP] warner
بَصِيرٌ	someone seen	وَعِيدٌ	threat
سَمِيعٌ	hearer	مُلْكٌ	dominion, sovereignty, kingdom
حَكَمَ/يَحْكُمُ	to adjudicate	وَكِيلٌ	[AP] trustee, guardian, witness to bargain, agent
حَاجِزٌ	[AP] barrier	سَاعَةٌ	hour
مُحْسِنٌ	kind	قَرِيبٌ	near
ذُرِّيَّةٌ	progeny, descendants	كُفْرٌ	disbelief
مُبِينٌ	clear, evident	آتٍ	[AP] coming
مَبْسُوطٌ	spread out, outstretched	مُحْضَرٌ	[PP⁴] presented
أَنْفَقَ/يُنْفِقُ	to spend	بَعِيدٌ	far away, distant
مَرَّةٌ	Once	أَمَرٌ	a distant term, time, place
إِمْسَاكٌ	[VN4] seizure, restraint, retaining	أَمَّا	as far, but, as to
تَسْرِيحٌ	[VN2] release	عُسْرٌ	[VN] hardship

318

أَصْلَحَ/يُصْلِحُ	IV to reform, reconstruct
قَدْرٌ	[VN] power
رَجِيْمٌ	thrown off, cursed
أَحَسَّ / يُحِسُّ	IV to perceive
أَنْصَارٌ	helper
حِكْمَةٌ	wisdom
حُسْنٌ	good
تَحْرِيرٌ	VN^2 set up free
تَبْشِيْرٌ	bearer of glad tiding
نَذِيْرٌ	warner
عَفَا / يَعْفُو	to forgive
أَجْرٌ	reward
زَوْجٌ	spouse
أَرَادَ / يُرِيْدُ	IV wish, have a mind, be willing
سَفَكَ / يَسْفِكُ	to shed blood
كَتَمَ / يَكْتُمُ	to conceal
أَوْحَى	IV to reveal

دِمَاءٌ	blood
خَطَأٌ	mistake
تَحْرِيرٌ	[VN2] emancipation
رَقَبَةٌ	neck, slave
مُؤْمِنٌ	[AP4] believer
أَشْرَكَ/يُشْرِكُ	IV to associate partner
مِيْزَانٌ	balance
أَنْزَلَ/ يُنْزِلُ	IV to reveal
دَرَى / يَدْرِي	to know
يُسْرٌ	ease
عَفَا / يَعْفُو	to pardon
وَهَبَ / يَهَبُ	to grant, to donate
صَرَّفَ / يُصَرِّفُ	II to set forth
وَعِيْدٌ	threat
أَنْقَذَ / يُنْقِذُ	IV to deliver, save, rescue
أَقْرَضَ / يُقْرِضُ	IV to loan, lend
كَرَّمَ / يُكَرِّمُ	II to honour, revere

سَوْفَ	used for future	وَدَّ / يَوَدُّ	to love, wish for, desire
وَجَدَ / يَجِدُ	to find	عَذَّبَ / يُعَذِّبُ	II to punish, chastise
أَصَابَ / يُصِيبُ	IV to hit, attain the purpose, to be right, to assail, to befall (calamity)	أَعْطَى / يُعْطِي	IV to give, present, offer
مُحْضَرٌ	PP[4] presented	رَضِيَ / يَرْضَى	to be pleased [TA4]
شَرَحَ / يَشْرَحُ	to uncover, spread out, made open	عُسْرٌ	hardship
أَمَدٌّ	space	يُسْرٌ	comfort
بَعِيدٌ	far	سَمَّى / يُسَمِّى	II to give name

METHOD OF TEACHING
LESSON 9

1. By retaining the same colours for radicals and additional letters the duals in the Perfect and the Imperfect can be introduced both on the magnetic board and overhead projector.

2. Students should be encouraged to consult the tables in the Appendix for dual verbs, and especially for their formation in weak verbs.

3. Personal Pronouns and the Pronoun suffix in their dual forms should be explained by examples. Students should consult the tables provided in the Appendix.

4. Guided questions can be asked to the students so as to enable them to give the dual forms of verbs, Personal Pronouns and the Pronoun Suffix.

5. Allow the students to construct sentences in which the nouns in their dual form are *muḍāf*.

6. With more examples the application of (سَـــ) and (سَوفَ) to the Imperfect can be explained.

7. To facilitate the students understanding of the formation of the derived form IV you should retain the same colours for the radicals and the additional letters both on the magnetic board and overhead projector for all five "pillars". Get the students to say these pillars in chorus. It is now possible from the root عَلِمَ to prepare 15 cards using the "five pillars". Five for the first form, five for the second form and again five for the fourth form.

8. Let the students identify all derived forms and their pillars from the text and ask them to give their reasons.
9. By means of a dictionary help the students to find out the meanings of the derived forms IV used in the text.

Lesson 9

Exercise No. 28

(1) Select the correct word(s) from the parenthesis to fill in the blanks in the following sentences.

(١) هُمَا .... إِلَى الْمَسْجِد للصَّلَوة.

(يَقْرَءَانِ، يَكْتُبَانِ، تَكْتُبَانِ، يَذْهَبَانِ)

(٢) بِنْتَان .... ذَاهِبَتَانِ مِنَ الْمَدْرَسَةِ إِلَى بَيْتِهِمَا.

(صَغِيرَتَيْنِ، جَمِيلَتَانِ، صَغِيرَانِ، عَالِمَانِ)

(٣) .... الْأَبَوَانِ يَرْجِعَانِ مِنَ الْحَرْثِ إِلَى الْبَيْتِ.

(ذَلِكَ، تِلْكَ، تَانِكَ، ذَانِكَ)

(٤) لَقِيتُ .... ذَوَيْ عِلْمٍ.

(وَلَدَيْنِ، أَبَوَانِ، بِنْتَانِ، أُخْتَانِ)

(٥) الْمُؤْمِنُ مَنْ .... بِالله.

(أَشْرَكَ، آمَنَ، كَفَرَ، تَرَكَ)

(٦) الْمُحْسِنُ مَنْ .... إِلَى النَّاسِ.

(أَشْرَكَ، أَحْسَنَ، ظَلَمَ، يُفْسِدُ)

(٧) الْكَافِرُ مَنْ .... بِالله.

(كَفَرَ، آمَنَ، أَسْلَمَ، أَعَانَ)

(٨) نَحْنُ .... مِنَ الْقُرْآن الْكَرِيْمِ.

(أَقْرَأُ، قَرَأْتُ، نَقْرَأُ، قَرَأْتُ)

322

(٩) .... الْبَيْتُ كَبِيرَان.

(كُرْسِيَّان، مَائِدَتَان، غُرْفَتَان، بَابَا)

(١٠) الظَّالِمَةُ .... إِثْماً عَظِيْماً.

(تَكْسِبُ، تَصُومُ، تَنْظُرُ، تَقْرَأُ)

(2) Put i'rāb

(١) داود و موسى عليهما السلام رسولان.

(٢) المعلم يعلم القراءة و الكتابة.

(٣) أطعمت الفقير فرضى عني و دعا لي.

(٤) أدخل الأب الولد الطويل في البيت.

(٥) أنا أحب الله حبا شديدا.

(3) Give the Perfect and Imperfect forms in $IIIM^2$, $IIIF^2$, IIM^2, IIF^2 and $I\ M^{2,3} + F^{2,3+}$ for the following verbs.

(١) ذَهَبَ (٢) قَرَأَ (٣) أَكَلَ (٤) أَدْخَلَ (٥) أَخْرَجَ
(٦) أَحْسَنَ (٧) حَسَّنَ (٨) فَهَّمَ (٩) أَشْرَكَ (١٠) آمَنَ

(4) Give the Perfect, the Imperfect, the verbal noun, the Active Participle, the Passive Participle for the Fourth Derived Form from the following roots:

(١) دَخَلَ   (٢) خَرَجَ   (٣) أَمِنَ   (٤) نَزَلَ   (٥) شَرِكَ

(5) Translate into Arabic

1. Allah does not oppress mankind.
2. The oppressor oppresses and he does not repent to Allah.
3. Two tall boys are returning to their house from the school.
4. The kind person is he who shows kindness to the people.
5. The believer is not afraid of people.
6. Allah has revealed the Qur'ān and He will protect it.
7. The reformer is he who reforms the people.
8. The corrupt person spreads corruption in the world.
9. Allah does not like the corrupt person and the corruption.
10. Allah loves kindness and reform.

  (6) From the Qur'ānic text of Lesson 9 identify the
      following:
  (a) Derived forms.
  (b) Dual nouns.

Phase Four

(**21**: 107)

(١) إِبْرَاهِيمُ (عَلَيْهِ السَّلَامُ) وَحَّدَ اللهَ تَوْحِيداً كَامِلاً وَمَا أَشْرَكَ فِي عِبَادَةِ اللهِ أَحَداً ، وَكَانَ حَنِيفاً مُسْلِماً.

(٢) الْمُنَافِقُ مَنْ يُنَافِقُ وَيُحِبُّ النِّفَاقَ.

(٣) النِّفَاقُ كِتْمَانُ الشَّرِّ فِي الْقَلْبِ وَإِظْهَارُ الْخَيْرِ بِاللِّسَانِ.

(٤) الْمُجَاهِدُ مَنْ يُجَاهِدُ فِي سَبِيلِ اللهِ وَلَا يَخَافُ لَوْمَةَ لَائِمٍ.

(٥) الْجِهَادُ نَوْعَانِ : جِهَادُ النَّفْسِ وَالْهَوَى وَجِهَادُ السَّيْفِ.

(٦) الْمُجَاهِدُ يُحِبُّ الْجِدَالَ وَالْقِتَالَ لِإِعْلَاءِ كَلِمَةِ الْحَقِّ.

(٧) الْمُسَافِرُ مَنْ يُسَافِرُ مِنْ بَلَدٍ إِلَى بَلَدٍ .

(٨) أَطْعَمْتُ الْمُسَافِرَ فَدَعَا لِي قَائِلاً: بَارَكَ اللهُ فِيكَ.

(٩) هَلْ تُسَافِرُ مَعَ أُمِّكَ إِلَى مَكَّةَ؟
نَعَمْ، نُسَافِرُ بِإِذْنِ اللهِ إِلَى مَكَّةَ لِلْحَجِّ .

(١٠) الْأَبُ وَالِابْنُ يُحَافِظَانِ عَلَى صَلَاتِهِمَا وَ لَا يَتْرُكَانِهَا.

(١١) هُمَا يُعَاوِنَانِ عَلَى الْخَيْرِ وَلَا يُعَاوِنَانِ عَلَى الْإِثْمِ.

(١٢) أَكْرَمْتُ الضَّيْفَ فَالضَّيْفُ مُكْرَمٌ.

﷽ UNIT 34 ﷽

(١) كَانَ ابْنِي يُجَالِسُ الْمُسِيءَ فَسَاءَ أَدَبُهُ ، فَلَعَلَّهُ يَتُوبُ
إِلَى اللهِ فَيُصْلِحُ عَمَلَهُ وَيُحَسِّنُ إِسْلَامَهُ .

(٢) كَانَ رَسُولُ اللهِ (ﷺ) يَقُولُ قَوْلاً صَادِقاً، وَكَانَ
يَأْمُرُ بِالْمَعْرُوفِ وَيَنْهَى عَنِ الْمُنْكَرِ.

(٣) كَانَ إِبْرَاهِيمُ (عليه السلام) يُنَاظِرُ الْمَلِكَ نَمْرُودَ فِي
التَّوْحِيدِ فَكَانَ يَهْزِمُهُ فِي الْمُنَاظَرَةِ.

﷽ UNIT 35 ﷽

(الْبَاءُ)	(الْأَلِفُ)
كَانَ زَيْدٌ عَالِماً	(١) زَيْدٌ عَالِمٌ
كَانَتْ فَاطِمَةُ صَالِحَةً	(٢) فَاطِمَةُ صَالِحَةٌ
لَيْسَ الرَّجُلُ قَوِيّاً	(٣) الرَّجُلُ قَوِيٌّ
لَيْسَت الْمَرْأَةُ ضَاحِكَةً	(٤) الْمَرْأَةُ ضَاحِكَةٌ
صَارَ الطَّالِبُ أُسْتَاذاً	(٥) الطَّالِبُ أُسْتَاذٌ
صَارَت الْأُمُّ ضَعِيفَةً	(٦) الْأُمُّ ضَعِيفَةٌ
ظَلَّ الْوَلَدُ نَائِماً	(٧) الْوَلَدُ نَائِمٌ
أَصْبَحَ أَحْمَدُ مَرِيضاً	(٨) أَحْمَدُ مَرِيضٌ
أَضْحَى الْقَارِئُ مُقْبِلاً	(٩) الْقَارِئُ مُقْبِلٌ
بَاتَ الْمَرِيضُ بَاكِياً	(١٠) الْمَرِيضُ بَاكٍ

(١١) كَانَ الْوَلَدُ صَغِيراً فَصَارَ شَاباً.

(١٢) كُنْتُ فَقِيراً فَأَغْنَانِي اللهُ مِنْ فَضْلِه.

(١٣) كُنْتُ جَاهِلاً فَعَلَّمَنِي الْمُعَلِّمُ الْقِرَاءَةَ وَالْكِتَابَةَ .

(١٤) كُنْتُ ضَالاًّ فَهَدَانِي اللهُ إِلَى الصِّرَاطِ الْمُسْتَقِيمِ.

(١٥) كَانَ مُحَمَّدٌ (ﷺ) رَسُولَ اللهِ.

(١٦) كَانَ مُوسَى (عليه السلام) رَسُولاً.

(١٧) صَارَ الْفَقِيرُ بِفَضْلِ اللهِ غَنِيّاً.

(١٨) صَارَ الْمُفْسِدُ مُصْلِحاً.

(١٩) أَضْحَى الْغَمَامُ كَثِيفاً.

(٢٠) ظَلَّ السَّارِقُ هَارِباً .

(٢١) بَاتَ الْمِصْبَاحُ مُنَوَّراً .

❈ UNIT 36 ❈

(١) أَنْتُمْ صَادِقُونَ وَهُنَّ صَادِقَاتٌ.

(٢) نَحْنُ جَاهِلُونَ وَهُنَّ عَالِمَاتٌ.

(٣) أَنْتُمْ مُحْسِنُونَ وَهُنَّ مُحْسِنَاتٌ.

(٤) أَنْتُمْ صَائِمُونَ وَأَنْتُنَّ صَائِمَاتٌ.

(٥) هُمْ مُؤْمِنُونَ وَهُنَّ مُؤْمِنَاتٌ .

(٦) أَنْتُمْ مُطِيعُونَ وَأَنْتُنَّ مُطِيعَاتٌ.

نَحْنُ مُصْلِحُونَ وَتَائِبُونَ إِلَى اللهِ. (٧)

أَنْتُنَّ شَاكِرَاتٌ وَعَابِدَاتٌ. (٨)

هَلْ أَنْتُمْ رَازِقُونَ؟ (٩)

لَا، اللهُ هُوَ الرَّازِقُ وَنَحْنُ شَاكِرُونَ وَعَابِدُونَ .

إِنَّا شَاكِرُونَ لَكُمْ إِحْسَانَكُمْ لَنَا. (١٠)

إِنَّ اللهَ رَازِقٌ وَمَا أَنْتُمْ بِرَازِقِينَ. (١١)

اللهُ هُوَ رَبُّنَا وَنَحْنُ عَلَى ذَلِكَ مِنَ الشَّاهِدِينَ (١٢)
وَالشَّاكِرِينَ.

أَمَا أَنْتُمْ خَائِفُونَ مِنْ عَذَابِ اللهِ؟ (١٣)

بَلَى، نَحْنُ خَائِفُونَ مِنْ عَذَابِ اللهِ .

إِنَّ اللهَ لَمَعَ الصَّادِقِينَ وَ الصَّادِقَاتِ وَالصَّابِرِينَ (١٤)
وَ الصَّابِرَات.

يُدْخِلُ اللهُ الْمُؤْمِنِينَ وَ الْمُؤْمِنَاتِ فِي الْجَنَّةِ الْعَالِيَةِ. (١٥)

"لَا يَرْحَمُ اللهُ مَنْ لَا يَرْحَمُ النَّاسَ". "ح" (١٦)

"الرَّاحِمُونَ يَرْحَمُهُمُ الرَّحْمَنُ". "ح" (١٧)

"إِنَّمَا الْمُؤْمِنُونَ إِخْوَةٌ". "ح" (١٨)

"الْغِنَى غِنَى النَّفْسِ" . "ح" (١٩)

"مَنْ قَاتَلَ لِتَكُونَ *كَلِمَةُ اللهِ هِيَ الْعُلْيَا فَهُوَ فِي سَبِيْلِ (٢٠)
اللهِ". "ح"

---

* See rule no. 83.

329

(٢١) "مَا أَطْعَمْتَ نَفْسَكَ فَهُوَ لَكَ صَدَقَةٌ، وَمَا أَطْعَمْتَ وَلَدَكَ فَهُوَ لَكَ صَدَقَةٌ، وَمَا أَطْعَمْتَ زَوْجَكَ فَهُوَ لَكَ صَدَقَةٌ، وَمَا أَطْعَمْتَ خَادِمَكَ فَهُوَ لَكَ صَدَقَةٌ". "ح"

(٢٢) "طَلَبُ الْعِلْمِ فَرِيضَةٌ عَلَى كُلِّ مُسْلِمٍ". . "ح"

(٢٣) "مَثَلُ الَّذِي يَذْكُرُ رَبَّهُ وَالَّذِي لاَ يَذْكُرُ رَبَّهُ مَثَلُ الْحَيِّ وَالْمَيِّتِ". "ح"

(٢٤) مَنْ صَلَّى عَلَيَّ وَاحِدَةً صَلَّى اللهُ عَلَيْهِ بِهَا عَشْراً. "ح"

(٢٥) وَاللهُ فِي عَوْنِ الْعَبْدِ مَادَامَ الْعَبْدُ فِي عَوْنِ أَخِيهِ. "ح"

(٢٦) اَللهُ أَفْرَحُ بِتَوْبَةِ عَبْدِهِ مِنْ أَحَدِكُمْ سُقِطَ** عَلَى بَعِيرِهِ وَقَدْ أَضَلَّهُ فِي أَرْضٍ فَلاَةٍ. "ح"

(٢٧) لَيْسَ مِنَّا مَنْ دَعَا إِلَى الْعَصَبِيَّةِ وَلَيْسَ مِنَّا مَنْ قَاتَلَ عَلَى عَصَبِيَّةٍ وَلَيْسَ مِنَّا مَنْ مَاتَ عَلَى عَصَبِيَّةٍ .ح"

(٢٨) إِنَّ أَحَبَّ الدِّينِ إِلَى اللهِ مَا دَاوَمَ عَلَيْهِ صَاحِبُهُ. "ح"

(٢٩) إِنَّ اللهَ يَقْبِضُ الْعِلْمَ بِقَبْضِ الْعُلَمَاءِ. "ح"

(٣٠) عَنِ ابْنِ عَبَّاسٍ رَضِيَ اللهُ عَنْهُ، أَنَّ رَسُوْلَ اللهِ (ﷺ) كَانَ يَقُوْلُ عِنْدَ الْكَرْبِ: لاَ إِلَـهَ إِلاَّ اللهُ الْعَظِيمُ الْحَلِيمُ ، لاَ إِلَـهَ إِلاَّ اللهُ رَبُّ الْعَرْشِ الْعَظِيمِ، لاَ إِلَهَ إِلاَّ اللهُ رَبُّ السَّمَاوَاتِ وَرَبُّ الْعَرْشِ الْكَرِيمِ. "ح"

** See rule no. 79.

(٣١) الْجِدُّ خَيْرٌ مِنَ الْكَسَلِ.   "م"

(٣٢) مَا هَلَكَ امْرُؤٌ عَنْ مَشُورَةٍ.   "م"

(٣٣) مَوْتُ الْعَالِمِ مَوْتُ كُلِّ الْعَالَمِ.   "م"

(٣٤) مَنْ أَطَاعَ غَضَبَهُ أَضَاعَ أَدَبَهُ.   "م"

(٣٥) إِذَا تَمَّ الْعَقْلُ نَقَصَ الْكَلَامُ.   "م"

(٣٦) مَنْ عَمِلَ دَائِماً أَكَلَ نَائِماً.   "م"

(٣٧) لِكُلِّ عَمَلٍ ثَوَابٌ.   "م"

(٣٨) التَّدْبِيرُ نِصْفُ الْمَعِيشَةِ.   "م"

(٣٩) الْحَسَدُ ثِقْلٌ لاَ يَضَعُهُ حَامِلُهُ.   "م"

(٤٠) الْحَرِيصُ مَحْرُومٌ.   "م"

331

GLOSSARY
LESSON 10

وَحَّدَ / يُوَحِّدُ	II to make into one
تَوْحِيدٌ	[VN] belief in the oneness of God
كَامِلٌ	[AP] perfect
عِبَادَةٌ	[VN] worship
حَنِيفٌ	upright person, true believer
مُنَافِقٌ	[AP^3] hypocrite
نَافَقَ / يُنَافِقُ	III to behave as hypocrite
نِفَاقٌ	[VN^3] hypocrisy
كِتْمَانٌ	[VN] secrecy, concealment
إِظْهَارٌ	[VN^4] presentation, exposition
مُجَاهِدٌ	[AP^3] fighter, freedom fighter
جَاهَدَ / يُجَاهِدُ	[III] to endeavor, to strive, to fight
لَوْمَةٌ	rebuke, blame
لَائِمٌ	[AP] blamer
نَوْعٌ	kind
سَيْفٌ	sword
جِدَالٌ	[VN^3] dispute
قِتَالٌ	[VN^3] battle, combat
إِعْلَاءٌ	[VN^4] uplift, raising, exaltation
مُسَافِرٌ	[AP^3] traveler

سَافَرَ / يُسَافِرُ	III to travel
أَطْعَمَ / يُطْعِم	IV to feed
إِذْنٌ	permission
عَاوَنَ / يُعَاوِن	III to help, to assist
أَكْرَمَ / يُكْرِمُ	IV to honour someone
ضَيْفٌ	guest
مُكْرَمٌ	[PP4] honoured
نَاظَرَ / يُنَاظِرُ	III to argue, to debate, to dispute with someone
هَزَمَ / يَهْزِمُ	to defeat, to vanquish
مُنَاظَرَةٌ	[VN3] debate, conversation
لَيْسَ	not to be, not to exist
صَارَ / يَصِيرُ	to become
ظَلَّ / يَظَلُّ	to be, to become, turn into
أَصْبَحَ / يُصْبِحُ	IV to enter into morning
مَرِيضٌ	sick
مُقْبِلٌ	[AP4] coming, advancing
أَضْحَى / يُضْحِي	IV to be, to become, to make forenoon
بَاتَ / يَبِيْتُ	to pass or spend the night, to stay over night
شَابٌّ	youth
أَغْنَى / يُغْنِي	IV to make free from want, to make rich, to enrich

333

غَنِيٌّ	wealthy, prosperous
غَمَامٌ	cloud
كَثِيفٌ	thick, dense
هَارِبٌ	[AP] runaway, fugitive
مِصْبَاحٌ	lamp
مُنَوَّرٌ	[PP^2] illuminated
هُمْ	III M^{3+} they
هُنَّ	[III F^3+] they
أَنْتُمْ	[II M^3+] you
أَنْتُنَّ	II F^{3+} you
نَحْنُ	[IM$^{2,3+}$,I, F$^{2,3+}$] we
عَالٍ	elevated
إِخْوَةٌ	M^{3+} brothers
صَدَقَةٌ	alms
فَرِيضَةٌ	obligatory
فَرِحَ/يَفْرَحُ	to be pleased
أَفْرَحُ	must pleased
فَلاَةٌ	waterless desert
عَصَبِيَّةٌ	fanaticism

دَاوَمَ/يُدَاوِمُ	to continue
أَحَبَّ	most lovable
جِدٌّ	toil
مَشُورَةٌ	consultation
أَطَاعَ / يُطِيعُ	IV to obey
أَضَاعَ / يُضِيعُ	IV to ruin, to let perish
دَائِمٌ	always
أَدَبٌ	good manners, humanity
تَمَّ / يَتِمُّ	to be or to become complete, completed
نَقَصَ / يَنْقُصُ	to decrease, to become less
تَدْبِيرٌ	[VN^2] planning, organisation
مَعِيشَةٌ	livelihood
حَسَدٌ	envy
ثِقْلٌ	weight, load
حَرِيصٌ	greedy
مَحْرُومٌ	[PP] deprived
أَجَادَ / يُجِيدُ	IV to do excellently something
سَادَ / يَسُودُ	to be or become master, to become head, to become chief

GRAMMATICAL THEMES
LESSON 10

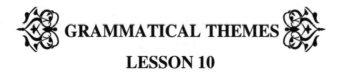

UNIT 33

ثُلَاثِي مَزِيدٌ فِيهِ : بَابُ فِعَالٌ / مُفَاعَلَةٌ

Derived Form III فِعَالٌ

The Third derived form has the significance of reciprocity and of making an effort to accomplish something.

The Formation:

Perfect:

It is formed from the First Form IIIM[1] (فَعَلَ) adding *Alif* after the radical *Fā'* (فَاعَلَ). The root جَلَسَ (to sit) in the Third derived form becomes جَالَسَ (to sit in the company of someone).

The other conjugations in the Perfect Indicative follow the pattern (فَاعَلَ) and their endings remain the same as for the Perfect in the First Form. (See TC under III)

Imperfect:

The formation of the Imperfect is based on the IIIM[1] pattern (يُفَاعِلُ). All prefixes and endings remain the same as in the First Form. (See TD under III)

Verbal Nouns:

The Verbal noun is formed on the pattern of فِعَالٌ and مُفَاعَلَةٌ . The Verbal Noun for جَالَسَ is مُجَالَسَةٌ
There are some roots for Verbal Nouns which take both patterns. e.g. جَاهَدَ (to strive) جِهَادٌ and مُجَاهَدَةٌ (struggle).

Active Participle:

The Active Participle is formed on the pattern of مُفَاعِلٌ

From جَاهَدَ the Active Participle is مُجَاهِدٌ (freedom fighter).

Passive Participle:

The Passive Participle is formed on the pattern of مُفَاعَلٌ

From هَاجَرَ (to migrate) the Passive Participle becomes مُهَاجَرٌ (migrated).

(For Verbal Nouns, Active and Passive Participles see TB under III)

Significances: Derived Form III

(a) It indicates the association of two or more persons with an action.

First Form	Meaning	Third Form	Meaning
أَكَلَ	(to eat)	آكَلَ	(to eat with someone)
شَرِبَ	(to drink)	شَارَبَ	(to drink in someone's company)
جَلَسَ	(to sit)	جَالَسَ	(to sit in the company of someone)

(b) To perform similar acts to share certain behavior.

شَرِكَ	(to share)	شَارَكَ	(to share something with someone)
قَتَلَ	(to kill)	قَاتَلَ	(to combat)

(c) Sometimes the reciprocity does not exist but gives a meaning which is similar to the Second and Fourth Forms.

بَرَكَ	(to kneel down)	بَارَكَ	(to give one's blessing)
هَجَرَ	(to abandon)	هَاجَرَ	(to emigrate)
نَفَقَ	(to sell well)	نَافَقَ	(to behave with hypocrisy)

338

(d) With reciprocity it imparts the meaning of competition.

First Form	Meaning	Third Form	Meaning
سَرَعَ	(to hurry)	سَارَعَ	(to compete with others for something)
سَبَقَ	(to go ahead of someone or something)	سَابَقَ	(to try to defeat or beat someone)

Example Analysis:

الْمُسْلِمُ مَنْ أَسْلَمَ وَجْهَهُ لله.

The Muslim is one who surrenders his face to Allah.

أَسْلَمَ (to surrender) is the Fourth Form Perfect (IIIM[1]) from

سَلِمَ (to be safe and sound). Its object is وَجْهَه .

الْمُسْلِمُ is the Active Participle from أَسْلَمَ (See TB under IV)

آمَنْتُ بِمَا أَنْزَلَ اللَّهُ عَلَى مُحَمَّدٍ (ﷺ) وَبِمَا أَنْزَلَ عَلَى مَنْ قَبْلَهُ.

I believed in what Allah has revealed to Muhammad (the blessings of Allah and peace be upon him) and what He has revealed to the messengers before him.

آمَنْتُ (I believed) is the Fourth Form Perfect weak (I M[1]+F[1]) from أَمِنَ (to be safe).

339

أَنْزَلَ (he revealed) is the Fourth Form Perfect sound (III M[1]) from نَزَلَ (to descend).

الْمُرْسَلِيْنَ is the sound plural in the genitive case because it is preceded by a preposition مِنْ (from). مُرْسَلٌ (sent) is the Passive Participle from أَرْسَلَ (to send).

(See TB under IV)

UNIT 34

The Imperfect and Past Continuous:

Rule No. 51

The Imperfect gives the meaning of Past Continuous when كَانَ and its conjugated forms, depending on the Imperfect form, precede the Imperfect.

Example Analysis:

كَانَ رَسُولُ اللهِ (ﷺ) يَقُولُ قَوْلاً صَادِقاً، وَكَانَ يَأْمُرُ

بِالْمَعْرُوفِ وَيَنْهَى عَنِ الْمُنْكَرِ.

The messenger of Allah (the blessings of Allah and peace be upon him) used to speak truthful words and he used to command for right conduct and forbid indecency.

كَانَ precedes the Imperfect يَقُولُ , يَأْمُرُ and يَنْهَى and agrees in IIIM[1]. Therefore, these three Imperfects give the meaning of the Past Continuous.

UNIT 35

كَانَ and its Sisters:

Rule No. 52

←

(كَانَ، لَيْسَ، صَارَ، ظَلَّ، أَصْبَحَ، أَضْحَى، بَاتَ) are the verbs.
When they precede the subjects they keep the subjects in the nominative case and change the predicates into the accusative case.

(Note these verbs are known as كَانَ and its sisters.)

Example Analysis:

Beneath (الْأَلِفُ) all sentences are nominal sentences which are comprised of subjects and predicates.

الرَّجُلُ، الطَّالِبُ، الْبِنْتُ، زَيْدٌ، فَاطِمَةُ are in the nominative case therefore, they carry *dammah*. The rest are predicates and they also carry *dammah*. أَحْمَدُ، الْقَارِىءُ، الْمَرِيْضُ

Beneath (الْبَاءُ) the same sentences are preceded by كَانَ and its sisters. Therefore, the predicates are changed into accusative case.

(a) Note in the above sentences كَانَ and its sisters agree with the subjects in both number and gender.

(b) With the exception of لَيْسَ which is confined to the Perfect, the rest of them are used in the Imperfect as well as the Imperative.

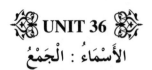

UNIT 36

الأَسْمَاءُ : الْجَمْعُ

Nouns: Plural

There are two kinds of plural nouns in Arabic: Sound and Broken.   Certain nouns take the sound plural form whilst others take the broken plural form. Nouns, which take the sound plural form, follow one of the four set patterns depending on their cases and genders. The broken plural form like the First Form verbal nouns for the formation of the plural accept various patterns which will be introduced later.   In this lesson only Sound plurals are examined.

جَمْعُ السَّالِمِ

Sound Plural

Rule No. 53

The sound plural form in the nominative case for a masculine gender is formed by adding وْنَ __ at the end in the genitive and accusative cases by adding يْنَ __ at the end.

The sound plural form in the nominative case for the feminine gender is formed by adding (‐اتٌ) (*ātun*) if the noun is indefinite and (‐اتُ) (*ātu*) if it is definite. In the genitive and accusative cases it is formed by adding (‐اتٍ) (*ātin*) if it is indefinite and (‐اتِ) (*āti*) if it is definite.

The prefixes of sound plural are as follows:

‐اتَ ، ‐اتُ ، ‐اتٌ ، ‐يْنَ ، ‐وْنَ

←

Sound Plural

	Masculine		Feminine	
	Nominative [Indefinite]	Genitive + Accusative [Indefinite]	Nominative [Indefinite]	Genitive + Accusative [Indefinite]
	مُسْلِمٌ+ـُوْنَ		مُسْلِمَةٌ + ـَاتٌ	مُسْلِمَةٌ + ـَاتٍ
	=	مُسْلِمٌ + ـِيْنَ	=	=
	مُسْلِمُونَ	=	مُسْلِمَاتٌ	مُسْلِمَات
		مُسْلِمِيْنَ		
	[Definite]	[Definite]	[Definite]	[Definite]
	الْمُسْلِمُونَ	الْمُسْلِمِيْنَ	الْمُسْلِمَةُ+ـَاتُ	الْمُسْلِمَةُ+ـَات
			=	=
			الْمُسْلِمَاتُ	الْمُسْلِمَاتِ

Note: In the above examples the letter *ta'* of *Muslimah* shall be deleted for the formation of the sound plural.

Personal Pronouns: Plural

IIIM[3+] هُمْ (they)   IIIF[3+] هُنَّ (they)

IIM[3+] أَنْتُمْ (you)   IIF[3+] أَنْتُنَّ (you)

النَّصُّ الْقُرآنِيُّ
Lesson 10

١. وَكَانَ ٱللَّهُ عَلِيمًا حَكِيمًا (170 :4)

٢. وَكَانَ ٱللَّهُ سَمِيعًا بَصِيرًا (134 :4)

٣. وَكَانَ ٱللَّهُ قَوِيًّا عَزِيزًا (25 :33)

٤. إِنَّ ٱللَّهَ كَانَ لَطِيفًا خَبِيرًا (34 :33)

٥. وَكَانَ ٱللَّهُ عَلَىٰ كُلِّ شَىْءٍ رَّقِيبًا (52 :33)

٦. وَكَانَ وَعْدُ رَبِّى حَقًّا (98 :18)

٧. مَن كَانَ يُرِيدُ ٱلْعِزَّةَ فَلِلَّهِ ٱلْعِزَّةُ جَمِيعًا (10 :35)

٨. مَّن كَانَ يُرِيدُ ثَوَابَ ٱلدُّنْيَا فَعِندَ ٱللَّهِ ثَوَابُ ٱلدُّنْيَا وَٱلْأَخِرَةِ وَكَانَ ٱللَّهُ سَمِيعًا بَصِيرًا (134 :4)

٩. يَغْفِرُ لِمَن يَشَاءُ وَيُعَذِّبُ مَن يَشَاءُ وَكَانَ ٱللَّهُ غَفُورًا رَّحِيمًا (14 :48)

١٠. كَانَ ٱلنَّاسُ أُمَّةً وَاحِدَةً (2: 213)

١١. أَلَيْسَ ٱللَّهُ بِكَافٍ عَبْدَهُ ۖ (39: 36)

١٢. أَلَيْسَ ٱلصُّبْحُ بِقَرِيبٍ (11: 81)

١٣. يَوْمَ يَكُونُ ٱلنَّاسُ كَٱلْفَرَاشِ ٱلْمَبْثُوثِ (101: 4)

١٤. وَيَقُولُ ٱلْكَافِرُ يَٰلَيْتَنِى كُنتُ تُرَٰبًا (78: 40)

١٥. وَكَانَتِ ٱمْرَأَتِى عَاقِرًا (19: 5)

١٦. وَكَانَ أَبُوهُمَا صَٰلِحًا (18: 82)

١٧. فَلَمَّا وَضَعَتْهَا قَالَتْ رَبِّ إِنِّى وَضَعْتُهَآ أُنثَىٰ وَٱللَّهُ أَعْلَمُ بِمَا وَضَعَتْ وَلَيْسَ ٱلذَّكَرُ كَٱلْأُنثَىٰ ۖ وَإِنِّى سَمَّيْتُهَا مَرْيَمَ وَإِنِّى أُعِيذُهَا بِكَ وَذُرِّيَّتَهَا مِنَ ٱلشَّيْطَٰنِ ٱلرَّجِيمِ (3: 36)

١٨. وَإِذَا سَأَلَكَ عِبَادِى عَنِّى فَإِنِّى قَرِيبٌ ۖ أُجِيبُ دَعْوَةَ ٱلدَّاعِ إِذَا دَعَانِ ۖ (2: 186)

١٩. وَهَٰذَا كِتَٰبٌ أَنزَلْنَٰهُ مُبَارَكٌ مُّصَدِّقُ ٱلَّذِى بَيْنَ يَدَيْهِ (6: 92)

٢٠. فَـَٔامَنَ لَهُۥ لُوطٌ ۘ وَقَالَ إِنِّى مُهَاجِرٌ إِلَىٰ رَبِّى ۚ إِنَّهُۥ هُوَ ٱلْعَزِيزُ ٱلْحَكِيمُ (29: 26)

٢١. وَنَادَىٰ نُوحٌ رَّبَّهُۥ فَقَالَ رَبِّ إِنَّ ٱبۡنِى مِنۡ أَهۡلِى وَإِنَّ

وَعۡدَكَ ٱلۡحَقُّ وَأَنتَ أَحۡكَمُ ٱلۡحَٰكِمِينَ (11: 45)

٢٢. مَالِ هَٰذَا ٱلۡكِتَٰبِ لَا يُغَادِرُ صَغِيرَةً وَلَا كَبِيرَةً إِلَّآ

أَحۡصَىٰهَا ۚ (18: 49)

٢٣. إِذۡ نَادَىٰ رَبَّهُۥ نِدَآءً خَفِيًّا (19: 3)

٢٤. وَنَادَىٰ فِرۡعَوۡنُ فِى قَوۡمِهِۦ قَالَ يَٰقَوۡمِ أَلَيۡسَ لِى مُلۡكُ

مِصۡرَ (43: 51)

٢٥. إِنَّ ٱلۡمُسۡلِمِينَ وَٱلۡمُسۡلِمَٰتِ وَٱلۡمُؤۡمِنِينَ

وَٱلۡمُؤۡمِنَٰتِ وَٱلۡقَٰنِتِينَ وَٱلۡقَٰنِتَٰتِ وَٱلصَّٰدِقِينَ

وَٱلصَّٰدِقَٰتِ وَٱلصَّٰبِرِينَ وَٱلصَّٰبِرَٰتِ وَٱلۡخَٰشِعِينَ

وَٱلۡخَٰشِعَٰتِ وَٱلۡمُتَصَدِّقِينَ وَٱلۡمُتَصَدِّقَٰتِ وَٱلصَّٰٓئِمِينَ

وَٱلصَّٰٓئِمَٰتِ وَٱلۡحَٰفِظِينَ فُرُوجَهُمۡ وَٱلۡحَٰفِظَٰتِ

وَٱلذَّٰكِرِينَ ٱللَّهَ كَثِيرًا وَٱلذَّٰكِرَٰتِ أَعَدَّ ٱللَّهُ لَهُم

مَّغۡفِرَةً وَأَجۡرًا عَظِيمًا (33: 35)

٢٦. ٱلصَّٰبِرِينَ وَٱلصَّٰدِقِينَ وَٱلۡقَٰنِتِينَ وَٱلۡمُنفِقِينَ

(3: 17)

٢٧. وَإِنَّكَ لَمِنَ ٱلْمُرْسَلِينَ (2: 252)

٢٨. إِنَّكَ مَيِّتٌ وَإِنَّهُم مَّيِّتُونَ (39: 30)

٢٩. وَمَا هُم بِخَٰرِجِينَ مِنَ ٱلنَّارِ (2: 167)

٣٠. وَيَتُوبَ ٱللَّهُ عَلَى ٱلْمُؤْمِنِينَ وَٱلْمُؤْمِنَٰتِ وَكَانَ ٱللَّهُ غَفُورًا

رَّحِيمًا (33: 73)

٣١. فَضَّلَ ٱللَّهُ ٱلْمُجَٰهِدِينَ بِأَمْوَٰلِهِمْ وَأَنفُسِهِمْ عَلَى

ٱلْقَٰعِدِينَ دَرَجَةً (4: 95)

٣٢. كَانَ ٱلنَّاسُ أُمَّةً وَٰحِدَةً فَبَعَثَ ٱللَّهُ ٱلنَّبِيِّۦنَ مُبَشِّرِينَ

وَمُنذِرِينَ (2: 213)

٣٣. إِنَّ ٱلصَّلَوٰةَ كَانَتْ عَلَى ٱلْمُؤْمِنِينَ كِتَٰبًا مَّوْقُوتًا (4: 103)

٣٤. إِنَّا لِلَّهِ وَإِنَّا إِلَيْهِ رَٰجِعُونَ (2: 156)

٣٥. إِنَّا نَحْنُ نَزَّلْنَا عَلَيْكَ ٱلْقُرْءَانَ تَنزِيلًا (76: 23)

٣٦. تَنزِيلُ ٱلْكِتَٰبِ لَا رَيْبَ فِيهِ مِن رَّبِّ ٱلْعَٰلَمِينَ (32: 2)

٣٧. وَتِلْكَ ٱلْأَيَّامُ نُدَاوِلُهَا بَيْنَ ٱلنَّاسِ (3: 140)

٣٨. لَا يُغَادِرُ صَغِيرَةً وَلَا كَبِيرَةً إِلَّآ أَحْصَىٰهَا ۚ وَوَجَدُواْ مَا عَمِلُواْ حَاضِرًا ۗ وَلَا يَظْلِمُ رَبُّكَ أَحَدًا (18: 49)

٣٩. وَٱلسَّـٰبِقُونَ ٱلسَّـٰبِقُونَ ۞ أُوْلَـٰٓئِكَ ٱلْمُقَرَّبُونَ (56: 10- 11)

٤٠. إِنَّ ٱللَّهَ لَا يَظْلِمُ ٱلنَّاسَ شَيْئًا وَلَـٰكِنَّ ٱلنَّاسَ أَنفُسَهُمْ يَظْلِمُونَ (10: 44)

٤١. إِنَّ ٱلْحَسَنَـٰتِ يُذْهِبْنَ ٱلسَّيِّـَٔاتِ (11: 114)

٤٢. لِلَّذِينَ أَحْسَنُواْ فِى هَـٰذِهِ ٱلدُّنْيَا حَسَنَةٌ ۗ (39: 10)

٤٣. ٱلتَّـٰٓئِبُونَ ٱلْعَـٰبِدُونَ ٱلْحَـٰمِدُونَ ٱلسَّـٰٓئِحُونَ ٱلرَّٰكِعُونَ ٱلسَّـٰجِدُونَ ٱلْأَٰمِرُونَ بِٱلْمَعْرُوفِ وَٱلنَّاهُونَ عَنِ ٱلْمُنكَرِ (9: 112)

٤٤. لَّقَدْ كَانَ لَكُمْ فِى رَسُولِ ٱللَّهِ أُسْوَةٌ حَسَنَةٌ لِّمَن كَانَ يَرْجُواْ ٱللَّهَ وَٱلْيَوْمَ ٱلْأَخِرَ (33: 21)

لَطِيفٌ	most subtle	غَادَرَ / يُغَادِرُ	III to leave, to leave behind
خَبِيرٌ	the ever aware	أَحْصَى / يُحْصِي	IV to count
رَقِيبٌ	[AP] watcher	نَادَى/يُنَادِي	to call
وَعْدٌ	promise	نِدَاءٌ	[VN³] call, cry
أَرَادَ/ يُرِيدُ	to desire	خَفِيٌّ	secret
لَيْسَ	not	قَانِتٌ	[AP] devout
قَرِيبٌ	near	صُبْحٌ	morning
كَافٍ	[AP] sufficient	صَابِرٌ	[AP] patient
فَرَاشٌ	moths, butterflies	خَاشِعٌ	[AP] humble, submissive
مَبْثُوثٌ	[PP] scattered	فَرْجٌ ج فُرُوجٌ	[VN] chastity (private part)
تُرَابٌ	soil, earth	أَعَدَّ / يُعِدُّ	IV to prepare, to make ready
ذُرِّيَّةٌ	progeny	مُنْفِقٌ	[AP⁴] one who spends
عَاقِرٌ	barren	مُرْسَلٌ	[PP⁴] sent (messenger)
أَعَاذَ / يُعِيذُ	IV to seek refuge	مَيِّتٌ	[AP] dead
أَجَابَ / يُجِيبُ	IV to answer	قَاعِدٌ	[AP] sitting
مُبَارَكٌ	[PP³] blessed	مَوْقُوتٌ	[PP] appointed, fixed, set (time)
مُهَاجِرٌ	[AP³] emigrant	فَضَّلَ/يُفَضِّلُ	II to cause to excel

349

حَاكِمٌ	[AP] judge	دَاوَلَ / يُدَاوِلُ	III to be in rotation, to change
مُجَاهِدٌ	[AP³] struggler	مُقَرَّبٌ	[AP] one who praises
حَاضِرٌ	[AP] present	سَائِحٌ	[AP] constant fasting
سَابِقٌ	[AP] antecedent, foregoing	رَاكِعٌ	[AP] bowing
مُقَرَّبٌ	[AP²] close companion	سَاجِدٌ	[AP] prostrating
أُسْوَةٌ	example, model, pattern		

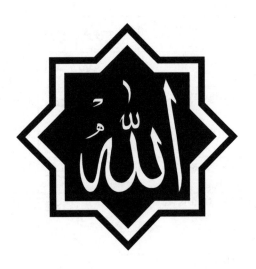

METHOD OF TEACHING
LESSON 10

1. Repeat steps 6 - 8 for the introduction of the Third derived form فَاعَلَ mentioned in the Method of Teaching Lesson 9.

2. For example analysis it is always better to use the overhead projector and a pointer for highlighting key words and phrases.

3. Ask the students to construct sentences using (كَانَ) with the Imperfect to give the meaning of the Past continuous.

4. Present the Arabic text on columns الألف and الباء on the overhead projector and take the following steps.

   (i) Cover the column الباء completely

   (ii) Highlight the subjects and predicate. At this stage it is easy for the students to recognise them.

   (iii) Cover the area up to the subjects of the column الباء

   making visible only predicate and ask the students to read what remains.

   (iv) Cover only *kāna* and its sisters.

   (v) Shift the sheet which covers *kāna* and its sisters making visible the first sentence and only indicating the effect of *kāna* on its predicate and ask the students to read this. Likewise gradually make all the sentences visible.

5. With the use of the two columns one for the nouns and the other for the additions on the magnetic board and overhead projector sound plurals can be effectively taught.

6. Assist the students to construct sound plurals by providing them with appropriate nouns, cases and genders.

7. Display the sound plural table on sound plural the overhead projector and with a pointer to highlight the variations.

351

Accusative	Genitive	Nominative		
مُسْلِماً	مُسْلِمٍ	مُسْلِمٌ	Singular	
مُسْلِمَيْن	مُسْلِمَيْن	مُسْلِمَان	Dual	
مُسْلِمِين	مُسْلِمِين	مُسْلِمُوْنَ	Plural	MASCULINE
الْمُسْلِمِين	الْمُسْلِمِين	الْمُسْلِمُوْنَ	Plural (Definite)	
مُسْلِمَةً	مُسْلِمَةٍ	مُسْلِمَةٌ	Singular	
مُسْلِمَتَيْن	مُسْلِمَتَيْن	مُسْلِمَتَان	Dual	
مُسْلِمَات	مُسْلِمَات	مُسْلِمَاتٌ	Plural	FEMININE
الْمُسْلِمَات	الْمُسْلِمَات	الْمُسْلِمَاتُ	Plural (Definite)	

Genitive	Accusative	Nominative			
ـٍ	ـاً	ـٌ	مُسْلِم	Singular	
ـَيْن	ـَيْن	ـَان	مُسْلِم +	Dual	
ـِيْن	ـِيْن	ـُوْنَ	مُسْلِم +	Plural	MASCULINE
ـِيْن	ـِيْن	ـُوْنَ	الْمُسْلِم +	Plural (Definite)	
ـٍ	ـً	ـٌ	مُسْلِمَة	Singular	
ـَيْن	ـَيْن	ـَان	+ مُسْلِمَة*	Dual	
ـَات	ـَات	ـَاتٌ	+ مُسْلِمَة**	Plural	FEMININE
ـَات	ـَات	ـَاتُ	+الْمُسْلِمَة**	Plural (Definite)	

NOTES:

* :- replace ' ة ' by ' ت '

** :- delete ' ة '

Lesson 10

Exercise No. 29

(1) Select the correct word(s) from the parenthesis to fill in the blanks in the following sentences.

(١)   أَرَأَيْتَ الظَّالِمَ الَّذى .... الإِنْسَانَ.

(يَنْصُرُ، يَفُوزُ، يُكَرِّمُ، يَظْلِمُ)

(٢)   الْمُسَافِرُ مَنْ .... مِنْ بَلَدٍ إِلَى بَلَدٍ.

(يُصَالِحُ، يَكْفُرُ، يَعْدِلُ، يُسَافِرُ)

(٣)   الْعَالِمُ حَيٌّ لاَ يَمُوتُ ....

(بِالْكَذِب، بِالْحُسْنِ، بِالنِّفَاقِ، بِالْمَوْت)

(٤)   الْكَافِرُونَ .... بِاللهِ وَ الْمُؤْمِنُونَ يُؤْمِنُونَ بِاللهِ.

(يَتَقَرَّبُونَ، يَكْفُرُونَ، يَصْدُقُونَ)

(٥)   .... الْمُسْلِمَات لَفَائِزَاتٌ.

(كَانَ، صَارَ، رَبَّاتُ، إِنَّ)

(٦)   اَلْأَبُ .... تَدْرِيسَ الْقُرْآن.

(يُحِبُّ، يَكْذِبُ، يَفُوزُ، يَقْرَأُ)

(٧)   الرَّجُلُ الْقَوِيُّ خَيْرٌ مِنَ الرَّجُلِ ....

(جَمِيْلٌ، صَادِقاً، الضَّعِيْف)

(٨)   الْمُنَافِقُونَ يَأْمُرُونَ ....

(بِالْمَعْرُوف، بِالإِصْلاَحِ، بِالْمُنْكَرِ، بِالْخَيْرِ)

السَّمَاءُ .... اْلأَرْضِ وَ اْلأَرْضُ .... السَّمَاءِ.

(فَوْقَ، تَحْتَ، مَعَ، أَمَامَ، خَلْفَ، قَبْلَ، بَعْدَ)

(٩)   هَذِهِ الْبِنْتُ .... أُمٌّ.

(صَالِحٌ، كَبِيرٌ، الْجَمِيلَةُ، الْقَصِيرُ)

(١٠)   أَنَا .... اللهَ وَ رَسُولَهُ (ﷺ) وَ لاَ أَعْصِيهِمَا.

(نُطِيعُ، أُطِيعُ، يُطِيعُ، أَطَعْتَ)

(١١)   .... الْمَرِيضَةُ ضَعِيفَةً.

(كَانَ، بَاتَ، أَضْحَى، صَارَتْ)

(١٢)   إِنَّ اللهَ لاَ يُحِبُّ الَّذِينَ يَكْذِبُونَ وَ ..... فِي الأَرْضِ.

(يُصْلِحُونَ، يُفْسِدُونَ، يَعْبُدُونَ)

(2) Put *irāb*.

(١)   هل تسافر من لندن إلى مكة للحج؟

(٢)   أنا أحب المجاهد لأنه يجاهد في سبيل الله.

(٣)   هما طالبان يسافران من بلد إلى بلد.

(٤)   كان الرسول (ﷺ) يحب الله حبا شديدا.

(٥)   كان إبراهيم (عليه السلام) رسولا صادقا.

(٦)   إن المؤمنين والمؤمنات لهم الجنة العالية جزاء في الآخرة.

(3) Give the perfect, the Imperfect, the Verbal Noun, the Active Participle and the Passive Participle for the Third Derived Form from the following roots.

(١)   حَفظَ (٢) سَفَرَ (٣) بَرَكَ (٤) شَرِكَ (٥) قَتَلَ

(4) Translate the following sentences into Arabic.

1. Allah loves the *Jihād* waged for the truth.
2. The travellers (M^{3+}) are truthful.
3. He was mislead then Allah guided him.
4. The corrupt woman by the grace of Allah became reformer.
5. Ismael was the son of Abraham and both were messengers (peace be upon them).
6. Two virtuous men are helping each other in kindness.
7. Verily Allah loves the truthful men and truthful women.
8. We are the worshippers and reformers.
9. The patient men and the patient women are successful.
10. The fasting women are truthful.

(5) From the Qur'ānic text of Lesson 10 identify the following:

(a) Derived Forms.
(b) Sound plurals (SP)

355

قُوٓا أَنفُسَكُمْ وَأَهْلِيكُمْ نَارًا 66:6

356

UNIT 37

(١) اللهُ هُوَ الَّذِي أَنْزَلَ الْقُرْآنَ وَ فِيهِ هُدًى لِلنَّاسِ.

(٢) الْمُسْلِمُ يَشْهَدُ أَنَّ اللهَ وَاحِدٌ وَ أَنَّ مُحَمَّداً رَسُولُ اللهِ (ﷺ).

(٣) الْمُنَادِي يُنَادِي لِلْحَقِّ فَلِمَاذَا أَنْتُم غَافِلُونَ، وَ لِمَاذَا لَا تَفْعَلُونَ الْخَيْرَ لَعَلَّكُمْ تُفْلِحُونَ.

(٤) الْكَافِرُونَ يَكْفُرُونَ بِاللهِ وَ الْمُؤْمِنُونَ يُؤْمِنُونَ بِاللهِ وَ هُمْ لَيْسُوا بِكَاذِبِينَ.

(٥) هَلْ أَنْتُمْ تَعْلَمُونَ مَا تَفْعَلُونَ؟

(٦) نَحْنُ نَدْرُسُ لُغَةَ الْقُرْآنِ الْكَرِيمِ وَنَعْلَمُ مَا نَفْعَلُ.

(٧) هَلْ هُنَّ مُنَافِقَاتٌ؟

نَعَمْ، هُنَّ مُنَافِقَاتٌ لِأَنَّهُنَّ نَافَقْنَ.

(٨) هَلْ عَمِلْتُنَّ عَمَلاً صَالِحاً لِوَجْهِ اللهِ؟

نَعَمْ، عَمِلْنَا عَمَلاً صَالِحاً لِوَجْهِ اللهِ.

(٩) الْكَافِرُونَ يَظُنُّونَ أَنَّهُمْ نَاجِحُونَ فِي الدُّنْيَا.

(١٠) كَانَ الْكَافِرُونَ يَعْصُونَ اللهَ وَ يَقْتُلُونَ الْمُرْسَلِينَ.

357

(١١) إِنَّ الَّذِينَ جَاهَدُوا سَيَهْدِيهِمُ اللهُ سَبِيلَهُ وَ إِنَّ اللهَ لَمَعَ الْمُحْسِنِينَ.

(١٢) ﴿إِنَّ الْمَوْتَ الَّذِي تَفِرُّونَ مِنْهُ فَإِنَّهُ مُلَاقِيكُمْ﴾

(١٣) الْمَوْتُ حَقٌّ فَلَا يَنْفَعُكُمُ الْفِرَارُ مِنْهُ شَيْئاً.

(١٤) الْمُؤْمِنُونَ يَأْمُرُونَ بِالْمَعْرُوفِ وَ يَنْهَوْنَ عَنِ الْمُنْكَرِ وَ يُسَارِعُونَ فِي الْخَيْرَاتِ.

(١٥) الْمُنَافِقُونَ يَأْمُرُونَ بِالْمُنْكَرِ وَ يَنْهَوْنَ عَنِ الْمَعْرُوفِ وَ يُسَارِعُونَ فِي السَّيِّئَاتِ.

(١٦) إِنَّ اللهَ لَا يُحِبُّ الَّذِينَ يَكْذِبُونَ وَ يُفْسِدُونَ فِي الْأَرْضِ بَعْدَ إِصْلَاحِهَا.

(١٧) أُولَئِكَ الْمُسْلِمُونَ لَا يَعْلَمُونَ شَيْئاً فَهُمْ جَاهِلُونَ.

(١٨) هَؤُلَاءِ الْمُنَافِقُونَ يُفَرِّقُونَ بَيْنَ الْمُسْلِمِينَ وَ يُحِبُّونَ الْفَسَادَ وَ الْعُدْوَانَ.

(١٩) نَحْنُ نُكْرِمُ الْمُعَلِّمَ وَ نُعَظِّمُهُ وَ نُحِبُّهُ.

(٢٠) تَكْرِيمُ الْمُعَلِّمِ وَ تَعْظِيمُهُ وَاجِبٌ عَلَيْنَا.

(٢١) قَالَ الشَّاعِرُ :

(٢٢) قُمْ لِلْمُعَلِّمِ وَفِّــهِ * تَبْجِيــلاً
كَادَ الْمُعَلِّمُ أَنْ يَكُونَ رَسُــوْلاً

---

* See rule no. 77.

(١) الْمُؤْمِنُونَ يَقْرَؤُونَ الْقُرْآنَ وَ يَتَدَبَّرُونَ فِي آيَاتِهِ.

(٢) الْقُرْآنُ يَأْمُرُ الْإِنْسَانَ بِتَدَبُّرِ آيَاتِهِ.

(٣) الرَّجُلُ يَتَقَرَّبُ إِلَى اللهِ بِالْعَمَلِ الصَّالِحِ.

(٤) نَحْنُ نَتَفَكَّرُ فِي خَلْقِ اللهِ.

(٥) زَيْدٌ مُتَوَكِّلٌ عَلَى اللهِ.

(٦) يُيَسِّرُ اللهُ عَمَلَ الْمُتَوَكِّلِ الصَّادِقِ وَ يُعْطِيهِ طُمَأْنِينَةً فِي الْقَلْبِ.

(٧) قُمْتُ فِي اللَّيْلِ فَتَوَضَّأْتُ وَ صَلَّيْتُ، وَ بَعْدَ الصَّلَاةِ دَعَوْتُ اللهَ دُعَاءً طَوِيلاً.

(٨) النِّسَاءُ تَوَضَّأْنَ وَ صَلَّيْنَ فِي بُيُوتِهِنَّ.

(٩) قَالَ رَسُولُ اللهِ (ﷺ):

"خَيْرُكُمْ مَنْ تَعَلَّمَ الْقُرْآنَ وَ عَلَّمَهُ"

(١٠) "كُلُّكُمْ رَاعٍ وَ كُلُّكُمْ مَسْؤُولٌ عَنْ رَعِيَّتِهِ".

(١١) "مَنْ تَشَبَّهَ بِقَوْمٍ فَهُوَ مِنْهُمْ".

(١٢) "الْمُسْلِمُ مَنْ سَلِمَ الْمُسْلِمُونَ مِنْ لِسَانِهِ وَ يَدِهِ".

(١٣) "لَيْسَ الشَّدِيدُ بِالصُّرَعَةِ إِنَّمَا الشَّدِيدُ مَنْ يَمْلِكُ نَفْسَهُ عِنْدَ الْغَضَبِ".

(١٤) "إِنَّ الْمَاهِرَ بِالْقُرْآنِ مَعَ السَّفَرَةِ الْكِرَامِ الْبَرَرَةِ".

(١٥) "خَيْرُكُمْ خَيْرُكُمْ لِأَهْلِهِ وَ أَنَا خَيْرُكُمْ لِأَهْلِي".

(١٦) تَعْلِيمُ الْمُتَعَلِّمِ طَرِيقُ التَّعَلُّمِ. "م"

(١٧) الْعَالِمُ وَ الْمُتَعَلِّمُ شَرِيكَانِ فِي الْخَيْرِ. "م"

(١٨) الْعَاقِلُ مَنْ كَلاَمُهُ قَلِيلٌ وَ عَمَلُهُ كَثِيرٌ. "م"

(١٩) مَنْ غَابَ خَابَ. "م"

(٢٠) لِكُلِّ قَدِيمٍ حُرْمَةٌ. "م"

(٢١) الْكِبْرُ قَائِدُ الْبُغْضِ. "م"

(٢٢) الْغَيْرَةُ مِنَ الإِيمَانِ. "م"

(٢٣) دَوَاءُ الدَّهْرِ الصَّبْرُ عَلَيْهِ. "م"

(٢٤) الْحُرُّ تَكْفِيهِ الإِشَارَةُ. "م"

(٢٥) خَيْرُ النَّاسِ لِلنَّاسِ خَيْرُهُمْ لِنَفْسِهِ. "م"

تَشَبَّهَ / يَتَشَبَّهُ	V to imitate, to copy	مُنَادٍ	[AP³] herald, crier
شَدِيدٌ	strong, powerful, forceful	عُدْوَانٌ	[VN] enmity, hostility
صُرَعَةٌ	[VN] wrestling	تَكْرِيمٌ	[VN²] honouring
غَضَبٌ	[VN] anger	وَاجِبٌ (عَلَى)	obligatory
مَاهِرٌ	[AP] skillful	تَدَبَّرَ / يَتَدَبَّرُ	V to reflect, to ponder
سَفَرَةٌ	literally journey, travel (angels)	تَدَبُّرٌ	[VN⁵] reflection
بَرَرَةٌ	reverent, dutiful	آيَةٌ ج آيَاتٌ	verse, sign
تَعْلِيمٌ	[VN²] education, teaching	تَقَرَّبَ / يَتَقَرَّبُ	V to come close, to get close to someone
مُتَعَلِّمٌ	[AP⁵] student	تَعَبَّدَ / يَتَعَبَّدُ	V to worship
غَابَ / يَغِيبُ	to be or to remain absent	إِسَاءَةٌ	[VN] offense, sin, insult
خَابَ / يَخِيبُ	to be unsuccessful, to be disappointed	تَفَكَّرَ / يَتَفَكَّرُ	V to reflect, to meditate
قَدِيمٌ	old	مُتَوَكِّلٌ	[AP⁵ one who relies
كِبْرٌ	pride	يَسَّرَ / يُيَسِّرُ	II to make easy
قَائِدٌ	leader	طُمَأْنِينَةٌ	tranquillity

361

تَوَضَّأَ / يَتَوَضَّأُ	V to perform ablution (*wuḍū*)	بُغْضٌ	hatred, hate
تَعَلَّمَ / يَتَعَلَّمُ	V to learn, to study	غَيْرَةٌ	self respect
رَاعٍ	[AP]shepherd, herdsman	دَوَاءٌ	remedy, medicine
مَسْؤُولٌ	[PP] questioned	رَعِيَّةٌ	herd, flock

إِنَّمَا يَخْشَى ٱللَّهَ مِنْ عِبَادِهِ ٱلْعُلَمَٰٓؤُاْ 35:28

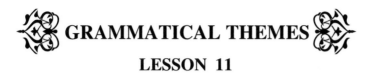

GRAMMATICAL THEMES
LESSON 11
UNIT 37

الأَفْعَالُ: الْجَمْعُ

Verbs: Plural

Formation

Perfect

Rule No. 54

When [وْا -ُ] is suffixed to the root it forms III M^{3+} and
when [نَ -ْ] is suffixed it forms III F^{3+}.

فَعَلُوا = فَعَلَ -ُ + وْا   III M^{3+} (they did)

فَعَلْنَ = فَعَلَ -ْ + نَ   III F^{3+} (they did)

Rule No. 55

When [تُمْ] is suffixed to the root it forms II M^{3+} and when
[تُنَّ] is suffixed it forms II F^{3+}.

فَعَلْتُمْ = فَعَلَ + تُمْ   II M^{3+} (you did)

فَعَلْتُنَّ = فَعَلَ + تُنَّ   II F^{3+} (you did)

(See TA under III M^{3+} F^{3+}; II M^{3+} F^{3+})

Imperfect:

Rule No. 56

When [نَ وْ ُ-] suffixed to III M^1 of the Imperfect it forms III M^{3+} and when [نَ ْ-] is suffixed it forms III F^{3+}.

يَفْعَلُوْنَ = يَفْعَلُ + ُ- وْ نَ   III M^{3+} (they are doing)

يَفْعَلْنَ = يَفْعَلُ + ْ- نَ   III F^{3+} (they are doing)

Rule No. 57

When [نَ وْ ُ-] is suffixed to II M^1 it forms II M^3+ and when [نَ ْ-] is suffixed it forms II F^3+.

تَفْعَلُوْنَ = تَفْعَلُ + ُ- وْ نَ   II M^{3+} (you are doing)

تَفْعَلْنَ = تَفْعَلُ + ْ- نَ   II F^{3+} (you are doing)

(See TA under III M^{3+} F^{3+}; II M^{3+} F^{3+}).

Example Analysis:

هَلْ عَمِلْتُنَّ عَمَلاً صَالِحاً لِوَجْهِ اللهِ؟

Did you [women] do virtuous deeds for the sake of Allah?

عَمِلْتُنَّ is the Perfect II F^{3+}

عَمَلاً is a Verbal Noun from عَمِلَ . It is a qualifying noun and the object, therefore it is in the accusative case.

لِ is a preposition.

وَجْه is in the genitive case because it is preceded by the preposition (لِ). It is the first noun of a 'construct phrase'.

اللهِ is the second noun of the 'construct phrase' therefore, it is definite and in the genitive case.

الْكَافِرُوْنَ يَكْفُرُوْنَ بِاللهِ وَالْمُؤْمِنُوْنَ يُؤْمِنُوْنَ بِاللهِ وَهُمْ لَيْسُوْا بِكَاذِبِيْنَ.

The disbelievers disbelieve in Allah and the believers believe in Allah and they are not liars.

الْكَافِرُوْنَ is the sound plural of the Active Participle in the nominative case.

يَكْفُرُوْنَ is the Imperfect III M^{3+}.

الْمُؤْمِنُوْنَ is the sound plural of the Active Participle of the Fourth Form آمَنَ. It is in the nominative case.

لَيْسُوْا is the Perfect III M^{3+}.

بِ is the preposition.

كَاذِبِيْنَ is the Active Participle sound plural (APM^{3+}). It is in the genitive case.

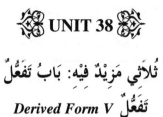

UNIT 38

ثُلاَثِيٌّ مَزِيدٌ فِيهِ: بَابُ تَفَعَّلَ
Derived Form V تَفَعَّلَ

Formation:

Perfect:

The Fifth derived Form is formed from the Second derived Form فَعَّلَ by prefixing تَ: تَفَعَّلَ

The other conjugations in the Perfect Indicative follow the pattern تَفَعَّلَ and their endings remain the same as for the Perfect in the First Form.

(See TC under V)

Imperfect:

The formation of the Imperfect is based on the III M[1] pattern يَتَفَعَّلُ. All prefixes and endings remain the same as in the First Form. (See TD under V)

Verbal Nouns:

The Verbal Noun is formed on the pattern of تَفَعُّلٌ. The Verbal Noun for تَطَوَّعَ (to do voluntarily) is تَطَوُّعٌ(voluntariness).

Active Participle:

The Active Participle is formed on the pattern of مُتَفَعِّل /

مُتَطَوِّعٌ (volunteer)

Passive Participle:

The Passive Participle is formed on the pattern of مُتَفَعَّل/

مُتَطَوَّعٌ (volunteered)

(For Verbal Nouns, and the Active and Passive Participles see
TB under V)

Significances: Derived Form V

(a) The Fifth derived Form expresses "the state into which the
object of the action denoted by the Second Form is brought by
that action, as its effect or result."[*]

أَدَّبْتُهُ فَتَأَدَّبَ.

I educated him so he received fine education.

كَسَّرْتُ الْقَلَمَ فَتَكَسَّرَ.

I broke the pen so it was broken.

(b) Sometimes it gives the same meaning as found in the First,
the Second and Fourth Forms.

تَكَلَّمَ to speak, to talk.

تَحَدَّثَ to discuss.

---

[*] W. Wright, *A Grammar of Arabic Language*, Third Edition, Cambridge
University Press, 1985 p.36

Example Analysis:

(١) الْمُؤْمِنُوْنَ يَقْرَأُوْنَ الْقُرْآنَ وَيَتَدَبَّرُوْنَ فِي آيَاتِهِ.

The believers are reading the Qur'ān and they are reflecting on its verses.

دَبَّرَ the Second derived Form means 'to make arrangements, prepare, to plan.'

تَدَبَّرَ the Fifth derived Form means 'to be organised, to be managed, to ponder, to reflect.'

تَدَبَّرَ is the result of دَبَّرَ .

(٥) زَيْدٌ مُتَوَكِّلٌ عَلَى الله.

Zayd is relying on Allah.

مُتَوَكِّلٌ is the Active Participle from the Fifth Form تَوَكَّلَ.

١. فَعَلَى ٱللَّهِ تَوَكَّلْتُ (10: 71)

٢. إِنِّى تَوَكَّلْتُ عَلَى ٱللَّهِ رَبِّى وَرَبِّكُمْ (11: 56)

٣. وَمَا تَوْفِيقِى إِلَّا بِٱللَّهِ عَلَيْهِ تَوَكَّلْتُ وَإِلَيْهِ أُنِيبُ (11: 88)

٤. وَسِعَ رَبُّنَا كُلَّ شَىْءٍ عِلْمًا عَلَى ٱللَّهِ تَوَكَّلْنَا (7: 89)

٥. رَبَّنَا عَلَيْكَ تَوَكَّلْنَا وَإِلَيْكَ أَنَبْنَا وَإِلَيْكَ ٱلْمَصِيرُ (60: 4)

٦. ٱلَّذِينَ صَبَرُواْ وَعَلَىٰ رَبِّهِمْ يَتَوَكَّلُونَ (16: 42)

٧. وَسِعَ رَبِّى كُلَّ شَىْءٍ عِلْمًا أَفَلَا تَتَذَكَّرُونَ (6: 80)

٨. كَذَٰلِكَ يُبَيِّنُ ٱللَّهُ لَكُمُ ٱلْآيَٰتِ لَعَلَّكُمْ تَتَفَكَّرُونَ (2: 266)

٩. وَمَن تَطَوَّعَ خَيْرًا فَإِنَّ ٱللَّهَ شَاكِرٌ عَلِيمٌ (2: 158)

١٠. تَكَادُ ٱلسَّمَٰوَٰتُ يَتَفَطَّرْنَ مِنْهُ (19: 90)

369

١١. وَيَوْمَ تَقُومُ ٱلسَّاعَةُ يَوْمَئِذٍ يَتَفَرَّقُونَ (30: 14)

١٢. وَنَحْنُ نَتَرَبَّصُ بِكُمْ (9: 52)

١٣. لَا تَكَلَّمُ نَفْسٌ إِلَّا بِإِذْنِهِ (11: 105)

١٤. وَتَقَطَّعُوا أَمْرَهُم بَيْنَهُمْ كُلٌّ إِلَيْنَا رَاجِعُونَ (21: 93)

١٥. لَّا يَتَكَلَّمُونَ إِلَّا مَنْ أَذِنَ لَهُ ٱلرَّحْمَٰنُ (78: 38)

١٦. فَيَتَعَلَّمُونَ مِنْهُمَا مَا يُفَرِّقُونَ بِهِ بَيْنَ ٱلْمَرْءِ وَزَوْجِهِ (2: 102)

١٧. لَآ إِكْرَاهَ فِي ٱلدِّينِ قَد تَّبَيَّنَ ٱلرُّشْدُ مِنَ ٱلْغَيِّ (2: 256)

١٨. وَمَن تَزَكَّىٰ فَإِنَّمَا يَتَزَكَّىٰ لِنَفْسِهِ وَإِلَى ٱللَّهِ ٱلْمَصِيرُ (35: 18)

١٩. وَيَتَجَنَّبُهَا ٱلْأَشْقَى ۞ ٱلَّذِى يَصْلَى ٱلنَّارَ ٱلْكُبْرَىٰ (87: 11-12)

٢٠. فَمَن تَعَجَّلَ فِي يَوْمَيْنِ فَلَآ إِثْمَ عَلَيْهِ وَمَن تَأَخَّرَ فَلَآ إِثْمَ عَلَيْهِ (2: 203)

٢١. وَمِنَ ٱلْأَعْرَابِ مَن يَتَّخِذُ مَا يُنفِقُ مَغْرَمًا وَيَتَرَبَّصُ بِكُمُ ٱلدَّوَآئِرَ (9: 98)

٢٢. أَمْ أَنزَلْنَا عَلَيْهِمْ سُلْطَـٰنًا فَهُوَ يَتَكَلَّمُ بِمَا كَانُوا بِهِۦ يُشْرِكُونَ (30: 35)

٢٣. وَلَا يَتَمَنَّوْنَهُۥ أَبَدًۢا بِمَا قَدَّمَتْ أَيْدِيهِمْ ۚ وَٱللَّهُ عَلِيمٌۢ بِٱلظَّـٰلِمِينَ (62: 7)

٢٤. ثُمَّ يَتَوَلَّىٰ فَرِيقٌ مِّنْهُمْ وَهُم مُّعْرِضُونَ (3: 23)

٢٥. تَتَنَزَّلُ عَلَيْهِمُ ٱلْمَلَـٰٓئِكَةُ (41: 30)

٢٦. كَلَّا سَوْفَ تَعْلَمُونَ ۝ ثُمَّ كَلَّا سَوْفَ تَعْلَمُونَ (102: 3-4)

٢٧. فَكَفَرُوا بِهِ ۖ فَسَوْفَ يَعْلَمُونَ (37: 170)

٢٨. سَوْفَ تَعْلَمُونَ مَن يَأْتِيهِ عَذَابٌ يُخْزِيهِ وَمَنْ هُوَ كَـٰذِبٌ (11: 93)

٢٩. وَيُطِيعُونَ ٱللَّهَ وَرَسُولَهُۥٓ ۚ أُوْلَـٰٓئِكَ سَيَرْحَمُهُمُ ٱللَّهُ (9: 71)

٣٠. فَسَوْفَ تَعْلَمُونَ مَن تَكُونُ لَهُۥ عَـٰقِبَةُ ٱلدَّارِ (6: 135)

٣١. ٱلَّذِينَ يَجْعَلُونَ مَعَ ٱللَّهِ إِلَـٰهًا ءَاخَرَ ۚ فَسَوْفَ يَعْلَمُونَ (15: 96)

٣٢. وَسَوْفَ يَعْلَمُونَ حِينَ يَرَوْنَ ٱلْعَذَابَ (25: 42)

٣٣. وَسَوْفَ يُؤْتِ ٱللَّهُ ٱلْمُؤْمِنِينَ أَجْرًا عَظِيمًا (4: 146)

٣٤. إِنَّهُ لَكَبِيرُكُمُ ٱلَّذِى عَلَّمَكُمُ ٱلسِّحْرَ فَلَسَوْفَ تَعْلَمُونَ
(26: 49)

٣٥. فَسَتَعْلَمُونَ مَنْ هُوَ فِى ضَلَلٍ مُّبِينٍ (67: 29)

٣٦. فَسَيَرَى ٱللَّهُ عَمَلَكُمْ وَرَسُولُهُۥ وَٱلْمُؤْمِنُونَ (9: 105)

٣٧. قَالَ كَلَّآ إِنَّ مَعِىَ رَبِّى سَيَهْدِينِ (26: 62)

٣٨. وَسَيَجْزِى ٱللَّهُ ٱلشَّـٰكِرِينَ (3: 144)

٣٩. وَٱلْمُؤْمِنُونَ بِٱللَّهِ وَٱلْيَوْمِ ٱلْأَخِرِ أُوْلَـٰئِكَ سَنُؤْتِيهِمْ أَجْرًا
عَظِيمًا (4: 162)

تَوَكَّلَ / يَتَوَكَّلُ	V to put trust
تَوْفِيقٌ	[VN²] success, hope
أَنَابَ / يُنِيْبُ	IV to repent, to turn to Allah
مَصِيرٌ	[VN] return, destination
تَذَكَّرَ / يَتَذَكَّرُ	V to remember, to receive admonition
بَيَّنَ / يُبَيِّنُ	II to expound
تَفَكَّرَ/يَتَفَكَّرُ	V to reflect
تَطَوَّعَ / يَتَطَوَّعُ	V to do voluntarily something
تَفَطَّرَ / يَتَفَطَّرُ	V to be split, to be broken into pieces
كَادَ/ يَكَادُ	to be on the point
تَفَرَّقَ / يَتَفَرَّقُ	V to become scattered
سَمَاءٌ/ج سَمَاوَاتٌ	heaven
تَرَبَّصَ/ يَتَرَبَّصُ	V to wait, to watch for an opportunity

تَقَطَّعَ / يَتَقَطَّعُ	V to sever or to become severed
إِكْرَاهٌ	[VN⁴] compulsion
رُشْدٌ	[VN] rectitude, discretion
غَيٌّ	error
غَنِيٌّ	self sufficient
تَزَكَّى / يَتَزَكَّى	V to be purified, to be chastened
تَجَنَّبَ / يَتَجَنَّبُ	V to keep away
أَشْقَى	wretched, unfortunate, [elative, see Rule No. 74]
تَعَجَّلَ / يَتَعَجَّلُ	V to haste
تَأَخَّرَ / يَتَأَخَّرُ	V to delay
أَعْرَابٌ	dwellers of the desert
اتَّخَذَ / يَتَّخِذُ	VIII to take
مَغْرَمٌ	[VN] forced loan, debt that must be settled
دَائِرَةٌ ج دَوَائِرُ	turn
بَأْسٌ ج بَأْسَاءُ	terror, punishment

ضَرٌّ ج ضَرَّاءُ	hurt
تَضَرَّعَ / يَتَضَرَّعُ	V to pray with humility
حِجَارَةٌ	stone
تَمَنَّى / يَتَمَنَّى	V to wish, raise hope
مُعْرِضٌ	[AP⁴] backslider
تَنَزَّلَ / يَتَنَزَّلُ	V to come down
عَاقِبَةٌ	end, consequence
سِحْرٌ	magic
أَطَاعَ / يُطِيعُ	IV to be obedient
كَلَّا	not at all

METHOD OF TEACHING
LESSON 11

1. The formation of Plurals both in the Perfect and the Imperfect can effectively be taught by retaining the three colours for the radicals with which the students are by now familiar and by adding a fourth black colour. The overhead projector proves to be very useful for this purpose.

2. Once the students have grasped the plurals in all three persons it is important to create confidence in their use. Thus their use can be achieved by selecting at least 20 roots on cards and preparing 14 small cards for the abbreviated forms in the three persons e.g. II M^1, III M^2, III M^{3+} etc.

3. Demonstrate one root and one small card containing the abbreviation and ask the students to give you the forms in the Perfect and the Imperfect. Continue to change the small cards.

4. Ask the students to use the Plural forms in their sentences.

5. Let the students identify the Plural forms clarifying their roots from the Qur'ānic text of the lesson.

6. Repeat steps 6 - 8 for the introduction of the Fifth derived Form تَفَعَّلَ, as mentioned in the Method of Teaching Lesson 9.

376

Lesson 11

Exercise No. 30

(1) Select the correct word(s) from the parentheses to fill in the blanks in the following sentences.

(١) الْمُؤْمِنُوْنَ ..... مَا يَتَيَسَّرُ مِنَ الْقُرْآنِ الْكَرِيْمِ.
(يَعْمَلُوْنَ ، يَتْلُوْنَ ، يَفْعَلُوْنَ ، يَنْصُرُوْنَ)

(٢) نَحْنُ .... فِيْ أَمْرِ دِيْنِنَا.
(نَتَحَدَّثُ ، نَأْكُلُ ، نَشْرَبُ ، نَذْهَبُ).

(٣) .... أُولُوْا الْعِلْمِ هُمُ الْفَائِزُوْنَ.
(هُنَّ ، أُولَئِكَ ، تِلْكَ ، هَذِهِ).

(٤) إِنَّ اللهَ لَمَعَ .... وَالْمُحْسِنَاتِ وَالْقَانِتِيْنَ وَالْقَانِتَاتِ.
(الظَّالِمِيْنَ ، الظَّالِمَاتِ ، الْكَافِرِيْنَ ، الْمُحْسِنِيْنَ)

(٥) .... مَنْ تَوَكَّلَ عَلَى اللهِ.
(الْكَافِرُ ، الْمُنَافِقُ ، الْمُتَوَكِّلُ ، الظَّالِمُ)

(٦) .... إِلَى اللهِ مِفْتَاحُ الْفَلَاحِ فِي الدُّنْيَا وَالآخِرَةِ.
(التَّقَرُّبُ ، الْعِلْمُ ، النَّجَاةُ ، الْمُؤْمِنُ).

(2) Put *I'rāb*

(١) نحن توكلنا على الله الذي يعلم الغيب والشهادة.

(٢) إن الله بما تعملون عليم.

(٣) أفلا تنظرون إلى الماء الذي تشربون؟

(٤) نحن نتكلم ونتحدث في هذا الأمر.

(٥) ما لكم لا تعبدون الله الذي خلقكم؟

(٦) المؤمنون يفعلون ما يقولون.

(٧) إن الذين جاهدوا لإعلاء كلمة الحق لهم الجنة جزاء بما كانوا يفعلون.

(٨) اولئك المؤمنون يتعلمون العلم.

(٩) نحن نؤمن باله واحد ودين واحد.

(١٠) هم ليسوا متشددين في أمر دينهم.

(١١) هؤلاء المؤمنات يقرأن ويفهمن ويتدبرن القرآن الكريم.

(3) Translate into Arabic.

1. Allah the Glorified and Exalted is One and He has revealed the Qur'ān.
2. The disbelievers do not fight in the way of Allah.
3. The believing women are reading the Qur'ān and they are reflecting on its verses.
4. The respect of parents is incumbent on us.

5. I put my trust in Allah alone and I reflect over His creation.
6. The travellers (M^{3+}) performed *wuḍū* (ablution) and prayed in the mosque.
7. We stood in the night Prayer and we asked Allah for guidance in this world and the Hereafter.
8. People don't like those who speak lies and prevail corruption on earth.
9. Do you (F^{3+}) know what they (M^{3+}) are doing in the mosque?
10. They (M^{3+}) are learning the Qur'ān from the teacher.

(4) From the Qur'ānic text of Lesson 11 identify Derived forms.

"The word from a Merciful Rabb is: Peace!" It can be read from both sides. (**36**: 58)

UNIT 39

(٢) هَؤُلَاءِ مُجَاهِدُونَ.	(١) الرِّجَالُ نَائِمُونَ.
(٤) الْمُؤْمِنُونَ يُجَاهِدُونَ.	(٣) أُولَئِكَ مُؤْمِنُونَ.
(٦) نَحْنُ تَائِبُونَ.	(٥) هُمْ فَائِزُونَ.
(٨) هُنَّ طَالِبَاتٌ.	(٧) هَؤُلَاءِ عَالِمَاتٌ.
(١٠) أُولَئِكَ صَائِمَاتٌ.	(٩) أَنْتُنَّ ذَاكِرَاتٌ.
(١٢) الْمُنَافِقَاتُ كَاذِبَاتٌ.	(١١) الْأُمَّهَاتُ صَادِقَاتٌ.

(١٣) أَنْتُمْ عَالِمُونَ وَأَنْتُنَّ عَالِمَاتٌ.

UNIT 40

(٢) اَلْأَزْهَارُ جَمِيْلَةٌ.	(١) اَلْبُيُوتُ طَوِيْلَةٌ.
(٤) اَلْقُلُوبُ خَاشِعَةٌ.	(٣) اَلْأَنْهَارُ جَارِيَةٌ.
(٦) اَلْقُلُوبُ خَشَعَتْ.	(٥) اَلْوُجُوهُ ضَاحِكَةٌ.
(٨) اَلْعُيُونُ دَمَعَتْ.	(٧) اَلْآذَانُ سَمِعَتْ.

باء	ألف
(٢) قَالَتِ النِّسَاءُ.	(١) قَالَ النِّسَاءُ.
(٤) قَالَتِ الْمَلَائِكَةُ.	(٣) قَالَ الْمَلَائِكَةُ.
(٦) قَالَتِ الْقَوْمُ.	(٥) قَالَ الْقَوْمُ.
(٨) جَاءَتِ النَّاسُ.	(٧) جَاءَ النَّاسُ.

(٢) تِلْكَ بُيُوتٌ.	(١) هَذِهِ بِحَارٌ.
(٤) تِلْكَ كُتُبٌ.	(٣) هَذِهِ قُلُوبٌ.
(٦) تِلْكَ أَبْوَابٌ.	(٥) هَذِهِ وُجُوهٌ.
(٨) تِلْكَ أَنْهَارٌ.	(٧) هَذِهِ مَسَاجِدُ.

(٢) صَامَتِ الْمُؤْمِنَاتُ.	(١) سَجَدَ الْمُصَلُّونَ.
(٤) صَلَّتِ الْمُسْلِمَاتُ.	(٣) قَامَ الْعَابِدُونَ.
(٦) فَهِمَ السَّامِعُونَ.	(٥) خَسِرَ النَّائِمُونَ.
(٨) بَقِيَتِ الْجَاهِلَاتُ.	(٧) مَاتَ الْعَالِمُونَ.
(١٠) مَاتَتِ الْمُنَافِقَاتُ.	(٩) تَابَ الْمُؤْمِنُونَ.

UNIT 44

(٢) كَتَبَتِ ٱلْأَقْلَامُ.   (١) سَقَطَتِ الْكَرَاسِيُّ.

(٤) جَمُلَتِ الْوُجُوهُ.   (٣) خَشَعَتِ الْقُلُوبُ.

(٦) كَثُرَتِ الذُّنُوْبُ.   (٥) كَتَبَتِ الْأَيْدِى.

UNIT 45

(٢) لَقِيْتُ مُصْلِحِي الْبَلَدِ.   (١) مُسْلِمُو بِرِيطَانِيَا.

(٤) مُكْرِمُو الضُّيُوفِ.   (٣) ظَالِمُو الْبَلَدِ.

(٦) كُتُبُ الطُّلَّابِ.   (٥) أَقْلَامُ الْبَنَاتِ.

(٨) بَنَاتُ الْأُمَّهَاتِ.   (٧) عَالِمَاتُ الْبَلَدِ.

(١٠) بُيُوتُ الْمُؤْمِنِيْنَ.   (٩) حَسَنَاتُ الصَّالِحِيْنَ.

(١٢) أَبْنَاءٌ مُطِيعُونَ.   (١١) الرِّجَالُ الصَّائِمُونَ.

(١٤) مُجَاهِدُونَ صَابِرُونَ.   (١٣) عِبَادٌ مُكْرَمُونَ.

UNIT 46

(٢) الْكُتُبُ السَّمَاوِيَّةُ.   (١) الْأَقْلَامُ الْقَصِيْرَةُ.

(٤) اَلْأَيَّامُ الْمَاضِيَةُ.   (٣) الْآلِهَةُ الْبَاطِلَةُ.

(٦) اَلْأَنْهَارُ الْجَارِيَةُ.   (٥) عُيُونٌ نَاظِرَةٌ.

(٨) آذَانٌ سَامِعَةٌ.   (٧) وُجُوهٌ ضَاحِكَةٌ.

(١) اللهُ الَّذي خَلَقَ الإِنْسَانَ مِنْ نَفْسٍ وَاحِدَةٍ وَخَلَقَ مِنْهَا زَوْجَهَا لِيَسْكُنَ* إِلَيْهَا.

(٢) خَلَقَ اللهُ مِنْ آدَمَ وَحَوَّاءَ رِجَالاً وَنِسَاءً كَثِيرِينَ.

(٣) الَّذِينَ آمَنُوا يَخْشَعُونَ لِرَبِّهِمْ وَيَعْبُدُونَهُ فِي اللَّيْلِ وَالنَّهَارِ وَيَتَفَكَّرُونَ فِي خَلْقِ السَّمَاوَاتِ وَالْأَرْضِ.

(٤) الْمُؤْمِنُونَ يَتَوَاصَوْنَ بِالْحَقِّ وَيَتَوَاصَوْنَ بِالصَّبْرِ.

(٥) الْمُؤْمِنُونَ يُقِيمُونَ الصَّلَاةَ وَيُؤْتُونَ الزَّكَاةَ وَيُؤْمِنُونَ بِالْغَيْبِ وَيَحْكُمُونَ بِكِتَابِ اللهِ.

(٦) الْمُؤْمِنُونَ لَا يَعْلَوْنَ فِي الْأَرْضِ وَيَكْرَهُونَ الْفَسَادَ فِيهَا.

(٧) الْمُؤْمِنُونَ يَتُوبُونَ إِلَى اللهِ وَيَذْكُرُونَهُ قِيَاماً وَقُعُوداً وَعَلَى جُنُوبِهِمْ.

(٨) الْمُؤْمِنُونَ يُجَاهِدُونَ فِي سَبِيلِ اللهِ بِأَمْوَالِهِمْ وَأَنْفُسِهِمْ وَيَسْعَوْنَ لِإِعْلَاءِ كَلِمَةِ اللهِ سَعْياً كَامِلاً وَعَلَى رَبِّهِمْ يَتَوَكَّلُونَ.

(٩) الْمُؤْمِنُونَ يَتَعَاوَنُونَ عَلَى الْخَيْرِ وَلَا يَتَعَاوَنُونَ عَلَى الْإِثْمِ وَالْفَسَادِ وَالشَّرِّ وَالْعُدْوَانِ.

(١٠) الْمُؤْمِنُونَ يَخْشَوْنَ رَبَّهُمْ بِالْغَيْبِ وَيُؤْمِنُونَ أَنَّهُمْ رَاجِعُونَ إِلَيْهِ بَعْدَ الْمَوْتِ.

(١١) أُولَئِكَ لَهُمْ أَجْرٌ كَبِيرٌ وَيَدْخُلُونَ الْجَنَّةَ وَهُمْ فِيهَا خَالِدُونَ.

* See rule no. 83

(١٢) إِنَّ الْمُشْرِكِينَ يَدْعُونَ مِنْ دُونِ الله مَا لاَ يَضُرُّهُمْ وَلاَ يَنْفَعُهُمْ وَيَقُولُونَ عَلَى الله كَذِباً.

(١٣) الْمُشْرِكُونَ يَعْبُدُونَ أَهْوَاءَهُمْ وَلاَ يُؤْمِنُونَ بِالْغَيْبِ وَالرُّسُلِ وَالْكُتُبِ وَالْمَلاَئِكَةِ.

(١٤) كَيْفَ يُمْكِنُ الْجَمْعُ بَيْنَ عِبَادَةِ الله وَعِبَادَةِ الْهَوَى؟

۞ UNIT 48 ۞

(١) كَانَ رَسُولُ الله (ﷺ) يَدْعُو إِلَى سَبِيلِ رَبِّهِ بِالْحِكْمَةِ وَ كَانَ يُوصِي النَّاسَ بِالْحَقِّ وَ الْخَيْرِ.

(٢) كَانَ الرَّسُولُ (ﷺ) يَنْهَى عَنِ التَّنَازُعِ وَ التَّخَاصُمِ وَ كَانَ يَحْكُمُ بِكِتَابِ الله.

(٣) كَانَ نَبِيُّ الله (ﷺ) يَأْمُرُ النَّاسَ بِالتَّعَاوُنِ وَ التَّصَالُحِ وَ عِبَادَةِ الله الْوَاحِدِ الْقَهَّارِ.

(٤) اللهُ هُوَ الَّذِي خَلَقَ الْإِنْسَانَ مِنَ الْأَرْضِ ثُمَّ يُعِيدُهُ فِيهَا ثُمَّ يُخْرِجُهُ مِنْهَا إِخْرَاجاً.

(٥) إِنَّ اللهَ تَبَارَكَ وَ تَعَالَى هُوَ الَّذِي خَلَقَ كُلَّ شَيْءٍ فَأَحْسَنَ خَلْقَهُ.

(٦) اَلْأَوْلاَدُ الصَّالِحُونَ يُطِيعُونَ اللهَ وَ الرَّسُولَ وَ يُطِيعُونَ آبَاءَهُمْ وَ أُمَّهَاتِهِمْ فِيمَا لَيْسَ فِيهِ مَعْصِيَةٌ رَبِّهِمْ.

(٧) اَلْأَبْنَاءُ الصَّالِحُونَ لَا يَقُولُونَ لِآبَائِهِمْ وَ أُمَّهَاتِهِمْ أُفٍّ وَ لَا يَنْهَرُونَهُمْ.

قَالَ رَسُولُ اللهِ (ﷺ):

(٨) اَلْمُسْلِمُ مَنْ سَلِمَ الْمُسْلِمُونَ مِنْ لِسَانِه وَ يَدِه.

(٩) إِنَّ اللهَ لَا يَنْظُرُ إِلَى صُوَرِكُمْ وَ أَمْوَالِكُمْ وَ لَكِنْ يَنْظُرُ إِلَى قُلُوبِكُمْ وَ أَعْمَالِكُمْ.

(١٠) اَلسَّاعِي عَلَى الْأَرْمَلَةِ وَ الْمِسْكِينِ كَالسَّاعِي فِي سَبِيلِ اللهِ.

(١١) مَنْ أَنْظَرَ مُعْسِراً أَوْ وَضَعَ عَنْهُ أَنْجَاهُ اللهُ مِنْ كُرَبِ يَوْمِ الْقِيَامَة.

(١٢) مَنْ يَضْمَنْ* لِي مَا بَيْنَ لَحْيَيْهِ وَ مَا بَيْنَ رِجْلَيْهِ أَضْمَنْ لَهُ الْجَنَّةَ.

(١٣) خَيْرُ الْأُمُورِ أَوْسَطُهَا.

(١٤) لَا يُصِيبُ الْمُؤْمِنَ شَوْكَةٌ فَمَا فَوْقَهَا إِلَّا رَفَعَهُ اللهُ بِهَا دَرَجَةً وَ حَطَّ عَنْهُ سَيِّئَةً.

(١٥) لَيْسَ الْمُؤْمِنُ بِالَّذِي يَشْبَعُ وَ جَارُهُ جَائِعٌ إِلَى جَنْبِهِ.

(١٦) إِنَّمَا الْأَعْمَالُ بِالنِّيَّات.

(١٧) لَوْ كَانَ لِابْنِ آدَمَ وَادِيَانِ مِنْ ذَهَبٍ لَابْتَغَى² ثَالِثَهُمَا.

(١٨) مِنْ حُسْنِ إِسْلَامِ الْمَرْءِ تَرْكُهُ مَا لَا يَعْنِيه.

(١٩) اَلدِّينُ النَّصِيحَةُ، لِلَّهِ، وَ لِكِتَابِهِ، وَ لِرَسُولِهِ، وَ لِأَئِمَّةِ الْمُسْلِمِينَ وَ عَامَّتِهِمْ.

* See rule no 73

(٢٠) النِّكَاحُ مِنْ سُنَّتِي فَمَنْ رَغِبَ عَنْ سُنَّتِي فَلَيْسَ مِنِّي.

(٢١) إِيَّاكُمْ وَالْحَسَدَ إِنَّ الْحَسَدَ يَأْكُلُ الْحَسَنَاتِ كَمَا تَأْكُلُ النَّارُ الْحَطَبَ.

(٢٢) إِذَا مَاتَ الْمَيِّتُ قَالَتِ الْمَلَائِكَةُ مَا قَدَّمَ وقَالَ بَنُوْ آدَمَ مَا خَلَّفَ.

(٢٣) تَعْدِلُ بَيْنَ اثْنَيْنِ صَدَقَةٌ وتُعِينُ الرَّجُلَ فِي دَابَّتِه فَتَحْمِلُهُ عَلَيْهَا وتَرْفَعُ لَهُ عَلَيْهَا مَتَاعَهُ صَدَقَةٌ وَالْكَلِمَةُ الطَّيِّبَةُ صَدَقَةٌ وبِكُلِّ خُطْوَةٍ تَمْشِيهَا إِلَى الصَّلَاةِ صَدَقَةٌ وتُمِيطُ الْأَذَى عَنِ الطَّرِيقِ صَدَقَةٌ.

(٢٤) لَا يَدْخُلُ الْجَنَّةَ مَنْ كَانَ فِي قَلْبِه مِثْقَالُ ذَرَّةٍ مِنْ كِبْرٍ. فَقَالَ رَجُلٌ: إِنَّ الرَّجُلَ يُحِبُّ أَنْ يَكُونَ ثَوْبُهُ حَسَنًا وَنَعْلُهُ حَسَنَةً قَالَ: إِنَّ اللهَ جَمِيلٌ يُحِبُّ الْجَمَالَ، الْكِبَرُ بَطْرُ الْحَقِّ وَغَمْطُ النَّاسِ.

◈

(٢٥) فِي سَعَةِ الْأَخْلَاقِ كُنُوزُ الْأَرْزَاقِ. "م"

(٢٦) بِئْسَ الشِّعَارُ الْحَسَدُ. "م"

(٢٧) الْحِقْدُ شَرُّ الْخِصَالِ. "م"

(٢٨) إِذَا تَخَاصَمَ اللِّصَّانِ ظَهَرَ الْمَسْرُوقُ. "م"

(٢٩) مَنْ أَدَّبَ أَوْلَادَهُ أَرْغَمَ حُسَّادَهُ. "م"

(٣٠) التَّوَاضُعُ شَبَكَةُ الشَّرَفِ. "م"

(٣١) مَنْ تَرَكَ الشَّهَوَاتِ عَاشَ حُرّاً. "م"

(٣٢) فِي بَعْضِ الْقُلُوبِ عُيُونٌ. "م"

(٣٣) النَّاسُ أَعْدَاءُ مَا جَهِلُوا. "م"

(٣٤) تُعَاشِرُوا كَالإِخْوَانِ وتَعَامَلُوا كَالأَجَانِبِ. "م"

(٣٥) مَنْ طَلَبَ العُلَا سَهِرَ اللَّيَالِي. "م"

(٣٦) مَنْ كَثُرَ كَلَامُهُ كَثُرَتْ أَخْطَاؤُهُ. "م"

(٣٧) تُعَاشِروا كَالإِخْوَانِ وتُعَامِلُوا كَالأَجَانِبِ. "م"

(٣٨) إِذَا شَاوَرْتَ العَاقِلَ صَارَ عَقْلُهُ لَكَ. "م"

"And the servants of the Merciful are those who walk upon the earth modestly and when the ignorant address them, they say: 'Peace'." (**25**: 63)

GLOSSARY
LESSON 12

رَجُلٌ / ج رِجَالٌ	man
بَيْتٌ / ج بُيُوتٌ	house
زَهْرَةٌ / ج أَزْهَارٌ	flower
نَهْرٌ / ج أَنْهَارٌ	river
قَلْبٌ / ج قُلُوبٌ	heart
خَشَعَ / يَخْشَعُ	to be humble
أُذُنٌ / ج آذَانٌ	ear
عَيْنٌ / ج عُيُونٌ	eye
دَمَعَ / يَدْمَعُ	to water (eye)
نِسَاءٌ	women
مَلَكٌ / مَلَائِكَةٌ	angel
قَوْمٌ / ج أَقْوَامٌ	people, nation
بَحْرٌ / ج بِحَارٌ	sea
كِتَابٌ / ج كُتُبٌ	book
وَجْهٌ / ج وُجُوهٌ	face
بَابٌ / ج أَبْوَابٌ	door
مَسْجِدٌ / ج مَسَاجِدُ	mosque
كُرْسِيٌّ / ج كَرَاسِيّ	chair
قَلَمٌ / ج أَقْلَامٌ	pen

يَدٌ / ج أَيْدٍ	hand
ذَنْبٌ / ج ذُنُوبٌ	sin
بِنْتٌ / ج بَنَاتٌ	girl
طَالِبٌ / ج طُلَّابٌ	[AP] student
ابْنٌ / ج أَبْنَاءٌ	son
ضَيْفٌ / ضُيُوفٌ	guest
	slave, servant
عَبْدٌ / ج عِبَادٌ	
	god
إِلَهٌ / ج آلِهَةٌ	
	day
يَوْمٌ / ج أَيَّامٌ	
سَكَنَ / يَسْكُنُ	to become tranquil, to be peaceful
تَوَاصَى / يَتَوَاصَى	VI to admonish each other
تَيَسَّرَ / يَتَيَسَّرُ	V to become easy
	to be high
عَلاَ / يَعْلُو	
كَرِهَ / يَكْرَهُ	to detest, to hate
أَوْصَى / يُوصِي	IV to advise, to counsel
تَنَازُعٌ	[VN⁶] fight, strive
تَخَاصُمٌ	[VN⁶] dispute, quarrel
تَعَاوُنٌ	[VN⁶] mutual cooperation
تَصَالُحٌ	[VN⁶] mutual reconciliation
الْقَهَّارُ	the Subduer

أَعَادَ / يُعِيْدُ	IV to cause to return, to bring back
تَبَارَكَ	VI blessed, exalted
تَعَالَى	VI Exalted
أُمٌّ / ج أُمَّهَاتٌ	mother
مَعْصِيَةٌ	disobedience
أُفٍّ	fie, a word of contempt
قِيَامٌ	standing
قُعُودٌ	sitting
جَنْبٌ / ج جُنُوبٌ	lit. beside, next to, reclining
تَعَاوَنَ / يَتَعَاوَنُ	VI to help, to assist one another
هَوَى / ج أَهْوَاءٌ	passion, longing, whim
أَمْكَنَ / يُمْكِنُ	IV to be possible
جَمْعٌ	[VN] combination
رَسُولٌ / ج رُسُلٌ	messenger
مَالٌ / ج أَمْوَالٌ	wealth
عَمَلٌ / ج أَعْمَالٌ	work
أَرْمَلَةٌ	widow
أَنْظَرَ / يُنْظِرُ	IV to grant a delay or respite to someone
مُعْسِرٌ	[AP⁴] (living) in straitened circumstances

أَنْجَى / يُنْجِي	IV to rescue save, to bring to safety someone
كَرَبٌ / ج كُرَبٌ	pain, anxiety
ضَمِنَ / يَضْمَنُ	to be or to become responsible or liable
لِحْى	jaw bones
أَوْسَطُ	middle
شَوْكَةٌ	thorn
دَرَجَةٌ	rank, degree
حَطَّ / يَحُطُّ	to put down, to set down
شَبِعَ / يَشْبَعُ	to satisfy ones appetite
جَارٌ	neighbour
جَائِعٌ	[AP] hungry
نِيَّةٌ / ج نِيَّاتٌ	intention
وَادٍ	valley
نَصِيحَةٌ	sincerity
نِكَاحٌ	marriage
سُنَّةٌ	legally binding, precedent, tradition

392

رَغِبَ [عَنْ]	to dislike, to detest
سَعَةٌ	wideness, affluence, power
خُلُقٌ / ج أَخْلاَقٌ	character
كَنْزٌ / ج كُنُوزٌ	treasure
رِزْقٌ / ج أَرْزَاقٌ	sustenance, subsistence
شِعَارٌ	characteristic
حِقْدٌ	hatred, malice
خَصْلَةٌ / ج خِصَالٌ	quality, peculiarity
تَخَاصَمَ / يَتَخَاصَمُ	VI to quarrel, to have a fight
لِصٌّ	thief
مَسْرُوقٌ	stolen
أَدَّبَ / يُؤَدِّبُ	II to refine, to educate someone
وَلَدٌ / ج أَوْلاَدٌ	boy, son
أَرْغَمَ / يُرْغِمُ	IV to coerce
حَاسِدٌ / ج حُسَّادٌ	[AP] envier
تَوَاضُعٌ	humility, humbleness
شَبَكَةٌ	net
شَرَفٌ	nobility, high rank
شَهْوَةٌ / ج شَهَوَاتٌ	passion, greed, lust
عَاشَ / يَعِيشُ	to live

393

عَدُوٌّ / ج أَعْدَاءٌ	enemy
أَجْنَبِيٌّ / ج أَجَانِبٌ	stranger
عَاشَرَ / يُعَاشِرُ	III to be on intimate terms
إِيَّاكُمْ	be ware
حَطَبٌ	wood
قَدَّمَ / يُقَدِّمُ	II to send forward
خَلَّفَ / يُخَلِّفُ	II to leave behind
دَابَّةٌ	beast of burden
أَمَاطَ / يُمِيطُ	to remove
خُطْوَةٌ	step
مَشَى / يَمْشِي	to walk
أَذًى	harmful (object)
مِثْقَالُ	weight
كَبَرٌ	pride
بَطَرٌ	arrogance
غَمْطٌ	hold in contempt

394

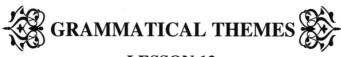

GRAMMATICAL THEMES

LESSON 12

جَمْعُ التَّكْسِيرِ

Broken Plural

Broken Plurals accept various patterns. Arabic dictionaries always provide singulars with their plurals if they are broken. Some of the prominent patterns are as follows:

Pattern	Singular	Meaning	Plural
فُعَلٌ	أُمَّةٌ	*Ummah* Community	أُمَمٌ
فُعُلٌ	كِتَابٌ	book	كُتُبٌ
فِعَالٌ	بَحْرٌ	sea	بِحَارٌ
فُعُوْلٌ	جِلْدٌ	skin	جُلُوْدٌ
فُعَّالٌ	صَانِعٌ	artisan	صُنَّاعٌ
أَفْعَالٌ	شَيْءٌ	thing	أَشْيَاءٌ
أَفْعِلَةٌ	زَمَانٌ	time	أَزْمِنَةٌ
فَوَاعِلُ	صَاعِقَةٌ	thunderbolt	صَوَاعِقُ
فَعَائِلُ	صَحِيْفَةٌ	scripture, book	صَحَائِفُ
فِعْلَانٌ	أَخٌ	brother	إِخْوَانٌ
فُعَلَاءُ	فَقِيرٌ	poor	فُقَرَاءُ
أَفْعِلَاءُ	صَدِيْقٌ	friend	أَصْدِقَاءُ
فَعَالَى	يَتِيْمٌ	orphan	يَتَامَى
فَعِيْلٌ	عَبْدٌ	servant, slave	عَبِيْدٌ

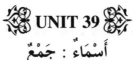

UNIT 39

أَسْمَاءٌ : جَمْعٌ

Rule No. 58   **Nouns : Plural**

In a nominative sentence, if the subject is the plural of an animate noun the predicate should be plural and shall agree with the gender of the subject.

Example Analysis:

In sentences 1 - 13 the subjects are:

الرِّجَالُ (the men), هَؤُلاَءِ (these), أُولَئِكَ (those),

الْمُؤْمِنُونَ (the believing men), هُمْ (they M³⁺), نَحْنُ (we)

هَؤُلاَءِ (these), هُنَّ (those F³⁺), أَنْتُنَّ (you F³⁺),

أُولَئِكَ (those), الأُمَّهَاتُ (the mothers), الْمُنَافِقَاتُ (the hypocrite

women), أَنْتُمْ (you M³⁺) أَنْتُنَّ (you F³⁺)

All nouns are animate plurals.
The predicates are:

مُجَاهِدُونَ (M³⁺ strugglers),	نَائِمُونَ (M³⁺ sleeping),
يُجَاهِدُونَ (M³⁺ they struggle),	مُؤْمِنُونَ (M³⁺ believing),
تَائِبُونَ (M³⁺ repenting),	فَائِزُونَ (M³⁺ successful),
طَالِبَاتٌ (F³⁺ students),	عَالِمَاتٌ (F³⁺ women scholars),
صَائِمَاتٌ (F³⁺ fasting),	ذَاكِرَاتٌ (F³⁺ remembering),
كَاذِبَاتٌ (F³⁺ liars),	صَادِقَاتٌ (F³⁺ truthful),
عَالِمَاتٌ (F³⁺ scholars)	عَالِمُونَ (M³⁺ scholars) and

All are plural and agree with the genders of their plurals.

Plural: Demonstrative Nouns

	Singular		Plural

Singular

هَذَا (M¹) + هَذِه (F¹)

ذَلِكَ (M¹) + تِلْكَ (F¹)

Plural

هَؤُلاَءِ (M³⁺ + F³⁺)

أُولَئِكَ (M³⁺ + F³⁺)

Rule No. 59

The Plurals for Demonstrative Nouns are used for both genders but their singular and dual forms also take into consideration the genders of the nouns.

هَؤُلاَءِ مُجَاهِدُونَ.

(2) These are strugglers.

هَؤُلاَءِ is the demonstrative noun in the plural for مُجَاهِدُونَ which is the sound plural in the nominative case. It is the Third Form Active Participle and it is a masculine noun used for human beings. Here هَؤُلاَءِ is used for masculine noun.

هَؤُلاَءِ عَالَمَاتٌ.

(7) These are scholars [women].

هَؤُلاَءِ is the demonstrative noun in the plural for عَالَمَاتٌ which is the sound plural in the nominative case. It is the First Form Active Participle and it is a feminine noun used for human beings. Here هَؤُلاَءِ is used for the feminine noun.

أُولَئِكَ مُؤْمِنُونَ.

(3) Those are believing men.

أُولَئِكَ is the demonstrative noun in plural for مُؤْمِنُونَ which is the sound plural in the nominative case. It is the Fourth Form Active Participle and it is a masculine noun used for human beings. Here أُولَئِكَ is used for masculine noun.

أُولَئِكَ صَائِمَاتٌ.

(10) Those are fasting women.

أُولَئِكَ is the demonstrative noun in the plural for صَائِمَاتٌ which is the sound plural in nominative case. It is the First Form Active Participle and it is a feminine noun used for human beings. Here, أُولَئِكَ is used for the feminine noun.

 UNIT 40

Rule No. 60

In a nominative sentence, if the subject is the plural of an inanimate noun the predicate is the singular feminine.

Example Analysis:

In examples 1-8 the subjects are:

الْبُيُوتُ (the houses),   الْأَزْهَارُ (the flowers),

الأَنْهَارُ (the rivers),   الْقُلُوبُ (the hearts),

الْوُجُوهُ (the faces),   الآذَانُ (the ears) and

الْعُيُونُ (the eyes).

All the nouns are inanimate plurals.

(Note parts of the human body when treated separately are regarded as inanimate. e.g. face, heart, ear, eye, hand etc.)

UNIT 41

Rule No. 61

If the subject is either human beings or angels and the broken plural, the verb is used as singular and can be either masculine or feminine.

Example Analysis:

The subjects under (ألف) and (بَاء) are the broken plural nouns. These are:

النِّسَاءُ (the women), الْمَلاَئِكَةُ (the angels),

الْقَوْمُ (the people) and النَّاسُ (the mankind).

Under (ألف) the verbs are singular masculine قَالَ III M[1]

and جَاءَ III M[1].

Under (بَاء) the same verbs are singular feminine. Both ألف

and بَاء are correct.

UNIT 42

Rule No. 62

If the predicate is the broken plural of an inanimate noun the subject is singular feminine.

Example Analysis:

In sentences 1 - 8 the predicates are:

بِحَارٌ (seas), بُيُوتٌ (houses), قُلُوبٌ (hearts),

أَبْوَابٌ (doors), وُجُوهٌ (faces), كُتُبٌ (books),

أَنْهَارٌ (rivers) and مَسَاجِدُ (mosques).

All the nouns are broken plural and inanimate. The subjects are:

تِلْكَ (that F¹) and هِيَ (she F¹) هَذِه (this F¹)

All are singular feminine.

🎕 UNIT 43 🎕

Rule No. 63

In a verbal sentence, if the subject is sound plural, the verb is singular and agrees with the gender of the subject.

Example Analysis:

In sentences 1 - 10 the subjects are:

الْمُؤْمِنَاتُ (F³⁺ believing women), الْمُصَلُّونَ (M³⁺ worshippers),

الْمُسْلِمَاتُ (F³⁺ Muslim women), الْعَابِدُونَ (M³⁺ worshippers),

السَّامِعُونَ (M³⁺ listening men), النَّائِمُونَ (M³⁺ sleeping men),

الْجَاهِلَاتُ (F³⁺ ignorant women), الْعَالِمُونَ (M³⁺ scholars men),

الْمُنَافِقَاتُ (F³⁺ hypocrite women) الْمُؤْمِنُونَ (M³⁺ believing men)

All the nouns are sound plural

The verbs are:

سَجَدَ (to prostrate III M¹)   قَامَ (to stand III M¹)

خَسِرَ (to incur a loss III M¹) فَهِمَ (to understand III M¹)

مَاتَ (to die III M¹)   تَابَ (to repent III M¹)

These are all singular masculine verbs because their subjects are sound masculine plurals. They agree with the genders of their subjects.

صَامَتْ (III F¹ from صَامَ to fast)

صَلَّتْ (III F¹ from صَلَّى to pray)

بَقِيَتْ (III F¹ from بَقِيَ to remain) and

مَاتَتْ (III F¹ from مَاتَ to die).

These are all singular feminine verbs because their subjects are sound feminine plurals. They agree with the genders of their subjects.

UNIT 44

Rule No. 64

If the subject is the broken plural of an inanimate noun the verb is singular feminine.

   Example Analysis:

   In sentences 1 - 6 the subjects are:

الْكَرَاسِيُّ (the chairs M³⁺)   اَلْأَقْلَامُ (the pens M³⁺)

الْقُلُوبُ (the hearts M³⁺)   الْوُجُوهُ (the faces M³⁺)

الْأَيْدِي (the hands F³⁺)   الذُّنُوْبُ (the sins M³⁺)

These are the broken plurals of inanimate nouns.
The verbs are:

سَقَطَتْ (III F¹ from سَقَطَ to fall), كَتَبَتْ (III F¹ from كَتَبَ to

write), خَشَعَتْ (III F¹ from خَشَعَ to become tender), جَمُلَتْ (III

F¹ from جَمُلَ to become beautiful) and كَثُرَتْ (III F¹ from كَثُرَ to

increase)

All these verbs are singular feminine because their subjects are
the broken plurals of inanimate nouns.

🏵 UNIT 45 🏵

Rule No. 65

The consonant " نْ " in the sound plural of the first noun of
the *Iḍāfah*, the 'Construct Phrase', is deleted.

Example Analysis:

Examples 7 - 9 are the *Iḍāfah*, 'Construct Phrases.' Their
first nouns are:

(i) [نَ]مُسْلِمُو (M³⁺ Muslims) is the sound plural of the First

Form verb. It is the first noun of the *Iḍāfah*, 'Construct

Phrase', therefore, its " نْ " is dropped. It becomes مُسْلِمُو .

The second noun of the *Iḍāfah* is بِرِيْطَانِيَا (Britain). It

means Muslims of Britain.

402

(ii) [نَ]مُصْلِحِي (M³⁺ reformers) is the sound plural and the Active Participle of the Fourth Form verb. It is in the accusative case because it is an object of لَقِيْتُ (I met). Again it is the first noun of the *Iḍāfah*, therefore, its " نَ " is dropped. It becomes مُصْلِحِي . The second noun of the *Iḍāfah* is الْبَلَد (the city). It means the reformers of the city.

(iii) [نَ]ظَالِمُو (M³⁺ oppressors) is the sound plural of the First Form verb. It is the first form noun of the *Iḍāfah*, 'Construct Phrase', therefore, its " نَ " is dropped. It becomes ظَالِمُو . The second noun of the *Iḍāfah* is الْبَلَد (the city). It means the oppressors of the city.

Rule No. 66

If the qualifying noun (*mawṣūf*) is the plural of the noun used for human beings, the adjective (*ṣifah*) is plural and agrees with the gender of the qualifying noun.

Example Analysis:

In example الرِّجَالُ الصَّائِمُونَ The fasting men الرِّجَالُ is the qualifying noun and الصَّائِمُونَ is its adjective. Since الرِّجَالُ is masculine and also the plural of a noun used for human beings, therefore, الصَّائِمُونَ its adjective is also in the plural and agrees with the gender of the qualifying noun الرِّجَالُ .

In example الْمُسْلِمَاتُ الْعَابِدَاتُ The worshipping women,

الْمُسْلِمَاتُ is the qualifying noun and الْعَابِدَاتُ is its adjective.

Since الْمُسْلِمَاتُ is feminine and the plural of a noun used for

human beings, therefore, الْعَابِدَاتُ its adjective is also in the

plural and agrees with the gender of the qualifying noun

(الْمُسْلِمَاتُ).

❧ UNIT 46 ❧

Rule No. 67

If the qualifying noun is the plural of an inanimate noun the adjective is in the singular feminine.

Example Analysis:

In sentences 1 - 8 the qualifying nouns are: الْأَقْلَامُ (the pens),

الْكُتُبُ (the books), الْآلِهَةُ (the gods), الأَيَّامُ (the days), عُيُونٌ

(eyes), الْأَنْهَارُ (the rivers) وُجُوهٌ (faces) and آذَانٌ (ears) are the

qualifying nouns and all of them are the plural of inanimate

nouns.

The adjectives in these sentences are:

السَّمَاوِيَّةُ (F¹ heavenly)	الْقَصِيرَةُ (F¹ short)
الْمَاضِيَةُ (F¹ past)	الْبَاطِلَةُ (F¹ false)
الْجَارِيَةُ (F¹ flowing)	نَاظِرَةٌ (F¹ seeing)
سَامِعَةٌ (F¹ listening)	ضَاحِكَةٌ (F¹ laughing)

All these adjectives are singular feminine because their qualifying nouns are the plurals of inanimate nouns.

UNIT 47

ثُلاَثِي مَزِيْدٌ فِيهِ : بَابُ تَفَاعُلٌ

تَفَاعُلٌ Derived Form VI

Formation:

The Sixth Form is formed from the Third Form (فَاعَلَ) by prefixing تَ (تَفَاعَلَ)

The other conjugations in the Perfect Indicative follow the pattern تَفَاعَلَ and their endings remain the same as for the Perfect in the First Form.

(See TC under VI)

Imperfect:

The formation of the Imperfect is based on the III M[1] pattern (يَتَفَاعَلُ) All prefixes and endings remain the same as in the First Form.

(See TD under VI)

Verbal Noun:

The Verbal Noun is formed on the pattern of تَفَاعُلٌ Verbal Noun for تَعَاوَنَ (to help or assist one another) is تَعَاوُنٌ (cooperation)

Active Participle:

The Active Participle is formed on the pattern of مُتَفَاعِلٌ /

مُتَعَاوِنٌ (cooperating)

Passive Participle:

The Passive Participle is formed on the pattern of
مُتَعَاوَنٌ / مُتَفَاعَلٌ (cooperated)

(For Verbal nouns, Active and Passive Participles see TB under VI)

Significances: Derived Form VI

Reciprocity, which is implied in some Third Forms, becomes distinct in the Sixth Form.

(a)   Third Form   Sixth Form

قَاتَلَ   to combat   تَقَاتَلَ to combat with
                              each other

نَادَى   to call   تَنَادَى to call each other

          to be or
شَارَكَ become   تَشَارَكَ to enter partnership
          partners

(b) It demonstrates pretenses:

تَمَارَضَ   he feigned illness

تَمَاوَتَ   he pretended to be dead

تَضَاحَكَ	he pretended to laugh
تَجَاهَلَ	he feigned ignorance
تَبَاكَى	he pretended to weep

(c) It sometimes emphasizes the importance:

تَعَاظَمَ الأَمْرَ   to find the matter great.

(d) Sometimes it accepts the influence of the Third Form فَاعَلَ

بَاعَدْتُهُ فَتَبَاعَدَ   I kept him at a distance so he kept away.

(e) Sometimes it indicates the same meaning as for the First Form:

تَعَالَى	to rise
تَكَامَلَ	to complete
تَكَاثَرَ	to increase

Example Analysis:

(٩) الْمُؤْمِنُونَ يَتَعَاوَنُونَ عَلَى الْخَيْرِ وَلاَ يَتَعَاوَنُونَ عَلَى الْإِثْمِ وَالْفَسَادِ وَالشَّرِّ وَالْعُدْوَان.

The believing men are helping each other in virtue and they do not assist each other in sin, corruption, evil and transgression.

يَتَعَاوَنُونَ is III M³⁺ from the Sixth derived Form.

407

UNIT 48

Rule No. 68

When the Perfect كَانَ appears with the Imperfect it changes into the Past Continuous and agrees with the gender and number of the Imperfect.

Example Analysis:

(٣) كَانَ نَبِيُّ اللهِ (ﷺ) يَأْمُرُ النَّاسَ بِالتَّعَاوِنِ وَالتَّصَالُحِ وَعِبَادَةِ اللهِ الْوَاحِدِ الْقَهَّارِ.

(3) The Prophet of Allah (may the blessings of Allah and peace be upon him) used to command mankind for mutual cooperation, reform and worship of Allah, the One the Almighty. The Imperfect يَأْمُرُ is followed by the Perfect.

Both agree in gender and number. The Imperfect يَأْمُرُ gives meaning of the Past Continuous.

النَّصُّ الْقُرآنِيُّ

Lesson 12

١. وُجُوهٌ يَوْمَئِذٍ نَّاعِمَةٌ ۝ لِّسَعْيِهَا رَاضِيَةٌ (8-9 :88)

٢. فِيهَا كُتُبٌ قَيِّمَةٌ (3 :98)

٣. اَلرِّجَالُ قَوَّامُونَ عَلَى ٱلنِّسَآءِ بِمَا فَضَّلَ ٱللَّهُ بَعْضَهُمْ عَلَىٰ

بَعْضٍ (34 :4)

٤. وَٱللَّهُ يَشْهَدُ إِنَّ ٱلْمُنَـٰفِقِينَ لَكَـٰذِبُونَ (1 :63)

٥. ٱلَّذِينَ تَتَوَفَّـٰهُمُ ٱلْمَلَـٰٓئِكَةُ ظَالِمِىٓ أَنفُسِهِمْ (28 :16)

٦. سُنَّتَ ٱللَّهِ ٱلَّتِى قَدْ خَلَتْ فِى عِبَادِهِۦ ۖ وَخَسِرَ هُنَالِكَ

ٱلْكَـٰفِرُونَ (85 :40)

٧. فَوَيْلٌ لَّهُم مِّمَّا كَتَبَتْ أَيْدِيهِمْ وَوَيْلٌ لَّهُم مِّمَّا يَكْسِبُونَ

(79 :2)

٨. سَيَجْعَلُ لَهُمُ ٱلرَّحْمَـٰنُ وُدًّا (96 :19)

٩. إِذْ قَالَتِ ٱلْمَلَـٰٓئِكَةُ يَـٰمَرْيَمُ إِنَّ ٱللَّهَ يُبَشِّرُكِ بِكَلِمَةٍ مِّنْهُ

(45 :3)

409

١٠. قُلُوبٌ يَوْمَئِذٍ وَاجِفَةٌ ۝ أَبْصَارُهَا خَاشِعَةٌ (8-9 :79)

١١. وُجُوهٌ يَوْمَئِذٍ خَاشِعَةٌ (2 :88)

١٢. وُجُوهٌ يَوْمَئِذٍ نَّاضِرَةٌ ۝ إِلَىٰ رَبِّهَا نَاظِرَةٌ (22-23 :75)

١٣. قَالُوٓاْ ءَأَنتَ فَعَلْتَ هَٰذَا بِـَٔالِهَتِنَا يَٰٓإِبْرَٰهِيمُ (62 :21)

١٤. فَأَخَذْنَٰهُم بِٱلْبَأْسَآءِ وَٱلضَّرَّآءِ لَعَلَّهُمْ يَتَضَرَّعُونَ (42 :6)

١٥. وَإِنَّ مِنَ ٱلْحِجَارَةِ لَمَا يَتَفَجَّرُ مِنْهُ ٱلْأَنْهَٰرُ (74 :2)

١٦. أُوْلَٰٓئِكَ سَوْفَ يُؤْتِيهِمْ أُجُورَهُمْ (152 :4)

١٧. وَٱلَّذِينَ ءَامَنُواْ وَعَمِلُواْ ٱلصَّٰلِحَٰتِ سَنُدْخِلُهُمْ جَنَّٰتٍ تَجْرِى مِن تَحْتِهَا ٱلْأَنْهَٰرُ (122 :4)

١٨. وَيُرْسِلُ ٱلصَّوَٰعِقَ فَيُصِيبُ بِهَا مَن يَشَآءُ (13 :13)

١٩. تِلْكَ ٱلرُّسُلُ فَضَّلْنَا بَعْضَهُمْ عَلَىٰ بَعْضٍ مِّنْهُم مَّن كَلَّمَ ٱللَّهُ وَرَفَعَ بَعْضَهُمْ دَرَجَٰتٍ (253 :2)

٢٠. يَٰصَٰحِبَىِ ٱلسِّجْنِ ءَأَرْبَابٌ مُّتَفَرِّقُونَ خَيْرٌ أَمِ ٱللَّهُ ٱلْوَٰحِدُ ٱلْقَهَّارُ (39 :12)

٢١. وَأَحَلَّ ٱللَّهُ ٱلْبَيْعَ وَحَرَّمَ ٱلرِّبَوٰاْ (275 :2)

٢٢. يَٰٓأَيُّهَا ٱلنَّبِىُّ لِمَ تُحَرِّمُ مَآ أَحَلَّ ٱللَّهُ لَكَ (1 :66)

٢٣. فَتَقَبَّلَهَا رَبُّهَا بِقَبُولٍ حَسَنٍ (37 :3)

بِسْمِ ٱللَّهِ ٱلرَّحْمَٰنِ ٱلرَّحِيمِ

٢٤. وَٱلْعَصْرِ ۝ إِنَّ ٱلْإِنسَٰنَ لَفِى خُسْرٍ ۝ إِلَّا ٱلَّذِينَ ءَامَنُواْ
وَعَمِلُواْ ٱلصَّٰلِحَٰتِ وَتَوَاصَوْاْ بِٱلْحَقِّ وَتَوَاصَوْاْ بِٱلصَّبْرِ (103:
1-3)

٢٥. ثُمَّ كَانَ مِنَ ٱلَّذِينَ ءَامَنُواْ وَتَوَاصَوْاْ بِٱلصَّبْرِ وَتَوَاصَوْاْ
بِٱلْمَرْحَمَةِ (17 :90)

٢٦. أَلَا لَهُ ٱلْخَلْقُ وَٱلْأَمْرُ ۗ تَبَارَكَ ٱللَّهُ رَبُّ ٱلْعَٰلَمِينَ (54 :7)

٢٧. تَبَٰرَكَ ٱلَّذِى بِيَدِهِ ٱلْمُلْكُ وَهُوَ عَلَىٰ كُلِّ شَىْءٍ قَدِيرٌ (1 :67)

٢٨. تَبَارَكَ ٱلَّذِى نَزَّلَ ٱلْفُرْقَانَ عَلَىٰ عَبْدِهِ لِيَكُونَ لِلْعَٰلَمِينَ
نَذِيرًا (1 :25)

٢٩. قَالُواْ سِحْرَانِ تَظَٰهَرَا وَقَالُواْ إِنَّا بِكُلٍّ كَٰفِرُونَ (48 :28)

٣٠. فَأَقْبَلَ بَعْضُهُمْ عَلَىٰ بَعْضٍ يَتَلَٰوَمُونَ (30 :68)

٣١. كَانُواْ لَا يَتَنَاهَوْنَ عَن مُّنكَرٍ فَعَلُوهُ (79 :5)

٣٢. إِنَّ ٱللَّهَ يَحْكُمُ مَا يُرِيدُ (1 :5)

411

قَيِّمٌ	eternal, lasting, guardian
قَوَّامٌ / ج قَوَّامُونَ	overseer, maintainer, carer
نَافَقَ / يُنَافِقُ	III to behave hypocritly
تَوَفَّى / يَتَوَفَّى	V to cause to die
سُنَّةٌ	dispensation, custom, practice, mode of conduct
نَهْرٌ / ج أَنْهَارٌ	river
خَلَا / يَخْلُو	to pass away (time), to be alone [TA⁴]
صَاعِقَةٌ / ج صَوَاعِق	thunder
وَيْلٌ	woe (an interjection) to express misfortune
وُدٌّ	love, affection
وَاجِفٌ	[AP] throbbing, palpitating
بَصَرٌ / ج أَبْصَارٌ	sight
أَحَلَّ / يُحِلُّ	IV to make lawful
حَرَّمَ / يُحَرِّمُ	II to make unlauful
نَاضِرٌ	[AP] shining, fresh
نَاظِرٌ	[AP] observer
بَأْسٌ ج بَأْسَاءُ	terror, tribulation, punishment
ضُرٌّ / ج ضَرَّاءُ	adversity

حِجَارَةٌ	stone
تَفَجَّرَ / يَتَفَجَّرُ	V to flow out
أَجْرٌ / ج أُجُورٌ	reward
صَاحِبٌ	companion
سِجْنٌ	prison
رَبٌّ / ج أَرْبَابٌ	lord, nourisher, guide, sustainer
مُتَفَرِّقٌ	[AP5] divers
عَصْرٌ	time
تَوَاصَى / يَتَوَاصَى	VI to enjoin each other, to admonish each other
تَبَارَكَ / يَتَبَارَكُ	VI blessed
مَرْحَمَةٌ	compassion
فُرْقَانٌ	criterion (of right and wrong)
أَقْبَلَ / يُقْبِلُ	IV to draw near
تَلاَوَمَ / يَتَلاَوَمُ	VI to blame each other
تَنَاهَى / يَتَنَاهَى	VI to forbid each other
مُنْكَرٌ	[PP4] what is strange to the human nature, false, wrong
تَظَاهَرَ / يَتَظَاهَرُ	VI to make a public demonstration, to support each other

413

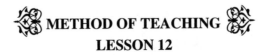

METHOD OF TEACHING
LESSON 12

1. Since Broken Plurals accept various patterns it is important to remove confusion and fear from the minds of the students about their use. To assist comprehension project various patterns gradually and their plural and singular forms on to the screen.

2. Indicate the roots in the Plural forms and compare these with its pattern. In this way it will become easy for students to recognise the Broken Plurals.

3. The *tanwīn* at the end of Broken Plurals clearly demonstrate that it is a noun. Point out their singular forms and ask the students to compare them. The change becomes obvious and this is helpful in the recognition of Broken Plurals.

4. هَؤُلَاءِ and أُولَئِكَ can be made clear by pointing out the students who are close and the students who are at a distance. If students are only few in number, photographs can be used to portray a crowd of people. For the distinction in these two forms a few interrogative sentences may enable students to recognise these demonstrative noun. Singular and dual forms can also be used. Repeat steps 6 - 8 for the introduction of the Sixth derived Form تَفَاعَلَ mentioned in the Method of Teaching Lesson 9.

5. Rule 60 – 67: cover the use of the Plural with different kinds of nouns. Experience suggests that if the students are first asked to read from the screen the rule and later on all subjects, predicates and other forms are pointed out on the screen the application of the rules in the examples becomes clear and easy.

Lesson 12

Exercise No.31

(1) Put *i'rāb*

(١) المؤمنون لا يتنازعون و لا يتخاصمون و يحكمون بكتاب الله.

(٢) المؤمنون لا يتحاكمون إلى الشياطين و يتعاونون على الخير و لا يتعاونون على الإثم و الشر.

(٣) كان رسول الله (ﷺ) يحكم بكتاب الله و كان يتفكر في خلق الله.

(٤) الذين آمنوا بالله و ملائكته و رسله و تواصوا بالحق و تواصوا بالخير، أولئك يدخلون الجنة، لهم فيها مساكن طيبة و أزواج مطهرة.

(٥) أحمد تاجر عنده بيوت عالية و غرفات واسعة و فاخرة.

(٦) أولو العلم أحياء و لو كانوا في التراب.

(٧) الظالم يظلم و لا يتوب إلى الله.

(٨) من هذا الرجل الصالح و ماذا يقول؟

(٩) إن السيرة الجميلة خير من الصورة الجميلة.

(١٠) هو يترك طعامه لوجه الله.

(١١) المسلم من سلم الناس من لسانه و يده.

(١٢) هو يقرأ من القرآن الذي هو كتاب الله.

(١٣) فتحت الأم باب البيت.

(١٤) اللهم يسره لي و لا تعسره.

(2) Translate into Arabic

1. Those scholars (F^{3+}) are sitting in their houses and are teaching the Qur'ān.
2. In the gardens the flowers are beautiful and the rivers are flowing in front of the houses.
3. Women said: In the mosque the worshippers have prostrated.
4. The sins have increased and the obedient people have decreased.
5. I believe in all heavenly books revealed to the messengers.
6. The disbelievers neither fear Allah nor pray nor reflect on Allah's creation.
7. The believing women hate both corruption and transgression.
8. The Prophet Moses (peace be upon him) used to prevent people from worshipping Pharaoh.
9. Mutual co-operation and reform are liked by Allah.
10. Allah the Exalted has created righteous parents for their obedient sons.

(3) From the Qur'ānic text of Lesson 12 identify the following:
   (a) Derived forms.
   (b) Broken plurals (BP)

النَّصُّ القُرآنِيُّ

Lesson 13

١. عَلَّمَ ٱلْإِنسَـٰنَ مَا لَمْ يَعْلَمْ (96: 5)

٢. أَلَمْ يَعْلَم بِأَنَّ ٱللَّهَ يَرَىٰ (96: 14)

٣. أَيَحْسَبُ أَن لَّمْ يَرَهُۥٓ أَحَدٌ ۝ أَلَمْ نَجْعَل لَّهُۥ عَيْنَيْنِ ۝

وَلِسَانًا وَشَفَتَيْنِ (90: 7-9)

٤. أَلَمْ نَشْرَحْ لَكَ صَدْرَكَ (94: 1)

٥. أَوَلَا يَذْكُرُ ٱلْإِنسَـٰنُ أَنَّا خَلَقْنَـٰهُ مِن قَبْلُ وَلَمْ يَكُ شَيْـًٔا

(19: 67)

٦. وَمَن لَّمْ يَحْكُم بِمَآ أَنزَلَ ٱللَّهُ فَأُوْلَـٰٓئِكَ هُمُ ٱلظَّـٰلِمُونَ

(5: 45)

٧. ثُمَّ أَنزَلَ ٱللَّهُ سَكِينَتَهُۥ عَلَىٰ رَسُولِهِۦ وَعَلَى ٱلْمُؤْمِنِينَ

وَأَنزَلَ جُنُودًا لَّمْ تَرَوْهَا (9: 26)

٨. أَلَمْ يَعْلَمُوٓا۟ أَنَّ ٱللَّهَ يَعْلَمُ سِرَّهُمْ وَنَجْوَىٰهُمْ وَأَنَّ ٱللَّهَ

عَلَّـٰمُ ٱلْغُيُوبِ (9: 78)

417

٩. الَّذِينَ ءَامَنُوا وَلَمْ يَلْبِسُوا إِيمَـٰنَهُم بِظُلْمٍ أُوْلَـٰئِكَ لَهُمُ الْأَمْنُ وَهُم مُّهْتَدُونَ (6: 82)

١٠. وَأَنزَلَ اللَّهُ عَلَيْكَ الْكِتَـٰبَ وَالْحِكْمَةَ وَعَلَّمَكَ مَا لَمْ تَكُن تَعْلَمُ وَكَانَ فَضْلُ اللَّهِ عَلَيْكَ عَظِيمًا (4: 113)

١١. أَلَمْ تَرَ أَنَّ اللَّهَ أَنزَلَ مِنَ السَّمَاءِ مَاءً فَأَخْرَجْنَا بِهِ ثَمَرَٰتٍ مُّخْتَلِفًا أَلْوَٰنُهَا (35: 27)

١٢. وَإِن تُؤْمِنُوا وَتَتَّقُوا فَلَكُمْ أَجْرٌ عَظِيمٌ (3: 179)

١٣. إِن تَكْفُرُوا فَإِنَّ اللَّهَ غَنِيٌّ عَنكُمْ وَلَا يَرْضَىٰ لِعِبَادِهِ الْكُفْرَ (39: 7)

١٤. وَإِن تُصْلِحُوا وَتَتَّقُوا فَإِنَّ اللَّهَ كَانَ غَفُورًا رَّحِيمًا (4: 129)

١٥. وَإِن تُبْدُوا مَا فِي أَنفُسِكُمْ أَوْ تُخْفُوهُ يُحَاسِبْكُم بِهِ اللَّهُ (2: 284)

١٦. فَإِنِ انتَهَوْا فَإِنَّ اللَّهَ غَفُورٌ رَّحِيمٌ (2: 192)

١٧. فَإِنِ انتَهَوْا فَإِنَّ اللَّهَ بِمَا يَعْمَلُونَ بَصِيرٌ (8: 39)

١٨. يَـٰٓأَيُّهَا ٱلَّذِينَ ءَامَنُوٓاْ إِن تَتَّقُواْ ٱللَّهَ يَجْعَل لَّكُمْ فُرْقَانًا وَيُكَفِّرْ عَنكُمْ سَيِّـَٔاتِكُمْ وَيَغْفِرْ لَكُمْ ۗ وَٱللَّهُ ذُو ٱلْفَضْلِ ٱلْعَظِيمِ (8: 29)

١٩. وَلِبَاسُ ٱلتَّقْوَىٰ ذَٰلِكَ خَيْرٌ (7: 26)

٢٠. وَمَن يُطِعِ ٱللَّهَ وَرَسُولَهُ فَقَدْ فَازَ فَوْزًا عَظِيمًا (33: 71)

٢١. مَّن يُطِعِ ٱلرَّسُولَ فَقَدْ أَطَاعَ ٱللَّهَ (4: 80)

٢٢. وَمَن يُشْرِكْ بِٱللَّهِ فَقَدْ ضَلَّ ضَلَٰلًا بَعِيدًا (4: 116)

٢٣. وَمَن يَدْعُ مَعَ ٱللَّهِ إِلَٰهًا ءَاخَرَ لَا بُرْهَٰنَ لَهُۥ بِهِۦ فَإِنَّمَا حِسَابُهُۥ عِندَ رَبِّهِۦٓ (23: 117)

٢٤. وَمَن يَكْفُرْ بِٱلْإِيمَٰنِ فَقَدْ حَبِطَ عَمَلُهُۥ وَهُوَ فِى ٱلْـَٔاخِرَةِ مِنَ ٱلْخَٰسِرِينَ (5: 5)

٢٥. وَمَن يَكْفُرْ بِٱللَّهِ وَمَلَـٰٓئِكَتِهِۦ وَكُتُبِهِۦ وَرُسُلِهِۦ وَٱلْيَوْمِ ٱلْـَٔاخِرِ فَقَدْ ضَلَّ ضَلَٰلًا بَعِيدًا (4: 136)

٢٦. وَمَن يَتَّخِذِ ٱلشَّيْطَٰنَ وَلِيًّا مِّن دُونِ ٱللَّهِ فَقَدْ خَسِرَ خُسْرَانًا مُّبِينًا (4: 119)

٢٧. وَمَن يَكُنِ ٱلشَّيْطَٰنُ لَهُۥ قَرِينًا فَسَآءَ قَرِينًا (4: 38)

٢٨. وَمَن يَعْصِ ٱللَّهَ وَرَسُولَهُۥ فَقَدْ ضَلَّ ضَلَٰلًا مُّبِينًا (33: 36)

٢٩. مَن يُضْلِلِ ٱللَّهُ فَلَا هَادِيَ لَهُۥ (7: 186)

٣٠. وَمَن يُؤْمِنۢ بِٱللَّهِ يَهْدِ قَلْبَهُۥ ۚ وَٱللَّهُ بِكُلِّ شَىْءٍ عَلِيمٌ (64: 11)

٣١. وَمَن يُطِعِ ٱللَّهَ وَرَسُولَهُۥ يُدْخِلْهُ جَنَّٰتٍ تَجْرِى مِن تَحْتِهَا ٱلْأَنْهَٰرُ خَٰلِدِينَ فِيهَا ۚ وَذَٰلِكَ ٱلْفَوْزُ ٱلْعَظِيمُ (4: 13)

٣٢. وَمَن يَتَّقِ ٱللَّهَ يَجْعَل لَّهُۥ مَخْرَجًا ۝ وَيَرْزُقْهُ مِنْ حَيْثُ لَا يَحْتَسِبُ ۚ وَمَن يَتَوَكَّلْ عَلَى ٱللَّهِ فَهُوَ حَسْبُهُۥ ۚ إِنَّ ٱللَّهَ بَٰلِغُ أَمْرِهِۦ ۚ قَدْ جَعَلَ ٱللَّهُ لِكُلِّ شَىْءٍ قَدْرًا (65: 2-3)

٣٣. وَمَن يُهَاجِرْ فِى سَبِيلِ ٱللَّهِ يَجِدْ فِى ٱلْأَرْضِ مُرَٰغَمًا كَثِيرًا وَسَعَةً ۚ وَمَن يَخْرُجْ مِنۢ بَيْتِهِۦ مُهَاجِرًا إِلَى ٱللَّهِ وَرَسُولِهِۦ ثُمَّ يُدْرِكْهُ ٱلْمَوْتُ فَقَدْ وَقَعَ أَجْرُهُۥ عَلَى ٱللَّهِ ۗ وَكَانَ ٱللَّهُ غَفُورًا رَّحِيمًا (4: 100)

٣٤. وَمَن يَهْدِ ٱللَّهُ فَهُوَ ٱلْمُهْتَدِ (17: 97)

٣٥. فَمَن يَعْمَلْ مِثْقَالَ ذَرَّةٍ خَيْرًا يَرَهُۥ ۝ وَمَن يَعْمَلْ مِثْقَالَ ذَرَّةٍ شَرًّا يَرَهُۥ (99: 7-8)

٣٦. وَمَن يَكْسِبْ إِثْمًا فَإِنَّمَا يَكْسِبُهُ عَلَىٰ نَفْسِهِ ۚ وَكَانَ اللَّهُ عَلِيمًا حَكِيمًا (111 :4)

٣٧. وَمَا تَفْعَلُوا۟ مِنْ خَيْرٍ يَعْلَمْهُ اللَّهُ (197 :2)

٣٨. وَمَا تُقَدِّمُوا۟ لِأَنفُسِكُم مِّنْ خَيْرٍ تَجِدُوهُ عِندَ اللَّهِ ۗ إِنَّ اللَّهَ بِمَا تَعْمَلُونَ بَصِيرٌ (110 :2)

٣٩. أَيْنَمَا تَكُونُوا۟ يُدْرِككُّمُ الْمَوْتُ (78 :4)

٤٠. أَيْنَ مَا تَكُونُوا۟ يَأْتِ بِكُمُ اللَّهُ جَمِيعًا (148 :2)

٤١. قَالَ رَبِّ إِنِّى وَهَنَ الْعَظْمُ مِنِّى وَاشْتَعَلَ الرَّأْسُ شَيْبًا وَلَمْ أَكُنۢ بِدُعَآئِكَ رَبِّ شَقِيًّا (4 :19)

٤٢. وَإِذْ قَالَ إِبْرَٰهِيمُ لِأَبِيهِ ءَازَرَ أَتَتَّخِذُ أَصْنَامًا ءَالِهَةً (74 :6)

٤٣. وَاتَّخَذَ اللَّهُ إِبْرَٰهِيمَ خَلِيلًا (125 :4)

٤٤. الَّذِينَ إِذَآ أَصَٰبَتْهُم مُّصِيبَةٌ قَالُوا۟ إِنَّا لِلَّهِ وَإِنَّآ إِلَيْهِ رَٰجِعُونَ ۞ أُو۟لَٰٓئِكَ عَلَيْهِمْ صَلَوَٰتٌ مِّن رَّبِّهِمْ وَرَحْمَةٌ ۖ وَأُو۟لَٰٓئِكَ هُمُ الْمُهْتَدُونَ (157-156 :2)

٤٥. وَكَانَ اللَّهُ عَلَىٰ كُلِّ شَىْءٍ مُّقْتَدِرًا (45 :18)

421

٤٦. إِنَّ فِى خَلْقِ ٱلسَّمَٰوَٰتِ وَٱلْأَرْضِ وَٱخْتِلَٰفِ ٱلَّيْلِ وَٱلنَّهَارِ لَءَايَٰتٍ لِّأُوْلِى ٱلْأَلْبَٰبِ (3: 190)

٤٧. إِنَّكُمْ يَوْمَ ٱلْقِيَٰمَةِ عِندَ رَبِّكُمْ تَخْتَصِمُونَ (39: 31)

٤٨. وَهُوَ ٱلَّذِى يُحْىِۦ وَيُمِيتُ وَلَهُ ٱخْتِلَٰفُ ٱلَّيْلِ وَٱلنَّهَارِ أَفَلَا تَعْقِلُونَ (23: 80)

٤٩. فَإِنَّهُمْ يَوْمَئِذٍ فِى ٱلْعَذَابِ مُشْتَرِكُونَ (37: 33)

٥٠. قَدْ ضَلُّوا۟ وَمَا كَانُوا۟ مُهْتَدِينَ (6: 140)

٥١. قَالَ لِمَنْ حَوْلَهُۥٓ أَلَا تَسْتَمِعُونَ (26: 25)

٥٢. لِكُلِّ ٱمْرِئٍ مِّنْهُم مَّا ٱكْتَسَبَ مِنَ ٱلْإِثْمِ (24: 11)

٥٣. لَهَا مَا كَسَبَتْ وَعَلَيْهَا مَا ٱكْتَسَبَتْ (2: 286)

٥٤. أَفَلَا يَتَدَبَّرُونَ ٱلْقُرْءَانَ وَلَوْ كَانَ مِنْ عِندِ غَيْرِ ٱللَّهِ لَوَجَدُوا۟ فِيهِ ٱخْتِلَٰفًا كَثِيرًا (4: 82)

حَسَبَ	to count, to reckon	لَوْنٌ / ج اَلْوَانٌ	colour
شَفَةٌ	lip	أَبْدَأَ / يُبْدِىءُ	IV to originate
صَدْرٌ / ج صُدُورٌ	breast	أَخْفَى / يُخْفِي	IV to conceal
سَكِينَةٌ	tranquility	حَاسَبَ / يُحَاسبُ	III to reckon
جُنْدٌ / ج جُنُودٌ	army	اِنْتَهَى / يَنْتَهِي	VIII to refrain
سِرٌّ / ج أَسْرَارٌ	secret	مُبِينٌ	clear, self-experience
نَجْوَى	secret conversation	حَبِطَ / يَحْبِطُ	to go in vain
عَلَّامٌ	well knowing	بُرْهَانٌ	proof
غَيْبٌ	hidden	خُسْرَانٌ	loss
اتَّقَى / يَتَّقِي	VIII to be pious, fear, ward off (evil), to be conscious of Allah, to keep duty to Allah	قَنَطَ / يَقْنَطُ	to despair
تَقْوَى	Allah fearing, Allah conscious, piety	قَرِينٌ	companion
أَمْنٌ	peace	وَلِيٌّ	protecting friend, defender
مُهْتَدٍ / مُهْتَدِي	[PP[8]] one who is guided	دُونَ	less than

423

اِشْتَعَلَ / يَشْتَعِلُ	VIII to become inflamed	اِسْتَمَعَ / يَسْتَمِعُ	VIII to hear
شَيْبٌ	grey hair, old age	اِخْتَصَمَ / يَخْتَصِمُ	VIII to contend, to dispute
شَقِيٌّ	unblessed	مُشْتَرِكٌ	[AP8] sharer
صَنَمٌ / ج أَصْنَامٌ	idol	حَوْلَ	[VN] around
خَلِيلٌ	friend	اِكْتَسَبَ / يَكْتَسِبُ	VIII to earn
صَلَاةٌ / ج صَلَوَاتٌ	Prayer	تَدَبَّرَ / يَتَدَبَّرُ	V to reflect
مُقْتَدِرٌ	[AP8] powerful	اِخْتِلَافٌ	[VN8] difference

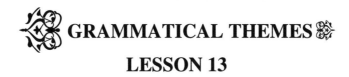

GRAMMATICAL THEMES
LESSON 13

UNIT 49

The endings of the Perfect never change but the endings of the Imperfect change either in the Jussive (*Majzūm*) and Subjunctive (*Manṣūb*) moods or in the case of emphasis with the consonant *Nūn* corroborative *Nūn* (*Nūn Mu'akkadah*). In this lesson the Imperfect Jussive mood is explained.

مُضَارِعٌ مَجْزُوْمٌ
Imperfect: Jussive mood

There are certain particles when they precede the Imperfect change the Imperfect into the Jussive mood. The Jussive mood is identified with a quiescent sign [̊—].

Rule No. 69

When the particle لَمْ (not) precedes the Imperfect a change in the meaning and form takes place.

Change in the meaning:

The Imperfect gives the meaning of the perfect negative.

Change in the form:

The final radical's *ḥarakah*, short vowel is changed into *sukūn* quiescent in the forms III M[1]; III F[1]; II M[1]; I M[1] + F[1];

425

I $M^2 + F^2 + M^{3+} + F^{3+}$ two *Nūns* of III F^{3+} and II F^{3+}.

Example Analysis:

Zayd did not go   زَيْدٌ لَمْ يَذْهَبْ.

يَذْهَبْ III M^1 is preceded by one of the Jussive particles

لَمْ therefore, the final radical (ب) accepts the *sukūn* quiescent sign and the Imperfect gives the meaning of the Perfect negative.

Zaynab did not go   زَيْنَبُ لَمْ تَذْهَبْ

تَذْهَبْ III F^1 is preceded by one of the Jussive particles

therefore, the final radical (ب) accepts *sukūn* the quiescent sign and the Imperfect gives the meaning of the Perfect negative.

You did not go.   أَنْتَ لَمْ تَذْهَبْ.

I did not go.   أَنَا لَمْ أَذْهَبْ.

We did not go.   نَحْنُ لَمْ نَذْهَبْ.

تَذْهَبْ II M^1, أَذْهَبْ I M^1 + F^1 and نَذْهَبْ I M^2 + F^2 + M^{3+} + F^{3+} all these Imperfects are preceded by (لَمْ), therefore, their final radical is quiescent and they give the meaning of the Perfect negative.

Rule No. 70

When the Jussive particle (لَمْ) precedes the Imperfect II F^{3+} and III F^{3+} both give the meaning of the Perfect negative but their forms remain the same.

Example Analysis:

The women did not go   النِّسَاءُ لَمْ يَذْهَبْنَ.

You women did not go   أَنْتُنَّ لَمْ تَذْهَبْنَ.

يَذْهَبْنَ III F^{3+} and تَذْهَبْنَ II F^{3+} remain the same but the meaning changes to the Perfect negative.

Rule No. 71

When the Jussive particle (لَمْ) precedes the Imperfect forms III M^2 and III F^2 the change occurs in their form and meaning. In both forms the final *Nūn* is dropped.

Example Analysis:

Zayd and Aḥmad did not go.   زَيْدٌ وَ أَحْمَدُ لَمْ يَذْهَبَا.

Zaynab and Fāṭimah did not go.   زَيْنَبُ وَ فَاطِمَةُ لَمْ تَذْهَبَا.

Because of the Jussive particle (لَمْ), the final *Nūn* of يَذْهَبَانِ (III M^2) and تَذْهَبَانِ (III F^2) is dropped and both become يَذْهَبَا and تَذْهَبَا. Their Perfect negative meaning remains.

Rule No. 72

When the Jussive particle (لَمْ) precedes the Imperfect forms III M^{3+}, II M^{3+} and II F^1 a change occurs in their forms. In these forms the *Nūn* is dropped.

Example Analysis:

The men did not listen.　　الرِّجَالُ لَمْ يَسْمَعُوا.

You men did not listen.　　أَنْتُمْ لَمْ تَسْمَعُوا.

You (F¹) did not listen.　　أَنْتِ لَمْ تَسْمَعِي.

The Imperfect forms يَسْمَعُونَ (III M³⁺), تَسْمَعُونَ (II M³⁺)

and تَسْمَعِينَ (II F¹), their final *Nūn* is dropped because these are

preceded by the Jussive particle (لَمْ) and they give the meaning

of the Perfect negative.

Jussive mood and the Weak Verbs
(A)

Aḥmad did not say.　　اَحْمَدُ لَمْ يَقُلْ.

Zaynab did not sleep.　　زَيْنَبُ لَمْ تَنَمْ.

Fāṭimah did not sell.　　فَاطِمَةُ لَمْ تَبِعْ.

I did not walk.　　أَنَا لَمْ أَسِرْ.

We were not afraid.　　نَحْنُ لَمْ نَخَفْ.

يَقُلْ is the changed form of يَقُوْلُ . Because of the

Jussive particle (لَمْ) the final radical *Lām* becomes quiescent

it leaves the medial radical (و) vowel quiescent; for articulation

it drops out. Similarly تَنَامُ becomes تَنَمْ , تَبِيْعُ becomes تَبِعْ , أَسِيْرُ

becomes أَسِرْ and نَخَافُ becomes نَخَفْ .

All medial vowels which are quiescent are dropped.

(B)

He did not give.   لَمْ يُعْطِ

He did not remain.   لَمْ يَبْقَ

He did not guide.   لَمْ يَهْتَدِ

He did not call.   لَمْ يَدْعُ

We did not hope.   لَمْ نَرْجُ

يُعْطِ is the changed form of يُعْطِي . Because of the Jussive particle (لَمْ) the final vowel (ي) is dropped. Similarly يَبْقَى becomes يَبْقَ , يَهْتَدِي becomes يَهْتَدِ , يَدْعُو becomes يَدْعُ and نَرْجُو becomes نَرْجُ .

N.B: In the jussive mood, 5 imperfect verbs which end with ḍammah shall be changed into sukún. All verbs which end with Nún, Núns shall be deleted except two Núns for women, IIIF^{3+} and IIF^{3+}.

✣ UNIT 50 ✣

Rule No. 73

When the underlined particles in the following sentences precede the Imperfect they change the Imperfect into the Jussive mood. Unlike the particle (لَمْ) the change occurs only in the form. These particles are generally conditional and the result of the condition is imparted in the Imperfect Jussive mood.

<u>إِنْ</u> تَجْتَهِدْ تَفُزْ.

(1) If you work hard you will succeed.

إِذْ مَا تَفْعَلْ تَنْدَمْ.

(2) If you do not work you will regret.

مَا تُنْفِقْ فِي سَبِيلِ اللهِ تَجِدْهُ عِنْدَ اللهِ.

(3) Whatever you spend in the way of Allah you will find it with Allah.

مَهْمَا تُنْفِقْ فِي الْبِرِّ تَنْفَعِ النَّاسَ.

(4) Whatsoever you spend in virtue you will benefit mankind.

مَنْ يَفْعَلْ خَيْراً يَفُزْ فِي الْآخِرَةِ.

(5) Whosoever does good succeeds in the Hereafter.

مَتَى تُسَافِرْ أُسَافِرْ.

(6) Whenever you travel I will travel.

أَيَّانَ تُنَادِ أُجِبْكَ.

(7) When you call I will answer you.

أَيْنَ تَذْهَبْ أَذْهَبْ مَعَكَ.

(8) Wherever you go I will go with you.

أَنَّى يَنْزِلِ الْعَالِمُ يُكْرِمْهُ النَّاسُ.

(9) Wherever the scholar descends people respect him.

حَيْثُمَا يَجْرِ مَاءُ الْمَطَرِ يُفِدْ.

(10)   Wherever the rainwater flows it benefits.

كَيْفَمَا أُعَامِلْ صَدِيْقِي يُعَامِلْنِي.

(11)   Howsoever I treat my friend he will treat me.

أَيَّ مَسْجِدٍ تَدْخُلْ تَسْلَمْ.

(12)   Whichever mosque you enter you feel secure.

Example Analysis:

إِنْ تَجْتَهِدْ تَفُزْ.

(1) If you work hard you will succeed.

(إِنْ if) is one of the Jussive particles, therefore, the Imperfect

(تَجْتَهِدْ) used for the condition is in the Jussive mood and its

result (تَفُزْ) is also in the Jussive mood.

إِذْ مَا تَفْعَلْ تَنْدَمْ.

(2) If you do not work you will regret.

إِذْ مَا when not is one of the Jussive particles, the

Imperfect (تَفْعَلْ) is used for the condition in the Jussive mood

and its result (تَنْدَمْ) is also in the Jussive mood.

حَيْثُمَا ، أَنَّى ، أَيْنَ ، أَيَّانَ ، مَتَى ، مَنْ ، مَهْمَا ، إِذْ مَا ،

مَا ، أَيَّ ، إِنْ and كَيْفَمَا

all are conditional Jussive particles. They have changed the
Imperfect forms, which indicate the condition, and the Imperfect
forms which provide the results of the conditions into the
Jussive moods.

431

UNIT 51

ثُلَاثِي مَزِيدٌ فِيهِ: بَابُ افْتِعَالٌ

*افْتِعَالٌ   *Derived Form VIII*

Formation:

It is formed by prefixing *Alif maksūr* after keeping the radical *Fā'* quiescent and *Tā'* before the radical *'Ayn* افْتَعَلَ

It is to be noted that certain exceptional changes occur in this form.

(i) When the radical *Fā'* is a vowel it changes into *Tā'*

أَخَذَ (I) becomes اتَّخَذَ (VIII) (to take something)

وَقَى (I) becomes اتَّقَى (VIII) (to be on one's guard, to be conscious of ones duty to Allah)

(ii) The consonant *Tā'* of افْتَعَلَ is changed to *ṭā'*.

طَلَعَ (I) becomes اطَّلَعَ (VIII) (to obtain information)

(iii) If the radical *Fā'* is *Ẓā'* then the consonant *ta'* of افْتَعَلَ changes into *ẓā'*.

ظَلَمَ (I) becomes اظَّلَمَ (VIII) (to suffer injustice)

(iv) If the radical *Fā'* is either *Dāl'*, *Dhāl'* or *Ẓā'* the consonant *Tā'* of افْتَعَلَ becomes *Dāl'*.

ذَكَرَ (I) becomes ادَّكَرَ (VIII) (to remember)

---

* A *ḥarakah* is deliberately placed under or above *hamzat al-waṣl* for the purposes of learning in this and subsequent lessons.

دَعَى (I) becomes ادَّعَى (VIII) (to lay claim)

زَادَ (I) becomes ازْدَادَ (VIII) (to grow)

(v) The *Alif* of this form is *Hamzat al-Waṣl* which remains silent when it combines with another word.

$$فَاجْتَمَعَ = فَ + اِجْتَمَعَ$$

The other conjugations in the Perfect Indicative follow the pattern of افْتَعَلَ and their endings remain the same as for the Perfect in the First Form.

(See Table C under VIII)

Imperfect:

The formation of the Imperfect is based on the III M[1] pattern (يَفْتَعِلُ). All prefixes and endings remain the same as in the First Form.

(See Table D under VIII)

Verbal Noun:

The Verbal Noun is formed on the pattern of افْتِعَالٌ .

The Verbal noun for انْتَظَرَ to wait for someone is

انْتِظَارٌ(waiting, wait).

Active Participle:

The Active Participle is formed on the pattern of مُفْتَعِلٌ /

مُنْتَظِرٌ (waiting)

Passive Participle:

The Passive Participle is formed on the pattern of مُفْتَعَل /

مُنْتَظَرٌ (waited)

(For verbal nouns, Active and Passive participles see TB under VIII)

Significances:

(a) It expresses the acceptance of the influence of the First Form verb.

جَمَعْتُ النَّاسَ فَآجْتَمَعُوا

I gathered the people so they got together.

مَنَعْتُ الرَّجُلَ فَأَمْتَنَعَ

I prevented the man so he refrained.

(b) It sometimes indicates mutual co-operation.

اِخْتَلَفُوا they disagreed with each other.

اِشْتَرَكُوا they associated with each other.

(c) It sometimes reflects exertion from the completion of a work.

كَسَبَ (I) to earn   اِكْتَسَبَ to earn with effort

حَمَلَ (I) to carry   اِحْتَمَلَ to carry with some effort

(d) It sometimes gives the same meaning as in the First Form.

اِقْتَرَبَ   to draw near

اِبْتَعَدَ   to go far

اِقْتَدَرَ   to have power

(e) Sometimes it imparts a completely new meaning

| اِغْتَسَلَ | to take bath |
| اِنْتَظَرَ | to wait |

Exercise No. 32

From the Qur'ānic Text of Lesson 13 identify the Imperfect Jussive.

Calligraphy on white marble.

✾ METHOD OF TEACHING ✾
LESSON 13

1. The Jussive mood is very important. It is something of a foundation because upon it depends the formation of the Subjunctives and the corroborative *Nūn*, Imperatives and Prohibitives. All efforts, therefore, should be made to ensure that the students understand the Jussive mood.

2. Rules 69-73 should be made clear after projecting these rules one after the other and explaining fully the changes, which occur in the Imperfect Forms.

3. Ask the students to construct a few sentences with the use of some of the Jussive particles.

4. In some roots the derived Form اِفْتَعَلَ behaves strangely.

    All these exceptional changes should be explained to the students.

5. Repeat steps 6-8 for the introduction of the Eighth Form (اِفْتَعَلَ)

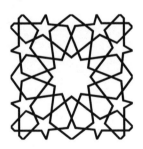

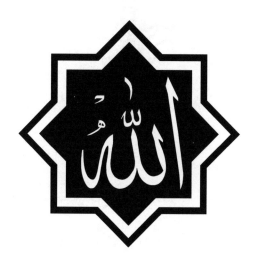

النَّصُّ القُرْآنِي

Lesson 14

١. وَٱلَّذِينَ ءَامَنُوٓاْ أَشَدُّ حُبًّا لِّلَّهِ (2: 165)

٢. وَلَذِكْرُ ٱللَّهِ أَكْبَرُ (29: 45)

٣. وَٱلْفِتْنَةُ أَكْبَرُ مِنَ ٱلْقَتْلِ (2: 217)

٤. وَٱلْفِتْنَةُ أَشَدُّ مِنَ ٱلْقَتْلِ (2: 191)

٥. فَلَمَّا رَءَا ٱلشَّمْسَ بَازِغَةً قَالَ هَٰذَا رَبِّى هَٰذَآ أَكْبَرُ (6: 78)

٦. وَمَآ أَمْرُ ٱلسَّاعَةِ إِلَّا كَلَمْحِ ٱلْبَصَرِ أَوْ هُوَ أَقْرَبُ (16: 77)

٧. وَمَنْ أَحْسَنُ دِينًا مِّمَّنْ أَسْلَمَ وَجْهَهُ لِلَّهِ وَهُوَ مُحْسِنٌ (4: 125)

٨. ءَأَنتُمْ أَشَدُّ خَلْقًا أَمِ ٱلسَّمَآءُ بَنَٰهَا (79: 27)

٩. وَٱتَّبِعُوٓاْ أَحْسَنَ مَآ أُنزِلَ إِلَيْكُم مِّن رَّبِّكُم (39: 55)

١٠. إِنَّنِى أَنَا ٱللَّهُ لَآ إِلَٰهَ إِلَّآ أَنَا۠ فَٱعْبُدْنِى وَأَقِمِ ٱلصَّلَوٰةَ لِذِكْرِىٓ (20: 14)

١١. أَطِيعُوا۟ ٱللَّهَ وَأَطِيعُوا۟ ٱلرَّسُولَ وَأُو۟لِى ٱلْأَمْرِ مِنكُمْ (4: 59)

١٢. يَٰٓأَيُّهَا ٱلَّذِينَ ءَامَنُوا۟ ٱرْكَعُوا۟ وَٱسْجُدُوا۟ وَٱعْبُدُوا۟

رَبَّكُمْ وَٱفْعَلُوا۟ ٱلْخَيْرَ لَعَلَّكُمْ تُفْلِحُونَ ۩

وَجَٰهِدُوا۟ فِى ٱللَّهِ حَقَّ جِهَادِهِۦ (22: 77-78)

١٣. يَٰٓأَيُّهَا ٱلَّذِينَ ءَامَنُوا۟ ٱتَّقُوا۟ ٱللَّهَ وَكُونُوا۟ مَعَ

ٱلصَّٰدِقِينَ (9: 119)

١٤. ٱدْعُ إِلَىٰ سَبِيلِ رَبِّكَ بِٱلْحِكْمَةِ وَٱلْمَوْعِظَةِ ٱلْحَسَنَةِ

وَجَٰدِلْهُم بِٱلَّتِى هِىَ أَحْسَنُ (16: 125)

١٥. قُلْ إِنَّ صَلَاتِى وَنُسُكِى وَمَحْيَاىَ وَمَمَاتِى لِلَّهِ رَبِّ

ٱلْعَٰلَمِينَ (6: 162)

١٦. حَٰفِظُوا۟ عَلَى ٱلصَّلَوَٰتِ وَٱلصَّلَوٰةِ ٱلْوُسْطَىٰ وَقُومُوا۟ لِلَّهِ

قَٰنِتِينَ (2: 238)

١٧. ٱعْدِلُوا۟ هُوَ أَقْرَبُ لِلتَّقْوَىٰ (5: 8)

١٨. كُونُواْ قَوَّٰمِينَ بِٱلْقِسْطِ شُهَدَآءَ لِلَّهِ وَلَوْ عَلَىٰٓ أَنفُسِكُمْ أَوِ ٱلْوَٰلِدَيْنِ وَٱلْأَقْرَبِينَ إِن يَكُنْ غَنِيًّا أَوْ فَقِيرًا فَٱللَّهُ أَوْلَىٰ بِهِمَا (4: 135)

١٩. وَإِذَا قُلْتُمْ فَٱعْدِلُواْ وَلَوْ كَانَ ذَا قُرْبَىٰ (6: 152)

٢٠. وَتَزَوَّدُواْ فَإِنَّ خَيْرَ ٱلزَّادِ ٱلتَّقْوَىٰ (2: 197)

٢١. وَبِٱلْوَٰلِدَيْنِ إِحْسَٰنًا إِمَّا يَبْلُغَنَّ عِندَكَ ٱلْكِبَرَ أَحَدُهُمَآ أَوْ كِلَاهُمَا فَلَا تَقُل لَّهُمَآ أُفٍّ وَلَا تَنْهَرْهُمَا وَقُل لَّهُمَا قَوْلاً كَرِيمًا ۝ وَٱخْفِضْ لَهُمَا جَنَاحَ ٱلذُّلِّ مِنَ ٱلرَّحْمَةِ (17: 23-24)

٢٢. وَيَسْـَٔلُونَكَ مَاذَا يُنفِقُونَ قُلِ ٱلْعَفْوَ (2: 219)

٢٣. خُذْ مِنْ أَمْوَٰلِهِمْ صَدَقَةً تُطَهِّرُهُمْ وَتُزَكِّيهِم بِهَا (9: 103)

٢٤. يَٰٓأَيُّهَا ٱلنَّاسُ كُلُواْ مِمَّا فِي ٱلْأَرْضِ حَلَٰلًا طَيِّبًا (2: 168)

٢٥. وَءَاتَى ٱلْمَالَ عَلَىٰ حُبِّهِۦ ذَوِى ٱلْقُرْبَىٰ وَٱلْيَتَٰمَىٰ وَٱلْمَسَٰكِينَ وَٱبْنَ ٱلسَّبِيلِ وَٱلسَّآئِلِينَ وَفِي ٱلرِّقَابِ (2: 177)

٢٦. وَأَنفَقُواْ مِمَّا رَزَقْنَٰهُمْ سِرًّا وَعَلَانِيَةً (35: 29)

٢٧. وَكُلُواْ مِمَّا رَزَقَكُمُ ٱللَّهُ حَلَٰلًا طَيِّبًا (5: 88)

٢٨. كُلُواْ مِن طَيِّبَٰتِ مَا رَزَقْنَٰكُمْ وَٱشْكُرُواْ لِلَّهِ (2: 172)

٢٩. فَـَٔاتِ ذَا ٱلْقُرْبَىٰ حَقَّهُۥ (30: 38)

٣٠. يَٰٓأَيُّهَا ٱلَّذِينَ ءَامَنُواْ ٱتَّقُواْ ٱللَّهَ وَذَرُواْ مَا بَقِىَ مِنَ

ٱلرِّبَوٰٓاْ إِن كُنتُم مُّؤْمِنِينَ (2: 278)

٣١. يَٰٓأَيُّهَا ٱلَّذِينَ ءَامَنُوٓاْ أَنفِقُواْ مِمَّا رَزَقْنَٰكُم مِّن قَبْلِ أَن

يَأْتِىَ يَوْمٌ لَّا بَيْعٌ فِيهِ وَلَا خُلَّةٌ وَلَا شَفَٰعَةٌ (2: 254)

٣٢. إِنَّمَا ٱلْمُؤْمِنُونَ إِخْوَةٌ فَأَصْلِحُواْ بَيْنَ أَخَوَيْكُمْ وَٱتَّقُواْ

ٱللَّهَ لَعَلَّكُمْ تُرْحَمُونَ (49: 10)

٣٣. وَٱعْتَصِمُواْ بِحَبْلِ ٱللَّهِ جَمِيعًا وَلَا تَفَرَّقُواْ (3: 103)

٣٤. وَمَآ ءَاتَىٰكُمُ ٱلرَّسُولُ فَخُذُوهُ وَمَا نَهَىٰكُمْ عَنْهُ فَٱنتَهُواْ

وَٱتَّقُواْ ٱللَّهَ إِنَّ ٱللَّهَ شَدِيدُ ٱلْعِقَابِ (7: 59)

٣٥. وَإِذَا قُلْتُمْ فَٱعْدِلُواْ وَلَوْ كَانَ ذَا قُرْبَىٰ (6: 152)

٣٦. وَأَوْفُواْ بِٱلْعَهْدِ إِنَّ ٱلْعَهْدَ كَانَ مَسْـُٔولًا (17: 34)

٣٧. يَٰٓأَيُّهَا ٱلَّذِينَ ءَامَنُوٓاْ أَوْفُواْ بِٱلْعُقُودِ (5: 1)

٣٨. يَـٰٓأَيُّهَا ٱلَّذِينَ ءَامَنُوا۟ ٱتَّقُوا۟ ٱللَّهَ وَقُولُوا۟ قَوْلًا سَدِيدًا
(33: 70)

٣٩. وَٱجْتَنِبُوا۟ قَوْلَ ٱلزُّورِ (22: 30)

٤٠. وَٱقْصِدْ فِى مَشْيِكَ وَٱغْضُضْ مِن صَوْتِكَ (31: 19)

٤١. وَذَرُوا۟ ظَـٰهِرَ ٱلْإِثْمِ وَبَاطِنَهُۥ (6: 120)

٤٢. يَـٰٓأَيُّهَا ٱلَّذِينَ ءَامَنُوٓا۟ إِنَّمَا ٱلْخَمْرُ وَٱلْمَيْسِرُ وَٱلْأَنصَابُ وَٱلْأَزْلَـٰمُ رِجْسٌ مِّنْ عَمَلِ ٱلشَّيْطَـٰنِ فَٱجْتَنِبُوهُ لَعَلَّكُمْ تُفْلِحُونَ (5: 90)

٤٣. وَقُلِ ٱعْمَلُوا۟ فَسَيَرَى ٱللَّهُ عَمَلَكُمْ (9: 105)

٤٤. يَـٰٓأَيُّهَا ٱلَّذِينَ ءَامَنُوا۟ قُوٓا۟ أَنفُسَكُمْ وَأَهْلِيكُمْ نَارًا (66: 6)

٤٥. وَأَوْفُوا۟ ٱلْكَيْلَ وَٱلْمِيزَانَ بِٱلْقِسْطِ (6: 152)

٤٦. خُذِ ٱلْعَفْوَ وَأْمُرْ بِٱلْعُرْفِ وَأَعْرِضْ عَنِ ٱلْجَـٰهِلِينَ (7: 199)

٤٧. يَـٰٓأَيُّهَا ٱلَّذِينَ ءَامَنُوا۟ ٱذْكُرُوا۟ ٱللَّهَ ذِكْرًا كَثِيرًا (33: 41)

٤٨. يَـٰٓأَيُّهَا ٱلَّذِينَ ءَامَنُوا۟ تُوبُوٓا۟ إِلَى ٱللَّهِ تَوْبَةً نَّصُوحًا (66: 8)

٤٩. قُلْ يَـٰعِبَادِىَ ٱلَّذِينَ أَسْرَفُوا۟ عَلَىٰٓ أَنفُسِهِمْ لَا تَقْنَطُوا۟ مِن رَّحْمَةِ ٱللَّهِ إِنَّ ٱللَّهَ يَغْفِرُ ٱلذُّنُوبَ جَمِيعًا (39: 53)

٥٠. قُل لِّلْمُؤْمِنِينَ يَغُضُّوا۟ مِنْ أَبْصَٰرِهِمْ وَيَحْفَظُوا۟ فُرُوجَهُمْ ۚ ذَٰلِكَ أَزْكَىٰ لَهُمْ ۗ (24: 30)

٥١. وَلَا تَهِنُوا۟ وَلَا تَحْزَنُوا۟ وَأَنتُمُ ٱلْأَعْلَوْنَ إِن كُنتُم مُّؤْمِنِينَ (3: 139)

٥٢. يَٰٓأَيُّهَا ٱلَّذِينَ ءَامَنُوا۟ لَا تَكُونُوا۟ كَٱلَّذِينَ كَفَرُوا۟ (3: 156)

٥٣. وَلَا تَقْرَبُوا۟ ٱلْفَوَٰحِشَ مَا ظَهَرَ مِنْهَا وَمَا بَطَنَ ۖ (6: 151)

٥٤. وَلَا تَأْكُلُوٓا۟ أَمْوَٰلَكُم بَيْنَكُم بِٱلْبَٰطِلِ وَتُدْلُوا۟ بِهَآ إِلَى ٱلْحُكَّامِ لِتَأْكُلُوا۟ فَرِيقًا مِّنْ أَمْوَٰلِ ٱلنَّاسِ بِٱلْإِثْمِ وَأَنتُمْ تَعْلَمُونَ (2: 188)

٥٥. وَلَا تَقْتُلُوٓا۟ أَوْلَٰدَكُمْ خَشْيَةَ إِمْلَٰقٍ ۖ نَّحْنُ نَرْزُقُهُمْ وَإِيَّاكُمْ ۚ إِنَّ قَتْلَهُمْ كَانَ خِطْـًٔا كَبِيرًا (17: 31)

٥٦. وَأَمَّا ٱلسَّآئِلَ فَلَا تَنْهَرْ (93: 10)

٥٧. فَأَمَّا ٱلْيَتِيمَ فَلَا تَقْهَرْ (93: 9)

٥٨. وَلَا تَجْعَلْ يَدَكَ مَغْلُولَةً إِلَىٰ عُنُقِكَ وَلَا تَبْسُطْهَا كُلَّ ٱلْبَسْطِ فَتَقْعُدَ مَلُومًا مَّحْسُورًا (17: 29)

443

٥٩. وَأَنفِقُواْ فِى سَبِيلِ ٱللَّهِ وَلَا تُلْقُواْ بِأَيْدِيكُمْ إِلَى ٱلتَّهْلُكَةِ
(2: 195)

٦٠. وَلَا تَقْتُلُواْ ٱلنَّفْسَ ٱلَّتِى حَرَّمَ ٱللَّهُ إِلَّا بِٱلْحَقِّ (17: 33)

٦١. وَلَا تَقْتُلُوٓاْ أَنفُسَكُمْ (4: 29)

٦٢. وَلَا تَقْرَبُواْ ٱلزِّنَىٰٓ إِنَّهُۥ كَانَ فَٰحِشَةً وَسَآءَ سَبِيلًا (17: 32)

٦٣. وَلَا تَمْشِ فِى ٱلْأَرْضِ مَرَحًا (17: 37)

٦٤. وَلَا تَيَمَّمُواْ ٱلْخَبِيثَ مِنْهُ تُنفِقُونَ (2: 267)

٦٥. يَٰٓأَيُّهَا ٱلَّذِينَ ءَامَنُواْ لَا يَسْخَرْ قَوْمٌ مِّن قَوْمٍ (49: 11)

٦٦. وَلَا تَجَسَّسُواْ وَلَا يَغْتَب بَّعْضُكُم بَعْضًا (49: 12)

٦٧. وَلَا تَنَابَزُواْ بِٱلْأَلْقَٰبِ (49: 11)

٦٨. وَلَا تَسُبُّواْ ٱلَّذِينَ يَدْعُونَ مِن دُونِ ٱللَّهِ فَيَسُبُّواْ ٱللَّهَ عَدْوًۢا بِغَيْرِ عِلْمٍ (6: 108)

٦٩. وَلَا تَجْهَرْ بِصَلَاتِكَ وَلَا تُخَافِتْ بِهَا وَٱبْتَغِ بَيْنَ ذَٰلِكَ سَبِيلًا (17: 110)

٧٠. فَلَا تَذْهَبْ نَفْسُكَ عَلَيْهِمْ حَسَرَٰتٍ إِنَّ ٱللَّهَ عَلِيمٌۢ بِمَا يَصْنَعُونَ (35: 8)

٧١. يَـٰٓأَيُّهَا ٱلَّذِينَ ءَامَنُوا۟ لَا تُحَرِّمُوا۟ طَيِّبَـٰتِ مَآ أَحَلَّ ٱللَّهُ لَكُمْ

وَلَا تَعْتَدُوٓا۟ إِنَّ ٱللَّهَ لَا يُحِبُّ ٱلْمُعْتَدِينَ (5: 87)

٧٢. وَلَا تَا۟يْـَٔسُوا۟ مِن رَّوْحِ ٱللَّهِ إِنَّهُۥ لَا يَا۟يْـَٔسُ مِن رَّوْحِ ٱللَّهِ

إِلَّا ٱلْقَوْمُ ٱلْكَـٰفِرُونَ (12: 87)

٧٣. يَـٰٓأَيُّهَا ٱلَّذِينَ ءَامَنُوا۟ لَا يَسْخَرْ قَوْمٌ مِّن قَوْمٍ عَسَىٰٓ أَن

يَكُونُوا۟ خَيْرًا مِّنْهُمْ وَلَا نِسَآءٌ مِّن نِّسَآءٍ عَسَىٰٓ أَن يَكُنَّ

خَيْرًا مِّنْهُنَّ وَلَا تَلْمِزُوٓا۟ أَنفُسَكُمْ وَلَا تَنَابَزُوا۟ بِٱلْأَلْقَـٰبِ

بِئْسَ ٱلِٱسْمُ ٱلْفُسُوقُ بَعْدَ ٱلْإِيمَـٰنِ وَمَن لَّمْ يَتُبْ

فَأُو۟لَـٰٓئِكَ هُمُ ٱلظَّـٰلِمُونَ (49: 11)

٧٤. فَلَا تَجْعَلُوا۟ لِلَّهِ أَندَادًا وَأَنتُمْ تَعْلَمُونَ (2: 22)

٧٥. وَلَا تَجْعَلُوا۟ ٱللَّهَ عُرْضَةً لِّأَيْمَـٰنِكُمْ (2: 224)

٧٦. إِنَّ ٱللَّهَ يَأْمُرُ بِٱلْعَدْلِ وَٱلْإِحْسَـٰنِ وَإِيتَآئِ ذِى ٱلْقُرْبَىٰ

وَيَنْهَىٰ عَنِ ٱلْفَحْشَآءِ وَٱلْمُنكَرِ وَٱلْبَغْىِ يَعِظُكُمْ

لَعَلَّكُمْ تَذَكَّرُونَ (16: 90)

٧٧. إِذَا ٱلسَّمَآءُ ٱنفَطَرَتْ ۝ وَإِذَا ٱلْكَوَاكِبُ ٱنتَثَرَتْ

(82: 1-2)

٧٨. تَكَادُ ٱلسَّمَوَاتُ يَتَفَطَّرْنَ مِنْهُ وَتَنشَقُّ ٱلْأَرْضُ (19: 90)

٧٩. ٱلسَّمَاءُ مُنفَطِرٌ بِهِ ۚ كَانَ وَعْدُهُ مَفْعُولاً (73: 18)

٨٠. ثُمَّ ٱرْجِعِ ٱلْبَصَرَ كَرَّتَيْنِ يَنقَلِبْ إِلَيْكَ ٱلْبَصَرُ خَاسِئًا وَهُوَ حَسِيرٌ (67: 4)

٨١. وَتَعَاوَنُواْ عَلَى ٱلْبِرِّ وَٱلتَّقْوَىٰ ۖ وَلَا تَعَاوَنُواْ عَلَى ٱلْإِثْمِ وَٱلْعُدْوَانِ ۚ (5: 2)

٨٢. وَسَيَعْلَمُ ٱلَّذِينَ ظَلَمُواْ أَيَّ مُنقَلَبٍ يَنقَلِبُونَ (26: 227)

٨٣. فَسَوْفَ تُحَاسَبُ حِسَابًا يَسِيرًا ۞ وَيَنقَلِبُ إِلَىٰ أَهْلِهِ مَسْرُورًا (84: 8-9)

٨٤. قَالُواْ إِنَّا إِلَىٰ رَبِّنَا مُنقَلِبُونَ (7: 125)

٨٥. وَإِنْ أَصَابَتْهُ فِتْنَةٌ ٱنقَلَبَ عَلَىٰ وَجْهِهِ خَسِرَ ٱلدُّنْيَا وَٱلْآخِرَةَ ۚ ذَٰلِكَ هُوَ ٱلْخُسْرَانُ ٱلْمُبِينُ (22: 11)

QUR'ANIC TEXT
VOCABULARY
LESSON 14

أَشَدُّ	most severe	عَفْوٌ	Forgiving
فِتْنَةٌ	temptation, sedition	زَكَّى/يُزَكِّي	II to purify, to clean
أَكْبَرُ	great	حَلَالٌ	lawful
بَازِغٌ	[AP] uprising	طَيِّبٌ	good
لَمْعٌ	twinkling	مِسْكِينٌ / ج مَسَاكِينٌ	poor
سَبِيلٌ/ ج سُبُلٌ	path, way, manner	ابْنُ السَّبِيلِ	wayfarer
جَادَلَ/يُجَادِلُ	III to quarrel, to dispute	سَائِلٌ	[AP] questioner, beggar
نُسُكٌ	slaughtering an animal by way of sacrifice	عَلَانِيَةٌ	openly
مَحْيَا	[VN] to live life	ذَرَى/ يَذْرُو	to disperse
مَمَاتٌ	death	قُرْبَى	kindred
وُسْطَى	middle	بَيْعٌ	[VN] selling and buying
أَقْرَبُ	most closed	خُلَّةٌ	friendship
أَقْرَبُونَ	kins, relatives	شَفَاعَةٌ	[VN] intercession
أَوْلَى	the nearest one	اعْتَصَمَ/يَعْتَصِمُ	VIII to hold fast

447

قُرْبَى	kinship	حَبْلٌ	rope
تَزَوَّدَ/يَتَزَوَّدُ	V to provide food for journey	عِقَابٌ	chastisement
كِلاَ	Both	عَدَلَ / يَعْدِلُ	to act justly
خَفَضَ	to depress, to lower	أَوْفَى/ يُوْفِي	to fulfill
جَنَاحٌ	wing	عَهْدٌ	fulfillment of (a promise)
ذُلٌّ	weakness	عَقْدٌ /ج عُقُودٌ	knot
اجْتَنَبَ/يَجْتَنِبُ	VIII to avoid	سَدِيْدٌ	straight to the point, proper
زُوْرٌ	falsehood	قَهَرَ/ يَقْهَرُ	to oppress, to force
قَصَدَ (فى)/ يَقْصِدُ	to adopt a middle course	مَغْلُولٌ	[PP] fettered
مَشْيٌ	walk	مَلُومٌ	[PP] blamed
غَضَّ/ يَغُضُّ	to lower the voice or eyes	مَحْسُورٌ	[PP] impoverished stripped off
صَوْتٌ	voice	تَهْلُكَةٌ	[VN] perdition
خَمْرٌ	wine	زِنًا	Adultery
مَيْسِرٌ	gambling	مَرَحٌ	Struttingly
نِصَابٌ /ج أَنْصَابٌ	idol, image, goal	تَيَمَّمَ/ يَتَيَمَّمُ	V to intend
زَلَمٌ/ ج أَزْلاَمٌ	an arrow without a head and feathers	خَبِيْثٌ	foul, evil, bad

رِجْسٌ	uncleanliness	سَخِرَ / يَسْخَرُ	to make fun of, to laugh at, to mock
مِيزَانٌ	weight, balance	تَجَسُّسُ	[VN²] to investigate, to spy
قِسْطٌ	justice	اِغْتَابَ / يَغْتَابُ	VIII to backbite
أَعْرَضَ (عَنْ)/ يُعْرِضُ	IV to turn away	سَبَّ / يَسُبُّ	to revile, to defame
نَصُوحٌ	true and sincere (repentance)	اِبْتَغَى / يَبْتَغِي	VIII to seek
فَاحِشَةٌ / ج فَوَاحِشٌ	vile deed	اِعْتَدَى / يَعْتَدِي	VIII to transgress
بَاطِلٌ	falsehood	مُعْتَدِ	[AP⁸] transgressor
إِمْلَاقٌ	[VN⁴] falling to poverty	يَئِسَ / يَيْأَسُ	to despair, to give up hope
أَدْلَى / يُدْلِي	IV to convey	رَوْحٌ	bounty, mercy
خَطَأً	mistake, wrong	عَسَى	may, well be, it may be
نَهَرَ / يَنْهَرُ	to floe, to repulse	لَمَزَ / يَلْمِزُ	to defame
لَقَبٌ / ج أَلْقَابٌ	nickname	تَنَابَزَ / يَتَنَابَزُ	VI to call each other in insulting name
فِسْقٌ / ج فُسُوقٌ	[VN] abomination, transgression	اِنْشَقَّ / يَنْشَقُّ	VII to rent asunder
نِدٌّ / ج أَنْدَادٌ	like, equal, match	مُنْفَطِرٌ	[AP⁷] split (one)
عُرْضَةٌ	a butt, an excuse	كَرَّةٌ	a return
يَمِينٌ / أَيْمَانٌ	oath, right hand	خَاسِئٌ	[AP] despised one

449

بَغْيٌ	[VN] oppressing	حَسِيرٌ	[AP] dim, dull, weary, exhausted
اِنْفَطَرَ/ يَنْفَطِرُ	VII to be broken	اِنْقَلَبَ/ يَنْقَلِبُ	VII to be turned round or over, to return
كَوْكَبٌ/ ج كُوَاكِبُ	star	مُنْقَلِبٌ	[AP⁷] returning
اِنْتَشَرَ/ يَنْتَشِرُ	VIII to disperse, to disseminate	مَسْرُورٌ	[PP] delighted
تَفَطَّرَ/ يَتَفَطَّرُ	V to be split, to be broken into pieces		

"Enter there in peace, secure." (**15**: 46)

450

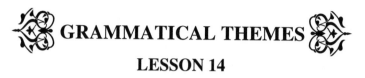

GRAMMATICAL THEMES
LESSON 14

أَفْعَلُ التَّفْضِيْلِ

The أَفْعَلُ of Superiority

Rule No. 74

When two things are compared with each other in their size, quality, inferiority or superiority, the noun on the pattern of أَفْعَلُ is used for both genders and is called the أَفْعَلُ of Superiority.

Example Analysis:

(١) اللهُ أَكْبَرُ

(1) Allah is Great.

(٢) زَيْدٌ أَصْغَرُ مِنْ أَحْمَدَ.

(2) Zayd is smaller than Aḥmad.

(٣) الْخَيْرُ أَحْسَنُ مِنَ الشَّرِّ.

(3) Virtue is better than vice.

(٤) الزَّيْتُونُ أَرْخَصُ مِنَ التِّيْنِ.

(4) The olive is cheaper than the fig.

(٥) الْعَالِمَاتُ أَفْضَلُ مِنَ الْجَاهِلَاتِ.

451

(5) The learned women are superior to the ignorant women.

In the above sentences the nouns أَرْخَصُ، أَحْسَنُ، أَصْغَرُ، أَكْبَرُ

And أَفْضَلُ are on the pattern of أَفْعَلُ and these are *Af'al al –*
Tafḍīl.

Note in sentence No. 5 it is used for feminine nouns.

Rule No. 75

When the أَفْعَلُ of superiority is used as definite it generally
gives the meaning of adjective.

(١) الْوَلَدُ الأَصْغَرُ. The small boy.

(٢) الْوَلَدُ الأَكْبَرُ The big boy.

In the above two sentences أَصْغَرُ and أَكْبَرُ are used as definites,
therefore, neither give the meaning of superiority but instead
both have become adjectives.

Note the feminine of أَفْعَلُ behaves along the pattern of فُعْلَى

(F) صُغْرَى/(M) أَصْغَرُ   (F); كُبْرَى   (M) أَكْبَرُ

(F) أُوْلَى / (M) أَوَّلُ   (F);عُظْمَى / (M) أَعْظَمُ

The plural of أَفْعَلُ (masculine) behaves on the pattern of أَفَاعِلُ
and أَفْعَلُونَ

(M³⁺) أَوَائِلُ / أَوَّلُونَ   (M¹) أَوَّلُ

(M³⁺) أَكَابِرُ / أَكْبَرُونَ   (M¹) أَكْبَرُ

الرِّجَالُ الأَكَارِمُ   The noble men

452

The plural of فُعْلَى (feminine) behaves on the pattern of

فُعْلَى and فُعْلَيَات

كُبَرٌ / كُبْرَيَاتٌ (M³⁺)   كُبْرَى (F¹)

أُوَلٌ / أُوْلَيَاتٌ (F³⁺)   أُوْلَى (F¹)

This is the great calamity.   هَذِهِ هِيَ الْمُصِيْبَةُ الْعُظْمَى

Rule No. 76

**If the noun on the pattern of أَفْعَل denotes the meaning of
colour, any defect in the human body or sickness then it is
not regarded as the noun of superiority.**

Example Analysis:

(1)   أَبْيَضُ (white),   أَسْوَدُ (black),   أَحْمَرُ (red),

أَخْضَرُ (green),   أَصْفَرُ (yellow)

All these nouns are on the pattern of أَفْعَل . Since they give the
meaning of colour, they are therefore, not the nouns of
superiority.

(2)   أَعْمَى (blind),   أَصَمُّ (deaf),   أَبْكَمُ (dumb),

أَعْوَرُ (one - eyed),   أَعْرَجُ (lame)

All these nouns are on the pattern of أَفْعَل. Since they give the
meaning of defects in the human body, they too therefore, are
not treated as nouns of superiority.

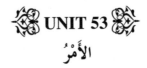

UNIT 53

الأَمْرُ

Amr: Imperative:

Formation:

The Imperative is formed from the Imperfect Jussive mood. The Jussive mood has already been treated in the previous lesson, and therefore the formation of Imperative will be easy to understand.

The Method of Making an Imperative:

Rule No. 77

The formation of the Imperative needs the six second person Imperfect Indicative forms (II M^1+M^2 +M^{3+}; II F^1+ F^2 + F^{3+}). First of all they should be changed into the Jussive mood. After that under a second change the initial *Tā'* should be deleted. In some verbs whatever is left over after these two changes is the Imperative while in some other verbs the left over form needs certain minor adjustments.

A

Meaning	Imperative	First Change (Jussive)	II Person Imperfect	Verbs in III Person
say	قُلْ	تَقُلْ	تَقُولُ	قَالَ / يَقُولُ
sell	بِعْ	تَبِعْ	تَبِيعُ	بَاعَ / يَبِيعُ
come	جِئْ	تَجِئْ	تَجِيءُ	جَاءَ / يَجِيءُ
promise	عِدْ	تَعِدْ	تَعِدُ	وَعَدَ / يَعِدُ
sleep	نَمْ	تَنَمْ	تَنَامُ	نَامَ / يَنَامُ
guard	قِ	تَقِ	تَقِي	وَقَى / يَقِي
command	مُرْ	تَأْمُرْ	تَأْمُرُ	أَمَرَ / يَأْمُرُ

454

call	نَادِ	تُنَاد تُنَادِى	نَادَى / يُنَادِى
move forward	تَقَدَّمْ	تَتَقَدَّمْ تَتَقَدَّمُ	تَقَدَّمَ/ يَتَقَدَّمُ

B

Enter	اُدْخُلْ	تَدْخُلْ تَدْخُلُ	دَخَلَ / يَدْخُلُ
be kind	اُلْطُفْ	تلْطُفْ تلْطُفُ	لَطَفَ/يَلْطُفُ
call	اُدْعُ	تَدْعُ تَدْعُو	دَعَا/يَدْعُو
write	اُكْتُبْ	تَكْتُبْ تَكْتُبُ	كَتَبَ/ يَكْتُبُ
come out	اُخْرُجْ	تَخْرُجْ تَخْرُجُ	خَرَجَ/يَخْرُجُ

In the above examples after the first change when the initial *tā'* is deleted it leaves the radical *Fā'* quiescent which presents some difficulty in reading the word. In order to over come this difficulty and for the sake of convenience in reading a *ḥamzat al-waṣl*, connecting *ḥamzah*, is added. The *ḥarakah*, short vowel sign on the *ḥamzat al - waṣl* is decided on the *ḥarakah* which the medial radical *'Ayn* carries. If the radical *'Ayn* carries *ḍammah* then generally *ḍammah* is placed on the *ḥamzat al-waṣl* for the convenience of reading. If it carries either *fathah* or *kasrah* then *kasrah* is placed under it. If any preceding letter joins it then *ḥamzat al - waṣl* remains silent but is nevertheless written.

In the examples under B *ḥamzat al-waṣl* carrying *ḍammah* in the (imperfect).

Note that *ḥarakah* is not placed neither under or on a *ḥamzat al-waṣl*. The *ḥarakah* is placed in these examples for learning purpose.

C

Meaning	Imperative	First Change (Jussive)	II Person Imperfect	Verbs in III Person
be pleased	اِرْضَ	تَرْضَ	تَرْضَى	رَضِيَ/يَرْضَى
guide	اهْدِ	تَهْدِ	تَهْدِي	هَدَى/يَهْدِي
struggle	اِسْعَ	تَسْعَ	تَسْعَى	سَعَى/يَسْعَى
Make something	اِصْنَعْ	تَصْنَعْ	تَصْنَعُ	صَنَعَ/يَصْنَعُ
ask	اِسْأَلْ	تَسْأَلْ	تَسْأَلُ	سَأَلَ/يَسْأَلُ
be patient	اِصْبِرْ	تَصْبِرْ	تَصْبِرُ	صَبَرَ/يَصْبِرُ
be merciful	اِرْحَمْ	تَرْحَمْ	تَرْحَمُ	رَحِمَ/يَرْحَمُ
read	اِقْرَأْ	تَقْرَأْ	تَقْرَأُ	قَرَأَ/يَقْرَأُ
take	اِتَّخِذْ	تَتَّخِذْ	تَتَّخِذُ	اِتَّخَذَ/يَتَّخِذُ

In the above examples the radical 'Ayn carries *fatḥah* or *kasrah* therefore, *hamzat al-waṣl* carries *kasrah* in the imperative.

D

Meaning	Imperative	First Change (Jussive)	II Person Imperfect	Verbs in III Person
prolong	أَطِلْ	تُطِلْ	تُطِيلُ	أَطَالَ/يُطِيلُ
help	أَعِنْ	تُعِنْ	تُعِينُ	أَعَانَ/يُعِينُ
light	أَوْقِدْ	تُوقِدْ	تُوقِدُ	أَوْقَدَ/يُوقِدُ
extinguish	أَطْفِئْ	تُطْفِئْ	تُطْفِئُ	أَطْفَأَ/يُطْفِئُ
send	أَرْسِلْ	تُرْسِلْ	تُرْسِلُ	أَرْسَلَ/يُرْسِلُ

In these examples, the imperative is made from the Fourth Form. In this form the initial *hamzah* is *hamzat al-qaṭ‛*, disjunctive *hamzah*. For distinction between the First and the Fourth Forms, a disjunctive *hamzah* is added in the Imperative.

E

take	أُوخُذْ/خُذْ	تَأْخُذْ	يَأْخُذُ	أَخَذَ/يَأْخُذَ
command	أُومُرْ/مُرْ	تَأْمُرْ	تَأْمُرُ	أَمَرَ/يَأْمُرُ
eat	أُوكُلْ/كُلْ	تَأْكُلْ	تَأْكُلُ	أَكَلَ/يَأْكُلُ
come	ائْتِ	تَأْتِ	تَأْتِي	أَتَى/يَأْتِي

F

pass	مُرَّ/اُمْرُرْ	تَمُرَّ	تَمُرُّ	مَرَّ/يَمُرُّ
touch	مُسَّ	تَمَسَّ	تَمَسُّ	مَسَّ/يَمَسُّ
draw tight	اُشْدُدْ	تَشُدَّ	تَشُدُّ	شَدَّ/يَشُدُّ
respect	اعْزُزْ	تَعِزَّ	تَعِزُّ	عَزَّ/يَعِزُّ

The examples under E and F present certain exceptional Imperative forms.

Conjugation of Imperative:

(A)		(B)	
قُلْ (II M¹)		اُدْخُلْ (II M¹)	
قُولاَ (II M²)		اُدْخُلاَ (II M²)	
قُولُوا (II M³⁺)		اُدْخُلُوا (II M³⁺)	
قُولِي (II F¹)		اُدْخُلِي (II F¹)	
قُولاَ (II F²)		اُدْخُلاَ (II F²)	
قُلْنَ (II F³⁺)		اُدْخُلْنَ (II F³⁺)	

(C)		(D)	
اِرْحَمْ (II M¹)		أَرسِلْ (II M¹)	
اِرْحَمَا (II M²)		أَرْسِلاَ (II M²)	
اِرْحَمُوا (II M³⁺)		أَرْسِلُوا (II M³⁺)	
اِرْحَمِى (II F¹)		أَرْسِلِى (II F¹)	
اِرْحَمَا (II F²)		أَرْسِلاَ (II F²)	
اِرْحَمْنَ (II F³⁺)		أَرْسِلْنَ (II F³⁺)	

UNIT 54

النَّهْيُ

Prohibition

Formation:

Rule No. 78

the Prohibition is also formed from the Imperfect Jussive mood. The particle (لا) is placed before the second person Jussive mood.

| Do not oppress | ظَلَمَ / يَظْلِمُ / تَظْلِمُ / تَظْلِمْ / لاتَظْلِمْ |

| | (M¹) لاَ تَظْلِمْ | (M²) لاَ تَظْلِمَا | (M³⁺)لاَ تَظْلِمُوْا |
| | (F¹) لاَ تَظْلِمِي | (F²)لاَ تَظْلِمَا | (F³⁺) لاَ تَظْلِمْنَ |

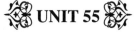

UNIT 55

ثُلاَثِي مَزِيْدٌ فِيْهِ: بَابُ انْفِعَالٌ

Derived Form VII انْفِعَالٌ

Formation:

It is formed by prefixing (انْ) to فَعَلَ = انْفَعَلَ
The other conjugations in the Perfect Indicative follow the pattern of انْفَعَلَ and their endings remain the same as for the Perfect in the First Form.

(See TC under VII)

Imperfect:

The formation of the Imperfect is based on the III M[1] pattern
(يَنْفَعِلُ). All prefixes and endings remain the same as in the
First Form.

(See TD under VII)

Verbal Noun:

The Verbal Noun is formed on the pattern of اِنْفِعَالٌ . The
verbal noun for اِنْقَلَبَ (to be changed) is اِنْقِلَابٌ (revolution)

Active Participle:

The Active Participle is formed on the pattern of مُنْقَلِبٌ/مُنْفَعِلٌ
 (overthrow)

Passive Participle:

The Passive Participle is formed on the pattern of مُنْقَلَبٌ/مُنْفَعَلٌ
(place of overthrow i.e. Hereafter)
(For verbal nouns, Active and Passive Participles see TB under
VII)

Significance:

It expresses the acceptance of the influence of the First Form
verb.

كَسَرَ (to break)   اِنْكَسَرَ (to get broken)

دَفَعَ (to push)   اِنْدَفَعَ (to burst forth)

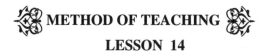

METHOD OF TEACHING
LESSON 14

1. After explaining the *Af'al al-Tafḍiīl* ask students to use these in their own sentences. Let them identify them in the Qur'ānic text and other *āyāt* which they know.

2. For the *Amr*, the Imperative Tables A - F should be gradually projected on the screen.

3. Give the students certain other roots which are not mentioned in Tables A - F but which they are already familiar to construct the imperatives. Ask them to give their reasons for the variations.

4. Similarly *Nahy* should be introduced.

Exercise No. 33

From the Qur'ānic text of Lesson 14 identify the Imperatives and Prohibitions.

"And the servants of the Merciful are those who walk upon the earth modestly and when the ignorant address them, they say: 'Peace'." (25: 63)

461

النَّصُّ الْقُرآنِيُّ
Lesson 15

١.   إِذَا ٱلشَّمْسُ كُوِّرَتْ ۝ وَإِذَا ٱلنُّجُومُ ٱنكَدَرَتْ ۝
وَإِذَا ٱلْجِبَالُ سُيِّرَتْ ۝ وَإِذَا ٱلْعِشَارُ عُطِّلَتْ ۝ وَإِذَا
ٱلْوُحُوشُ حُشِرَتْ ۝ وَإِذَا ٱلْبِحَارُ سُجِّرَتْ ۝ وَإِذَا
ٱلنُّفُوسُ زُوِّجَتْ ۝ وَإِذَا ٱلْمَوْءُۥدَةُ سُئِلَتْ ۝ بِأَيّ
ذَنبٍ قُتِلَتْ ۝ وَإِذَا ٱلصُّحُفُ نُشِرَتْ ۝ وَإِذَا ٱلسَّمَآءُ
كُشِطَتْ ۝ وَإِذَا ٱلْجَحِيمُ سُعِّرَتْ ۝ وَإِذَا ٱلْجَنَّةُ
أُزْلِفَتْ ۝ عَلِمَتْ نَفْسٌ مَّآ أَحْضَرَتْ (81: 1-14)

٢.   أَفَلَا يَعْلَمُ إِذَا بُعْثِرَ مَا فِى ٱلْقُبُورِ ۝ وَحُصِّلَ مَا فِى
ٱلصُّدُورِ (100: 9-10)

٣.   فَإِذَا جَآءَ أَمْرُ ٱللَّهِ قُضِىَ بِٱلْحَقِّ (40: 78)

٤.   قُتِلَ ٱلْإِنسَـٰنُ مَآ أَكْفَرَهُۥ (80: 17)

462

٥. خُلِقَ مِن مَّاءٍ دَافِقٍ ۞ يَخْرُجُ مِنۢ بَيْنِ ٱلصُّلْبِ وَٱلتَّرَآئِبِ
(86: 6-7)

٦. كُتِبَ لَهُم بِهِۦ عَمَلٌ صَٰلِحٌ (9: 120)

٧. كُنتُمْ خَيْرَ أُمَّةٍ أُخْرِجَتْ لِلنَّاسِ تَأْمُرُونَ بِٱلْمَعْرُوفِ
وَتَنْهَوْنَ عَنِ ٱلْمُنكَرِ وَتُؤْمِنُونَ بِٱللَّهِ (3: 110)

٨. يَٰٓأَيُّهَا ٱلَّذِينَ ءَامَنُوا۟ كُتِبَ عَلَيْكُمُ ٱلصِّيَامُ كَمَا كُتِبَ
عَلَى ٱلَّذِينَ مِن قَبْلِكُمْ لَعَلَّكُمْ تَتَّقُونَ (2: 183)

٩. إِنَّمَا كَانَ قَوْلَ ٱلْمُؤْمِنِينَ إِذَا دُعُوٓا۟ إِلَى ٱللَّهِ وَرَسُولِهِۦ
لِيَحْكُمَ بَيْنَهُمْ أَن يَقُولُوا۟ سَمِعْنَا وَأَطَعْنَا ۚ وَأُو۟لَٰٓئِكَ هُمُ
ٱلْمُفْلِحُونَ (24: 51)

١٠. وَأُمِرْتُ لِأَعْدِلَ بَيْنَكُمُ ۖ (42: 15)

١١. إِنَّمَا ٱللَّهُ إِلَٰهٌ وَٰحِدٌ ۖ سُبْحَٰنَهُۥٓ أَن يَكُونَ لَهُۥ وَلَدٌ
(4: 171)

١٢. قُلْ إِنِّىٓ أُمِرْتُ أَنْ أَكُونَ أَوَّلَ مَنْ أَسْلَمَ ۖ (6:14)

١٣. فَلَا تَتَّبِعُوا۟ ٱلْهَوَىٰٓ أَن تَعْدِلُوا۟ (4: 135)

١٤. إِنَّمَا يُرِيدُ ٱلشَّيْطَٰنُ أَن يُوقِعَ بَيْنَكُمُ ٱلْعَدَٰوَةَ وَٱلْبَغْضَآءَ
فِى ٱلْخَمْرِ وَٱلْمَيْسِرِ وَيَصُدَّكُمْ عَن ذِكْرِ ٱللَّهِ وَعَنِ ٱلصَّلَوٰةِ ۖ
(5: 91)

١٥. وَأَن تُشْرِكُوا بِٱللَّهِ مَا لَمْ يُنَزِّلْ بِهِۦ سُلْطَٰنًا (7: 33)

١٦. قَالَ يَٰمُوسَىٰٓ أَتُرِيدُ أَن تَقْتُلَنِي كَمَا قَتَلْتَ نَفْسًا بِٱلْأَمْسِ (28: 19)

١٧. قَالَ رَبِّ إِنِّىٓ أَعُوذُ بِكَ أَنْ أَسْـَٔلَكَ مَا لَيْسَ لِى بِهِۦ عِلْمٌ (11: 47)

١٨. فَعَسَى ٱللَّهُ أَن يَأْتِىَ بِٱلْفَتْحِ أَوْ أَمْرٍ مِّنْ عِندِهِۦ (5: 52)

١٩. قَالَ مَا مَنَعَكَ أَلَّا تَسْجُدَ إِذْ أَمَرْتُكَ (7: 12)

٢٠. وَمَا كَانَ لِنَفْسٍ أَن تُؤْمِنَ إِلَّا بِإِذْنِ ٱللَّهِ (10: 100)

٢١. وَمَا كَانَ لِنَفْسٍ أَن تَمُوتَ إِلَّا بِإِذْنِ ٱللَّهِ كِتَٰبًا مُّؤَجَّلًا (3: 145)

٢٢. وَلَا يَأْبَ كَاتِبٌ أَن يَكْتُبَ كَمَا عَلَّمَهُ ٱللَّهُ (2: 282)

٢٣. وَمَا يَكُونُ لَنَآ أَن نَّعُودَ فِيهَآ إِلَّآ أَن يَشَآءَ ٱللَّهُ (7: 89)

٢٤. وَلَا يَأْبَ كَاتِبٌ أَن يَكْتُبَ كَمَا عَلَّمَهُ ٱللَّهُ (2: 282)

٢٥. وَمَن يَبْتَغِ غَيْرَ ٱلْإِسْلَٰمِ دِينًا فَلَن يُقْبَلَ مِنْهُ وَهُوَ فِى ٱلْآخِرَةِ مِنَ ٱلْخَٰسِرِينَ (3: 85)

٢٦. وَإِن كُنتُمْ فِى رَيْبٍ مِّمَّا نَزَّلْنَا عَلَىٰ عَبْدِنَا فَأْتُوا بِسُورَةٍ

مِّن مِّثْلِهِۦ وَٱدْعُوا شُهَدَآءَكُم مِّن دُونِ ٱللَّهِ إِن كُنتُمْ

صَـٰدِقِينَ ۞ فَإِن لَّمْ تَفْعَلُوا وَلَن تَفْعَلُوا فَٱتَّقُوا ٱلنَّارَ

ٱلَّتِى وَقُودُهَا ٱلنَّاسُ وَٱلْحِجَارَةُ ۖ أُعِدَّتْ لِلْكَـٰفِرِينَ

(2: 23-24)

٢٧. وَذَا ٱلنُّونِ إِذ ذَّهَبَ مُغَـٰضِبًا فَظَنَّ أَن لَّن نَّقْدِرَ عَلَيْهِ

فَنَادَىٰ فِى ٱلظُّلُمَـٰتِ أَن لَّآ إِلَـٰهَ إِلَّآ أَنتَ سُبْحَـٰنَكَ إِنِّى

كُنتُ مِنَ ٱلظَّـٰلِمِينَ (21: 87)

٢٨. وَإِذْ قُلْتُمْ يَـٰمُوسَىٰ لَن نُّؤْمِنَ لَكَ حَتَّىٰ نَرَى ٱللَّهَ جَهْرَةً

(2: 55)

٢٩. قَالُوا يَـٰمُوسَىٰٓ إِنَّ فِيهَا قَوْمًا جَبَّارِينَ وَإِنَّا لَن نَّدْخُلَهَا

حَتَّىٰ يَخْرُجُوا مِنْهَا فَإِن يَخْرُجُوا مِنْهَا فَإِنَّا دَٰخِلُونَ

(5: 22)

٣٠. وَمَن يُرِدِ ٱللَّهُ فِتْنَتَهُۥ فَلَن تَمْلِكَ لَهُۥ مِنَ ٱللَّهِ شَيْـًٔا

(5:41)

٣١. مَن كَانَ يَظُنُّ أَن لَّن يَنصُرَهُ ٱللَّهُ فِى ٱلدُّنْيَا وَٱلْأَخِرَةِ

(22:15)

٣٢. وَلَا يَحْزُنكَ ٱلَّذِينَ يُسَـٰرِعُونَ فِى ٱلْكُفْرِ ۚ إِنَّهُمْ لَن يَضُرُّوا

ٱللَّهَ شَيْـًٔا ۗ (3: 176)

465

٣٣. ذَٰلِكَ بِأَنَّهُمْ قَالُوا لَن تَمَسَّنَا ٱلنَّارُ إِلَّا أَيَّامًا مَّعْدُودَتٍ
(3: 24)

٣٤. وَلَن يَجْعَلَ ٱللَّهُ لِلْكَٰفِرِينَ عَلَى ٱلْمُؤْمِنِينَ سَبِيلًا (4: 141)

٣٥. وَلَا تَمْشِ فِي ٱلْأَرْضِ مَرَحًا ۖ إِنَّكَ لَن تَخْرِقَ ٱلْأَرْضَ

وَلَن تَبْلُغَ ٱلْجِبَالَ طُولًا (17: 37)

٣٦. وَمَا كَانَ ٱللَّهُ لِيُعْجِزَهُۥ مِن شَىْءٍ فِي ٱلسَّمَٰوَٰتِ وَلَا فِي

ٱلْأَرْضِ (35: 44)

٣٧. وَكَذَٰلِكَ جَعَلْنَٰكُمْ أُمَّةً وَسَطًا لِّتَكُونُوا شُهَدَآءَ عَلَى

ٱلنَّاسِ (2: 143)

٣٨. لَّمْ يَكُنِ ٱللَّهُ لِيَغْفِرَ لَهُمْ وَلَا لِيَهْدِيَهُمْ سَبِيلًا (4: 137)

٣٩. فَمَا كَانَ ٱللَّهُ لِيَظْلِمَهُمْ وَلَٰكِن كَانُوا أَنفُسَهُمْ يَظْلِمُونَ
(9: 70)

٤٠. وَمَا كَانَ ٱللَّهُ لِيُطْلِعَكُمْ عَلَى ٱلْغَيْبِ وَلَٰكِنَّ ٱللَّهَ يَجْتَبِى مِن

رُّسُلِهِۦ مَن يَشَآءُ ۖ فَـَٔامِنُوا بِٱللَّهِ وَرُسُلِهِۦ ۚ وَإِن تُؤْمِنُوا

وَتَتَّقُوا فَلَكُمْ أَجْرٌ عَظِيمٌ (3: 179)

٤١. فَمَا كَانَ ٱللَّهُ لِيَظْلِمَهُمْ وَلَٰكِن كَانُوا أَنفُسَهُمْ يَظْلِمُونَ
(9: 70)

٤٢. قَالَ لَمْ أَكُن لِّأَسْجُدَ لِبَشَرٍ خَلَقْتَهُۥ مِن صَلْصَٰلٍ مِّنْ حَمَإٍ مَّسْنُونٍ (15: 33)

٤٣. تَدْعُونَنِى لِأَكْفُرَ بِٱللَّهِ وَأُشْرِكَ بِهِۦ مَا لَيْسَ لِى بِهِۦ عِلْمٌ (40: 42)

٤٤. لِّيَغْفِرَ لَكَ ٱللَّهُ مَا تَقَدَّمَ مِن ذَنۢبِكَ وَمَا تَأَخَّرَ (48: 2)

٤٥. لِيَعْلَمَ أَنِّى لَمْ أَخُنْهُ بِٱلْغَيْبِ (12: 52)

٤٦. قَالَ إِنَّمَآ أَنَا۠ رَسُولُ رَبِّكِ لِأَهَبَ لَكِ غُلَٰمًا زَكِيًّا (19: 19)

٤٧. وَإِذَا تَوَلَّىٰ سَعَىٰ فِى ٱلْأَرْضِ لِيُفْسِدَ فِيهَا وَيُهْلِكَ ٱلْحَرْثَ (2: 205)

٤٨. هُوَ ٱلَّذِى جَعَلَ ٱلشَّمْسَ ضِيَآءً وَٱلْقَمَرَ نُورًا وَقَدَّرَهُۥ مَنَازِلَ لِتَعْلَمُوا۟ عَدَدَ ٱلسِّنِينَ وَٱلْحِسَابَ (10: 5)

٤٩. فَرَدَدْنَٰهُ إِلَىٰٓ أُمِّهِۦ كَىْ تَقَرَّ عَيْنُهَا وَلَا تَحْزَنَ (28: 13)

٥٠. فَأَثَٰبَكُمْ غَمًّۢا بِغَمٍّ لِّكَيْلَا تَحْزَنُوا۟ عَلَىٰ مَا فَاتَكُمْ (3: 153)

٥١. وَمِنكُم مَّن يُرَدُّ إِلَىٰٓ أَرْذَلِ ٱلْعُمُرِ لِكَىْ لَا يَعْلَمَ بَعْدَ عِلْمٍ شَيْـًٔا (16: 70)

٥٢. كَىْ لَا يَكُونَ دُولَةًۢ بَيْنَ ٱلْأَغْنِيَآءِ مِنكُمْ (59: 7)

٥٣. إِنَّ ٱللَّهَ لَا يُغَيِّرُ مَا بِقَوْمٍ حَتَّىٰ يُغَيِّرُوا۟ مَا بِأَنفُسِهِمْ

(13: 11)

٥٤. وَمَا كُنَّا مُعَذِّبِينَ حَتَّىٰ نَبْعَثَ رَسُولًا (17: 15)

٥٥. لَن تَنَالُوا۟ ٱلْبِرَّ حَتَّىٰ تُنفِقُوا۟ مِمَّا تُحِبُّونَ (3: 92)

٥٦. وَلَا تُقَٰتِلُوهُمْ عِندَ ٱلْمَسْجِدِ ٱلْحَرَامِ حَتَّىٰ يُقَٰتِلُوكُمْ فِيهِ

(2: 191)

٥٧. فَلَا تَتَّخِذُوا۟ مِنْهُمْ أَوْلِيَآءَ حَتَّىٰ يُهَاجِرُوا۟ فِى سَبِيلِ ٱللَّهِ

(4: 89)

٥٨. وَمَا يُعَلِّمَانِ مِنْ أَحَدٍ حَتَّىٰ يَقُولَآ إِنَّمَا نَحْنُ فِتْنَةٌ فَلَا

تَكْفُرْ (2: 102)

٥٩. فَأَجِرْهُ حَتَّىٰ يَسْمَعَ كَلَٰمَ ٱللَّهِ (9: 6)

٦٠. وَلَا يَدْخُلُونَ ٱلْجَنَّةَ حَتَّىٰ يَلِجَ ٱلْجَمَلُ فِى سَمِّ ٱلْخِيَاطِ

(7: 40)

٦١. وَلَا تَقُولَنَّ لِشَا۟ىْءٍ إِنِّى فَاعِلٌ ذَٰلِكَ غَدًا ۝ إِلَّآ أَن

يَشَآءَ ٱللَّهُ (18: 23-24)

٦٢. وَلَنَجْزِيَنَّ ٱلَّذِينَ صَبَرُوٓا۟ أَجْرَهُم بِأَحْسَنِ مَا كَانُوا۟

يَعْمَلُونَ (16: 96)

٦٣. وَلَنَبْلُوَنَّكُمْ حَتَّىٰ نَعْلَمَ ٱلْمُجَٰهِدِينَ مِنكُمْ (47: 31)

٦٤. لَا تَحْسَبَنَّ ٱلَّذِينَ يَفْرَحُونَ بِمَا أَتَوا وَّيُحِبُّونَ أَن يُحْمَدُوا بِمَا لَمْ يَفْعَلُوا فَلَا تَحْسَبَنَّهُم بِمَفَازَةٍ مِّنَ ٱلْعَذَابِ (188 :3)

٦٥. ٱلْحَقُّ مِن رَّبِّكَ فَلَا تَكُونَنَّ مِنَ ٱلْمُمْتَرِينَ (147 :2)

٦٦. يَٰأَيُّهَا ٱلَّذِينَ ءَامَنُوا ٱتَّقُوا ٱللَّهَ حَقَّ تُقَاتِهِۦ وَلَا تَمُوتُنَّ إِلَّا وَأَنتُم مُّسْلِمُونَ (102 :3)

٦٧. فَلَا تَكُونَنَّ مِنَ ٱلْجَٰهِلِينَ (6:35)

٦٨. قَالَ ءَامَنتُمْ لَهُۥ قَبْلَ أَنْ ءَاذَنَ لَكُمْ إِنَّهُۥ لَكَبِيرُكُمُ ٱلَّذِى عَلَّمَكُمُ ٱلسِّحْرَ فَلَأُقَطِّعَنَّ أَيْدِيَكُمْ وَأَرْجُلَكُم مِّنْ خِلَٰفٍ وَلَأُصَلِّبَنَّكُمْ فِى جُذُوعِ ٱلنَّخْلِ وَلَتَعْلَمُنَّ أَيُّنَا أَشَدُّ عَذَابًا وَأَبْقَىٰ (71 :20)

٦٩. وَلَا تَحْسَبَنَّ ٱللَّهَ غَٰفِلًا عَمَّا يَعْمَلُ ٱلظَّٰلِمُونَ (42 :14)

٧٠. يَوْمَ تَبْيَضُّ وُجُوهٌ وَتَسْوَدُّ وُجُوهٌ فَأَمَّا ٱلَّذِينَ ٱسْوَدَّتْ وُجُوهُهُمْ أَكَفَرْتُم بَعْدَ إِيمَٰنِكُمْ فَذُوقُوا ٱلْعَذَابَ بِمَا كُنتُمْ تَكْفُرُونَ (106 :3)

469

QUR'ANIC TEXT
VOCABULARY
LESSON 15

كَوَّرَ / يُكَوِّرُ	II to make round, to roll up
انْكَدَرَ / يَنْكَدِرُ	VII to fall, to shout out
جَبَلٌ / ج جِبَالٌ	mountain
سَيَّرَ / يُسَيِّرُ	II to set in motion
عِشَارٌ	she camel
عَطَّلَ / يُعَطِّلُ	II to despoil, to leave unprotected
وَحْشٌ / ج وُحُوشٌ	wild beast
حَشَرَ / يَحْشُرُ	to gather, to assemble
سَجَّرَ / يُسَجِّرُ	II to cause to overflow
زَوَّجَ / يُزَوِّجُ	II to pair, to join in pairs or couples
الْمَوْؤُودَةُ	(girl) buried alive
صَحِيفَةٌ / ج صُحُفٌ	scripture, book, writ
كَشَطَ / يَكْشُطُ	to take off (the cover, veil), to strip, to scrap
جَحِيمٌ	hell
سَعَّرَ / يُسَعِّرُ	II to provoke, to light the fire
أَزْلَفَ / يُزْلِفُ	IV to bring near, to cause to approach
بَعْثَرَ / يُبَعْثِرُ	(quadriliteral verb) to overturn
قَبْرٌ / ج قُبُورٌ	grave
حَصَّلَ / يُحَصِّلُ	II to attain, to obtain something
دَافِقٌ	[AP] dripping

470

صُلْبٌ	breast bone
تِرْبٌ / ج تَرَائِبُ	breast bone, upper part of chest
صِيَامٌ	fasting
عَدَاوَةٌ	enmity
بَغْضَاءُ	hatred
صَدَّ / يَصُدُّ	to oppose, to turn away, divert
سُلْطَانٌ	authority
أَوْقَعَ / يُوقِعُ	IV to bring about
الأَمْسِ	yesterday
مُؤَجَّلٌ	[PP^2] fixed term
أَبَى / يَأْبَى	to refuse, to reject
رَيْبٌ	doubt
وَقُودٌ	fuel
أَعَدَّ / يُعِدُّ	IV to prepare, make ready
ذُوالنُّونِ	literary 'Lord of the Fish' - Jonah
مُغَاضِبٌ	[AP^3] in state of anger
جَبَّارٌ	strong, powerful, tyrant, rebellious, giant, compeller
ظَهِيرٌ	[AP] helper
مُجْرِمٌ	sinner
حَزِنَ / يَحْزَنُ	to grieve

مَعْدُودٌ	[PP] counted
خَرَقَ / يَخْرِقُ	to tear, to rend tear apart
أَعْجَزَ / يُعْجِزُ	IV to become incapable, to become powerless
أَضَاعَ / يُضِيْعُ	IV to waste, to neglect, to loose
أَطْلَعَ / يُطْلِعُ	IV to cause some one to know
اجْتَبَى / يَجْتَبِي	VIII to select
صَلْصَالٌ	ringing clay
حَمَأٍ	clay
مَسْنُوْنٌ	[PP] moulded
خَانَ / يَخُونُ	to defraud, to be treacherous
زَكِيٌّ	pure
سَنَةٌ / ج سِنِيْنَ	year
حِسَابٌ	reckoning
قَرَّ / يَقِرُّ	to be fixed in a place
أَثَابَ / يُثِيْبُ	IV to reward recompense
غَمٌّ	sorrow
فَاتَ / يَفُوتُ	to pass, to escape, to lose
أَرْذَلُ	the nearest one
كَيْ	so that, in order that
دُوْلَةٌ	exclusively confined

غَنِيٌّ / ج أَغْنِيَاءُ	rich
غَيَّرَ / يُغَيِّرُ	II to alter, to change
مُعَذِّبٌ	[AP²] treats with punishment
أَجَارَ / يُجِيرُ	IV to employ, to hire
سَمٌّ	the eye of needle
خِيَاطٌ	needle
جُوْعٌ	hunger
نَقْصٌ	[VN] diminution
مُصِيبَةٌ	calamity
حَسِبَ / يَحْسَبُ	to think, consider
مَفَازَةٌ	place of safety, place of refuge
تُقَاةٌ	fearing
خِلَافٌ	opposite side
صَلَّبَ / يُصَلِّبُ	II to crucify
جِذْعٌ / ج جُذُوْعٌ	Stem, trunk
نَخْلٌ	tree
أَبْقَى / يُبْقِي	IV more lasting one
ابْيَضَّ / يَبْيَضُّ	IX to become white
اسْوَدَّ / يَسْوَدُّ	IX to become black
ذَاقَ / يَذُوْقُ	to taste, experience
نَجْمٌ / ج نُجُوْمٌ	star
وَلَجَ / يَلِجُ	to enter, to penetrate, to go through

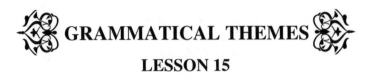

GRAMMATICAL THEMES

LESSON 15

✿ UNIT 56 ✿

الْفِعْلُ الْمَبْنِيُّ لِلْمَجْهُول: الْمَاضِي وَ الْمُضَارِعُ

Passive: Perfect and Imperfect

So far the Perfect Indicative and the Imperfect Indicative have been presented and their passive forms deliberately avoided for the sake of better comprehension of the Indicative forms.

Passive Perfect:

Formation:

Rule No. 79

The Passive Perfect in sound triliteral is formed by
(i) placing *ḍammah* on the radical *Fā'*
(ii) placing *kasrah* under the radical *'Ayn*
(iii) keeping the radical *Lām* intact and its endings as in the indicative form.

(Sound)

فَعَلَ (he did)   فُعِلَ (it was done)

كَتَبَ (he wrote)   كُتِبَ (it was written)

(Weak)

هَدَى (he guided)   هُدِيَ (he was guided)

سَأَلَ (he asked)   سُئِلَ (he was asked)

474

| Zayd hit Ḥāmid. | ضَرَبَ زَيْدٌ حَامداً. |
| Ḥāmid was hit. | ضُرِبَ حَامِدٌ. |

Rule No. 80

If the medial radical is a vowel then the radical *Fā'* accepts *kasrah* instead of *fatḥah* and the medial radical remains quiescent.

| جَاءَ (he came) | جِيءَ (he was brought) |
| قَالَ (he said) | قِيلَ (it was said) |

Imperfect:

Rule No. 81

The formation of the Passive Imperfect accommodates the following changes:

All signs of the Imperfect which precede the Imperfect carry *ḍammah*
• **the radical *'Ayn* carries *fatḥah***
• **the endings remain the same.**
• **the Imperfect Passive accepts the Jussive and the Subjunctive moods.**

(Sound)

| يَفْعَلُ (he does) | يُفْعَلُ (it will be done) |
| يَكْتَبُ (he writes) | يُكْتَبُ (it will be written) |

(Weak)

| يَهْدِي (he guides) | يُهْدَى (he will be guided) |
| يَسْأَلُ (he asks) | يُسْأَلُ (he will be asked) |

| Zayd hits Ḥāmid. | (١) يَضْرِبُ زَيْدٌ حَامِداً. |
| Ḥāmid is being hit. | (٢) يُضْرَبُ حَامِدٌ. |

Rule No. 82

If the medial radical is a vowel then it changes into *Alif*.

يَجِيءُ (he comes)   يُجَاءُ (he will be brought)

يَقُولُ (he says)   يُقَالُ (it will be said)

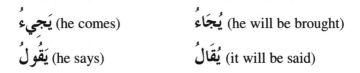

UNIT 57

مُضَارِعٌ مَنْصُوبٌ

Subjunctive Mood [‑]

Rule No. 83

(حَتَّى، كَيْ، إِذَنْ، لَنْ، أَنْ، لِ) are the Subjunctive particles
(*al-Ḥurūf al-Nāṣibah*). When they precede the Imperfect
it changes the Imperfect into the Subjunctive mood. This
mood is identified by the *fatḥah* sign. The following
changes take place:

(i)   the final *dammah* is changed into *fatḥah* in III M[1],
III F[1], IIM[1] and I M[1] + F[1], IM[2, 3+] + F[2,3+]

(ii)   there is no change in IIIF[3]+ and IIF[3+]

(iii)   the consonant *Nūn* is dropped from III M[2], III F[2],
III M[3+], IIM[3+] and II F[1].

476

Examples:

(١) عَلَيْكَ أَنْ تَفْعَلَ الْخَيْرَ وَ تَتْرُكَ الشَّرَّ.

(٢) لَنْ يَنَالَ الْوَلَدُ الْكَسْلاَنُ رِضَا الْمُعَلِّمِ.

(٣) إِنْ تَجْتَهِدْ إِذَنْ تَنَالَ رِضَا الْمُعَلِّمِ.

(٤) جِئْتُ كَيْ أُعَلِّمَ الْقُرْآنَ الْكَرِيمَ.

(٥) قَالَ الْكَافِرُونَ لِرَسُولِ اللهِ (صَلَّى اللهُ عَلَيْهِ وَسَلَّمَ) لَنْ نُؤْمِنَ لَكَ حَتَّى تَأْتِيَنَا بِكِتَابٍ مِنَ السَّمَاءِ.

(1)   It is necessary for you that you do good and leave evil.
(2)   The lazy boy will never get the pleasure of the teacher.
(3)   If you work hard only then you will get the pleasure of the teacher.
(4)   I came so that I could teach you the noble Qur'an.
(5)   The disbelievers said to the Messenger of Allah (blessing of Allah and peace be upon him) we shall never believe until you bring for us a book from the heaven.

In the above sentences كَيْ، إِذَنْ، لَنْ، أَنْ and حَتَّى are the subjunctive particles. They appear before the Imperfects تَفْعَلَ، تَأْتِيَ، نُؤْمِنَ، أُعَلِّمَ، تَنَالَ، يَنَالَ therefore, their final *dammah* is changed into *fathah*.

UNIT 58

النُّونُ الْمُؤَكِّدَةُ

Emphasis with the corroborative *Nūn*

Emphasis is gained by adding either *Nūn mushaddadah* (نّْ)

or *Nun sākinah* (نْ) to the endings of the Imperfects either in the

Jussive or the Subjunctive moods.

لَيَفْعَلَ + نّ   =   لَيَفْعَلَنَّ   (he should do)

لَيَكْتُبَ + نّ   =   لَيَكْتُبَنَّ   (he should write)

لَيَفْعَلَ + نْ   =   لَيَفْعَلَنْ   (he should do)

لَيَكْتُبَ + نْ   =   لَيَكْتُبَنْ   (he should write)

The underlined verbs in the Qur'ānic text provide examples of
this emphasis with the Corroborative *Nūn*.

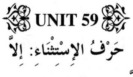

UNIT 59

حَرْفُ الإِسْتِثْنَاءِ: إِلَّا

The Exceptive Particle إِلَّا

Rule No. 84

If in a sentence where the Exceptive Particle إِلَّا is used and
the negative meaning does not exist then the noun which
follows إِلَّا carries *fatḥah* /accusativeness.

Examples:

(١) لَقِيتُ الطُّلَّابَ إلاَّ وَلَدَكَ.

I met the students except your son.

(٢) جَاءَ الرِّجَالُ إلاَّ أَخَاكَ.

The people came except your brother.

(٣) صَلَّت الْمُؤْمِنَاتُ إلاَّ الْمُنَافِقَاتِ.

The believing women prayed except the hypocrite women.

(٤) لاَ إِلَهَ إِلاَّ اللهُ.

There is no god except Allah.

(٥) لَنْ أَشْرَبَ إلاَّ لَبَنًا.

I shall not drink anything except milk.

(٦) لَمْ يَقُومُوا إِلاَّ زَيْدٌ

They did not stand except Zayd.

In the above first sentences the exceptive particle إِلاَّ is not preceded by any negative meaning, therefore, all three nouns, which follow, remain in the accusative case.

In sentences 4 - 6, the exceptive particle إِلاَّ is preceded by a negative meaning, therefore, all three nouns which follow retain their own cases.

UNIT 60

ثُلاثِي مَزِيدٌ فِيْهِ: بَابُ إِفْعِلاَلٌّ

Derived Form IX   إِفْعِلاَلٌّ

Formation:

It is formed by prefixing *Alif maksūr* after making the radical *Fā'* quiescent and placing *shaddah* on the radical *Lām*

اِفْعَلَّ

The other conjugations in the Perfect Indicative follow the pattern of اِفْعَلَّ and their endings remain the same as for the Perfect in the First Form.

(See TC under IX)

Imperfect

The formation of the Imperfect is based on the III M[1] pattern

(يَفْعَلُّ) . All prefixes and endings remain the same as in the First Form.

(See TD under IX)

Verbal Nouns:

The Verbal Noun is formed on the pattern of اِفْعِلاَلٌ / اِحْمِرَارٌ (reddening)

Active Participle:

The Active Participle is formed on the pattern of مُفْعَلٌّ / مُحْمَرٌّ (reddening)

480

[N.B. The use of this form is very limited. This form does not give the Passive Participle.]

(For the Verbal Noun and Active Participle see TC^2 under IX).

Significances:

The Ninth Form is derived from noun adjectives denoting colour, defect or condition.

بَيَّضْتُهُ فَابْيَضَّ   I made it white so it became white.

سَوَّدْتُهُ فَاسْوَدَّ   I made it black so it became black.

حَمَّرْتُهُ فَاحْمَرَّ   I made it red so it became red.

خَضَّرْتُهُ فَاخْضَرَّ   I made it green so it became green.

صَفَّرْتُهُ فَاصْفَرَّ   I made it yellow so it became yellow.

Exercise No. 34

From the Qur'ānic text of lesson 15 identify the following:
- (a) Perfect and Imperfect passive
- (b) Derived forms
- (c) Subjunctive mood

❧ METHOD OF TEACHING ❧
LESSON 15

1. After explaining the Passive forms both in the Perfect and the Imperfect, encourage the students to read and translate all the Passive forms already mentioned in the Table A after projecting these one after the other onto the screen. With this method the students may grasp the changes which occur in these forms and especially in weak verbs.

2. Assist the students to use a few Passive forms both in the Perfect and the Imperfect in their own sentences.

3. If all the changes which take place in the formation of the Subjunctive mood are related with the changes in the Jussive mood with which the students are already acquainted, they will be able to comprehend the Subjunctive mood more easily and quickly.

4. Project the full conjugation of the Corroborative *Nūn* mentioned in TA Nos. 14 - 15 and ask the students to translate.

5. Project the first three examples of إِلَّا on the screen and point out that these three sentences are not preceded by any negative meaning. Encourage the students to point out the negative forms which are preceded with إِلَّا

النَّصُّ الْقُرآنِيُّ

Lesson 16

١. وَٱلصُّبْحِ إِذَآ أَسْفَرَ (74: 34)

٢. وَٱلصُّبْحِ إِذَا تَنَفَّسَ (81: 18)

٣. أَلَيْسَ ٱلصُّبْحُ بِقَرِيبٍ (11: 81)

٤. إِنَّ قُرْءَانَ ٱلْفَجْرِ كَانَ مَشْهُودًا (17: 78)

٥. سَلَٰمٌ هِيَ حَتَّىٰ مَطْلَعِ ٱلْفَجْرِ (97: 5)

٦. مِّن قَبْلِ صَلَوٰةِ ٱلْفَجْرِ وَحِينَ تَضَعُونَ ثِيَابَكُم مِّنَ ٱلظَّهِيرَةِ

وَمِنْ بَعْدِ صَلَوٰةِ ٱلْعِشَآءِ (24: 58)

٧. وَٱذْكُرِ ٱسْمَ رَبِّكَ بُكْرَةً وَأَصِيلًا (76: 25)

٨. فَأَوْحَىٰ إِلَيْهِمْ أَن سَبِّحُوا۟ بُكْرَةً وَعَشِيًّا (19: 11)

٩. وَٱلنَّهَارِ إِذَا جَلَّىٰهَا (91: 3)

483

١٠. هُوَ ٱلَّذِى جَعَلَ لَكُمُ ٱلَّيْلَ لِتَسْكُنُواْ فِيهِ وَٱلنَّهَارَ مُبْصِرًا

(10: 67)

١١. إِنَّ فِى ٱخْتِلَفِ ٱلَّيْلِ وَٱلنَّهَارِ وَمَا خَلَقَ ٱللَّهُ فِى ٱلسَّمَوَتِ

وَٱلْأَرْضِ لَأَيَتٍ لِّقَوْمٍ يَتَّقُونَ (10: 6)

١٢. وَهُوَ ٱلَّذِى جَعَلَ لَكُمُ ٱلَّيْلَ لِبَاسًا وَٱلنَّوْمَ سُبَاتًا وَجَعَلَ

ٱلنَّهَارَ نُشُورًا (25: 47)

١٣. وَمِن رَّحْمَتِهِ جَعَلَ لَكُمُ ٱلَّيْلَ وَٱلنَّهَارَ لِتَسْكُنُواْ فِيهِ

وَلِتَبْتَغُواْ مِن فَضْلِهِ (28: 73)

١٤. وَٱلَّيْلِ إِذْ أَدْبَرَ (74: 33)

١٥. وَٱلضُّحَىٰ ۝ وَٱلَّيْلِ إِذَا سَجَىٰ (93: 1-2)

١٦. وَٱلَّيْلِ إِذَا يَسْرِ (89: 4)

١٧. وَٱلَّيْلِ إِذَا يَغْشَىٰ (92: 1)

١٨. وَلَهُ ٱلْحَمْدُ فِى ٱلسَّمَوَتِ وَٱلْأَرْضِ وَعَشِيًّا وَحِينَ تُظْهِرُونَ

(30: 18)

١٩. كَأَنَّهُمْ يَوْمَ يَرَوْنَهَا لَمْ يَلْبَثُواْ إِلَّا عَشِيَّةً أَوْ ضُحَىٰهَا (79: 46)

٢٠. ٱلنَّارُ يُعْرَضُونَ عَلَيْهَا غُدُوًّا وَعَشِيًّا (40: 46)

٢١. لَّا يَسْمَعُونَ فِيهَا لَغْوًا إِلَّا سَلَـٰمًا ۖ وَلَهُمْ رِزْقُهُمْ فِيهَا بُكْرَةً وَعَشِيًّا (19: 62)

٢٢. وَمَا أَنزَلْنَا عَلَىٰ عَبْدِنَا يَوْمَ ٱلْفُرْقَانِ (8: 41)

٢٣. إِذَا نُودِىَ لِلصَّلَوٰةِ مِن يَوْمِ ٱلْجُمُعَةِ (62: 9)

٢٤. يَوْمَ تَجِدُ كُلُّ نَفْسٍ مَّا عَمِلَتْ مِنْ خَيْرٍ مُّحْضَرًا (3: 30)

٢٥. فَإِنِّي أَخَافُ عَلَيْكُمْ عَذَابَ يَوْمٍ كَبِيرٍ (11: 3)

٢٦. ٱلْيَوْمَ أَكْمَلْتُ لَكُمْ دِينَكُمْ (5: 3)

٢٧. يَوْمَ لَا تَمْلِكُ نَفْسٌ لِّنَفْسٍ شَيْئًا ۖ وَٱلْأَمْرُ يَوْمَئِذٍ لِّلَّهِ (82: 19)

٢٨. وَأَنَّكَ لَا تَظْمَؤُا۟ فِيهَا وَلَا تَضْحَىٰ (20: 119)

٢٩. أَوَأَمِنَ أَهْلُ ٱلْقُرَىٰ أَن يَأْتِيَهُم بَأْسُنَا ضُحًى وَهُمْ يَلْعَبُونَ (7: 98)

٣٠. قَالُوٓا۟ أَءِذَا مِتْنَا وَكُنَّا تُرَابًا وَعِظَـٰمًا أَءِنَّا لَمَبْعُوثُونَ (23: 82)

٣١. وَٱلَّذِينَ إِذَا فَعَلُوا۟ فَـٰحِشَةً أَوْ ظَلَمُوٓا۟ أَنفُسَهُمْ ذَكَرُوا۟ ٱللَّهَ (3: 135)

٣٢. ءَآلْـٰٔنَ وَقَدْ عَصَيْتَ قَبْلُ وَكُنتَ مِنَ ٱلْمُفْسِدِينَ (10: 91)

٣٣. قَالَ إِنِّي تُبْتُ ٱلْـٰٔنَ (4: 18)

٣٤. ٱلْـٰٔنَ جِئْتَ بِٱلْحَقِّ (2: 71)

٣٥. يَسْئَلُونَ أَيَّانَ يَوْمُ ٱلدِّينِ (51: 12)

٣٦. يَسْئَلُ أَيَّانَ يَوْمُ ٱلْقِيَمَةِ (75: 6)

٣٧. وَمَا يَشْعُرُونَ أَيَّانَ يُبْعَثُونَ (27: 65)

٣٨. يَسْئَلُونَكَ عَنِ ٱلسَّاعَةِ أَيَّانَ مُرْسَىٰهَا (7: 187)

٣٩. وَيَقُولُونَ مَتَىٰ هَـٰذَا ٱلْوَعْدُ إِن كُنتُمْ صَـٰدِقِينَ (10: 48)

٤٠. يَتْلُونَ ءَايَـٰتِ ٱللَّهِ ءَانَآءَ ٱلَّيْلِ وَهُمْ يَسْجُدُونَ (3: 113)

٤١. أَمَّنْ هُوَ قَـٰنِتٌ ءَانَآءَ ٱلَّيْلِ سَاجِدًا وَقَآئِمًا (39: 9)

٤٢. وَمِنْ ءَانَآىِٕ ٱلَّيْلِ فَسَبِّحْ وَأَطْرَافَ ٱلنَّهَارِ لَعَلَّكَ تَرْضَىٰ (20: 130)

٤٣. وَجَآءُوٓ أَبَاهُمْ عِشَآءً يَبْكُونَ (12: 16)

٤٤. وَبِٱلْأَسْحَارِ هُمْ يَسْتَغْفِرُونَ (51: 18)

٤٥. قَالَ يَـٰمُوسَىٰٓ أَتُرِيدُ أَن تَقْتُلَنِى كَمَا قَتَلْتَ نَفْسًا بِٱلْأَمْسِ (28: 19)

٤٦. وَمَا تَدْرِى نَفْسٌ مَّاذَا تَكْسِبُ غَدًا (31: 34)

٤٧. وَلْتَنظُرْ نَفْسٌ مَّا قَدَّمَتْ لِغَدٍ (59: 18)

٤٨. فَمَن شَهِدَ مِنكُمُ ٱلشَّهْرَ فَلْيَصُمْهُ (2: 185)

٤٩. شَهْرُ رَمَضَانَ ٱلَّذِىٓ أُنزِلَ فِيهِ ٱلْقُرْءَانُ (2: 185)

٥٠. فِى كُلِّ عَامٍ (126 :9)

٥١. وَمَآ أَمْرُ ٱلسَّاعَةِ إِلَّا كَلَمْحِ ٱلْبَصَرِ (77 :16)

٥٢. فَسُبْحَنَ ٱللَّهِ حِينَ تُمْسُونَ وَحِينَ تُصْبِحُونَ (17 :30)

٥٣. وَلَهُ ٱلْحَمْدُ فِى ٱلسَّمَوَتِ وَٱلْأَرْضِ وَعَشِيًّا وَحِينَ
تُظْهِرُونَ (18 :30)

٥٤. وَسَوْفَ يَعْلَمُونَ حِينَ يَرَوْنَ ٱلْعَذَابَ (42 :25)

٥٥. وَدَخَلَ ٱلْمَدِينَةَ عَلَىٰ حِينِ غَفْلَةٍ مِّنْ أَهْلِهَا (15 :28)

٥٦. هُوَ ٱلَّذِى يُصَوِّرُكُمْ فِى ٱلْأَرْحَامِ كَيْفَ يَشَآءُ (6 :3)

٥٧. وَمِنَ ٱلَّيْلِ فَسَبِّحْهُ وَإِدْبَرَ ٱلنُّجُومِ (49 :52)

٥٨. كُلَّ مَا جَآءَ أُمَّةً رَّسُولُهَا كَذَّبُوهُ (44 :23)

٥٩. وَرُسُلًا قَدْ قَصَصْنَهُمْ عَلَيْكَ مِن قَبْلُ وَرُسُلًا لَّمْ
نَقْصُصْهُمْ عَلَيْكَ (164 :4)

٦٠. لِلَّهِ ٱلْأَمْرُ مِن قَبْلُ وَمِنْ بَعْدُ (4 :30)

٦١. وَأُمِرْتُ لِأَنْ أَكُونَ أَوَّلَ ٱلْمُسْلِمِينَ (12 :39)

٦٢. كُلُواْ وَتَمَتَّعُواْ قَلِيلاً (46 :77)

٦٣. وَذَكَرُواْ ٱللَّهَ كَثِيرًا (227 :26)

٦٤. قُلْ هُوَ ٱللَّهُ أَحَدٌ (1 :112)

٦٥. وَأَنَّ ٱلْمَسَـٰجِدَ لِلَّهِ فَلَا تَدْعُوا۟ مَعَ ٱللَّهِ أَحَدًا (18 :72)

٦٦. مَّا كَانَ مُحَمَّدٌ أَبَآ أَحَدٍ مِّن رِّجَالِكُمْ وَلَـٰكِن رَّسُولَ ٱللَّهِ (33 :40)

٦٧. إِذَا حَضَرَ أَحَدَكُمُ ٱلْمَوْتُ حِينَ ٱلْوَصِيَّةِ ٱثْنَانِ ذَوَا عَدْلٍ مِّنكُمْ (5 :106)

٦٨. قَالَتْ إِحْدَىٰهُمَا يَـٰٓأَبَتِ ٱسْتَـْٔجِرْهُ (28 :26)

٦٩. ثَمَـٰنِيَةَ أَزْوَٰجٍ مِّنَ ٱلضَّأْنِ ٱثْنَيْنِ وَمِنَ ٱلْمَعْزِ ٱثْنَيْنِ قُلْ ءَآلذَّكَرَيْنِ حَرَّمَ أَمِ ٱلْأُنثَيَيْنِ أَمَّا ٱشْتَمَلَتْ عَلَيْهِ أَرْحَامُ ٱلْأُنثَيَيْنِ نَبِّـُٔونِى بِعِلْمٍ إِن كُنتُمْ صَـٰدِقِينَ ۝ وَمِنَ ٱلْإِبِلِ ٱثْنَيْنِ وَمِنَ ٱلْبَقَرِ ٱثْنَيْنِ قُلْ ءَآلذَّكَرَيْنِ حَرَّمَ أَمِ ٱلْأُنثَيَيْنِ (6 :144-143)

٧٠. إِذْ أَخْرَجَهُ ٱلَّذِينَ كَفَرُوا۟ ثَانِىَ ٱثْنَيْنِ إِذْ هُمَا فِى ٱلْغَارِ (9 :40)

٧١. فَمَن لَّمْ يَجِدْ فَصِيَامُ شَهْرَيْنِ مُتَتَابِعَيْنِ تَوْبَةً مِّنَ ٱللَّهِ (4 :92)

٧٢. وَلَهُنَّ ٱلرُّبُعُ مِمَّا تَرَكْتُمْ إِن لَّمْ يَكُن لَّكُمْ وَلَدٌ (4 :12)

٧٣. فَإِن كَانَ لَهُۥ إِخْوَةٌ فَلِأُمِّهِ ٱلسُّدُسُ (4: 11)

٧٤. فَإِن كَانَ لَكُمْ وَلَدٌ فَلَهُنَّ ٱلثُّمُنُ مِمَّا تَرَكْتُمْ (4: 12)

٧٥. سَيَقُولُونَ ثَلَٰثَةٌ رَّابِعُهُمْ كَلْبُهُمْ (18: 22)

٧٦. لَّوْلَا جَآءُو عَلَيْهِ بِأَرْبَعَةِ شُهَدَآءَ (24: 13)

٧٧. فَشَهَٰدَةُ أَحَدِهِمْ أَرْبَعُ شَهَٰدَٰتٍ بِٱللَّهِ (24: 6)

٧٨. وَيَقُولُونَ خَمْسَةٌ سَادِسُهُمْ كَلْبُهُمْ رَجْمًۢا بِٱلْغَيْبِ (18: 22)

٧٩. وَلَا خَمْسَةٍ إِلَّا هُوَ سَادِسُهُمْ (58: 7)

٨٠. وَكَانَ فِى ٱلْمَدِينَةِ تِسْعَةُ رَهْطٍ يُفْسِدُونَ فِى ٱلْأَرْضِ (27:48)

٨١. إِنَّ رَبَّكُمُ ٱللَّهُ ٱلَّذِى خَلَقَ ٱلسَّمَٰوَٰتِ وَٱلْأَرْضَ فِى سِتَّةِ أَيَّامٍ (7: 54)

٨٢. قُلْ مَن رَّبُّ ٱلسَّمَٰوَٰتِ ٱلسَّبْعِ وَرَبُّ ٱلْعَرْشِ ٱلْعَظِيمِ (23: 86)

٨٣. وَٱلْبَحْرُ يَمُدُّهُۥ مِنۢ بَعْدِهِۦ سَبْعَةُ أَبْحُرٍ مَّا نَفِدَتْ كَلِمَٰتُ ٱللَّهِ (31: 27)

٨٤. وَيَقُولُونَ سَبْعَةٌ وَثَامِنُهُمْ كَلْبُهُمْ (18: 22)

٨٥. سَخَّرَهَا عَلَيْهِمْ سَبْعَ لَيَالٍ وَثَمَٰنِيَةَ أَيَّامٍ حُسُومًا (69: 7)

٨٦. وَأَنزَلَ لَكُم مِّنَ ٱلْأَنْعَمِ ثَمَنِيَةَ أَزْوَجٍ (6 :39)

٨٧. وَلَقَدْ ءَاتَيْنَا مُوسَىٰ تِسْعَ ءَايَتٍ بَيِّنَتٍ (101 :17)

٨٨. مَن جَآءَ بِٱلْحَسَنَةِ فَلَهُ عَشْرُ أَمْثَالِهَا (160 :6)

٨٩. تِلْكَ عَشَرَةٌ كَامِلَةٌ (196 :2)

٩٠. إِنِّى رَأَيْتُ أَحَدَ عَشَرَ كَوْكَبًا وَٱلشَّمْسَ وَٱلْقَمَرَ رَأَيْتُهُمْ لِى سَجِدِينَ (4 :12)

٩١. إِنَّ عِدَّةَ ٱلشُّهُورِ عِندَ ٱللَّهِ ٱثْنَا عَشَرَ شَهْرًا فِى كِتَبِ ٱللَّهِ (36 :9)

٩٢. وَبَعَثْنَا مِنْهُمُ ٱثْنَىْ عَشَرَ نَقِيبًا (12 :5)

٩٣. وَقَطَّعْنَهُمُ ٱثْنَتَىْ عَشَرَةَ أَسْبَاطًا أُمَمًا (160 :7)

٩٤. وَوَعَدْنَا مُوسَىٰ ثَلَثِينَ لَيْلَةً وَأَتْمَمْنَهَا بِعَشْرٍ (142 :7)

٩٥. وَإِذْ وَعَدْنَا مُوسَىٰ أَرْبَعِينَ لَيْلَةً (51 :2)

٩٦. فَتَمَّ مِيقَتُ رَبِّهِ أَرْبَعِينَ لَيْلَةً (142 :7)

٩٧. فَمَن لَّمْ يَسْتَطِعْ فَإِطْعَامُ سِتِّينَ مِسْكِينًا (4 :58)

٩٨. ثُمَّ فِى سِلْسِلَةٍ ذَرْعُهَا سَبْعُونَ ذِرَاعًا فَٱسْلُكُوهُ (32 :69)

٩٩. فَٱجْلِدُوهُمْ ثَمَنِينَ جَلْدَةً وَلَا تَقْبَلُوا۟ لَهُمْ شَهَدَةً أَبَدًا (4 :24)

١٠٠. إِنَّ هَـٰذَآ أَخِى لَهُۥ تِسْعٌ وَتِسْعُونَ نَعْجَةً وَلِىَ نَعْجَةٌ وَٰحِدَةٌ
(38: 23)

١٠١. فَأَمَاتَهُ ٱللَّهُ مِا۟ئَةَ عَامٍ ثُمَّ بَعَثَهُۥ (2: 259)

١٠٢. وَلَبِثُوا۟ فِى كَهْفِهِمْ ثَلَٰثَ مِا۟ئَةٍ سِنِينَ وَٱزْدَادُوا۟ تِسْعًا (18: 25)

١٠٣. إِن يَكُن مِّنكُمْ عِشْرُونَ صَٰبِرُونَ يَغْلِبُوا۟ مِا۟ئَتَيْنِ (8: 65)

١٠٤. فَلَبِثَ فِيهِمْ أَلْفَ سَنَةٍ إِلَّا خَمْسِينَ عَامًا (29: 14)

١٠٥. وَإِنَّ يَوْمًا عِندَ رَبِّكَ كَأَلْفِ سَنَةٍ مِّمَّا تَعُدُّونَ (22: 47)

١٠٦. فَٱسْتَجَابَ لَكُمْ أَنِّى مُمِدُّكُم بِأَلْفٍ مِّنَ ٱلْمَلَٰئِكَةِ

مُرْدِفِينَ (8: 9)

١٠٧. يُمْدِدْكُمْ رَبُّكُم بِخَمْسَةِ ءَالَٰفٍ مِّنَ ٱلْمَلَٰئِكَةِ مُسَوِّمِينَ (3: 125)

١٠٨. تَعْرُجُ ٱلْمَلَٰئِكَةُ وَٱلرُّوحُ إِلَيْهِ فِى يَوْمٍ كَانَ مِقْدَارُهُۥ

خَمْسِينَ أَلْفَ سَنَةٍ (70: 4)

١٠٩. أَلَمْ تَرَ إِلَى ٱلَّذِينَ خَرَجُوا۟ مِن دِيَٰرِهِمْ وَهُمْ أُلُوفٌ (2: 243)

١١٠. فَٱعْلَمْ أَنَّهُۥ لَآ إِلَٰهَ إِلَّا ٱللَّهُ وَٱسْتَغْفِرْ لِذَنۢبِكَ (47: 19)

١١١. وَيَٰقَوْمِ ٱسْتَغْفِرُوا۟ رَبَّكُمْ ثُمَّ تُوبُوٓا۟ إِلَيْهِ (11: 52)

١١٢. وَٱسْتَغْفِرُواْ ٱللَّهَ إِنَّ ٱللَّهَ غَفُورٌ رَّحِيمٌ (73: 20)

١١٣. وَمَن يَعْمَلْ سُوٓءًا أَوْ يَظْلِمْ نَفْسَهُۥ ثُمَّ يَسْتَغْفِرِ ٱللَّهَ يَجِدِ ٱللَّهَ غَفُورًا رَّحِيمًا ۞ وَمَن يَكْسِبْ إِثْمًا فَإِنَّمَا يَكْسِبُهُۥ عَلَىٰ نَفْسِهِۦ وَكَانَ ٱللَّهُ عَلِيمًا حَكِيمًا (4: 110-111)

١١٤. فَأَمَّا ٱلَّذِينَ ءَامَنُواْ فَزَادَتْهُمْ إِيمَـٰنًا وَهُمْ يَسْتَبْشِرُونَ (9: 124)

١١٥. وَإِذَا سَأَلَكَ عِبَادِى عَنِّى فَإِنِّى قَرِيبٌ أُجِيبُ دَعْوَةَ ٱلدَّاعِ إِذَا دَعَانِ فَلْيَسْتَجِيبُواْ لِى وَلْيُؤْمِنُواْ بِى لَعَلَّهُمْ يَرْشُدُونَ (2: 186)

١١٦. وَٱلَّذِينَ يَدْعُونَ مِن دُونِهِۦ لَا يَسْتَجِيبُونَ لَهُم بِشَىْءٍ (13: 14)

١١٧. إِنَّهُۥ لَا يُحِبُّ ٱلْمُسْتَكْبِرِينَ (16: 23)

١١٨. وَوَيْلٌ لِّلْكَـٰفِرِينَ مِنْ عَذَابٍ شَدِيدٍ ۞ ٱلَّذِينَ يَسْتَحِبُّونَ ٱلْحَيَوٰةَ ٱلدُّنْيَا عَلَى ٱلْأَخِرَةِ وَيَصُدُّونَ عَن سَبِيلِ ٱللَّهِ وَيَبْغُونَهَا عِوَجًا أُوْلَـٰٓئِكَ فِى ضَلَـٰلٍ بَعِيدٍ (14: 2-3)

١١٩. وَإِذَا تُتْلَىٰ عَلَيْهِ ءَايَـٰتُنَا وَلَّىٰ مُسْتَكْبِرًا كَأَن لَّمْ يَسْمَعْهَا (31: 7)

١٢٠. وَزِنُواْ بِٱلْقِسْطَاسِ ٱلْمُسْتَقِيمِ (17: 35)

١٢١. وَإِذَا قُرِئَ ٱلْقُرْءَانُ فَٱسْتَمِعُوا لَهُ وَأَنصِتُوا لَعَلَّكُمْ

تُرْحَمُونَ (7: 204)

١٢٢. ٱلَّذِينَ يَسْتَمِعُونَ ٱلْقَوْلَ فَيَتَّبِعُونَ أَحْسَنَهُۥ (39: 18)

١٢٣. فَٱسْتَبِقُوا ٱلْخَيْرَٰتِ (5: 48)

١٢٤. وَأَنَّ هَٰذَا صِرَٰطِى مُسْتَقِيمًا فَٱتَّبِعُوهُ وَلَا تَتَّبِعُوا ٱلسُّبُلَ

فَتَفَرَّقَ بِكُمْ عَن سَبِيلِهِۦ (6: 153)

١٢٥. يَٰٓأَيُّهَا ٱلَّذِينَ ءَامَنُوا لَا تَدْخُلُوا بُيُوتًا غَيْرَ بُيُوتِكُمْ

حَتَّىٰ تَسْتَأْنِسُوا وَتُسَلِّمُوا عَلَىٰٓ أَهْلِهَا (24: 27)

493

QUR'ĀNIC TEXT
VOCABULARY
LESSON 16

أَسْفَرَ / يَسْفِرُ	IV to shine (dawn) enter at the time of dawn
تَنَفَّسَ / يَتَنَفَّسُ	V to breathe
مَطْلَعٌ	the time of rising
وَضَعَ / يَضَعُ	to lay down, to put down something
جَلَّى / يُجَلِّى	II to bring in light, to glorify, to make clear
تَجَلَّى / يَتَجَلَّى	V to unveil (face or glory)
مُبْصِرَةٌ	clear
سُبَاتٌ	repose, rest
نُشُورٌ	[VN] resurrection
أَدْبَرَ / يُدْبِرُ	IV to turn back
سَجَى / يَسْجُوْ	to be calm, to be covered with darkness
غَشِيَ / يَغْشَى	to cover, to conceal
أَظْهَرَ / يُظْهِرُ	IV to enter upon the time of noon
ظَمِئَ / يَظْمَأُ	to be thirsty
مُرْسَى	arrival, anchorage
غَفْلَةٌ	[VN] negligence, unawareness

494

صَوَّرَ / يُصَوِّرُ	II to shape, to form fashion
رَحِمٌ / ج أَرْحَامٌ	womb
إِدْبَارٌ	setting
كُلَّمَا	as often as
قَصَّ / يَقُصُّ	to tell, to narrate, to recount
تَمَتَّعَ / يَتَمَتَّعُ	V to enjoy, to relish
مَسْجِدٌ / ج مَسَاجِدُ	mosque
نِصْفٌ	half
إِحْدَى	F[1] one
وَصِيَّةٌ	bequest, legacy
اثْنَانِ / اثْنَيْنِ	two
ثَانِي	second
غَارٌ	cave
مُتَتَابِعٌ	[AP[6]] successive (one following another)
تَوْبَةٌ	repentance
أَدْنَى	nearest
ثُلُثٌ	one third
رُبْعٌ	one fourth
سُدُسٌ	one sixth

ثُمُنٌ	one eighth
ثَلاثَةٌ	three
أَرْبَعَةٌ	four
خَمْسَةٌ	five
سَادِسٌ	sixth
سِتَّةٌ	six
رَهْطٌ	group, company
سَبْعٌ	seven
مَدَّ / يَمُدُّ	to stretch
نَفَدَ / يَنْفَدُ	to exhaust
ثَمَانِيَةٌ	eight
حُسُومٌ	in succession
أَنْعَامٌ	cattle
تِسْعٌ	nine
عَشْرٌ	ten
أَحَدَ عَشَرَ	eleven
عِدَّةٌ	some number, lit. counting, to count
نَقِيبٌ	warden, captain
سِبْطٌ / ج أَسْبَاطٌ	tribe, lit. a tree full of branches, grandson

مِيْقَاتٌ	an ordained time of place
أَرْبَعُوْنَ	forty
إِطْعَامٌ	[VN⁴] feeding
سِلْسِلَةٌ	chain
ذِرَاعٌ / ج أَذْرُعٌ	length
سَلَكَ / يَسْلُكُ	to travel on a road, to make a way
ثَمَانِيْنَ	eighty
جَلْدَةٌ	stripe
أَبَدًا	forever
تِسْعُوْنَ	ninety
نَعْجَةٌ	ewe
مِئَةٌ	hundred
كَهْفٌ	cave
اِزْدَادَ / يَزْدَادُ	VIII to grow, to be growing, to be increasing
عِشْرُوْنَ	twenty
أَلْفٌ / ج أُلُوفٌ	one thousand
مُمِدٌّ	[AP⁴] one who helps
مُرْدَفٌ	[AP⁴] come in succession
أَمَدَّ / يُمِدُّ	IV to help, assist

سُوءٌ	evil
أَجَابَ / يُجِيبُ	IV to reply, to answer
اِسْتَجَابَ / يَسْتَجِيبُ	X to accept
مُسْتَكْبِرٌ	[AP10] arrogant (stiff necked)
عِوَجٌ	crookedness
وَزَنَ / يَزِنُ	to weigh
قِسْطَاسٌ	balance
مُسْتَقِيمٌ	[AP10] right, straight
اِسْتَمَعَ / يَسْتَمِعُ	VIII to hear
أَنْصَتَ / يُنْصِتُ	IV to keep quite in order to listen to
اِسْتَأْخَرَ / يَسْتَأْخِرُ	X to remain behind
اِسْتَقْدَمَ / يَسْتَقْدِمُ	X to seek to go in advance

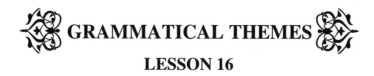

GRAMMATICAL THEMES

LESSON 16

UNIT 61

ظَرْفُ الزَّمَان وَالْمَكَان

Adverb of Time and Place

Rule No. 85

The noun, which denotes the meaning of time, is known as the Adverb of Time (ẓarf zamān)

Examples:

الصُّبْحُ (the morning)   الْفَجْرُ (the dawn)   الْعِشَاءُ (the night)

بُكْرَةً (morning)   أَصِيْلٌ (evening)   النَّهَارُ (the day)

اللَّيْلُ (the night)   الضُّحَى (the morning hours)

الظُّهْرُ (the noon)   غُدُوٌّ (morning)   يَوْمٌ (day)

إِذَا (when)   الآنَ (now)   أَيَّانَ (when)

مَتَى (when)   آنَاءَ (during)   سَحَرٌ (dawn)

الأَمْسِ (yesterday)   غَدًا (tomorrow)   شَهْرٌ (month)

عَامٌ (year)   السَّاعَةُ (the hour)   حِيْنٌ (time)

Note the Qur'ānic text incorporates the Adverbs of Time (Ẓurūf al-Zamān)

Rule No. 86

The noun, which denotes the meaning of place, is known as the Adverbs of Place (*ẓurf Makān*)

Examples:

مَسْجِدٌ (mosque)   مَنْزِلٌ (house)

It is formed on the pattern of مَفْعَلٌ or مَفْعِلٌ

Examples:

مَعْبَدٌ (place of worship, temple)

مَجْلِسٌ (council meeting, seat)

Unit 62 includes the names of the calendar Months and Week days.

 **UNIT 62**

الأَعْدَادُ

Numbers

Numbers vary in their usage depending upon their counting objects. They are on the whole quite interesting.

Rule No. 87

One and Two numbers in their counting work similar to the *ṣifah*, adjective, therefore, they agree with the nouns counted for in number, gender, case, definiteness and indefiniteness.

Examples:

(1) وَلَدٌ وَاحِدٌ (one boy)   بَيْتٌ وَاحِدٌ (one house)

(2) بِنْتٌ وَاحِدَةٌ (one girl)   غُرْفَةٌ وَاحِدَةٌ (one room)

Example Analysis:

(1) وَاحِدٌ is (M¹ AP¹) agrees with وَلَدٌ (M¹), the noun counted for in number, gender, case and indefiniteness.

(2) وَاحِدَةٌ is (F¹ AP¹) agrees with بِنْتٌ (F¹), the noun counted for in number, gender, case and indefiniteness.

Examples:

(1) وَلَدَانِ اثْنَانِ (two boys)   بَيْتَانِ اثْنَانِ   (two houses)

(2) بِنْتَانِ اثْنَتَانِ (two girls)   غُرْفَتَانِ اثْنَتَانِ   (two rooms)

(1) اثْنَانِ is (M²) agrees with وَلَدَانِ (M²) the noun counted for in number, gender, case and indefiniteness.

(2) اثْنَتَانِ is (F²) agrees with بِنْتَانِ (F²) the noun counted for in number, gender, case and indefiniteness.

(Note أَحَدٌ (M¹) and إِحْدَى (F¹) means one, both are nouns cannot be used as adjectives.

أَحَدُ الْبُيُوت (one of the houses)

إِحْدَى الْغُرُفَات (one of the rooms)

اثْنَانِ (M²) and اثْنَتَانِ (F²) are also nouns and duals but they also form adverbal and possessive nouns.

Rule No. 88

If the nouns counted for amount to between 3 and 10 and are masculine then with these nouns feminine numbers are used and again if these nouns are feminine then masculine numbers are used.

(1) ثَلاثَةُ رِجَالٍ (three men)   خَمْسَةُ بُيُوتٍ (five houses)

(2) ثَلَاثُ غُرُفَاتٍ (three rooms)   خَمْسُ بَنَاتٍ (five girls)

(1) رِجَالٌ is (M³⁺) therefore, the number ثَلَاثَةٌ in the feminine is used.

(2) غُرُفَاتٌ is (F³⁺) therefore, the number ثَلَاثُ in the masculine is used.

Feminine	Masculine	
وَاحِدَةٌ	وَاحِدٌ	(١)
إِحْدَى	أَحَدٌ	
اثْنَتَان	اثْنَان	(٢)
ثَلَاثٌ	ثَلَاثَةٌ	(٣)
أَرْبَعٌ	أَرْبَعَةٌ	(٤)
خَمْسٌ	خَمْسَةٌ	(٥)
سِتٌّ	سِتَّةٌ	(٦)
سَبْعٌ	سَبْعَةٌ	(٧)
ثَمَانٍ	ثَمَانِيَةٌ	(٨)
تِسْعٌ	تِسْعَةٌ	(٩)
عَشْرٌ	عَشَرَةٌ	(١٠)

Rule No. 89

When between 11 and 19 numbers are used for the counting of nouns, special adjustments are made:

(i) numbers 1 - 9 at their end accept *fathah*

(ii) number 10 (عَشَرَ) at its end accepts *fathah*

(iii) the consonant *Nūn* is dropped from اثْنَان and

اثْنَتَان

Rule No. 90

If the noun for counting is masculine then Table A is used and if it is feminine then Table B is used and the noun counted for is used in the singular.

Table B (Feminine)	Table A (Masculine)
إحْدَى عَشْرَةَ	(١١) أَحَدَ عَشَرَ
اثْنَتَا عَشْرَةَ	(١٢) اثْنَا عَشَرَ
ثلاثَ عَشْرَةَ	(١٣) ثَلاثَةَ عَشَرَ
أرْبَعَ عَشْرَةَ	(١٤) أرْبَعَةَ عَشَرَ
خَمْسَ عَشْرَةَ	(١٥) خَمْسَةَ عَشَرَ
ستَّ عَشْرَةَ	(١٦) ستَّةَ عَشَرَ
سَبْعَ عَشْرَةَ	(١٧) سَبْعَةَ عَشَرَ
ثَمانيَ عَشْرَةَ	(١٨) ثَمانيَةَ عَشَرَ
تسْعَ عَشْرَةَ	(١٩) تسْعَةَ عَشَرَ

Examples:

(1) ثَلاثَةَ عَشَرَ مُعَلِّمًا (13 teachers M^{3+})

(2) ثَلاثَ عَشْرَةَ بنْتًا (13 girls)

Example Analysis:

(1) The noun for counting is مُعَلِّمًا which is masculine, therefore, it is used as singular and in ثَلَاثَةَ عَشَرَ both numbers carry fathah.

(2) The noun for counting is بِنْتًا which is feminine, therefore, it is used as singular and in ثَلَاثَ عَشَرَةَ both numbers carry fathah.

Rule No. 91

The counting of tens is also done with the following figures depending on their cases. If the case is in the nominative (ـُ ونَ) is used and if the case is in the accusative and genitive (ـِ ينَ) is used. There is no change in gender.

Accusative + Genitive   Nominative

عِشْرِيْنَ	(٢٠) عِشْرُونَ	
ثَلَاثِيْنَ	(٣٠) ثَلَاثُونَ	(٢١) وَاحِدٌ وَعِشْرُونَ
أَرْبَعِيْنَ	(٤٠) أَرْبَعُونَ	(٢٢) إِثْنَان وَعِشْرُونَ
خَمْسِيْنَ	(٥٠) خَمْسُونَ	(٢٣) ثَلَاثَةٌ وَعِشْرُونَ
سِتِّيْنَ	(٦٠) سِتُّونَ	(٢٤) أَرْبَعَةٌ وَعِشْرُونَ
سَبْعِيْنَ	(٧٠) سَبْعُونَ	(٢٥) خَمْسَةٌ وَعِشْرُونَ
ثَمَانِيْنَ	(٨٠) ثَمَانُونَ	
تِسْعِيْنَ	(٩٠) تِسْعُونَ	

504

Rule No. 92

The compound numbers from 21 to 99 are formed according
to the following pattern.

Feminine	Masculine
٣٢ اثْنَتَان وَثلاَثُونَ بِنْتاً.	٢١ واَحِدٌ وَعِشْرُونَ مُعَلِّمًا.
٦٥ خَمْسٌ وَ سِتُّونَ أُمًّا.	٤٣ ثَلاَثَةٌ وَ أَرْبَعُونَ رَجُلاً.

Rule No. 93

The noun counted for after مِئَة (hundred) أَلْفٌ and
(thousand) remains in the singular and carries *kasrah*.

لَيْلَةُ اَلْقَدْرِ خَيْرٌ مِنْ أَلْفِ شَهْرٍ

The Night of Power is better than a thousand months. (**97**: 3)

أَرْبَعَةُ آلاَفٍ وَخَمْسُ مِئَةٍ وَاثْنَانِ وَتِسْعُونَ رَجُلاً.

Four thousand five hundred and ninety - two men.

(١٠٠) مِئَةٌ

(٢٠٠) مِئَتَان

(٣٠٠) ثَلاَثُ مِئَةٍ

(١٠٠٠) أَلْفٌ

(٢٠٠٠) أَلْفَان/أَلْفَيْن

(٣٠٠٠) ثَلاَثَةُ آلاَفٍ

Other counting,

	F	M
First	أُوْلَى	(١) أَوَّلٌ
Second	ثَانِيَةٌ	(٢) ثَانِي
Third	ثَالِثَةٌ	(٣) ثَالِثٌ
Fourth	رَابِعَةٌ	(٤) رَابِعٌ
Fifth	خَامِسَةٌ	(٥) خَامِسٌ
Sixth	سَادِسَةٌ	(٦) سَادِسٌ
Seventh	سَابِعَةٌ	(٧) سَابِعٌ
Eighth	ثَامِنَةٌ	(٨) ثَامِنٌ
Ninth	تَاسِعَةٌ	(٩) تَاسِعٌ
Tenth	عَاشِرَةٌ	(١٠) عَاشِرٌ

[Note this counting method is used throughout this book for all lessons]

1/2	(١) نِصْفٌ
1/3	(٢) ثُلُثٌ
1/4	(٣) رُبُعٌ
1/5	(٤) خُمُسٌ
1/6	(٥) سُدُسٌ
1/7	(٦) سُبُعٌ
1/8	(٧) ثُمُنٌ

(٨) تُسْعٌ   1/9

(٩) عُشْرٌ   1/10

Names of Week Days   أَسْمَاءُ أَيَّامِ الأُسْبُوعِ

(٥) يَوْمُ الْخَمِيسِ	(١) يَوْمُ الأَحَدِ
(٦) يَوْمُ الْجُمُعَةِ	(٢) يَوْمُ الإِثْنَيْنِ
(٧) يَوْمُ السَّبْتِ	(٣) يَوْمُ الثَّلاثَاءِ
	(٤) يَوْمُ الأَرْبِعَاءِ

Names of Months   أَسْمَاءُ الشُّهُورِ

(٧) رَجَبُ	(١) مُحَرَّمٌ
(٨) شَعْبَانُ	(٢) صَفَرٌ
(٩) رَمَضَانُ	(٣) رَبِيعُ الأَوَّلُ
(١٠) شَوَّالُ	(٤) رَبِيعُ الآخَرِ
(١١) ذُو الْقَعْدَةِ	(٥) جُمَادَى الأُولَى
(١٢) ذُو الْحِجَّةِ	(٧) جُمَادَى الآخِرَة

507

UNIT 63

ثُلاَثِي مَزِيدٌ فِيْهِ: بَابُ اسْتَفْعَلَ

Derived Form X اِسْتَفْعَلَ

Formation:

It is formed by prefixing اسْتَ by making the radical *Fā'*

quiescent. اسْتَفْعَلَ

The other conjugations in the Perfect Indicative follow the

pattern of اسْتَفْعَلَ and their endings remain the same as for the

Perfect in the First Form.

(See TC under X)

Imperfect:

The formation of the Imperfect is based on the III M[1] pattern

يَسْتَفْعِلُ. All prefixes and endings remain the same as in the

First Form.

(See TD under X)

[Note there are certain changes similar to those
mentioned in lesson 9 for the Fourth Form if the root is weak.]

Verbal Noun:

The Verbal Noun is formed on the pattern of اِسْتِفْعَالٌ

اِسْتِنْصَارٌ / (seeking assistance)

Active Participle:

The Active Participle is formed on the pattern of مُسْتَفْعِلٌ /

مُسْتَنْصِرٌ (seeker of assistance)

Passive Participle:

The Passive Participle is formed on the pattern of مُسْتَفْعَلٌ /

مُسْتَنْصَرٌ (helped)

Significances:

Certain verbs in the Tenth Form denote pleading and requesting.

اسْتَغْفَرَ	to seek forgiveness
اسْتَعَانَ	to seek help
اسْتَتَابَ	to seek repentance
اسْتَعْلَمَ	to seek knowledge

(b) The facility provided in the Fourth Form is further expanded:

Fourth Form		Tenth Form	
أَسْلَمَ	to surrender	اسْتَسْلَمَ	to surrender completely
أَعَدَّ	to prepare	اسْتَعَدَّ	to prepare oneself

(c) Sometime it is used for the consideration of a special characteristic in a thing.

اسْتَعْظَمَهُ	to find him great
اسْتَخَفَّهُ	to consider it as light
اسْتَجْهَلَهُ	to consider him as ignorant

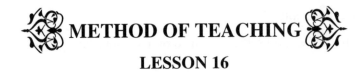

METHOD OF TEACHING

LESSON 16

1. Project the Qur'ānic text onto the screen and encourage the students to identify the Adverbs of Time.

2. Encourage the students to identify from the previous lessons the Adverbs of Place.

3. Rules 86 - 92 govern the use of numbers. Each rule and its examples should be projected onto the screen and explained. Ask the students to use these numbers in their sentences.

4. Project the Qur'ānic text onto the screen and encourage the students to point out the numbers giving their reasons for the same.

5. For teaching the Derived Form X repeat the method mentioned in Lesson 8.

General Exercise

Classify the following words into Perfect, Imperfect, Verbal, Noun, Active Participle, Passive Participle and Imperative and use them in your own sentences.

(A)

(١) مَنْصُورٌ	(٢) مُعَلِّمٌ	(٣) تَعْلِيمٌ	(٤) يَمْنَعُوْنَ
(٥) إِيمَانٌ	(٦) يُنْزِلُ	(٧) نَصَرْتُ	(٨) خَشِيَ
(٩) مَقْبُولٌ	(١٠) نَائِمٌ	(١١) السَّامِعُ	(١٢) هِجْرَةٌ
(١٣) مُشَارَكَةٌ	(١٤) مَرْحُوْمٌ	(١٥) رَاضٍ	(١٦) تَنْزِيْلٌ
(١٧) أَرْسَلْنَا	(١٨) قَادِرٌ	(١٩) قَضَى	(٢٠) يُصَدِّقُ
(٢١) قَارِئٌ	(٢٢) مُرْسَلٌ	(٢٣) فَهِمْنَ	(٢٤) فَتَحَ
(٢٥) فَانٍ	(٢٦) إِرْسَالٌ	(٢٧) قِتَالٌ	(٢٨) يَفِرُّ
(٢٩) مُنَظِّمٌ	(٣٠) الْفَاتِحُ	(٣١) اسْتَنْصَرَ	(٣٢) فَتْحٌ
(٣٣) يَسْتَمِعُ	(٣٤) مَنْهِيٌّ	(٣٥) يَعْلَمُ	(٣٦) مُنْتَظَرٌ
(٣٧) يَنْظُرُوْنَ	(٣٨) نَاصِرٌ	(٣٩) تَكْتُبِيْنَ	(٤٠) نَصْرٌ
(٤١) أُنْصُرْ	(٤٢) اسْمَعْ	(٤٣) يُكَبِّرُ	(٤٤) يُسَبِّحُ

(B)

(١) يُوَحِّدُ	(٢) أَقْرَأُ	(٣) نُصِرَ	(٤) جَالِسٌ
(٥) شِرْكٌ	(٦) مَخْلُوقٌ	(٧) مُنْتَظِرٌ	(٨) مَظْلُوْمٌ
(٩) رَحْمَةٌ	(١٠) مُتَكَلِّمٌ	(١١) نِفَاقٌ	(١٢) غَائِبٌ
(١٣) أَصْدُقُ	(١٤) تَأَخَّرَ	(١٥) جَزَاءٌ	(١٦) مَقْتُوْلَةٌ
(١٧) بَصِيرٌ	(١٨) اِخْتِلَافٌ	(١٩) كُلْ	(٢٠) عَلِّمْ

(٢١) اقْرَأْ (٢٢) كَرِيْمٌ (٢٣) صَدَقْتُنَّ (٢٤) فَهِمْتَ

(٢٥) شُكْرٌ (٢٦) يُحِبُّ (٢٧) مُنَادٍ (٢٨) اصْبِرُوْا

(٢٩) كُنْ (٣٠) مُؤْمِنٌ (٣١) لَاقٍ (٣٢) السَّاعِي

(٣٣) مُعَامَلَةٌ (٣٤) يَكْذِبُ (٣٥) نَسْمَعُ (٣٦) مُسْلِمٌ

(٣٧) يَفْهَمُ (٣٨) كَاذِبٌ (٣٩) احْسَانٌ (٤٠) مَعْلُوْمٌ

512

۞ مُخْتَارَاتٌ مِنَ الْقُرْآنِ الْكَرِيمِ ۞

Selection from the Qur'ān

بِسْمِ ٱللَّهِ ٱلرَّحْمَٰنِ ٱلرَّحِيمِ

ٱلْحَمْدُ لِلَّهِ رَبِّ ٱلْعَٰلَمِينَ ۞ ٱلرَّحْمَٰنِ ٱلرَّحِيمِ ۞ مَٰلِكِ يَوْمِ ٱلدِّينِ ۞ إِيَّاكَ نَعْبُدُ وَإِيَّاكَ نَسْتَعِينُ ۞ ٱهْدِنَا ٱلصِّرَٰطَ ٱلْمُسْتَقِيمَ ۞ صِرَٰطَ ٱلَّذِينَ أَنْعَمْتَ عَلَيْهِمْ غَيْرِ ٱلْمَغْضُوبِ عَلَيْهِمْ وَلَا ٱلضَّآلِّينَ ۞

(1: 1-7)

١. ٱللَّهُ لَآ إِلَٰهَ إِلَّا هُوَ ٱلْحَيُّ ٱلْقَيُّومُ لَا تَأْخُذُهُۥ سِنَةٌ وَلَا نَوْمٌ لَّهُۥ مَا فِي ٱلسَّمَٰوَٰتِ وَمَا فِي ٱلْأَرْضِ مَن ذَا ٱلَّذِى يَشْفَعُ عِندَهُۥٓ إِلَّا بِإِذْنِهِۦ يَعْلَمُ مَا بَيْنَ أَيْدِيهِمْ وَمَا خَلْفَهُمْ وَلَا يُحِيطُونَ بِشَىْءٍ مِّنْ عِلْمِهِۦٓ إِلَّا بِمَا شَآءَ وَسِعَ كُرْسِيُّهُ ٱلسَّمَٰوَٰتِ وَٱلْأَرْضَ وَلَا يَئُودُهُۥ حِفْظُهُمَا وَهُوَ ٱلْعَلِىُّ ٱلْعَظِيمُ (2: 255)

See the headings of the presented Qur'anic themes in the translation (Appendix 6)

513

٢. هُوَ ٱللَّهُ ٱلَّذِى لَا إِلَٰهَ إِلَّا هُوَ عَٰلِمُ ٱلْغَيْبِ وَٱلشَّهَٰدَةِ هُوَ ٱلرَّحْمَٰنُ ٱلرَّحِيمُ ﴿٢٢﴾ هُوَ ٱللَّهُ ٱلَّذِى لَا إِلَٰهَ إِلَّا هُوَ ٱلْمَلِكُ ٱلْقُدُّوسُ ٱلسَّلَٰمُ ٱلْمُؤْمِنُ ٱلْمُهَيْمِنُ ٱلْعَزِيزُ ٱلْجَبَّارُ ٱلْمُتَكَبِّرُ سُبْحَٰنَ ٱللَّهِ عَمَّا يُشْرِكُونَ ﴿٢٣﴾ هُوَ ٱللَّهُ ٱلْخَٰلِقُ ٱلْبَارِئُ ٱلْمُصَوِّرُ لَهُ ٱلْأَسْمَآءُ ٱلْحُسْنَىٰ يُسَبِّحُ لَهُ مَا فِى ٱلسَّمَٰوَٰتِ وَٱلْأَرْضِ وَهُوَ ٱلْعَزِيزُ ٱلْحَكِيمُ

(59: 22-24)

٣. سَبَّحَ لِلَّهِ مَا فِى ٱلسَّمَٰوَٰتِ وَٱلْأَرْضِ وَهُوَ ٱلْعَزِيزُ ٱلْحَكِيمُ ﴿١﴾ لَهُ مُلْكُ ٱلسَّمَٰوَٰتِ وَٱلْأَرْضِ يُحْىِۦ وَيُمِيتُ وَهُوَ عَلَىٰ كُلِّ شَىْءٍ قَدِيرٌ ﴿٢﴾ هُوَ ٱلْأَوَّلُ وَٱلْأَخِرُ وَٱلظَّٰهِرُ وَٱلْبَاطِنُ وَهُوَ بِكُلِّ شَىْءٍ عَلِيمٌ ﴿٣﴾ هُوَ ٱلَّذِى خَلَقَ ٱلسَّمَٰوَٰتِ وَٱلْأَرْضَ فِى سِتَّةِ أَيَّامٍ ثُمَّ ٱسْتَوَىٰ عَلَى ٱلْعَرْشِ يَعْلَمُ مَا يَلِجُ فِى ٱلْأَرْضِ وَمَا يَخْرُجُ مِنْهَا وَمَا يَنزِلُ مِنَ ٱلسَّمَآءِ وَمَا يَعْرُجُ فِيهَا وَهُوَ مَعَكُمْ أَيْنَ مَا كُنتُمْ وَٱللَّهُ بِمَا تَعْمَلُونَ بَصِيرٌ ﴿٤﴾ لَهُ مُلْكُ ٱلسَّمَٰوَٰتِ وَٱلْأَرْضِ وَإِلَى ٱللَّهِ

تُرْجَعُ ٱلْأُمُورُ ۞ يُولِجُ ٱلَّيْلَ فِى ٱلنَّهَارِ وَيُولِجُ ٱلنَّهَارَ فِى ٱلَّيْلِ ۚ وَهُوَ عَلِيمٌۢ بِذَاتِ ٱلصُّدُورِ (57: 1-6)

٤.   ٱللَّهُ نُورُ ٱلسَّمَـٰوَٰتِ وَٱلْأَرْضِ ۚ مَثَلُ نُورِهِۦ كَمِشْكَوٰةٍ فِيهَا مِصْبَاحٌ ۖ ٱلْمِصْبَاحُ فِى زُجَاجَةٍ ۖ ٱلزُّجَاجَةُ كَأَنَّهَا كَوْكَبٌ دُرِّىٌّ يُوقَدُ مِن شَجَرَةٍ مُّبَـٰرَكَةٍ زَيْتُونَةٍ لَّا شَرْقِيَّةٍ وَلَا غَرْبِيَّةٍ يَكَادُ زَيْتُهَا يُضِىٓءُ وَلَوْ لَمْ تَمْسَسْهُ نَارٌ ۚ نُّورٌ عَلَىٰ نُورٍ ۗ يَهْدِى ٱللَّهُ لِنُورِهِۦ مَن يَشَآءُ ۚ وَيَضْرِبُ ٱللَّهُ ٱلْأَمْثَـٰلَ لِلنَّاسِ ۗ وَٱللَّهُ بِكُلِّ شَىْءٍ عَلِيمٌ (24: 35)

٥.   قُل لَّوْ كَانَ ٱلْبَحْرُ مِدَادًا لِّكَلِمَـٰتِ رَبِّى لَنَفِدَ ٱلْبَحْرُ قَبْلَ أَن تَنفَدَ كَلِمَـٰتُ رَبِّى وَلَوْ جِئْنَا بِمِثْلِهِۦ مَدَدًا (18: 109)

٦.   وَلَوْ أَنَّمَا فِى ٱلْأَرْضِ مِن شَجَرَةٍ أَقْلَـٰمٌ وَٱلْبَحْرُ يَمُدُّهُۥ مِنۢ بَعْدِهِۦ سَبْعَةُ أَبْحُرٍ مَّا نَفِدَتْ كَلِمَـٰتُ ٱللَّهِ ۗ إِنَّ ٱللَّهَ عَزِيزٌ حَكِيمٌ (31: 27)

٧. بَدِيعُ ٱلسَّمَٰوَٰتِ وَٱلْأَرْضِ ۖ وَإِذَا قَضَىٰ أَمْرًا فَإِنَّمَا يَقُولُ لَهُۥ كُن فَيَكُونُ (2: 117)

٨. أَوَلَمْ يَرَ ٱلَّذِينَ كَفَرُوٓا۟ أَنَّ ٱلسَّمَٰوَٰتِ وَٱلْأَرْضَ كَانَتَا رَتْقًا فَفَتَقْنَٰهُمَا ۖ وَجَعَلْنَا مِنَ ٱلْمَآءِ كُلَّ شَىْءٍ حَىٍّ ۖ أَفَلَا يُؤْمِنُونَ (21: 30)

٩. خَلَقَ ٱلسَّمَٰوَٰتِ بِغَيْرِ عَمَدٍ تَرَوْنَهَا ۖ وَأَلْقَىٰ فِى ٱلْأَرْضِ رَوَٰسِىَ أَن تَمِيدَ بِكُمْ وَبَثَّ فِيهَا مِن كُلِّ دَآبَّةٍ ۚ وَأَنزَلْنَا مِنَ ٱلسَّمَآءِ مَآءً فَأَنۢبَتْنَا فِيهَا مِن كُلِّ زَوْجٍ كَرِيمٍ ۝ هَٰذَا خَلْقُ ٱللَّهِ فَأَرُونِى مَاذَا خَلَقَ ٱلَّذِينَ مِن دُونِهِۦ ۚ بَلِ ٱلظَّٰلِمُونَ فِى ضَلَٰلٍ مُّبِينٍ (31: 10-11)

١٠. وَإِنَّ يَوْمًا عِندَ رَبِّكَ كَأَلْفِ سَنَةٍ مِّمَّا تَعُدُّونَ (22: 47)

١١. وَلَقَدْ خَلَقْنَا ٱلْإِنسَٰنَ مِن سُلَٰلَةٍ مِّن طِينٍ ۝ ثُمَّ جَعَلْنَٰهُ نُطْفَةً فِى قَرَارٍ مَّكِينٍ ۝ ثُمَّ خَلَقْنَا ٱلنُّطْفَةَ عَلَقَةً

فَخَلَقْنَا ٱلْعَلَقَةَ مُضْغَةً فَخَلَقْنَا ٱلْمُضْغَةَ عِظَـٰمًا فَكَسَوْنَا

ٱلْعِظَـٰمَ لَحْمًا ثُمَّ أَنشَأْنَـٰهُ خَلْقًا ءَاخَرَ فَتَبَارَكَ ٱللَّهُ أَحْسَنُ

ٱلْخَـٰلِقِينَ

(23: 12-14)

١٢. يَـٰٓأَيُّهَا ٱلنَّاسُ إِنَّا خَلَقْنَـٰكُم مِّن ذَكَرٍ وَأُنثَىٰ وَجَعَلْنَـٰكُمْ

شُعُوبًا وَقَبَآئِلَ لِتَعَارَفُوٓا۟ إِنَّ أَكْرَمَكُمْ عِندَ ٱللَّهِ أَتْقَىٰكُمْ

إِنَّ ٱللَّهَ عَلِيمٌ خَبِيرٌ (49: 13)

١٣. ٱللَّهُ ٱلَّذِى سَخَّرَ لَكُمُ ٱلْبَحْرَ لِتَجْرِىَ ٱلْفُلْكُ فِيهِ بِأَمْرِهِۦ

وَلِتَبْتَغُوا۟ مِن فَضْلِهِۦ وَلَعَلَّكُمْ تَشْكُرُونَ ۝ وَسَخَّرَ لَكُم مَّا

فِى ٱلسَّمَـٰوَٰتِ وَمَا فِى ٱلْأَرْضِ جَمِيعًا مِّنْهُ إِنَّ فِى ذَٰلِكَ

لَءَايَـٰتٍ لِّقَوْمٍ يَتَفَكَّرُونَ (45: 12-13)

١٤. أَتَىٰٓ أَمْرُ ٱللَّهِ فَلَا تَسْتَعْجِلُوهُ سُبْحَـٰنَهُ وَتَعَـٰلَىٰ عَمَّا

يُشْرِكُونَ ۝ يُنَزِّلُ ٱلْمَلَـٰٓئِكَةَ بِٱلرُّوحِ مِنْ أَمْرِهِۦ عَلَىٰ

مَن يَشَآءُ مِنْ عِبَادِهِۦٓ أَنْ أَنذِرُوٓا۟ أَنَّهُۥ لَآ إِلَـٰهَ إِلَّآ أَنَا۠

517

فَٱتَّقُونِ ۝ خَلَقَ ٱلسَّمَـٰوَٰتِ وَٱلْأَرْضَ بِٱلْحَقِّ تَعَـٰلَىٰ عَمَّا يُشْرِكُونَ ۝ خَلَقَ ٱلْإِنسَـٰنَ مِن نُّطْفَةٍ فَإِذَا هُوَ خَصِيمٌ مُّبِينٌ ۝ وَٱلْأَنْعَـٰمَ خَلَقَهَا ۗ لَكُمْ فِيهَا دِفْءٌ وَمَنَـٰفِعُ وَمِنْهَا تَأْكُلُونَ ۝ وَلَكُمْ فِيهَا جَمَالٌ حِينَ تُرِيحُونَ وَحِينَ تَسْرَحُونَ ۝ وَتَحْمِلُ أَثْقَالَكُمْ إِلَىٰ بَلَدٍ لَّمْ تَكُونُوا۟ بَـٰلِغِيهِ إِلَّا بِشِقِّ ٱلْأَنفُسِ ۚ إِنَّ رَبَّكُمْ لَرَءُوفٌ رَّحِيمٌ ۝ وَٱلْخَيْلَ وَٱلْبِغَالَ وَٱلْحَمِيرَ لِتَرْكَبُوهَا وَزِينَةً ۚ وَيَخْلُقُ مَا لَا تَعْلَمُونَ ۝ وَعَلَى ٱللَّهِ قَصْدُ ٱلسَّبِيلِ وَمِنْهَا جَآئِرٌ ۚ وَلَوْ شَآءَ لَهَدَىٰكُمْ أَجْمَعِينَ ۝ هُوَ ٱلَّذِىٓ أَنزَلَ مِنَ ٱلسَّمَآءِ مَآءً ۖ لَّكُم مِّنْهُ شَرَابٌ وَمِنْهُ شَجَرٌ فِيهِ تُسِيمُونَ ۝ يُنۢبِتُ لَكُم بِهِ ٱلزَّرْعَ وَٱلزَّيْتُونَ وَٱلنَّخِيلَ وَٱلْأَعْنَـٰبَ وَمِن كُلِّ ٱلثَّمَرَٰتِ ۗ إِنَّ فِى ذَٰلِكَ لَأَيَةً لِّقَوْمٍ يَتَفَكَّرُونَ

(16: 1-11)

١٥. الٓمٓر ۚ تِلْكَ ءَايَـٰتُ ٱلْكِتَـٰبِ ۗ وَٱلَّذِىٓ أُنزِلَ إِلَيْكَ مِن رَّبِّكَ ٱلْحَقُّ وَلَـٰكِنَّ أَكْثَرَ ٱلنَّاسِ لَا يُؤْمِنُونَ ۝ ٱللَّهُ ٱلَّذِى

رَفَعَ ٱلسَّمَـٰوَٰتِ بِغَيْرِ عَمَدٍ تَرَوْنَهَا ۖ ثُمَّ ٱسْتَوَىٰ عَلَى ٱلْعَرْشِ ۖ وَسَخَّرَ ٱلشَّمْسَ وَٱلْقَمَرَ ۖ كُلٌّ يَجْرِى لِأَجَلٍ مُّسَمًّى ۚ يُدَبِّرُ ٱلْأَمْرَ يُفَصِّلُ ٱلْـَٔايَـٰتِ لَعَلَّكُم بِلِقَآءِ رَبِّكُمْ تُوقِنُونَ ۞ وَهُوَ ٱلَّذِى مَدَّ ٱلْأَرْضَ وَجَعَلَ فِيهَا رَوَٰسِىَ وَأَنْهَـٰرًا ۖ وَمِن كُلِّ ٱلثَّمَرَٰتِ جَعَلَ فِيهَا زَوْجَيْنِ ٱثْنَيْنِ ۖ يُغْشِى ٱلَّيْلَ ٱلنَّهَارَ ۚ إِنَّ فِى ذَٰلِكَ لَـَٔايَـٰتٍ لِّقَوْمٍ يَتَفَكَّرُونَ ۞ وَفِى ٱلْأَرْضِ قِطَعٌ مُّتَجَـٰوِرَٰتٌ وَجَنَّـٰتٌ مِّنْ أَعْنَـٰبٍ وَزَرْعٌ وَنَخِيلٌ صِنْوَانٌ وَغَيْرُ صِنْوَانٍ يُسْقَىٰ بِمَآءٍ وَٰحِدٍ وَنُفَضِّلُ بَعْضَهَا عَلَىٰ بَعْضٍ فِى ٱلْأُكُلِ ۚ إِنَّ فِى ذَٰلِكَ لَـَٔايَـٰتٍ لِّقَوْمٍ يَعْقِلُونَ ۞ ۞ وَإِن تَعْجَبْ فَعَجَبٌ قَوْلُهُمْ أَءِذَا كُنَّا تُرَٰبًا أَءِنَّا لَفِى خَلْقٍ جَدِيدٍ ۗ أُو۟لَـٰٓئِكَ ٱلَّذِينَ كَفَرُوا۟ بِرَبِّهِمْ ۖ وَأُو۟لَـٰٓئِكَ ٱلْأَغْلَـٰلُ فِىٓ أَعْنَاقِهِمْ ۖ وَأُو۟لَـٰٓئِكَ أَصْحَـٰبُ ٱلنَّارِ ۖ هُمْ فِيهَا خَـٰلِدُونَ ۞ وَيَسْتَعْجِلُونَكَ بِٱلسَّيِّئَةِ قَبْلَ ٱلْحَسَنَةِ وَقَدْ خَلَتْ مِن قَبْلِهِمُ ٱلْمَثُلَـٰتُ ۗ وَإِنَّ رَبَّكَ لَذُو مَغْفِرَةٍ لِّلنَّاسِ عَلَىٰ ظُلْمِهِمْ ۖ وَإِنَّ رَبَّكَ لَشَدِيدُ ٱلْعِقَابِ ۞ وَيَقُولُ ٱلَّذِينَ كَفَرُوا۟ لَوْلَآ أُنزِلَ عَلَيْهِ ءَايَةٌ مِّن رَّبِّهِۦٓ ۗ إِنَّمَآ أَنتَ

مُنذِرٌ وَلِكُلِّ قَوْمٍ هَادٍ ۝ اللَّهُ يَعْلَمُ مَا تَحْمِلُ كُلُّ

أُنثَىٰ وَمَا تَغِيضُ ٱلْأَرْحَامُ وَمَا تَزْدَادُ وَكُلُّ شَيْءٍ عِندَهُ

بِمِقْدَارٍ ۝ عَٰلِمُ ٱلْغَيْبِ وَٱلشَّهَٰدَةِ ٱلْكَبِيرُ ٱلْمُتَعَالِ

۝ سَوَآءٌ مِّنكُم مَّنْ أَسَرَّ ٱلْقَوْلَ وَمَن جَهَرَ بِهِۦ وَمَنْ هُوَ

مُسْتَخْفٍ بِٱلَّيْلِ وَسَارِبٌ بِٱلنَّهَارِ ۝ لَهُۥ مُعَقِّبَٰتٌ مِّنۢ

بَيْنِ يَدَيْهِ وَمِنْ خَلْفِهِۦ يَحْفَظُونَهُۥ مِنْ أَمْرِ ٱللَّهِ إِنَّ ٱللَّهَ

لَا يُغَيِّرُ مَا بِقَوْمٍ حَتَّىٰ يُغَيِّرُوا۟ مَا بِأَنفُسِهِمْ وَإِذَآ أَرَادَ ٱللَّهُ

بِقَوْمٍ سُوٓءًا فَلَا مَرَدَّ لَهُۥ وَمَا لَهُم مِّن دُونِهِۦ مِن وَالٍ ۝

هُوَ ٱلَّذِى يُرِيكُمُ ٱلْبَرْقَ خَوْفًا وَطَمَعًا وَيُنشِئُ

ٱلسَّحَابَ ٱلثِّقَالَ ۝ وَيُسَبِّحُ ٱلرَّعْدُ بِحَمْدِهِۦ

وَٱلْمَلَٰٓئِكَةُ مِنْ خِيفَتِهِۦ وَيُرْسِلُ ٱلصَّوَٰعِقَ فَيُصِيبُ بِهَا مَن

يَشَآءُ وَهُمْ يُجَٰدِلُونَ فِى ٱللَّهِ وَهُوَ شَدِيدُ ٱلْمِحَالِ ۝

لَهُۥ دَعْوَةُ ٱلْحَقِّ وَٱلَّذِينَ يَدْعُونَ مِن دُونِهِۦ لَا يَسْتَجِيبُونَ

لَهُم بِشَىْءٍ إِلَّا كَبَٰسِطِ كَفَّيْهِ إِلَى ٱلْمَآءِ لِيَبْلُغَ فَاهُ وَمَا هُوَ

بِبَٰلِغِهِۦ وَمَا دُعَآءُ ٱلْكَٰفِرِينَ إِلَّا فِى ضَلَٰلٍ ۝ وَلِلَّهِ

يَسْجُدُ مَن فِى ٱلسَّمَٰوَٰتِ وَٱلْأَرْضِ طَوْعًا وَكَرْهًا وَظِلَٰلُهُم

بِٱلْغُدُوِّ وَٱلْأَصَالِ ۞ ۩ قُلْ مَن رَّبُّ ٱلسَّمَـٰوَٰتِ وَٱلْأَرْضِ قُلِ ٱللَّهُ ۚ قُلْ أَفَٱتَّخَذْتُم مِّن دُونِهِۦ أَوْلِيَآءَ لَا يَمْلِكُونَ لِأَنفُسِهِمْ نَفْعًا وَلَا ضَرًّا ۚ قُلْ هَلْ يَسْتَوِى ٱلْأَعْمَىٰ وَٱلْبَصِيرُ أَمْ هَلْ تَسْتَوِى ٱلظُّلُمَـٰتُ وَٱلنُّورُ ۗ أَمْ جَعَلُوا۟ لِلَّهِ شُرَكَآءَ خَلَقُوا۟ كَخَلْقِهِۦ فَتَشَـٰبَهَ ٱلْخَلْقُ عَلَيْهِمْ ۚ قُلِ ٱللَّهُ خَـٰلِقُ كُلِّ شَىْءٍ وَهُوَ ٱلْوَٰحِدُ ٱلْقَهَّـٰرُ ۞ أَنزَلَ مِنَ ٱلسَّمَآءِ مَآءً فَسَالَتْ أَوْدِيَةٌۢ بِقَدَرِهَا فَٱحْتَمَلَ ٱلسَّيْلُ زَبَدًا رَّابِيًا ۚ وَمِمَّا يُوقِدُونَ عَلَيْهِ فِى ٱلنَّارِ ٱبْتِغَآءَ حِلْيَةٍ أَوْ مَتَـٰعٍ زَبَدٌ مِّثْلُهُۥ ۚ كَذَٰلِكَ يَضْرِبُ ٱللَّهُ ٱلْحَقَّ وَٱلْبَـٰطِلَ ۚ فَأَمَّا ٱلزَّبَدُ فَيَذْهَبُ جُفَآءً ۖ وَأَمَّا مَا يَنفَعُ ٱلنَّاسَ فَيَمْكُثُ فِى ٱلْأَرْضِ ۚ كَذَٰلِكَ يَضْرِبُ ٱللَّهُ ٱلْأَمْثَالَ ۞ لِلَّذِينَ ٱسْتَجَابُوا۟ لِرَبِّهِمُ ٱلْحُسْنَىٰ ۚ وَٱلَّذِينَ لَمْ يَسْتَجِيبُوا۟ لَهُۥ لَوْ أَنَّ لَهُم مَّا فِى ٱلْأَرْضِ جَمِيعًا وَمِثْلَهُۥ مَعَهُۥ لَٱفْتَدَوْا۟ بِهِۦٓ ۚ أُو۟لَـٰٓئِكَ لَهُمْ سُوٓءُ ٱلْحِسَابِ وَمَأْوَىٰهُمْ جَهَنَّمُ ۖ وَبِئْسَ ٱلْمِهَادُ

(13: 1-18)

521

١٦. يَـٰٓأَيُّهَا ٱلَّذِينَ ءَامَنُوٓاْ ءَامِنُواْ بِٱللَّهِ وَرَسُولِهِۦ وَٱلْكِتَـٰبِ ٱلَّذِى نَزَّلَ عَلَىٰ رَسُولِهِۦ وَٱلْكِتَـٰبِ ٱلَّذِىٓ أَنزَلَ مِن قَبْلُ وَمَن يَكْفُرْ بِٱللَّهِ وَمَلَـٰٓئِكَتِهِۦ وَكُتُبِهِۦ وَرُسُلِهِۦ وَٱلْيَوْمِ ٱلْأَخِرِ فَقَدْ ضَلَّ ضَلَـٰلًۢا بَعِيدًا (4: 136)

١٧. قُولُوٓاْ ءَامَنَّا بِٱللَّهِ وَمَآ أُنزِلَ إِلَيْنَا وَمَآ أُنزِلَ إِلَىٰٓ إِبْرَٰهِـۧمَ وَإِسْمَـٰعِيلَ وَإِسْحَـٰقَ وَيَعْقُوبَ وَٱلْأَسْبَاطِ وَمَآ أُوتِىَ مُوسَىٰ وَعِيسَىٰ وَمَآ أُوتِىَ ٱلنَّبِيُّونَ مِن رَّبِّهِمْ لَا نُفَرِّقُ بَيْنَ أَحَدٍ مِّنْهُمْ وَنَحْنُ لَهُۥ مُسْلِمُونَ (2: 136)

١٨. قُلْ ءَامَنَّا بِٱللَّهِ وَمَآ أُنزِلَ عَلَيْنَا وَمَآ أُنزِلَ عَلَىٰٓ إِبْرَٰهِيمَ وَإِسْمَـٰعِيلَ وَإِسْحَـٰقَ وَيَعْقُوبَ وَٱلْأَسْبَاطِ وَمَآ أُوتِىَ مُوسَىٰ وَعِيسَىٰ وَٱلنَّبِيُّونَ مِن رَّبِّهِمْ لَا نُفَرِّقُ بَيْنَ أَحَدٍ مِّنْهُمْ وَنَحْنُ لَهُۥ مُسْلِمُونَ (3: 84)

١٩. مَّنِ ٱهْتَدَىٰ فَإِنَّمَا يَهْتَدِى لِنَفْسِهِۦ ۖ وَمَن ضَلَّ فَإِنَّمَا يَضِلُّ عَلَيْهَا ۚ وَلَا تَزِرُ وَازِرَةٌ وِزْرَ أُخْرَىٰ ۗ وَمَا كُنَّا مُعَذِّبِينَ حَتَّىٰ نَبْعَثَ رَسُولاً (17: 15)

٢٠. يَٰبَنِىٓ ءَادَمَ إِمَّا يَأْتِيَنَّكُمْ رُسُلٌ مِّنكُمْ يَقُصُّونَ عَلَيْكُمْ ءَايَٰتِى ۙ فَمَنِ ٱتَّقَىٰ وَأَصْلَحَ فَلَا خَوْفٌ عَلَيْهِمْ وَلَا هُمْ يَحْزَنُونَ ۞ وَٱلَّذِينَ كَذَّبُوا۟ بِـَٔايَٰتِنَا وَٱسْتَكْبَرُوا۟ عَنْهَآ أُو۟لَٰٓئِكَ أَصْحَٰبُ ٱلنَّارِ ۖ هُمْ فِيهَا خَٰلِدُونَ (7: 35-36)

٢١. وَمَآ أَرْسَلْنَا قَبْلَكَ مِنَ ٱلْمُرْسَلِينَ إِلَّآ إِنَّهُمْ لَيَأْكُلُونَ ٱلطَّعَامَ وَيَمْشُونَ فِى ٱلْأَسْوَاقِ ۗ وَجَعَلْنَا بَعْضَكُمْ لِبَعْضٍ فِتْنَةً أَتَصْبِرُونَ ۗ وَكَانَ رَبُّكَ بَصِيرًا (25: 20)

٢٢. وَلِكُلِّ أُمَّةٍ رَّسُولٌ ۖ فَإِذَا جَآءَ رَسُولُهُمْ قُضِىَ بَيْنَهُم بِٱلْقِسْطِ وَهُمْ لَا يُظْلَمُونَ (10: 47)

٢٣. سُنَّةَ مَن قَدْ أَرْسَلْنَا قَبْلَكَ مِن رُّسُلِنَا ۖ وَلَا تَجِدُ لِسُنَّتِنَا

تَحْوِيلًا (17: 77)

٢٤. يَا أَيُّهَا ٱلنَّبِيُّ إِنَّا أَرْسَلْنَاكَ شَهِدًا وَمُبَشِّرًا وَنَذِيرًا ۞

وَدَاعِيًا إِلَى ٱللَّهِ بِإِذْنِهِ وَسِرَاجًا مُّنِيرًا ۞ وَبَشِّرِ ٱلْمُؤْمِنِينَ

بِأَنَّ لَهُم مِّنَ ٱللَّهِ فَضْلًا كَبِيرًا ۞ (33: 45-47)

٢٥. وَمَا أَرْسَلْنَاكَ إِلَّا كَافَّةً لِّلنَّاسِ بَشِيرًا وَنَذِيرًا وَلَكِنَّ

أَكْثَرَ ٱلنَّاسِ لَا يَعْلَمُونَ ۞ (34: 28)

٢٦. وَمَا خَلَقْتُ ٱلْجِنَّ وَٱلْإِنسَ إِلَّا لِيَعْبُدُونِ (51: 56)

٢٧. قُلْ أَمَرَ رَبِّي بِٱلْقِسْطِ ۖ وَأَقِيمُوا وُجُوهَكُمْ عِندَ كُلِّ

مَسْجِدٍ وَٱدْعُوهُ مُخْلِصِينَ لَهُ ٱلدِّينَ ۚ كَمَا بَدَأَكُمْ تَعُودُونَ

(7: 29)

٢٨. إِنَّمَا يَعْمُرُ مَسَٰجِدَ ٱللَّهِ مَنْ ءَامَنَ بِٱللَّهِ وَٱلْيَوْمِ ٱلْأَخِرِ وَأَقَامَ ٱلصَّلَوٰةَ وَءَاتَى ٱلزَّكَوٰةَ وَلَمْ يَخْشَ إِلَّا ٱللَّهَ فَعَسَىٰٓ أُوْلَٰٓئِكَ أَن يَكُونُوا۟ مِنَ ٱلْمُهْتَدِينَ (9: 18)

٢٩. يَٰٓأَيُّهَا ٱلنَّاسُ ضُرِبَ مَثَلٌ فَٱسْتَمِعُوا۟ لَهُۥٓ إِنَّ ٱلَّذِينَ تَدْعُونَ مِن دُونِ ٱللَّهِ لَن يَخْلُقُوا۟ ذُبَابًا وَلَوِ ٱجْتَمَعُوا۟ لَهُۥ وَإِن يَسْلُبْهُمُ ٱلذُّبَابُ شَيْـًٔا لَّا يَسْتَنقِذُوهُ مِنْهُ ضَعُفَ ٱلطَّالِبُ وَٱلْمَطْلُوبُ ﴿٧٣﴾ مَا قَدَرُوا۟ ٱللَّهَ حَقَّ قَدْرِهِۦٓ إِنَّ ٱللَّهَ لَقَوِىٌّ عَزِيزٌ ﴿٧٤﴾ ٱللَّهُ يَصْطَفِى مِنَ ٱلْمَلَٰٓئِكَةِ رُسُلًا وَمِنَ ٱلنَّاسِ إِنَّ ٱللَّهَ سَمِيعٌۢ بَصِيرٌ ﴿٧٥﴾ يَعْلَمُ مَا بَيْنَ أَيْدِيهِمْ وَمَا خَلْفَهُمْ وَإِلَى ٱللَّهِ تُرْجَعُ ٱلْأُمُورُ ﴿٧٦﴾ يَٰٓأَيُّهَا ٱلَّذِينَ ءَامَنُوا۟ ٱرْكَعُوا۟ وَٱسْجُدُوا۟ وَٱعْبُدُوا۟ رَبَّكُمْ وَٱفْعَلُوا۟ ٱلْخَيْرَ لَعَلَّكُمْ تُفْلِحُونَ ۩ ﴿٧٧﴾ وَجَٰهِدُوا۟ فِى ٱللَّهِ حَقَّ جِهَادِهِۦ هُوَ ٱجْتَبَىٰكُمْ وَمَا جَعَلَ عَلَيْكُمْ فِى ٱلدِّينِ مِنْ حَرَجٍ مِّلَّةَ أَبِيكُمْ إِبْرَٰهِيمَ هُوَ سَمَّىٰكُمُ ٱلْمُسْلِمِينَ مِن قَبْلُ وَفِى هَٰذَا

لِيَكُونَ ٱلرَّسُولُ شَهِيدًا عَلَيْكُمْ وَتَكُونُوا۟ شُهَدَآءَ عَلَى

ٱلنَّاسِ فَأَقِيمُوا۟ ٱلصَّلَوٰةَ وَءَاتُوا۟ ٱلزَّكَوٰةَ وَٱعْتَصِمُوا۟ بِٱللَّهِ

هُوَ مَوْلَىٰكُمْ فَنِعْمَ ٱلْمَوْلَىٰ وَنِعْمَ ٱلنَّصِيرُ (73-78 :22)

٣٠. ٱلرَّحْمَٰنُ ﴿١﴾ عَلَّمَ ٱلْقُرْءَانَ ﴿٢﴾ خَلَقَ ٱلْإِنسَٰنَ ﴿٣﴾

عَلَّمَهُ ٱلْبَيَانَ ﴿٤﴾ ٱلشَّمْسُ وَٱلْقَمَرُ بِحُسْبَانٍ ﴿٥﴾

وَٱلنَّجْمُ وَٱلشَّجَرُ يَسْجُدَانِ ﴿٦﴾ وَٱلسَّمَآءَ رَفَعَهَا وَوَضَعَ

ٱلْمِيزَانَ ﴿٧﴾ أَلَّا تَطْغَوْا۟ فِى ٱلْمِيزَانِ ﴿٨﴾ وَأَقِيمُوا۟

ٱلْوَزْنَ بِٱلْقِسْطِ وَلَا تُخْسِرُوا۟ ٱلْمِيزَانَ ﴿٩﴾ وَٱلْأَرْضَ

وَضَعَهَا لِلْأَنَامِ ﴿١٠﴾ فِيهَا فَٰكِهَةٌ وَٱلنَّخْلُ ذَاتُ ٱلْأَكْمَامِ

﴿١١﴾ وَٱلْحَبُّ ذُو ٱلْعَصْفِ وَٱلرَّيْحَانُ ﴿١٢﴾ فَبِأَيِّ ءَالَآءِ

رَبِّكُمَا تُكَذِّبَانِ ﴿١٣﴾ خَلَقَ ٱلْإِنسَٰنَ مِن صَلْصَٰلٍ

كَٱلْفَخَّارِ ﴿١٤﴾ وَخَلَقَ ٱلْجَآنَّ مِن مَّارِجٍ مِّن نَّارٍ ﴿١٥﴾

فَبِأَيِّ ءَالَآءِ رَبِّكُمَا تُكَذِّبَانِ ﴿١٦﴾ رَبُّ ٱلْمَشْرِقَيْنِ وَرَبُّ

ٱلْمَغْرِبَيْنِ ﴿١٧﴾ فَبِأَيِّ ءَالَآءِ رَبِّكُمَا تُكَذِّبَانِ ﴿١٨﴾ مَرَجَ

ٱلْبَحْرَيْنِ يَلْتَقِيَانِ ﴿١٩﴾ بَيْنَهُمَا بَرْزَخٌ لَّا يَبْغِيَانِ ﴿٢٠﴾

فَبِأَيِّ ءَالَآءِ رَبِّكُمَا تُكَذِّبَانِ ۞ يَخْرُجُ مِنْهُمَا اللُّؤْلُؤُ

وَالْمَرْجَانُ ۞ فَبِأَيِّ ءَالَآءِ رَبِّكُمَا تُكَذِّبَانِ ۞ وَلَهُ

الْجَوَارِ الْمُنشَئاتُ فِي الْبَحْرِ كَالْأَعْلَمِ ۞ فَبِأَيِّ ءَالَآءِ

رَبِّكُمَا تُكَذِّبَانِ ۞ كُلُّ مَنْ عَلَيْهَا فَانٍ ۞ وَيَبْقَىٰ وَجْهُ

رَبِّكَ ذُو الْجَلَلِ وَالْإِكْرَامِ (55:1-27)

٣١. يَٰبَنِى إِسْرَءِيلَ اذْكُرُواْ نِعْمَتِىَ الَّتِى أَنْعَمْتُ عَلَيْكُمْ وَأَوْفُواْ

بِعَهْدِى أُوفِ بِعَهْدِكُمْ وَإِيَّىَ فَارْهَبُونِ ۞ وَءَامِنُواْ بِمَآ

أَنزَلْتُ مُصَدِّقًا لِّمَا مَعَكُمْ وَلَا تَكُونُواْ أَوَّلَ كَافِرٍ بِهِۦ ۖ وَلَا

تَشْتَرُواْ بِـَٔايَٰتِى ثَمَنًا قَلِيلًا وَإِيَّىَ فَاتَّقُونِ ۞ وَلَا تَلْبِسُواْ

الْحَقَّ بِالْبَٰطِلِ وَتَكْتُمُواْ الْحَقَّ وَأَنتُمْ تَعْلَمُونَ ۞

وَأَقِيمُواْ الصَّلَوٰةَ وَءَاتُواْ الزَّكَوٰةَ وَارْكَعُواْ مَعَ الرَّٰكِعِينَ ۞

۞ أَتَأْمُرُونَ النَّاسَ بِالْبِرِّ وَتَنسَوْنَ أَنفُسَكُمْ وَأَنتُمْ تَتْلُونَ

الْكِتَٰبَ أَفَلَا تَعْقِلُونَ ۞ وَاسْتَعِينُواْ بِالصَّبْرِ وَالصَّلَوٰةِ

وَإِنَّهَا لَكَبِيرَةٌ إِلَّا عَلَى الْخَٰشِعِينَ ۞ الَّذِينَ يَظُنُّونَ أَنَّهُم

مُّلَٰقُواْ رَبِّهِمْ وَأَنَّهُمْ إِلَيْهِ رَٰجِعُونَ (2: 40-46)

527

٣٢. يَـٰٓأَيُّهَا ٱلَّذِينَ ءَامَنُوا۟ ٱتَّقُوا۟ ٱللَّهَ حَقَّ تُقَاتِهِۦ وَلَا تَمُوتُنَّ إِلَّا وَأَنتُم مُّسْلِمُونَ ۝ وَٱعْتَصِمُوا۟ بِحَبْلِ ٱللَّهِ جَمِيعًا وَلَا تَفَرَّقُوا۟ وَٱذْكُرُوا۟ نِعْمَتَ ٱللَّهِ عَلَيْكُمْ إِذْ كُنتُمْ أَعْدَآءً فَأَلَّفَ بَيْنَ قُلُوبِكُمْ فَأَصْبَحْتُم بِنِعْمَتِهِۦٓ إِخْوَٰنًا وَكُنتُمْ عَلَىٰ شَفَا حُفْرَةٍ مِّنَ ٱلنَّارِ فَأَنقَذَكُم مِّنْهَا كَذَٰلِكَ يُبَيِّنُ ٱللَّهُ لَكُمْ ءَايَـٰتِهِۦ لَعَلَّكُمْ تَهْتَدُونَ ۝ وَلْتَكُن مِّنكُمْ أُمَّةٌ يَدْعُونَ إِلَى ٱلْخَيْرِ وَيَأْمُرُونَ بِٱلْمَعْرُوفِ وَيَنْهَوْنَ عَنِ ٱلْمُنكَرِ وَأُو۟لَـٰٓئِكَ هُمُ ٱلْمُفْلِحُونَ ۝ وَلَا تَكُونُوا۟ كَٱلَّذِينَ تَفَرَّقُوا۟ وَٱخْتَلَفُوا۟ مِنۢ بَعْدِ مَا جَآءَهُمُ ٱلْبَيِّنَـٰتُ وَأُو۟لَـٰٓئِكَ لَهُمْ عَذَابٌ عَظِيمٌ ۝ يَوْمَ تَبْيَضُّ وُجُوهٌ وَتَسْوَدُّ وُجُوهٌ فَأَمَّا ٱلَّذِينَ ٱسْوَدَّتْ وُجُوهُهُمْ أَكَفَرْتُم بَعْدَ إِيمَـٰنِكُمْ فَذُوقُوا۟ ٱلْعَذَابَ بِمَا كُنتُمْ تَكْفُرُونَ ۝ وَأَمَّا ٱلَّذِينَ ٱبْيَضَّتْ وُجُوهُهُمْ فَفِى رَحْمَةِ ٱللَّهِ هُمْ فِيهَا خَـٰلِدُونَ ۝ تِلْكَ ءَايَـٰتُ ٱللَّهِ نَتْلُوهَا عَلَيْكَ بِٱلْحَقِّ وَمَا ٱللَّهُ يُرِيدُ ظُلْمًا لِّلْعَـٰلَمِينَ ۝ وَلِلَّهِ مَا فِى ٱلسَّمَـٰوَٰتِ وَمَا فِى ٱلْأَرْضِ وَإِلَى

اللَّهِ تُرْجَعُ ٱلْأُمُورُ ۞ كُنتُمْ خَيْرَ أُمَّةٍ أُخْرِجَتْ لِلنَّاسِ

تَأْمُرُونَ بِٱلْمَعْرُوفِ وَتَنْهَوْنَ عَنِ ٱلْمُنكَرِ وَتُؤْمِنُونَ

بِٱللَّهِ ۗ وَلَوْ ءَامَنَ أَهْلُ ٱلْكِتَبِ لَكَانَ خَيْرًا لَّهُم مِّنْهُمُ

ٱلْمُؤْمِنُونَ وَأَكْثَرُهُمُ ٱلْفَسِقُونَ ۞ لَن يَضُرُّوكُمْ

إِلَّا أَذًى ۖ وَإِن يُقَتِلُوكُمْ يُوَلُّوكُمُ ٱلْأَدْبَارَ ثُمَّ لَا

يُنصَرُونَ ﹕

(3: 102- 111)

٣٣. هُوَ ٱلَّذِى أَرْسَلَ رَسُولَهُۥ بِٱلْهُدَىٰ وَدِينِ ٱلْحَقِّ لِيُظْهِرَهُۥ

عَلَى ٱلدِّينِ كُلِّهِۦ وَلَوْ كَرِهَ ٱلْمُشْرِكُونَ ۞ يَٰٓأَيُّهَا ٱلَّذِينَ

ءَامَنُواْ هَلْ أَدُلُّكُمْ عَلَىٰ تِجَٰرَةٍ تُنجِيكُم مِّنْ عَذَابٍ أَلِيمٍ ۞

تُؤْمِنُونَ بِٱللَّهِ وَرَسُولِهِۦ وَتُجَٰهِدُونَ فِى سَبِيلِ ٱللَّهِ بِأَمْوَٰلِكُمْ

وَأَنفُسِكُمْ ۚ ذَٰلِكُمْ خَيْرٌ لَّكُمْ إِن كُنتُمْ تَعْلَمُونَ ۞ يَغْفِرْ لَكُمْ

ذُنُوبَكُمْ وَيُدْخِلْكُمْ جَنَّٰتٍ تَجْرِى مِن تَحْتِهَا ٱلْأَنْهَٰرُ

وَمَسَٰكِنَ طَيِّبَةً فِى جَنَّٰتِ عَدْنٍ ۚ ذَٰلِكَ ٱلْفَوْزُ ٱلْعَظِيمُ ۞

وَأُخْرَىٰ تُحِبُّونَهَا ۖ نَصْرٌ مِّنَ ٱللَّهِ وَفَتْحٌ قَرِيبٌ ۗ وَبَشِّرِ

ٱلْمُؤْمِنِينَ ۞ يَٰٓأَيُّهَا ٱلَّذِينَ ءَامَنُواْ كُونُوٓاْ أَنصَارَ ٱللَّهِ كَمَا

529

قَالَ عِيسَى ٱبْنُ مَرْيَمَ لِلْحَوَارِيِّنَ مَنْ أَنصَارِىٓ إِلَى ٱللَّهِ ۖ قَالَ ٱلْحَوَارِيُّونَ نَحْنُ أَنصَارُ ٱللَّهِ ۖ فَـَٔامَنَت طَّآئِفَةٌ مِّنۢ بَنِىٓ إِسْرَٰٓءِيلَ وَكَفَرَت طَّآئِفَةٌ ۖ فَأَيَّدْنَا ٱلَّذِينَ ءَامَنُوا۟ عَلَىٰ عَدُوِّهِمْ فَأَصْبَحُوا۟ ظَٰهِرِينَ (61: 9-14) ۝

٣٠. وَقَضَىٰ رَبُّكَ أَلَّا تَعْبُدُوٓا۟ إِلَّآ إِيَّاهُ وَبِٱلْوَٰلِدَيْنِ إِحْسَٰنًا ۚ إِمَّا يَبْلُغَنَّ عِندَكَ ٱلْكِبَرَ أَحَدُهُمَآ أَوْ كِلَاهُمَا فَلَا تَقُل لَّهُمَآ أُفٍّ وَلَا تَنْهَرْهُمَا وَقُل لَّهُمَا قَوْلًا كَرِيمًا ۝ وَٱخْفِضْ لَهُمَا جَنَاحَ ٱلذُّلِّ مِنَ ٱلرَّحْمَةِ وَقُل رَّبِّ ٱرْحَمْهُمَا كَمَا رَبَّيَانِى صَغِيرًا ۝ رَّبُّكُمْ أَعْلَمُ بِمَا فِى نُفُوسِكُمْ ۚ إِن تَكُونُوا۟ صَٰلِحِينَ فَإِنَّهُۥ كَانَ لِلْأَوَّٰبِينَ غَفُورًا ۝ وَءَاتِ ذَا ٱلْقُرْبَىٰ حَقَّهُۥ وَٱلْمِسْكِينَ وَٱبْنَ ٱلسَّبِيلِ وَلَا تُبَذِّرْ تَبْذِيرًا ۝ إِنَّ ٱلْمُبَذِّرِينَ كَانُوٓا۟ إِخْوَٰنَ ٱلشَّيَٰطِينِ ۖ وَكَانَ ٱلشَّيْطَٰنُ لِرَبِّهِۦ كَفُورًا ۝ وَإِمَّا تُعْرِضَنَّ عَنْهُمُ ٱبْتِغَآءَ رَحْمَةٍ مِّن رَّبِّكَ تَرْجُوهَا فَقُل لَّهُمْ قَوْلًا مَّيْسُورًا ۝ وَلَا تَجْعَلْ يَدَكَ مَغْلُولَةً إِلَىٰ عُنُقِكَ وَلَا تَبْسُطْهَا كُلَّ ٱلْبَسْطِ

530

فَتَقْعُدَ مَلُومًا مَّحْسُورًا ۝ إِنَّ رَبَّكَ يَبْسُطُ ٱلرِّزْقَ لِمَن

يَشَآءُ وَيَقْدِرُ إِنَّهُۥ كَانَ بِعِبَادِهِۦ خَبِيرًۢا بَصِيرًا ۝ وَلَا

تَقْتُلُوٓا۟ أَوْلَٰدَكُمْ خَشْيَةَ إِمْلَٰقٍ نَّحْنُ نَرْزُقُهُمْ وَإِيَّاكُمْ إِنَّ

قَتْلَهُمْ كَانَ خِطْـًٔا كَبِيرًا ۝ وَلَا تَقْرَبُوا۟ ٱلزِّنَىٰٓ إِنَّهُۥ كَانَ

فَٰحِشَةً وَسَآءَ سَبِيلًا ۝ وَلَا تَقْتُلُوا۟ ٱلنَّفْسَ ٱلَّتِى حَرَّمَ

ٱللَّهُ إِلَّا بِٱلْحَقِّ وَمَن قُتِلَ مَظْلُومًا فَقَدْ جَعَلْنَا لِوَلِيِّهِۦ

سُلْطَٰنًا فَلَا يُسْرِف فِّى ٱلْقَتْلِ إِنَّهُۥ كَانَ مَنصُورًا ۝

وَلَا تَقْرَبُوا۟ مَالَ ٱلْيَتِيمِ إِلَّا بِٱلَّتِى هِىَ أَحْسَنُ حَتَّىٰ يَبْلُغَ

أَشُدَّهُۥ وَأَوْفُوا۟ بِٱلْعَهْدِ إِنَّ ٱلْعَهْدَ كَانَ مَسْـُٔولًا ۝

وَأَوْفُوا۟ ٱلْكَيْلَ إِذَا كِلْتُمْ وَزِنُوا۟ بِٱلْقِسْطَاسِ ٱلْمُسْتَقِيمِ ذَٰلِكَ

خَيْرٌ وَأَحْسَنُ تَأْوِيلًا ۝ وَلَا تَقْفُ مَا لَيْسَ لَكَ بِهِۦ عِلْمٌ

إِنَّ ٱلسَّمْعَ وَٱلْبَصَرَ وَٱلْفُؤَادَ كُلُّ أُو۟لَٰٓئِكَ كَانَ عَنْهُ مَسْـُٔولًا

۝ وَلَا تَمْشِ فِى ٱلْأَرْضِ مَرَحًا إِنَّكَ لَن تَخْرِقَ ٱلْأَرْضَ

وَلَن تَبْلُغَ ٱلْجِبَالَ طُولًا ۝ كُلُّ ذَٰلِكَ كَانَ سَيِّئُهُۥ

عِندَ رَبِّكَ مَكْرُوهًا ۝ ذَٰلِكَ مِمَّآ أَوْحَىٰٓ إِلَيْكَ رَبُّكَ مِنَ

ٱلْحِكْمَةِ ۗ وَلَا تَجْعَلْ مَعَ ٱللَّهِ إِلَـٰهًا ءَاخَرَ فَتُلْقَىٰ فِى جَهَنَّمَ

مَلُومًا مَّدْحُورًا (17: 23-39)

٣٥. الٓمٓ ۞ أَحَسِبَ ٱلنَّاسُ أَن يُتْرَكُوٓا۟ أَن يَقُولُوٓا۟ ءَامَنَّا

وَهُمْ لَا يُفْتَنُونَ ۞ وَلَقَدْ فَتَنَّا ٱلَّذِينَ مِن قَبْلِهِمْ ۖ

فَلَيَعْلَمَنَّ ٱللَّهُ ٱلَّذِينَ صَدَقُوا۟ وَلَيَعْلَمَنَّ ٱلْكَـٰذِبِينَ ۞

أَمْ حَسِبَ ٱلَّذِينَ يَعْمَلُونَ ٱلسَّيِّـَٔاتِ أَن يَسْبِقُونَآ ۚ سَآءَ مَا

يَحْكُمُونَ ۞ مَن كَانَ يَرْجُوا۟ لِقَآءَ ٱللَّهِ فَإِنَّ أَجَلَ ٱللَّهِ

لَـَٔاتٍ ۚ وَهُوَ ٱلسَّمِيعُ ٱلْعَلِيمُ ۞ وَمَن جَـٰهَدَ فَإِنَّمَا يُجَـٰهِدُ

لِنَفْسِهِۦٓ ۚ إِنَّ ٱللَّهَ لَغَنِىٌّ عَنِ ٱلْعَـٰلَمِينَ ۞ وَٱلَّذِينَ ءَامَنُوا۟

وَعَمِلُوا۟ ٱلصَّـٰلِحَـٰتِ لَنُكَفِّرَنَّ عَنْهُمْ سَيِّـَٔاتِهِمْ وَلَنَجْزِيَنَّهُمْ

أَحْسَنَ ٱلَّذِى كَانُوا۟ يَعْمَلُونَ ۞ وَوَصَّيْنَا ٱلْإِنسَـٰنَ

بِوَٰلِدَيْهِ حُسْنًا ۖ وَإِن جَـٰهَدَاكَ لِتُشْرِكَ بِى مَا لَيْسَ لَكَ

بِهِۦ عِلْمٌ فَلَا تُطِعْهُمَآ ۚ إِلَىَّ مَرْجِعُكُمْ فَأُنَبِّئُكُم بِمَا كُنتُمْ

تَعْمَلُونَ ۞ وَٱلَّذِينَ ءَامَنُوا۟ وَعَمِلُوا۟ ٱلصَّـٰلِحَـٰتِ

لَنُدْخِلَنَّهُمْ فِى ٱلصَّـٰلِحِينَ ۞ وَمِنَ ٱلنَّاسِ مَن يَقُولُ

ءَامَنَّا بِٱللَّهِ فَإِذَا أُوذِيَ فِى ٱللَّهِ جَعَلَ فِتْنَةَ ٱلنَّاسِ كَعَذَابِ

ٱللَّهِ وَلَئِن جَآءَ نَصْرٌ مِّن رَّبِّكَ لَيَقُولُنَّ إِنَّا كُنَّا مَعَكُمْ

أَوَلَيْسَ ٱللَّهُ بِأَعْلَمَ بِمَا فِى صُدُورِ ٱلْعَٰلَمِينَ ۝ وَلَيَعْلَمَنَّ

ٱللَّهُ ٱلَّذِينَ ءَامَنُواْ وَلَيَعْلَمَنَّ ٱلْمُنَٰفِقِينَ   (29: 1-11)

٣٦. وَلَا تَحْسَبَنَّ ٱلَّذِينَ قُتِلُواْ فِى سَبِيلِ ٱللَّهِ أَمْوَٰتَۢا بَلْ أَحْيَآءٌ

عِندَ رَبِّهِمْ يُرْزَقُونَ ۝ فَرِحِينَ بِمَآ ءَاتَىٰهُمُ ٱللَّهُ مِن

فَضْلِهِۦ وَيَسْتَبْشِرُونَ بِٱلَّذِينَ لَمْ يَلْحَقُواْ بِهِم مِّنْ خَلْفِهِمْ

أَلَّا خَوْفٌ عَلَيْهِمْ وَلَا هُمْ يَحْزَنُونَ ۝ ۝ يَسْتَبْشِرُونَ

بِنِعْمَةٍ مِّنَ ٱللَّهِ وَفَضْلٍ وَأَنَّ ٱللَّهَ لَا يُضِيعُ أَجْرَ ٱلْمُؤْمِنِينَ
(3: 169-171)

٣٧.

إِنَّ ٱلَّذِينَ قَالُواْ رَبُّنَا ٱللَّهُ ثُمَّ ٱسْتَقَٰمُواْ تَتَنَزَّلُ عَلَيْهِمُ

ٱلْمَلَٰٓئِكَةُ أَلَّا تَخَافُواْ وَلَا تَحْزَنُواْ وَأَبْشِرُواْ بِٱلْجَنَّةِ ٱلَّتِى

كُنتُمْ تُوعَدُونَ ۝ نَحْنُ أَوْلِيَآؤُكُمْ فِى ٱلْحَيَوٰةِ ٱلدُّنْيَا

وَفِى ٱلْأَخِرَةِ ۖ وَلَكُمْ فِيهَا مَا تَشْتَهِىٓ أَنفُسُكُمْ وَلَكُمْ فِيهَا

مَا تَدَّعُونَ ۝ نُزُلًا مِّنْ غَفُورٍ رَّحِيمٍ ۝ وَمَنْ أَحْسَنُ

533

قَوْلاً مِّمَّن دَعَا إِلَى ٱللَّهِ وَعَمِلَ صَلِحًا وَقَالَ إِنَّنِي مِنَ
ٱلْمُسْلِمِينَ ۝ وَلَا تَسْتَوِى ٱلْحَسَنَةُ وَلَا ٱلسَّيِّئَةُ ٱدْفَعْ
بِٱلَّتِي هِيَ أَحْسَنُ فَإِذَا ٱلَّذِي بَيْنَكَ وَبَيْنَهُ عَدَاوَةٌ كَأَنَّهُ
وَلِيٌّ حَمِيمٌ ۝ وَمَا يُلَقَّهَا إِلَّا ٱلَّذِينَ صَبَرُوا وَمَا يُلَقَّهَا
إِلَّا ذُو حَظٍّ عَظِيمٍ ۝ وَإِمَّا يَنزَغَنَّكَ مِنَ ٱلشَّيْطَنِ نَزْغٌ
فَٱسْتَعِذْ بِٱللَّهِ إِنَّهُ هُوَ ٱلسَّمِيعُ ٱلْعَلِيمُ   (41: 30-36)

٣٨. فَلَا يَسْتَطِيعُونَ تَوْصِيَةً وَلَا إِلَى أَهْلِهِمْ يَرْجِعُونَ ۝
وَنُفِخَ فِي ٱلصُّورِ فَإِذَا هُم مِّنَ ٱلْأَجْدَاثِ إِلَى رَبِّهِمْ
يَنسِلُونَ ۝ قَالُوا يَوَيْلَنَا مَنْ بَعَثَنَا مِن مَّرْقَدِنَا هَـٰذَا
مَا وَعَدَ ٱلرَّحْمَٰنُ وَصَدَقَ ٱلْمُرْسَلُونَ ۝ إِن
كَانَتْ إِلَّا صَيْحَةً وَٰحِدَةً فَإِذَا هُمْ جَمِيعٌ لَّدَيْنَا مُحْضَرُونَ
۝ فَٱلْيَوْمَ لَا تُظْلَمُ نَفْسٌ شَيْئًا وَلَا تُجْزَوْنَ إِلَّا مَا
كُنتُمْ تَعْمَلُونَ ۝ إِنَّ أَصْحَبَ ٱلْجَنَّةِ ٱلْيَوْمَ فِي شُغُلٍ
فَكِهُونَ ۝ هُمْ وَأَزْوَٰجُهُمْ فِي ظِلَلٍ عَلَى ٱلْأَرَآئِكِ
مُتَّكِئُونَ ۝ لَهُمْ فِيهَا فَكِهَةٌ وَلَهُم مَّا يَدَّعُونَ ۝ سَلَمٌ

534

قَوْلًا مِّن رَّبٍّ رَّحِيمٍ ۝ وَٱمْتَـٰزُوا۟ ٱلْيَوْمَ أَيُّهَا ٱلْمُجْرِمُونَ

۝ ۞ أَلَمْ أَعْهَدْ إِلَيْكُمْ يَـٰبَنِىٓ ءَادَمَ أَن لَّا تَعْبُدُوا۟

ٱلشَّيْطَـٰنَ إِنَّهُ لَكُمْ عَدُوٌّ مُّبِينٌ ۝ وَأَنِ ٱعْبُدُونِى هَـٰذَا

صِرَٰطٌ مُّسْتَقِيمٌ ۝ وَلَقَدْ أَضَلَّ مِنكُمْ جِبِلًّا كَثِيرًا

أَفَلَمْ تَكُونُوا۟ تَعْقِلُونَ ۝ هَـٰذِهِۦ جَهَنَّمُ ٱلَّتِى كُنتُمْ

تُوعَدُونَ ۝ ٱصْلَوْهَا ٱلْيَوْمَ بِمَا كُنتُمْ تَكْفُرُونَ

۝ ٱلْيَوْمَ نَخْتِمُ عَلَىٰٓ أَفْوَٰهِهِمْ وَتُكَلِّمُنَآ أَيْدِيهِمْ وَتَشْهَدُ

أَرْجُلُهُم بِمَا كَانُوا۟ يَكْسِبُونَ (36: 50-65)

٣٩. لِّلَّهِ مَا فِى ٱلسَّمَـٰوَٰتِ وَمَا فِى ٱلْأَرْضِ وَإِن تُبْدُوا۟ مَا فِىٓ

أَنفُسِكُمْ أَوْ تُخْفُوهُ يُحَاسِبْكُم بِهِ ٱللَّهُ فَيَغْفِرُ لِمَن يَشَآءُ

وَيُعَذِّبُ مَن يَشَآءُ وَٱللَّهُ عَلَىٰ كُلِّ شَىْءٍ قَدِيرٌ ۝

ءَامَنَ ٱلرَّسُولُ بِمَآ أُنزِلَ إِلَيْهِ مِن رَّبِّهِۦ وَٱلْمُؤْمِنُونَ كُلٌّ

ءَامَنَ بِٱللَّهِ وَمَلَـٰٓئِكَتِهِۦ وَكُتُبِهِۦ وَرُسُلِهِۦ لَا نُفَرِّقُ بَيْنَ

أَحَدٍ مِّن رُّسُلِهِۦ وَقَالُوا۟ سَمِعْنَا وَأَطَعْنَا غُفْرَانَكَ رَبَّنَا

وَإِلَيْكَ ٱلْمَصِيرُ ۝ لَا يُكَلِّفُ ٱللَّهُ نَفْسًا إِلَّا وُسْعَهَا

535

لَهَا مَا كَسَبَتْ وَعَلَيْهَا مَا ٱكْتَسَبَتْ رَبَّنَا لَا تُؤَاخِذْنَا إِن

نَّسِينَآ أَوْ أَخْطَأْنَا ۚ رَبَّنَا وَلَا تَحْمِلْ عَلَيْنَآ إِصْرًا كَمَا

حَمَلْتَهُۥ عَلَى ٱلَّذِينَ مِن قَبْلِنَا ۚ رَبَّنَا وَلَا تُحَمِّلْنَا مَا لَا

طَاقَةَ لَنَا بِهِۦ ۖ وَٱعْفُ عَنَّا وَٱغْفِرْ لَنَا وَٱرْحَمْنَآ ۚ أَنتَ

مَوْلَىٰنَا فَٱنصُرْنَا عَلَى ٱلْقَوْمِ ٱلْكَٰفِرِينَ (2: 284-286)

٤٠. سُبْحَٰنَ رَبِّكَ رَبِّ ٱلْعِزَّةِ عَمَّا يَصِفُونَ ﴿١٨٠﴾ وَسَلَٰمٌ

عَلَى ٱلْمُرْسَلِينَ ﴿١٨١﴾ وَٱلْحَمْدُ لِلَّهِ رَبِّ ٱلْعَٰلَمِينَ (37:

180-182)

Āyah (2: 268) is written with gold and silver thread embroidery.

536

Appendix

(4: 135)

Appendix 1

1. Table (A1-A18) (TA)

IMPERFECT PASSIVE WEAK	IMPERFECT INDICATIVE WEAK	PERFECT PASSIVE WEAK	PERFECT INDICATIVE WEAK	IMPERFECT PASSIVE SOUND	IMPERFECT INDICATIVE SOUND	PERFECT PASSIVE SOUND	PERFECT INDICATIVE SOUND	PERSON + NUMBER + GENDER
A1	A1	A1	A1	A	A	A	A	
يُلْقَى	يَلْقَى	قُضِيَ	قَضَى	يُفْعَلُ	يَفْعَلُ	فُعِلَ	فَعَلَ	III M¹
يُلْقَيانِ	يَلْقَيانِ	قُضِيا	قَضَيا	يُفْعَلانِ	يَفْعَلانِ	فُعِلا	فَعَلا	III M²
يُلْقَوْنَ	يَلْقَوْنَ	قُضُوا	قَضَوْا	يُفْعَلُونَ	يَفْعَلُونَ	فُعِلُوا	فَعَلُوا	III M³⁺
تُلْقَى	تَلْقَى	قُضِيَتْ	قَضَتْ	تُفْعَلُ	تَفْعَلُ	فُعِلَتْ	فَعَلَتْ	III F¹
تُلْقَيانِ	تَلْقَيانِ	قُضِيَتا	قَضَتا	تُفْعَلانِ	تَفْعَلانِ	فُعِلَتا	فَعَلَتا	III F²
يُلْقَيْنَ	يَلْقَيْنَ	قُضِينَ	قَضَيْنَ	يُفْعَلْنَ	يَفْعَلْنَ	فُعِلْنَ	فَعَلْنَ	III F³⁺
تُلْقَى	تَلْقَى	قُضِيتَ	قَضَيْتَ	تُفْعَلُ	تَفْعَلُ	فُعِلْتَ	فَعَلْتَ	II M¹
تُلْقَيانِ	تَلْقَيانِ	قُضِيتُما	قَضَيْتُما	تُفْعَلانِ	تَفْعَلانِ	فُعِلْتُما	فَعَلْتُما	II M²⁺
تُلْقَوْنَ	تَلْقَوْنَ	قُضِيتُم	قَضَيْتُم	تُفْعَلُونَ	تَفْعَلُونَ	فُعِلْتُم	فَعَلْتُم	II F¹
تُلْقَيْنَ	تَلْقَيْنَ	قُضِيتِ	قَضَيْتِ	تُفْعَلِينَ	تَفْعَلِينَ	فُعِلْتِ	فَعَلْتِ	II F2
تُلْقَيْنَ	تَلْقَيْنَ	قُضِيتُنَّ	قَضَيْتُنَّ	تُفْعَلْنَ	تَفْعَلْنَ	فُعِلْتُنَّ	فَعَلْتُنَّ	II F³⁺
أُلْقَى	أَلْقَى	قُضِيتُ	قَضَيْتُ	أُفْعَلُ	أَفْعَلُ	فُعِلْتُ	فَعَلْتُ	I M¹ + F¹
نُلْقَى	نَلْقَى	قُضِينا	قَضَيْنا	نُفْعَلُ	نَفْعَلُ	فُعِلْنا	فَعَلْنا	I M²,³⁺ + F²,³⁺

Appendix 1

TABLE A (TA)

IMPERFECT PASSIVE WEAK	IMPERFECT INDICATIVE WEAK	PERFECT PASSIVE WEAK	PERFECT INDICATIVE WEAK	IMPERFECT PASSIVE WEAK	IMPERFECT INDICATIVE WEAK	PERFECT PASSIVE WEAK	PERFECT INDICATIVE WEAK	PERSON + NUMBER + GENDER
A3	A3	A3	A3	A2	A2	A2	A2	
يَرْضَى	يَرْضَى	رُضِيَ	رَضِيَ	يُجَاءُ	يَجِيءُ	جِيءَ	جَاءَ	III M¹
يُرْضَيَان	يَرْضَيَان	رُضِيَا	رَضِيَا	يُجَاءَان	يَجِيئَان	جِيئَا	جَاءَا	III M²
يُرْضَوْنَ	يَرْضَوْنَ	رُضُوا	رَضُوا	يُجَاؤُونَ	يَجِيئُونَ	جِيئُوا	جَاؤُوا	III M³⁺
تُرْضَى	تَرْضَى	رُضِيَتْ	رَضِيَتْ	تُجَاءُ	تَجِيءُ	جِيئَتْ	جَاءَتْ	III F¹
تُرْضَيَان	تَرْضَيَان	رُضِيَتَا	رَضِيَتَا	تُجَاءَان	تَجِيئَان	جِيئَتَا	جَاءَتَا	III F²
يُرْضَيْنَ	يَرْضَيْنَ	رُضِينَ	رَضِينَ	يُجَأْنَ	يَجِئْنَ	جِئْنَ	جِئْنَ	III F³⁺
تُرْضَى	تَرْضَى	رُضِيتَ	رَضِيتَ	تُجَاءُ	تَجِيءُ	جُئْتَ	جِئْتَ	II M¹
تُرْضَيَان	تَرْضَيَان	رُضِيتُمَا	رَضِيتُمَا	تُجَاءَان	تَجِيئَان	جُئْتُمَا	جِئْتُمَا	II M²
تُرْضَوْنَ	تَرْضَوْنَ	رُضِيتُمْ	رَضِيتُمْ	تُجَاؤُونَ	تَجِيئُونَ	جُئْتُمْ	جِئْتُمْ	II M³⁺
تُرْضَيْنَ	تَرْضَيْنَ	رُضِيتِ	رَضِيتِ	تُجَائِينَ	تَجِيئِينَ	جُئْتِ	جِئْتِ	II F¹
تُرْضَيَان	تَرْضَيَان	رُضِيتُمَا	رَضِيتُمَا	تُجَاءَان	تَجِيئَان	جُئْتُمَا	جِئْتُمَا	II F²
تُرْضَيْنَ	تَرْضَيْنَ	رُضِيتُنَّ	رَضِيتُنَّ	تُجَأْنَ	تَجِئْنَ	جُئْتُنَّ	جِئْتُنَّ	II F³⁺
أُرْضَى	أَرْضَى	رُضِيتُ	رَضِيتُ	أُجَاءُ	أَجِيءُ	جُئْتُ	جِئْتُ	I M¹ + F¹
نُرْضَى	نَرْضَى	رُضِينَا	رَضِينَا	نُجَاءُ	نَجِيءُ	جُئْنَا	جِئْنَا	I M²,³⁺ +F²,³⁺

539

PERSON + NUMBER + GENDER	PERFECTE INDICATIVE WEAK A4	PERFECT PASSIVE WEAK A4	IMPERFECT INDICATIVE WEAK A4	IMPERFECT PASSIVE WEAK A4	PERFECT INDICATIVE WEAK A5	PERFECT PASSIVE WEAK A5	IMPERFECT INDICATIVE WEAK A5	IMPERFECT PASSIVE WEAK A5
III M^1								
III M^2								
III M^{3+}								
III F^1								
III F^2								
III F^{3+}								
II M^1								
II M^2								
II M^{3+}								
II F^1								
II F^2								
II F^{3+}								
I $M^1 + F^1$								
I $M^{2,3+} + F^{2,3+}$								

TABLE A (TA)

540

Appendix 1

PERSON + NUMBER + GENDER	PERFECT INDICATIVE WEAK (A6)	PERFECT PASSIVE WEAK (A6)	IMPERFECT INDICATIVE WEAK (A6)	IMPERFECT PASSIVE WEAK (A6)	PERFECT INDICATIVE WEAK (A7)	PERFECT PASSIVE WEAK (A7)	IMPERFECT INDICATIVE WEAK (A7)	IMPERFECT PASSIVE WEAK (A7)
III M¹	A6	A6	A6	A6	A7	A7	A7	A7
III M²								
III M³⁺								
III F¹								
III F²								
III F³⁺								
II M¹								
II M²								
II M³⁺								
II F¹								
II F²								
II F³⁺								
I M¹ + F¹								
I M²,³⁺ + F²,³⁺								

(TABLE A (TA))

541

	IMPERFECT PASSIVE WEAK A9	IMPERFECT INDICATIVE WEAK A9	PERFECT PASSIVE WEAK A9	PERFECT INDICATIVE WEAK A9	IMPERFECT PASSIVE WEAK A8	IMPERFECT INDICATIVE WEAK A8	PERFECT PASSIVE WEAK A8	PERFECT INDICATIVE WEAK A8	PERSON + NUMBER + GENDER
									III M¹
									III M²
									III F¹
									III F²
									III M³⁺
E									II M¹
L									II M²
B									II F¹
A									II F²
T									II M³⁺
									II F³⁺
A									II M²·³⁺ + F³⁺
									I M¹ + F¹
(TA)									I M²·³⁺ +F²·³⁺

542

	IMPERFECT PASSIVE WEAK	IMPERFECT INDICATIVE WEAK	PERFECT PASSIVE WEAK	PERFECT INDICATIVE WEAK	IMPERFECT PASSIVE WEAK	IMPERFECT INDICATIVE WEAK	PERFECT PASSIVE WEAK	PERFECT INDICATIVE WEAK	PERSON + NUMBER + GENDER
	A11	A11	A11	A11	A10	A10	A10	A10	
T	يُوقَى	يَقِي	وُقِيَ	وَقَى	يُرَى	يَرَى	رُئِيَ	رَأَى	III M¹
A	يُوقَيَان	يَقِيَان	وُقِيَا	وَقَيَا	يُرَيَان	يَرَيَان	رُئِيَا	رَأَيَا	III M²
B	يُوقُونَ	يَقُونَ	وُقُوا	وَقَوْا	يُرَوْنَ	يَرَوْنَ	رُؤُوا	رَأَوْا	III M³⁺
L	تُوقَى	تَقِي	وُقِيَتْ	وَقَتْ	تُرَى	تَرَى	رُئِيَتْ	رَأَتْ	III F¹
E	تُوقَيَان	تَقِيَان	وُقِيَتَا	وَقَتَا	تُرَيَان	تَرَيَان	رُئِيَتَا	رَأَتَا	III F²
	يُوقَيْنَ	يَقِيْنَ	وُقِيْنَ	وَقَيْنَ	يُرَيْنَ	يَرَيْنَ	رُئِيْنَ	رَأَيْنَ	III F³⁺
A	تُوقَى	تَقِي	وُقِيْتَ	وَقَيْتَ	تُرَى	تَرَى	رُئِيْتَ	رَأَيْتَ	II M¹
	تُوقَيَان	تَقِيَان	وُقِيْتُمَا	وَقَيْتُمَا	تُرَيَان	تَرَيَان	رُئِيْتُمَا	رَأَيْتُمَا	II M²
(TA)	تُوقُونَ	تَقُونَ	وُقِيْتُمْ	وَقَيْتُمْ	تُرَوْنَ	تَرَوْنَ	رُئِيْتُمْ	رَأَيْتُمْ	II M³⁺
	تُوقَيْنَ	تَقَيْنَ	وُقِيْتِ	وَقَيْتِ	تُرَيْنَ	تَرَيْنَ	رُئِيْتِ	رَأَيْتِ	II F¹
	تُوقَيَان	تَقِيَان	وُقِيْتُمَا	وَقَيْتُمَا	تُرَيَان	تَرَيَان	رُئِيْتُمَا	رَأَيْتُمَا	II F²
	تُوقَيْنَ	تَقَيْنَ	وُقِيْتُنَّ	وَقَيْتُنَّ	تُرَيْنَ	تَرَيْنَ	رُئِيْتُنَّ	رَأَيْتُنَّ	II F³⁺
	أُوقَى	أَقِي	وُقِيْتُ	وَقَيْتُ	أُرَى	أَرَى	رُئِيْتُ	رَأَيْتُ	I M¹ + F¹
	نُوقَى	نَقِي	وُقِيْنَا	وَقَيْنَا	نُرَى	نَرَى	رُئِيْنَا	رَأَيْنَا	I M²,³⁺ +F²,³⁺

Appendix 1

PERSONAL PRONOUN SUFFIX	PERSONAL PRONOUN	PROHABATIVE	IMPERFECT SUBJUNCTIVE WITH نْ	IMPERFECT SUBJUNCTIVE WITH نْ	IMPERFECT SUBJUNCTIVE WITH لْ	IMPERFECT JUSSIVE	PERSON + NUMBER + GENDER
A18	A17	A16	A15	A14	A13	A12	
ـهُ ...	هُوَ			تَفْعَلَنْ	لِيَفْعَلَنْ	يَفْعَلْ	III M¹
ـهُمَا ...	هُمَا			تَفْعَلَانْ	لِيَفْعَلَا	يَفْعَلَا	III M²
ـهُمْ ...	هُمْ		تَفْعَلُنْ	تَفْعَلُونْ	لِيَفْعَلُوا	يَفْعَلُوا	III M³⁺
ـهَا ...	هِيَ		تَفْعَلَنْ	تَفْعَلَنْ	لِتَفْعَلْ	تَفْعَلْ	III F¹
ـهُمَا ...	هُمَا			تَفْعَلَانْ	لِتَفْعَلَا	تَفْعَلَا	III F²
ـهُنَّ ...	هُنَّ		تَفْعَلْنَانْ	تَفْعَلْنَانْ	لِيَفْعَلْنَ	يَفْعَلْنَ	III F³⁺
ـكَ ...	أَنْتَ	لَا تَفْعَلَنْ	تَفْعَلَنْ	تَفْعَلَنْ		تَفْعَلْ	II M¹
ـكُمَا ...	أَنْتُمَا	لَا تَفْعَلَا	تَفْعَلَانْ	تَفْعَلَانْ		تَفْعَلَا	II M²
ـكُمْ ...	أَنْتُمْ	لَا تَفْعَلُوا	تَفْعَلُنْ	تَفْعَلُونْ		تَفْعَلُوا	II M³⁺
ـكِ ...	أَنْتِ	لَا تَفْعَلِي	تَفْعَلِنْ	تَفْعَلِنْ		تَفْعَلِي	II F¹
ـكُمَا ...	أَنْتُمَا	لَا تَفْعَلَا		تَفْعَلَانْ		تَفْعَلَا	II F²
ـكُنَّ ...	أَنْتُنَّ	لَا تَفْعَلْنَ	تَفْعَلْنَانْ	تَفْعَلْنَانْ		تَفْعَلْنَ	II F³⁺
ـنِي ...	أَنَا		تَفْعَلَنْ	تَفْعَلَنْ		أَفْعَلْ	I M¹ + F¹
ـنَا ...	نَحْنُ		نَفْعَلَنْ	نَفْعَلَنْ		نَفْعَلْ	I M²,³⁺ + F²,³⁺

544

Appendix 2

Appendix 2 Table B (TB)

DERIVED FORMS

NUMBER	PERFECT 1	IMPERFECT 2	VERBAL NOUN 3	ACTIVE PARTICIPLE 4	PASSIVE PARTICIPLE 5	PERFECT PASSIVE 6	IMPERFECT PASSIVE 7
II	فَعَّلَ	يُفَعِّلُ	تَفْعِيل	مُفَعِّل	مُفَعَّل	فُعِّلَ	يُفَعَّلُ
III	فاعَلَ	يُفاعِلُ	فِعال / مُفاعَلة	مُفاعِل	مُفاعَل	فوعِلَ	يُفاعَلُ
IV	أَفْعَلَ	يُفْعِلُ	إفْعال	مُفْعِل	مُفْعَل	أُفْعِلَ	يُفْعَلُ
V	تَفَعَّلَ	يَتَفَعَّلُ	تَفَعُّل	مُتَفَعِّل	مُتَفَعَّل	تُفُعِّلَ	يُتَفَعَّلُ
VI	تَفاعَلَ	يَتَفاعَلُ	تَفاعُل	مُتَفاعِل	مُتَفاعَل	تُفوعِلَ	يُتَفاعَلُ
VII	اِنْفَعَلَ *	يَنْفَعِلُ	اِنْفِعال	مُنْفَعِل	مُنْفَعَل		يُنْفَعَلُ
VIII	اِفْتَعَلَ *	يَفْتَعِلُ	اِفْتِعال	مُفْتَعِل	مُفْتَعَل	اُفْتُعِلَ	يُفْتَعَلُ
IX	اِفْعَلَّ *	يَفْعَلُّ	اِفْعِلال	مُفْعَلّ			
X	اِسْتَفْعَلَ *	يَسْتَفْعِلُ	اِسْتِفْعال	مُسْتَفْعِل	مُسْتَفْعَل	اُسْتُفْعِلَ	يُسْتَفْعَلُ

* Note the *kasrah* placed under *hamzat al-wasl* for the sake of learning.

545

Appendix 3 Table (C) (TC) Perfect   Derived Form

X	IX	VIII	VII	VI	V	IV	III	II	GENDER
اِسْتَفْعَلَ	اِفْعَلَّ	اِفْتَعَلَ	اِنْفَعَلَ	تَفاعَلَ	تَفَعَّلَ	أَفْعَلَ	فاعَلَ	فَعَّلَ	III M¹
اِسْتَفْعَلا	اِفْعَلّا	اِفْتَعَلا	اِنْفَعَلا	تَفاعَلا	تَفَعَّلا	أَفْعَلا	فاعَلا	فَعَّلا	III M²
اِسْتَفْعَلوا	اِفْعَلّوا	اِفْتَعَلوا	اِنْفَعَلوا	تَفاعَلوا	تَفَعَّلوا	أَفْعَلوا	فاعَلوا	فَعَّلوا	III M³⁺
اِسْتَفْعَلَتْ	اِفْعَلَّتْ	اِفْتَعَلَتْ	اِنْفَعَلَتْ	تَفاعَلَتْ	تَفَعَّلَتْ	أَفْعَلَتْ	فاعَلَتْ	فَعَّلَتْ	III F¹
اِسْتَفْعَلَتا	اِفْعَلَّتا	اِفْتَعَلَتا	اِنْفَعَلَتا	تَفاعَلَتا	تَفَعَّلَتا	أَفْعَلَتا	فاعَلَتا	فَعَّلَتا	III F²
اِسْتَفْعَلْنَ	اِفْعَلَلْنَ	اِفْتَعَلْنَ	اِنْفَعَلْنَ	تَفاعَلْنَ	تَفَعَّلْنَ	أَفْعَلْنَ	فاعَلْنَ	فَعَّلْنَ	III F³⁺
اِسْتَفْعَلْتَ	اِفْعَلَلْتَ	اِفْتَعَلْتَ	اِنْفَعَلْتَ	تَفاعَلْتَ	تَفَعَّلْتَ	أَفْعَلْتَ	فاعَلْتَ	فَعَّلْتَ	II M¹
اِسْتَفْعَلْتُما	اِفْعَلَلْتُما	اِفْتَعَلْتُما	اِنْفَعَلْتُما	تَفاعَلْتُما	تَفَعَّلْتُما	أَفْعَلْتُما	فاعَلْتُما	فَعَّلْتُما	II M²
اِسْتَفْعَلْتُمْ	اِفْعَلَلْتُمْ	اِفْتَعَلْتُمْ	اِنْفَعَلْتُمْ	تَفاعَلْتُمْ	تَفَعَّلْتُمْ	أَفْعَلْتُمْ	فاعَلْتُمْ	فَعَّلْتُمْ	II M³⁺
اِسْتَفْعَلْتِ	اِفْعَلَلْتِ	اِفْتَعَلْتِ	اِنْفَعَلْتِ	تَفاعَلْتِ	تَفَعَّلْتِ	أَفْعَلْتِ	فاعَلْتِ	فَعَّلْتِ	II F¹
اِسْتَفْعَلْتُما	اِفْعَلَلْتُما	اِفْتَعَلْتُما	اِنْفَعَلْتُما	تَفاعَلْتُما	تَفَعَّلْتُما	أَفْعَلْتُما	فاعَلْتُما	فَعَّلْتُما	II F²
اِسْتَفْعَلْتُنَّ	اِفْعَلَلْتُنَّ	اِفْتَعَلْتُنَّ	اِنْفَعَلْتُنَّ	تَفاعَلْتُنَّ	تَفَعَّلْتُنَّ	أَفْعَلْتُنَّ	فاعَلْتُنَّ	فَعَّلْتُنَّ	II F³⁺
اِسْتَفْعَلْتُ	اِفْعَلَلْتُ	اِفْتَعَلْتُ	اِنْفَعَلْتُ	تَفاعَلْتُ	تَفَعَّلْتُ	أَفْعَلْتُ	فاعَلْتُ	فَعَّلْتُ	I M¹ + F¹
اِسْتَفْعَلْنا	اِفْعَلَلْنا	اِفْتَعَلْنا	اِنْفَعَلْنا	تَفاعَلْنا	تَفَعَّلْنا	أَفْعَلْنا	فاعَلْنا	فَعَّلْنا	I M²,³⁺ + F²,³⁺

Appendix 4

4 Table D (TD) Imperfect   **Derived Form**

X	IX	VIII	VII	VI	V	IV	III	II	GENDER
									III M[1]
									III M[2]
									III M[3+]
									III F[1]
									III F[2]
									III F[3+]
									II M[1]
									II M[2]
									II M[3+]
									II F[1]
									II F[2]
									II F[3+]
									I M[1]
									I M[2,3+]
									I M[1] + F[1]
									I M[2,3+] + F[2,3+]

547

First Form : Five Pillars
Lesson 2

Appendix E 5

Passive Participle	Active Participle	Verbal Noun	Imperfect	Perfect	Meaning	No.
مَعْلُومٌ	عَالِمٌ/عَلِيمٌ	عِلْمٌ	يَعْلَمُ	عَلِمَ	to know	1
مَجْهُولٌ	جَاهِلٌ	جَهْلٌ	يَجْهَلُ	جَهِلَ	to remain ignorant	2
مَصْدُوقٌ	صَادِقٌ	صِدْقٌ	يَصْدُقُ	صَدَقَ	to speak the truth	3
مَكْتُوبٌ	كَاتِبٌ	كِتَابَةٌ	يَكْتُبُ	كَتَبَ	to write	4
مَقْرُوءٌ	قَارِئٌ	قِرَاءَةٌ	يَقْرَأُ	قَرَأَ	to read	5
مَدْخُولٌ	دَاخِلٌ	دُخُولٌ	يَدْخُلُ	دَخَلَ	to enter	6
	خَارِجٌ	خُرُوجٌ	يَخْرُجُ	خَرَجَ	to come out	7
مَأْكُولٌ	آكِلٌ	أَكْلٌ	يَأْكُلُ	أَكَلَ	to eat	8
مَشْرُوبٌ	شَارِبٌ	شُرْبٌ	يَشْرَبُ	شَرِبَ	to drink	9
	جَالِسٌ	جُلُوسٌ	يَجْلِسُ	جَلَسَ	to sit	10
مَسْمُوعٌ	سَامِعٌ/سَمِيعٌ	سَمْعٌ	يَسْمَعُ	سَمِعَ	to listen	11
مَكْذُوبٌ	كَاذِبٌ	كَذِبٌ	يَكْذِبُ	كَذَبَ	to speak lie	12
	ذَاهِبٌ	ذَهَابٌ	يَذْهَبُ	ذَهَبَ	to go	13
	ضَعِيفٌ	ضُعْفٌ	يَضْعُفُ	ضَعُفَ	to become weak	14

Lesson 3

Passive Participle	Active Participle	Verbal Noun	Imperfect	Perfect	Meaning	No.
مَخْلُوقٌ	خَالِقٌ	خَلْقٌ	يَخْلُقُ	خَلَقَ	to create	15
	نَازِلٌ	نُزُولٌ	يَنْزِلُ	نَزَلَ	to descend	16
	كَافِرٌ	كُفْرٌ	يَكْفُرُ	كَفَرَ	to hide	17
مَفْهُومٌ	فَاهِمٌ / فَهِيمٌ	فَهْمٌ	يَفْهَمُ	فَهِمَ	to understand	18
	رَاجِعٌ	رُجُوعٌ	يَرْجِعُ	رَجَعَ	to return	19

Lesson 4

Passive Participle	Active Participle	Verbal Noun	Imperfect	Perfect	Meaning	No.
مَحْمُودٌ	حَامِدٌ	حَمْدٌ	يَحْمَدُ	حَمِدَ	to praise	20
مَهْلُوكٌ	هَالِكٌ	هَلَاكٌ	يَهْلِكُ	هَلَكَ	to perish	21
مَقُولٌ	قَائِلٌ	قَوْلٌ	يَقُولُ	قَالَ	to say [A¹]	22
	صَائِمٌ	صَوْمٌ	يَصُومُ	صَامَ	to fast [A¹]	23
	قَائِمٌ	قِيَامٌ	يَقُومُ	قَامَ	to stand [A¹]	24
	كَائِنٌ	كَوْنٌ	يَكُونُ	كَانَ	to be [A¹]	25
	نَائِمٌ	نَوْمٌ	يَنَامُ	نَامَ	to sleep [A¹]	26
	جَاءٍ	مَجِيءٌ	يَجِيءُ	جَاءَ	to come [A²]	27

Lesson 5

Passive Participle	Active Participle	Verbal Noun	Imperfect	Perfect	Meaning	No.
مَغْسُولٌ	غَاسِلٌ	غُسْلٌ	يَغْسِلُ	غَسَلَ	to wash	28
مَقْتُولٌ	قَاتِلٌ	قَتْلٌ	يَقْتُلُ	قَتَلَ	to kill	29
مَعْبُودٌ	عَابِدٌ	عِبَادَةٌ	يَعْبُدُ	عَبَدَ	to worship	30
مَأْمُورٌ	آمِرٌ	أَمْرٌ	يَأْمُرُ	أَمَرَ	to command	31
	تَائِبٌ	تَوْبَةٌ	يَتُوبُ	تَابَ	to repent [A¹]	32

	فَائِزٌ	فَوْزٌ	يَفُوزُ	فَازَ	to be successful [A6]	33
مَدْعُوٌّ	دَاعٍ	دَعْوَةٌ/دُعَاءٌ	يَدْعُو	دَعَا	to call [A4]	34
	فَانٍ	فَنَاءٌ	يَفْنَى	فَنِيَ	to perish [A3]	35
مَرْضِيٌّ	رَاضٍ	رِضَاءٌ	يَرْضَى	رَضِيَ	to be pleased [A3]	36
	سَاعٍ	سَعْيٌ	يَسْعَى	سَعَى	To struggle [A5]	37
مَنْهِيٌّ	نَاهٍ	نَهْيٌ	يَنْهَى	نَهَى	to prevent [A5]	38
مَهْدٍ	هَادٍ	هُدًى	يَهْدِي	هَدَى	to guide [A6]	39
مَسْؤُوْلٌ	سَائِلٌ	سُؤَالٌ	يَسْأَلُ	سَأَلَ	to ask [A9]	40
مَسُوقٌ	سَائِقٌ	سِيَاقَةٌ	يَسُوقُ	سَاقَ	to drive [A1]	41
مَذَاقٌ	ذَائِقٌ	ذَوْقٌ	يَذُوقُ	ذَاقَ	to taste [A1]	42
	ظَاهِرٌ	ظُهُورٌ	يَظْهَرُ	ظَهَرَ	to appear	43
مَحْفُوظٌ	حَافِظٌ/حَفِيظٌ	حِفْظٌ	يَحْفَظُ	حَفِظَ	to protect	44
مَوْسُوعٌ	وَاسِعٌ	وُسْعٌ	يَسَعُ	وَسِعَ	to be wide/spacious	45
مَظْلُومٌ	ظَالِمٌ	ظُلْمٌ	يَظْلِمُ	ظَلَمَ	to oppress	46
	سَائِقٌ	سُوقٌ	يَسُوقُ	سَاقَ	to drive [A1]	47
مَشْهُودٌ	شَاهِدٌ	شُهُودٌ	يَشْهَدُ	شَهِدَ	to witness	48

Lesson 6

	عَاصٍ	عِصْيَانٌ	يَعْصِي	عَصِي	to disobey [A6]	49
مَنْصُورٌ	نَاصِرٌ/نَصِيرٌ	نَصْرٌ	يَنْصُرُ	نَصَرَ	to help	50
مَرْزُوقٌ	رَازِقٌ	رِزْقٌ	يَرْزُقُ	رَزَقَ	to provide sustenance	51
	نَافِعٌ	نَفْعٌ	يَنْفَعُ	نَفَعَ	to benefit	52
مَطْلُوبٌ	طَالِبٌ	طَلَبٌ	يَطْلُبُ	طَلَبَ	to seek	53
مَتْرُوكٌ	تَارِكٌ	تَرْكٌ	يَتْرُكُ	تَرَكَ	to give renounce	54
	جَاعِلٌ	جَعْلٌ	يَجْعَلُ	جَعَلَ	to make	55
مَفْتُوحٌ	فَاتِحٌ	فَتْحٌ	يَفْتَحُ	فَتَحَ	to open to conquer	56

مَفْرُورٌ	فَارٌّ	فِرَارٌ	يَفِرُّ	فَرَّ	to escape/ to flee from [A8]	57
	وَالِجٌ	وُلُوجٌ	يَلِجُ	وَلَجَ	to penetrate	58
مَضْرُوبٌ	ضَارِبٌ	ضَرْبٌ	يَضْرِبُ	ضَرَبَ	to beat	59
	سَاقِطٌ	سُقُوطٌ	يَسْقُطُ	سَقَطَ	to fall	60
مَحْمُولٌ	حَامِلٌ	حَمْلٌ	يَحْمِلُ	حَمَلَ	to bear/carry	61
مَكْسُوبٌ	كَاسِبٌ	كَسْبٌ	يَكْسِبُ	كَسَبَ	to earn	62
مَخُوفٌ	خَائِفٌ	خَوْفٌ	يَخَافُ	خَافَ	to dread/fear [A2]	63
مَمْلُوكٌ	مَالِكٌ/مَلِيكٌ	مُلْكٌ	يَمْلِكُ	مَلَكَ	to possess	64
مَدْرُوْءٌ	دَارِءٌ	دَرْءٌ	يَدْرَأُ	دَرَأَ	to revert	65
مَشَاءٌ	شَاءٍ	مَشِيئَةٌ	يَشَاءُ	شَاءَ	to will	66
مَخْتُومٌ	خَاتِمٌ	خَتْمٌ/خِتَامٌ	يَخْتِمُ	خَتَمَ	to seal	67
	مَرِيضٌ	مَرَضٌ	يَمْرَضُ	مَرِضَ	to be sick	68
	شَافٍ	شِفَاءٌ	يَشْفِي	شَفَى	to heal/cure [A3]	69
مَفْطُورٌ	فَاطِرٌ	فَطْرٌ	يَفْطُرُ	فَطَرَ	to create	70
	كَامِلٌ	كَمَالٌ	يَكْمُلُ	كَمُلَ	to complete	71
مَمْرُورٌ	مَارٌّ	مُرُورٌ	يَمُرُّ	مَرَّ (ب/عَلَى)	to pass by	72
مُعَاذٌ	عَائِذٌ	عَوْذٌ/عِيَاذٌ	يَعُوذُ	عَاذَ	to seek refuge [A1]	73
مُلَاقٍ	لَاقٍ	لِقَاءٌ	يَلْقَى	لَقِيَ	to meet [A3]	74
	بَاكٍ	بُكَاءٌ	يَبْكِي	بَكَى	to cry [A6]	75
	بَاقٍ	بَقَاءٌ	يَبْقَى	بَقِيَ	to remain/ survive [A3]	76
مَنْسِيٌّ	نَاسٍ	نِسْيَانٌ	يَنْسَى	نَسِيَ	to forget [A3]	77
	خَاشٍ	خَشْيَةٌ	يَخْشَى	خَشِيَ	to be afraid [A3]	78
	عَائِدٌ	عَوْدٌ/مَعَادٌ	يَعُودُ	عَادَ	to return [A1]	79
	بَالٍ	بَلَاءٌ	يَبْلُو	بَلَا	to test [A4]	80
	مَيِّتٌ	مَوْتٌ	يَمُوتُ	مَاتَ	to die [A1]	81
مَرْأَى	رَاءٍ	رُؤْيَةٌ	يَرَى	رَأَى	to see [A10]	82

مَرْجُوٌّ	رَاجٍ	رَجَاءٌ	يَرْجُو	رَجَا	to hope [A4]	83

Lesson 7

مَشْكُوكٌ	شَاكٌّ	شَكٌّ	يَشُكُّ	شَكَّ	to doubt	84
مَرْحُومٌ	رَاحِمٌ/رَحِيمٌ	رَحْمَةٌ	يَرْحَمُ	رَحِمَ	to have mercy	85
	صَالِحٌ	صَلَاحٌ	يَصْلُحُ	صَلَحَ	to be good	86
مَذْكُورٌ	ذَاكِرٌ	ذِكْرٌ	يَذْكُرُ	ذَكَرَ	to remember	87
	صَابِرٌ	صَبْرٌ	يَصْبِرُ	صَبَرَ	to exercise patience	88
مُشَدَّدٌ	شَدِيدٌ	شِدَّةٌ	يَشُدُّ	شَدَّ	to be firm	89
مَسْفُوكٌ	سَافِكٌ	سَفْكٌ	يَسْفُكُ	سَفَكَ	to shed blood	90
مَخْفِيٌّ	خَافٍ	خَفَاءٌ	يَخْفَى	خَفِيَ	to be hidden [A3]	91
مَشْكُورٌ	شَاكِرٌ	شُكْرٌ	يَشْكُرُ	شَكَرَ	to thank/be thankful	92
	وَاقِعٌ	وُقُوعٌ	يَقَعُ	وَقَعَ	to come to pass	93
مَبْسُوطٌ	بَاسِطٌ	بَسْطٌ	يَبْسُطُ	بَسَطَ	to spread	94
مَقْضِيٌّ	قَاضٍ	قَضَاءٌ	يَقْضِى	قَضَى	to decree	95
مَوْجُودٌ	وَاجِدٌ	وُجُودٌ	يَجِدُ	وَجَدَ	to find	96
مَتْبُوعٌ	تَابِعٌ	تَبَاعٌ	يَتْبَعُ	تَبِعَ	to follow	97
	لَاعِبٌ	لَعْبٌ	يَلْعَبُ	لَعِبَ	to play	98
	خَاسِرٌ	خُسْرَانٌ	يَخْسِرُ	خَسِرَ	to earn loss	99
	رَامٍ	رَمْيٌ	يَرْمِى	رَمَى	to throw [A6]	100
	جَمِيلٌ	جَمَالٌ	يَجْمُلُ	جَمُلَ	to be beautiful	101
	قَصِيرٌ	قَصْرٌ	يَقْصُرُ	قَصُرَ	to be short	102
	طَوِيلٌ	طُولٌ	يَطُولُ	طَالَ	to be long	103
	كَبِيرٌ	كِبْرٌ	يَكْبُرُ	كَبُرَ	to be big	104
	كَرِيمٌ	كَرَامَةٌ	يَكْرُمُ	كَرُمَ	to be noble	105
	عَظِيمٌ	عِظَمٌ	يَعْظُمُ	عَظُمَ	to be grand	106
	قَوِيٌّ	قُوَّةٌ	يَقْوَى	قَوِيَ	to be strong [A3]	107

مَحْكُومٌ	حَاكِمٌ	حُكْمٌ	يَحْكُمُ	حَكَمَ	to judge	108
	بَاطِلٌ	بُطْلَانٌ	يَبْطُلُ	بَطَلَ	to become vain	109
مَصْنُوعٌ	صَانِعٌ	صُنْعٌ	يَصْنَعُ	صَنَعَ	to make	110
	غَنِيٌّ	غَنَاءٌ	يَغْنَى	غَنِيَ	to be rich[A³]	111
مَيْسُورٌ	يَاسِرٌ	يُسْرٌ	يَيْسِرُ	يَسَرَ	to be easy	112
مَقْدُورٌ	قَادِرٌ/قَدِيرٌ	قُدْرَةٌ	يَقْدِرُ	قَدَرَ	to decide	113
	خَصِيمٌ	خُصُومَةٌ	يَخْصِمُ	خَصَمَ	to quarrel	114
مَفْضُولٌ	فَاضِلٌ	فَضْلٌ	يَفْضُلُ	فَضَلَ	to be excellent	115
	غَائِبٌ	غَيْبٌ	يَغِيبُ	غَابَ	to be absent[A²]	116
	لَطِيفٌ	لُطْفٌ	يَلْطُفُ	لَطُفَ	to be kind	117
	خَبِيرٌ	خَبْرٌ	يَخْبُرُ	خَبَرَ	to know well	118
	نَعِيمٌ	نَعْمَةٌ	يَنْعَمُ	نَعِمَ	to live in comfort	119
	فَاسِدٌ	فَسَادٌ	يَفْسُدُ	فَسَدَ	to be corrupt	120
مَقْدُومٌ	قَادِمٌ	قُدُومٌ	يَقْدُمُ	قَدَمَ	to precede	121
	خَاسِرٌ	خُسْرَانٌ	يَخْسِرُ	خَسِرَ	to incur a loss	122
	لَاعِبٌ	لَعْبٌ	يَلْعَبُ	لَعِبَ	to play	123
مَحْسُوبٌ	حَاسِبٌ/حَسِيبٌ	حِسَابٌ	يَحْسُبُ	حَسَبَ	to count	124
	عَزِيزٌ	عِزًّا	يَعِزُّ	عَزَّ	to be respected	125
مَثْبُوتٌ	ثَابِتٌ	ثَبَاتٌ	يَثْبُتُ	ثَبَتَ	to stand firm	126
مَلُومٌ	لَآئِمٌ	لَوْمٌ	يَلُومُ	لَامَ	to blame	127
مَعْمُولٌ	عَامِلٌ	عَمَلٌ	يَعْمَلُ	عَمِلَ	to work	128
مَنْظُورٌ	نَاظِرٌ	نَظَرٌ	يَنْظُرُ	نَظَرَ	to look	129
مَأْلُومٌ	أَلِيمٌ	أَلَمٌ	يَأْلَمُ	أَلِمَ	to be in pain	130
		عَذْبٌ	يَعْذُبُ	عَذُبَ	to impede	131
	آثِمٌ	إِثْمٌ	يَأْثَمُ	أَثِمَ	to sin	132
	وَحِيدٌ	وَحْدٌ	يَحِدُّ	وَحَدَ	to be singular	133
	قَوِيٌّ	قُوَّةً	يَقْوَى	قَوِيَ	to be/become strong	134
مَطْعُومٌ	طَاعِمٌ	طَعْمٌ	يَطْعَمُ	طَعِمَ	to eat	135

مَفْعُولٌ	فَاعلٌ	فَعْلٌ	يَفْعَلُ	فَعَلَ	to do	136
	عَادلٌ	عَدْلٌ	يَعْدلُ	عَدَلَ	to act justly	137
وَاقٍ	وَقى	وَقَايَةٌ	يَقى	وَقى	to protect [A[11]]	138
	عَالٍ	عُلُوٌّ	يَعْلُو	عَلاَ	to elevate [A[4]]	139
	بَانٍ	بُنْيَانٌ	يَبْنَى	بَنَى	to build [A[6]]	140
مَعْرُوفٌ	عَارفٌ	مَعْرِفَةٌ	يَعْرَفُ	عَرَفَ	to knew	141
مَغْضُوبٌ	غَاضبٌ	غَضْبٌ	يَغْضبُ	غَضبَ	to be/become angry	142
	عَاصٍ	عُصْيَانٌ	يَعْصَى	عَصَى	to disobey	143

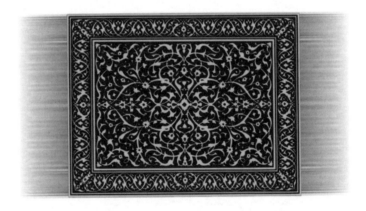

Appendix F 6

DERIVED FORM II
Lesson 8

باب تَفْعِيلٌ

Passive Participle	Active Participle	Verbal Noun	Imperfect	Perfect	No
مُنَزَّلٌ	مُنَزِّلٌ	تَنْزِيلٌ	يُنَزِّلُ	نَزَّلَ	1
مُعَلَّمٌ	مُعَلِّمٌ	تَعْلِيمٌ	يُعَلِّمُ	عَلَّمَ	2
مُبَلَّغٌ	مُبَلِّغٌ	تَبْلِيغٌ	يُبَلِّغُ	بَلَّغَ	3
مُقَرَّبٌ	مُقَرِّبٌ	تَقْرِيبٌ	يُقَرِّبُ	قَرَّبَ	4
مُبَعَّدٌ	مُبَعِّدٌ	تَبْعِيدٌ	يُبَعِّدُ	بَعَّدَ	5
مُطَهَّرٌ	مُطَهِّرٌ	تَطْهِيرٌ	يُطَهِّرُ	طَهَّرَ	6
مُرَتَّلٌ	مُرَتِّلٌ	تَرْتِيلٌ	يُرَتِّلُ	رَتَّلَ	7
مُصَدَّقٌ	مُصَدِّقٌ	تَصْدِيقٌ	يُصَدِّقُ	صَدَّقَ	8
مُكَذَّبٌ	مُكَذِّبٌ	تَكْذِيبٌ	يُكَذِّبُ	كَذَّبَ	9
مُحَقَّرٌ	مُحَقِّرٌ	تَحْقِيرٌ	يُحَقِّرُ	حَقَّرَ	10
مُذَلَّلٌ	مُذَلِّلٌ	تَذْلِيلٌ	يُذَلِّلُ	ذَلَّلَ	11
مُضَعَّفٌ	مُضَعِّفٌ	تَضْعِيفٌ	يُضَعِّفُ	ضَعَّفَ	12
مُسَلَّمٌ	مُسَلِّمٌ	تَسْلِيمٌ	يُسَلِّمُ	سَلَّمَ	13
مُطَوَّلٌ	مُطَوِّلٌ	تَطْوِيلٌ	يُطَوِّلُ	طَوَّلَ	14
مُرَكَّبٌ	مُرَكِّبٌ	تَرْكِيبٌ	يُرَكِّبُ	رَكَّبَ	15
مُسَمَّعٌ	مُسَمِّعٌ	تَسْمِيعٌ	يُسَمِّعُ	سَمَّعَ	16
مُخَوَّفٌ	مُخَوِّفٌ	تَخْوِيفٌ	يُخَوِّفُ	خَوَّفَ	17
مُكَتَّبٌ	مُكَتِّبٌ	تَكْتِيبٌ	يُكَتِّبُ	كَتَّبَ	18
مُكَسَّرٌ	مُكَسِّرٌ	تَكْسِيرٌ	يُكَسِّرُ	كَسَّرَ	19
مُغَسَّلٌ	مُغَسِّلٌ	تَغْسِيلٌ	يُغَسِّلُ	غَسَّلَ	20
مُقَتَّلٌ	مُقَتِّلٌ	تَقْتِيلٌ	يُقَتِّلُ	قَتَّلَ	21
مُكَفَّرٌ	مُكَفِّرٌ	تَكْفِيرٌ	يُكَفِّرُ	كَفَّرَ	22
مُبَشَّرٌ	مُبَشِّرٌ	تَبْشِيرٌ	يُبَشِّرُ	بَشَّرَ	23
مُقَدَّرٌ	مُقَدِّرٌ	تَقْدِيرٌ	يُقَدِّرُ	قَدَّرَ	24

Passive Participle	Active Participle	Verbal Noun	Imperfect	Perfect	No.
مُفَكَّرٌ	مُفَكِّرٌ	تَفْكِيرٌ	يُفَكِّرُ	فَكَّرَ	25
مُسَوًّى	مُسَوِّي	تَسْوِيَةٌ	يُسَوِّي	سَوَّى	26
مُسَبَّحٌ	مُسَبِّحٌ	تَسْبِيحٌ	يُسَبِّحُ	سَبَّحَ	27
مُسَخَّرٌ	مُسَخِّرٌ	تَسْخِيرٌ	يُسَخِّرُ	سَخَّرَ	28
مُسَمًّى	مُسَمِّي	تَسْمِيَةٌ	يُسَمِّي	سَمَّى	29
مُكَلَّمٌ	مُكَلِّمٌ	تَكْلِيمٌ	يُكَلِّمُ	كَلَّمَ	30
مُقَدَّمٌ	مُقَدِّمٌ	تَقْدِيمٌ	يُقَدِّمُ	قَدَّمَ	31
مُكَلَّفٌ	مُكَلِّفٌ	تَكْلِيفٌ	يُكَلِّفُ	كَلَّفَ	32
مُوَسَّعٌ	مُوَسِّعٌ	تَوْسِيعٌ	يُوَسِّعُ	وَسَّعَ	33
مُخَلَّقٌ	مُخَلِّقٌ	تَخْلِيقٌ	يُخَلِّقُ	خَلَّقَ	34
مُعَرَّفٌ	مُعَرِّفٌ	تَعْرِيفٌ	يُعَرِّفُ	عَرَّفَ	35
مُقَوَّمٌ	مُقَوِّمٌ	تَقْوِيمٌ	يُقَوِّمُ	قَوَّمَ	36
مُدَرَّسٌ	مُدَرِّسٌ	تَدْرِيسٌ	يُدَرِّسُ	دَرَّسَ	37
مُضَلَّلٌ	مُضَلِّلٌ	تَضْلِيلٌ	يُضَلِّلُ	ضَلَّلَ	38
مُحَسَّنٌ	مُحَسِّنٌ	تَحْسِينٌ	يُحَسِّنُ	حَسَّنَ	39
مُعَظَّمٌ	مُعَظِّمٌ	تَعْظِيمٌ	يُعَظِّمُ	عَظَّمَ	40
مُوَفَّقٌ	مُوَفِّقٌ	تَوْفِيقٌ	يُوَفِّقُ	وَفَّقَ	41
مُدَبَّرٌ	مُدَبِّرٌ	تَدْبِيرٌ	يُدَبِّرُ	دَبَّرَ	42
مُزَيَّنٌ	مُزَيِّنٌ	تَزْيِينٌ	يُزَيِّنُ	زَيَّنَ	43
مُسَرَّحٌ	مُسَرِّحٌ	تَسْرِيحٌ	يُسَرِّحُ	سَرَّحَ	44
مُحَرَّرٌ	مُحَرِّرٌ	تَحْرِيرٌ	يُحَرِّرُ	حَرَّرَ	45
مُصَرَّفٌ	مُصَرِّفٌ	تَصْرِيفٌ	يُصَرِّفُ	صَرَّفَ	46
مُكَرَّمٌ	مُكَرِّمٌ	تَكْرِيمٌ	يُكَرِّمُ	كَرَّمَ	47
مُوَحَّدٌ	مُوَحِّدٌ	تَوْحِيدٌ	يُوَحِّدُ	وَحَّدَ	48
مُنَوَّرٌ	مُنَوِّرٌ	تَنْوِيرٌ	يُنَوِّرُ	نَوَّرَ	49
مُعَذَّبٌ	مُعَذِّبٌ	تَعْذِيبٌ	يُعَذِّبُ	عَذَّبَ	50
مُوَقَّتٌ	مُوَقِّتٌ	تَوْقِيتٌ	يُوَقِّتُ	وَقَّتَ	51

Passive Participle	Active Participle	Verbal Noun	Imperfect	Perfect	No
مُبَيَّنٌ	مُبَيِّنٌ	تَبْيِينٌ	يُبَيِّنُ	بَيَّنَ	52
مُؤَدَّبٌ	مُؤَدِّبٌ	تَأْدِيبٌ	يُؤَدِّبُ	أَدَّبَ	53
مُفَضَّلٌ	مُفَضِّلٌ	تَفْضِيلٌ	يُفَضِّلُ	فَضَّلَ	54
مُقَدَّمٌ	مُقَدِّمٌ	تَقْدِيمٌ	يُقَدِّمُ	قَدَّمَ	55
مُكَوَّرٌ	مُكَوِّرٌ	تَكْوِيرٌ	يُكَوِّرُ	كَوَّرَ	56
مُسَيَّرٌ	مُسَيِّرٌ	تَسْيِيرٌ	يُسَيِّرُ	سَيَّرَ	57
مُسَجَّرٌ	مُسَجِّرٌ	تَسْجِيرٌ	يُسَجِّرُ	سَجَّرَ	58
مُزَوَّجٌ	مُزَوِّجٌ	تَزْوِيجٌ	يُزَوِّجُ	زَوَّجَ	59
مُسَعَّرٌ	مُسَعِّرٌ	تَسْعِيرٌ	يُسَعِّرُ	سَعَّرَ	60
مُحَصَّلٌ	مُحَصِّلٌ	تَحْصِيلٌ	يُحَصِّلُ	حَصَّلَ	61
مُغَيَّرٌ	مُغَيِّرٌ	تَغْيِيرٌ	يُغَيِّرُ	غَيَّرَ	62
مُجَلًّى	مُجَلٍّ	تَجَلٍّ	يُجَلِّي	جَلَّى	63
مُيَسَّرٌ	مُيَسِّرٌ	تَيْسِيرٌ	يُيَسِّرُ	يَسَّرَ	64
مُحَدَّثٌ	مُحَدِّثٌ	تَحْدِيثٌ	يُحَدِّثُ	حَدَّثَ	65
مُؤَجَّلٌ	مُؤَجِّلٌ	تَأْجِيلٌ	يُؤَجِّلُ	أَجَّلَ	66
مُصَوَّرٌ	مُصَوِّرٌ	تَصْوِيرٌ	يُصَوِّرُ	صَوَّرَ	67

DERIVED FORM IV
Lesson 9
باب إِفْعَالٌ

Passive Participle	Active Participle	Verbal Noun	Imperfect	Perfect	No
مُسْلَمٌ	مُسْلِمٌ	إِسْلَامٌ	يُسْلِمُ	أَسْلَمَ	68
مُنْزَلٌ	مُنْزِلٌ	إِنْزَالٌ	يُنْزِلُ	أَنْزَلَ	69
مُدْخَلٌ	مُدْخِلٌ	إِدْخَالٌ	يُدْخِلُ	أَدْخَلَ	70

Passive Participle	Active Participle	Verbal Noun	Imperfect	Perfect	No
مُخْرَجٌ	مُخْرِجٌ	إِخْرَاجٌ	يُخْرِجُ	أَخْرَجَ	71
مُشْرَكٌ	مُشْرِكٌ	إِشْرَاكٌ	يُشْرِكُ	أَشْرَكَ	72
مُؤْمَنٌ	مُؤْمِنٌ	إِيمَانٌ	يُؤْمِنُ	آمَنَ	73
مُحْيَى	مُحْيِي	إِحْيَاءٌ	يُحْيِي	أَحْيَى	74
مَمَاتٌ	مُمِيتٌ	إِمَاتَةٌ	يُمِيتُ	أَمَاتَ	75
مُحْسَنٌ	مُحْسِنٌ	إِحْسَانٌ	يُحْسِنُ	أَحْسَنَ	76
مُفْسَدٌ	مُفْسِدٌ	إِفْسَادٌ	يُفْسِدُ	أَفْسَدَ	77
مُصْلَحٌ	مُصْلِحٌ	إِصْلَاحٌ	يُصْلِحُ	أَصْلَحَ	78
مُكْثَرٌ	مُكْثِرٌ	إِكْثَارٌ	يُكْثِرُ	أَكْثَرَ	79
مُبْعَدٌ	مُبْعِدٌ	إِبْعَادٌ	يُبْعِدُ	أَبْعَدَ	80
مُورَثٌ	مُورِثٌ	إِيرَاثٌ	يُورِثُ	أَوْرَثَ	81
مُنْفَقٌ	مُنْفِقٌ	إِنْفَاقٌ	يُنْفِقُ	أَنْفَقَ	82
مُمْسَكٌ	مُمْسِكٌ	إِمْسَاكٌ	يُمْسِكُ	أَمْسَكَ	83
مُضَلٌّ	مُضِلٌّ	اضْلَالٌ	يُضِلُّ	أَضَلَّ	84
مُوحَى	مُوحِي	إِيحَاءٌ	يُوحِي	أَوْحَى	85
مُرْسَلٌ	مُرْسِلٌ	إِرْسَالٌ	يُرْسِلُ	أَرْسَلَ	86
مُدْرَيٌ	مُدْرِيٌ	إِدْرَاءٌ	يُدْرِي	أَدْرَى	87
مُنْقَذٌ	مُنْقِذٌ	إِنْقَاذٌ	يُنْقِذُ	أَنْقَذَ	88
مُحَسٌّ	مُحِسٌّ	إِحْسَاسٌ	يُحِسُّ	أَحَسَّ	89
مُقْرَضٌ	مُقْرِضٌ	إِقْرَاضٌ	يُقْرِضُ	أَقْرَضَ	90
مُرَادٌ	مُرِيدٌ	إِرَادَةٌ	يُرِيدُ	أَرَادَ	91
مُصَابٌ	مُصِيبٌ	إِصَابَةٌ	يُصِيبُ	أَصَابَ	92
مُعَاذٌ	مُعِيذٌ	إِعَاذَةٌ	يُعِيذُ	أَعَاذَ	93
مُكْرَمٌ	مُكْرِمٌ	إِكْرَامٌ	يُكْرِمُ	أَكْرَمَ	94
مُحْضَرٌ	مُحْضِرٌ	إِحْضَارٌ	يُحْضِرُ	أَحْضَرَ	95
مُعْطَى	مُعْطِي	إِعْطَاءٌ	يُعْطِي	أَعْطَى	96

مُظْهَرٌ	مُظْهِرٌ	إِظْهَارٌ	يُظْهِرُ	أَظْهَرَ	97
مُطْعَمٌ	مُطْعِمٌ	إِطْعَامٌ	يُطْعِمُ	أَطْعَمَ	98
مُصْبَحٌ	مُصْبِحٌ	إِصْبَاحٌ	يُصْبِحُ	أَصْبَحَ	99
مُضْحَى	مُضْحِي	إِضْحَاءٌ	يُضْحِي	أَضْحَى	100
مُطَاعٌ	مُطِيعٌ	إِطَاعَةٌ	يُطِيعُ	أَطَاعَ	101
مُضَاعٌ	مُضِيعٌ	إِضَاعَةٌ	يُضِيعُ	أَضَاعَ	102
مُجَادٌ	مُجِيدٌ	إِجَادَةٌ	يُجِيدُ	أَجَادَ	103
مُجَابٌ	مُجِيبٌ	إِجَابَةٌ	يُجِيبُ	أَجَابَ	104
مُحْصَى	مُحْصِي	إِحْصَاءٌ	يُحْصِي	أَحْصَى	105
مُذْهَبٌ	مُذْهِبٌ	إِذْهَابٌ	يُذْهِبُ	أَذْهَبَ	106
مُعَدٌّ	مُعِدٌّ	إِعْدَادٌ	يُعِدُّ	أَعَدَّ	107
مُفْلَحٌ	مُفْلِحٌ	إِفْلَاحٌ	يُفْلِحُ	أَفْلَحَ	108
مُنْكَرٌ	مُنْكِرٌ	إِنْكَارٌ	يُنْكِرُ	أَنْكَرَ	109
مُنَابٌ	مُنِيبٌ	إِنَابَةٌ	يُنِيبُ	أَنَابَ	110
مُكْرَهٌ	مُكْرِهٌ	إِكْرَاهٌ	يُكْرِهُ	أَكْرَهَ	111
مُقَامٌ	مُقِيمٌ	إِقَامَةٌ	يُقِيمُ	أَقَامَ	112
مُعْلَى	مُعْلِي	إِعْلَاءٌ	يُعْلِي	أَعْلَى	113
مُمْكَنٌ	مُمْكِنٌ	إِمْكَانٌ	يُمْكِنُ	أَمْكَنَ	114
مُعَادٌ	مُعِيدٌ	إِعَادَةٌ	يُعِيدُ	أَعَادَ	115
مُنْظَرٌ	مُنْظِرٌ	إِنْظَارٌ	يُنْظِرُ	أَنْظَرَ	116
مُنْجَى	مُنْجِي	إِنْجَاءٌ	يُنْجِي	أَنْجَى	117
مُوصَى	مُوصِي	إِيصَاءٌ	يُوصِي	أَوْصَى	118
مُبْدَئٌ	مُبْدِئٌ	إِبْدَاءٌ	يُبْدِئُ	أَبْدَأَ	119
مُخْفَى	مُخْفِي	إِخْفَاءٌ	يُخْفِي	أَخْفَى	120
مُعْرَضٌ	مُعْرِضٌ	إِعْرَاضٌ	يُعْرِضُ	أَعْرَضَ	121
مُدْلَى	مُدْلِي	إِدْلَاءٌ	يُدْلِي	أَدْلَى	122
مُزْلَفٌ	مُزْلِفٌ	إِزْلَافٌ	يُزْلِفُ	أَزْلَفَ	123
مُوقَعٌ	مُوقِعٌ	إِيقَاعٌ	يُوقِعُ	أَوْقَعَ	124

Passive Participle	Active Participle	Verbal Noun	Imperfect	Perfect	No
مُعْجَزٌ	مُعْجِزٌ	إعْجَازٌ	يُعْجِزُ	أَعْجَزَ	125
مُطْلَعٌ	مُطْلِعٌ	إطْلَاعٌ	يُطْلِعُ	أَطْلَعَ	126
مُثَابٌ	مُثِيبٌ	إثَابَةٌ	يُثِيبُ	أَثَابَ	127
مُجَارٌ	مُجِيرٌ	إجَارَةٌ	يُجِيرُ	أَجَارَ	128
مُبْقَى	مُبْقِي	إبْقَاءٌ	يُبْقِي	أَبْقَى	129
مُغْنَى	مُغْنِي	إغْنَاءٌ	يُغْنِي	أَغْنَى	130
مُدْبَرٌ	مُدْبِرٌ	إدْبَارٌ	يُدْبِرُ	أَدْبَرَ	131
مُرْدَفٌ	مُرْدِفٌ	إرْدَافٌ	يُرْدِفُ	أَرْدَفَ	132
مُسْفَرٌ	مُسْفِرٌ	إسْفَارٌ	يُسْفِرُ	أَسْفَرَ	133

DERIVED FORM III
Lesson 10

مُفَاعَلَةٌ /باب فِعَالٌ

Passive Participle	Active Participle	Verbal Noun	Imperfect	Perfect	No
مُنَافَقٌ	مُنَافِقٌ	مُنَافَقَةٌ/نفَاقٌ	يُنَافِقُ	نَافَقَ	134
مُجَاهَدٌ	مُجَاهِدٌ	مُجَاهَدَةٌ/جِهَادٌ	يُجَاهِدُ	جَاهَدَ	135
مُجَادَلٌ	مُجَادِلٌ	مُجَادَلَةٌ/جِدَالٌ	يُجَادِلُ	جَادَلَ	136
مَقَاتَلٌ	مُقَاتِلٌ	مُقَاتَلَةٌ/قِتَالٌ	يُقَاتِلُ	قَاتَلَ	137
مَسَافَرٌ	مُسَافِرٌ	مُسَافَرَةٌ	يُسَافِرُ	سَافَرَ	138
مُحَافَظٌ	مُحَافِظٌ	مُحَافَظَةٌ/حِفَاظٌ	يُحَافِظُ	حَافَظَ	139
مَعَاوَنٌ	مُعَاوِنٌ	مُعَاوَنَةٌ	يُعَاوِنُ	عَاوَنَ	140
مُجَالَسٌ	مُجَالِسٌ	مُجَالَسَةٌ	يُجَالِسُ	جَالَسَ	141
مُنَاظَرٌ	مُنَاظِرٌ	مُنَاظَرَةٌ	يُنَاظِرُ	نَاظَرَ	142
مُؤَاكَلٌ	مُؤَاكِلٌ	مُؤَاكَلَةٌ	يُؤَاكِلُ	آكَلَ	143

Passive Participle	Active Participle	Verbal Noun	Imperfect	Perfect	No
مُشَارَبٌ	مُشَارِبٌ	مُشَارَبَةٌ	يُشَارِبُ	شَارَبَ	144
مُشَارَكٌ	مُشَارِكٌ	مُشَارَكَةٌ	يُشَارِكُ	شَارَكَ	145
مُبَارَكٌ	مُبَارِكٌ	مُبَارَكَةٌ	يُبَارِكُ	بَارَكَ	146
مُهَاجَرٌ	مُهَاجِرٌ	مُهَاجَرَةٌ	يُهَاجِرُ	هَاجَرَ	147
مُسَابَقٌ	مُسَابِقٌ	مُسَابَقَةٌ	يُسَابِقُ	سَابَقَ	148
مُنَادَى	مُنَادٍ	مُنَادَاةٌ/نِدَاءٌ	يُنَادِي	نَادَى	149
مُدَاوَلٌ	مُدَاوِلٌ	مُدَاوَلَةٌ	يُدَاوِلُ	دَاوَلَ	150
مُغَادَرٌ	مُغَادِرٌ	مُغَادَرَةٌ	يُغَادِرُ	غَادَرَ	151
مُسَارَعٌ	مُسَارِعٌ	مُسَارَعَةٌ	يُسَارِعُ	سَارَعَ	152
مُحَاسَبٌ	مُحَاسِبٌ	مُحَاسَبَةٌ	يُحَاسِبُ	حَاسَبَ	153
مُتَابَعٌ	مُتَابِعٌ	مُتَابَعَةٌ	يُتَابِعُ	تَابَعَ	154

DERIVED FORM V
Lesson 11
باب تَفَعُّلٌ

Passive Participle	Active Participle	Verbal Noun	Imperfect	Perfect	No
مُتَدَبَّرٌ	مُتَدَبِّرٌ	تَدَبُّرٌ	يَتَدَبَّرُ	تَدَبَّرَ	155
مُتَقَرَّبٌ	مُتَقَرِّبٌ	تَقَرُّبٌ	يَتَقَرَّبُ	تَقَرَّبَ	156
مُتَفَكَّرٌ	مُتَفَكِّرٌ	تَفَكُّرٌ	يَتَفَكَّرُ	تَفَكَّرَ	157
مُتَوَكَّلٌ	مُتَوَكِّلٌ	تَوَكُّلٌ	يَتَوَكَّلُ	تَوَكَّلَ	158
مُتَوَضَّئٌ	مُتَوَضِّئٌ	تَوَضُّؤٌ	يَتَوَضَّأُ	تَوَضَّأَ	159
مُتَعَلَّمٌ	مُتَعَلِّمٌ	تَعَلُّمٌ	يَتَعَلَّمُ	تَعَلَّمَ	160
مُتَشَبَّهٌ	مُتَشَبِّهٌ	تَشَبُّهٌ	يَتَشَبَّهُ	تَشَبَّهَ	161
مُتَعَبَّدٌ	مُتَعَبِّدٌ	تَعَبُّدٌ	يَتَعَبَّدُ	تَعَبَّدَ	162

561

Passive Participle	Active Participle	Verbal Noun	Imperfect	Perfect	No
مُتَذَكَّرٌ	مُتَذَكِّرٌ	تَذَكُّرٌ	يَتَذَكَّرُ	تَذَكَّرَ	163
مُتَطَوَّعٌ	مُتَطَوِّعٌ	تَطَوُّعٌ	يَتَطَوَّعُ	تَطَوَّعَ	164
مُتَفَطَّرٌ	مُتَفَطِّرٌ	تَفَطُّرٌ	يَتَفَطَّرُ	تَفَطَّرَ	165
مُتَفَرَّقٌ	مُتَفَرِّقٌ	تَفَرُّقٌ	يَتَفَرَّقُ	تَفَرَّقَ	166
مُتَرَبَّصٌ	مُتَرَبِّصٌ	تَرَبُّصٌ	يَتَرَبَّصُ	تَرَبَّصَ	167
مُتَقَطَّعٌ	مُتَقَطِّعٌ	تَقَطُّعٌ	يَتَقَطَّعُ	تَقَطَّعَ	168
مُتَزَكًّى	مُتَزَكٍّ	تَزَكٍّ	يَتَزَكَّى	تَزَكَّى	169
مُتَبَيَّنٌ	مُتَبَيِّنٌ	تَبَيُّنٌ	يتبين	تَبَيَّنَ	170
مُتَكَلَّمٌ	مُتَكَلِّمٌ	تَكَلُّمٌ	يَتَكَلَّمُ	تَكَلَّمَ	171
مُتَجَنَّبٌ	مُتَجَنِّبٌ	تَجَنُّبٌ	يَتَجَنَّبُ	تَجَنَّبَ	172
مُتَعَجَّلٌ	مُتَعَجِّلٌ	تَعَجُّلٌ	يَتَعَجَّلُ	تَعَجَّلَ	173
مُتَأَخَّرٌ	مُتَأَخِّرٌ	تَأَخُّرٌ	يَتَأَخَّرُ	تَأَخَّرَ	174
مُتَيَسَّرٌ	مُتَيَسِّرٌ	تَيَسُّرٌ	يتيسر	تَيَسَّرَ	175
مُتَنَزَّلٌ	مُتَنَزِّلٌ	تَنَزُّلٌ	يَتَنَزَّلُ	تَنَزَّلَ	176
مُتَضَرَّعٌ	مُتَضَرِّعٌ	تَضَرُّعٌ	يَتَضَرَّعُ	تَضَرَّعَ	177
مُتَفَجَّرٌ	مُتَفَجِّرٌ	تَفَجُّرٌ	يَتَفَجَّرُ	تَفَجَّرَ	178
مُتَوَفًّى	مُتَوَفٍّ	تَوَفٍّ	يَتَوَفَّى	تَوَفَّى	179
مُتَيَمَّمٌ	مُتَيَمِّمٌ	تَيَمُّمٌ	يتيمم	تَيَمَّمَ	180
مُتَزَوَّدٌ	مُتَزَوِّدٌ	تَزَوُّدٌ	يَتَزَوَّدُ	تَزَوَّدَ	181
مُتَجَلًّى	مُتَجَلٍّ	تَجَلٍّ	يَتَجَلَّى	تَجَلَّى	182
مُتَمَتَّعٌ	مُتَمَتِّعٌ	تَمَتُّعٌ	يتمتع	تَمَتَّعَ	183
مُتَنَفَّسٌ	مُتَنَفِّسٌ	تَنَفُّسٌ	يَتَنَفَّسُ	تَنَفَّسَ	184

DERIVED FORM VI
Lesson 12
باب تَفَاعُلٌ

Passive Participle	Active Participle	Verbal Noun	Imperfect	Perfect	No
مُتَعَاوَنٌ	مُتَعَاوِنٌ	تَعَاوُنٌ	يَتَعَاوَنُ	تَعَاوَنَ	185
مُتَخَاصَمٌ	مُتَخَاصِمٌ	تَخَاصُمٌ	يَتَخَاصَمُ	تَخَاصَمَ	186
مُتَعَالَى	مُتَعَالِي	تَعَالٍ	يَتَعَالَى	تَعَالَى	187
مُتَصَالَحٌ	مُتَصَالِحٌ	تَصَالُحٌ	يَتَصَالَحُ	تَصَالَحَ	188
مُتَبَارَكٌ	مُتَبَارِكٌ	تَبَارُكٌ	يَتَبَارَكُ	تَبَارَكَ	189
مُتَلَاوَمٌ	مُتَلَاوِمٌ	تَلَاوُمٌ	يَتَلَاوَمُ	تَلَاوَمَ	190
مُتَظَاهَرٌ	مُتَظَاهِرٌ	تَظَاهُرٌ	يَتَظَاهَرُ	تَظَاهَرَ	191
مُتَنَاهَى	مُتَنَاهِي	تَنَاهٍ	يَتَنَاهَى	تَنَاهَى	192
مُتَنَابَزٌ	مُتَنَابِزٌ	تَنَابُزٌ	يَتَنَابَزُ	تَنَابَزَ	193
مُتَتَابَعٌ	مُتَتَابِعٌ	تَتَابُعٌ	يَتَتَابَعُ	تَتَابَعَ	194

DERIVED FORM VIII
Lesson 13
باب اِفْتِعَالٌ

Passive Participle	Active Participle	Verbal Noun	Imperfect	Perfect	No
مُتَّقَى	مُتَّقِي	اِتِّقَاءٌ	يَتَّقِي	اتَّقَى	195
مُهْتَدَى	مُهْتَدِي	اهْتِدَاءٌ	يَهْتَدِي	اهْتَدَى	196
مُشْتَعَلٌ	مُشْتَعِلٌ	اشْتِعَالٌ	يَشْتَعِلُ	اشْتَعَلَ	197
مُقْتَدَرٌ	مُقْتَدِرٌ	اقْتِدَارٌ	يَقْتَدِرُ	اقْتَدَرَ	198
مُسْتَمَعٌ	مُسْتَمِعٌ	اسْتِمَاعٌ	يَسْتَمِعُ	اسْتَمَعَ	199
مُخْتَصَمٌ	مُخْتَصِمٌ	اخْتِصَامٌ	يَخْتَصِمُ	اخْتَصَمَ	200
مُشْتَرَكٌ	مُشْتَرِكٌ	اشْتِرَاكٌ	يَشْتَرِكُ	اشْتَرَكَ	201

Passive Participle	Active Participle	Verbal Noun	Imperfect	Perfect	No
مُظَّلَمٌ	مُظَّلِمٌ	اظَّلَامٌ	يَظَّلِمُ	اظَّلَمَ	202
مُطَّلَعٌ	مُطَّلِعٌ	اطِّلَاعٌ	يَطَّلِعُ	اطَّلَعَ	203
مُتَّخَذٌ	مُتَّخِذٌ	اتِّخَاذٌ	يَتَّخِذُ	اتَّخَذَ	204
مُدَّكَرٌ	مُدَّكِرٌ	ادِّكَارٌ	يَدَّكِرُ	ادَّكَرَ	205
مُجْتَمَعٌ	مُجْتَمِعٌ	اجْتِمَاعٌ	يَجْتَمِعُ	اجْتَمَعَ	206
مُنْتَظَرٌ	مُنْتَظِرٌ	انْتِظَارٌ	يَنْتَظِرُ	انْتَظَرَ	207
مُكْتَسَبٌ	مُكْتَسِبٌ	اكْتِسَابٌ	يَكْتَسِبُ	اكْتَسَبَ	208
مُمْتَنَعٌ	مُمْتَنِعٌ	امْتِنَاعٌ	يَمْتَنِعُ	امْتَنَعَ	209
مُقْتَرَبٌ	مُقْتَرِبٌ	اقْتِرَابٌ	يَقْتَرِبُ	اقْتَرَبَ	210
مُبْتَعَدٌ	مُبْتَعِدٌ	ابْتِعَادٌ	يَبْتَعِدُ	ابْتَعَدَ	211
مُخْتَلَفٌ	مُخْتَلِفٌ	اخْتِلَافٌ	يَخْتَلِفُ	اخْتَلَفَ	212
مُشْتَرَكٌ	مُشْتَرِكٌ	اشْتِرَاكٌ	يَشْتَرِكُ	اشْتَرَكَ	213
مُحْتَمَلٌ	مُحْتَمِلٌ	احْتِمَالٌ	يَحْتَمِلُ	احْتَمَلَ	214
مُعْتَصَمٌ	مُعْتَصِمٌ	اعْتِصَامٌ	يَعْتَصِمُ	اعْتَصَمَ	215
مُجْتَنَبٌ	مُجْتَنِبٌ	اجْتِنَابٌ	يَجْتَنِبُ	اجْتَنَبَ	216
مُبْتَغًى	مُبْتَغِي	ابْتِغَاءٌ	يَبْتَغِي	ابْتَغَى	217
مُعْتَدًى	مُعْتَدِي	اعْتِدَاءٌ	يَعْتَدِي	اعْتَدَى	218
مُنْتَشَرٌ	مُنْتَشِرٌ	انْتِشَارٌ	يَنْتَشِرُ	انْتَشَرَ	219

DERIVED FORM VII
Lesson 14

باب إِنْفِعَالٌ

Passive Participle	Active Participle	Verbal Noun	Imperfect	Perfect	No
مُنْفَطَرٌ	مُنْفَطِرٌ	إِنْفِطَارٌ	يَنْفَطِرُ	إِنْفَطَرَ	220

Passive Participle	Active Participle	Verbal Noun	Imperfect	Perfect	No
مُنْشَقٌّ	مُنْشَقٌّ	إِنْشِقَاقٌ	يَنْشَقُّ	إِنْشَقَّ	221
مُتَقَلَّبٌ	مُنْقَلَبٌ	إِنْقِلَابٌ	يَنْقَلَبُ	إِنْقَلَبَ	222
مُنْكَسَرٌ	مُنْكَسَرٌ	إِنْكِسَارٌ	يَنْكَسِرُ	إِنْكَسَرَ	223
مُنْدَفَعٌ	مُنْدَفَعٌ	إِنْدِفَاعٌ	يَنْدَفِعُ	إِنْدَفَعَ	224
مُنْكَدِرٌ	مُنْكَدِرٌ	إِنْكِدَارٌ	يَنْكَدِرُ	إِنْكَدَرَ	225

DERIVED FORM IX
Lesson 15

باب إِفْعِلَالٌ

Active Participle	Verbal Noun	Imperfect	Perfect	No
مُبَيِّضٌ	ابْيِضَاضٌ	يَبْيَضُّ	ابْيَضَّ	226
مُسْوَدٌّ	اسْوِدَادٌ	يَسْوَدُّ	اسْوَدَّ	227
مُحْمَرٌّ	احْمِرَارٌ	يَحْمَرُّ	احْمَرَّ	228
مُصْفَرٌّ	اصْفِرَارٌ	يَصْفَرُّ	اصْفَرَّ	229
مُخْضَرٌّ	اخْضِرَارٌ	يَخْضَرُّ	اخْضَرَّ	**230**

DERIVED FORM X
Lesson 16

باب إِسْتِفْعَالٌ

Passive Participle	Active Participle	Verbal Noun	Imperfect	Perfect	No
مُسْتَجَابٌ	مُسْتَجِيبٌ	اسْتِجَابٌ	يَسْتَجِيبُ	اسْتَجَابَ	231
مُسْتَكْبَرٌ	مُسْتَكْبِرٌ	اسْتِكْبَارٌ	يَسْتَكْبِرُ	اسْتَكْبَرَ	232

Passive Participle	Active Participle	Verbal Noun	Imperfect	Perfect	No
مُسْتَجَارٌ	مُسْتَجِيرٌ	اسْتِجَارٌ	يَسْتَجِيرُ	اسْتَجَارَ	233
مُسْتَقْدَمٌ	مُسْتَقْدِمٌ	اسْتِقْدَامٌ	يَسْتَقْدِمُ	اسْتَقْدَمَ	234
مُسْتَغْفَرٌ	مُسْتَغْفِرٌ	اسْتِغْفَارٌ	يَسْتَغْفِرُ	اسْتَغْفَرَ	235
مُسْتَنْصَرٌ	مُسْتَنْصِرٌ	اسْتِنْصَارٌ	يَسْتَنْصِرُ	اسْتَنْصَرَ	236
مُسْتَعْلَمٌ	مُسْتَعْلِمٌ	اسْتِعْلَامٌ	يَسْتَعْلِمُ	اسْتَعْلَمَ	237
مُسْتَعَدٌّ	مُسْتَعِدٌّ	اسْتِعْدَادٌ	يَسْتَعِدُّ	اسْتَعَدَّ	238
مُسْتَسْلَمٌ	مُسْتَسْلِمٌ	اسْتِسْلَامٌ	يَسْتَسْلِمُ	اسْتَسْلَمَ	239

The *āyah* (**48**: 29) is carved on wood.

566

APPENDIX

G 7

Qur'ānic Text Translation in English

LESSON 5

1   He is the First and the Last, and the Evident and the Imminent and He is the Knower of everything. (**57**: 3)

2   God in the sky and God in the earth (**43**: 84)

3   ...and the Word of Allah (**9**: 40)

4   And your Lord is a Warden over every–thing. (**34**: 21)

5   Allah is the Creator of everything. (**39**: 62)

6   Is there any creator other than Allah (**35**: 3)

7   ...and Allah's earth is spacious. (**39**: 10)

8   And there shall come every soul, with whom will be a driver and a witness. (**50**: 21)

9   ...there came the affair of Allah. (**57**: 14)

10 And the stupor of death will come in Truth (**50**: 19)

11 Every soul shall taste death (**3**: 185)

12 And he entered his garden, while he was a wrong–doer (**18**: 35)

13 'I am Joseph and this is my brother' (**12**: 90)

14 And a witness from her own household bore witness (**12**: 26)

15 'Are you the one who has done this' (**21**: 62)

16 Muhammad is the Messenger of Allah (**8**: 29)

17 'This is a mercy from my Lord' (**18**: 98)

18 Is there any other god along with Allah? (**27**: 63)

19 …in the way of Allah (**2**: 154)

LESSON 6

1 And of mankind is he who worships Allah upon the very edge (**22**: 11)

2 The Prophet said: 'My Lord knows the Word in the heavens' (**21**: 4)

3 'He knows what is spoken aloud' (**21**: 110)

4 He knows what penetrates into the earth and what comes forth from it (**34**: 2)

5 Not a leaf falls but He knows it (**6**: 59)

6 Allah knows what every female bears (**13**: 8)

7 …nor does a female conceive or bring forth but with His knowledge. (**41**: 47)

8 He knows what each soul earns. (**13**: 42)

9 …none knows their interpretation save Allah. (**3**: 7)

10 You know what is in my mind, and I do not know what is in Your mind. (**5**: 116)

11 And no person earns anything save against himself (**6**: 164)

12 And as for him who dreaded standing before his Lord, and restrained

his soul from desires. (**79**: 40)

13 'I possess no power of benefit or hurt to myself save as Allah wills[371]; (**7**: 188)

14 ...then who will succour me against Allah, if I disobey Him? (**11**: 63)

15 ...and your Lord wrongs not anyone. (**18**: 49)

16 And it will avert the chastizement from her (**24**: 8)

17 'And why should I not worship Him alone Who has originated me' (**36**: 22)

18 On the Day when man shall flee from his brother, • And his mother and father (**80**: 34-35)

19 Man, on that Day, shall say: 'Whither to flee?' (**75**: 10)

20 Then Pharaoh denied the Messenger (**73**: 16)

21 'I have sought refuge in my Lord' (**44**: 20)

22 ...then who will succour me against Allah, if I disobey Him? (**11**: 63)

23 Allah guides whom He will (**2**: 213)

24 My Lord comprehends everything in His knowledge. (**6**: 80)

25 ...light upon light. Allah guides unto His Light whom He will. (**24**: 35)

26 Allah says the Truth and He guides the way. (**33**: 4)

27 This is the Guidance of Allah with which He guides whomsoever He wish. (**6**: 88)

28 And He it is Who has created the night and the day, the sun and the moon (**21**: 33)

29 Every moving thing Allah has created of water (**24**: 45)

30 ...has made for you the day a resurrection (**25**: 47)

31 ...and has placed therein a lamp and a moon enlightening. (**25**: 61)

32 ...and has made the sun for a lamp (**71**: 16)

33 He it is Who has made the sun a glow and the moon a light (**10**: 5)

34 He has created everything and He is the Knower of everything.
    (**6**: 101)

35 ...and has sealed up his hearing and his heart and has set up a
    covering on his sight (**45**: 23)

36 ...has created man from water (**25**: 54)

37 'And when I sicken, then He heals me. (**26**: 80)

LESSON 7

1   In the name of Allah, the Compassionate, the Merciful. (**27**: 30)

2   ...verily my Lord is Merciful, Loving. (**11**: 90)

3   Surely it is He Who is Relenting, Merciful. (**2**: 37)

4   Verily Allah is unto mankind, Clement, Merciful. (**22**: 65)

5   ...surely the Mercy of Allah is nigh (**7**: 56)

6   ...verily my Lord is over everything a Guardian. (**11**: 57)

7   Verily honour is wholly Allah's. He is the Hearer, the Knower.
     (**10**: 65)

8   'The affair is wholly Allah's.' (**3**: 154)

9   …and that verily with Him is a mighty reward. (**8**: 28)

10 …and God there is none save Allah, and surely Allah it is Who is Mighty, Wise. (**3**: 62)

11 Surely Allah! Naught is hidden from Him in the earth or in the heaven. (**3**: 5)

12 Whosoever gives thanks only gives thanks for his own soul, and whosoever is ungrateful, then my Lord is Self–sufficient, Munificent.'(**27**: 40)

13 …surely that is easy for Allah. (**29**: 19)

14 Verily My earth is wide (**29**: 56)

15 He creates whatever He will, and Allah is Potent over everything. (**5**: 17)

16 His is the kingdom, His is the praise, and He is Potent over everything. (**64**: 1)

17 Surely Allah does not wrong anyone a grain's weight (**4**: 40)

18 Allah guides whom He will to a straight path. (**2**: 213)

19 …and that the grace is in Allah's hand. (**57**: 29)

20 And had your Lord willed He would surely have made mankind of a single community (**11**: 118)

21 …how Allah has propounded the similitude of the clean Word? It is like a clean tree, its roots firmly fixed, and its branches reaching the heaven; (**14**: 24)

22 And naught there is hidden in the heaven and the earth but it is in a Book manifest. (**27**: 75)

23 Allah! There is no god but He, the Living, the Sustainer (**2**: 255)

24 …and Allah is the Possessor of mighty grace. (**2**: 105)

25 'Allah's is the east and the west; He guides whom He will to the straight path.' (**2**: 142)

26 In Allah's succour, He succours whom He will. And He is the Mighty, the Merciful. (**30**: 5)

27 He creates what He will, and He is the Knower, the Potent. (**30**: 54)

28 He has created man from a drop, and lo! He is a disputant open. (**16**: 4)

29 Will not He Who has created know? He is the Subtle, the Aware. (**67**: 14)

30 And Allah shall relent towards whom He pleases; and Allah is Knowing, Wise. (**9**: 15)

31 Allah has placed abundant good therein. (**4**: 19)

32 Allah has made the Ka'ba, the Sacred House, a maintenance for mankind (**5**: 97)

33 Have you killed an innocent person not in return for a person? (18: 74)

34 In a lofty Garden •   No vain discourse they shall hear therein, (**88**: 10-11)

35 And when you look them you behold delight and a magnificent dominion. (**76**: 20)

36 A questioner has questioned about chastizement about to befall, (**70**: 1)

37 That is a mighty achievement. (**10**: 64)

38 Verily, herein is a Sign to him who fears the torment of the Hereafter. (**11**: 103)

39 That it is the speech brought by an honourable envoy.   •   And it is not the speech of a poet. (**69**: 40-1)

40 Verily your Lord extends the provision for whom He will, and measures it out (**17**: 30)

41 ...that the ship sails into the sea by the favour of Allah (**31**: 31)

42 She said: 'Lord! I have wronged my soul' (**27**: 44)

43 ...he said: 'I know that surely Allah is Potent over everything'. (**2**: 259)

44 Whenever Zacharia entered the apartment to see her, he found provision by her. He said: 'O Maryam! Whence have you this?' She said: 'This is from before Allah.' Surely Allah provides for whom He will without stint. (**3**: 37)

45 Surely the True Faith with Allah is Islam (**3**: 19)

46 Verily Allah commands justice and well–doing (**16**: 90)

47 ...life for life, eye for eye, nose for nose, ear for ear, tooth for tooth (**5**: 45)

48 ...and that Allah is Knower of everything. (**5**: 97)

49 ...verily my Lord is Subtle to whom He will. Verily He, only He, is the Knowing, the Wise. (**12**: 100)

50 Verily your Lord! He is the Great Creator, the Knower. (**15**: 86)

51 All praise be to Allah Who has bestowed on me, despite old age, Ishmael and Isaac. (**14**: 39)

52 Who can intercede with Him, save by His leave? (**2**: 255)

53 He is Allah, there is no god but He, the Knower of the Unseen and the seen, He is the Compassionate, the Merciful. (**59**: 22)

54 ...that whoso kills a person, except for a person, or for corruption in the land, it shall be as if he had killed all mankind (**5**: 32)

55 ...whosoever follows me is of me, and whoever disobeys me then verily You are Forgiving, Merciful. (**14**: 36)

56 And had your Lord willed He would surely have made mankind of a single community; and they will not cease differing. (**11**: 118)

57 ...and the life of this world is but a vain bauble. (**57**: 20)

58 ...threw you not when you threw, but Allah threw (**8**: 17)

59 Verily Allah is the Knower of everything. (**58**: 7)

60 Verily Qarun was of the people of Moses (**28**: 76)

61 Verily I am going to my Lord (**37**: 99)

62 ...that you are Allah's Messenger (**63**: 1)

63 Verily my Lord is the Hearer of supplication. (**14**: 39)

64 And verily it is the Truth of absolute certainty. (**69**: 51)

65 You are in your old–time illusion.' (**12**: 95)

66 Verily man is in loss. (**103**: 2)

67 Verily the chastizement of your Lord is sure to overtake. (**52**: 7)

68 Assuredly did Allah show a true vision to His Messenger in very Truth (**48**: 27)

69 ...this Qur'an is an admonition. (**74**: 54)

70 That it is an honoured Recitation. (**56**: 77)

71 Verily it is a discourse decisive. (**86**: 13)

72 Verily Allah is the Lord of Grace for mankind (**40**: 61)

LESSON 8

1   Whoso is an enemy to Gabriel – then surely it is he who has brought down this Revelation, by Allah's command (**2**: 97)

2   ...surely Allah announces to you John!, confirming the Word from Allah (**3**: 39)

3   He neither believed nor prayed. •   Indeed, he belied (**75**: 30-1)

4   And Allah measures the night and the day. (**73**: 20)

5   Surely he considered and devised. (**74**: 18)

6   Who has created the universe and then proportioned it •   And Who has disposed and then guided it (**87**: 2-3)

7   Hallows Allah whatsoever is in the heavens and the earth, and He is the Mighty, the Wise. (**57**: 1)

8   And the thunder hallows His glory (**13**: 13)

9   Surely everyone knows his prayer and his hallowing (**24**: 41)

10 ...and hath subjected the sun and the moon, each running unto an appointed term (**3**:26)

11 You exalt whom You will, and You abase whom You will (**3**:26)

12 And whosoever brings the Truth and whosoever gives credence to it (**39**: 33)

13 ...and to Moses Allah spoke directly. (**4**: 164)

14 The Revelation of the Book is from Allah, the Mighty, the Wise. (**46**: 2)

15 …that it has been sent down by your Lord in Truth (**6**: 114)

16 And He shall teach him the Book and wisdom and the Torah and the Gospel. (**3**: 48)

17 …the sun and the moon according to a reckoning. That is the disposition of the Mighty, the Knowing. (**6**: 96)

18 What will make you deny the Requital? (**95**: 7)

19 …a Day whereon man will see what he has sent forth (**78**: 40)

20 Man will say: 'Would that I had sent before for this life on mine.' (**89**: 24)

21 And this is a Book confirming it in Arabic speech (**46**: 12)

22 And that Allah may succour you with a mighty succour. (**48**: 3)

23 Verily for you is the day a prolonged occupation. (**73**: 7)

24 And honourable word and forgiveness are better than alms followed by injury (**2**: 263)

25 …for which Allah has sent down no warranty (**7**: 71)

26 Allah charges not a soul excepting according to its capacity. (**2**: 286)

LESSON 9

1 The likeness of the two parties is as the blind and deaf, and the seeing and hearing (**11**: 24)

2 And as to David and Solomon, recall when they gave judgment regarding the tillage (**21**: 78)

3 …and has set a barrier between the two seas (**27**: 62)

4   …and of their offspring some are well–doers, and some who wrong themselves manifestly. (**37**: 113)

5   Aye! His hands are both wide open: He expends however He wills. (**5**: 64)

6   Divorce is twice; thereafter either retaining her honorably or releasing her kindly. (**2**: 229)

7   Will You place therein one who will act corruptly therein and shed blood (**2**: 30)

8   And a believing man of Pharaoh's household, hiding his Faith, said: (**40**: 28)

9   Why then was there not a town which believed, so that its Faith might have profited, except the people of Jonah? (**10**: 98)

10 'But, He is Allah, my Lord, and with my Lord I do not join anyone. (**18**: 38)

11 All praise to Allah Who has sent down to His bondsman the Book (**18**: 1)

12 Allah it is Who has sent down the Book with the Truth and the balance (**42**: 17)

13 I believe in whatsoever Allah has sent down of the Book (**42**: 15)

14 …you know not what the Book was, nor what the Faith (**42**: 52)

15 That is part of that wisdom which your Lord has revealed to you (**17**: 39)

16 But Allah bears witness by that which he has sent down to you. He sent it down with His own knowledge. (**4**:166)

17 Is the recompense for good other than good? (**55**: 60)

18 And as for him who believes and works righteously, for him will be a goodly reward (**18**: 88)

19 ...but whosoever pardons and is reconciled, his reward is on Allah (**42**: 40)

20 ...then repents and amends, then verily He is Forgiving, Merciful. (**6**: 54)

21 ...and he who kills a Believer by mischance, on him is the setting free of a believing slave (**4**: 92)

22 Verily We! We have sent you with the Truth, as a bearer of glad tidings and as a warner (**35**: 24)

23 ...and bestowed on him John and We made sound for him his spouse. (**21**: 90)

24 Verily We have sent it down on the Night of Power. (**97**: 1)

25 And what will make you know what the Night of Power is? (**97**: 2)

26 And thus We have sent it down, an Arabic recitation, and propounded variously therein of the threats (**20**: 113)

27 And We have sent down the Book to you with Truth and confirming what has preceded it of the Book (**5**: 48)

28 As your Lord had caused you to go forth from your houses for a right cause (**8**: 5)

29 Lord I have need of the good which You may send down for me. (**28**: 24)

30 ...will you rescue him who is in the Fire? (**39**: 19)

31 Who is he that will lend Allah a goodly loan (**57**: 11)

32 'How shall Allah quicken it after its death? (**2**: 259)

33 Verily Allah performs whatsoever He intends. (**22**: 14)

34 Verily Allah ordains what He will. (**5**: 1)

35 It is but an admonition (**6**: 90)

36 Allah has sent down from the heaven water, then He revives the earth by it after its death (**16**: 65)

37 And assuredly We have honoured the Children of Adam (**17**: 70)

38 Allah said: 'As to My chastisement, I afflict therewith whom I will, and as to My mercy, it comprehends everything.' (**7**: 156)

39 Shall there, then, be one whose breast Allah has expanded for Islam, so that he follows a light from His Lord (**39**: 22)

40 Has there come to you the story of Abraham's honoured guests? (**51**: 24)

41 And We sent not a Messenger but with the speech of his people (**14**: 4)

42 Then when she bore her, she said: 'My Lord! Surely I bore a female – And Allah knew best what she had borne – and the male is not as the female, and surely I have named her Maryam, and I commit her and her progeny to You for protection from Satan the accursed'. (**3**: 36)

43 And Pharaoh proclaimed among his people saying: 'My people! Is not mine the kingdom of Egypt (**43**: 51)

44 You are but a warner, and of everything Allah is a Trustee. (**11**: 12)

45 And what shall make you know? Haply the hour may be nigh. (**42**: 17)

46 The when Jesus perceived infidelity in them, he said: 'Who will be my helper unto Allah?' (**3**: 52)

47 Whosoever hopes for the meeting with Allah, then Allah's term is surely coming, and He is the Hearer, the Knower. (**29**: 5)

48 A Day whereon no soul will own aught of power for any other soul, and the command will be wholly Allah's. (**82**: 19)

49 The Day when each soul shall find presented whatever it has worked of good and whatever it has worked of evil, it would like that there were between it and that Day wide space. (**3**: 30)

50 And whoever has been blind in this world will be blind in the Hereafter (**17**: 72)

51 ...that whoso kills a person, except for a person, or for corruption in the land, it shall be as if he had killed all mankind (**5**: 32)

52 He said: 'As for him who does wrong presently we shall chastize him (**18**: 87)

53 And soon shall your Lord give unto you so that you shall be well–pleased. (**93**: 5)

54 Allah will soon appoint ease for hardship. (**65**: 7)

55 ...we shall speak to him some thing easy of our affair (**18**: 88)

LESSON 10

1   ...and Allah is ever Knowing, Wise. (**4**: 170)

2   ...and Allah is ever Hearing, Seeing. (**4**: 134)

3   Allah is ever Strong, Mighty. (**33**: 25)

4   Verily Allah is ever Subtle, Aware.' (**33**: 34)

5   ...and Allah is ever Watcher over everything. (**33**: 52)

6   ...and the promise of my Lord is ever True.' (**18**: 98)

7   Whosoever desires glory, then all glory is Allah's. (**35**: 10)

8   He who seeks the reward of this world, with Allah is the reward of this

world and the Hereafter, and Allah is ever Hearing, Seeing. (**4**: 134)

9 He forgives whomsoever He will, and chastizes whomsoever He will; and Allah is ever Forgiving, Merciful. (**48**: 14)

10 Mankind was one community (**2**: 213)

11 Is Allah not sufficient for His bondsmen? (**39**: 36)

12 …is not morning nigh? (**11**: 81)

13 A Day when mankind shall become as moths scattered. (**101**: 4)

14 …and the infidel will say: 'Would that I had been dust!'(**78**: 40)

15 …and my wife has been barren (**19**: 5)

16 …and their father was righteous (**18**: 82)

17 Then when she bore her, she said: 'My Lord! Surely I bore a female – And Allah knew best what she had borne – and the male is not as the female, and surely I have named her Maryam, and I commit her and her progeny to You for protection from Satan the accursed'. (**3**: 36)

18 And when My bondsmen ask you regarding Me, then surely I am nigh. I answer the call of the caller, when he calls Me (**2**: 186)

19 And this is a Book We have sent down, blessed and confirming what has been before it (**6**: 92)

20 And Lot believed in him. And he said: 'Verily I will flee to my Lord; verily He is the Mighty, the Wise.' (**29**: 26)

21 And Noah cried to his Lord, and said: 'Lord! Verily my son is of my household, and Your promise is the Truth, and You are the Greatest of rulers.' (**11**: 45)

22 What ails this Book that it leaves not any misdeed, small or great, but it has comprehended it! (**18**: 49)

23 Recall when he cried unto his Lord with a low tone. (**19**: 3)

24 And Pharaoh proclaimed among his people saying: 'My people! Is not mine the kingdom of Egypt' (**43**: 51)

25 Verily the Muslim men and Muslim women, and the believing men and the believing women, and the devout men and the devout women, and the men of veracity, and the women of veracity, and the persevering men and the persevering women, and the men of humility and the women of humility and the almsgiving men and the almsgiving women, and the fasting men and the fasting women, and the men who guard their modesty and the women who guard their modesty, and the Allah-remembering men and the Allah remembering women: Allah hath prepared for them forgiveness and mighty hire. (**33**:35)

26 The steadfast ones and the truthful ones and the devout ones and the spenders in charity (**3**: 17)

27 …and, surely, you are one of the envoys. (**2**: 252)

28 Verily you are mortal and they are mortals. (**39**: 30)

29 …and they shall not be coming forth from the Fire. (**2**: 167)

30 And Allah will relent towards the believing men and women, and Allah is ever Forgiving, Merciful.(**33**: 73)

31 And Allah has preferred the strivers above the holders back with a mighty reward. (**4**: 95)

32 Mankind was one community thereafter Allah raised Prophets as bearers of glad tidings and warners (**2**: 213)

33 …verily the prayer is prescribed to Believers at definite times. (**4**: 103)

34 Surely we are Allah's and surely to Him we shall return (**2**: 156)

35 Verily it is We Who have revealed to you the Qur'an a gradual revelation. (**76**: 23)

36 Revelation of this Book of which there is no doubt, is from the Lord of the worlds. (**32**: 2)

37 These are the changes which We cause to follow one another, for mankind (**3**: 140)

38 it leaves not any misdeed, small or great, but it has comprehended it!' And they shall find present all that they had wrought; and your Lord wrongs not anyone. (**18**: 49)

39 And the preceders are the preceders • Those shall be brought nigh. (**56**: 10-11)

40 Verily, Allah does not wrong in aught, but mankind wrong themselves. (**10**: 44)

41 ...verily virtues obliterate vices (**11**: 114)

42 For those who do good in this world there is good (**39**: 10)

43 They are those who repent, who worship, who praise, who fast constantly, who bow down, who prostrate themselves, who bid the reputable and forbid the disreputable (**9**: 112)

44 Assuredly there has been an excellent pattern for you in the Messenger of Allah, for him who hopes in Allah and the Last Day (**33**: 21)

LESSON 11

1 ...on Allah I rely (**10**: 71)

2 I rely on Allah, my Lord and your Lord. (**11**: 56)

3 ...and my hope is not a success save with Allah; in Him I rely and to Him I turn in repentance. (**11**: 88)

4 ...everything our Lord comprehends in His knowledge, in Allah we

place our trust. (**7**: 89)

5 Our Lord! In You we put our trust and to you we turn and to You is our journeying. (**60**: 4)

6 They are those who bear in patience, and in their Lord they trust. (**16**: 42)

7 My Lord comprehends everything in His knowledge. Will you not then be admonished? (**6**: 80)

8 Thus does Allah expound to you His Signs that haply you may ponder. (**2**: 266)

9 And whosoever does good voluntarily, then surely Allah is Appreciative, Knowing. (**2**: 158)

10 The heavens are well–nigh rent there at. (**19**: 90)

11 On the Day whereon the Hour arrives, that day they will be separated. (**30**: 14)

12 …we also are with you awaiting. (**9**: 52)

13 …no soul shall speak save by His leave. (**11**: 105)

14 And they split up their affair among them, all shall return to Us. (**21**: 93)

15 …they will not be able to speak, except whom the Compassionate gives leave. (**78**: 38)

16 But they did learn from the twain that with which they might separate man from his wife (**2**: 102)

17 No compulsion is there in Religion. Surely rectitude has become distinct from error. (**2**: 256)

18 And whosoever becomes clean, becomes clean only for himself; and to Allah is the return. (**35**: 18)

19 And the wretched shuns it • He who shall roast into the Great Fire, (**87**: 11-12)

20 Then whoso hastens away even in two days, on him is no sin, and whoso stays on, on him is no sin. (**2**: 203)

21 And among the desert–dwellers is one who takes what he spends as a fine, and waits for evil turns of fortune for you. (**9**: 98)

22 Or, have We sent to them any authority, so that it speaks of what they have been associating with Him? (**30**: 35)

23 And they will never wish for it, because of what their hands have sent forward. And Allah is the Knower of the wrong-doers. (**62**: 7)

24 Then a party of them turns away unheeding. (**3**: 23)

25 ...on them will descend the angels (**41**: 30)

26 Lo! You shall soon know • Again lo! You shall soon know. (**102**: 3-4)

27 Yet they disbelieve therein; presently they shall come to know. (**37**: 170)

28 ...presently you will know on whom comes a chastisement, humiliating him and who is a liar. (**11**: 93)

29 ...and obey Allah and His Messenger. Those! Allah will surely show mercy to them; verily, Allah is Mighty, Wise. (**9**: 71)

30 ...presently you shall know what will be the happy end of the abode (**6**: 135)

31 Who set up along with Allah another god; presently they shall know. (**15**: 96)

32 Presently they shall know, when they see the torment (**25**: 42)

33 ...and soon shall Allah give the Believers a mighty reward. (**4**: 146)

34 Surely he is your chief who taught you magic; so you shall surely come to know (**26**: 49)

35 And soon you will know who it is that is in manifest error.' (**67**: 29)

36 Allah holds your work, and so does His Messenger and the Believers (**9**: 105)

37 Moses said: 'By no means! With me is my Lord; He shall guide me.' (**26**: 62)

38 And surely Allah will recompense the grateful. (**3**: 144)

39 ...and the Believers in Allah and the Last Day — it is those to whom We shall soon give a mighty wage. (**4**: 162)

LESSON 12

1 Faces on that Day shall be delighted •   Well–pleased with their end– eavour, (**88**: 8-9)

2 Wherein there are eternal discourses. (**98**: 3)

3 Men are overseers over women, by reason of that wherewith Allah has made one of them excel over another (**4**: 34)

4 Allah also bears witness that the hypocrites are liars indeed. (**63**: 1)

5 Those whom the angels cause to die while they are wronging themselves (**16**: 28)

6 This is Allah's dispensation that has been in regard to His bondsmen. And lost were the infidels then and there. (**40**: 85)

7 Woe then to them for what their hands have written, and woe to them for that they earn thereby! (**2**: 79)

8   ...the Compassionate will assign for them affection. (**19**: 96)

9   Recall when the angels said: 'O Maryam, surely Allah announces to you a word from Him (**3**: 45)

10 Hearts that Day will be throbbing • Their looks will be downcast. (**79**: 8-9)

11 Faces on that Day shall be downcast (**88**: 2)

12 Faces on that Day shall be radiant • Looking towards their Lord. (**75**: 22-23)

13 They said: 'Are you the one who has done this to our gods, O Abraham?' (**21**: 62)

14 We seized them with adversity and distress, that haply they may humble themselves. (**6**: 42)

15 …and surely of stones there are some from which rivers gush forth (**2**: 74)

16 …soon We shall give them their wages (**4**: 152)

17 And those who believe and work righteous works soon We shall admit them to Gardens beneath which rivers flow (**4**: 122)

18 He sends the thunderbolts and smites with them whomsoever He will. (**13**: 13)

19 These Messengers! We have preferred some of them above others; to some Allah spoke directly; and some He raised in rank. (**2**: 253)

20 'O my two fellow prisoners! Are sundry lords better or Allah the One, the Subduer? (**12**: 39)

21 …whereas Allah has allowed trade and has forbidden usury. (**2**: 275)

22 O Prophet! Why do you forbid for you what Allah has allowed to you (**66**: 1)

23 Then her Lord accepted her with goodly acceptance (**3**: 37)

24 By the time • Verily man is in loss • But not those who believe and work righteous deeds, and enjoin upon each other the Truth and enjoin upon each other steadfastness. (**103**: 1-3)

25 Then he became one of those who believed and enjoined on each other steadfastness and enjoined on each other compassion. (**90**: 17)

26 Verily! His is the creation and the command. Blessed is Allah, the Lord of the Worlds. (**7**:54)

27 Blessed be He, in Whose hand is the Sovereignty, and He is Potent over everything. (**67**: 1)

28 Blessed be He Who has sent down the Criterion to His bondsman that he may be a warner to the worlds. (**25**: 1)

29 They say: 'Two magics supporting each other.' And they say: 'We are disbelievers in all such things.' (**28**: 48)

30 Then they turned to each other reproaching. (**68**: 30)

31 They were wont not to desist from the evil they committed. (**5**: 79)

32 Verily Allah ordains what He will. (**5**: 1)

LESSON 13

1 Has taught man what he knew not. (**96**: 5)

2 Does he not know that Allah sees? (**96**: 14)

3 Does he suppose that no one has seen him • Have We not made for him two eyes • And a tongue and two lips, (**90**: 7-9)

4 Have We not opened for you your breast? (**94**: 1)

5 Does not man remember that We created him before he was anything? (**19**: 67)

6   And he who does not judge according to what Allah has sent down, it is they who are the wrong–doers. (**5**: 45)

7   Thereafter, did Allah send down His calm upon His Messenger and upon the Believers; and He sent down the hosts that you did not see (**9**: 26)

8   Know they not that Allah knows their secret and their whisper, and that Allah is the Knower of things Unseen? (**9**: 78)

9   'It is those who believe and do not confound their belief with wrong–doing. These! Theirs is the security and they are the guided.' (**6**: 82)

10   And Allah has sent down to you the Book and wisdom, and has taught you what you know not; and the Grace of Allah on you is ever Mighty. (**4**: 113)

11   Do you not see that   Allah sends down water from the sky, and then We thereby bring fruit of diverse hues? (**35**: 27)

12   …and if you believe and fear, yours shall be a mighty reward. (**3**: 179)

13   If you disbelieve, then verily Allah is independent of you. And He does not approve of infidelity in His bondsmen. (**39**: 7)

14   And if you effect reconciliation and fear Allah, then Allah is ever Forgiving, Merciful. (**4**: 129)

15   and whether you reveal what is in your mind or hide it, Allah will reckon with you therefore (**2**: 284)

16   Then if they desist, then surely Allah is Forgiver, Merciful. (**2**: 192)

17   So if they now desist, then Allah is the Beholder of what they are doing. (**8**: 39)

18   O you who believe! If you fear, Allah, He will make for you a distinction and will expiate for you your misdeeds and forgive you; and Allah is the Owner of Mighty Grace. (**8**: 29)

19   …and the garment of piety that is the best. (**7**: 26)

20 …and whoso obeys Allah and His Messenger, he has indeed accomplished a great achievement. (**33**: 71)

21 He who obeys the Messenger has indeed obeyed Allah (**4**: 80)

22 …and he who associates aught with Allah has certainly strayed far away. (**4**: 116)

23   And whosoever calls along with Allah unto another god, of whom he has no proof, then his reckoning is only with his Lord (**23**: 117)

24 And whoso rejects the Faith, his work will surely come to naught, and in the Hereafter he will be of the losers. (**5**: 5)

25 …and he who disbelieves in Allah and His angels and His Books and His Messengers and the Last Day, has strayed far away. (**4**: 136)

26 And he who takes Satan instead of Allah, for a friend, shall surely suffer a manifest loss. (**4**: 119)

27 …and whoso has for him Satan as a companion, a vile companion has he. (**4**: 38)

28 And whoso disobeys Allah and His Messenger have strayed manifestly. (**33**: 36)

29 Whoso Allah sends astray, no guide is then for him (**7**: 186)

30 And whoso believes in Allah his heart He guides, and Allah is the Knower of everything. (**64**: 11)

31 …and whoever obeys Allah and His Messenger, him He shall admit into the Gardens beneath which rivers flow, as abiders therein; and that is mighty achievement. (**4**: 13)

32 And whoso fears Allah He makes an outlet for him ◆ And He provides for him from whence he never reckons. And whoso puts his trust in Allah, He will suffice him. Verily Allah is sure to attain His purpose, and has assigned to everything a measure. (**65**: 2-3)

33 And he who migrates in the way of Allah shall find in the earth plentiful refuge and amplitude; and he who goes forth from his house as a fugitive unto Allah and His Messenger, and death overtakes him, his reward has surely devolved upon Allah, and Allah is ever Forgiving, Merciful. (**4**: 100)

34 And whom Allah guides he is the rightly-guided (**17**: 97)

35 Then whosoever has worked good of an atom's weight shall see it
•   And whosoever has worked ill of an atom's weight shall see it.
(**99**: 7-8)

33 And whosoever earns a sin, only against his own soul he earns it and Allah is ever Knowing, Wise. (**4**:111)

37 …and whatever good you do Allah shall know it (**2**: 197)

38 …and whatever of good you send forth for your souls you shall find with Allah; surely Allah is Beholder of what you do. (**2**: 110)

39 Death shall overtake you wheresoever you may be (**4**: 78)

40 Wherever you may be, Allah shall bring you all together (**2**: 148)

41 He said: 'Lord! My bones have waxen feeble and the head is glistening with hoariness, and I have not yet been in my prayer to You, my Lord! Unblest. (**19**: 4)

42 Recall when Abraham said to his father: 'Azar, take you idols for gods.' (**6**: 74)

43 And Allah has taken Abraham for a friend. (**4**: 125)

44 Who, when an affliction afflicts them, say: 'Surely we are Allah's and surely to Him we shall return'. •   They are the ones on whom shall be benediction from their Lord and mercy, and they are the ones who are guided. (**2**: 156-157)

45 And Allah is Potent over everything . (**18**: 45)

46 Verily in the creation of the heavens and the earth[244] and in the alternation of the night and the day are Signs for men of understanding. (**3**: 190)

47 Then on the Day of Resurrection you shall be contending before your Lord. (**39**: 31)

48 And He it is Who gives life and cause to die; and His is the alternation of night and day; will you not then reflect? (**23**: 80)

49 So on the Day they all will be sharers in the torment. (**37**: 33)

50 …surely they have strayed and have not become the guided ones. (**6**: 140)

51 Pharaoh said to those around him in amazement: 'Do you not hear?' (**26**: 25)

52 Unto everyone of them shall be what he has earned of the sin (**24**: 11)

53 For it shall be the good it earns, and against it the evil it earns (**2**: 286)

54 Do they not then ponder on the Qur'an? Were it from other than Allah they would surely find therein many a contradiction. (**4**: 82)

LESSON 14

1 And those who believe are strongest in love of Allah. (**2**: 165)

2 …and remembrance of Allah is the highest. (**29**: 45)

3 …and mischief is far more grievous than bloodshed. (**2**: 217)

4 …and mischief is more grievous than bloodshed. (**2**: 191)

5 Then when he saw the sun rising up, he said: 'This is my Lord! This is the greatest.' (**6**: 78)

6 …and the affair of the Hour will be not but as a flash of the eye. Or it is even nearer (**16**: 77)

7 And who can be better in Religion than he who submits his face to Allah, and is sincere (**4**: 125)

8 Are you harder to create or the sky He has built? (**79**: 27)

9 And follow the best of what has been sent down to you from your Lord (**39**: 55)

10 'And I! I am Allah. No god is there but I, so worship Me and establish prayer for My remembrance. (**20**: 14)

11 Obey Allah and obey the Messenger and men of authority from amongst you (**4**: 59)

12 O you who believe! Bow down and prostrate yourselves and worship your Lord, and do good; haply you may thrive • And strive hard for Allah as is due unto him hard striving. (**22**: 77-78)

13 O you who believe! Fear Allah and be with the truthful. (**9**: 119)

14 Call you them to the way of your Lord with wisdom and goodly exhortation, and argue with them with what is best. (**16**: 125)

15 Say: 'Surely my prayer and my rites and my life and my death are all for Allah, Lord of the worlds. (**6**: 162)

16 Be watchful over the prayers, and the middle prayer, and stand up to Allah truly devout. (**2**: 238)

17 …act fairly; that is nigh unto piety. (**5**: 8)

18 Be you maintainers of equity and bearers of testimony for Allah's sake, though it be against yourselves or your parents or kindred. Be he rich or poor Allah is Higher unto either (**4**: 135)

19 And when you speak, be fair, even though it be against a kinsman (**6**: 152)

20 And take provision for the journey; surely the best provision is piety (**2**: 197)

21 …say not unto them: 'fie!', and browbeat them not, and speak to them a respectful speech. • And lower unto them the wing of meekness out of mercy (**17**: 23-24)

22 And they ask you as to what they shall spend. Say: 'Redundant

portion'. (**2**: 219)

23 Take you alms of their riches; thereby you will cleanse them and purify them (**9**: 103)

24 O mankind! Eat of whatever is on the earth lawful and good (**2**: 168)

25 …and gives of his substance, for love of Him, to kindred and orphans and the needy and the wayfarer and the beggars and for redeeming necks (**2**: 177)

26 …and expend of that with which We have provided them, secretly and in open (**35**: 29)

27 And eat of that with which Allah has provided you as lawful and good (**5**: 88)

28 O you who believe! Eat of the good things with which We have provided you and return thanks to Allah (**2**: 172)

29 So give you to the kinsman his due (**30**: 38)

30 O you who believe! Fear Allah and waive what has yet remained of the usury due to you, if you are Believers. (**2**: 278)

31 O you who believe! Spend of what We have provided you before the Day arrives when there shall be neither trading nor friendship nor intercession. (**2**: 254)

32 The faithful are but brethren; so affect reconciliation between your brethren and fear Allah that haply mercy may be shown to you. (**49**: 10)

33 And hold fast, all of you to the cord of Allah, and separate not (**3**: 103)

34 Take whatsoever the Messenger gives you, and refrain from whatsoever he forbids you. And fear Allah; verily Allah is Stern in chastizing. (**59**: 7)

35 And when you speak, be fair, even though it be against a kinsman. (**6**: 152)

36 And fulfil the covenant; verily the covenant shall be questioned.
(**17**: 34)

37 O you who believe! Fulfill your obligations. (**5**: 1)

38 O you who believe! Fear Allah, and speak a straight speech. (**33**: 70)

39 …and avoid the falsehood – (**22**: 30)

40 And be you modest in your gait and lower your voice (**31**: 19)

41 Leave the outside sin and its inside. (**6**: 120)

42 O you who believe! Wine and gambling and stone altars and divining
arrows are only an abomination, a handiwork of Satan; so shun it, that
haply you may thrive. (**5**: 90)

43 And say you: 'Work on! Allah holds your work (**9**: 105)

44 O you who believe! Guard yourselves and your households against a
Fire (**66**: 6)

45 …and fill up the measure and balance with equity (**6**: 152)

46 Show forgiveness and enjoin what is honourable and turn away from
the ignorant. (**7**: 199)

47 O you who believe! Remember Allah oft. (**33**: 41)

48 O you who believe! Turn to Allah with a sincere repentance. (**66**: 8)

49 Say: 'My bondsmen who have committed extravagance against
themselves; despair not of the mercy of Allah'; verily Allah will
forgive the sins altogether. (**39**: 53)

50 Say to the faithful that they lower their sights and guard their private
parts; that is cleaner for them. (**24**: 30)

51 And do not faint nor grieve, you shall triumph, if you are Believers.
(**3**: 139)

52 O you who believe! Be not like those who disbelieve (**3**: 156)

53 …and approach not indecencies, whether openly or in secret (**6**: 151)

54 And do not devour your riches among yourselves in vanity, nor convey them to the judges that you may thereby devour a portion of other people's riches sinfully while you know. (**2**: 188)

55 Kill not your offspring for fear of want. We provide for them and for yourselves; their killing is a great crime. (**17**: 31)

56 And as to the beggar, chide him not; (**93**: 10)

57 Wherefore as to the orphan be not you overbearing unto him; (**93**: 9)

58 Let not your hand be chained to your neck, nor stretch it forth to its extremity, lest you sit down reproached, impoverished. (**17**: 29)

59 And spend in the way of Allah and do not cast yourselves with your hands in perdition (**2**: 195)

60 And do not kill anyone whom Allah has forbidden except by right (**17**: 33)

61 …and kill not yourselves (**4**: 29)

62 And do not approach adultery; it is ever an abomination and vile as a pathway. (**17**: 32)

63 And do not you walk on earth struttingly (**17**: 37)

64 …and seek not the vile of it to spend (**2**: 267)

65 O you who believe! Let not one group scoff at another group (**49**: 11)

66 And spy not, nor backbite one another (**49**: 12)

67 And do not traduce one another, nor revile one another by odious appellations (**49**: 11)

68 Revile not those whom they invoke besides Allah, lest they may revile Allah spitefully without knowledge. (**6**: 108)

69 And shout not your prayer, nor speak it low, but seek a midway.' (**17**: 110)

70 ...so let not your souls expire after them in sighings. Verily Allah is the Knower of what they perform. (**35**: 8)

71 O you who believe! Forbid not to yourselves the good things Allah has allowed to you, and trespass not; verily Allah does not love the trespassers. (**5**: 87)

72 ...and despair not of the mercy of Allah; none despair of the mercy of Allah except a people disbelieving.' (**12**: 87)

73 O you who believe! Let not one group scoff at another group; perchance they may be better than they are, nor let some women scoff at other women, perchance the latter may be better than they are. And do not traduce one another, nor revile one another by odious appellations; ill is the name of sin after belief. And whosoever will not repent, then those are the wicked. (**49**: 11)

74 ...set not up compeers to Allah, while you know. (**2**: 22)

75 And make not Allah a butt of your oaths (**2**: 224)

76 Verily Allah commands justice and well–doing and giving to kindred; and He prohibits lewdness and wickedness and oppression. He exhorts you that haply you may be admonished. (**16**: 90)

77 When the sky is cleft •   And when the stars are scattered, (**82**: 1-2)

78 The heavens are well–nigh rent thereat and the earth cleft and the mountains well–nigh fell down (**19**: 90)

79 And the sky will be split therein, His promise is certainly to be accomplished. (**73**: 18)

80 Then repeat your look twice over and your look will return to you dim and drowsy. (**67**: 4)

81 Cooperate with one another in virtue and piety, and do not cooperate in sin and transgression. (**5**: 2)

82 And those who do wrong, shall presently come to know by what overturning they are being overturned. (**26**: 227)

83 His account will presently be taken by an easy reckoning • And he shall return to his people joyfully. (**84**: 8-9)

84 They said: 'Verily to our Lord we are turning, (**7**: 125)

85 ...if there befalls him a trial, he turns round on his face. He loses both this world and the Hereafter, that indeed is a manifest loss. (**22**: 11)

LESSON 15

1 When the sun shall be wound round • And the stars shall dart down • And when the mountains shall be made to pass away • And when the she-camels big with young shall be abandoned • And when the wild beasts shall be gathered together • And when the seas shall be filled • And when the souls shall be paired • And when the girl buried alive shall be questioned • For what sin she was slain • And when the Writs shall be laid open • And when the sky shall be stripped off • And when the Scorch shall be set Ablaze • And when the Garden shall be brought near • Then every soul shall know what it has presented.(**81**: 1-14)

2 Knows he not – when that which in the graves shall be ransacked? And there shall be brought to light that which is in the breasts. (**100**: 9-10)

3 So when comes the command of Allah, Judgement will be given with Truth (**40**: 78)

4 Perish man! How ingrate he is! (**80**: 17)

5 Created from a water dripping • That issues from between the loins

and the breast bones. (**86**: 6-7)

6 …a good deed is thereby written (**9**: 120)

7 You are the best community ever sent forth to mankind; you enjoin good and forbid evil, and you believe in Allah (**3**: 110)

8 O you who believe! Ordained for you is fasting, even as it was ordained for those before you, that haply you will be God–fearing.[12] (**2**:183)

9 The only saying of the believers when they were called to Allah and His apostle that he might judge between them was that they said: we hear and we obey. And these! They are the very ones blissful. (**24**: 51)

10 …and I am commanded that I should do justice between you (**42**: 15)

11 Allah is but the One God; hallowed be He that there should be up to Him a son! (**4**: 171)

12 Say: I am commanded that I be the first who surrenders himself (**6**:14)

13 …so follow not the caprice, lest you may deviate. (**4**: 135)

14 Satan only seeks to breed enmity and spite among you by means of wine and gambling and would keep you from the remembrance of Allah and from prayer (**5**: 91)

15 …and that you associate aught with Allah that for which He has sent down no warranty (**7**: 33)

16 …he said: 'O Moses! Would you slay me as you did slay a person yesterday? (**28**: 19)

17 Noah said: 'Lord! I take refuge with You lest I may ask You that of which I have no knowledge. (**11**: 47)

18 But may be Allah may bring a victory or some other affair from Himself (**5**: 52)

19 Allah said: 'What prevented you, that you should not make obeisance, when I commanded you? (**7**: 12)

20 It is not for any soul that it should believe save with Allah's will (**10**: 100)

21 It is not open to any person to die except by Allah's will at a time recorded. (**3**: 145)

22 ...and let not the scribe refuse to write according as Allah has taught him. (**2**: 282)

23 It is not for us to return to it unless Allah should (so) will (**7**:89)

24 ...and let not the scribe refuse to write according as Allah hath taught him (**2**:282)

25 And whosoever will seek a religion other than Islam, it shall not be accepted of Him, and he shall be of the losers in the Hereafter. (**3**:85)

26 And if you are in doubt concerning what We have sent down upon our bondman then bring a chapter like it, and call upon your witnesses, besides Allah, if you are truthful. • But if you do not, and you cannot, then dread the fire whose fuel is men and stones, prepared for the disbelievers. (**2**:23-24)

27 And as to Dhu al-Nun, recall when he departed with anger and imagined that We have no power over him, and then he cried in the layer of darkness: 'There is no God but you! Hallowed be you! Verily I have been of the wrong-doers.' (**21**:87)

28 And recall that time you said: O Musa! We will not believe in you until we see Allah openly (**2**: 55)

29 They said: 'O Moses! Verily therein are a people high–handed and we shall never march to it so long as they do not depart: if they depart, we shall certainly march to it.' (**5**: 22)

30 And you shall not avail against Allah in aught anyone whom Allah wishes to try. (**5**:41)

31 Whosoever has been imagining that Allah will not make him triumphant in this world and the Hereafter (**22**: 15)

32 And let not those grieve you who have turned towards infidelity; verily they shall not harm Allah at all. (**3**: 176)

33 This is because they say: 'The Fire shall not touch us save a few days numbered (**3**: 24)

34 ...and Allah shall not make a way for the infidels against the Believers. (**4**: 141)

35 And do not you walk on earth struttingly; verily you will not by any means rend the earth, nor can you attain the mountains in stature. (**17**: 37)

36 Allah is not such that naught in the heavens and the earth can frustrate Him. (**35**: 44)

37 And thus We have made you a community justly–balanced, that you might be witnesses to mankind (**2**: 143)

38 Allah shall not forgive them nor guide them on the way. (**4**: 137)

39 So Allah was not the One to wrong them, but themselves they were wont to wrong. (**9**: 70)

40 And Allah is not to acquaint you with the Unseen but Allah chooses him whom He will of His Messengers. Believe therefore in Allah and His Messengers: and if you believe and fear, yours shall be a mighty reward. (**3**: 179)

41 So Allah was not the One to wrong them, but themselves they were wont to wrong. (**9**: 70)

42 He said: 'It was not for me that I should prostrate myself before a human being whom You have created from ringing clay of moulded loam.' (**15**: 33)

43 'You call me for this, that I should blaspheme against Allah, and associate with Him that of which I have no knowledge (**40**: 42)

44 That He may forgive you of your sins, past and future (**48**: 2)

45 ...that he may know that I did not betray him in secret (**12**: 52)

46 He said: 'I am but an envoy of your Lord, and have come to bestow on you a boy, faultless.' (**19**: 19)

47 And when he turns away he speeds through the land so that he may make mischief therein and destroy the tillage (**2**: 205)

48 He it is Who has made the sun a glow and the moon a light, and has determined mansions for her that you may know the number of the years and the reckoning. (**10**: 5)

49 So We restored him to his mother that she might be comforted and not grieve (**28**: 13)

50 Then He caused grief to overtake you for grief, so that you might not grieve for what you might lose (**3**: 153)

51 Of you are some who are brought back to the meanest of age, so that they know not aught (**16**: 70)

52 ...so that it may not be confined to the rich among you. (**59**: 7)

53 Verily Allah alters not what is with a people, until you alter what is within them. (**13**: 11)

54 And We do not chastize until We have raised a Messenger. (**17**: 15)

55 You cannot attain virtue unless you spend of what you love and whatever you spend (**3**: 92)

56 And do not fight them near the Sacred Mosque unless they fight you therein (**2**: 191)

57 So do not take friends from among them unless they migrate for the sake of Allah (**4**: 89)

58 To none did the twain teach it until they had said: 'We are but a

temptation, so blaspheme not. (**2**: 102)

59 ...grant him protection, that he may hear the Word of Allah (**9**: 6)

60 ...nor will they enter the Garden until a camel passes through the eye of a needle. (**7**: 40)

61 And never say you of a thing: 'I am going to do that in the morning'
   • Except with this reservation that Allah so will. (**18**: 23-24)

62 ...and We will surely recompense those who have been patient, their reward for the best of what they have been working. (**16**: 96)

63 And of a surety We shall put you to the proof till We know the valiant among you (**47**: 31)

64 Imagine you not that those who exult in what they have brought about and love to be praised for what they have not done, imagine not you that they shall be secured from the torment. (**3**: 188)

65 The Truth is from your Lord; do not then be of the doubters. (**2**: 147)

66 O you who believe! Fear Allah with fear due to Him, and do not die except you be Muslims. (**3**: 102)

67 ...so be not then you of the ignorant. (**6**: 35)

68 Pharaoh said: 'What! Did you believe in Him before I gave you leave? Surely he is your chief who taught you magic. So I will surely cut off your hands and feet on the opposite sides; and surely crucify you on the trunks of palm–trees; and you will surely know which of us is sterner in torment and more lasting.' (**20**: 71)

69 Do not consider Allah heedless of what the wrong–doers do (**14**: 42)

70 On the Day when some faces will become whitened and other faces will become blackened. Then as for those whose faces shall have become blackened: did you disbelieve after your profession of belief? Taste the torment for you have been disbelieving. (**3**: 106)

LESSON 16

1   And by the morning when it brightens. (**74**: 34)

2   And by the morning when it shines forth. (**81**: 18)

3   …is not morning nigh?' (**11**: 81)

4   …verily the recitation at the dawn is ever borne witness to. (**17**: 78)

5   It is all peace till the rising of the dawn. (**97**: 5)

6   …before the dawn–prayer, and when you lay aside your garments at noon–day and after the night prayer (**24**: 58)

7   And remember you the name of your Lord, every morning and evening. (**76**: 25)

8   …and he beckoned to them: 'Hallow your Lord morning and evening. (**19**: 11)

9   By the day when it glorifies the sun, (**91**: 3)

10   He it is Who has appointed for you the night that you may repose therein and the day enlightening. (**10**: 67)

11   Verily in the alternation of night and day and in what Allah has created in the heavens and the earth are surely Signs to a people who fear God. (**10**: 6)

12   And it is He who has made for you the night a covering, and the sleep a repose, and has made the day a resurrection. (**25**: 47)

13   It is of His mercy that He has made for you night and day, that in them you may have repose and that you may seek of His Grace (**28**: 73)

14   And by the night when it withdraws. (**74**: 33)

15   By the morning brightness • By the night, when it darkens. (**93**: 1-2)

16   And by the night when it departs, (**89**: 4)

17   By the night when it envelops, (**92**: 1)

18   And His is all praise in the heavens and the earth, and at the sun's setting and decline and when you enter the noon. (**30**: 18)

19   ...it will appear to them as though they had not tarried save an evening or the morning. (**79**: 46)

20   The Fire! They are exposed thereto morning and evening (**40**: 46)

21   They shall not hear therein any vain word, but they shall hear only peace; and they shall have therein their provision morning and evening. (**19**: 62)

22   ...and what We sent down upon Our bondsmen on the day of distinction (**8**: 41)

23   When the call is made to the prayer on Friday (**62**: 9)

24   The Day when each soul shall find presented whatever it has worked of good (**3**: 30)

25   I fear for you the torment of a Great Day. (**11**: 3)

26   This day I have perfected your Religion for you (**5**: 3)

27   A Day whereon no soul will own aught of power for any other soul, and the command will be wholly Allah's. (**82**: 19)

28   'Nor that you shall thirst here nor shall you suffer from the sun.' (**20**: 119)

29   Or, are the people of towns then secure that Our wrath would not visit them by daylight while they are disporting themselves? (**7**: 98)

30   They say: 'When we are dead and have become dust and bones, shall

we be raised up indeed? (**23**: 82)

31   And those who, when they have committed a misdeed or wronged themselves, remember Allah (**3**: 135)

32   Now indeed! While you have rebelled afore, and was of the corrupters! (**10**: 91)

33   ...and he says: 'Now I repent' (**4**: 18)

34   'You have now brought the Truth.' (**2**: 71)

35   They ask: 'When is the Day of Requital coming?' (**51**: 12)

36   He questions, when will be the Day of Resurrection? (**75**: 6)

37   ...nor can they perceive when they will be raised.' (**27**: 65)

38   They ask you concerning the Hour and when it is to come? (**7**: 187)

39   And they say: 'When is coming that promise, if you say sooth?' (**10**: 48)

40   ...reciting the Revelations of Allah in the watches of night while they prostrate themselves. (**3**: 113)

41   Is he who is devout in the watches of the night prostrating himself and standing (**39**: 9)

42   ...and hallow the praise of your Lord before sunrise and before sunset; and hallow Him in parts of the night and the ends of the day, haply you will be pleased. (**20**: 130)

43   And they came to their father at nightfall, weeping. (**12**: 16)

44   And in the dawns they used to pray for forgiveness. (**51**: 18)

45   ...he said: 'O Moses! Would you slay me as you did slay a person yesterday? (**28**: 19)

46   And no person knows what he will earn on the morrow (**31**: 34)

47   ...and let every soul look to what it sends forward for the morrow
     (**59**: 18)

48   So whoso of you witnesses the month, he shall fast it (**2**: 185)

49   The month of Ramadan: in it was sent down the Qur'an (**2**: 185)

50   ...every year (**9**: 126)

51   ...and the affair of the Hour will be not but as a flash of the eye
     (**16**: 77)

52   So hallow Allah when you enter the night and when you enter the
     morning. (**30**: 17)

53   And His is all praise in the heavens and the earth, and at the sun's
     setting and decline and when you enter the noon. (**30**: 18)

54   Presently they shall know, when they see the torment (**25**: 42)

55   And he entered the city at a time of the unawareness of its
     inhabitants (**28**: 15)

56   He it is Who fashions you in the wombs as He will (**3**: 6)

57   And hallow Him in the night and at the declining of the stars.
     (**52**: 49)

58   But no sooner did there come to a community their Messenger than
     they belied him. (**23**: 44)

59   Messengers, some of whom We have narrated to you before and of
     others of whom We have not narrated to you (**4**: 164)

60   Allah's is the command, before and after (**30**: 4)

61   'And I am bidden this, in order that I may be the first of those who
     submit.' (**39**: 12)

62   Eat and drink but little (**77**: 46)

63   …and remember Allah much (**26**: 227)

64   Say: He is Allah, the One. (**112**: 1)

65   And prostrations* are for Allah, so do not call along with Allah anyone. (**72**: 18)

66   Muhammad is not the father of any of your males, but a Messenger of Allah (**33**: 40)

67   …when you are face to face with death, at the making of a bequest shall be that of two equitable persons from among you (**5**: 106)

68   And said one of them: 'Father hire him (**28**: 26)

69   Allah has created eight pairs; of the sheep a twain, of the goats a twain. Say: 'Is it the two males He has forbidden or the two females, or what the wombs of the females contain? Declare to me with knowledge, if you are truth–tellers.' •   Of the camels He has created a twain and of the oxen a twain. Say: 'Is it the two males He has forbidden or the two females, or what the wombs of the females contain? (**6**: 143-144)

70   …when those who disbelieved banished him; the second of the two; when the twain were in a cave (**9**: 40)

71   Then whoso does not find the wherewithal, on him is the fasting for two months in succession; a penance from Allah. (**4**: 92)

72   And they will have a fourth of what you may leave if you have no child (**4**: 12)

73   …but if he have brothers, then his mother will have a sixth (**4**: 11)

74   …but if you have a child then they will have an eighth of what you may leave (**4**: 12)

---

* mosques

75   Presently they will say: There were three, the fourth being their dog. (**18**: 22)

76   And since they could not produce four witnesses (**24**: 13)

77   ...the testimony of one of them shall be to aver four times by Allah (**24**: 6)

78   They were five, the sixth being their dog — guessing at the unknown (**18**: 22)

79   ...nor among five but He is their sixth (**58**: 7)

80   And there were nine of a group in the city, who spread corruption in the land (**27**: 48)

81   In Truth your Lord is Allah Who created the heavens and the earth in six days (**7**: 54)

82   Say: 'Who is the Lord of the seven heavens and Lord of the Mighty Throne?' (**23**: 86)

83   ...with seven more seas to help it, the Words of Allah could not be exhausted (**31**: 27)

84   ...and they will say: 'They were seven, the eight being their dog. (**18**: 22)

85   To which He subjected them for seven nights and eight days in succession (**69**: 7)

86   ...and of the cattle He sent down unto you eight kinds (**39**: 6)

87   And assuredly We gave Moses nine manifest Signs (**17**: 101)

88   Whoso will come with a virtue, for him there shall be ten like thereof (**6**: 160)

89   ...these are ten days complete (**2**: 196)

90   I have seen eleven stars and the sun and the moon; I have seen them

prostrating themselves before me.' (**12**: 4)

91 Verily, the number of months with Allah is twelve months ordained in the Writ of Allah (**9**: 36)

92 ...and We raised from amongst them twelve leaders. (**5**: 12)

93 And We divided them into twelve tribes as nations. (**7**: 160)

94 And We treated with Moses thirty nights, and We completed them with ten (**7**: 142)

95 And recall when We treated with Moses forty nights (**2**: 51)

96 And We treated with Moses thirty nights, and We completed them with ten (**7**: 142)

97 ...and on him who is unable to do so is the feeding of sixty indigent ones. (**58**: 4)

98 Then fasten him with a chain seventy cubits long. (**69**: 32)

99 ...scourge them with eighty stripes and accept not their testimony for ever. (**24**: 4)

100 'Verily this my brother has ninety–nine ewes while I have a solitary ewe (**38**: 23)

101 Thereupon Allah made him dead for a hundred years and then raised him up (**2**: 259)

102 And they stayed in their cave three hundred years and added nine. (**18**: 25)

103 If there be twenty of you steadfast, they will overcome two hundred (**8**: 65)

104 Then he stayed among them for a thousand years, less fifty years (**29**: 14)

105 And a day with the Lord is a thousand years of what you compute.

(**22**: 47)

106 He answered you: 'Surely I am about to succour you with a thousand angels, rank on rank.' (**8**: 9)

107 …your Lord shall reinforce you with five thousand angels marked. (**3**: 125)

108 Thereby the angels ascend to Him and also the Spirit; on a Day whose space is fifty thousand years. (**70**: 4)

109 Have you not looked at those who went forth from their dwellings, and they were in their thousands (**2**: 243)

110 So know you that there is no god save Allah, and ask forgiveness for your fault (**47**: 19)

111 'O my people ask forgiveness of your Lord, then repent to Him (**11**: 52)

112 And beg forgiveness of Allah; verily Allah is Forgiving. Merciful. (**73**: 20)

113 And he who works an evil or wrongs his own soul and thereafter begs forgiveness of Allah, shall find Allah Forgiving, Merciful
   •   And he who earns a sin, only against his own soul earns it; and Allah is ever Knowing, Wise. (**4**: 110-111)

114 As for the faithful it has increased them in Faith and they rejoice. (**9**: 124)

115 And when My bondsmen ask you regarding Me, then surely I am nigh. I answer the call of the caller, when he calls Me; so let them answer Me and believe in Me, haply they may be directed. (**2**: 186)

116 …and those whom they call upon beside Him answer them not at all (**13**: 14)

117 verily He loves not the stiff–necked. (**16**: 23)

118 …and woe be to the infidels because of a ·severe torment •   Those

who prefer the life of this world to the Hereafter, and hinder people from the way of Allah and seek crookedness therein, these are in far–off error. (**14**: 2-3)

119   And when Our Revelations are recited to him, he turns away in pride as though he did not hear that at all (**31**: 7)

120   …and weigh with an even balance (**17**: 35)

121   So when the Qur'an is recited, listen to it and keep silence; haply you may be shown mercy. (**7**: 204)

122   Who listen to the Word and follow the excellent thereof. (**39**: 18)

123   Hasten therefore to virtues (**5**: 48)

124   'This is My path, straight; follow it then, and do not follow other ways; that will deviate you from His way. (**6**: 153)

125   O you who believe! Do not enter houses other than your own until you have asked leave and invoked peace on their inmates. (**24**: 27)

MUKHTARAT

The Opening Chapter:

1   In the name of Allah, the Compassionate, the Merciful • All Praise unto Allah, Lord of the worlds • The Compassionate, the Merciful • Sovereign of the Day of Reckoning • You alone we Worship, and of You alone we seek help. Guide us to the path straight. The path of those whom You have favored. Not of those whom indignation brought down, nor of the astray. (**1**: 1-7)

al-Tawhid, Oneness of Allah:

2   Allah! There is no god but He, the Living, the Sustainer, slumber seizes Him not, nor sleep. His is whatever is in the heavens and whatever is on the earth. Who can intercede with Him, save by His leave? He knows whatever was before them and whatever shall be after them. And they encompass naught of His knowledge, save what

He wills. His Throne comprehends the heavens and the earth; and the guarding of both wearies Him not, and He is the High, the Supreme. (**2**: 255)

3   He is Allah, there is no god but He, the Knower of the Unseen and the seen, He is the Compassionate, the Merciful. • He is Allah, there is no god but He, the Sovereign, the Holy, the Author of Safety, the Giver of Peace, the Protector, the Mighty, the Mender, the Majestic. Hallowed be Allah from what they associate • He is Allah, the Creator, the Maker, The Fashioner; His are the Excellent Names. Him hallows whatsoever is in the heavens and the earth, and He is the Mighty, the Wise. (**59**: 22-24)

4   Hallows Allah whatsoever is in the heavens and the earth, and He is the Mighty, the Wise • His is the dominion of the heavens and the earth; He gives life and causes death; and He is Potent over everything • He is the First and the Last, and the Evident and the Imminent and He is the Knower of everything • He it is Who created the heavens and the earth in six days; then He established Himself on the Throne. He knows whatsoever plunges into the earth, and whatsoever comes forth therefrom, and whatsoever descends from the heaven, and whatsoever ascends thereto; and He is with you wheresoever you be; and Allah is Beholder of whatever you do • His is the dominion of the heavens and the earth, and to Allah will all affairs be brought back • He plunges the night into the day, and plunges the day into the night, and He is the Knower of whatsoever is in the breasts. (**57**: 1-6)

5   Allah is the Light of the heavens and the earth; the likeness of His Light is as a niche wherein is a lamp; the lamp is in a glass; the glass is as though it is a star brilliant; lit from a tree blest, an olive, neither of the east nor of the west; its very oil will shine forth, even though no fire touched it; light upon light. Allah guides unto His Light whom He will. Allah propounds similitudes for mankind; and verily Allah is the Knower of everything. (**24**: 35)

Allah the Omnipotent:

6   Say: 'Were the oceans to become ink for the Words of my Lord the ocean would surely exhaust before the Words of my Lord exhausted, even though We brought another ocean for support.' (**18**: 109)

7   And if whatever trees are on the earth were pens, and sea were ink, with seven more seas to help it, the Words of Allah could not be exhausted; verily Allah is Mighty, Wise. (**31**: 27)

Allah the Creator of the Universe:

8   The Originator of the heavens and the earth, and whenever He decrees an affair, He merely says to it, 'Be', and it becomes. (**2**: 117)

9   Have not those who disbelieved considered that the heavens and the earth were closed up, then We rent them? And We have made of water everything living, will they not then believe? (**21**: 30)

10 He has created the heavens that you see without pillars and has cast firm mountains in the earth lest it move away with you, and He has scattered thereon every kind of animal. And We send down water from the sky and We make all manner of goodly growth therein • This is the creation of Allah. Show me what those beside Allah have created. Aye! The ungodly are in manifest error. (**31**: 10-11)

11 And a day with the Lord is a thousand years of what you compute. (**22**: 47)

Allah the Creator of Mankind:

12 Assuredly We created man out of an extract of clay • Thereafter We made him a sperm in a safe receptacle • Thereafter We made the sperm a clot; then We made the clot a lump of flesh; then We made the lump of flesh bones; then We clothed the bones with flesh; thereafter We brought him forth as another creature. Blest be then Allah, the Best of Creators. (**23**: 12-14)

13 Mankind! Verily We! We have created you of a male and a female, and We have made you nations and tribes that you might know one another. Verily the noble of you with Allah is the most pious of you. Verily Allah is Knowing, Wise. (**49**: 13)

Allah has Subjugated the Universe for the Service of Mankind:

14 Allah it is Who has subjected the sea to you that ships may run on it by His command, and that you may seek of His grace, and that haply

you may return thanks •   And He has subjected to you whatsoever is in the heavens and whatsoever is on the earth, the whole from Himself. Verily herein are Signs for a people who ponder. (**45**: 12-13)

15 The affair of Allah comes, so do not seek to hasten it. Hallowed be He and Exalted above what they associate •   He sends down the angels with the Spirit by His command upon whosoever of His bondsmen He wills; warn that there is no god but I, so fear Me •   He has created the heavens and the earth with a purpose. Exalted is He above what they associate •   He has created man from a drop, and lo! He is a disputant open •   And the cattle! He has created them. For you in them there is warmth and other profits and of them you eat •   And for you there is a beauty in them as you drive them at the eventide and as you drive them out to pasture •   And they bear your loads to a city which you could not reach except with the travail of your souls; verily your Lord is kind, Merciful •   And He has created horses and mules and asses that you may ride them, and as an adornment; and He creates what you do not know •   And upon Allah is the direction of the way, and of that is some crooked, and had He willed, He would have guided you all •   He it is Who sends down from the heaven water for you, from which is drinking and from which is vegetation from which you pasture your herds •   He grows thereby the corn and olive and date palms and grapes and all manner of fruit. Verily in that is a Sign for a people who ponder. (**16**: 1-11)

16 Alif.Lam.Mim.Ra. These are the verses of the Book. And what is sent down to you from your Lord is the Truth, but most of the people believe not •   Allah it is Who has raised the heavens without the pillars you can see, then He established Himself on the Throne and subjected the sun and the moon to Himself, each running to a determined period. He directs the affairs and details the Signs, that haply you may be convinced of the meeting with your Lord •   And He it is Who has stretched the earth, and placed therein firm mountains and rivers, and of every fruit He has placed therein two in pairs. He covers the night with the day; verily in that are Signs for a people who ponder •   And in the earth are regions adjoining and gardens of vine and corn–fields, and palm–trees, clustered and single, watered by the same water; yet some We make excel others in food. Verily in that are Signs for a people who reflect •   And should you marvel, then marvellous is their saying: 'When we have become dust, shall we be in a new creation?' These are they who disbelieved in

615

their Lord; and these! Shackles round their necks; and these shall be the fellows of the Fire as abiders therein • And they ask you to hasten the evil before the good, while examples have already gone forth before them. And your Lord is Owner of forgiveness to mankind despite their wrong–doing; and verily your Lord is Severe in requital • And those who disbelieve say: 'Why is not a Sign sent down to him from his Lord?' You are but a warner, and to every people there is a guide • Allah knows what every female bears and what the wombs want and what they exceed, and with Him everything is in due measure. • Knower of the hidden and the manifest! The Great, the Exalted! • Alike to Him is he among you who hides the Word and he who proclaims it, and he who hides himself in the night and he who goes about freely in the day • For each one are attendant angels, before him and behind him. They guard him with Allah's command. Verily Allah alters not what is with a people, until you alter what is within them. And when Allah intends evil to a people, there is no turning it back, nor is there for them any patron, beside Him • He it is Who shows lightening to you for inspiring fear and hope, and brings up the heavy clouds • And the thunder hallows His glory, and so do the angels, in awe of Him, and He sends the thunderbolts and smites with them whomsoever He will. They dispute concerning Allah, and He is strong in prowess • To Him alone is the True Call; and those whom they call upon beside Him answer them not at all, save as is answered one stretching out his palms to water that it may reach his mouth, while it will reach him not. And the supplication of infidels goes only astray • And to Allah bows whosoever is in the heavens and the earth, willingly or unwillingly, and also their shadows in the mornings and the evenings • Say you: 'Who is the Lord of the heavens and the earth?' Say you: 'Allah.' Say you: 'Have you then taken beside Him, patrons who own neither benefit nor hurt to themselves?' Say you: 'Are there the blind and the seeing alike or are darkness and light alike?' Or have they set up associates with Allah, who have created as He has created, so that the creation has become dubious to them? Say: 'Allah is the creator of everything; and He is the One, the Subduer.' • He sends down water from the heaven, so that the valleys flow according to their measure; then the torrent bears the scum on top; and from that over which they kindle a fire seeking ornaments or goods arises a scum like thereto: thus Allah propounds the Truth and falsity. Then as for the scum, it departs as rubbish, and as for that which benefits mankind, it lasts on the earth; thus does Allah propound similitudes • For those who answer their Lord is ordained good. And as for those who do not answer their Lord, if they had all that is in the earth together with its like, they would ransom themselves with that. These! For them shall be an evil reckoning; and their resort is Hell, a hapless bed! (**13**: 1-18)

The Articles of Faith:

17 O you who believe! Believe in Allah and His Messenger and the Book He has sent down to His Messenger and the Book He sent down formerly; and he who disbelieves in Allah and His angels and His Books and His Messengers and the Last Day, has strayed far away. (**4**: 136)

18 Say: 'We believe in Allah and what has been sent down to us and what was sent down to Abraham and Ishmael and Isaac and Jacob and the tribes and what was given to Moses and 'Isa, and what was given to the Prophets[93] from their Lord! We make no difference between any of them, and to Him we are submissive'. (**2**: 136)

Faith on the Messengers:

19 Say: 'We believe in Allah and in what has been sent down to us, and what was sent down to Abraham and Ishmael, and Isaac and Jacob and the tribes, and what was given to Moses and Jesus and other Prophets from their Lord: we discriminate against none of them, and to Him we are submissive.' (**3**: 84)

Humans are Responsible for their Own Deeds:

20 Whoso is guided, it is only for himself that he is guided, and whoso strays it is only against his soul that he strays; and not one laden bears the load of another. And We do not chastize until We have raised a Messenger. (**17**: 15)

Guidance through the Messengers:

21 O Children of Adam! If there came to you Messengers from among you, recounting My Signs to you, then whoever shall fear Allah and act right, on them shall come no fear, nor shall they grieve • And those who belie Our Signs and are stiff–necked, against them – they shall be fellows of the Fire and therein they shall be abiders. (**7**: 35-36)

The Characteristics of the Messengers:

22 And We have not sent before you any of the Messengers but they did eat food and did walk about in the market-places. And We have made some of you a temptation to some others; will you have patience? And your Lord is a Beholder. (**25**: 20)

All People of the World, in the Past were Blessed with Messengers:

23 For each community there has been sent a Messenger, and when their Messenger has arrived, the affair between them is decreed in equity, and they are not wronged. (**10**: 47)

24 This was Our dispensation with those whom We sent before you of Our Messengers and you will not find a change in this Our dispensation. (**17**: 77)

The Noble Character of the Prophet Muḥammad ﷺ:

25 O Prophet! We have verily sent you as a witness and a bearer of glad tidings and a warner • And a summoner unto Allah by His command, and a luminous lamp • And bear you to the faithful the glad tidings that there is for them a great grace from Allah. (**33**: 45-47)

26 And We have not sent you save as a bearer of glad tiding and a warner to all mankind; yet most mankind do not know. (**34**: 28)

The Worship:

27 And I have not created the *jinn* and mankind but that they should worship Me, (**51**: 56)

Sincerity in Worship:

28 Say: 'My Lord has enjoined equity, and that you shall set your faces aright at every prostration, and call on Him, making Faith pure for Him. Even as He has begun you, you shall be brought back.' (**7**: 29)

29 They only shall tend Allah's mosques who believe in Allah and the Last Day and establish prayer and give the poor–rate and fear none save Allah. They may be among the guided ones. (**9**: 18)

The Commandments and Prohibitions:

30 O mankind! A similitude is propounded; listen to it. Verily those whom you call upon beside Allah can by no means create a single fly, even though all of them assembled for that; and if a fly were to snatch away aught from them, they cannot retain it. Feeble indeed are the seeker and the sought! • They have not estimated Allah His rightful estimate; verily Allah is Strong, Mighty • Allah chooses Messengers from the angels and mankind; Verily Allah is Hearing, Beholding • He knows what is before them and what is behind them, and to Allah are returned all affairs • O you who believe! Bow down and prostrate yourselves and worship your Lord, and do good; haply you may thrive • And strive hard for Allah as is due unto him hard striving. He has distinguished you, and has not laid upon you any narrowness in Religion: the Faith of your father Abraham. He has named you Muslim before, and in this, that the Messenger may be witness against you and that you may be witnesses against mankind. So establish the prayer and pay the poor–rate, and hold fast by prayer to Allah. He is your Patron — an Excellent Patron and an Excellent Helper! (**22**: 73-78)

Allah Consciousness, Unity and Commanding in what is Right and Preventing from Wrong:

31 The Compassionate • He taught the Qur'an • He created man • He taught him distinctness • The sun and the moon are in the reckoning ✦ And herbs and trees do obeisance • And the sky! He has elevated it and set the balance • That you should not trespass in respect of the balance • And observe the weight with equity, and do not make the balance deficient • And the earth: He has laid it for the creatures • Therein are fruit and palm trees sheathed • And grain chaffed and other food • Which, then, of the benefits of your Lord will you twain deny? • He created man from potter's clay • And has created the *jinn* from a flame of fire • Which, then, of the benefits of your Lord will you twain deny? • He is Lord of the two easts and the two wests • Which, then, of the benefits of your Lord will you twain deny? • He has let loose the two oceans • In

between them is a barrier they cannot pass • Which, then, of the benefits of your Lord will you twain deny? • There come forth from the two the pearl and the coral • Which, then, of the benefits of your Lord will you twain deny? • His are the ships slanted like mountains in the sea • Which, then, of the benefits of your Lord will you twain deny? • Everyone who is thereon is mortal • And there will remain the Face of your Lord, Owner of Majesty and Beneficence. (**55**: 1-27)

32 O Children of Israel! Remember My favour wherewith I favoured you, and fulfil My covenant, and I shall fulfil your covenant, and dread Me alone • And believe in what I have sent down confirming what is with you, and be not the first to disbelieve therein. And barter not My Signs for a small price, and fear Me alone • And confound not the Truth with falsehood, nor conceal the Truth while you know • And establish prayer, and give the poor–rate and bow down with those who bow. • Do you enjoin mankind to piety and forget yourselves while you read the Book? Do you not understand? • And seek help in patience and prayer, and surely it is hard, save to the meek • Who know, that surely they are going to meet their Lord, and that surely to Him they are going to return. (**2**: 40-46)

33 O you who believe! Fear Allah with fear due to Him, and do not die except you be Muslims • And hold fast, all of you to the cord of Allah, and separate not. And remember Allah's favour to you in that you were enemies, and He joined your hearts together, so you became brethren by His favour; and you were on the brink of a pit of Fire and He rescued you from it. Thus, does Allah expound to you His Revelations that perhaps you may remain guided • And let there be among you a community calling others to good and commanding equity and forbidding evil. And it is these who are blissful • And be not as those who separated and differed among themselves after there had come to them evidence. These are the ones for whom shall be a mighty torment • On the Day when some faces will become whitened and other faces will become blackened. Then as for those whose faces shall have become blackened: did you disbelieve after your profession of belief? Taste the torment for you have been disbelieving • And as for those whose faces shall have become whitened they shall be in Allah's mercy; therein they shall abide • These are Revelations of Allah, We rehearse them to you with Truth; and Allah intends not wrong to His creatures • Allah's is whatever is in the heavens and in the earth; and to Allah are

committed all affairs • You are the best community ever sent forth
to mankind; you enjoin good and forbid evil, and you believe in
Allah. Now if the People of the Book have Faith, it were better for
them; among them some are Believers, and most of them are ungodly.
(**3**: 102-110)

The Religion of Truth:

34 He it is Who has sent His Messenger with Guidance and true Faith,
that He may make it triumph over every other faith, though the
associates may be averse • O you who believe! Shall I direct you to
a trade which will deliver you from an afflictive torment? • It is;
believe in Allah and His Messenger and strive in the cause of Allah
with your riches and lives. That is best for you if you only know! ✦ He
will forgive you your sins, and make you enter the Gardens with
running rivers, and happy abodes in the Everlasting Gardens. That is
a great achieve-ment • And also another bliss which you love:
succour from Allah and a swift victory. And bear you the glad tidings
to the faithful • O you who believe! Be Allah's helpers, even as
Jesus, son of Maryam, said to the disciples: 'Who shall be my helpers
for Allah?' The disciples said: 'We are Allah's helpers.' Then a party
of the Children of Israel believed, and another party disbelieved. Then
We streng-thened those who believed against their foe; so they
became triumphant. (**61**: 9-14)

Kindness to Parents and Social Ethics:

35 And your Lord has decreed that you should worship none but Him,
and show kindness to parents; and if either of them or both of them
attain old age with you, say not unto them: 'pooh!', and browbeat
them not, and speak to them a respectful speech • And lower unto
them the wing of meekness out of mercy, and say: Lord! Have mercy
on the twain as they brought me up when young • Your Lord is the
Best knower of what is in your souls; if you have been righteous, then
He is unto you Penitent, Forgiving • And give you to the kinsman
his due, and also to the needy and wayfarer; and squander not in
squandering • Truly the squanderers are the brethren of the devils,
and the Devil is ever ungrateful to his Lord • And if you turn away
from them awaiting a mercy from your Lord which you hope, then
speak to them a gentle word • Let not your hand be chained to your
neck, nor stretch it forth to its extremity, lest you sit down reproached,

impoverished • Verily your Lord extends the provision for whom He will, and measures it out, He is in respect of His creatures Aware, Beholder • Kill not your offspring for fear of want. We provide for them and for yourselves; their killing is a great crime • And do not approach adultery; it is ever an abomination and vile as a pathway • And do not kill anyone whom Allah has forbidden except by right, and whoever is killed wrongfully. We have surely given his next–of–kin authority; so let him not exceed killing; verily he is ever succoured • And do not approach the substance of an orphan save with what is best, until he reaches the age of strength. And fulfil the covenant; verily the covenant shall be questioned • And give full measure when you measure, and weigh with an even balance, that is good, and the best interpretation • And do not you go after that of which you have no knowledge; verily the hearing and the sight and the hearts, each of them shall be questioned about • And do not you walk on earth struttingly; verily you will not by any means rend the earth, nor can you attain the mountains in stature • Each of these! Their vice is to your Lord ever detestable • That is part of that wisdom which your Lord has revealed to you, and set not up you along with Allah another god, lest you be cast into Hell reproved, damned.(**17**: 23-39)

The Righteous Deeds:

36 Alif.Lam.Mim • Do people think that they shall be left alone because they say: 'We believe'; and that they shall not be tested? • And assuredly We have tested those who were before them. So Allah will surely know those who are true and will surely know the liars • Or do those who work ill–deeds think that they will outstrip Us? Ill do they judge! • Whosoever hopes for the meeting with Allah, then Allah's term is surely coming, and He is the Hearer, the Knower ♦ And whosoever strives, strives only for himself, verily Allah is Independent of the worlds • And whosoever believes and works righteous deeds, We shall purge away the evil deeds from them, and shall recompense them the best of what they have been working • And We have enjoined on man kindness to parents, but if they strive to make you associate with Me that of which you have no knowledge, do not obey them; to Me is your return, and I shall declare to you what you have been doing • And those who believe and work righteous deeds We shall surely make them enter among the righteous • Of mankind are some who say, 'we believe in Allah', then if they are afflicted in the way of Allah, they take the persecution

of men as the torment of Allah, and then, if succour comes from your Lord they say, 'verily we have been with you'. Is not Allah the best Knower of what is in the breasts of the creatures? • And surely Allah will come to know those who believe, and surely He will come to know the hypocrites. (**29**: 1-11)

The Martyrs are the Successful:

37 And reckon you not those slain in the way of Allah as dead. Nay, they are alive and with their Lord, and provided for • Exulting in what Allah has granted them of His grace. And they rejoice in those who have not yet joined them from behind, in the thought that no fear shall come to them nor shall they grieve • They rejoice at the favour of Allah and His Grace and that Allah wastes not the reward of the Believers. (**3**: 169-171)

Allah Helps the Believers:

38 Verily those who said: 'Our Lord is Allah', and have thereafter stood by it on them will descend the angels saying: 'Fear not, nor grieve, and rejoice at the glad–tidings of the Garden which you have been promised.' • We have been your friends in the life of the world, and are such in the Hereafter; herein whatsoever you desire shall be yours and whatsoever you call for shall be yours • An entertainment for you from your Lord, the Forgiving, the Merciful • And who is better in speech than he who summons unto Allah and works righteously, and says: 'Verily I am of the Muslims?' • Good and evil cannot be equal. Repeal evil with what is goodly, then behold! He, between whom and you was enmity, will be as though he was a warm friend • And none attains that except those who are patient; and none attains that except the owner of mighty good fortune • And if there stirs you an incitement from Satan, then seek refuge in Allah. Verily He! He is the Hearer, the Knower. (**41**: 30-36)

The Life Hereafter:

39 And they will not be able to make a disposition, nor to their family will they return • And the Trumpet will be blown, and lo! From their tombs they shall be hastening to their Lord • They will say: 'Ah woe to us! Who has roused us from our sleeping–place?' This is what the Compassionate had promised, and truly spake the sent ones • It shall

be but one shout; and lo! They shall all be brought together before Us
• Today no soul shall be wronged at all; nor shall you be requited
but for what you have been doing • Verily the dwellers of the
Garden today shall be happily employed • They and their mates
shall be reclining on couches in shade • Theirs shall be fruit therein,
and theirs shall be whatsoever they ask for • Peace shall be the
Word from the Lord Merciful • And separate yourselves, this Day,
O you culprits! • Children of Adam! Did I not enjoin you, that you
shall not serve Satan; verily he is your manifest foe? • And that, you
shall worship Me! This is the straight path • And yet he has
assuredly led astray a great multitude of you. Why do you not reflect?
• There is Hell which you were promised • Roast therein today for
that you have been disbelieving • Today We will seal up their
mouths, and their hands shall speak to Us and their feet shall bear
witness to what they have been earning. (**36**: 50-65)

al-Tawḥīd, **The Articles of Faith and Supplication:**

40 Allah's is whatever is in the heavens and whatever is in the earth, and
    whether you reveal what is in your mind or hide it, Allah will reckon
    with you therefore, then He will forgive whom He will and torment
    whom He will, and Allah is Potent over everything • The
    Messenger believes in what is sent down to him from his Lord, and
    so do the Believers. They all believe in Allah and His angels and His
    Books and His Messengers, saying: 'We discriminate not against any
    of His Messengers.' And they say: 'We hear and obey; Your
    forgiveness, our Lord! And to You is our return.' • Allah charges
    not a soul excepting according to its capacity. For it shall be the
    good it earns, and against it the evil it earns: Our Lord! Reckon with
    us not if we forget or err. Our Lord! Burden us not like unto those
    You burdened before us. Our Lord! Impose not on us that for which
    we have not strength. And pardon us, forgive us, and have mercy on
    us. You are our Master, so make us triumph over the disbelieving
    people. (**2**: 284-286)

41 Hallowed be your Lord, the Lord of Majesty, from what they associate to
    Him! And peace be unto the sent ones. And all praise to Allah, the
    Lord of the worlds! (**37**: 180-182)

624

APPENDIX
H8
Glossary of Grammatical Terms[1]

Where an example is partly in italics and partly in roman type, it is the words in roman that exemplify the term being defined.

absolute used independently of its customary grammatical relationship or construction, e.g. Weather permitting, *I will come.*

accusative grammatical case indicating the object of an action.

active applied to a verb whose subject is also the source of the action of the verb, e.g. *We* saw *him*; opposite of **passive**.

adjective a word that names an attribute, used to describe a noun or pronoun, e.g. small *child, it is* small.

adverb a word that modifies an adjective, verb, or another adverb, expressing a relation of place, time, circumstance, manner, cause, degree, etc., e.g. *gently, accordingly, now, here why.*

affirmative saying 'yes'.

agree to have the same grammatical number, gender, case or person as another word.

animate denoting a living being.

article a/an (**indefinite** article) or *the* (**definite** article).

case the form (**subjective**, **objective**, or **possessive**) of a noun or pronoun, expressing relation to some other word.

conditional designating (1) a clause which expresses a condition, or (2) a mood of the verb used in the consequential clause of a conditional sentence, e.g. (1) *if he had come*, (2) *I* should have seen *him.*

conjugation inflect (a verb), various forms of a verb related to third person, second person and first person etc.

conjunctive connecting.

consonant (1) a speech sound in which breath is at least partly obstructed, combining with vowel to form a syllable; (2) a letter usually used to represent (1); e.g. ewe is written with vowel +

---

[1] Extracts taken form: E. S. C. Weiner and J. M. Hawkins, *The Oxford Guide to the English Language*, Oxford University Press, 1984

consonant + vowel, but is pronounced as consonant (y) + vowel (oo).

demonstrative showing

diphthong a group of two letters standing for a single sound, e.g. *ea* in *head*, gh in cough; Literature: a typographical symbol consisting of two letters joined together, e.g. *fi*, *fl*. The term *diphthong* is best restricted to the sense for which there is no synonym.

feminine the gender proper to female beings.

future the tense of a verb referring to an event yet to happen: simple future, e.g. *I shall go*; future in the past, referring to an event that was yet to happen at a time prior to the time of speaking, e.g. *He said he would go*.

genitive grammatical case showing source or possession.

glottal sound produced by sudden explosive release of breath from behind the closed glottis.

hollow empty within, not solid.

imperative the mood of a verb expressing command, e.g. Come *here!*

inanimate opposite of **animate**.

interjection process of interjecting.

intransitive designating a verb that does not take a direct object, e.g. *I must* think.

interrogation question closely.

jussive expressing command.

masculine the gender proper to male beings.

nominal designating a phrase or clause that is used like a noun, e.g. What you need *is a drink.*

nominative a form noun used when it is the subject of a verb.

object a noun or its equivalent governed by an active transitive verb, e.g. *I will take* that one.

objective the case of pronoun typically used when the pronoun is the object of a verb or governed by a preposition, e.g. *me*, *him.*

participle the part of a verb used like an adjective but retaining some verbal qualities (tense and government of an object) and also used to form compound verb forms.

passive designating a form of the verb by which the verbal action is attributed to the person or thing to whom it is actually directed (i.e. the logical object is the grammatical subject), e.g. *He* was seen *by us*; opposite of **active**.

perfect a tense denoting completed action or action viewed in relation to the present, e.g. *I* have finished *now*; perfect infinitive, e.g. *He seems* to have finished *now*.

person one of the three classes of personal pronouns or verbs-forms, denoting the person speaking (first person), the person spoken to (second person), and the person or thing spoken about (third person).

plural denoting more than one.

possessive the case of a noun or a pronoun indicating possession, e.g. *John's*; **possessive pronoun**, e.g. my, his.

predicate the part of a clause consisting of what is said of the subject, including verb + complement or object.

prefix a verbal element placed at the beginning of a word to quality its meaning, e.g. *ex-, non-*.

preposition a word governing a noun or pronoun, expressing the relation of the latter to other words, e.g. *seated* at *the table*.

present a tense expressing action now going on or habitually performed in past and future, e.g. *He* commutes *daily*.

prohibition forbid (n.).

pronoun a word used instead of a noun to designate (without naming) a person or thing already known or indefinite, e.g. *I, you, he,* etc., *anyone, something,* etc.

qualify (of an adjective or adverb) to attribute some quality to (a noun or adjective/verb).

subject the element in a clause (usually noun or its equivalent) about which something is predicted (the latter is the **predicate**).

subjective the case of a pronoun typically used when the pronoun is the subject of a clause.

subjunctive the mood of a verb denoting what is imagined, wished, or possible, e.g. *I insist that it* be *finished*.

suffix a verbal element added at the end of a word to form a derivative, e.g. *–ation, -ing, -itis, -ize*.

superlative the form of an adjective or adverb expressing the highest or a very high degree of a quality, e.g. *brave, worst*.

transitive designating a verb that takes a direct object, e.g. *I* said *nothing*.

Triliteral root: It is comprising of three radical letters

verb a part of speech that predicates.

vowel (1) an open speech sound made without audible friction and capable of forming a syllable with or without a consonant; (2) a letter usually used to represent (1), e.g. *a, e, i, o, u*.

APPENDIX
(I) 9
Key to Exercises 1-35

(Phase one)

Exercise No.1

←

ب، ث، ت، ث، ب

ت ،

Exercise No.2

ح، ت، ث، ج، خ، ب، ح، ث، ت

Exercise No.3

ذ، ت، د، ح، ث، خ، ذ، د، ث، خ

Exercise No.4

ز، ح، د، ذ، ر، ت، ث، ج، ب، خ، ز

Exercise No.5

خ، س، ج، ش، ب، ر، د، ث، ذ، ب، ح، ز، ش، ب، ذ، ت،
س، ش، ح، خ، ج، ر، ز

Exercise No.6

س، ص،د، ض، ت، ث، ج، ح، ب، خ، ش ، ذ، ر، ز، ث،
ح، خ، ر، ز، ج، د، ذ، ص، ض، س، ش، ب، ت

Exercise No.7

ض، ر، ز، ب، ت، س، ش، خ، ث، ج، ح، ظ، ط

628

Exercise No.8

ت، ب، ث، غ، د، ذ، س، ش، ط، ظ، ح، ز، ض، ط، خ

Exercise No.9

ف، ك، ق، ل، م، ن، و، ح، ي، ع، ء، غ، ط، ظ

ص، ض، ت، ث، خ، هـ، و

Exercise No.11

(١) جَ (٢) عُ (٣) ب (٤) ذُ (٥) ثِ (٦) شَ (٧) سِ (٨) سُ (٩) كِ (١٠) وُ (١١) قَ

(١٢) فِ (١٣) زُ (١٤) يَ (١٥) و (١٦) لُ (١٧) مُ (١٨) هُ (١٩) خَ (٢٠) حِ (٢١) غِ

(٢٢) نَ (٢٣) كُ (٢٤) ظَ (٢٥) قُ (٢٦) خِ (٢٧) مِ (٢٨) طَ (٢٩) طُ (٣٠) ذَ (٣١) ه

(٣٢) حَ (٣٣) وَ (٣٤) تُ (٣٥) طِ (٣٦) صَ (٣٧) شِ

Exercise No.12

(١) بَسَطَ (٢) نَظَرَ (٣) ضَحِكَ (٤) طَمِعَ (٥) تُبِعَ (٦) ثَمَرَ (٧) جَهِلَ

(٨) عَرَفَ (٩) حَنَثَ (١٠) خَيَّرَ (١١) دَسَرَ (١٢) ذَوَقَ (١٣) صَدَفَ (١٤) رَحِمَ

(١٥) رَزَقَ (١٦) سُطِرَ (١٧) فُتِحَ (١٨) ضُبِطَ (١٩) شَرِبَ (٢٠) أَكَلَ

Exercise No.13

(١) قَرَءْتُمْ (٢) سَتَعْلَمُ (٣) جَهْلُكَ (٤) قَضَيْتَ (٥) كَمْ لَبِثْتُمْ (٦) عَبْدُكَ

(٧) نَحْمَدُكَ (٨) مِنْ قَبْلِكُمْ (٩) أَرْسَلْتُمْ (١٠) فَرَغْتُمْ (١١) أَمِنْتُمْ

(١٢) لَمْ أَضْرِبْ (١٣) لَمْ يَكْذِبْ (١٤) أَمْرُكُمْ (١٥) أَجْرُكُمْ

Exercise No.14

(١) أَهَلَّنَا (٢) أَكَلَهَا (٣) أَرْضَنَا (٤) بِسِحْرِهِم (٥) تَكَادُ (٦) بَيْنَهُمَا

(٧) إِذَا (٨) لَأَنَا (٩) بِمَا (١٠) تَبْسُطُهَا (١١) عَرَضْنَا (١٢) غَزْلَهَا (١٣) أَصْوَافِهَا

(١٤) أَوْبَارِهَا (١٥) أَشْعَارِهَا

Exercise No.15

(١) نَاطِقِينَ (٢) مُسْلِمِينَ (٣) قَانِطِينَ (٤) يُوْعَدُ (٥) مُشْرِكِينَ (٦) نَاصِرِينَ

(٧) مِنْ بَعْدِهِ (٨) بِعِبَادِهِ (٩) جَاهِلِينَ (١٠) ظَهْرِهِ (١١) بَعْدَ ظُلْمِهِ

Exercise No.16

(١) ثُوْ (٢) زُوْ (٣) سُوْ (٤) شُوْ (٥) صُوْ (٦) زُوء (٧) غُوْ (٨) لُوْ (٩) نُوْ

(١٠) تُفْلِحُوْنَ (١١) دَاخِلُوْنَ (١٢) يَصْنَعُوْنَ (١٣) يُنْظَرُوْنَ (١٤) يَسْتَهْزِءُوْنَ

(١٥) يَشْعُرُوْنَ (١٦) يُلْحِدُوْنَ (١٧) يُبْصِرُوْنَ (١٨) مُسْلِمُوْنَ (١٩) دَرَجَاتُكُمْ

(٢٠) عَمَلُهُ (٢١) فِكْرُهُ (٢٢) نُورُهُ (٢٣) يَسْتَغْفِرُوْنَكُمْ (٢٤) شَهَادَتُهُ

(٢٥) قَوْمُهُ

Exercise No.17

(١) السَّمَاوَاتُ (٢) الدِّيْنُ (٣) الْجِنُّ (٤) الشَّمْسُ (٥) سَخَّرَ (٦) يُنَجِّيْكُمْ

(٧) الظَّالِمُونَ (٨) الْبَرُّ (٩) النَّاسُ (١٠) النَّارُ (١١) الذَّاكِرُونَ (١٢) الضَّلَالُ

(١٣) الْحَقُّ (١٤) يُحِبُّونَهُمْ (١٥) إِنَّكُمْ (١٦) يَظُنُّونَ (١٧) عَلَّمَ (١٨) حَرَّمْنَا

(١٩) بِمُعَذِّبِينَ (٢٠) حَجَّ (٢١) جَهَنَّمَ

Exercise No.18

(١) رَقِيبًا (٢) قَدِيْرًا (٣) قَابِض (٤) مُجِيْبًا (٥) مُبِيْنًا (٦) جَلِيْلٍ (٧) وَارِثُوْنَ

(٨) وَاسِعًا (٩) جَمِيْعٍ (١٠) حَقًّا (١١) جَمِيْعًا (١٢) غَافِرٌ

Lesson 1

Exercise No. 19

1: Construction of sentences:

أَ هَذَا كُرْسِيٌّ؟	أَ هَذَا كِتَابٌ؟	أَ هَذَا قَلَمٌ؟
هَلْ هَذَا وَلَدٌ؟	هَلْ هَذَا أَبٌ؟	هَلْ هَذَا رَجُلٌ؟
أَ هَذه زَهْرَةٌ؟	أَ هَذه مَائِدَةٌ؟	أَ هَذه غُرْفَةٌ؟
هَلْ هَذه بِنْتٌ؟	هَلْ هَذه امْرَأَةٌ؟	هَلْ هَذه أُمٌّ؟
هَلْ هَذه يَدٌ؟	هَلْ هَذه شَمْسٌ؟	هَلْ هَذه سَمَاءٌ؟

هُوَ أَبٌ.	هُوَ رَجُلٌ.	هُوَ وَلَدٌ.
هِيَ أُمٌّ.	هِيَ امْرَأَةٌ.	هِيَ بِنْتٌ.

2: Translation into Arabic:

نَعَمْ، هُوَ رَجُلٌ.	هَلْ هُوَ رَجُلٌ؟
نَعَمْ، هَذه زَهْرَةٌ.	هَلْ هَذه زَهْرَةٌ؟
لاَ، هَذه يَدٌ.	هَلْ هَذه عَيْنٌ؟
هَذَا رَجُلٌ.	مَنْ هَذَا؟
هِيَ أُمٌّ.	مَنْ هِيَ؟
لاَ، هَذه كَأْسٌ.	هَلْ هَذَا بَابٌ؟

لاَ،هَذه امْرَأَةٌ.	أ هَذه بنْتٌ؟
	هِيَ أُمٌّ وَهُوَ أَبٌ.

Lesson 2

Exercise No. 20

1: Construction of sentences:

أ هَذه الْجَنَّةُ؟	هَلْ هَذا الثَّوْبُ؟	أ هَذَا الـــتُّرَابُ؟
أ هَذَا النَّهَارُ؟	أ ذَلكَ الهُدَى؟	هَلْ هَذَا الْحَرْثُ؟
هَلْ هَذه الظُّلْمَةُ؟	أ تلْكَ الْفُلْكُ؟	هَلْ هَذَا اللَّيْلُ؟
أ ذَلكَ الذَّهَبُ؟	هَلْ هَذَا الصِّرَاطُ؟	أ هَذَا الطَّعَامُ ؟
		أ تلْكَ الدُّنْيَا؟

هُوَ دَخَلَ.	هُوَ كَاذبٌ.	هُوَجَلَسَ.	هُوَ فَعَلَ.
هِيَ جَلَسَتْ.	هِيَ خَرَجَتْ.	هِيَ ذَهَبَتْ.	هُوَ ضَعُفَ.
أَنْتَ صَدَقْتَ.	أَنْتَ جَلَسْتَ.	أَنْتَ كَذَبْتَ.	أَنْتَ سَمِعْتَ.

أَنَا عَالِـمٌ.	أَنَا قَارِئٌ.	أَنَا صَادِقٌ.	أَنْتَ جَهِلْتَ.
			أَنَا جَاهِلٌ.

2: Translation into Arabic:

هَذَا الثَّوبُ وَ تِلْكَ الفُلْكُ.	2	هَذَا التُّـرَاب وَ هَذِه الجَنَّةُ.	1
هَذِه الْيَدُ وَ ذَلِكَ الذَّهَبُ.	4	هَذِه الظُّلْمَةُ وَ ذَلِكَ النُّور.	3
هَذِه الدُّنْيَا وَ تِلْكَ السَّمَاءُ.	6	تِلْكَ الكَأْسُ وَ هَذِه زَهْرَةٌ.	5
عَلِمَ اللَّهُ وَ عَلِمَ الرَّسُولُ (ﷺ).	8	هَذِه طَرِيقٌ وَ تِلْكَ الفُلْكُ.	7
الأَبُ قَرَأَ وَ الْبِنْتُ سَمِعَتْ.	10	هِيَ أَكَلَتْ وَ شَرِبَتْ.	9
نَعَمْ كَتَبْتُ وَ قَرَأْتُ.	12	هَلْ كَتَبْتَ وَ قَرَأْتَ .	11
الْبِنْتُ قَارِئَةٌ وَ الْوَلَدُ سَامِعٌ.	14	خَرَجَ الكَاذِبُ وَ ذَهَبَ.	13
		كَتَبَ الْعَالِمُ وَ قَرَأَ الْكَاتِبُ.	15

3: Active participate singular, masculine, feminine, definite and indefinite:

دَخَلَ ، خَرَجَ ، ذَهَبَ ، ضَعُفَ

فَعَلَ	فَاعِلٌ	فَاعِلَةٌ	الفَاعِلُ	الفَاعِلَةُ
قَرَأَ	قَارِئٌ	قَارِئَةٌ	الْقَارِئُ	الْقَارِئَةُ
سَمِعَ	سَامِعٌ	سَامِعَةٌ	السَّامِعُ	السَّامِعَةُ
عَلِمَ	عَالِمٌ	عَالِمَةٌ	الْعَالِمُ	الْعَالِمَةُ
جَهِلَ	جَاهِلٌ	جَاهِلَةٌ	الْجَاهِلُ	الجَاهِلَةُ
كَتَبَ	كَاتِبٌ	كَاتِبَةٌ	الْكَاتِبُ	الْكَاتِبَةُ
صَدَقَ	صَادِقٌ	صَادِقَةٌ	الصَّادِقُ	الصَّادِقَةُ
كَذَبَ	كَاذِبٌ	كَاذِبَةٌ	الْكَاذِبُ	الْكَاذِبَةُ
أَكَلَ	آكِلٌ	آكِلَةٌ	الآكِلُ	الآكِلَةُ
شَرِبَ	شَارِبٌ	شَارِبَةٌ	الشَّارِبُ	الشَّارِبَةُ
جَلَسَ	جَالِسٌ	جَالِسَةٌ	الْجَالِسُ	الْجَالِسَةُ

Lesson 3

Exercise No. 21

1: Fill in the blank :

١.   هِيَ كَاتِبَةٌ بِـالْقَلَمِ.

٢.   ذَهَبْتُ مِنَ الْبَيْتِ إِلَى الْمَسْجِدِ.

٣.   قَرَأْتُ مِنَ الْكِتَابِ.

٤.   الْوَلَدُ خَرَجَ مِنَ الْبَيْتِ.

٥.   الْفُلْكُ فِي الْبَحْرِ.

٦.   الْكَأْسُ عَلَى الْمَائِدَةِ.

٧.   الْعَالِمُ جَالِسٌ عَلَى الْكُرْسِيِّ.

٨.   هُوَ أَكَلَ بِالْيَدِ.

٩.   أَنَا جَالِسٌ فِي الْمَسْجِدِ.

(2)   Translation into Arabic:

١. أَيْنَ الْبِنْتُ؟ اَلْبِنْتُ فِي غُرْفَتِهَا.

٢. اَللّٰهُ هُوَالْخَالِقُ وهُوَالْعَالِمُ و أَنَا جَاهِلٌ.

٣. مِنْ أَيْنَ دَخَلْتَ فِي الْبَيْتِ؟ دَخَلْتُ مِنْ الْبَابِ.

٤. مَنْ أَنت مَنْ هُوَ ومَنْ هِيَ؟

٥. بِمَ كَتَبْتَ؟ كَتَبْتُ بِالْقَلَمِ.

٦. اَلْأَرْضُ لِلّه وأَنَا لِلّه.

٧. يَا أَيُّهَا الْوَلَدُ مِنْ أَيْنَ ذَهَبْتَ؟

٨. رَجَعْتُ إِلَى الْبَيْتِ وجَلَسْتُ عَلَى الكُرْسِيِّ.

٩. عَلاَمَ جَلَسْتَ؟ جَلَسْتُ عَلَى الكُرْسِيِّ فِي غُرْفَتِي.

Lesson 4

Exercise No. 22

(1) Construction of sentences:

١. ذَهَبْتُ إِلَى بَيْتِ الله.

٢. قَرَأْتُ مِنَ القُرْآنِ فِي صَلاَةِ الفَجْرِ.

٣. سُورَةُ الرَّحْمَنِ مِنَ القُرْآنِ.

٤. ذَهَبْتُ مَعَ وَلَدِه.

٥. اِسْمِي عَبْدُاللهِ.

(2) The i'rāb

(١)   مَا اسْمُكَ؟

اِسْمِي أَحْمَدُ.

(٢)   الْكَافِرُ مَنْ كَفَرَ بِاللهِ.

(٣)   هُوَ أَبُوهُ وَهُوَ أَخِي.

(٤)   قَرَأْتُ مِنْ كِتَابِ اللهِ.

(٥)   هَذَا الْكِتَابُ لِمَسْجِدِي.

(٦)   أَنَا عَبْدُ اللهِ وَهُوَ كَافِرٌ بِاللهِ.

(٧)   مَنْ رَبُّ السَّمَاءِ وَرَبُّ الْأَرْضِ؟

(٨)   الْقُرْآنُ كِتَابُ اللهِ.

(٩)   أَيْنَ مَالُ الْأَبِ؟
       مَالُ الْأَبِ فِي بَيْتِهِ.

(١٠)   مِنْ ظُلْمَةِ اللَّيْلِ إِلَى ضِيَاءِ النَّهَارِ

(3) Translation into Arabic:

١. هَلْ قَرَأْتَ مِنْ كِتَابِ اللهِ؟ نَعَمْ قَرَأْتُ مِنْ كِتَابِ
   اللهِ.

٢. يَا وَلَدُ مَا اسْمُكَ؟ مَنْ أَنْتَ؟ وَأَيْنَ بَيْتُكَ؟

٣. أَنَا فِي بَيْتِي وَ أَنْتَ فِي بَيْتِكَ.

٤. هَلْ ذَهَبْتَ إِلَى بَيْتِ أَخِيكَ؟

٥. أَكَلْتُ طَعَامِي بِيَدِي فِي غُرْفَةِ الطَّعَامِ.

٦. جَزَاءُ الْجَنَّةِ وَعَذَابُ النَّارِ مِنَ اللهِ.

٧. أَنَا مَعَ اللهِ وَهُوَ رَبُّ السَّمَاءِ وَ الْأَرْضِ.

٨. قُلْتُ أَنَا صَائِمٌ لِوَجْهِ اللهِ. قَالَ أَنْتَ صَائِمٌ.

٩. قَالَ رَسُولُ اللهِ صَلَّى اللهُ عَلَيْهِ وَسَلَّمَ: الْأَرْضُ مَسْجِدٌ.

١٠. قَامَ فِي مَسْجِدِ الرَّسُولِ صَلَّى اللهُ عَلَيْهِ وَسَلَّمَ.

Lesson 5

Exercise No. 23

(1) III F[1], II M[1], II F[1], I M[1]+F[1]:

كَانَ، سَعَى، فَازَ، تَابَ، دَعَا، هَدَى، نَهَى.

كُنْتُ	كُنْتِ	كُنْتَ	كَائَتْ	كَانَ
سَعَيْتُ	سَعَيْتِ	سَعَيْتَ	سَعَتْ	سَعَى
فُزْتُ	فُزْتِ	فُزْتَ	فَازَتْ	فَازَ
تُبْتُ	تُبْتِ	تُبْتَ	تَابَتْ	تَابَ
دَعَوْتُ	دَعَوْتِ	دَعَوْتَ	دَعَتْ	دَعَا
هَدَيْتُ	هَدَيْتِ	هَدَيْتَ	هَدَتْ	هَدَى
نَهَيْتُ	نَهَيْتِ	نَهَيْتَ	نَهَتْ	نَهَى

(2) Fill in the blank:

(١)   أَكَلْتُ قَبْلَ الصَّلَاةِ .

كِتَابِي عِنْدَ وَلَدِهِ .

(٢)   السَّمَاءُ فَوْقَ الْأَرْضِ .

638

(٣) الأَرْضُ تَحْتَ السَّمَاءِ .

(٤) شَرِبْتُ مَعَ الطَّعَامِ .

(٥) ذَهَبْتُ مَعَ وَلَدِي .

(٦) الْمَسْجِدُ أَمَامَ بَيْتِي، وَحَرْثِي خَلْفَ بَيْتِي .

(3) The *i'rab*

(١) ذَهَبْتُ إِلَى الْمَسْجِدِ لِلصَّلَاةِ مَعَ أَبِي .

(٢) هَلْ رَضِيتَ بِاللهِ ؟

نَعَمْ، رَضِيتُ بِاللهِ وَهُوَ وَخَالِقِي السَّمَاءُ مَخْلُوقَةُ

الله .

(٣) ذَهَبْتُ إِلَى الْمَسْجِدِ قَبْلَ الصَّلَاةِ وَرَجَعْتُ إِلَى

الْبَيْتِ بَعْدَ الصَّلَاةِ .

(٤) اَللهُ هُوَ الْمَعْبُودُ وَأَنَا عَبْدُ اللهِ .

(٥) أَمَا نَهَيْتَ ؟ بَلَى، نَهَيْتُ .

(٦) هَلْ كَتَبْتَ ؟ لَا، مَا كَتَبْتُ .

(4) Construction of sentences:

١: اَلْكِتَابُ مَكْتُوبٌ. ٢: اَلطَّعَامُ مَأْكُولٌ. ٣: اَلْوَلَدُ مَضْرُوبٌ ٤:

اَلْأَرْضُ مَخْلُوقَةٌ.

٥: اَلْمَاءُ مَشْرُوبٌ

639

(5) Translation into Arabic:

١: يَااللَّهُ أَنْتَ خَلَقْتَني وَ أَنَا مَخْلُوقٌ. ٢: بَيْتي أَمَامَ المَسْجِدِ وَ حَرْثي خَلْفَ المَسْجِد.

٣: هَل أَكَلْتَ قَبْلَ الصَّلاَةِ أَمْ بعْدَ الصَّلاَةِ. ٤: اَلسَّمَاءُ فَوْقَ الفُلْك والمَاءُ تَحْتَ الفُلْك.

٥: كِتَابي عِنْدَكَ. (مَعَكَ) ٦:ذَهَبْتُ مَعَ أَبي إِلَى الْجَنَّة

٧: مَا دَخَلْتُ في الحَرْث. ذَهَبْتُ إِلَى المَّسْجِدِ للصَّلاَة.

٨: أَمَا كَفَرَ بِالشَّيْطانِ؟ نَعَمْ كَفَرْبه.

٩:أَمَرْتَني بِالْخَيْرِ.

١٠ : الْكِتَابُ مَكْتُوبٌ وَمَقْرُوْءٌ.

(6) Active Participle and Passive Participle [singular, masculine, feminine, definite, and indefinite]:

فَعَلَ، قَرَأَ، سَمِعَ، عَلِمَ، جَهِلَ، كَتَبَ، صَدَقَ، كَذَبَ، أَكَلَ، شَرِبَ

الْفَاعِلَةُ	الْفَاعِلُ	فَاعِلَةٌ	فَاعِلٌ	فَعَلَ
الْقَارِئَةُ	الْقَارِئُ	قَارِئَةٌ	قَارِئٌ	قَرَأَ
السَّامِعَةُ	السَّامِعُ	سَامِعَةٌ	سَامِعٌ	سَمِعَ
الْعَالِمَةُ	الْعَالِمُ	عَالِمَةٌ	عَالِمٌ	عَلِمَ

الْجَاهِلَةُ	الْجَاهِلُ	جَاهِلَةٌ	جَاهِلٌ	جَهِلَ
الْكَاتِبَةُ	الْكَاتِبُ	كَاتِبَةٌ	كَاتِبٌ	كَتَبَ
الصَّادِقَةُ	الصَّادِقُ	صَادِقَةٌ	صَادِقٌ	صَدَقَ
الْكَاذِبَةُ	الْكَاذِبُ	كَاذِبَةٌ	كَاذِبٌ	كَذَبَ
الآكِلَةُ	الآكِلُ	آكِلَةٌ	آكِلٌ	أَكَلَ
الشَّارِبَةُ	الشَّارِبُ	شَارِبَةٌ	شَارِبٌ	شَرِبَ
الْجَالِسَةُ	الْجَالِسُ	جَالِسَةٌ	جَالِسٌ	جَلَسَ

Passive Participle [singular, masculine, feminine, definite, and indefini

الْمَفْعُولَةُ	الْمَفْعُولُ	مَفْعُولَةٌ	مَفْعُولٌ
الْمَقْرُوءَةُ	الْمَقْرُوءُ	مَقْرُوءَةٌ	مَقْرُوءٌ
الْمَسْمُوعَةُ	الْمَسْمُوعُ	مَسْمُوعَةٌ	مَسْمُوعٌ
الْمَعْلُومَةُ	الْمَعْلُومُ	مَعْلُومَةٌ	مَعْلُومٌ
الْمَجْهُولَةُ	الْمَجْهُولُ	مَجْهُولَةٌ	مَجْهُولٌ
الْمَكْتُوبَةُ	الْمَكْتُوبُ	مَكْتُوبَةٌ	مَكْتُوبٌ
الْمَصْدُوقَةُ	الْمَصْدُوقُ	مَصْدُوقَةٌ	مَصْدُوقٌ
الْمَكْذُوبَةُ	الْمَكْذُوبُ	مَكْذُوبَةٌ	مَكْذُوبٌ
الْمَأْكُولَةُ	الْمَأْكُولُ	مَأْكُولَةٌ	مَأْكُولٌ
الْمَشْرُوبَةُ	الْمَشْرُوبُ	مَشْرُوبَةٌ	مَشْرُوبٌ

(7) Identification of 'Construct Phrases':

٣: كَلِمَةُ ٱللَّهِ	: بِكُلِّ شَىْءٍ
٥: خَلْقُ كُلِّ شَىْءٍ	٤: رَبُّكَ ، كُلِّ شَىْءٍ
٧: أَرْضُ الله	٦: غَيْرُ ٱللَّهِ
٩: أَمْرُ ٱللَّهِ	٨: كُلُّ نَفْسٍ
١: كُلُّ نَفْسٍ ذَآئِقَةُ ٱلْمَوْتِ	١٠: سَكْرَةُ ٱلْمَوْتِ
١٣: أَخِى	١٢: جَنَّتَهُ، لِنَفْسِهِ
١٦: رَّسُولُ ٱللَّهِ	١٤: أَهْلِهَا
١٩: سَبِيلِ ٱللَّهِ	١٧: رَبِّي

Lesson 6

Exercise No. 24

(1) Fill in the blank :

(١) غَسَلْتُ الثَّوْبَ فَالثَّوْبُ مَغْسُوْلٌ.

(٢) أَكَلْتُ الطَّعَامَ فَالطَّعَامُ مَأْكُوْلٌ.

(٣) شَرِبْتُ الْمَاءَ فَالْمَاءُ مَشْرُوبٌ.

(٤) نَصَرْتُ الرَّجُلَ فَالرَّجُلُ مَنْصُورٌ.

(٥) ضَرَبَ الْأَبُ الْوَلَدَ فَالْوَلَدُ مَضْرُوبٌ.

(٦) حَفِظَ الرَّجُلُ الْبَيْتَ فَالْبَيْتُ مَحْفُوْظٌ.

(٧) كَتَبْتُ الْكِتَابَ فَالْكِتَابُ مَكْتُوبٌ.

(٨) فَتَحْتُ الْبَابَ فَالْبَابُ مَفْتُوْحٌ.

(٩) غَسَلْتُ الْعَيْنَ فَالْعَيْنُ مَغْسُوْلَةٌ.

(١٠) فَرَّ الْوَلَدُ مِنَ الْبَيْتِ فَالْوَلَدُ فَارٌّ.

(2) The i'rāb

(١) لَقِيَ زَيْدٌ رَجُلاً.

(٢) فَتَحْتُ الْقُرْآنَ فَالْقُرْآنُ مَفْتُوْحٌ.

(٣) هَلْ قَرَأْتَ الْكِتَابَ؟

مَا قَرَأْتُ الْكِتَابَ.

(٤) الْوَلَدُ يَقْرَأُ الْقُرْآنَ والْأُمُّ تَسْمَعُهُ.

(٥) الْبِنْتُ تَشْرَبُ الْمَاءَ والْوَلَدُ يَشْرَبُ اللَّبَنَ.

(٦) أَنْتَ تَذْهَبُ إِلَى الْمَدْرَسَةِ وأَنْتِ تَأْكُلِيْنَ الطَّعَامَ.

(٧) أَنَا أَكْتُبُ الْكِتَابَ وبِنْتِي تَجْلِسُ عَلَى الْكُرْسِي أَمَامِي.

(٨) الْبِنْتُ تَعُوْدُ مِنَ الْمَسْجِدِ وتَقْرَأُ الْقُرْآنَ فِي الْبَيْتِ.

(٩) النَّفْسُ تَلُوْمُ عَلَى الشَّرِّ وتَرْضَى بِالْخَيْرِ.

643

(١٠) هَلْ أَنْتَ تَعْصِينَ اللهَ وَالرَّسُولَ (ﷺ)؟

(١١) أَنَا أَرْجُوْ مِنْكَ خَيْراً.

(١٢) هُوَ يَتْلُوْ القُرْآنَ وَيَبْكِي.

(١٣) تَرَى فِي الدُّنْيَا خَيْراً وَشَرّاً.

(١٤) هَلْ تَرْضَى بِجَزَائِي لَكَ؟

(١٥) أَنْتَ تَمُوْتُ وَالدُّنْيَا تَفْنَى.

(١٦) هُوَ يَسْعَى وَيَقُوْلُ: أَنَا فَائِزٌ فِي الدُّنْيَا.

(١٧) يَقُوْل الإِنْسَانُ يَوْمَئِذٍ أَيْنَ المَفَرُّ.

(3) The Imperfect:

٤: يَفْهَمُ	٣: تَعْلَمُ	٢: أَكْتُبُ	١: تَقْرَئِينَ
٨: يَجْلِسُ	٧: تَجْهَلُ	٦: أَنْصُرُ	٥: تَسْمَعُ
١٢: تَقُوْلُ	١١: أَتْلُوْ	١٠: تَخْرُجِيْنَ	٩: تَدْخُلُ
١٦: تَعْصِي	١٥: يَرْجُوْ	١٤: تَرَى	١٣: تَدْعِيْنَ
٢٠: أَسْعَى	١٩: تَفُوْزِيْنَ	١٨: تَفْنَى	١٧: تَخْشَى
٢٤: تَبْكِيْنَ	٢٣: أَثُوْبُ	٢٢: يَهْدِي	٢١: تَلُوْمُ
٢٨: تَكُوْنِيْنَ	٢٧: أَعُوْدُ	٢٦: يَرْضَى	٢٥:

644

			تَمُوتُ

(4) Translation into Arabic:

١ : الطَّعَامُ مَأْكُولٌ وَالْيَدُ مَغْسُولَةٌ

٢ : شَرِبَت الأُمُّ اللَّبَنَ وَ شَرِبَ الأَبُ المَاءَ.

٣ : أَذْهَبُ إِلَى المَسْجِد للصَّلاَة.

٤ : هَل تَقْرَأُ الْكِتَابَ؟

٥ : هَلْ تَغْسِلِينَ غُرْفَةَ الطَّعَامِ؟

٦ : هَلْ أَبُوكَ وَأَخُوْهُ فِي الْمَسْجِد.

٧ : اسْمُ كِتَاب رَبِّي الْقُرْآنُ.

٨ : أَنَا أَعْبُدُ اللهَ وَهُوَ رَبِّي.

٩ : هِيَ تَكْتُبُ وَ أَنَا أَقْرَأُ.

١٠ : أَدْخُلُ فِي بَيْت ابْنِي.

١١ : هَلْ تَقْرَأُ الْقُرْآنَ فِي بَيْتِكَ؟ نَعَمْ أَقْرَأُ الْقُرْآنَ فِي بَيْتِي.

١٢ : هُوَ يَبْكِي وَ يَتُوبُ إِلَى الله.

١٣ : هَلْ تَعُوْدُ إِلَى بَيْتِكَ مِنْ مَسْجِدالنَّبِيِّ(ﷺ)؟

١٤ : نَعَمْ، أَعُوْدُ بَعْدَ الصَّلاَة.

١٥ : هَلْ تَعْصِينَ اللهَ وَ رَسُوْلَهُ؟ لاَ، أَ عْصِيْ اللهَ وَ رَسُوْلَهُ (ﷺ).

١٦ : أَقْرَأُ الْقُرْآنَ وَ أَتُوبُ إِلَى الله.

١٧ : الْجَاهِلُ يَطْلُبُ الدُّنْيَا وَ يَرْضَى بِالدُّنْيَا.

١٨ : يَسْعَى الْعَالِمُ لِلْآخِرَة.

١٩ : هُوَ لاَ يَعْبُدُ مَخْلُوقَ اللّه.

٢٠ : تَعْبُدُ اللّهَ وَ تَرْجِعُ إِلَيْهِ.

(5) Idenfication of Imperfect and Object :

١ : يَعْبُدُ (Imperfect)، اللّهَ (Object)

٢ : يَعْلَمُ (Imperfect)، الْقَوْلَ (Object)

٣ : يَعْلَمُ (Imperfect)، الْجَهْرَ (Object)

٤ : يَعْلَمُ، يَلِجُ، تَخْرُجُ (Imperfect)

٥ : تَسْقُطُ، يَعْلَمُ (Imperfect)

٦ : يَعْلَمُ، تَحْمِلُ (Imperfect)

٧ : تَحْمِلُ، تَضَعُ (Imperfect)

٨ : يَعْلَمُ، تَكْسِبُ (Imperfect)

٩ : يَعْلَمُ (Imperfect)، تَأْوِيلَهُ (Object)

١٠ : تَعْلَمُ، أَعْلَمُ (Imperfect)

١١ : تَكْسِبُ (Imperfect)

١٢: مَقَامَ، ٱلنَّفْسَ (Object)

١٣: أَمْلِكُ (Imperfect)، نَفْعًا، ضَرًّا (Object)

١٤: يَنصُرُانِى (Imperfect+ Object)

١٥: يَظْلِمُ (Imperfect)، أَحَدًا (Object)

١٦: يَدْرَؤُاْ (Imperfect)، ٱلْعَذَابَ (Object)

١٧: أَعْبُد (Imperfect)

١٨: يَفِرُّ (Imperfect)، ٱلْمَرْءُ (Object)

١٩: يَقُولُ (Imperfect)

٢٠: ٱلرَّسُولَ (Imperfect)

٢٢: يَنصُرُانِى (Imperfect+ Object)

٢٣: يَهْدِى، يَشَآءُ (Imperfect)، مَن (Object)

٢٤: كُلَّ ، عِلْمًا (Imperfect)

٢٥: يَهْدِى، يَشَآءُ (Imperfect)، مَن (Object)

٢٦: يَقُولُ، يَهْدِى (Imperfect)، ٱلْحَقَّ، ٱلسَّبِيلَ (Object)

٢٧: يَهْدِى، (Imperfect)

٢٨: ٱلَّيْلَ (Object)

647

٢٩ :كُلَّ (Object)

٣٠ :ٱلنَّهَارَ، نُشُورًا (Object)

٣١ :سِرَاجًا (Object)

٣٢ ٱلشَّمْسَ ، سِرَاجًا (Object)

٣٣ :ٱلشَّمْسَ ، ضِيَاءً (Object)

٣٤ :كُلَّ (Object)

٣٥ :غِشَوَةً (Object)

٣٦ :بَشَرًا (Object)

٣٧ :يَشْفِينِ . (Object +Imperfect)

Lesson 7

Exercise No.25

(1) Fill in the blank:

(١)   هَذَا رَجُلٌ صَالِحٌ.

(٢)   هَذِه الْبِنْتُ جَمِيلَةٌ.

(٣)   ذَهَبْتُ إِلَى الْمَسْجِدِ مَعَ رَجُلٍ طَوِيْلٍ.

(٤)   رَأَيْتُ الْبَيْتَ الْكَبِيْرَ.

(٥)   كَتَبْتُ بِالْقَلَمِ الصَّغِيْرِ.

(2) The *i'rāb*

١) تَكْسِبُ الظَّالِمَةُ إِثْماً عَظِيماً.

٢) النَّفْسُ الْمُطْمَئِنَّةُ خَيْرٌ مِنْ النَّفْسِ اللائِمَةِ.

٣) هَلْ تَشُكِّينَ فِي كِتَابِ اللهِ؟

٤) أَنَا لاَ أَشُكُّ فِي كِتَابِ اللهِ.

٥) هَلْ تُحِبُّ اللهَ الوَاحِدَ؟

٦) أَنَا أُحِبُّ اللهَ السَّمِيعَ العَلِيمَ.

٧) القُرْآنُ الكَرِيمُ كِتَابُ اللهِ.

٨) رَجُلٌ قَوِيٌّ خَيْرٌ مِنْ رَجُلٍ ضَعِيفٍ.

٩) بِنْتٌ جَمِيلَةٌ صَادِقَةٌ.

١٠) الْوَلَدُ الصَّغِيرُ يَقْرَأُ كِتَابَ اللهِ فِي غُرْفَتِهِ.

١١) إِنَّ اللهَ سَمِيعٌ عَلِيمٌ.

١٢) لَيْتَنِي سَمِعْتُ قَوْلَكَ.

١٣) إِنَّ رَبَّكَ هُوَ الذِي خَلَقَ وَهَدَى.

١٤) إِنَّ الْمَرْأَةَ الْجَمِيلَةَ الَّتِي تَقْرَأُ القُرْآنَ تَفُوزُ فِي الدُّنْيَا وَالآخِرَةِ.

١٥) إِنَّ اللهَ لاَ يَأْمُرُ بِالشَّرِّ وَلَكِنَّهُ يَأْمُرُ بِالْخَيْرِ.

١٦) لَعَلَّ الوَلَدَ الَّذِي يَسْعَى يَفُوزُ فِي سَعْيِهِ.

١٧) إِنَّ اللهَ لَمَعَ الرَّجُلِ الصَّالِحِ.

(١٨)   إِنَّ مُحَمَّداً لَرَسُوْلُ الله (ﷺ).

(١٩)   أَنَا أَعْبُدُ اللهَ كَأَنِّـي أَرَاهُ.

(٢٠)   إِنَّ اللهَ لاَ يَظْلِمُ الإِنْسَانَ ولَكِنَّ الإِنْسَانَ يَظْلِمُ نَفْسَهُ.

(3) Translation into Arabic:

١: يَا أَخِي أَيْنَ تَذهَبُ هَلْ تَرْضَى عَنِّي.

٢: صِحَّةُ ابْنِ أَخِي طَيِّبَةٌ.

٣: الْوَلَدُ الْقَصِيْرُ يَقْرَأُ الْقُرْآنَ الْكَرِيْمَ وَ أُمَّهُ الْعَالِمَةُ تَسْمَعُهُ.

٤: أَبٌ طَوِيْلٌ يَذْهَبُ إِلَى مَسْجِد النَّبِي للصَّلاَةِ.

٥: رَأَيْتُ الزَّهْرَةَ الْجَمِيْلَةَ عَلَى الْمَائِدَةِ الْكَبِيْرَة.

٦: هِيَ تُحِبُّ اللهَ السَّمِيْعَ العَلِيْمَ.

٧: زَيْدٌ يَظْلِمُ رَجُلاً طَوِيلاً واسْمُهُ أَحْمَدُ

٨: هَلْ تَشُكُّ فِي كِتَاب الله.

٩: وَلَدٌ عَالِمٌ خَيْرٌ مِنْ وَلَد جَاهِلٍ.

١٠: بِنْتٌ جَمِيْلَةٌ تَقْرَأُ الْقُرْآنَ الْكَرِيْمَ.

١١: وَلَدٌ قَوِيٌّ يَعْمَلُ فِي حَرْث الأَبِ.

١٢: النَّفْسُ الْمُطْمَئِنَّةُ تَدْخُلُ الْجَنَّةَ.

١٣: إِنَّ مُوْسَى عَلَيْه السَّلاَمُ رَسُولُ الله.

١٤: إِنَّ رَبَّكَ لَيَعْلَمُ مَا تَقُوْلُ وَتَسْمَعُ.

١٥: إِنَّ الْعَالِمَ لاَ يَمُوْتُ بِمَوْتِه وَلَكِنَّ الْجَاهِلَ يَمُوْتُ.

١٦: اَلْمَرْأَةُ الَّتِي تَقْرَأُ الْقُرْآنَ أُخْتِي.

١٧: اَلْوَلَدُ الطَّوِيلُ الَذِي يَقْرَأُ الْقُرْآنَ لَفَائِزٌ.

١٨:أَنَا أُحِبُّ اللهَ وَإِنَّ اللهَ خَالِقِي وَ خَالِقُكَ.

(4) Identification of the adjectives (Adj.), predicate of إِنَّ and her sisters:

1. الرَّحْمَنِ، الرَّحِيمِ (Adj.)

2. رَحِيمٌ، وَدُودٌ (Predicate)

3. التَّوَّابُ الرَّحِيمُ (Predicate)

4. رَءُوفٌ رَحِيمٌ (Predicate)

5. قَرِيبٌ (Predicate)

6. حَفِيْظٌ (Predicate)

7. السَّمِيعُ الْعَلِيمُ (Predicate)

9. عَظِيْمٌ (Adj.)

10. الْعَزِيْزُ الْحَكِيْمُ (Predicate)

12. غَنِيٌّ كَرِيْمٌ (Predicate)

13. يَسِيْرٌ (Predicate)

14. وَاسِعَةٌ (Predicate)

18. مُسْتَقِيمٍ (Adj.)

20. وَاحِدَةً (Adj.)

651

21. طَيِّبَةً، طَيِّبَةٍ، ثَابِتٌ   (Adj.)

22. مُبِين   (Adj.)

23. الحَيُّ القَيُّومُ   (Adj.)

24. العَظِيمِ   (Adj.)

25. مُسْتَقِيمٍ   (Adj.)

28. مُبِينٌ   (Adj.)

31. كَثِيراً   (Adj.)

32. الْحَرَامَ   (Adj.)

33. زَكِيَّةً   (Adj.)

34. عَالِيَة   (Adj.)

35. كَبِيراً   (Adj.)

36. وَاقِعٍ   (Adj.)

37. العَظِيْمِ   (Adj.)

39. كَرِيْمٍ   (Adj.)

43. قَدِيْرٌ   (Predicate)

48. عَلِيْمٌ   (Predicate)

49. لَطِيفٌ، العَلِيْمُ الحَكِيْمُ   (Predicate)

50. الْخَلَّقُ العَلِيْمُ   (Predicate)

55. غَفُوْرٌ رَّحِيْمٌ   (Predicate)

56. وَاحِدَةٌ   (Adj.)

57. اَلدُّنْيَا   (Adj.)

57. لَعِبٌ   (Predicate)

59. عَلِيْمٌ   (Predicate)

62. لَرَسُولُهُ   (Predicate)

63. لَسَمِيْعٌ   (Predicate)

64. اليَقِيْنِ   (Predicate)

65. القَدِيْمِ   (Adj.)

67. لَوَاقِع   (Predicate)

69. تَذْكِرَة   (Predicate)

70. كَرِيْمٌ   (Adj.)

71. فَضْلٌ   (Adj.)

72. لَذُوْ فَضْلٍ   (Predicate)

Lesson 8

Exercise No. 27

(1) Construction of sentences using إِنَّ and her sisters:

١ : إِنَّ اللهَ يَعْلَمُ وَ أَنَالاَ أَعْلَمُ.

٢ : إِنَّ زَيْدًارَجُلٌ عَالِمٌ.

٣ : إِنَّ الْقُرْآنَ الْكَرِيْمَ كِتَابُ اللّهِ.

٤ : إِنَّ اللهَ جَمِيلٌ.

٥ : إِنَّ الْعِلْمَ يَنْفَعُ النَّاسَ.

(2) Construction of sentences using the Second Derived Form:
فَعَّلَ.

١ : الْمُعَلِّمُ يُعَلِّمُني الْقُرْآنَ الْكَرِيمَ ٢ : أَحْمَدُ يُكَرِّمُ الضَّيْفَ.

٣ : نَزَّلَ اللَّهُ الْقُرْآنَ تَنْزِيلاً. ٤ : حَرَّمَ اللَّهُ الْمُنْكَرَ

٥ : أَنَا أُعَلِّمُ الطَّالِبَ الْقُرْآنَ الْكَرِيمَ.

(3) Construct of the sentences:

هَذَانِ أَبَوَانِ. هَاتَانِ عَيْنَانِ. ذَانِكَ قَلَمَانِ.

تَانِكَ يَدَانِ. هَذَانِ وَلَدَانِ. هَاتَانِ عَلاَمَتَانِ.

ذَانِكَ كِتَابَانِ. تَانِكَ جَنَّتَانِ. هَذَانِ كُرْسِيَّانِ.

هَاتَانِ بِنْتَانِ. ذَانِكَ خُبْزَانِ. تَانِكَ كَأْسَانِ.

هَذَانِ بَحْرَانِ. هَاتَانِ زَهْرَتَانِ. ذَانِكَ رَجُلاَنِ.

تَانِكَ امْرَأَتَانِ. هَاتَانِ غُرْفَتَانِ. تَانِكَ مَائِدَتَانِ. تَانِكَ فُلْكَانِ.

هَذَان	
هَاتَان	عَيْنَان، أَبَوَان، مَائِدَتَان، قَلَمَان، يَدَان، وَلَدَان، عَلَامَتَان،
ذَانِكَ	كِتَابَان، جَنَّتَان، بِنْتَان، كَأْسَان، كُرْسِيَّان، فُلْكَان،
تَانِكَ	خُبْزَان، غُرْفَتَان، بَحْرَان، زَهْرَتَان، رَجُلَان، امْرَأَتَان

(4) Fill in the blank:

(١)   هُوَ يَشْكُرُ اللهَ شُكْرًا كَثِيرًا.

(٢)   هُوَ يَقُومُ فِي صَلَاةِ اللَّيْلِ قِيَامًا طَوِيلاً.

(٣)   مَاتَ أَبِي فَصَبَرْتُ صَبْرًا جَمِيلاً.

(٤)   حَفِظْتُ الْقُرْآنَ حِفْظًا قَوِيًّا.

(٥)   ذَكَرْتُ اللهَ ذِكْرًا كَثِيرًا.

(5) Put i‘rāb

(١)   قَامَ أَحْمَدُ فِي اللَّيْلِ وَذَكَرَ اللهَ ذِكْراً كَثِيراً.

(٢)   الظَّالِمُ يَظْلِمُ ظُلْماً كَثِيراً.

(٣)   هَاتَانِ عَلَامَتَان وَهَذَانِ رَجُلَانِ قَصِيرَانِ.

(٤)   نَزَّلَ اللهُ الْقُرْآنَ تَنْزِيلاً.

(٥)   أَنَا مُعَلِّمُ الْقُرْآنِ وَمُبَلِّغُ الْإِسْلَامِ.

(٦)   هُوَ يُصَلِّي الصَّلَاةَ لِذِكْرِ اللهِ.

(٧) هَلْ أَنْتَ تُحِبُّ اللهَ السَّمِيعَ الْعَلِيمَ؟

(٨) أَنَا مُدَرِّسٌ أُدَرِّسُ ابْنِي الْقِرَاءَةَ وَالْكِتَابَةَ.

(٩) مَنْ يُصَلِّي الصَّلَاةَ بِخُشُوعٍ يَفُوزْ فِي الدُّنْيَا وَالآخِرَةِ.

(١٠) اَلْقُرْآنَ تَنْـزِيلٌ مِنَ اللهِ وَأَنَا أُحِبُّهُ.

(5) Translation into Arabic:

١ : ذَانِكَ الْقَلَمَانِ عَلَى الْمَائِدَةِ.

٢ : عَيْنَانِ جَمِيلَتَانِ وَكَبِيرَتَانِ.

٣ : وَلَدَانِ صَغِيرَانِ يَجْلِسَانِ عَلَى مَائِدَتَيْنِ.

٤ : أَعْبُدُاللهَ لِأَنِّي أُحِبُّ اللهَ حُبًّا كَثِيرًا.

٥ : الصَّلَاةُ لِتَطْهِيرِ الْقَلْبِ. (الروح).

٦ : غَضِبْتُ غَضَبًا شَدِيدًا لِأَنَّهُ كَذَبَ.

٧ : نَزَّلَ اللهُ الْقُرْآنَ إِلَى رَسُولِه (ﷺ).

٨ : تَحْقِيرُ الْإِنْسَانِ عَمَلٌ قَبِيحٌ.

٩ : تَدْرِيسُ الْقُرْآنِ عَمَلٌ جَمِيلٌ.

١٠ : يَا اللَّهُ أَدْعُو الصَّبْرَ.

(6) Identification of Derived form II Perfect, Imperfect and Verbal Noun:

1. نَزَّلَ Perf² IIIM¹

    مُصَدِّقًا AP² M¹

2. يُبَشِّرُكَ Imp² III M¹

    مُصَدِّقًا AP² M¹

3. صَدَّقَ Perf² IIIM¹

    كَذَّبَ Perf² IIIM¹

4. يُقَدِّرُ Imp² III M¹

5. فَكَّرَ Perf² IIIM¹

    قَدَّرَ Perf² IIIM¹

6. فَسَوَّىٰ Perf² IIIM¹

    قَدَّرَ Perf² IIIM¹

7. سَبَّحَ Perf² IIIM¹

8. يُسَبِّحُ Imp² III M¹

9. تَسْبِيحَ(هُ) VN²

10. سَخَّرَ Perf² IIIM¹

    مُسَمَّى IIAP² M¹

11. تُعِزُّ Imp² II M¹

    تُذِلُّ Imp² II M¹

12. صَدَّقَ Perf² IIIM¹

13. كَلَّمَ Perf² IIIM¹

    تَكْلِيمًا VN²

14. تَنزِيلُ VN²

15. مُنَزَّلٌ PP²

16. (يُعَلِّمُهُ) Imp² III M¹

17. تَقْدِيرٌ VN²

18. (يُكَذِّبُكَ) Imp² III M¹

19. قَدَّمَتْ Perf² III F¹

20. قَدَّمْتُ Perf² IM¹ +F¹

21. مُصَدِّقٌ AP² M¹

25. نَزَّلَ Perf² IIIM¹

26. يُكَلِّفُ Imp² III M¹

Lesson 9

Exercise No. 28

(1) Fill in the blank:

(١) هُمَا يَذْهَبَانِ إِلَى الْمَسْجِدِ لِلصَّلَوةِ.

(٢) بِنْتَانِ جَمِيلَتَانِ ذَاهِبَتَانِ مِنَ الْمَدْرَسَةِ إِلَى بَيْتِهِمَا.

(٣) . ذَلِكَ الْأَبَوَانِ يَرْجِعَانِ مِنَ الْحَرْثِ إِلَى الْبَيْتِ.

(٤) لَقِيْتُ وَلَدَيْنِ ذَوَيْ عِلْمٍ.

(٥) الْمُؤْمِنُ مَنْ آمَنَ بِاللهِ.

(٦) الْمُحْسِنُ مَنْ أَحْسَنَ إِلَى النَّاسِ.

(٧) الْكَافِرُ مَنْ كَفَرَ بِاللهِ.

(٨) نَحْنُ نَقْرَأُ مِنَ الْقُرْآنِ الْكَرِيْمِ.

(٩) بَابَا الْبَيْتِ كَبِيرَانِ.

(١٠) الظَّالِمَةُ تَكْسِبُ إِثْماً عَظِيْماً.

(2) The *i'rāb*

(١) دَاوُدُ وَ مُوسَى عَلَيْهِمَا السَّلاَمُ رَسُوْلاَنِ.

(٢) اَلْمُعَلِّمُ يُعَلِّمُ الْقِرَاءَةَ وَ الْكِتَابَةَ.

(٣) أَطْعَمْتُ الْفَقِيرَ فَرَضِيَ عَنِّي وَ دَعَا لِي.

(٤) أَدْخَلَ الْأَبُ الْوَلَدَ الطَّوِيْلَ فِي الْبَيْتِ.

(٥) أَنَا أُحِبُّ اللهَ حُبّاً شَدِيداً..

(3) : The Perfect and Imperfect Form in IIIM^2, IIIF^2, IIM^2, IIF^2 and I M^{2,3} + F$^{2,3+}$ for the following verbs.

Perfect form in IIIM^2, IIIF^2, IIM^2, IIF^2 and I M^{2,3} + F$^{2,3+}$:

I M^{2,3} + F$^{2,3+}$	IIF^2	IIM^2	IIIF^2	IIIM^2	Verbs
ذَهَبْنَا	ذَهَبْتِ	ذَهَبْتَ	ذَهَبَتَا	ذَهَبَا	ذَهَبَ
قَرَأْنَا	قَرَأْتِ	قَرَأْتَ	قَرَأَتَا	قَرَآ	قَرَأَ
أَدْخَلْنَا	أَدْخَلْتِ	أَدْخَلْتَ	أَدْخَلَتَا	أَدْخَلَا	أَدْخَلَ
أَخْرَجْنَا	أَخْرَجْتِ	أَخْرَجْتَ	أَخْرَجَتَا	أَخْرَجَا	أَخْرَجَ
أَحْسَنَّا	أَحْسَنْتِ	أَحْسَنْتَ	أَحْسَنَتَا	أَحْسَنَا	أَحْسَنَ
حَسَّنَّا	حَسَّنْتِ	حَسَّنْتَ	حَسَّنَتَا	حَسَّنَا	حَسَّنَ
فَهَّمْنَا	فَهَّمْتِ	فَهَّمْتَ	فَهَّمَتَا	فَهَّمَا	فَهَّمَ
أَشْرَكْنَا	أَشْرَكْتِ	أَشْرَكْتَ	أَشْرَكَتَا	أَشْرَكَا	أَشْرَكَ
آمَنَّا	آمَنْتِ	آمَنْتَ	آمَنَتَا	آمَنَا	آمَنَ

Imperfect form in IIIM^2, IIIF^2, IIM^2, IIF^2 and I M^{2,3} + F$^{2,3+}$

I M^{2,3} + F$^{2,3+}$	IIF^2	IIM^2	IIIF^2	IIIM^2	Verbs
نَذْهَبُ	تَذْهَبَانِ	تَذْهَبَانِ	تَذْهَبَانِ	يَذْهَبَانِ	يَذْهَبُ
نَقْرَأُ	تَقْرَآنِ	تَقْرَآنِ	تَقْرَآنِ	يَقْرَآنِ	يَقْرَأُ

نَأْكُلُ	تَأْكُلاَن	تَأْكُلاَن	يَأْكُلاَن	يَأْكُلُ
نُدْخِلُ	تُدْخِلاَن	تُدْخِلاَن	يُدْخِلاَن	يُدْخِلُ
نُخْرِجُ	تُخْرِجَان	تُخْرِجَان	يُخْرِجَان	يُخْرِجُ
نُحْسِنُ	تُحْسِنَان	تُحْسِنَان	يُحْسِنَان	يُحْسِنُ
نُحَسِّنُ	تُحَسِّنَان	تُحَسِّنَان	يُحَسِّنَان	يُحَسِّنُ
نُفَهِّمُ	تُفَهِّمَان	تُفَهِّمَان	يُفَهِّمَان	يُفَهِّمُ
نُشْرِكُ	تُشْرِكَان	تُشْرِكَان	يُشْرِكَان	يُشْرِكُ
نُؤْمِنُ	تُؤْمِنَان	تُؤْمِنَان	يُؤْمِنَان	يُؤْمِنُ

(١) ذَهَبَ (٢) قَرَأَ (٣) أَكَلَ (٤) أَدْخَلَ (٥) أَخْرَجَ

(٦) أَحْسَنَ (٧) حَسَّنَ (٨) فَهَّمَ (٩) أَشْرَكَ (١٠) آمَنَ

(4) The Perfect, the Imperfect, the verbal noun, the Active Participle, the Passive Participle for the Fourth Derived Form:

(١) دَخَلَ (٢) خَرَجَ (٣) أَمِنَ (٤) نَزَلَ (٥) شَرِكَ

Fourth Derived Form

Passive Participle	Active Participle	Verbal noun	Imperfect	Perfect	Derived forms. IV
مُدْخَلٌ	مُدْخِلٌ	إِدْخَالٌ	يُدْخِلُ	أَدْخَلَ	أَدْخَلَ
مُخْرَجٌ	مُخْرِجٌ	إِخْرَاجٌ	يُخْرِجُ	أَخْرَجَ	أَخْرَجَ
مُؤْمَنٌ	مُؤْمِنٌ	إِيمَانٌ	يُؤْمِنُ	آمَنَ	آمَنَ

660

أَنْزَلَ	أَنْزَلَ	يُنْزِلُ	إِنْزَالٌ	مُنْزِلٌ	مُنْزَلٌ
أَشْرَكَ	أَشْرَكَ	يُشْرِكُ	إِشْرَاكٌ	مُشْرِكٌ	مُشْرَكٌ

(5) Translation into Arabic:

١ : لاَ يَظْلِمُ اللهُ الإِنْسَانَ.

٢ : اَلظَّالِمُ يَظْلِمُ وَلاَ يَتُوبُ إِلى الله.

٣ : وَلَدَانِ طَوِيلَانِ يَرْجِعَانِ إِلى بَيْتِهِمَا مِنْ الْمَدْرَسَةِ.

٤ : اَلرَّجُلُ الْكَرِيمُ الَّذي يُظْهِرُ كَرَمَهُ لِلنَّاسِ.

٥ : اَلْمُؤْمِنُ لاَ يَخَافُ مِنَ النَّاسِ.

٦ : اَللهُ نَزَّلَ الْقُرْآنَ وَهُوَ يَحْفَظُهُ.

٧ : اَلْمُصْلِحُ مَنْ يُصْلِحُ النَّاسَ.

٨ : اَلشَّخْصُ الْفَاسِدُ يَنْشُرُ الْفَسَادَ في الْعَالَمِ.

٩ : لاَ يُحِبُّ اللهُ الشَّخْصَ الْفَاسِدَ وَ الْفَسَادَ.

١٠ : يُحِبُّ اللهُ الرَّحْمَةَ وَ الإِصْلاَحَ.

(6) Identification of Derived form and Dual noun: ($M^{2+} + F^2$) :

1. اَلْفَرِيقَيْن N M^2

2. تَحَكُمَانِ
Imperfect III M^2

3. اَلْبَحْرَيْنِ N M^2

5. يَدَاهُ NF^2

مَبْسُوطَتَانِ NF^2

6. مَرَّتَانِ N F^2

4. مُحْسِنٌ AP^4 M^1

5. يُنْفِقُ Imp^4 III M^1

6. فَإِمْسَاكٌ VN^4

تَسْرِيحٌ VN^2

بِإِحْسَنٍ VN^4

15. أَوْحَى Perf^4 IIIM^1

16. أَنزَلَ Perf^4 IIIM^1

أَنزَلَهُ Perf^4 IIIM^1

17. ٱلْإِحْسَنِ VN^4

ٱلْإِحْسَنُ VN^4

18. ءَامَنَ Perf^4 IIIM^1

19. أَصْلَحَ Perf^4 III M^1

20. أَصْلَحَ Perf^4 III M^1

21. فَتَحْرِيرُ VN^2

مُّؤْمِنَةٍ VN^4 F^1

22. أَرْسَلْنَ(ـلَكَ) Perf^4 I M^{1+} I F^{1+}

23. أَصْلَحْنَا Perf^4 I M^{2+} I F^{2+}

24. أَنزَلْنَ(ـهُ) Perf^4 I M^{2+} +I F^{2+}

25. أَدْرَرٰ(ـلَكَ) Perf^4 III M^1

26. أَنزَلْنَ(ـهُ) Perf^4 I M^{2+} +I F^{2+}

صَرَّفْنَا Perf^2 I M^{2+} +I F^{2+}

27. أَنزَلْنَا Perf^4 I M^{2+} +I F^{2+}

مُصَدِّقًا AP^2 M^1

28. أَخْرَجَكَ Perf^4 III M^1

29. أَنزَلْتَ Perf^4 II M^1

30. تُنقِذُ Imp^4 II M^1

31. يُقْرِضُ Imp^4 IIIM^1

32. يُحْى Imp^4 IIIM^1

33. يُرِيدُ Imp^4 IIIM^1

34. يُرِيدُ Imp^4 IIIM^1

36. أَنزَلَ Perf^4 IIIM^1

فَأَحْيَا Perf^4 IIIM^1

37. كَرَّمْنَا Perf^2 I M^{2+} +I F^{2+}

38. أُصِيبُ Imp^4 I M^1 +I F^1

39. (لِ)لِلإِسْلَمِ VN^4

41. (نَا)أَرْسَلْ Perf^4 I M^{1+} +I F^{1+}

42. (تُهَا)سَمَّيْ Perf^2 I M^1 +I F^1

أُعِيذُهَا Imp^4 I M^1 +I F^1

43. نَادَى Perf^3 IIIM^1

45. (لِمَكَ)يُدْرِي Imp^4 III M^1

46. أَحَسَّ Perf^4 IIIM^1

49. مُحْضَرًا PP^4

50. أَعْمَىٰ Perf^4 IIIM^1

أَعْمَىٰ Perf^4 IIIM^1

52. (ه)نُعَذِّبُ Imp^2 I M^{1+} +I F^1

53. (لِمَكَ)يُعْطِي Imp^4 III M^1

664

Lesson 10

Exercise No. 29

(1) Fill in the blank:

(١) أَرَأَيْتَ الظَّالِمَ الَّذِى يَظْلِمُ الإِنْسَانَ.

(٢) الْمُسَافِرُ مَنْ يُسَافِرُ مِنْ بَلَدٍ إِلَى بَلَدٍ.

(٣) الْعَالِمُ حَيٌّ لاَ يَمُوتُ بِالْمَوْتِ.

(٤) الْكَافِرُونَ يَكْفُرُونَ بِاللهِ وَ الْمُؤْمِنُونَ يُؤْمِنُونَ بِاللهِ.

(٥) إِنَّ الْمُسْلِمَاتِ لَفَائِزَاتٌ.

(٦) اَلْأَبُ يُحِبُّ تَدْرِيسَ الْقُرْآنِ.

(٧) الرَّجُلُ الْقَوِيُّ خَيْرٌ مِنَ الرَّجُلِ الضَّعِيفِ.

(٨) الْمُنَافِقُونَ يَأْمُرُونَ بِالْمُنْكَرِ.

(٩) السَّمَاءُ فَوْقَ الْأَرْضِ وَ الْأَرْضُ تَحْتَ السَّمَاءِ.

(١٠) هَذِهِ الْبِنْتُ الْجَمِيلَةُ أُمٌّ.

(١١) أَنَا أُطِيعُ اللهَ وَ رَسُولَهُ (ﷺ) وَ لاَ أَعْصِيهُمَا.

(١٢) صَارَتِ الْمَرِيضَةُ ضَعِيفَةً.

(١٣) إِنَّ اللهَ لاَ يُحِبُّ الَّذِينَ يَكْذِبُونَ وَ يُفْسِدُونَ فِي الْأَرْضِ.

(2) The *i'rāb*.

(١) هَلْ تُسَافِرُ مِنْ لَنْدَنَ إِلَى مَكَّةَ لِلْحَجِّ؟

665

(٢) أَنَا أُحِبُّ الْمُجَاهِدَ لِأَنَّهُ يُجَاهِدُ فِي سَبِيلِ اللهِ.

(٣) هُمَا طَالِبَانِ يُسَافِرَانِ مِنْ بَلَدٍ إِلَى بَلَدٍ.

(٤) كَانَ الرَّسُولُ (ﷺ) يُحِبُّ اللهَ حُبّاً شَدِيداً.

(٥) كَانَ إِبْرَاهِيمُ (الْعَلَيْهِ) رَسُوْلاً صَادِقاً.

(٦) إِنَّ الْمُؤْمِنِينَ وَالْمُؤْمِنَاتِ لَهُمُ الْجَنَّةُ الْعَالِيَةُ جَزَاءٌ فِي الْآخِرَةِ.

(3) Perfect, Imperfect, Verbal Noun, Active Participle and Passive Participle for the Third Derived Form:

(١) حَفِظَ (٢) سَفَرَ (٣) بَرَكَ (٤) شَرِكَ (٥) قَتَلَ

Third Derived Form

Passive Participle	Active Participle	Verbal noun	Imperfect	Perfect	Derived forms. III
مُحَافَظٌ	مُحَافِظٌ	مُحَافَظَةٌ	يُحَافِظُ	حَافَظَ	حَافَظَ
مُسَافَرٌ	مُسَافِرٌ	مُسَافَرَةٌ	يُسَافِرُ	سَافَرَ	سَافَرَ
مُبَارَكٌ	مُبَارِكٌ	مُبَارَكَةٌ	يُبَارِكُ	بَارَكَ	بَارَكَ
مُشَارَكٌ	مُشَارِكٌ	مُشَارَكَةٌ	يُشَارِكُ	شَارَكَ	شَارَكَ
مُقَاتَلٌ	مُقَاتِلٌ	مُقَاتَلَةٌ	يُقَاتِلُ	قَاتَلَ	قَاتَلَ

666

(4) Translation into Arabic:

١: اَللهُ يُحِبُّ الْجِهَادَ في سَبِيلِ الْحَقِّ.

٢: اَلْمُسَافِرُوْنَ صَادِقُوْنَ

٣: هُوَ كَانَ ضَالاًّ ثُمَّ هَدَاهُ اللهُ.

٤: اَلْمَرْأَةُ الْفَاسِدَةُ بِرَحْمَةِ اللهِ أَصْبَحَتْ مُصْلِحَةً.

٥: كَانَ إِسْمَاعِيْلُ وَلَدَ إِبْرَاهِيْمَ وَ كِلاَهُمَا كَانَا نَبِيَّيْنِ.

٦: رَجُلاَنِ فَاضِلاَنِ يُسَاعِدَانِ بَعْضُهُمَاالْبَعْضِ بِمَوَدَّةٍ.

٧: إِنَّ اللهَ يُحِبُّ الرَّجُلَ الصَّادِقَ وَالْمَرْأَةُ الصَّادِقَةَ

٨: نَحْنُ عَابِدُوْنَ وَمُصْلِحُوْنَ.

٩: اَلصَّابِرُ وَ الصَّابِرَةُ نَاجِحَانِ

١٠: اَلنِّسَاءُ الصَّائِمَاتُ صَادِقَاتٌ

667

(5) Identification of Derived Form and Sound Plural (SP):

23. نَادَىٰ Perf^3 IIIM^1	7. يُرِيدُ Imp^4 IIIM^1
نِدَآءً VN^3	8. يُرِيدُ Imp^4 IIIM^1
24. نَادَىٰ Perf^3 IIIM^1	9. يُعَذِّبُ Imp^2 IIIM^1
25. ٱلْمُسْلِمِينَ SP	17. (سَمَّيْ(تُهَا Perf^2 I M^1+I F^1
ٱلْمُسْلِمَتِ SP	أُعِيذُهَا Imp^4 I M^1+I F^1
ٱلْمُؤْمِنِينَ SP	18. أُجِيبُ Imp^4 I M^1+I F^1
ٱلْمُؤْمِنَتِ SP	19. أَنزَلْنَهُ Perf^4 I M^{2+}+I F^{2+}
ٱلْقَنِتِينَ SP	مُبَارَكٌ AP^3 + PP^3 M^1
ٱلْقَنِتَتِ SP	مُصَدِّقٌ AP^2 M^1
ٱلصَّدِقِينَ SP	20. فَـَامَنَ Perf^4 IIIM^1
ٱلْخَشِعَتِ SP	مُهَاجِرٌ AP^3 M^1
ٱلصَّدِقِينَ SP	21. نَادَىٰ Perf^3 IIIM^1
ٱلصَّدِقَتِ SP	22. يُغَادِرُ Imp^3 IIIM^1
	أَحْصَنَهَا Perf^4 IIIM^1

27. SP ٱلْمُرْسَلِينَ

28. SP مَّيِّتُونَ

29. SP بِخَٰرِجِينَ

30. SP ٱلْمُؤْمِنِينَ

SP ٱلْمُؤْمِنَٰتِ

31. SP ٱلْمُجَٰهِدِينَ

SP ٱلْقَٰعِدِينَ

32. SP ٱلنَّبِيِّنَ

SP مُبَشِّرِينَ

SP مُنذِرِينَ

33. SP ٱلْمُؤْمِنِينَ

35. Perf² IIIM¹ نَزَّلْنَا

VN² تَنزِيلًا

36. VN² تَنزِيلُ

37. Imp³ I M²+I F² نُدَاوِل(ُهَا)

25. SP ٱلصَّٰبِرِينَ

SP ٱلصَّٰبِرَٰتِ

SP ٱلْخَٰشِعِينَ

SP ٱلْخَٰشِعَٰتِ

SP ٱلْمُتَصَدِّقِينَ

SP ٱلْمُتَصَدِّقَٰتِ

SP ٱلصَّٰٓئِمِينَ

SP ٱلصَّٰٓئِمَٰتِ

SP ٱلْحَٰفِظِينَ

ٱلْحَٰفِظَٰتِ

SP ٱلذَّٰكِرِينَ

SP ٱلذَّٰكِرَٰتِ

26. SP ٱلصَّٰبِرِينَ

SP ٱلصَّٰدِقِينَ

SP ٱلْقَٰنِتِينَ

38. يُغَادِرُ Imp[3] IIIM[1]

أَحْصَنَهَا Perf[4] IIIM[1]

39. اَلسَّبِقُونَ SP

اَلسَّبِقُونَ SP

اَلْمُقَرَّبُونَ SP

41. اَلْحَسَنَٰتِ SP

اَلسَّيِّئَاتِ S.P

43. اَلتَّئِبُونَ SP

اَلْعَٰبِدُونَ SP

اَلْحَٰمِدُونَ SP

اَلسَّٰئِحُونَ SP

اَلرَّٰكِعُونَ SP

اَلسَّٰجِدُونَ SP

اَلْأَٰمِرُونَ SP

اَلنَّاهُونَ SP

670

(4) Identification of Derived Form

1. تَوَكَّلْتُ Perf⁵ I M¹⁺   12. نَتَرَبَّصُ Imp⁵ IM²⁺+F²⁺

2. تَوَكَّلْتُ Perf⁵ I M¹+ F¹   13. تَكَلَّمُ Perf⁵ III M¹

3. تَوْفِيقِيَ VN²   14. تَقَطَّعُوا Perf⁵ III M³⁺

    تَوَكَّلْتُ Perf⁵ I M¹+ F¹   15. يَتَكَلَّمُونَ Imp⁵ IIIM³⁺

    أُنِيبُ Imp⁴ I M¹+ F¹   16. فَيَتَعَلَّمُونَ Imp⁵ IIIM³⁺

4. تَوَكَّلْنَا Perf⁵ I M²⁺+ F²   يُفَرِّقُونَ Imp² IIIM³⁺

5. تَوَكَّلْنَا Perf⁵ I M²⁺+F²   17. تَبَيَّنَ Perf⁵ III M¹

    أَنَبْنَا Perf⁴ I M²⁺+F²⁺   18. تَزَكَّىٰ Perf⁵ III M¹

6. يَتَوَكَّلُونَ Imp⁵ IIIM³·   يَتَزَكَّىٰ Imp⁵ IIIM¹

7. تَتَذَكَّرُونَ Imp⁵ IIM³⁺   19. يَتَجَنَّبُهَا Imp⁵ IIIM¹

8. يُبَيِّنُ Imp² IIIM¹   20. تَعَجَّلَ Perf⁵ III M¹

    تَتَفَكَّرُونَ Imp⁵ IIM³·   تَأَخَّرَ Perf⁵ III M¹

9. تَطَوَّعَ Imp⁵ IIIM¹   21. يَتَّخِذُ Imp⁸ IIIM¹

10. يَتَفَطَّرْنَ Imp⁵ IIIM¹   يُنْفِقُ Imp⁴ IIIM¹

          يَتَرَبَّصُ Imp⁵ IIIM¹

11. يَتَفَرَّقُونَ Imp⁵ IIIM

22. أَنزَلْنَا Perf^4 I M^{2+} + F^{2+}

يَتَكَلَّمُ Imp^5 IIIM^1

يُشْرِكُونَ Imp^4 IIIM^{3+}

23. يَتَمَنَّوْنَهُ Imp^5 IIIM^{3+}

قَدَّمَتْ Perf^2 III F^1

24. يَتَوَلَّى Imp^5 IIIM^1

مُعْرِضُونَ AP^4 IIIM^{3+}

25. تَتَنَزَّلُ Imp^5 IIIF^1

28. تُخْزِيهِ Imp^4 IIIM^1

29. يُطِيعُونَ Imp^4 IIIM^1

34. عَلَّمَكُمُ Perf^2 III M^1

Lesson 11

Exercise No. 30

(1) Fill in the blank:

(١)   الْمُؤْمِنُوْنَ يَتْلُوْنَ مَا يَتَيَسَّرُ مِنَ الْقُرْآنِ الْكَرِيْمِ.

(٢)   نَحْنُ نَتَحَدَّثُ فِيْ أَمْرِ دِيْنِنَا.

(٣)   أُولَئِكَ أُولُوْا الْعِلْمِ هُمُ الْفَائِزُوْنَ.

(٤)   إِنَّ اللهَ لَمَعَ الْمُحْسِنِيْنَ وَالْمُحْسِنَاتِ وَالْقَانِتِيْنَ
وَالْقَانِتَاتِ.

(٥)   الْمُتَوَكِّلُ مَنْ تَوَكَّلَ عَلَى اللهِ.

(٦)   التَّقَرُّبُ إِلَى اللهِ مِفْتَاحُ الْفَلَاحِ فِي الدُّنْيَا
وَالآخِرَةِ.

(2) The *i'rāb*

(١)   نَحْنُ تَوَكَّلْنَا عَلَى اللهِ الَّذِي يَعْلَمُ الْغَيْبَ وَالشَّهَادَةَ.

(٢)   إِنَّ اللهَ بِمَا تَعْمَلُوْنَ عَلِيْمٌ.

(٣)   أَفَلَا تَنْظُرُوْنَ إِلَى الْمَاءَ الَّذِي تَشْرَبُوْنَ؟

(٤)   نَحْنُ نَتَكَلَّمُ وَنَتَحَدَّثُ فِي هَذَا الأَمْرِ.

(٥)   مَا لَكُمْ لَا تَعْبُدُوْنَ اللهَ الَّذِي خَلَقَكُمْ؟

(٦)   الْمُؤْمِنُوْنَ يَفْعَلُوْنَ مَا يَقُوْلُوْنَ.

673

(٧) إِنَّ الَّذِينَ جَاهَدُوا لِإِعْلَاءِ كَلِمَةِ الْحَـقِّ لَهُمُ الْجَنَّةُ جَزَاءً بِمَا كَانُوا يَفْعَلُوْنَ.

(٨) أُولَئِكَ الْمُؤْمِنُوْنَ يَتَعَلَّمُوْنَ الْعِلْمَ.

(٩) نَحْنُ نُؤْمِنُ بِإِلَهٍ وَاحِدٍ وَدِينٍ وَاحِدٍ.

(١٠) هُمْ لَيْسُوا مُتَشَدِّدِينَ فِي أَمْرِ دِينِهِمْ.

(١١) هَؤُلَاءِ الْمُـؤْمِنَاتُ يَقْرَأْنَ وَيَفْهَمْنَ وَيَتَدَبَّرْنَ الْقُرْآنَ الْكَرِيمَ.

(3) Translation into Arabic:

١: اَللهُ سُبْحَانَهُ وَ تَعَالَى وَاحِدٌ وَهُوَ نَزَّلَ الْقُرْآنَ.

٢: اَلْكُفَّارُ لَا يُحَارِبُوْنَ فِي سَبِيْلِ اللهِ.

٣: اَلْمَرْأَةُ الْمُسْلِمَةُ تَقْرَأُ الْقُرْآنَ وَ تَنْعَكِسُ عَلَى آيَاتِهَا.

٤: احْتِرَامُ الْوَالِدَيْنِ وَاجِبٌ عَلَيْنَا.

٥: أَتَوَكَّلُ عَلَى اللهِ فَقَطْ وَ أَتَفَكَّرُ فِي مَخْلُوْقَاتِه.

٦: تَوَضَّأَ الْمُسَافِرُوْنَ وَ صَلُّوا فِي الْمَسْجِدِ.

٧: صَلَّيْنَا قِيَامَ اللَّيْلِ وَ سَأَلْنَا اللهَ الْهِدَايَةَ فِي الدُّنْيَا وَ الآخِرَةِ.

٨: لَا يُحِبُّ النَّاسُ أُولَئِكَ الَّذِينَ يَكْذِبُوْنَ وَيَطْغَوْنَ فَسَاداً فِي الأَرْضِ.

٩: هَلْ تَعْرِفْنَ مَا يَفْعَلُوْنَ فِي الْمَسْجِدِ.

١٠: هُمْ يَتَعَلَّمُوْنَ الْقُرْآنَ مِنْ الأُسْتَاذِ.

(4) Identification of Derived F

1. تَوَكَّلْتُ Perf^5 I M^1+ F^1

2. تَوَكَّلْتُ Perf^5 I M^1+ F^1

3. تَوْفِيقِيَ VN^2

تَوَكَّلْتُ Perf^5 I M^1+ F^1

أُنِيبُ Imp^4 I M^1+ F^1

4. تَوَكَّلْنَا Perf^5 I M^{2+}+ F^{2+}

5. تَوَكَّلْنَا Perf^5 I M^{2+}+ F^{2+}

أَنَبْنَا Perf^4 I M^{2+}+ F^{2+}

6. يَتَوَكَّلُونَ Imp^5 IIIM^{3+}

7. تَتَذَكَّرُونَ Imp^5 IIM^{3+}

8. يُبَيِّنُ Imp^2 IIIM^1

تَتَفَكَّرُونَ Imp^5 IIM^{3+}

9. تَطَوَّعَ Imp^5 IIIM^1

10. يَتَفَطَّرْنَ Imp^5 IIIM^1

11. يَتَفَرَّقُونَ Imp^5 IIIM^{3+}

12. نَتَرَبَّصُ Imp^5 IM^{2+} +F^{2+}

13. تَكَلَّمُ Perf^5 III M^1

14. تَقَطَّعُوا Perf^5 III M^{3+}

15. يَتَكَلَّمُونَ Imp^5 IIIM^{3+}

16. فَيَتَعَلَّمُونَ Imp^5 IIIM^{3+}

يُفَرِّقُونَ Imp^2 IIIM^{3+}

17. تَبَيَّنَ Perf^5 III M^1

18. تَزَكَّىٰ Perf^5 III M^1

يَتَزَكَّىٰ Imp^5 IIIM^1

19. يَتَجَنَّبُهَا Imp^5 IIIM^1

20. تَعَجَّلَ Perf^5 III M^1

تَأَخَّرَ Perf^5 III M^1

21. يَتَّخِذُ Imp^8 IIIM^1

يُنفِقُ Imp^4 IIIM^1

يَتَرَبَّصُ Imp^5 IIIM^1

22. أَنزَلْنَا Perf[4] I M[2+] + F[2+]

يَتَكَلَّمُ Imp[5] IIIM[1]

يُشْرِكُونَ Imp[4] IIIM[3+]

23. يَتَمَنَّوْنَهُ Imp[5] IIIM[3+]

قَدَّمَتْ Perf[2] III F[1]

24. يَتَوَلَّى Imp[5] IIIM[1]

مُعْرِضُونَ AP[4] IIIM[3+]

25. تَتَنَزَّلُ Imp[5] IIIF[1]

28. تُخْزِيهِ Imp[4] IIIM[1]

29. يُطِيعُونَ Imp[4] IIIM[1]

34. عَلَّمَكُمُ Perf[2] III M[1]

Lesson 12

Exercise No.31

(1) The i'rāb

(١) اَلْمُؤْمِنُوْنَ لاَ يَتَنَازَعُوْنَ وَ لاَ يَتَخَاصَمُوْنَ وَ يَحْكُمُوْنَ بكِتَاب الله.

(٢) اَلْمُؤْمِنُوْنَ لاَ يَتَحَاكَمُوْنَ إلى الشَّيَاطِيْنِ وَ يَتَعَاوَئُوْنَ عَلَى الخَيْرِ وَ لاَ يَتَعَاوَئُوْنَ عَلَى الْإِثْمِ وَ الشَّرِّ.

(٣) كَانَ رَسُوْلُ الله (ﷺ) يَحْكُمُ بكِتَاب الله وَ كَانَ يَتَفكَّرُ في خَلْقِ الله.

(٤) اَلَّذِينَ آمَنُوْا باللهِ وَ مَلاَئِكَتِه وَ رُسُلِه وَ تَوَاصَوْا بالْحَقِّ وَ تَوَاصَوْا بالْخَيْرِ، أُوْلَئكَ يَدْخُلُوْنَ الْجَنَّةَ، لَهُمْ فِيْهَا مَسَاكِنَ طَيِّبَةٌ وَ أَزْوَاجٌ مُطَهَّرَةٌ.

(٥) أَحْمَدُ تَاجِرٌ عِنْدَهُ بُيُوْتٌ عَالِيَةٌ وَ غُرُفَاتٌ وَاسِعَةٌ وَ فَاخِرَةٌ.

(٦) أُوْلُوْ الْعِلْمِ أَحْيَاءٌ وَ لَوْ كَانُوْا في التُّرَابِ.

(٧) اَلظَّالِمُ يَظْلِمُ وَ لاَ يَتُوْبُ إلى الله.

(٨) مَنْ هَذَا الرَّجُلُ الصَّالِحُ وَ مَاذَا يَقُوْلُ؟

(٩) إنَّ السِّيْرَةَ الْجَمِيْلَةَ خَيْرٌ مِنْ الصُّوْرَةِ الْجَمِيْلَةِ.

(١٠) هُوَ يَتْرُكُ طَعَامَهُ لِوَجْهِ الله.

(١١) اَلْمُسْلِمُ مَنْ سَلِمَ النَّاسُ مِنْ لِسَانِه وَ يَدِه.

(١٢) هُوَ يَقْرَأُ مِنَ الْقُرآنِ الَّذِي هُوَ كِتَابُ الله.

677

(١٣) فَتَحَتْ الأُمُّ بَابَ الْبَيْت.

(١٤) اللَّهُمَّ يَسِّرْهُ لِي وَ لاَ تُعَسِّرْهُ.

(2) Translation into Arabic

١: أُولئكَ الْعَالِمَاتُ يَجْلِسْنَ فِي بُيُوتِهِنَّ و يُدَرِّسْنَ الْقُرْآنَ.

٢: فِي الْحَدَائِقَ أَزْهَارٌ جَمِيلَةٌ وَ الأَنْهَارُ تَجْرِي أَمَامَ الْبُيُوت.

٣: قَالَتْ النِّسَاءُ: اَلْمُصَلُّوْنَ يَرْكَعُوْنَ فِي الْمَسْجِد.

٤: زَادَتْ الآثَامُ وَانْخَفَضَ عَدَدُ النَّاسِ الْمُطِيْعِيْنَ.

٥: أُوْمِنُ بِجَمِيْعِ الْكُتُبِ السَّمَاوِية نَزَلَتْ عَلَى الرُّسُل.

٦: اَلْكُفَّارُ لاَ يَخَافُوْنَ اللهَ وَلاَ يَعْبُدُوْنَهُ وَلاَ يَتَأَمَّلُوْنَ فِي خَلْقِه.

٧: اَلنِّسَاءُ الْمُؤْمِنَاتُ يَكْرَهْنَ الْفَسَادَ وَالتَّجَاوُزَ.

٨: كَانَ النَّبِيُّ مُوْسَى يَمْنَعُ النَّاسَ مِنْ عِبَادَة فِرْعَوْنَ.

٩: اَلْمُسَاعَدَةُ الْمُتَبَادَلَةُ وَ الاِصْلاَحُ مَحْبُوْبٌ عِنْدَاللهِ.

١٠: خَلَقَ اللهُ سُبْحَانَهُ وَتَعَالَى وَالِدَيْنِ صَالِحَيْنِ لأَبْنَائِهِمَا الْمُطِيْعِيْنَ.

(3) Identification of Derived Form and Broken Plural (BP):

1. وُجُوهٌ BP

2. كُتُبٌ BP

3. ٱلرِّجَالُ BP

ٱلنِّسَآءِ BP

فَضَّلَ Perf[2] III M[1]

5. تَتَوَفَّىٰهُم Imp[5] IIIF[1]

ٱلْمَلَـٰٓئِكَةُ BP

6. عِبَادِ BP

7. بِأَيْدِيهِمْ BP

9. ٱلْمَلَـٰٓئِكَةُ BP

(ك)يُبَشِّرُ Imp[2] IIIM[1]

10. قُلُوبٌ BP

أَبْصَـٰرُهَا BP

11. وُجُوهٌ BP

12. وُجُوهٌ BP

13. بِعَاهَتِنَا BP

14. يَتَضَرَّعُونَ Imp^5 IIIM^{3+}

15. كَٱلْحِجَارَةِ BP

يَتَفَجَّرُ Imp^5 IIIM^{3+}

ٱلْأَنْهَـٰرُ BP

16. أُجُورَهُمْ BP

17. ٱلْأَنْهَـٰرُ BP

18. وَيُرْسِلُ Imp^4 IIIM^1

ٱلصَّوَٰعِقَ BP

فَيُصِيبُ Imp^5 IIIM^{3+}

19. فَضَّلْنَا Perf^2 I M^{2+} + F^{2+}

كَلَّمَ Perf^2 III M^1

20. أَرْبَاب BP

مُتَفَرِّقُونَ AP^5 IIIM^{3+}

21. أَحَلَّ Perf^2 III M^1

حَرَّمَ Perf^2 III M^1

22. تُحَرِّمُ Imp^2 IIM^1

أَحَلَّ Perf^4 III M^1

23. فَتَقَبَّلَهَا Perf^5 III M^1

24. تَوَاصَوْا۟ Perf^6 III M^{3+}

تَوَاصَوْا۟ Perf^6 III M^{3+}

25. تَوَاصَوْا۟ Perf^6 III M^{3+}

تَوَاصَوْا۟ Perf^6 III M^{3+}

26. تَبَارَكَ Perf^6 III M^1

27. تَبَارَكَ Perf^6 III M^1

28. تَبَارَكَ Perf^6 III M^1

نَزَّلَ Perf^2 III M^1

29. تَظَـٰهَرَا Perf^6 III M^1

30. يَتْلَوَمُونَ Imp^6 IIIM^{3+}

31. يَتَنَاهَوْنَ Imp^6 IIIM^{3+}

32. يُرِيدُ Imp^4 IIIM^1

Lesson 13

Exercise No. 32

Identification of Imperfect Jussive mood:

10. أَنزَلَ	1. عَلَّمَ
عَلَّمَكَ	لَمْ يَعْلَمْ
لَمْ تَكُن	2. لَمْ يَعْلَمْ
11. لَمْ تَرَ	3. لَمْ يَرَ
أَنزَلَ	لَمْ نَجْعَل
فَأَخْرَجْنَا	4. لَمْ نَشْرَحْ
12. إِن تُؤْمِنُواْ	5. لَمْ يَكُ
تَتَّقُواْ	6. لَمْ تَحْكُم
13. إِن تَكْفُرُواْ	أَنزَلَ
14. إِن تُصْلِحُواْ	7. أَنزَلَ
تَتَّقُواْ	أَنزَلَ
15. إِن تُبْدُوا	لَمْ تَرَوَهَا
تُخْفُوهُ	8. لَمْ يَعْلَمُواْ
يُحَاسِبْكُم	9. لَمْ يَلْبِسُواْ
16. فَإِن ٱنتَهَوْاْ	مُّهْتَدُونَ

681

17. فَإِنِ ٱنتَهَوٰاْ	30. مَن يُؤْمِن
18. إِن تَتَّقُواْ	يَهْدِ
تَجْعَل	31. مَن يُطِعِ
يُكَفِّرْ	يُدْخِلْهُ
يَغْفِرْ	32. مَن يَتَّقِ
20. مَن يُطِعِ	تَجْعَل
21. مَن يُطِعِ	يَرْزُقْهُ
أَطَاعَ	مَن يَتَوَكَّلْ
22. مَن يُشْرِكْ	33. مَن يُهَاجِرْ
23. مَن يَدْعُ	تَجِدْ
24. مَن يَكْفُرْ	مَن تَخْرُجْ
25. مَن يَكْفُرْ	يُدْرِكْهُ
26. مَن يَكُنِ	34. مَن يَهْدِ
27. مَن يَتَّخِذِ	ٱلْمُهْتَدِ
28. مَن يَعْصِ	35. فَمَن يَعْمَلْ
29. مَن يُضْلِلِ	مَن يَعْمَلْ

45. مُقْتَدِرًا	36. مَن يَكْسِبْ
46. ٱخْتِلَفِ	37. مَا تَفْعَلُواْ
47. تَخْتَصِمُونَ	يَعْلَمْهُ
48. تُحْيِ	38. مَا تُقَدِّمُواْ
يُمِيتُ	تَجِدُوهُ
ٱخْتِلَفُ	39. أَيْنَمَا تَكُونُواْ
49. مُشْتَرِكُونَ	يُدْرِككُّمُ
50. مُهْتَدِينَ	40. أَيْنَمَا تَكُونُواْ
51. تَسْتَمِعُونَ	يَأْتِ
52. ٱكْتَسَبْ	41. ٱشْتَعَلَ
53. ٱكْتَسَبَتْ	لَمْ أَكُنْ
54. يَتَدَبَّرُونَ	42. تَتَّخِذُ
لَوَجَدُواْ	43. ٱتَّخَذَ
ٱخْتِلَفًا	44. أَصَبَتْهُم
	مُصِيبَةٌ
	ٱلْمُهْتَدُونَ

683

Lesson 14

Exercise No. 33

Identification of Imperative and Prohibition:

7. أَسْلَمَ

مُحْسِنٌ

9. اَتَّبِعُواْ

10. فَاَعْبُدَنِي

أَقِمِ

11. أَطِيعُواْ

أَطِيعُواْ

12. اَرْكَعُواْ

اَسْجُدُواْ

اَعْبُدُواْ

اَفْعَلُواْ

وَجَهِدُواْ

جِهَادِه

13. اَتَّقُواْ

كُونُواْ

14. اَدْعُ

جَادِلْهُم

15. قُلْ

16. حَافِظُواْ

قُومُواْ

17. اَعْدِلُواْ

18. كُونُواْ

19. فَاَعْدِلُواْ

20. تَزَوَّدُواْ

12. إِحْسَنًا

فَلَا تَقُل

لَا تَنْهَرْهُمَا

قُل

اَخْفِضْ

22. يُنفِقُونَ

قُلِ

23. خُذْ

تُطَهِّرُهُمْ

24. كُلُواْ

26. أَنفَقُواْ

27. كُلُواْ

28. كُلُواْ

ٱشْكُرُواْ

29. فَئَاتِ

30. ٱتَّقُواْ

ذَرُواْ

31. أَنفَقُواْ

32. فَأَصْلِحُواْ

ٱتَّقُواْ

33. ٱعْتَصِمُواْ

لاَ تَفَرَّقُواْ

34. فَخُذُوهُ

فَٱنتَهُواْ

ٱتَّقُواْ

35. فَٱعْدِلُواْ

36. أَوْفُواْ

37. أَوْفُواْ

38. ٱتَّقُواْ

قُولُواْ

39. ٱجْتَنِبُواْ

40. ٱقْصِدْ

ٱغْضُضْ

41. ذَرُواْ

42. ٱجْتَنِبُواْ

685

43. قُلِ	58. وَلَا تَبْسُطْ وَلَا تَجْعَلْ
اعْمَلُوا	
44. قُوٓا۟	59. أَنفِقُوا
45. أَوْفُوا۟	وَلَا تُلْقُوا
46. خُذِ ، أَعْرِض	60. وَلَا تَقْتُلُوا۟
47. اذْكُرُوا۟	
48. تُوبُوٓا۟	
49. قُلْ ، لَا تَقْنَطُوا	
50. قُل	
51. وَلَا تَهِنُوٓا۟	
وَلَا تَحْزَنُوا۟	
52. لَا تَكُونُوا۟	
53. وَلَا تَقْرَبُوا۟	
54. وَلَا تَأْكُلُوٓا۟	
55. وَلَا تَقْتُلُوا	
56. فَلَا تَنْهَرْ	
57. فَلَا تَقْهَرْ	

Lesson 15

Exercise No. 34

Identification of perfect passive, imperfect passive and derived forms:

1. كُوِّرَتْ Perf² III F¹ Passive M¹ Passive

2. بُعْثِرَ Perf² III M¹ Passive

حُصِّلَ Perf III M¹ Passive

حُصِّلَ Perf III M¹ Passive

سُيِّرَتْ Perf² III F¹ Passive

4. قُتِلَ Perf III M¹

انكَدَرَتْ Perf² III F¹ Passive

6. كُتِبَ Perf III M¹

عُطِّلَتْ Perf² III F¹ Passive M¹ Passive

8. كُتِبَ Perf III

حُشِرَتْ Perf² III F¹ Passive M¹ Passive

كُتِبَ Perf III

سُجِّرَتْ Perf² III F¹ Passive AP+M³⁺SP

تَتَّقُونَ Perf⁸⁺ II

زُوِّجَتْ Perf² III F¹ Passive

9. دُعُواْ Imp⁴ III F¹

سُئِلَتْ Perf III F¹ Passive

أَطَعْنَا Perf⁴ I M²³⁺ F²³⁺

قُتِلَتْ Perf⁴ III F¹ Passive M³⁺SP

المُفْلِحُونَ AP⁴

أُزْلِفَت Perf⁴ III F¹ Passive M¹⁺F¹

10. أُمِرْتُ Perf I

أَحْضَرَتْ Perf^4 III F^1

3. قُضِيَ Perf III M^1 Passive

أَكْفَرَهُ Perf^4 III M^1

5. خُلِقَ Perf III M^1 Passive

7. أُخْرِجَتْ Perf^4 III F^1 Passive

كُتِبَ Perf III M^1 Passive

تَتَّقُونَ Perf^{8+} II AP+M^{3+}SP

تُؤْمِنُونَ Imp^4 III F^1

Identification of subjunctive mood :

11. أَسْلَمَ Perf^4 III M^1 F^1 Passive

12. يُوقِعَ Imp^4 III

13. تُشْرِكُواْ Imp^4 II M^{3+}

14. تُرِيْدُ Imp^4 II M^1

15. تُؤْمِنَ Imp^4 II M^1

16. مُؤَجَّلاً PP2 M^1

17. عَلَّمَهُ Perf^2 III M^1

18. عَلَّمَهُ Perf^2 III

19. يُقْبَلَ Imp^4 II M^1 Passive M$^{2,3+}$ F$^{2,3+}$

20. نَزَّلْنَا Perf^2 I

أُعِدَّتْ Perf^4 III F^1 Passive

21. مُغَضِباً AP^3 M^1 M$^{2,3+}$ F$^{12,3+}$

22. نُؤْمِنَ Imp^4 I

نَادَى Perf^3 III M^1

23. يُرد Imp^4 III M^1 M^{3+} SP

25. لِيُعْجِزَهُ Imp^4 III M^1

26. لِيُطْلِعَكُمْ Imp^4 III M^1 M^2

يَجْتَبى Imp^8 III M^1 M^{3+}

تُؤْمِنُوا Imp^4 II M^{3+} III M^1 Passive

تَتَّقُوا Imp^4 II M^{3+} M^{3+} SP

47. لأَكْفُرَ Imp^4 I M^{1+} F^1 III F^1

44. تَقَدَّمَ Perf^5 III M^1 F^1

تَأَخَّرَ Perf^5 III M^1 III F^1

47. تَوَلَّى Perf^5 III M^1

يُفْسِدَ Imp^4 III M^1

يُهْلِكَ Imp^4 III M^1

48. قَدَّرَهُ Perf^2 III M^1

53. يُغَيِّرُ Imp^2 III M^1

24. الْمُؤْمِنينَ AP^4

58. يُعَلِّمَان Imp^3 II

64. يُحِبُّونَ Imp III

يُحْمَدُوا Imp

66. مُسْلِمُونَ AP^{4+}

70. تَبْيَضُّ Imp^9

تَسْوَدُّ Imp^9 III

اسْوَدَّتْ Imp^9

54. مُعَذِّبِينَ APL³⁺ SP

يُغَيِّرُوا Imp III M³⁺

55. تُحِبُّونَ تُنْفِقُواْ Imp⁴ II M³⁺

56. تُقَتِّلُوهُمْ Imp³ II M³⁺

يُقَتِّلُوكُم Imp³ III M³⁺

يُقَتِّلُوكُمْ Imp³ III M³⁺

تُحِبُّونَ Imp⁴ II M³⁺

57. تَتَّخِذُوا Imp³ II M³⁺

يُهَاجِرُواْ Imp³ III M³⁺

63. المُجَاهِدِينَ AP³⁺ M³⁺ SP

65. المُمْتَرِينَ AIP⁴ M³⁺ SP

Lesson 16

Exersice No. 35

Identificationof adverb of time and place.

1. الصُّبْحِ	2. الصُّبْحِ
3. الصُّبْحِ	4. الفَجْرِ
5. الفَجْرِ	6. الفَجْرِ، الظَّهِيرَة، العشَآء
7. بُكْرَةً، أَصِيلاً	8. بُكْرَةً، عَشِيّاً
9. اَلنَّهَارَ	10. الَّيْلَ، النَّهَارَ
11. الَّيْلَ، النَّهَارَ	12. الَّيْلَ، النَّهَارَ
13. الَّيْلَ، النَّهَارَ	14. الَّيْلَ
15. الضُّحَى، الَّيْلَ	16. الَّيْلَ
17. الَّيْلَ	18. عَشِيّاً
19. عَشِيَّةً ضُحـَاهَا	20. غُدُوّاً وَعَشِيّاً
21. بُكْرَةً وَعَشِيّاً	22. يَوْمَ
23. يَوْمِ الْجُمُعَة	24. يَوْمَ
25. يَوْمٍ	26. الْيَوْمَ
27. يَوْمَ يَوْمَئِذٍ	28. تَظْمَؤُاْ
29. ضُحىً	30. إذا
31. إذا	32. الْئِنَ

691

34. الْئَنَ   33. الْئَنَ

36. أَيَّانَ   35. أَيَّانَ

39. مَتَى   37. أَيَّانَ

41. ءانَآءَ الَّيْل   40. ءانَآءَ الَّيْل

43. عشَاءً   42. ءانَآىءَ الَّيْلِ

45. بِالْأَمْسِ   44. الأَسْحَارِ

47. غَدٍ   46. غَداً

49. شَهْرُ رَمَضانَ   48. الشَّهْرَ

51. السَّاعَةِ   50. عَامٍ

53. عَشِيّاً، حِيْنَ   52. حِيْنَ، حِيْنَ

55. حِيْنِ   54. حِيْنَ

57. الَّيْل   56. يُصَوِّرُكُمْ

59. قَبْلُ   58. كُلُّ

61. قَلِيلاً   60. بَعْد قَبْلُ

62. كَثِيراً

Identification of Derived Form:

93. قَطَّعْنَ___هُمْ Perf² I   8. أَوْحَى Perf⁴ III M¹ M^{2,3+} F^{2,3+}

94. وعَدْنَا أَتْمَمْنَ___هَا   9. جَلَّ___هَا Perf² III M¹

105. تَعُدُّونَ Imp^2 II M^{3+}

106. اسْتَجَابَ Perf^{10} III

107. مُرْدِفِينَ AP^4 M^3 SP

114. يَسْتَبْشِرُونَ Imp^{10} III

115. أُجِيبُ Imp^4 I M^{1+}F^1

117. الْمُسْتَكْبِرِينَ AP^4 M^{3+}

118. يَسْتَجِيبُونَ Imp^{10} III

119. مُسْتَكْبِرًا PP^{10} M^1

120. الْمُسْتَقِيمِ AP^{10} M^1

121. تُرْحَمُونَ Imp^4 III M^{3+}

122. يَسْتَمِعُونَ Imp^{10} III

يَتَّبِعُونَ Imp^8 III M^{3+}

124. مُسْتَقِيماً AP^{10} M^1

تَفَرَّقَ Perf^5 III M^1

125. تُسَلِّمُوا Imp^2 II M^{3+}

11. اخْتَلَفَ AP^8 M^1

يَتَّقُونَ Imp^8 III M^{3+}

13. لَتَبْتَغُوا Imp^8 III M^{3+}

14. أَدْبَرَ Perf^4 III M^1
M^{3+}

18. تُظْهِرُونَ Imp^4 III M^{3+}

20. يُعْرَضُونَ Imp^4 III M^{3+}
SP

22. أَنْزَلْنَا Perf^4 III M^{3+}
M^{3+}

24. مُحْضَرًا PP^4 M^1

26. أَكْمَلْتُ Perf^4 I M^{1+}F^1

32. الْمُفْسِدِينَ AP^4 M^{3+}F^{3+}

37. يُبْعَثُونَ Imp^4 III M^{3+} Passive
M^{3+}

38. مُرْسَـهَا PP^4 M^1

49. أُنْزِلَ Imp^4 III M^1

52. تُمْسُونَ Imp^4 III M^{3+}

تُضْبِحُونَ Imp^4 III M^{3+}

52. تُظْهِرُونَ Imp^4 III M^{3+}

54. يَعْلَمُونَ يَرَوْنَ

56. يُصَوِّرُكُمْ Imp[4] III M[3+]

58. كَذَّبُوهُ Perf[2] III M[3+]

61. أُمِرْتُ Perf[2] I M[1+] F[1] Passive

الْمُسْلِمِينَ AP[4] M[3+]

62. كُلُواْ تَمَتَّعُواْ

69. اشْتَمَلَتْ Perf[8] III F[1]

85. سَخَّرَهَا Perf[2] III M[1]

86. أَنْزَلَ Perf[4] III M[1]

APPENDIX
J10
Divine Prophecy;

A Reflection on the Qurā'nic *Āyah*, Verse, *Sūrat al-Ḥijr*, 15 :9

إِنَّا نَحْنُ نَزَّلْنَا ٱلذِّكْرَ وَإِنَّا لَهُۥ لَحَفِظُونَ

***"Verily We! It is We Who have revealed the reminder and
We are its Guardian!" (15 :9)***

Historical Background for the Revelation:

Out of 114 Qurā'nic *Suwar* (sing. *Sūrah*) Chapters, 86 were
revealed in Makkah and the remaining 28 were revealed in
Madinah. *Sūrat al-Ḥijr* was revealed during the Makkan
period when the hostility against the early Muslims and the
barbaric persecution and even brutal execution by the
Makkan polytheists was the order of the day. The number
of Muslims under the fold of Islam was small and majority
of them were poor and weak. The Prophet Muḥammad
(ﷺ) implemented a 'non-violence' policy and instructed
his followers to remain peaceful, calm and exercise
patience. He even permitted a few to migrate to the
neighbouring country of Abyssinia to witness freedom and
peace for the practice of their faith. Under such precarious
conditions the above mentioned *Āyah* was revealed to the
Prophet (ﷺ) which clearly contains a divine prophecy
referred to in the *Āyah* for safeguarding the Qurā'n from
any corruption. At the time of its revelation belief in the
materialisation of the prophecy in the future was very
difficult.

Grammatical Analysis of the *Āyah*:

For the better comprehension of the Divine prophecy it is essential to analyse the revealed Word. The *Āyah* contains a message which has been promulgated with the use of plural by the Sovereign Lord of the Universe, Almighty Allah. Almost all seven revealed words categorically reflect the Majesty of Allah. This particular Majestic message, like other messages addressed to the entire mankind, is to make them fully aware of their rights and responsibilities. The prophecy is conveyed in a remarkable style. In this style His Majesty, Allah, establishes the Truth with emphasis and great force for it is highly essential for humans to follow a Divine programme of human life (i.e. the Qurā'n) for their material as well as spiritual prosperity.

Divine prophecy commences with an emphasis in the use of an article *inna*, verily, We, which is followed by a pronoun suffix *wa*, stands for *Allah*. Immediately after that another personal masculine plural pronoun *naḥnu*, We, stands for *Allah* is followed by the second derived form verb, *nazzala*. It is a derived form from the tri-literal verb *nazala*, which means to descend. The second derived form in Arabic is noted for causative effect, it means to cause something to descend. It is *Allah* who has caused the Qurā'n to descend. This verb is suffixed with *nā*, first person plural which means We, invariably referring to *Allah*.

Al-Dhikr, the reminder, is the object in Arabic grammar which represents none except *Allah's* Word (i.e. the Qurā'n). *Wa*, a particle for conjunction is followed by the emphasis with which the *Ayah* of the prophecy started with *innā*, We, verily. It is mentioned again establishing only *Allah's* authority. *La* is a preposition which is prefixed to the third person masculine pronoun *hū* referring to *al-dhikr*, Word of *Allah* (the Qurā'n). With the prefix of *la* used for emphasis to *ḥāfiẓūn*, guardian, sound plural masculine in nominative case. It is one of the attributes of *Allah*.

Conclusion:

- It is bewildering to note that the *Āyah* of prophecy contains seven short words which include only twenty seven letters and eight times Allah is categorically referred to (in the grammatical analysis this reference to Allah is emphasized by presenting it in italics).

- The Qurā'n claims time and time again that it is a revelation from Allah. It was revealed to the heart of the final Messenger Prophet Muhammad (ﷺ) from 'al-Lawḥ al-Maḥfūz', the Preserved Tablet through the archangel Gabriel. The Prophet (ﷺ) was the 'Sayyid al-Ḥuffāẓ' the leader of millions who have memorised the entire Qurā'n throughout the centuries. Some among them have even kept the genealogy of teachers in this exercise which go back to the Prophet (ﷺ). Special biographical dictionaries have been contributed preserving their life for this privilege.

- It is amazing that the revealed text is guarded by its Guardian Almighty Allah throughout the ages from all corruption. Divine prophecy contained in the *Āyah* stands today as it was yesterday and it prophecies with great emphasis that it will remain so for tomorrow.

- The Qurā'n confirms this truth and it has been attested unanimously by all schools of Muslim thought throughout Muslim history:

"Falsehood cannot come to it (i.e. the Qurā'n) from before it or from behind it. It is a revelation from the One, the Wise and Praiseworthy". (Sūrat Fuṣṣilat 41: 42)

698

Islam: The Qur'anic Overview

by Dr Muhammad Ibrahim H.I. Surty

- **272 pages, hardback, beautifully illustrated in full colour on art paper**

- **It presents 41 Qur'anic themes with definitions and benefits**

- **Provides references from around one third of the Qur'an.**

- **It can be used as a guide book for the comprehension of Muslim faith and practice, as well as Muslim culture and civilisation**

- **Published by QAF: Qur'anic Arabic Foundation**

- **Subsidised price only £5.99**

The Science of Reciting the Qur'an
(with three audio CDs)

by Dr Muhammad Ibrahim H. I. Surty

- **The first teaching manual of its kind in English which enables one to learn and improve recitation.**
- **An Islamic Foundation publication**
- **Price: £22.50**

QAF: Qur'anic Arabic Foundation

Registered Charity No. 1027642
Founded in Birmingham, England in 1994.

Aims

(a) To promote the teaching of Qur'anic Arabic and the comprehension of the Qur'an.

(b) To develop methods and techniques for teaching and learning of the Qur'an and Qur'anic Arabic and for this purpose develop literature.

(c) To organise and arrange training courses, symposia, seminars, workshops, conferences and the exchange of scholars for the teaching and comprehension of the Qur'an and its sciences.

(d) To establish a resource centre for Qur'anic teaching, a library of the Qur'anic sciences and the *Sunnah*, and a *Bayt al-Qur'an* – The House of Wisdom and Peace.

(e) To plan and develop post-doctoral research on specific projects for Qur'anic sciences with the assistance of internationally renowned scholars.

(f) To promote knowledge, wisdom, peace and unity.

**552B Coventry Road, Small Heath, Birmingham,
B10 0UN, England, U.K.
Tel: 0121 771 1894   Fax: 0121 476 8428
Email: qaf@blueyonder.co.uk
www.qaf.org.uk**

About the author

Dr Muhammad Ibrahim H. I Surty,
(b. 1941) B.A (Hons.) MA (Bom), PhD (London)

Dr Surty served several years in the University of Sokoto
as Reader and Head of the Department of Islamic Studies. He is
a retired senior lecturer, Department of Theology and Religion,
University of Birmingham and the founder and Chairman of
QAF Charity.

His works include • *Adab al-Qāḍī* two vols • *The Qur'ān
and al-Shirk* • A Course in *'Ilm al-Tajwīd*.: The Science of
Reciting the *Qur'ān* (with three audio CDs) • *Muslims'
Contribution to Development of Hospitals* • *The Qur'ānic
concept of God* • *The Most Comprehensive Qur'ānic verse on
Socio Economic Ethics and its Relevance to Modern Life Islam*:
• *Islam the Qur'ānic Overview* • *Qur'ānic Arabic: A Manual
Teaching Arabic Through the Qur'ān (with DVDs covering all
16 Lesson)s*. He has contributed several articles on different
Islamic themes in the literary journals. He has participated in a
number of international seminars.

About the Book

- The course with DVDs is the first of its kind in the world.

- The fruit of several years of teaching and research at Universities and the Muslim Community in Britain.

- Teaches Arabic in a remarkably short period of time.

- DVDs include scores of audio visual aids with colour coding, classroom interaction which provide great assistance for the comprehension, reading, writing and teaching Arabic.

- Provides a key to 35 exercises.

- Each lesson contains a glossary and a method of teaching.

- Includes useful tables and diagrams based on rich Qur'ānic vocabulary and hundreds of references to the Qur'ān.

- Includes formation of 93 simple grammatical rules and example analysis.

- Contains 63 small units based on graded progression and all grammatical themes are supported by extensively designed text and the Qur'ānic text.

- Teaches Arabic through the Qur'ānic.

An Urdu Translation of Quranic Arabic
By
Dr Muhammad Ibrahim H. I. Surty

Paper Back
487 pp Price: £7.50 + postage